Years of Change

European History 1890–1945

Robert Wolfson

Hodder & Stoughton

A MEMBER OF THE HODDER HEADLINE GROUP

British Library Cataloguing in Publication Data

Wolfson, Robert
  Years of change
  1. Europe – History, 1871–1918
  2. Europe – History, 20th century
  I. Title
  940.2   D935

ISBN 0 7131 0273 X

First published 1978
Impression number   24 23 22 21 20 19 18 17
Year   1998   1997   1996   1995   1994

Printed in Great Britain for Hodder & Stoughton Educational,
a division of Hodder Headline Plc, 338 Euston Road,
London NW1 3BH by Clays Ltd, St Ives plc

Preface

This book is written for those in the 16+ age range who are studying this period in detail for the first time. It is intended to be a workbook rather than a reading book. It is expected that readers will take notes on much of the text, and a considerable number of exercises have been included. The text and exercises have been written with the view that history lessons have too often been used for teaching narrative, and text books for analysis, when the reverse can be more effective. The text is therefore intended to provide the basis of a narrative, and the exercises the beginnings of analysis.

Acknowledgements

The author would like to acknowledge the help of Dr. C.M. Andrew of Corpus Christi College, Cambridge, with reference to the material on France and the post-1918 period.

Sources are given at the head of each extract. Acknowledgement is due to the following for permission to reproduce copyright material:

Mrs Sarah G. Osgood for extracts from *the Fall of France*, trans. S.M. Osgood; National Bureau of Economic Research, N.Y. for an extract from G. Bry's *Wages in Germany, 1870–1945*; Hutchinson Publishing Group for extracts from Benito Mussolini's *My Autobiography*; Columbia University Press for an extract from F. Ernst's *The Germans and their Modern History*; Methuen & Co. Ltd for extracts from C. Seton-Watson's *Italy from Liberalism to Fascism 1870–1925* and Oxford University Press for extracts from *Documents in the Political History of the European Continent 1815–1919*, ed. G.A. Kertesz (1968).

Thanks also to Mr W.G. McDougall for his correction of inaccuracies in chapter VII.

Contents

XV An Outline of World War II in Europe

List of Tables

List of Maps

List of Diagrams

Introduction

(a) General

The impetus to write this book came from two sources. As a student of history, I often found it difficult to get full value from the analytical works recommended to me as I had little outline knowledge of the simple facts of the subjects I was studying. My first aim therefore has been to provide a factual account of the events of the period for those studying it for the first time. In so doing, I have endeavoured to play down, but not to eliminate, analytical aspects in the text and to organize it in a clear, straightforward manner. Consequently, I have adopted a 'country by country' approach, since, in my experience, this is the way it is generally taught and examined, rather than a thematic scheme. In addition, I have divided each chapter into political, economic and diplomatic (foreign policy) history for ease of reference. In so doing, I would be the first to accept the falsity of such divisions in many cases.

My second impetus has come as a teacher of history in secondary schools. Students at the 16+ level are required, in examinations, to write analytical essays, yet there is little to teach them how to do this. Existing books seem either factual accounts of a simple kind aimed at first level examinations with the emphasis on factual recall, or highly analytical works most suited to undergraduate or even graduate level where students have already acquired analytical skills. Consequently, through the exercises at the end of each chapter, I have endeavoured to bridge the gap between these two types of book.

In addition, I have been infuriated as both student and teacher by authors who use complex phrases and concepts that are well beyond the comprehension of their readers. I have tried, but no doubt in many cases failed, to avoid this pitfall. One teacher commented that 'most books seem to be written for some hypothetical being who doesn't get tired, is endowed with a colossal IQ, has a brilliant tutor, endless time and no exams to worry about'. This book is written, I hope, for more normal human beings.

I have chosen to take 1890 rather than 1870 as my starting point for a number of reasons. Primarily, this is a book about the first half of the twentieth century. Since any student of history has to study the period immediately preceding that with which he is chiefly interested, I have in many cases taken the narrative back to 1870. Had I chosen 1870 as my

1

starting date, I would have been forced to examine the events of the 1850s and 1860s. This would have given the book too great an emphasis on the nineteenth rather than the twentieth century. Secondly, the 1890s were, in a number of respects, a starting point for reigns and events that were to have a crucial bearing on the twentieth century; Bismarck resigned as Chancellor of Germany in 1890 and Nicholas II became Tsar of Russia in 1894. Similarly, many of the issues and disputes that were ultimately to be resolved in World War I had their foundations, though not their origins, in the 1890s.

(b) Preliminary areas of study

Obviously, there are many influences on a work such as this. In particular, I have been impressed by the Open University's approach to the teaching and learning of history. In some respects, I hope that this work could be used in a similar way to the material prepared by the OU and that the student could, through careful note-taking and completion of the exercises, teach him or herself with the aid of this book. Because I have been so influenced by the OU approach, I would strongly recommend students and teachers to study the Open University Humanities Foundation Course Units 5–8—'What History Is and Why it is Important', 'Primary Sources', 'Basic Problems of Writing History' and 'Common Pitfalls in Historical Writing'. These will give students a better appreciation of both why and how to study history. In particular, Unit 7 will help students who have already studied some history to distinguish between different types of history—narrative, analysis and description. These books are now readily available and their use for three or four weeks at the start of a course in modern European History will pay dividends for the whole course.

One other area of preliminary study is important. Few students at the 16+ level will have experience of the study of constitutions, which form the vital frameworks in which decisions are made and policies determined. Therefore some knowledge of the nature of constitutions will be of great value, especially an understanding of the different types of executive, legislature, election systems and judiciaries that exist. Such knowledge might be acquired by a brief comparative study of the present American and British constitutions or by a simulation exercise, such as 'Colonial Government in America' by B. Barker (published by Academic and Business Monographs Ltd, 1976).

(c) Bibliographies and Documents

There is an obvious trend in history teaching at all levels towards the use of primary source material. I have tried to cater for this by including sections of documentary work with a number of documents relating to a key event or period, such as the Dreyfus affair or Weimar Germany, rather than many single documents on many different periods and topics. I have done this in the belief that documentary work should not consist of a brief perusal of many documents, but rather that it should be thorough. Obviously, this approach has made it impossible to include documents on many topics. However, there are collections readily available that I would recommend for those who intend to take a closer look at the documents of the period. The Open University have published collections of documents on the international affairs of the period; these form a part of the Arts Third Level course *War and Society* and are Block II, Unit 5 'Collection of Nineteenth- and Twentieth-century Documents Part I' and Block VI 'Collection of Nineteenth- and Twentieth-century Documents Part II'. A substantial collection is to be found in *Documents in the Political History of the European Continent 1815–1939* selected and edited by G.A. Kertesz (Oxford University Press, 1968). Others are to be found in the American paperback Anvil Series, edited by L.L. Snyder and published by van Nostrand, and in the Longman 'Seminar Studies in History' series.

I have included bibliographies at the end of each chapter relating to the topic concerned. I have endeavoured to keep these brief and relevant, so that they are used rather than ignored. In addition, there are many general works that include chapters on all or many of the subjects covered by this book. Of these, I have found the following most useful and would recommend that they be available at least for reference. Historical atlases will be of great value, such as *Muir's Historical Atlas* (Philip, 1968) and *A Sketch-map History of the Great Wars and After* by I. Richards, J.B. Goodson and J.A. Morris (Harrap, 1961). A most useful reference book, particularly for the less well-known countries, is *An Encyclopaedia of World History* edited by W.L. Langer (Harrap, 1968). For background and considerable insight into the personalities of the rulers, John Elliot *Fall of Eagles* (BBC, 1974) is both entertaining and valuable. *Europe in the Twentieth Century*, edited by J.M. Roberts (Macdonald, 1970), originally published as a magazine series ('History of the Twentieth Century'), provides considerable detail, written by leading historians, on all aspects of the period. J.H. Clapham, *The Economic Development of France and Germany, 1815–1914* (C.U.P., 1936) and C.M. Cipolla (ed.), *The Fontana Economic History of Europe*, Volumes 3 and 4, (Fontana, 1973) will provide a background on the economic history of the period. Textbooks that include chapters on all the major events of the period include: T.K. Derry and T.L. Jarman, *The European World 1870–1961* (Bell, 1972), A.J. Grant and H. Temperley, *History of Europe 1789–1950* (Longman, 1952), K. Perry, *Modern European History Made Simple* (Allen, 1976), J.M. Roberts, *Europe 1880–1945* (Longman, 1945), A.J.P. Taylor, *The Struggle for Mastery in Europe 1848–1918* (OUP, 1954), D. Thomson, *Europe since Napoleon* (Pelican, 1966) and A. Wood, *Europe 1815–1945* (Longman, 1964).

(d) Essay-writing skills
Almost all exams contain at least some essay questions and in many cases the ability to write an historical essay is regarded as the main, or even sole, criterion for examination success. To assist in the development

of essay writing skills, I have included a number of essay titles at the end of each chapter and several exercises designed specifically to develop the skills required in essay writing. Before embarking on these, it is worth noting that almost all essay titles (especially in examinations) fall into one of four categories. Your ability to identify these separate types of essay, and to construct answers according to their different needs, will therefore be important. The four types are:

(1) 'List' questions that require you to list, usually, causes and/or effects of a particular event or series of events. For example, they may ask you to 'account for' (list the *reasons*) the outbreak of war in 1914, 'explain' why there were revolutions in Russia in 1917 or identify the 'effects' or 'consequences' of Fascist rule in Italy. This type of question requires a series of paragraphs that put forward a number, or 'list', of the different reasons, effects etc.

(2) 'Yes/No' questions that ask you to consider a particular judgement or point of view and decide whether or not you agree with it. Often, these questions are the easiest to identify as they can, logically, be answered by the words 'yes' or 'no'. They are sometimes disguised by the word 'Discuss', which is used as an alternative to 'Do you agree?'. For instance, you may be asked to 'discuss' the view that 'the rise of Hitler was primarily the result of the depression' or whether you 'agree' that 'Austria-Hungary was doomed by the nationalities problem'. These questions require you to consider all the arguments that support the view expressed (the 'Yes' arguments), and all those that refute it (the 'No' arguments) and then draw some conclusions.

(3) 'Importance' questions: these ask you to consider the importance or significance of a particular event or person, and usually include one of these two words in the title, though they are also disguised as 'To what extent ...'. For example, you might be asked to consider the 'significance' of the Spanish Civil War in the international affairs or the 1930s, or the extent to which Hitler was responsible for the outbreak of World War II. (In these terms, they are very similar to Yes/No type questions.) Importance questions are slightly harder than the other categories, in that they require you not only to identify the ways in which the person/event *was* important, but also in what ways he/it was *not* important and, logically, *what else* was of importance. They therefore require a three-part answer, whereas the other types require one and two parts respectively.

(4) 'Compare and/or contrast' questions: these used to be much favoured by examiners, but seem to be going out of fashion now. These ask you to compare and/or contrast two people or two countries or events. For example, they may ask you to 'compare Russia in 1923 and 1937' or compare and contrast 'socialism in France and Germany before the Great War'. They (obviously) require an answer that points out both similarities and differences.

Obviously, this analysis does not cover all eventualities, but the vast majority of essay questions fall into one of these categories. Once they have been identified, you can write the answer appropriate to the particuular type of question. Nearly all the essays included in the exercises in this book have been written with these categories in mind, and can be identified with one of them.

Essay planning is vital to successful essay writing. To aid this, you will find a number of exercises and schemes outlined in this book. In particular, the essay planning exercise at the end of the chapter IV (page 87) should give you some ideas in the early stages of your study.

I Austria-Hungary 1890–1914

1. Introduction

For centuries, Central Europe had been dominated by Austria-Hungary. Maps 1 and 2 illustrate the extent of this mighty Empire. Almost fifty million people, from the Adriatic coast to modern day Poland, and from the Swiss border to the Ukraine, lived under the rule of the Habsburg family. Yet while the other powers prospered, Austria-Hungary foundered. Politicians and observers both inside and outside the Empire spoke and wrote constantly of its impending downfall. In 1848–9, a revolt in Hungary had been suppressed with great difficulty, while defeat in Northern Italy in 1859 had forced the Emperor to make concessions to minority national groups. Modern historians too write of the 'weakness' of the Empire, and some have coupled it with Turkey, 'the sick man of Europe'. The study of the Habsburg Empire therefore provides the historian with an opportunity to consider the concept of the 'weakness' of a state.

The strength or weakness of the Empire was of considerable importance, not only to its inhabitants but also to the other European powers. Territorially, it was the second largest power on the Continent after Russia. Geographically, it bordered the Mediterranean and encompassed vital trade routes, most notably that which followed the Danube across south-east Europe to Constantinople. Most importantly, Austria-Hungary bordered the Balkans. By 1900, this was the only area of Europe whose political future remained uncertain; the rest of Europe was controlled by established powers within agreed and settled frontiers. Parts of the Balkans were still under Turkish rule *(see Map 3)*; most observers were convinced that this would soon be ended and those parts freed for the taking. The rest was made up of 'new' states which had gained their independence from Turkey during the nineteenth century. The governments of these new states of Greece, Serbia and Bulgaria were not firmly established and their attachments to the existing great powers were uncertain. Austria-Hungary's interests in the Balkans were twofold. Firstly, she was determined to maintain and expand her influence there and to win her share of the Turkish Empire. Secondly, if she too weakened, there would be an opportunity for the Balkan states, especially Serbia, to expand northwards and seize parts of Austria-Hungary. These associations between the Habsburg Empire and the Balkans were to prove crucial for all Europe.

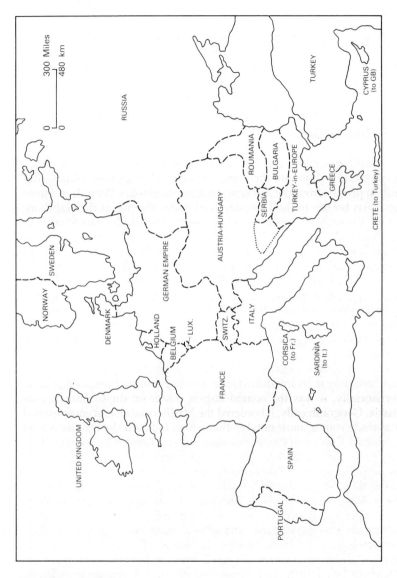

Map 1 Europe in 1890

The governance of Austria-Hungary highlights two problems shared in varying degrees by other European powers at this time. The Empire was ruled by a traditional monarchy in a time and place that was modernizing rapidly; to what extent could such a form of government survive? Secondly, and more acutely, it was faced by the problem of ruling many people of many nationalities. Its handling or mishandling of this situation was to prove a second crucial issue for all Europe.

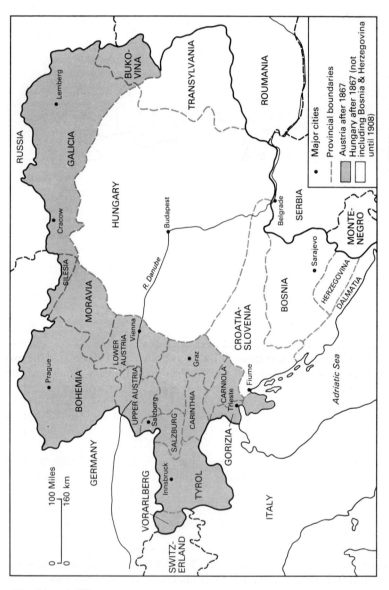

Map 2 Austria-Hungary

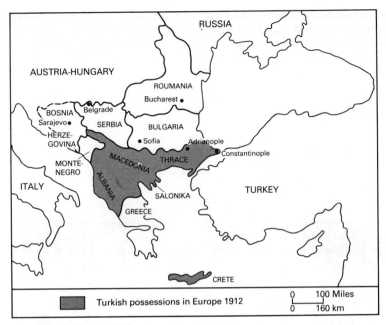

Map 3 The Balkans in 1912

2. The Constitutional Organization of the State

Until 1867, the Habsburgs survived the many challenges to their authority over the Empire. The Magyars, who lived in the Eastern half of the Empire, were increasingly dissatisfied with this situation and campaigned for greater autonomy (control over their own affairs). As a result, the 'Ausgleich', or Compromise, of 1867 was drawn up. This created the two separate but equal kingdoms of Austria and Hungary, known as the 'Dual Monarchy'. Austria was to be ruled by an Emperor and Hungary by a King. The King and Emperor were in fact to be a single person, Franz Josef. The constitutional arrangements (summarized in Diagram 1) were complicated, to allow for Hungary's new autonomy while maintaining the ancient links.

The old Empire was divided along the river Leitha and each half had its own Ministers and Parliament with control over all matters within their boundaries. In Austria the Patent of 1861 remained in force: the lower house had 203 members elected by a complicated four-class system through which one class, the wealthy landowners, were assured a majority. Franchise qualifications deprived the poorer classes of the right to vote. A reform of 1896 extended the franchise and increased the membership of the lower house to 425. Only in 1907 was universal manhood suffrage introduced. In Hungary too the franchise was restricted and the 453 deputies were elected only by Magyar taxpayers until the reforms of

1908. These provided for universal suffrage, but also included a literacy qualification, so that only those who could read and write Magyar were entitled to vote. As a result, less than 7% of the population had the right to vote, and the domination of the Magyars remained absolute.

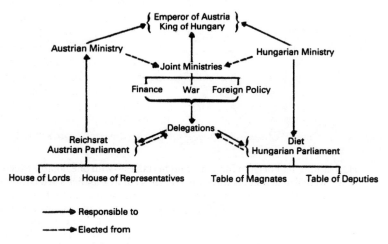

Diagram 1. The constitutional organization of Austria-Hungary

The Joint Ministers controlled foreign policy and war. The third Joint Ministry, finance, was only to administer the budgets required by the other two. The Joint Ministers were responsible to the two Delegations. Each Kingdom provided sixty delegates, twenty from the upper house, forty from the lower. The Delegations met separately though in the same city—Vienna one year, Budapest the next. The Joint Ministers explained their policies and financial needs to the Delegations, whose approval was required in order to direct the two parliaments to provide the necessary finance. Austria, the wealthier of the two, provided 70% of the Joint Budget. The Delegations communicated with each other in writing and met only when a vote was called. This never happened. The Austrian Delegation always consisted of a number of nationalities while the Hungarian one was wholly Magyar. Consequently, the Magyars needed only one vote from the Austrian Delegation to be sure of winning any vote. As they were always certain of getting this, the Joint Ministers made certain of Magyar support before approaching the Austrian Delegation. There was no joint Prime Minister or Cabinet.

The Magyars found little to satisfy them in these new arrangements. They disliked the common army whose German insignia and words of command were a reminder of Austrian domination. Equally, they feared Russia as their one-time conqueror and leading Slav power and felt that the common foreign policy was not sufficiently anti-Russian. Since the Austrians were also dissatisfied and hoped one day to reassert their old authority over the whole Empire, conflict was inevitable.

3. Political Background

(a) The Emperor

Much depended on the ability of the Emperor to maintain stability and order both in and between his two Kingdoms. Franz Josef had become Emperor in 1848, at the age of eighteen, when his lunatic uncle, Ferdinand I, was persuaded to abdicate. Franz Josef had an unshakeable belief in his divine right to rule over an empire that was his dynastic inheritance and which he believed had been given personally to the Habsburgs by God. Since his power was divine and in no way derived from his people, he had no responsibility to obey the 'General Will' of the people. His powers were limited by the arrangements of 1867, but he still had the right to declare and conclude war, call and dismiss Parliaments and appoint ministers. Elliott, in *Fall of Eagles*, describes his approach to life.

> His training had been in the army and his tastes—with one notable exception—were frugal and his ways austere. He slept in a soldier's bed beside a wooden camp washstand. He rose at dawn. His mind was as efficient and limited as a quarter-master's, his sense of protocol and authority absolute. His mother told him that his task was to restore and maintain order and discipline, and he devoted his life to it. His relaxations were music, hunting and reading the Army List. The exception to it all was his lifelong lechery; he was still capable of rape in his sixties, and in his youth his mother encouraged promiscuity to avoid the danger of an unsuitable permanent liaison. In all other circumstances he was remote: shy, sensitive, correct, polite and unattainable.

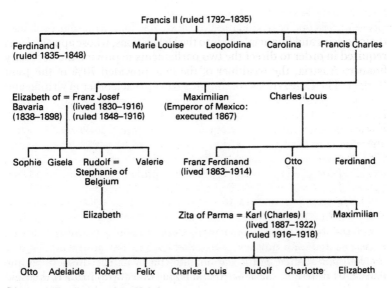

Diagram 2. Family tree of the Habsburgs

His marriage to the beautiful Elizabeth of Bavaria in 1854 turned into tragedy; she loathed the life of the court and left her husband, who adored her, as often as possible. Her own life ended tragically in 1898 when she was assassinated by an Italian anarchist. The couple had four children, three girls who could not inherit the Empire (one of them died young in any case) and a boy named Rudolf. Rudolf turned out to be an unsuitable heir; he drank and took drugs, and inherited his father's sexual appetite. In 1889 he died at Mayerling in a suicide pact with a lover. This made Franz Josef's nephew, Franz Ferdinand, heir to the throne. He was a distant and unpopular man. He was an advocate of the Trialist solution to the Empire's problems—the creation of a third kingdom of the Slavs in the South-west of the country. He therefore had few supporters among the traditionally-minded Germans and Magyars. He had married a Czech, Sophie Chotek, who was not considered sufficiently high born for their children to be heirs to the throne (hence the marriage is known as a morganatic one). The Emperor's family did little to ease his problems.

(b) The nationalities problem

The nationalities problem dominated Habsburg politics throughout the period 1890–1914. There was rivalry and hostility between the Austrians, who were racially German, and the Hungarians, who were Magyars. The Magyars hated being ruled by the Emperor of Austria and regarded the 1867 Ausgleich with contempt. They were eager to form a completely independent country. Until they could do so, they intended to wield as much power as they could through the Joint Ministries and the Delegations.

Racial group	Austrian half	Hungarian half
Germans	9 950 266	2 037 435
Magyars	10 974	10 050 575
Czechs	6 435 983	
Poles	4 967 984	
Ruthenes	3 518 854	472 587
Italians	768 422	
Roumanians	275 115	2 949 032
Slovaks		1 967 970
Slovenes ⎫ South	1 252 940	
Serbs ⎬ Slavs		1 106 471
Croats ⎭	783 334	1 833 162
Others		469 255
Approximate total:	28 000 000	21 000 000

Table 1. Distribution of population of Austria-Hungary according to 1910 Census

The main feature of the nationalities problem was the number and variety of different national groups living in the Empire. Table 1 enumerates the different races; this is based on the 1910 census, which obtained its figures on the basis of language and so probably exaggerated the number of Germans and Magyars. Diagram 3 shows the approximate location of the different races; obviously a more detailed map would show more accurately the confusion of races in some areas.

The nineteenth century was the age of the nation state when each separate nationality was being organized into its own state. The Greeks, Germans, Italians and, to a degree, the Magyars, had all achieved this by 1890. Many Czechs and Poles believed their numbers, traditions and location were such that they too should have their own state. At the very least, they demanded a measure of independence from the central government. For example, they wanted to have national universities and to use their own language in local government. Other races, especially the Serbs, Croats and Slovenes, all of whom were of Slav origin, wanted not only civil rights but also the opportunity to join with another country, Serbia, to form a South Slav federation. Others, particularly the Italians and Roumanians, were, like the Serbs, minority groups with an existing state to whom they could look for leadership. In addition, many groups within the different races had different aims; for example, some Croats were contented citizens of the Habsburg Empire, others wanted to join with Serbia while others wanted their own Croat state. The Emperor was therefore faced by a range of complex demands and problems.

Diagram 3. Location of nationalities within the Austro-Hungarian Empire

To complicate the issue further, many areas were of mixed population. In the large province of Bohemia, the population of seven millions was

13

divided approximately into 63% Czechs and 37% Germans; if the official language was Czech, a large minority would be dissatisfied, if it was German, the majority would be. In Bukovina, with a population of less than a million, 39% were Ruthenian, 34% Roumanian, 21% German, 5% Polish and 1% Magyar. In such areas, 'fair' legislation was impossible.

The approach to the complexities of the nationalities problem differed in the two halves of the Empire. In Austria, the Germans were outnumbered about 2 to 1 by other nationalities. In the Reichsrat, representatives were usually chosen on the basis of nationality rather than political party. In the 1911 Reichsrat, after universal suffrage had been introduced, there were 185 Germans, eighty-two Czechs, eighty-one Social Democrats, seventy-one Poles, thirty-seven Serbs and Croats, thirty Ruthenes, sixteen Italians, five Rumanians and nine others. Even before universal suffrage, Austrian Ministries were usually coalitions. Count Taaffe, Prime Minister from 1879 until 1893, was German and had Czech and Polish support while Count Badeni, Prime Minister in the late 1890s, was a Pole with Czech and German support. Because of their numbers, the Czechs and Poles were usually represented in the government and won concessions. For example, the Badeni Language Ordinance of 1897 gave parity between German and other languages. In turn, those races that were never in the government, especially the Serbs and Croats, believed their interests to be neglected. Generally, the Austrian Germans were tolerant of the different races over which they ruled.

The Magyars had an altogether different policy. In 1868 a liberal Nationalities Law had been passed, allowing the minorities considerable rights of language and custom. This was soon ignored and the minority races were suppressed. The Magyars ensured their own domination. At the turn of the century, they provided over 90% of state officials, local government officers, doctors and judges, although they were in a minority in the whole population. In the Diet of 1910, they occupied 405 of the 413 seats in the House of Representatives. The opposition claimed that troops had been used in 380 constituencies. In 1894 the Roumanian National Party was dissolved as 'unconstitutional'. At the same time, a policy of 'Magyarization' was undertaken to bring the minority races into line. This was especially true in the field of education. Magyar was made compulsory in all schools in 1883, even if there were no Magyars among either staff or pupils. The Apponyi Law of 1907 made teachers liable to dismissal if their pupils did not know Magyar. Outside schools, local traditions, festivals and costumes were suppressed, if necessary by force. Whereas the Austrians allowed a degree of freedom and representation, the Magyars did not.

4. Political History 1890–1914

The detailed political history of this period is extremely complicated. At any time, there were two prime Ministers and governments as well as the Joint Ministries and the King-Emperor himself. He often chose not to replace ministers for some months, while in Hungary there were occasions when the King's appointee was opposed by a Parliamentary leader. Consequently, it is not possible to make a simple list of political rulers or to follow chronologically the experience of the different ministries. Instead, this section examines the major themes and crises of the period.

Although the constitutional arrangements give the appearance of democratic government, Austria-Hungary remained an autocracy in many respects. A large police force was widely in evidence and the press, though not censored, was often bribed and bullied into loyalty. Personal freedoms, such as the right of association and the right to trial by jury, were limited. The Reichsrat's power over ministers was minimal, since ministers owed their loyalty more to the Emperor than to a Parliamentary majority. In any case, the restricted franchises ensured the preeminence of the aristocracy. The 1896 Reforms in Austria had added over five million voters; yet they had only seventy-two deputies while the other 1·7 million voters had 353 deputies.

Austrian governments were plagued by the constant rivalries between the nationalities. Until 1893, Count Taaffe maintained the support of German, Polish and Czech conservatives (the 'Iron Ring') by a series of minor concessions, such as additional language rights and local government posts. The opposition of the more radical Young Czechs, who won thirty-seven seats in the 1891 election, led to upheavals, and military law was declared in Prague in 1893. Taaffe considered extending the franchise, in the belief that the masses would be conservative, but the idea so alarmed his conservative supporters that Franz Josef dismissed him.

There followed two years of confusion. The Emperor decided not to appoint his own minister, but to allow Parliament to agree on a leader from its own ranks. This proved impossible as the different nationalities could not come to agreement. The chief argument was between the Germans and the Slovenes over the language to be used in the grammar school at Celje (Cilli). If Slovene was allowed there, the Germans, eager to uphold their influence in Slovenia and to make as few concessions as possible to the minorities, would vote against the government. If it was not, then the Slovenes, supported by the other Slavs, would do so. The issue dominated politics in 1894 and led to the fall of the government in June 1895 when a grant was given for Slovene classes. Franz Josef decided to choose his own man again.

Count Badeni, the Polish governor of Galicia, became Prime Minister. Like Taaffe, he relied on the Poles, Germans and Czechs for support. In 1897 he decreed that from 1901 both Czech and German should be used in the Bohemian civil service. This would give the Czechs a virtual monopoly since most educated Czechs spoke both languages whereas few Germans spoke Czech. Moreover, the Slovenes demanded similar rights. The German Nationalist Party was furious; ink pots were thrown in the Reichsrat and there was rioting in the streets. Badeni was dismissed and in 1899 his language laws dropped; there were riots in Czech areas. Badeni's successor, Ernst von Körber, did not even attempt to rule through Parliament. Instead, he invoked article 14 of the 1867 Constitution and ruled by decree until 1907. In that year, universal suffrage was introduced. The Germans lost heavily, and Ruthenes, Poles, Czechs and Slovenes all gained seats.

Two political parties stood out among the twenty-eight that were now represented. The Social Democratic party, founded in 1888, had won eleven seats in the Reichsrat even before the electoral reform of 1907. Thereafter, it was the largest single party with over eighty seats, and was especially strong in the North of the country, among the largest industrial centres. However, it proved difficult to uphold the idea of international brotherhood in a political climate dominated by nationalism. As early as 1910 the Czechs broke away to form their own party, which soon joined with other Czech deputies in creating the disturbances that led to the proroguement of the Reichsrat in the years before the Great War. The Christian Socialists, the other leading party, had been founded in the 1890s by Karl Lueger, mayor of Vienna. They drew their support from Austria itself and were opposed to liberalism and Marxism. Anti-semitism was also one of their platforms, but Lueger himself had said 'I will decide who is Jewish'—poor, patriotic Jews were quite safe. Christian Socialism was essentially an attempt by lower-middle-class Germans to put their case against the capitalists, the non-Catholics and the enemies of the Emperor. Nationality, however, remained the key difference between the deputies.

In Hungary, three issues dominated internal politics. The first was whether or not to permit civil marriage, an issue of considerable importance at the time, and one that distracted politicians from other matters. Secondly, the policy of 'Magyarization' was continued. By far the most important problem, however, was the relationship with Austria. The economic arrangements of the 'Ausgleich' were renewed every ten years, which led to considerable argument in 1897. The Liberal party, led first by Count Koloman Tisza and then by his son Stephen, supported the 1867 compromise, and sought to strengthen Hungary within it. The Independence party, led by Francis Kossuth (son of Louis Kossuth), opposed the Ausgleich and sought greater autonomy. In 1903, this party refused to support an increase in the size and budget of the joint army unless Magyar insignia and words of command were authorized for Magyar regiments. This was tantamount to demanding a separate Hungarian army and was rejected outright by Franz Josef, who was already faced by decree government in Austria. In the elections of 1905, the Independence party won a majority. Since they still refused to approve an increase in the army, Franz Josef appointed his own Prime Minister, Baron Fejerváry, and sent troops to disperse the Hungarian

Parliament. In this moment of truth, the Independents were unable to mobilize enough support to oppose this 'royal dictatorship'. Negotiations followed, in which the King threatened to introduce universal suffrage unless the Independents gave way. Since this would give the vote to millions of non-Magyars, and thus destroy the Magyar dominance, they surrendered and approved the army bill. Two years later, in 1908, universal suffrage was introduced, but it was based on Magyar literacy tests and so enabled the nobility to maintain their domination. Tisza once again became Prime Minister and in the years before the war the old relationship was restored.

1889	Suicide of Crown Prince Rudolf
1891	Renewal of Triple Alliance with Germany and Italy
	Gains in elections by Young Czech party
1893	Resignation of Count Taaffe as Austrian Prime Minister
1894	Parliamentary despite over language rights in Celje
1896	Franchise reform in Austria
1897	Badeni's language laws, followed by demonstrations and Badeni's resignation
	Agreement with Russia to maintain the status quo in the Balkans
1898	Assassination of the Empress Elizabeth at Geneva
1899	Repeal of Badeni's language reforms
1900	Körber Prime Minister of Austria
1903 ⎧	Constitutional crises. In Austria, parliamentary government proves impossible
⎪	and decree laws passed. In Hungary, the refusal of the Independence Party to
⎨	approve the military budget and their successes in the 1905 election leads to
⎪	the appointment of a non-parliamentary ministry and troops in
1906 ⎩	Budapest.
1906	Opening of 'Pig War' with Serbia
1907	Universal suffrage introduced in Austria
1908	Universal suffrage, with literacy qualifications, introduced in Hungary
	Annexation of Bosnia and Herzegovina
	New commercial agreement with Serbia ends 'Pig War'
1912	First Balkan War
1913	Second Balkan War
1914	Assassination of Franz Ferdinand at Sarajevo
	Outbreak of World War I

Table 2. Date chart of chief events in Austria-Hungary 1890–1914

The other issue in Hungary was the position of the Croats. Since they were in such an overwhelming majority in the south-west corner of the kingdom, they had been given their own provincial Diet and far more autonomy than any other minority in Hungary. Their position there was complicated by the fact that some of their number were in Austria, and by rivalry with the Serbs. While the Croats were Roman Catholics and looked to the West, the Serbs were Orthodox and in many respects almost Eastern. In 1903 there were demonstrations following the Emperor's refusal to meet petitioners from Dalmatia and Istria. In 1905 a conference demanded the unification of Croat provinces in the two halves of the Empire. When the Emperor dissolved the provincial Diet by decree, Croatian hostility was assured. Croats increasingly looked to Serbia for leadership against the Empire, and in so doing gave some credence to the belief, widely held in the Austrian government, that Serbia was plotting to seize Croatia. Following the annexation of Bosnia-Herzegovina in 1908 *(see pages 139–142)*, the idea of a South Slav kingdom was given extra impetus, and many Croats were prepared to settle their differences with the Serbs in exchange for freedom from Habsburg rule. By the time of the Balkan wars, Croatian discontent had become a matter of international diplomacy rather than internal politics.

5. Economic History

The economy of Austria-Hungary was dualist. That is to say, it was clearly divided between an industrial area and an agricultural sector, roughly corresponding to the two Kingdoms, Austria being industrial and Hungary agricultural. In such circumstances, the union of the two countries was advantageous, since it facilitated trade between the two sectors. However, the economic arrangements were reviewed every ten years, giving each side an opportunity to press for more favourable terms of trade.

In Austria, there were a number of centres of industry that developed rapidly in the nineteenth century. Bohemia had large deposits of coal and iron ore, both of which were exploited in large quantities. Almost a third of the population there was employed in industry in 1890—the highest proportion for any area in the Empire. Further south, there were considerable cotton and textile industries, and timber resources were exploited throughout Austria. Vienna itself was an industrial centre, but predominantly of light industry. Here were situated the Zeiss optical industry, the Porsche car works and a number of small arms factories.

In contrast, Hungary was almost exclusively agricultural. In 1890, it was estimated that almost 95% of Magyars derived their living from agriculture. The land was generally owned in enormous estates, one of which, belonging to the Esterhazy family, spread over more than half a million acres. The landowners had little desire to develop new methods, and were united in their hostility to industrial development, with the result that the vast majority of wage earning peasants lived in terrible poverty. Illiteracy was the norm and infant mortality among the highest in Europe. Hungary has been likened to the Southern States of the USA in the nineteenth century; in each, a small ruling oligarchy lived a life of luxury in splendid mansions while others laboured on their behalf. In Hungary, however, the crop was grain, not cotton. In 1900, Hungary was the third largest exporter of grain in the world, behind only the USA and Russia.

This dualist pattern is perhaps too great a simplification. In the first place, there was considerable agricultural activity in Austria; only about 20% of the population lived in towns of over 5000 in 1890, leaving the vast majority in the countryside. Secondly, Hungary was not totally non-industrial. In 1893 there were some 400 factories in Budapest (compared with forty in 1846), where flour milling, distilling and ship building were the chief industries. In 1906, half the equipment for London's Piccadilly Underground line came from Budapest, while Hungary was unchallenged as the world's leading manufacturer of electric milking machines. So although dualism was the chief feature of the economy of the Habsburg Empire, there were considerable exceptions to the overall pattern.

Two important questions remain: how 'backward' was the economy at the turn of the century? And how did her production levels relate to those of the rest of the world? Statistics for Austria-Hungary are notoriously difficult to find, and the use of those for the successor states is hazardous as they are eager to show both the necessity and achievements of nationalism. Tables 3, 4 and 5 provide some indications of Austria-Hungary's place in the world economy.

USA	5·10
Great Britain	4·01
Germany	3·85
France	1·59
Austria-Hungary	*1·17*
Italy	0·35
Russia	0·32

Table 3. Coal production per head of population (tons) in 1913

USA	27·8
Germany	14·1
Great Britain	9·1
France	4·1
Russia	3·0
Austria-Hungary	*2·1*
Italy	0·6

Table 4. Pig iron consumption (millions of tons) in 1910

Agriculture:	Wheat 39%	Potatoes 47%	Sugar beet 21% in Austria 180% in Hungary
Industry:	Soft coal 85%	Iron 144%	Steel 133% (261% in in Bohemia)

Table 5. Percentage increases in production in Austria-Hungary 1893–1913

Austria-Hungary was not in the front rank of world producers at this time, but at the same time she was in most respects ahead of the weakest European countries, Italy and Russia, although Russia was rapidly catching up by 1914. In 1901, there were over 36 000 kilometres of railway track in Austria-Hungary, compared with 49 000 in Russia, an area five times as large. In addition, Table 5 illustrates that the period before the Great War was one of considerable economic expansion, especially in heavy industry.

The economic differences between the two halves of the Empire only served to exacerbate their political differences. As far as the Austrians were concerned, the agricultural areas of Hungary were a burden on their resources. The regionalism of the economy also highlighted some of the nationalities grievances. For example, the Czechs who formed the bulk of the population in industrial Bohemia could justifiably claim that they would be better off independent, since they could then take full advantage of their wealth.

6. Foreign Policy

The chief aim of Austro-Hungarian foreign policy was to ensure the influence of the Habsburgs in the Balkans and, simultaneously, minimize Russian influence there (see Map 3). This did not necessarily mean that Austria-Hungary intended actually to take land from the Turkish Empire, but rather to make sure that any new regimes established there were friendly towards her. If the opportunity to take land arose, so much the better. Since Russia's intentions were identical, a great power conflict was perhaps inevitable, although each endeavoured to conceal their intentions and in 1897 signed an agreement to maintain the status quo in the Balkans.

The Balkan problem was complicated by the rise of the Serbian state, which by 1900 was acting quite independently of any great power. Serbia represented the two things most feared by Austria-Hungary—the possibility of Russian influence in the Balkans and Slav nationalism in the north Balkans, which included the southern part of the Empire. In the period after 1903 Serbian support for Croats and Slovenes, as well as Serbs, in the Empire was growing, at least in the minds of Habsburg politicians.

To assist her in her opposition to Russian and Serbian influence, and to help her maintain her world power position, Austria-Hungary relied on the friendship of Germany. This was sealed by two treaties before 1890—the Dreikaiserbund of 1873 with Germany and Russia and the Triple Alliance of 1882 with Germany and Italy. By the latter, Austria-Hungary and Germany agreed to come to each other's assistance in the event of a Russian attack on either of them. The balance of the German alliance changed considerably during the period; whereas in the 1870s Germany was glad of the friendship of an established world power, by 1914 Austria-Hungary was almost wholly dependent on the help of Europe's greatest military power.

What of the Empire's relations with the other powers? Italy, as a co-signatory of the Triple Alliance, should have been friendly. However, there was considerable disagreement over the treatment of Italians living in the Empire and over Austria-Hungary's control of the South Tyrol. Britain's attitude was dictated by two factors—as Germany's closest ally, Austria-Hungary was treated with some suspicion; secondly, the Balkans might threaten European peace and therefore Britain was interested in Austrian actions there. France's attitude was similar, though her consistent hostility towards Germany made her less friendly. With these factors in mind, Austro-Hungarian actions in the Balkans can be examined.

In 1903 the pro-Russian Karadjordjević dynasty came to power in Serbia. This, combined with the threat of Serbia acting as the centre of South Slav opposition to the monarchy *and* the possibility of a victorious war bringing prestige to the Crown, led Austro-Hungarian politicians to adopt an aggressively hostile attitude towards Serbia. In 1906, the existing tariff arrangements between the two countries were not renewed. As Serbia's main export of pigs was excluded from the Empire, this was known as the 'Pig War'. This lasted until 1908 when a new commercial treaty was signed which committed Serbia to higher imports from the Empire. In 1906, Aehrenthal became Joint Foreign Minister. He was keen to annex the provinces of Bosnia and Herzegovina which had been occupied and governed by the Empire since 1878 but still technically belonged to Turkey. Annexation would enable Austria-Hungary to suppress Slav opposition in the provinces more easily and pierce Serbian pride by ending her hopes of winning them. If annexation led to war with Serbia, so much the better, since the Serbian army would be no match for Austria-Hungary, provided that Russia did not join the conflict. When Aehrenthal won Izvolsky's (the Russian Foreign Minister) approval for the annexation in return for a promise to support Russia's claim to be allowed to use the Straits, the stage was set.

On 5 October 1908 Aehrenthal announced the annexation of the provinces. This precipitated an international crisis, since it was tantamount to seizing the territory of another power. Moreover, the Russian government denied Izvolsky's deal and threatened military support for Serbia. Germany's support for Austria-Hungary was therefore crucial; her promise of military assistance made both Serbia and Russia unlikely to risk war, and both accepted Austria-Hungary's action. Turkey was paid compensation and the provinces became a part of the Empire.

The annexation did not have the desired effect of establishing once and for all Habsburg domination in the north Balkans. It served instead to bring the conflict with Russia into the open and make each power more determined than ever to win the next round. To this end, Austria-Hungary signed a secret treaty with Bulgaria and war plans were drawn up. Russia was equally determined not to be pushed around by Germany and Austria-Hungary again. Even more importantly, Serbia openly supported South Slav opposition to the Habsburgs and did nothing to stop terrorist organizations forming in her towns to operate in the Southern provinces of the Empire. The most famous of these was the

Black Hand, founded in 1911 in Serbia for operations in Bosnia, where a number of Imperial officials were assassinated. Moreover, Serbia's power and prestige grew with her victories in the First Balkan War *(see page 142)*. When Bulgaria attacked Serbia in the Second Balkan War, partly as a result of the encouragement of Austro-Hungarian diplomats, Serbia was again victorious and her prestige reached new heights. By 1914, almost all Austro-Hungarian politicians, with the exception of Tisza, were convinced of the need for a preventive war against Serbia; Princip's assassination of Franz Ferdinand at Sarajevo provided them with just the excuse they sought (see Chapter VI).

7. Bibliography

The standard English history of Austria-Hungary is *The Habsburg Monarchy, 1809–1918* by A.J.P. Taylor (Hamish Hamilton, 1960) and this will provide the detail required. Other useful works include O. Jaszi, *The Dissolution of the Habsburg Monarchy* (Univ. of Chicago, 1929), A.J. May, *The Habsburg Monarchy 1867–1914* (Harvard University Press, 1960) and C.A. Macartney, *The Habsburg Empire 1790–1918* (Weidenfeld & Nicolson, 1971).

8. Discussion Points and Exercises

A   *This section consists of questions that might be used for discussion (or written answers) as a way of expanding on the chapter and testing understanding of it:*
1   Why were the Balkans a focus of European attention by 1900?
2   How suitable a person does Franz Josef seem as Emperor of Austria-Hungary?
3   What do you understand by the 'nationalities problem'?
4   How important an issue was universal suffrage in the Empire?
5   Which policy seems to have been more successful—Austrian toleration of the minorities or the Hungarian policy of 'Magyarization'?
6   Why were the South Slavs a greater problem to the government than larger nationalities like the Czechs and Poles?
7   How dualist was the economy?
8   Why were Austro-Hungarian politicians so hostile to Serbia?
9   What were the arguments in favour and against the annexation of Bosnia and Herzegovina?
10   How did the Balkan Wars affect Austria-Hungary's attitude to the Balkans?

B   *This section is intended to illustrate some of the problems faced by the government:*
1   Write a report for the Emperor outlining the problems caused by the multiplicity of nationalities in the Empire and suggesting possible solutions to them. Include maps, charts and diagrams.

2 Write a report for the Austro-Hungarian Foreign Office in 1897 examining Austria-Hungary's position in the Balkans and mapping out likely developments for the next ten years, not only in the Balkan states but also in the attitude of the great powers, including Turkey, to them.

C *This section suggests two ways in which you might compare Austria-Hungary with other European countries in this period:*
1 Compare the constitutional organization of Austria-Hungary with that of France.
2 Compare the economic condition of Austria-Hungary in this period with that of Germany and Italy in tabular form.

D *Essay questions:*
1 'Of all the nationalities, the Magyars caused the most problems.' Do you agree?
2 Examine the motives & achievements of Austro-Hungarian policies towards the Balkans from 1890 to 1914.

9. Austria-Hungary: Strength or Weakness?

The introduction to this chapter suggested that Austria-Hungary provided the historian with an opportunity to consider the concept of the strength of a nation. This exercise is intended to do this. Throughout, you should consider the features and potential strength and weakness of a nation in the decade before the Great War.

(a) On the left hand side are listed some of the important features of any nation at that time, on which its prosperity and survival will depend. Add other features that you would consider come into this category. You could also reorder them, putting those features you consider most important at the top of the list, and so on down.
(b) In the two right hand columns state what you would expect to find in each a strong and a weak nation; often, these will simply be the converse of each other. This has been done for the first feature, the army *(see overleaf)*.

Draw three columns as below.

Features	Strong nation	Weak nation
Army	Numerous (?) Well-equipped and trained United and loyal Able officers, selected on merit	Small (?) Ill-equipped and trained Disunited and disloyal Incompetent officers, selected by wealth?
Other military factors		
Agricultural organization and production		
Balance of trade		
Suffrage		
Censorship and repression		

(c) Now make brief notes on Austria-Hungary under each of the headings in the first column, and compare these notes with the features you have listed in the 'weak' and 'strong' columns to reach a decision about the state of Austria-Hungary.

(d) Use these notes and charts to write an essay in answer to the question, 'Was Austria-Hungary a strong nation in the decade before the Great War?'

II France 1890–1914

1. Introduction

France is often regarded as the poor relation of the great powers in this period. Although her economy did not match that of Germany or Britain, she remained well ahead of most other powers in this field. In other respects, such as the size of her army and the expansion of her Empire, France remained well in the fore-front of world affairs. The image of apparent weakness is the result of the dominance of a single issue for much of the period; that issue was the 'Dreyfus affair', which started in 1894 and was not ended until twelve years later. Because of its obvious significance to the era, a considerable part of this chapter, including a documentary exercise, is devoted to the affair.

2. The Constitutional Organization of the State

The Third Republic of France was proclaimed on 5 September 1870, following the defeat of France by Prussia at Sedan in the midst of civil war between the people of Paris, who formed a 'commune' in 1871, and the army of the government of the National Assembly at Versailles. In May 1871 the government troops, led by General Gallifet, defeated the Parisians, some 30 000 of whom died during the struggle. Thereafter the more right wing National Assembly government, led first by Thiers and then by the monarchist Marshal MacMahon, was accepted as the government of the Third Republic. The Republic thus came into being under a traditional right-wing government whose first action had been to suppress an uprising by the left.

There was no formal written constitution by which the Republic was governed. Instead, a number of laws were passed, mainly in 1875, which provided most of the offices and instruments of government. These laws for the government of the Republic were passed by a National Assembly that contained a majority of anti-Republicans.

As head of state there was to be a President. He was to be chosen every seven years by the members of the legislature, not by the general public. He was given the power to appoint and dismiss ministers, negotiate treaties, suggest laws to the legislature and, with the approval of the Upper house (Senate), dissolve the Lower house (Chamber). Although he did not have the power of veto over legislation, his powers were very considerable. In fact, however, tradition and the people who held the office made it more of a figurehead than the monarchists, who framed the law, had intended.

The legislature was to consist of the Senate and the Chamber of Deputies. At first, the Senate had seventy-five life members chosen by the Assembly, which dissolved itself after passing these laws, and 255 members elected by an electoral college. Later, however, all members of the Senate were chosen by this body. The Chamber started life with 526 members, which had risen to 586 by 1914. These were elected by universal male suffrage in single member constituencies, except for the periods 1885–9 and 1919–28. If no candidate won a majority in the first ballot held, then a second ballot was held, thus assuring that each deputy elected could claim to have the majority of his constituents behind him.

Government was to be executed by a Council of Ministers (similar to the British Cabinet) who needed the support of the Senate and Chamber to govern. There was no 'Prime Minister', but the President of the Council of Ministers is normally referred to as such. He was appointed by the President, and then chose the members of his council for himself.

3. Political Background: Republicans against Monarchists

On the 30 January 1875 the continued life of the Republic was assured when the National Assembly voted in favour of a successive elected Presidency. However, the measure was only carried by 353 votes to 352; in other words, it was almost the case that the Republic was ended and a monarchy restored within five years of its foundation. This close division between those in favour and those against the Republic is well shown by the voting figures practically throughout the period 1870–1914. There were many Frenchmen, and many politicians (or rather, deputies and senators—the word 'politicien' was regarded as an insult), who wanted to see a royal dynasty back in control of France. At first, they hoped to restore one of the two men who claimed a right to the throne—the Count of Chambord or the Count of Paris; but, despite brief flirtations with the idea, both of these refused to be put forward.

Later, the hopes of the monarchists centred on anyone who might provide the firm, old-fashioned leadership they wanted. Immediately before 1890 their hopes reached a peak with General Georges Boulanger. Paradoxically, Boulanger was appointed Minister of War in 1886 specifically because he was considered a supporter of the Republic. Indeed, he started work in a way most pleasing to Republicans, improving living conditions among the troops and sacking leading monarchist officers, such as the Duke of Aumale, the uncle of the Count of Paris. However, during 1887 he seemed to be growing in power and prestige. His supporters put his name forward as a candidate for a by-election in the Department of the Seine and, even though he was technically ineligible to stand, he won 100 000 votes. In January 1887 Bismarck had referred to him as the greatest obstacle to good relations between France and Germany (following an incident over an alleged French spy); this was excellent news to French right wingers, who loved to displease Bismarck. Indeed, they saw Boulanger as a possible leader of a campaign to regain the 'lost provinces' of Alsace and Lorraine, that had been taken by Germany in 1871. The government of Rouvier decided Boulanger was becoming too popular, and sent him to a military command in the Auvergne, well away from the centre of events. His departure was marked by a demonstration by Parisians at the station, trying to prevent his going.

In December 1887 the President (Grévy) and Prime Minister (Rouvier) were forced to resign following revelations that Grévy's son-in-law, Daniel Wilson, had been selling military honours and decorations. People could see only too clearly that a Republic allowed the 'wrong sort of people' into power; what was needed was someone who would provide firm, honourable leadership—someone like Boulanger. The Duchess of Uzès, a leading monarchist, sent 25 000 francs to Boulanger and 3 million to a National Committee of monarchists. With the prestige of the Republic so low, Boulanger's chances of seizing power for himself or a monarchist claimant seemed better than ever.

In March 1888 he resigned from the army, so making himself eligible for election and enabling him to concentrate on politics. Under the electoral system then in operation, it was possible for one man to stand and win in as many constituencies as he was able. So, during 1888, Boulanger won four by-elections. Then, in January 1889, he stood for election in the Department of the Seine and won 245 000 votes—a majority of 80 000. The one time heart of the Left and the Republic— Paris itself—had voted for the Nationalist/monarchist candidate, Boulanger. The streets of Paris were filled with people rejoicing at his victory, and many (members of the government included) expected him to march on the Elysée Palace and announce that he had taken over the government. Instead, for reasons best known to himself, he spent the night elsewhere in the company of his mistress, Madame de Bonnemain, and the threat to the Republic disintegrated. Later, he was charged with endangering national security, whereon, rather than appealing to his supporters and making an issue of the case, he fled to Brussels where he committed suicide over the grave of his mistress on 1 April 1891.

The details of this crisis well illustrate the problems of the Republic. Because there were so many people opposed to the idea of a President and ministers rather than a king, any error on the part of the officers of the Republic—like the Wilson Scandal—was used to recreate anti-Republican feeling. Equally, because it had made no attempt to regain the provinces lost to Germany, the Republic looked weak and 'true Frenchmen' would turn to those who preached revenge on the Germans. These two potential weaknesses of the Republic remained important throughout its life, and were exploited by its opponents.

In fact, the Boulanger crisis ended in profit not loss to the Republic, which entered the 1890s with more support than for many years. For Boulanger had faded to ridicule and, led by the Church, many monarchists turned to give their support to the Republic. This was the movement known as 'Ralliément'. It started on 12 November 1890 when Charles Cardinal Lavigerie, the head of the Church in French North Africa, when toasting French naval officers at Algiers said it was the duty of all citizens to 'rally' to support the government. These sentiments were echoed by other Churchmen, and with the support of the Church, traditionally an opponent of Republicanism and a bastion of monarchism, the officers of the Republic could look to the 1890s with renewed confidence.

4. Political History

(a) The 1890s
Despite its promising start, this decade turned out to be not one of revitalized confidence, but one in which the virtues and vices of Republicanism were raked over again and again, as a result of two scandals that shook the Republic violently.

(i) The Panama Scandal
Following their success as designers and engineers of the Suez Canal, the French had established a Panama Canal Company to build a canal through the isthmus of Panama to link the Pacific and Atlantic oceans, bringing both profit and honour to France. The President of the Company was Ferdinand de Lesseps, the architect of the Suez Canal. The Chamber had given loans to the Company and approved the issues of shares in the Company, and by 1888 thousands of Frenchmen had invested in the Company, to the tune of 1500 million francs. However, the Company had grossly underestimated the difficulties involved in building a canal through the malarial swamps of Panama and had spent many of their funds on a corrupt and inefficient administration. In 1889 the Company was declared bankrupt and 830 000 investors had lost their money.

For four years little more was heard of the failed Company. But by 1892 it had become clear that there was more to the collapse than met the eye. It was obvious that the company had been in difficulties in 1888—*before* the Chamber had approved a bill for a further 600 million francs to be raised by the sale of shares. Why, therefore, had the deputies approved the bill, and why had the press been so keen on the idea? Rumours of bribery abounded, and it became known that two German Jews, Baron Jacques de Reinach and Cornelius Hertz (an American citizen), had been responsible for paying deputies and journalists to support the company. Reinach committed suicide, threatened with blackmail by Hertz. Then Delahaye, a deputy who had supported Boulanger, claimed to have cheque stubs showing that 150 deputies had been paid, and demanded that they should be tried. Even the Finance Minister, Rouvier, was implicated and resigned, admitting he had received money but saying, 'What I have done all politicians worthy of the name have done before me.' Clemenceau, a leading Radical politician, was accused, but acquitted in an impeachment case, of being behind Hertz. Even the British government was hauled in, being implicated by its refusal to extradite Hertz from Bournemouth.

Eventually, in February 1893, a trial was held in which four directors, including de Lesseps, his son and the engineer Gustave Eiffel, and a former Minister of Public Works were found guilty. They were sentenced to pay large fines and serve prison sentences, but the prison terms were set aside by the 'Cour de cassation', France's highest court of appeal, on the grounds that it was more than three years since the crime had been committed.

The details of this affair are less important than its significance. People had been bribed in an effort to uphold the honour of the Republic, and had been found out. The old question arose—what kind of Republic was it that needed bribery to uphold its prestige? Again, the opponents had an opportunity to criticize the Republic but, again, they failed—in this case because their evidence was too slender and they offered no viable alternative. Yet, as Lord Bryce wrote in 1920:

> Panama created an atmosphere of suspicion which lasted for years, like the smoke that continues to hang over the spot where a high explosive shell has struck the ground....Nothing similar has occured since, yet the memory of Panama has remained to be used as a reproach against Parliamentary government.

(ii) The Dreyfus Affair

In 1894 the Ministry of War realized that military secrets were being given to the Germans. On 22 December temporary Staff-Captain Alfred Dreyfus, the only Jew in the Ministry and personally unpopular with his colleagues, was found guilty of selling secrets (to whom was not specified) and was sentenced to be degraded and deported to Devil's Island for life. Press and politicians alike—both Republicans and their opponents— were delighted that the honour of the Army had been preserved and justice done so swiftly and efficiently.

In 1897 Major Georges Picquart, the new chief of Intelligence in the French Army, having been sent some new documents, the 'petit bleu', became convinced that Dreyfus had been found guilty when the real agent was Major Count Walsin-Esterhazy, an ex-Austrian Army officer. (These documents can be seen on page 46.) When Picquart told his superiors of his suspicions he was told by General Gonse, second-in-command of the General Staff, to keep it to himself. Shortly afterwards he was posted to a command in Tunis. Before going, though, he had passed his news on to a journalist, who in turn informed Scheurer-Kestner, the Vice-President of the Senate. In fact, Scheurer-Kestner had already been told by Dreyfus' brother, Mathieu, and Bernard Lazare, a Jewish journalist, that the handwriting on the 'bordereau', the original document by which Dreyfus had been convicted, matched that of Esterhazy. Esterhazy himself urged that he should be put on trial. On 11

January 1898 he was tried and acquitted by a military tribunal, and Picquart was dismissed from the army.

Two days later the affair really came to life with the publication of the article 'J'Accuse' in *L'Aurore*, the paper edited by Clemenceau. The article was written by the leading novelist of the day, Emile Zola, and was an open letter to the President of the Republic, Felix Faure. In it, he accused five generals and two other officers of having known of Dreyfus' innocence and deliberately permitted his conviction. The article had a tremendous impact—200 000 copies were sold in Paris alone—and suddenly France was a divided nation. On one side were the Dreyfusards, who not only believed that Dreyfus was innocent but also that he should be shown to be innocent. On the other were the anti-Dreyfusards, who believed that even if Dreyfus was innocent (which to them was by no means certain) a retrial was against the honour of the army and the Republic; Dreyfus should suffer for the honour of his country. Zola's article led to a libel case in which he was found guilty and both fined and imprisoned for a year. Meanwhile the press continued the argument, the Dreyfusards led by Clemenceau and Jaurès presenting their handwriting experts while the anti-Dreyfusards presented theirs.

In July 1898 Cavaignac, the new Minister of War, presented new evidence of Dreyfus' guilt—three papers, two initialled 'D' and the third signed 'Dreyfus'; conclusive proof for the anti-Dreyfusards.

Then Cavaignac's own handwriting expert admitted that he had been wrong, and that the writing was actually that of Colonel Henry, the new Chief of Intelligence. Henry admitted his guilt, and committed suicide before he was brought for trial, while General Boisdeffre, the Chief of the General Staff, resigned. The innocence of Dreyfus was all but proven, and was hardly the issue any longer. Clemenceau later said, 'From this moment the discussion ceased to be whether or not Dreyfus was guilty but began to turn on whether or not Jews were birds of ill-omen, whether it was bad for the country and the army that a court martial might have been in error, and so forth. Arguments of that sort can drag on till the world itself comes to an end.'

Clemenceau was not strictly correct, for the affair of Dreyfus' guilt was not yet over. A retrial was held in August 1899 (during which the defence lawyer Labori was shot) and, by five votes to two, the judges found Dreyfus 'guilty with extenuating circumstances' but reduced his life sentence to ten years. The decision was obviously ludicrous: *If* he was guilty, which he obviously was not, then ten years was hardly a fit punishment for treason; and if he was not, then why say he was? The new Prime Minister, Waldeck-Rousseau, tried to correct the judgement by having President Loubet pardon Dreyfus. Many Dreyfusards, like Jaurès, as well as Dreyfus' own family, were satisfied by this, for the Captain was now free, and the victory won in fact, if not in law. Some however persisted that Dreyfus should be *proved* innocent. Eventually, on 12 July 1906, the 'Cour de cassation' set aside all previous judgements and found Dreyfus innocent. He was decorated and raised to the rank of Major, thus finally ending 'L'Affaire' that had split France so fiercely at the turn of the century.

Why had the case so divided France? And how important were the divisions that it created? To take the first question: it had aroused anger and indignation because it was a scandal involving the Republican government in a most tender spot, the army. Scandals, as the Wilson and Panama cases had shown, always aroused opposition to the Republic. But the involvement of the army made it even worse. For the army was, to many Frenchmen, crucial to France's present and future, since it would lead to France's recovery of Alsace and Lorraine from Germany. It must therefore be impeccable (in the literal meaning of the word, free from sin) and, perhaps more importantly, be seen to be so—and the Dreyfus case showed that it was not. Traditionally, like the Church, the army was an upholder of the monarchy, with titled officers who supported a strong, non-democratic central government. The army in the French Republic was always a paradox—was its loyalty to the Republican government that commanded it, or to the re-establishment of the old regime? This question was obviously brought out and debated at length during the case.

More important, however, was the division of Frenchmen into Dreyfusards and anti-Dreyfusards during the case. For it was obvious that the two sides had quite different ideas about government and the Republic. The Republic had been founded on the ideas of liberty and the Rights of Man—that is, men should have the right to vote, to speak and associate freely, to have a free press and so forth. They should be protected by a just legal system, and they should not be persecuted on grounds of class, race or religion. Dreyfus was a Jew and an 'outsider'; he was not of the family and background of most army officers. To those who saw the Republic as the protector of man's freedoms, the persecution of Dreyfus was an outrage that went against all that they stood for. On the other side were those who considered the greatness of France more important than the freedom of the individual, and therefore the army and its honour of paramount importance. Not only was France so important, but also its national religion, Catholicism; so to anti-Dreyfusards, non-Catholics, and especially Jews, were actually enemies of the state.

Nearly a century later, these events and arguments may seem irrelevant. Yet to Frenchmen in 1899 they mattered desperately—what was the Third Republic to be? A means of making France strong enough to defeat Germany, whatever the cost in individual freedom? Or a republic where the liberty of man was to live? It was for these issues that Frenchmen fought—and fight they did during the case; some fought duels, others fought street battles, while some right wingers even assaulted President Loubet. Leading politicians staked their reputations and careers on his innocence; others, like Barrès and Maurras, went on standing for the anti-Dreyfusard principles even after the case. Eventually, in the elections of 1902 and in the 'Cour de cassation' in 1906, the Dreyfusards won—but the arguments continued.

Finally, how important was the case? This can best be seen in two ways. In purely practical terms, it did make some difference. In the decade after the case, there were some reforms of a 'Republican' nature, most notably reducing the power of the Church; since the monastic orders, who were the main subjects of the reforms, had supported the case against Dreyfus, and since the reforms led to greater religious toleration, they can be seen broadly as a result of the case. Also, the Chambers elected in 1902 and 1906 were more left wing and Dreyfusards, suggesting that the case had influenced political opinion, though the elections of 1910 and 1914 reversed this trend. On a different level, the case perhaps resolved the true nature of the Third Republic—the freedom of the individual was to be more important than the honour of the state. Democracy was to be upheld and justice preserved. Historians may argue that in the long run this actually weakened France, since it meant that the government never had the strength to enforce firm but unpopular measures—like rearmament or the extension of conscription—but equally it meant that France remained in the forefront of democracy.

(b) 1900–14

The date chart (Table 6) hints at the preoccupations of France before the Great War—the relationship of Church and State, the growth of socialism, both as a parliamentary movement and in unions, clashes and crises with Germany and the inevitable changes of government that are the political hallmark of the Third Republic. Rather than look at these events purely chronologically, this section is divided into three parts—one on each of these themes (the clashes with Germany are covered separately under Foreign Policy).

(i) Church and State

The relationship between the Church and the State was always of great importance to the governments of the Republic. The Roman Catholic Church had usually supported the monarchy and strong central government, and, as in Italy, opposed the extension of democracy. Was it therefore right that, in a Republic whose ideals were essentially humanist rather than Christian, the Church should have such extensive influence in society, through its control over education and through the teaching and preaching of the religious Orders, the Congregations, and have such close connections to the State government, through the appointment and payment of bishops and priests by the State government?

During the 1890s Church and State were on friendly terms. In 1892, Pope Leo XIII issued an Encyclical to try to persuade monarchists to accept Republican government rather than campaign for the restoration of the monarchy. It seemed that the Church notables had accepted the fact of the Republic and were prepared to work within it; after all, it was a Churchman who issued the call for a Ralliément after the Boulanger affair.

The Dreyfus affair, however, reopened old wounds. Many traditional Churchmen, and most notably the religious Orders, sided against Dreyfus.

Following their victory in both the affair and the elections of 1902, many Radicals saw the opportunity of reducing the power of the Church in the State. This was done by three important pieces of legislation. During the affair itself, in 1901, the Associations Law was passed. This forbade the formation of any Congregation without a law defining its activities. All unauthorized congregations were to be dissolved. As a result of this some 3000 unauthorized schools were closed until they applied for, and received,

1900	Ten-hour day made compulsory in all establishments employing both men and women
1901	Associations Law requiring religious congregations to be authorized
1902	General election won by centre-left Radicals and Republicans who had supported Dreyfus
	Prime Minister Waldeck Rousseau resigns on grounds of ill-health (died of cancer, 1904) and because of opposition in the Chamber. Replaced by Emile Combes, a supporter of the anit-clerical legislation
1904	Visit of President Loubet to the King of Italy
	Signature of 'Entente Cordiale'
1905	Law separating Church and State passed
	Crisis with Germany over Morocco leading to Algeciras Conference and resignation of Delcassé
	Foundation of the united Socialist party, the 'Section Française de l'Internationale Ouvrière'
1906	Presidential election won by Armand Fallières
	General election maintains predominance of centre-left, and Georges Clemenceau becomes Prime Minister
	Old age pensions approved by the Chamber
	Ministry of Labour established
	CGT votes against all political affiliations and approves a motion describing all social legislation as insulting
1907	Strike of vineyard workers
1909	Strike of Paris postal workers put down by the use of troops
1910	Strike of railway workers put down by troops, leading to calls for a general strike
	General election shows swing to the right
1911	Strike by vineyard workers
	Second Moroccan crisis leads to resignation of Caillaux and Poincaré's appointment as Prime Minister
1913	Poincaré wins Presidential election
	Succession of short-lived ministries—five between January 1913 and June 1914
	Law passed increasing period of conscription from two years to three
1914	General election confirms earlier swing to right-wing parties
	Outbreak of World War I leads to formation of Government of National Unity led by René Viviani

Table 6. Date chart of main events in France 1900–14

authorization. Then, in 1904, all teaching by the Congregations was forbidden and control of education was taken over by the State through the Université. Finally in 1905, after a year's debate, a bill for the separation of Church and State was passed. This permitted complete liberty of conscience (no one *had* to belong to any Church or follow any set religion) and ended all links between the Church and the State—the government would no longer appoint or pay any priests. All property belonging to the Church was to be confiscated and only older priests, not only Catholic, but also Protestant and Jewish, would receive a pension from the state. Thus the relationship as settled by the Concordat of 1801 was ended and France became, by law, a lay State, so ending one of the debates that had divided Frenchmen for thirty years.

(ii) The development of socialism

As in the rest of Europe, this period saw the rapid development of a socialist movement, both inside and outside Parliament. It did, however, differ from the rest of Europe in that the Trade Union movement remained independent from the political parties, as the result of a vote taken in 1905. Like the rest of Europe, though, the Socialist parties were split, though in 1905 they joined together.

During the 1890s there was considerable socialist activity and a number of socialist political groups were formed. In 1891 Government troops had fired on left-wing demonstrators, including women and children, some of whom had been killed. This 'massacre of Fourmies' did much to arouse socialist hostility towards the government, as did anarchist activity, which reached a peak in June 1894 when President Carnot was stabbed at Lyons by an Italian anarchist, Santo Caserio. There were three chief socialist organizations by the end of the 1890s—the 'Parti Socialiste Révolutionnaire', the 'Parti Ouvrier Socialiste Révolutionnaire' and local groups, known as Socialist Federations, who joined together in 1896 to form the 'Fédération des Socialistes Independants de France', whose policies tended to be more moderate than the others. It was a member of the Socialist Federation of the Seine, Alexandre Millerand, who caused a great stir in the Socialist world by joining Waldeck-Rousseau's cabinet in 1899 as Minister of Commerce. He thereby created in France the revolutionary/revisionist (reformist) split that tormented the German socialists—should socialists join in Parliamentary governments, or should they work wholeheartedly for the overthrow of the bourgeois state and all that it stood for, including Parliamentary government? (See page 67.)

In 1901 the Socialists were reorganized into two parties, each led by one of the great Socialist leaders. Jules Guesde led the PSDF ('Parti Socialiste de France') while his rival Jean Jaurès led the more moderate PSF ('Parti Socialiste Française'). The PSDF represented the revolutionary wing of the movement, while the PSF accepted the reformist view that participation in Parliamentary Government was necessary and desirable. However, when the Second International (of all Socialist parties throughout the world) voted against reformism *and* that the French socialist parties should unite, Jaurès accepted the decision and agreed that the new united party—the SFIO ('Section Française de l'Internationale Ouvrière')—should adopt a revolutionary programme. In fact, except during the war, none of its members ever did join French governments until 1936, although it did accept democracy to the extent of putting up candidates for election to the Chamber. By 1914 it was the second largest single party in the Chamber. These various splits and coalitions of the left are shown in Diagram 4 (the more extreme parties are on the left, the more moderate on the right).

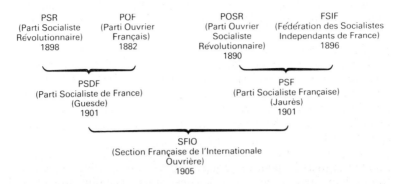

Diagram 4. Socialist parties in France 1880–1910

Despite the ever increasing representation of the Socialists in Parliament, there was little legislation of a socialist nature. As Minister of Commerce, Millerand did his best, with the introduction of state-paid factory inspectors, and an office that became the Ministry of Labour, as well as the ten-hour act of 1900. However, although they were approved by the Chamber in 1906, old age pensions were not introduced until 1910, by which time the Senate had considerably altered their value and structure. Income tax, too, was approved by the Chamber but opposition, notably by Poincaré and Rouvier, meant that it was not enacted until 1914 and then postponed with the outbreak of war. Therefore, there was not as much legislation of a socialist nature as might be expected when the Socialist party was strong and the Radicals in power.

However, many socialists, and especially Trade Unionists, would have been proud of this record. For their campaign was for direct action against the bourgeois state, a policy approved by the 1905 Congress of the CGT ('Confédération Générale du Travail') which voted that social legislation was insulting and that working men should use the general strike against the state. In so doing they were following the 'syndicalist' ideas of Georges Sorel, and so organized a number of strikes in the following years (see Table 6). These certainly brought the hoped-for confrontation with the government, but in all cases the government was victorious. Clemenceau's government used troops to force the postal workers back, and had a law passed forbidding civil servants the right to strike, while Briand, Prime Minister during the rail strike of 1910, called the strikers into the army as reservists, and thus made them subject to military law, and so unable to strike. The effects of these strikes were to embitter the socialists, who gained nothing, and force many middle-class people away from socialism to the safe harbours of the right, as the elections of 1910 demonstrated.

Finally, however, it is important not to overestimate the French socialism at this time. Only half the Trade Unions were even members of the CGT, and it has been estimated that there were only some 400 000 resolute syndicalists out of a population of eleven million working-class people. As long as the Socialist movement was split between unions and politicians, and, within each, between reformists and revolutionaries, it could never be as great a force as its German counterpart.

(iii) French politics

French politics in the Third Republic are extremely complex, but a study of the list of Prime Ministers and of the election results *(Tables 7, 8, 9)* will show that governments came and went with remarkable frequency. In addition, political parties were fragmentary, and became more so. However, some names recur often, if not frequently, in the list of ministers, and there were few elections despite the frequent changes of government. These peculiarities of French politics require further examination.

Date of election	Name	Term of office
30 January 1879	Jules Grévy	Served full term and reelected, but resigned over the Wilson scandal
3 December 1887	Sadi Carnot	Assassinated at Lyons by Italian anarchist, 24 June 1894
25 June 1894	Jean Casimir-Perier	Resigned
15 June 1895	Felix Faure	Died in office, while entertaining his mistress
16 February 1899	Emile Loubet	Served full term
18 February 1906	Armand Fallières	Served full term
18 February 1913	Raymond Poincaré	Served full term

Table 7. Presidents of France 1870–1921

French Prime Ministers were rarely the representative of the largest or majority party in the Chamber. Instead, they were chosen by the President as the man most likely to command support in both Parliament and the country. Sometimes, for example in 1899 when Waldeck-Rousseau was appointed after a twelve-day interval, Presidents found it difficult to find such a man. Often, as in the case of Clemenceau in 1909 who resigned over a report on the state of the Navy, Premiers resigned over trivial issues. Resignation did *not* lead to an election, but merely to the search for a new man. French Prime Ministers should not be equated with British ones as the leaders of the majority party in the Parliament, nor with German Chancellors as the personal servants of the Kaiser. Rather, they were leading members of a governmental team, and only in rare cases, such as Clemenceau in 1917–19, the real rulers of the country.

Similarly, French political parties should not be equated with other European ones. Many politicians were members, or had links with, more than one party and it is only possible to determine who belonged to what by the way they voted in the Chamber. Except for three or four very broad groupings—Republicans, Radicals and Socialists—political parties and labels had little relevance to French deputies. Deputies saw themselves not as representatives of a party, but as representatives of the area in which they lived. In the period 1870–1940, 90% of deputies were

Date of appointment	Name
2 February 1889	Pierre-Emmanuel Tirard
17 March 1890	Charles de Freycinet
29 February 1892	Emile Loubet
14 December 1892	Alexandre Ribot
30 March 1893	Charles Dupuy
3 December 1893	Jean Casimir-Perier
29 May 1894	Charles Dupuy
26 January 1895	Alexandre Ribot
30 October 1895	Leon Bourgeois
30 April 1896	Jules Méline
28 June 1898	Henri Brisson
31 October 1898	Charles Dupuy
22 June 1899	Pierre Waldeck-Rousseau
7 June 1902	Emile Combes
24 January 1905	Maurice Rouvier
14 March 1906	Jean Sarrien
23 October 1906	Georges Clemenceau
25 July 1909	Aristide Briand
5 March 1911	Ernest Monis
29 June 1911	Joseph Caillaux
14 January 1912	Raymond Poincaré
21 January 1913	Aristide Briand
21 March 1913	Louis Barthou
10 December 1913	Gaston Doumergue
9 June 1914	Alexandre Ribot
14 June 1914	René Viviani

Table 8. Prime Ministers of France 1889–1914

	1889	1893	1898	1902	1906	1910	1914
Right of Centre parties (1)	210	102	100	163	107	228	223
Republicans (also known as Right Radicals)	350	279	235	175	119	105	96
Radicals		153	180	192	278	145	164
Socialists (2)		31	55	45	71	100	103

Table 9. Political representation in the French Chamber of Deputies 1889–1911. As the text explains, French political parties cannot be compared with those of other countries. This table can therefore be taken only as an approximate guide.

(1) This includes a range of parties, including Boulangists in 1889, Ralliés in 1893 and 1898, Nationalists in 1902, Progressives and others
(2) This includes some independent socialists not affiliated to the SFIO

elected in the département in which they lived, a very different situation from Britain. In the period 1898–1940, one third of all French deputies were simultaneously local mayors while another third were members of their local councils. The deputy was seen as and acted as the representative of the people of his own area, and not as the member of a political party.

Finally, the recurrence of names deserves further comment. Historians have often commented on the paradox that French governments changed frequently and yet French politics remained apparently stable. This is explained by the fact that although governments changed, the people in government did not. In the period 1870–1940, of 4892 deputies elected, more than two-thirds served only one or two terms (i.e. four or eight years) but 496 were elected five or more times, and were therefore in the Chamber for anything over twenty years, so providing a small but substantial group of really experienced deputies. The same pattern is seen with ministers—120, out of a total of 561 were ministers five or more times. When it is also seen that three-quarters of ministers and over half the deputies were from the professions (lawyers, academics, doctors, journalists, engineers or civil servants) one important reason for the political stability of France is apparent. France was ruled by a smallish group of very experienced politicians from the professional classes.

5. Economic History

During this period France either remained or fell behind her main European rivals. Whereas in 1800 French industrial production ranked second only to Britain, by 1936 she had only 4½% of world industrial production, compared with Britain's 9%, Germany's 11% and the USA's 45%. In 1913 France had only 3·5 million horse-power employed in industry—less than half the amount of Britain or Germany. Tables 10 and 11 below illustrate a similar trend in heavy industry.

	UK	Germany	France
1880	7875	2729	1725
1890	8033	4037	1970
1900	9003	7549	2714
1910	10380	14793	4032

Table 10. Pig iron (annual production in thousands of metric tons)

	UK	Germany	France
1880	1320	660	388
1890	3637	2161	566
1900	5130	6645	1565
1910	6374	13698	3506

Table 11. Steel (annual production in thousands of metric tons)

Similar figures for coal production show France in an even worse light; in 1913 she produced 41 million tons, compared with Germany's 279 and Britain's 287. All the indices point to France's apparent backwardness—in the production of essential heavy goods, in the use of modern equipment and in her share of total world production.

However, it is essential to add some riders to this general picture of the backwardness of France. Firstly, Germany was undergoing a period of very rapid growth, with an average growth rate of 36% p.a. 1840–1910, while Britain's industrialization was thoroughly completed by the mid-nineteenth century. It is not therefore surprising to find France behind these two. If instead of comparing France to Germany and Britain, she was compared to Italy or Russia, the picture would be quite different. Secondly, if the economic development of France in this period is compared with her earlier development, the picture is again different. Between 1895 and 1914 there was a growth rate of some 9% p.a., while some new industries, like bicycles and motor cars, showed particularly rapid development. Even heavy industry was expanding faster than ever, as Tables 10 and 11 can be used to show. Between 1890 and 1900 steel output trebled, and then doubled again during the next decade. The French economy was not stagnant, nor declining—it was simply not expanding as rapidly as others.

Nonetheless, some explanation of France's comparative tardiness is required. Firstly, France did lack some of the stimulants to expansion so evident in the expansion of the German economy at the same time. One of these was the lack of raw materials, especially coal. Between 1870 and 1914 raw materials accounted for 60% of all of France's imports. Equally, the loss of Lorraine deprived France of most of the iron ore deposits she possessed as well as 80% of her machine tool industry, while there were no deposits of copper, lead, zinc or tin available to French industry. Another factor that had stimulated German industry was her growing population; this, too was lacking in France, as Table 12 below shows:

France		Germany	
1851	35 783 000	1855	36 113 644
1896	38 517 975	1890	49 428 470
1910	39 192 000	1910	64 925 993

Table 12. Population of France and Germany 1850–1910

A third factor that had greatly advanced German industry was the application of inventions to industrial purposes and in this too France lagged behind. Although there were many fine pure scientists in France, they seemed unable to apply their ideas to practical purposes, such as the chemical industry or transport system.

France also lacked the capital to develop her economy to the fullest capacity. This was not because there was no money available, but rather because much of it was invested overseas. Some of this money went on the establishment and development of French colonies, but far more went directly to foreign governments. For example, thousands of millions of francs were lost on the Panama Canal venture. In 1911 a loan was raised for the government of Paraguay and only later was it learnt that Paraguay was at war, had recently undergone four revolutions and had no way of repaying the interest on the loan. Even more French money went to Russia, mainly earmarked for military or semi-military purposes to build up Russia as a potential ally against Germany. By 1914 one-third of all foreign capital in Russia was French and in all one quarter of all French investment went to Russia—two-thirds of it to be lost forever. This emphasis on overseas investment undoubtedly deprived the French economy of much of the money that it required.

However, it has been argued that many French people did not want to industrialize. Instead, many Frenchmen, especially outside the towns, a category that included most politicians, would have said that they wanted France to remain an agricultural country. Indeed, it did just this, as Table 13 below illustrates. France remained predominantly rural far longer than either of its chief rivals.

UK	Urban	Rural	France	Urban	Rural	Germany	Urban	Rural
1861	62·3	37·3	1851	25·0	75·0	1875	39·0	61·0
1891	72·0	28·0	1891	37·4	62·6	1890	47·0	53·0
1911	78·1	21·9	1911	44·2	55·8	1910	60·0	40·0

Table 13. Distribution of total population between urban and rural area (in percentages)

Not only was France predominantly agricultural, but also agriculture went through a period of depression for the decade after 1882; the wine industry was especially badly hit at this time by an attack of greenfly, 'phylloxera vastata', whose effects cost twice as much as the war against Prussia. In addition, many of the factories that there were in France were small family businesses, rather than mighty combines or cartels. In 1896 only 151 firms in France had a work force of more than 1000 men, whereas half a million firms had an average work force of 5·5 men. There were neither the entrepreneurs nor entrepreneurial attitudes that were needed to provide the transport system, apply the inventions, build the factories or sell the goods if there was to be an economic boom on Germanic lines.

6. Foreign Policy

(a) Colonial policy
The Third Republic pursued an ambitious colonial policy, as a result of which she attained considerable possessions and influence. Jules Ferry

had initiated the policy in the 1880s, and the two areas that interested him—North-west Africa and South-east Asia—remained the main areas of activity for French colonialism *(see Map 4)*. In 1881 French troops occupied Tunis and, by the Treaty of Bardo, established a protectorate there. Thereafter, French influence was extended in North Africa, primarily in Algeria and Morocco. In West Africa, a number of coastal settlements had been established with local chiefs' agreement during the mid-nineteenth century. From there, a series of protectorates were formed in French Guinea (1893), Ivory Coast (1893) and Dahomey (1894). Expeditions and missions northwards extended the size of these protectorates by 1899 and in 1904 they were formally reorganized as French West Africa, with a single Governor-General at the capital of Dakar. This incorporated Senegal, French Guinea, Ivory Coast, Dahomey, Upper Senegal and Niger. Further South, an expedition under Savargnan de Brazza had been sent to the northern Congo in 1880, where a protectorate based on Brazzaville had been founded. This too was extended by expeditions northwards and by 1895 there were plans to extend the colony eastwards. Some even hoped that a central belt of French colonies might eventually be established from the Congo to French Somaliland on the eastern coast. These plans necessitated the capture of parts of the southern Sudan, and eventually led to the Fashoda crisis of 1898 *(see page 131)*. Like the western possessions, France's central African colonies were eventually joined together when, in 1910, the colonies of Gabon, the Middle Congo and Ubanghi-Shari became French Equatorial Africa. During the last twenty years of the nineteenth century, France had acquired and organized an enormous African Empire, covering some three million square miles.

The French were equally concerned to establish their influence in the Far East *(see Map 12, page 131)*. As a result of the Treaty of Tientsin (1885) following a short war (reverses during which led to Ferry's downfall), the Chinese government recognized the French protectorate over Tonkin. Further concessions were won from the Chinese in 1898 when they allowed the French to construct a railway to Yunnan-fu and gave them a ninety-nine year lease on Kwangchowan. By the turn of the century, therefore, the French government had acquired two major colonial spheres of influence.

However, these colonial achievements should not be exaggerated. Although the area under French rule was gigantic, many of the areas were relatively useless—such as the Sahara Desert—or difficult to exploit for economic gain. In addition, relatively few resources of men and money were invested in the Empire: colonial investments accounted for only 10% of France's total foreign investments. Far more went to Russia.

(b) European policy

The overriding aim of French foreign policy was 'Revanche' (or 'return match'), by which Frenchmen meant the recapture of the provinces of Alsace and Lorraine, taken by Germany in 1871. Most foreign policy

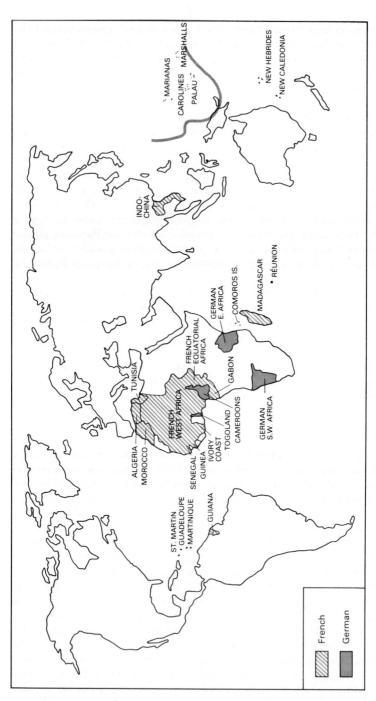

Map 4 German and French Colonies

debates centred around the means to this end, and statesmens' policies ranged from Caillaux, who sought commercial co-operation with Germany as a way to the peaceful reoccupation of the provinces, to those like Déroulède, who sought reconquest at the earliest moment. The majority were agreed that France would not be able to attack Germany until she had allies to help her. Consequently, the period 1890–1910 was primarily one in which alliances were sought and made.

Agreement with Britain seemed unlikely. Interests in Africa brought the two into conflict, while the possibility of an Anglo-German agreement in the 1890s put a British alliance almost out of the question.

Instead, republican France turned to autocratic Russia. The French were keener on this alliance than were the Russians, for it provided them with a military ally to divert Germany's attention. The Russians were less keen on such a commitment, and when General Boisdeffre took a draft military convention to St Petersburg in 1892, the Russians altered it considerably and even then only agreed to the proposals in principle, not in detail. However, further negotiations and exchanges of diplomatic notes led to the full acceptance of the convention, which was raised to the status of a treaty in January 1894. By it, each agreed that if the other was attacked by Germany, it would attack Germany, or if the forces of the Triple Alliance mobilized, then both would mobilize their forces. In 1899 a visit by Delcassé, the French Foreign Minister from 1898 to 1905, to St Petersburg led to the previous arrangements being made indefinite (rather than lasting as long as the Triple Alliance). In 1912 a naval convention was added, and in 1913 a military protocol by which both powers should mobilize if either were attacked by Germany 'without there being need for preliminary agreement'. Despite their political differences, France and Russia recognized their common interest against Germany and built a firm alliance on this foundation.

As well as Russia, France was able to come to considerable agreement with Italy, although, as a member of the Triple Alliance, she was ostensibly an enemy. In 1898 a commercial treaty ended the tariff war, and in 1900 agreement was reached over North Africa when Italy recognized France's rights in Morocco in exchange for French recognition of Italian claims to Tripoli. Then, in 1902, Italy assured France that if she was attacked by one of her (Italy's) allies, she (Italy) would remain neutral. So although Italy remained a member of the Triple Alliance she was actually in agreement with the chief enemy of that alliance, France.

Delcassé, whose term as Foreign Minister lasted for seven years and five governments, remained convinced of the need for an alliance with Britain, as much to prevent an Anglo-German alliance as to use Britain against Germany. The first agreements with Britain were reached over Africa. France recognized Britain's 'privileged position' in Egypt and Britain in turn accepted French rights in Morocco. These agreements led to the 'Entente Cordiale' of 1904 which reinforced the settlements over Africa and added to them an agreement that France would surrender her claim to the coast of Newfoundland in exchange for land near French

Gambia; in addition an agreement was made on the frontiers of Siam and disputes over Madagascar and the New Hebrides were settled. Thereafter, military discussions began in January 1906. Britain refused to promise support to France in the event of an attack by Germany but agreed to more general discussions on co-operation should it be needed, thereby creating the 'moral obligation' of Britain to France. Hereafter, France could reckon to at least equal the might of the Triple Alliance if not, bearing in mind the attitude of Italy and the Anglo-Russian alliance of 1907, outweigh it.

In the decade before the outbreak of the Great War France was involved in two major crises with the other great powers, notably Germany, over her position in Morocco. These arose in 1905 and 1911 and are more fully described on page 81. As far as France was concerned, her primary interests in both cases were to maintain her influence in Morocco, and, especially, to show her ability to stand up to Germany. The French position in the first crisis was considerably weakened by Russia's involvement in a war with Japan, thus making it impossible for France to take a tough line against Germany even to the extent of threatening war, which was what Delcassé planned (and was therefore forced to resign when the rest of Rouvier's cabinet realized how impossible this was). However, at the Algeçiras Conference of 1906, only Austria-Hungary stood by Germany and the French could be pleased with the outcome. In the second crisis of 1911, the Socialist-Radical Prime Minister, Caillaux, was prepared to meet Germany's demands for a part of the French Congo in exchange for recognizing France's control over Morocco. The Chamber unwillingly agreed, but much indignation was aroused over this 'sell-out' and Caillaux was forced to resign.

There followed a distinct revival in nationalist feeling and hostility towards Germany. Despite their alliances, France had never actually sought war with Germany, which they might have done in 1908 or 1911. However, between 1912 and 1914 extensive preparations were made. Military parades, dropped at the time of the Dreyfus affair, were revived, the high command reorganized, military aircraft developed and, in 1913, the military protocol with Russia signed. A three-year military service was enacted, extending the term that conscripts served from two years, despite the opposition of the left. These policies were largely on the initiative of the Prime Minister, Raymond Poincaré, who was elected President in 1913. He was from Lorraine, and historians have long argued as to whether or not he was actually preparing for war against Germany next time the opportunity arose. Certainly the German High Command thought he was. On the other hand his policies can be interpreted as a determination to reinforce France so that she would not be forced to 'give way' to Germany again. Nonetheless, on the outbreak of war in August 1914 France had never been readier (though not for the type of war that came). Interestingly, though, the chief interests of the French people in the summer of 1914 were domestic rather than foreign —the debate over income tax, the trial of Madame Caillaux for the murder of a newspaper editor and the assassination by a nationalist of the socialist leader, Jean Jaurès.

7. Bibliography

A most useful introductory book, which follows the history of the Third Republic chronologically rather than thematically, and which includes a number of documents, is *The Third French Republic 1870–1940* by L. Derfler (Van Nostrand, 1966). Another good book with which to start is *Clemenceau and the Third French Republic* by J. Hampden Jackson (English University Press, 1946) in the 'Teach Yourself History' series. The standard works, which deal with the subject in a more detailed and analytical fashion, include *The Development of Modern France 1870–1935* by D.W. Brogan (Hamish Hamilton, 1967), *France 1814–1940* by J.P.T. Bury (Methuen, 1954), *A History of Modern France*, Volume III 1871–1962 by A. Cobban (Penguin, 1972) and *Democracy in France* by D. Thomson (OUP, 1958).

8. Discussion Points and Exercises

A   *This section consists of questions that might be used for discussion (or written answers) as a way of expanding on the chapter and testing understanding of it:*

1   Why was it peculiar that the Republic was first ruled by right-wingers?
2   Why was the President given such extensive powers?
3   Why did the French 'love to displease Bismarck'?
4   What weaknesses of the Republic did the Boulanger crisis bring to the fore?
5   Why did French politicians accept money during the Panama scandal?
6   Why were army chiefs so keen to cover up their mistake in convicting Dreyfus?
7   Why was the position of the Church taken so seriously?
8   What conditions led to the development of the socialist parties in the late nineteenth century?
9   Compare the ruling élite of France with that of Germany.
10   Examine the effects of France's economic conditions on politics and foreign policy.
11   Why did France invest overseas so extensively?
12   Why was 'Revanche' such a key issue to French governments?
13   Why was it both unusual and likely that France sought an alliance with Russia?
14   How aggressive was French foreign policy immediately before 1914?

B *This section suggests two exercises which will help you to understand the problems and motives of the people involved in the events you have been studying:*

1 If you were a newspaper editor in the 1890s (fix the actual date for yourself), would you have supported or opposed the Republic? Write an editorial that you might have published on this subject.

2 Write a report on French foreign policy for either the British Prime Minister or the German Chancellor (as a British or German foreign office official) at any time between 1900 and 1914. Again, date your report accurately.

C *This section suggests two ways in which you might compare France with the rest of Europe in the period:*

1 Draw up a chart or diagram comparing French socialism with socialist developments in any one other European country.

2 In the chapter on Austria-Hungary, the concept of 'weakness' was discussed at some length. How does France measure up to the scales you devised then?

D *Essay questions:*

1 How influential was the French Labour movement compared with the German one before 1914?

2 Why, and in what ways, was France so deeply divided by the Dreyfus affair?

3 'French foreign policy was based on a false belief in France's continuing power and influence.' Do you agree?

9. Documentary Exercise on the Dreyfus Affair

Study the following documents relating to the affair.

A. The 'Bordereau' (1894)
(Source: F.C. Conybeare, *The Dreyfus Case,* quoted in Kertesz, pp.323–4)

This was the major evidence against Dreyfus and was found in the German military attaché's office in Paris.

> Sir,
>   though I have no news to indicate that you wish to see me, nevertheless I am sending you some interesting items of information.
> (1) A note on the hydraulic brake of the 120, and on the way in which this piece behaved.
> (2) A note on the covering troops (some modifications will be entailed by the new plan).
> (3) A note on a modification in artillery formations.
> (4) A note relative to Madagascar.
> (5) The project of a firing manual for field artillery, 14 March 1894.
> This last document is extremely difficult to procure, and I can only have it at my disposal during a very few days. The Minister of War has sent a

limited number of copies to the several corps, and these corps are responsible for the return of it after the manoeuvres. If, then, you would like to take out of it whatever interests you, and hold it afterwards at my disposal, I will take it, unless, indeed you would like me to have it copied 'in extenso', and then send the copy to your address.

I am just setting off to the manoeuvres.

B. The degradation of Dreyfus, 5 January 1895

(Source: M. Paleologue, 'An Intimate Journal of the Dreyfus Case', quoted in Derfler, *The Third French Republic*)

The 'execution' parade took place at 8.45 am, in the great court of the École Militaire, which was full of troops. In accordance with the provision of the military penal code, a detachment had been sent by every regiment of the Paris garrison. The morning was icy. Outside the gate, in the Place de Fontenoy, an enormous crowd, contained with difficulty by the police, was chafing, whistling and shouting: 'Death to the Jews!', 'Death to the traitor!', 'Death to Judas!'

Nine o'clock struck. General Darras, on horseback, followed by his staff, drew his sword. There was a roll of drums. 'Attention! Shoulder arms!' In a terrifying silence, in which thousands of men seemed to be holding their breath, Dreyfus appeared at the right-hand corner of the court, in the midst of four gunners and a corporal, with sabre in hand and revolver on his belt. He advanced firmly, head high, looking as if he were in command of the escort. The general stood in his stirrups and, holding his sword aloft, said: 'Alfred Dreyfus, you are no longer worthy to carry arms. In the name of the French people, we degrade you!' A warrant officer, a giant of a man, Sergeant-Major Bouxin, approached the condemned man as he stood there motionless and, with angry gestures, tore the braid from his cap and sleeves, the buttons from his jacket, his shoulder straps, all his marks of rank, and threw them in the mud. When Dreyfus' uniform had been torn to tatters, the giant took his sabre and scabbard and broke them over his knee. The fearful ordeal seemed interminable . . .

When the giant had completed his revolting task, Dreyfus shouted: 'You have just degraded an innocent man. By the head of my wife and children, I swear that I am innocent!'

Dreyfus stepped back between his escort. He was then marched the whole length of the lined-up troops, which was a long way, for at least four thousand men were on parade. During this Calvary, Dreyfus did not for one moment falter or revolt. Twice I heard him shout 'I am innocent'. When he reached the end of the courtyard, two gendarmes seized him, handcuffed him, and put him in a Black Maria, which trotted quickly away.

C. The 'Petit-bleu' (1896)

(Source: F.C. Conybeare, *op. cit.*)

This was the major piece of evidence against Esterhazy in 1897–8, but was countered by the forged evidence of Major Henry at Esterhazy's trial in 1898. 'Petit-bleu' means a telegram letter.

Address: M. le Commandant Esterhazy, 27 Rue de la Bienfaisance, Paris.
Text: I await before everything a more detailed explanation than what

you gave me the other day in regard to the question at issue. In consequence I beg you to give it me in writing so that I may judge if I can continue my relations with the firm R . . . or not.

D. The Zola letter 'J'accuse', 13 January 1898

I accuse Lieutenant-Colonel Du Paty de Clam of having been the diabolical worker of the judicial error, unconsciously, I would like to believe, and of afterwards having defended his unhappy work for three years, by the most irrelevant and blameworthy machinations. I accuse General Mercier of being an accomplice, at the very least by weakness of spirit, to one of the greatest inequities this ccentury. I accuse General Billot of having had in his hands certain proofs of Dreyfus' innocence and having suppressed them. . . . I accuse Generals Boisdeffre and Gonse of being accomplices to the same crime, one doubtless motivated by clerical passion, the other by that esprit de corps which makes the War Office an unassailable Holy Ark. I accuse General Pellieux and Major Ravary of having conducted a wicked investigation. . . . I accuse the three handwriting experts . . . of having made false and fraudulent reports, unless a medical report finds them stricken by diseased views and judgements. I accuse the War Office of having led an abominable press campaign, especially in the *Eclair* and in the *Echo de Paris*, to mislead public opinion and to conceal their blunder. I accuse, finally, the first Court Martial of having broken the law in condemning the accused on secret evidence, and I accuse the second Court Martial of having concealed this illegality, on orders, and committing, in turn, the juridicial crime of knowingly acquitting a guilty man. In making these accusations, I am aware that I put myself under the jurisdiction of articles 30 and 31 of the press law which punishes libel offences. I willingly expose myself to it. As for the people whom I have accused, I do not know them; I have never seen them, I bear them no hatred or bitterness. The act that I have accomplished here is only a revolutionary means to hasten the revelation of truth and justice. I have only one passion, enlightenment, in the name of humanity which has suffered so and has a right to happiness. My inflamed protest is only the cry of my soul. Let someone therefore indict me at the court of assizes and let the investigation take place in full daylight! I am waiting!

Much of the value of these documents will be gained from discussion. To give some structure to such discussion, consider each of the following questions:

1 Why would the 'bordereau' have caused such a stir in 1894?
2 Why did the authorities choose to degrade Dreyfus as described in B?
3 Was the decision to degrade him like this a wise one?
4 Why did Dreyfus himself find it so difficult to prove his own innocence?
5 How convincing does the 'petit-bleu' seem as evidence against Esterhazy?
6 Zola attributes a number of motives to the behaviour of the generals he accuses; what are these?
7 What did Zola hope to achieve through the publication of this letter?

III Italy 1890–1914

1. Italy in 1890

(a) Problems resulting from unification

The unification of Italy as a single Kingdom, the 'Risorgimento', was only completed in 1870 when Rome was captured and became a part of the new Kingdom. This unification, led by the Kingdom of Piedmont, had left the new government with three major problems, none of which had been satisfactorily resolved before 1890. Firstly, there were still many Italians living outside the boundaries of the new Kingdom, especially in the Tyrol, Trentino and Istria, all of which were a part of the Austro-Hungarian empire. The desire of the Italian government to draw these Italians, known collectively as 'Italia Irredenta', into the kingdom was bound to make relations with Italy's most immediate and most powerful neighbour, the Habsburg Empire, difficult.

Secondly, many Italians within the new Kingdom were not won over to the theory or practice of unification. To them, it had brought neither riches nor prestige, but rather a series of new taxes and new laws that restricted rather than enhanced their wealth and freedom. Not surprisingly, they resented the new central government.

Most importantly, the papacy was opposed to the new regime. Pope Pius IX refused to accept the Law of Guarantees (1871) which defined the relationship between Church and State and virtually gave the Pope power as a separate head of state within Italy, and an income equivalent to what he had received from his territories. Rejecting it, he instructed true Catholics to have nothing to do with the new regime which had made him the 'prisoner of the Vatican'. His successor, Leo XIII, (1878–1903) was regarded as more liberal (he did, for instance, instruct French Catholics to support the republic) but still, in an Encyclical of 1898, insisted that Italian Catholics should take no part in politics as long as the papacy remained in its 'intolerable position'. Since the Pope was widely respected and revered in a country as loyally Catholic as Italy, the new united government found his opposition a continual thorn in its side.

(b) Economic background

Unification had also led to economic problems, for it had left a huge debt that could only be removed by huge taxes. Until its abolition in 1884, the grist tax on bread made the central government especially unpopular. The debt also hampered the efforts of local government to raise sufficient capital to invest in education and public services. As this was a period in which the role of local government in Europe as a whole was expanding, with the provision of simple services like street lighting and pavements, this shortage was a serious handicap.

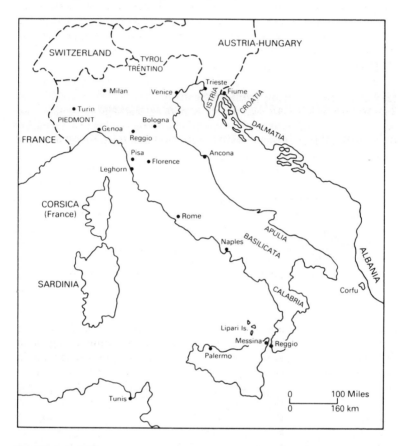

Map 5 Italy in 1890

Moreover, Italy in 1890 was a predominantly poor country, in which the majority of the population consisted of agricultural peasants. Of these, only 10% owned or shared their own land, leaving the rest as hired labourers, who competed for such work as was available in a time of slump *and* increasing population. It increased by four million between 1880 and 1900. Not surprisingly, wages were very low and poverty widespread. Again, the problem was worsened by unification, for with it had come free trade throughout the kingdom; this had lowered the price for the South's agricultural products and ended such industry as there had been in the South. The Italian economy became increasingly dualist with an industrial North and agricultural South, wherein the problems seemed ever increasing, for the annual value of the national agricultural product only once reached its 1880 level before 1901, while the spread of phylloxera from France ruined the vineyards. In the poorer areas, illiteracy was commonplace (75% in Basilicata in 1901) and as the franchise was based on literacy, the South remained under-represented. It was not surprising that emigration was high, the Mafia flourished and there were frequent outbreaks of peasant violence, which simply involved increased government expenditure in suppressing them.

2. Constitutional Organization of the State

Italy during this period was a constitutional monarchy, the structure of which is summarized in Diagram 5.

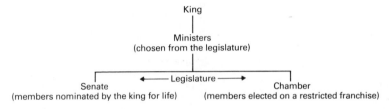

Diagram 5. The constitutional organization of Italy

This structure generally assured the King's government of control, and even if a vote in the legislature went against the government, a general election did not necessarily follow. Even in elections, the government in power was virtually certain of victory because of the restrictions on the franchise and its control of the electorate *(see below)*. Nevertheless, governments were shortlived, as Table 14 below demonstrates, and had an average life of less than two years throughout this period. This was largely the result of the successive governments' inability to cope with the country's problems, but also both reflected and encouraged the lack of national unity and the regional differences in the Kingdom.

The franchise was restricted throughout this period. In 1882 it was extended from about 600 000 to two million by reducing the age limit from 25 to 21 and lowering the tax paying requirements from 40 to 19 lire. A literacy test was still held, but this did at least bring some lower-middle-class people into the electorate. In 1912 the franchise was further extended. The vote was given to all male literates over 21 and illiterates on completion of military service or at the age of thirty. As a result of this, the electorate was increased to 8·6 million—24% of the population,

rather than 3·3%. However, elections rarely resembled modern democratic elections, since the prefects in charge of the sixty-nine provinces of
Italy were regarded as government servants. They were appointed by
the government in Rome and were offered favours, in the form of jobs, in
return for satisfactory election results; as constituences usually had less
than 5000 voters the prefects were usually able to satify their political
masters.

Kings

1878–1900 Umberto (Humbert) I (assassinated)
1900–1946 Victor Emmanuel III (son of Umberto I)

Prime Ministers

Date of assuming office	Name
May 1881	Agostini Depretis
August 1887	Francesco Crispi
February 1891	Marquis Antonio di Rudini
May 1892	Giovanni Giolitti
December 1893	Francesco Crispi
March 1896	Marquis Antonio di Rudini
June 1898	General Luigi Pelloux
June 1900	Giuseppe Saracco
February 1901	Giuseppe Zanardelli
November 1903	Giovanni Giolitti
March 1905	Alessandro Fortis
February 1906	Sidney Sonnino
May 1906	Giovanni Giolitti
December 1909	Sidney Sonnino
March 1910	Luigi Luzzatti
March 1911	Giovanni Giolitti
March 1914	Antonio Salandra

Table 14. Political officers of the Kingdom of Italy 1890–1914

3. The Ministries of Crispi 1887–91 and 1893–6

Francesco Crispi combined the jobs of Prime Minister, Foreign Minister
and Minister of the Interior when he was in office, so Italian policies can
be genuinely identified as his own at this time. He had been a revolutionary supporter of Garibaldi at the time of the 'Risorgimento', but was
regarded as more moderate by the time he took office. Nonetheless, he
began with a number of reforms, in local government, prisons and
sanitation. The traditional source of Church income, the ecclesiastical
tithes, were abolished and religious education in elementary schools was
no longer compulsory. He showed his less liberal side in handling
opposition to the government. On the introduction of higher taxes in
1893, a number of leagues of peasants and townsmen, called 'fasci', were

formed in Sicily, demanding lower taxes. Crispi's answer was to strike more than 800 000 people from the electoral rolls and, in 1894, ban anarchist and socialist parties. The prefect of Palermo province was sacked for allowing a socialist to be elected and 50 000 troops were sent to Sicily to enforce martial law. He even suspended Parliament for six months in order to forestall any questioning of his decisions. In his domestic policies, therefore, Crispi may be said to have started on a reformist note, but, faced with opposition, resorted to suppression as a solution.

Crispi regarded his foreign policy as the key to his own success and the future prosperity of Italy. At this point, it is worth considering Italian foreign policy in general, for it was bound by certain unalterable facts that hampered not only Crispi, but also Salandra during World War I and, even more painfully, Mussolini in his relations with Hitler. Firstly, Italy is very vulnerable in a military sense, and became more so during the twentieth century. As a peninsula, she was always open to attack from three sides by sea while her northern defence of mountains was increasingly useless as modern technology advanced. Secondly, her two northern neighbours, France and Austria-Hungary, were in various forms, enemies of each other almost continuously during the period 1882–1945. If Italy joined one of the European alliances, she almost certainly ensured that she had made an enemy of one northern neighbour. Thirdly, as Churchill realized in 1942, Italy's vulnerability made her an attractive route for attacking into central Europe. The seas and mountains that had been such a defence in the time of the Roman Empire were of little use in the conditions of modern warfare.

In the 1880s, though, such considerations were only just beginning to bear. So far as Crispi was concerned, recently united Italy was on the threshold of becoming a real world power, and he would achieve for her what Bismarck had for Germany. To this end, he was determined to strengthen Italy's links with Germany and Austria-Hungary, with whom she had joined in the Triple Alliance in 1882, so that the three Central European powers would be the masters of Europe. He also embarked on a tariff war with France; each country imposed high import duties on goods coming from the other, thus discouraging trade between the two by forcing the price of imports up.

Another route to world power in the late nineteenth century was colonialism, and Crispi was an enthusiastic follower of this. In 1890 he proclaimed Eritrea, on the horn of Africa, an Italian colony (see Map 6). At the same time, he did all he could to extend Italian influence in Ethiopia. From 1887 the Italian government supported Menelek, the king of Shoa, in his fight against Johannes, the Ethiopian 'king of kings'. When the latter died in 1889, Menelek became 'king of kings' and signed the treaty of Uccialli with the Italian government. By this, the Italians understood that Menelek had accepted an Italian protectorate over Ethiopia, but, in 1891, Menelek rejected this interpretation and refused to accept the instructions of the Italian government. By 1895, Crispi had decided that action was necessary to enforce Italy's decisions. Consequently, an

Italian army advanced into Ethiopia from Eritrea but was defeated at Amba Alagi by Ras Makonen, who then captured the Italian fortress of Makallé (20 January 1896). This was a disaster: a European army was not only failing to conquer an African country easily but had actually been defeated. Crispi, eager to restore the country's confidence, ordered General Baratieri to advance and win a victory. The general, against his own better judgement which told him to wait and prepare more thoroughly, did as he was told. On 1 March 1896 his 25 000 troops engaged 100 000 Ethiopians under Menelek at Adowa. The Italian army was easily beaten, and those not killed were held for ransom money. When the news reached Italy, Crispi immediately resigned, his foreign policy in ruins. The new government asked for peace and in October, 1896, signed the treaty of Addis Ababa, by which they recognized the independence of Ethiopia and promised to restrict their activities to Eritrea. This was indeed a meagre reward for the cost in high taxation, soldiers' lives and ignominy in Europe at suffering defeat at the hands of a black power.

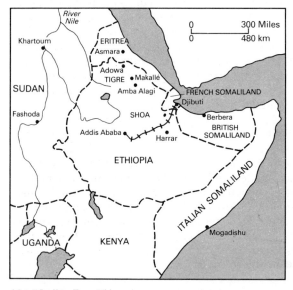

Map 6 Italian East Africa

4. Years of Disaster 1896–1900

If the Crispi era had been inauspicious, even worse was to follow. Many regions suffered virtually famine conditions for this period. There were serious bread riots, which reached a peak in the 'Fatti di Maggio'—May Riots—of 1898, when there was street fighting in Milan, in which two soldiers and eighty civilians were, according to the official figures, killed and 450 wounded. The violence was not restricted to the major cities, but extended to all areas. Fortunato described it as follows:

> An assault on the town hall, devastation and destruction of the tax registers; then the arrival of police or soldiers, volleys of stones from the crowd, opening of fire by the troops. The crowd retreats cursing, leaving its dead and wounded on the ground. Then questions in the Chamber, transfers of officials, resignation of the mayor, trial and conviction of the arrested, and quiet returns. A few weeks or months pass, and suddenly in another commune the story repeats itself.

Martial law was declared in thirty provinces and 400 000 soldiers were under arms. This was the climax of a period in which land had been seized by peasants and an attempt had been made on the King's life.

The government of Rudini was quite unable to deal with this unrest, and he gave way to General Pelloux, who promised severe measures to restore order. He brought in a Public Safety Law which promised drastic suppression; it was opposed by the radicals in Parliament and, having failed to amend the Chamber's procedures to get it passed, Pelloux appealed to the electorate in a general election in 1900. In this election, an unprecedented 200 opposition candidates were elected (a good indication of the government's loss of control) and Pelloux resigned. The people had voted against suppression, but this in effect meant inaction, for the government failed to do anything to relieve either the misery or the rioting, both of which continued. On 29 July 1900 King Umberto I was assassinated at Monza by the anarchist Gastano Bresci, an event which actually heralded the beginning of the end of the unrest. For his son, Victor Emmanuel III, was regarded as more liberal, and appointed the liberal, Zanardelli, as his prime minister. Although the strikes were not ended, they were at least industrial disputes rather than bread riots.

The only positive achievements of this period lay in the field of foreign affairs, where peace was made with France. The agreement was heralded by a settlement of 1896, by which Italy gave up her claims to Tunis, where France was attempting to extend her influence. Then in 1898 a commercial treaty was signed bringing the tariff war to an end, and in 1900 a second colonial agreement was signed; by this, Italy gave the French a free hand to do as they liked in Morocco while France gave Italy a free hand in Tripoli.

5. The Ministries of Giolitti 1903–14

For the decade before the Great War, Italy at last seemed to prosper. Industrial production all but doubled; from a base of 100 for 1896–1900, it rose to 167 between 1906 and 1910 and to 183 between 1911 and 1915. Foreign trade increased by 115%. New industries, notably cars and the electrical and chemical firms, expanded and exported. The political climate, too, was quieter, as the standard of living rose, so the frequency and intensity of strikes declined.

Much of the credit for this improvement must go to Giolitti, who was either Prime Minister or patron of the Prime Minister for all but 220 days of the period 1903–14. He had been Prime Minister in 1892–3, but had been forced to resign as the result of a financial scandal; he even had to leave the country for a time. Nonetheless, by the turn of the century he was back in office as Minister of the Interior in Zanardelli's government from 1900–1903. He adopted a new policy towards labour unrest, insisting that the government should remain neutral unless the law was actually broken or vital supplies threatened. Consequently, there was an upsurge in union activity, and the number of strikes rose from 410, involving some 43 000 workers, in 1900, to 1671, involving over 400 000, in 1901. However, these were not the political confrontations of the 1890s, but economic strikes aimed at, and generally achieving, higher wages; the workers were not to be left out of Italy's new prosperity. Giolitti's tolerance was not unbounded, though. In 1902 he forced the railway employers to accept a settlement to avoid a strike, and he gave his approval, on the other side, to the 'proletarian massacres' (as they were called by the left). These were incidents in which demonstrators and strikers were shot by the police, and they resulted in forty deaths between 1901 and 1904. It was one such incident that led to the general strike of September 1904, which Giolitti faced as Prime Minister.

Giolitti was shrewd enough to realize that the strike had limited support. He let it run its course—only four days—and then called a general election. As he expected, the left fared badly in the aftermath of the strike, and the restricted electorate returned government supporters in great numbers—399 of them against 169 opponents, compared with 296 to 202 in 1900. The new Pope, Pius X, even gave his approval for Catholics to vote in constituencies where their support would help to keep the Socialists out. Giolitti's new government introduced a number of reforms. Taxes on foodstuffs were reduced, legislation for the improvement of working conditions was passed and, in 1912, the franchise was reformed *(see page 51)*. Giolitti also improved relations with the papacy, by permitting religious instruction in schools where it was approved by the local council. For the first time, the government appeared actually to be tackling the country's problems rather than simply suppressing the protests that were produced by them.

However, the problems of Italy were by no means over. As the country became more industrialized, so the dualist nature of the economy became more apparent, since most of the new industries were in the North. The poverty of the South remained and was actually worsened by an accident of nature; in 1908 there was an earthquake in South Calabria and East Sicily, as a result of which a tidal wave destroyed the towns of Reggio and Messina with an estimated 15 000 dead. Emigration remained high, especially in the South. About half of Italy's emigrants came from the South, although it provided less than half the population *(see Table 15)*. Political problems remained. In 1912 the PSI rejected the reformist policies adopted by their leader, Bissolati, and many recommended more violent opposition to the state—a policy that came to fruition in 1914 *(see pages 59–61)*. Democracy, too, remained a sham, even after the extension of the franchise, for many constituencies were regarded as the personal property of their deputy, and in many others the prefects continued with their old practices—changing votes after they were cast, bribing (half the note would be given before the vote was cast, the other half after) and even using dead men's names on electoral rolls.

| Years | | Number of emigrants in thousands | | | Percentage of southerners: | |
		To European and Mediterranean countries	Overseas	Total	to Europe	Overseas
1891–1900	annual averages	129	154	283	32%	54%
1901–05		245	309	554		74%
1906–10		258	394	651	47%	71%
1911		271	263	534	38%	
1912		308	403	711	—	69%
1913		313	560	873	47%	

Table 15. Emigration from Italy 1890–1914   This table is taken from Seton-Watson, *Italy from Liberalism to Fascism.* It should be noted that much of the emigration was temporary, and it has been estimated that between 1900 and 1914 between three and four hundred thousand Italians returned to Italy each year.

Giolitti's foreign policy became increasingly active, especially in 1911 –12, when he followed the views of extreme nationalists like Enrico Corradini and Gabriele D'Annunzio. This time the object of Italy's attention was Tripoli in North Africa *(see Map 7)*. By Tripoli is meant not only the town of Tripoli but also the large area of North Africa to its south—modern day Libya—all of which was a part of the Ottoman (Turkish) Empire. Italy had won the agreement of most other European powers to her acquisition of this area—Germany and Austria-Hungary in 1887, Great Britain in 1890, France in 1900 and Russia in 1909—but had not been able to make any positive moves towards its acquisition. However, in 1911, when the other great powers were preoccupied with the second Moroccan crisis *(see page 82)*, the Italian government acted. An ultimatum was sent to the Turkish government claiming that Tripoli was in a 'state of neglect and disorder' that threatened Italian lives. When Turkey rejected this ultimatum, Italian troops were sent (5 October 1911) and the annexation of Tripoli was announced on 5 November.

The conquest proved less easy than expected. In Tripolitania the Arabs put up a stiff resistance, which in turn led to severe reprisals on the local population. The government was terrified of repeating the debacle of 1896, so that 100 000 troops were sent there to cope with 35 000 Arabs.

In turn, this meant that many soldiers spent most of their time sitting bored in camps, many of them suffering from cholera. By December 1911 it was clear that the war would not easily be won in Tripolotania itself, and this necessitated diplomatic action to enable Italy to extend the war to Turkey itself. As a result, several attacks were launched in the Dardanelles, and in May 1912 thirteen Dodecanese islands, including Rhodes, were occupied. By that summer the coastal strip of Tripolitania was occupied, and the Turks, fearful of attacks from the newly formed Balkan League *(see page 142)* agreed to peace talks. By the treaty of Ouchy (made definite by the treaty of Lausanne), Tripoli was given to Italy on condition that the Sultan of Turkey could still appoint the caliph (religious leader) and that Italy left Rhodes and the other occupied islands. Giolitti had not undertaken the war with enthusiasm, but had won some credit from it; at least this time Italy's goal had been achieved and there had been no humiliation.

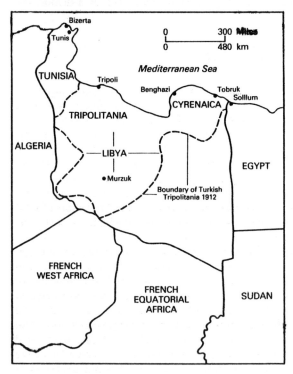

Map 7 Italian Lybia

However, the cost of the war had been high—1300 million lire—and had necessitated high taxation. There had not been many casualties—1500 killed in action, 1900 by disease and 4000 wounded—but the size of the army sent had meant that many families had seen their breadwinners conscripted for little purpose. The government fared badly in the election of 1913, when once again the opposition increased its representation, and in early 1914 popular discontent reached new heights. On 9 March there was a general strike in Rome to protest against the high taxes caused by the cost of the war, and popular discontent reached a peak in June of that year. An anti-military demonstration in Ancona led to riots and a general strike affecting many parts of the country *(see page 61)*. During this, 'Red Week', many government officials went into hiding and several towns declared themselves independent communes. In the Romagna, an independent republic was even proclaimed. It took a week for government troops to restore order, and thereafter, although Italy proclaimed her neutrality at the outbreak of the Great War, both people and government were preoccupied with the affairs of Europe. Nonetheless, it is significant that Italy in 1914 was experiencing the same disquiet that she had had in 1898; the 'Giolittian Era' may have achieved much, but Italy was still far from being either an industrial or a democratic country.

6. Italian Socialism 1900–14

Italian socialists had played their part in the disruption of the 1890s. During the period of repression, the party—the 'Partito Socialista Italiano'—had, along with the anarchists and other left-wing groups, been outlawed. This ban, of 1894, actually reinvigorated the party, which polled three times as many votes in the 1895 election as it had in 1892. Fifteen deputies were elected, three of whom were serving prison sentences at the time. In 1896 Rudini's policy of appeasement towards the left led to the release of these leaders and the launching of the party newspaper, *Avanti*, on Christmas Day. However, the May Riots of 1898 had led to a renewed period of suppression, during which the party was again put under pressure.

The Party Congress at Rome in 1900 saw the first attempt of the party to resolve the inevitable reformist—revolutionary split that had, as elsewhere *(see page 67)*, developed during the 1890s. The party drew up two programmes—a list of maximum demands that were their eventual aim and a minimum programme that identified the immediate policies. The party chose the reformist line by adopting the minimum programme, for the time being, and the moderate leaders, Turati and Bissolati, urged support for Giolitti's policies towards strikes. In fact, these two were invited to join Giolitti's government in November 1903, but turned down the offer for fear of exaggerating the differences between the left and the right of the party. It was this balance that was to dominate the party throughout the period up to the outbreak of war.

The moderate leadership faced opposition from two quarters. Within the party opposition was led by Enrico Ferri. He was a great orator who believed that reformism would achieve little, and that more forceful action was needed. In 1903 he replaced Bissolati as editor of *Avanti* and from this post led a series of virulent attacks on the government. Further to the left were the syndicalists, who regarded acceptance of reformism as tantamount to acceptance of capitalism and all that went with it. Led by a Naples journalist, Labriola, the syndicalists urged an active policy of strikes and violence through their paper, *L'Avanguardista Socialista*, which had a large following in the northern industrial centres. Until 1909 these left-wing elements of the party had considerable success. They dominated the Congress at Bologna in 1904 and led the general strike of September that year. Their policies were moderated by the 1906 Congress, which instead opted for a middle line proposed by Ferri as a compromise between the two wings of the party, but the outbreak of a new wave of strikes in 1907–8 brought them to prominence again. An agricultural strike in Parma in May 1908 lasted for two months and was only ended after violence with blacklegs, barricades in the streets and a police attack on the Chamber of Labour. This strike marked both the climax and the beginning of the end of syndicalist support, since it frightened off many socialists from the path of violence and confrontation.

Thereafter, until 1914, the party was dominated by the reformists. The 1908 Florence Congress of the party adopted the reformist programme, and in 1909 the party won forty-one seats in the election (they had previously had twenty-nine). The leaders—Turati and Bissolati—openly supported Giolitti, and were again invited to join the government, but again refused for fear of splitting the party, in 1911. By this time, the party was assured of the support of many of the newly prosperous working classes and had become similar in many respects to the British Labour Party. It also had the support of the General Confederation of Labour (the CGL) that had been founded in 1906. Although the party deputies murmured their disapproval at the invasion of Tripoli, they were in general loyal government supporters over other measures, such as the franchise reform of 1911.

This reformist trend was met by a reaction from the left of the party. Although the 1910 Congress reiterated its support for the reformist programme of 1908, there was a sizeable vote against it–6000 votes against 13 000. Southerners such as Salvemini felt that the party was ignoring the needs of the South, which had remained poor and backward, in favour of backing the claims of northern industrial workers. Others were attracted by the arguments of Mussolini, who led an attack on the reformists at the 1912 Congress, which resulted in the expulsion of Bissolati and three other moderate leaders. At that Congress, the party readopted a left-wing programme, demanding the class struggle, republicanism and an end to co-operation with the government. Mussolini, leader of this trend, became the new editor of *Avanti*. The revolutionary syndicalists also underwent a revival at this time. Their veteran leader, Malatesta, returned from exile after fourteen years, in 1913, and in the same year there were renewed strikes, including two general strikes in Milan.

The new pre-eminence of the left reached its height in the early summer of 1914. In April the party Congress at Ancona was once again dominated by the left, and repeated the programme of 1912. On 7 June, again in Ancona, a demonstration against militarism, nationalism and capitalism was held on Constitution Day. Clashes with police led to the deaths of three demonstrators. This provided the left with the excuse it was looking for. A general strike was called, and there was widespread, but unco-ordinated, disorder, especially in Emilia and the Marche. Stations, churches and great estates were attacked, public buildings seized and, in many areas, taxes abolished by decree. After two days the general strike was called off, but it was some time before order was restored. The reformist deputies dissociated themselves from the actions, and supported a motion of Turati that 'the emancipation of the prolet-ariat is not to be achieved by outbursts of disorganized mobs'. It was significant that they had little control over events during this 'Red Week', which was dominated rather by the extra-parliamentary left and the revolutionary syndicalists.

7. Bibliography

The two best-known and most useful books on Italy are *Italy* by D. Mack-Smith (Univ. of Michigan Press, 1959) and *Italy from Liberalism to Fascism: 1870–1925* by C. Seton-Watson (Methuen, 1967).

8. Discussion Points and Exercises

A   *This section consists of questions that might be used for discussion (or written answers) as a way of expanding on the chapter and testing understanding of it:*
1   Why did some Italians dislike their new Kingdom?
2   How was the Italian economy affected by unification?
3   Were short-lived governments inevitable?
4   What foreign policy options in Europe have been open and desirable to Italian governments in the twentieth century?
5   What did Crispi hope to achieve by taking Ethiopia?
6   Why were the late 1890s so disastrous?
7   Compare Giolitti's achievements with those of his predecessors.
8   Why did Italy attack Tripoli in 1911?
9   Why did Italian socialism become increasingly moderate, and then lurch leftwards again after 1912?

B   *This exercise is intended to show you some of the problems faced by the govern-ments at this time:*
1   Write a report for King Victor Emmanuel on his accession to the throne, outlining the major social and economic problems facing his country and suggesting possible solutions to them.

C *This section suggests ways in which you might compare Italy with other European countries at this time:*

1 Was Italy a particularly 'strong' or 'weak' country at this time?
2 Compare socialism in Italy with French and/or German socialism.
3 Compare Italian colonial aims and achievements with those of France and/or Germany.

D *Essays:*

1 How successful were Italian governments in solving the country's problems before 1914?
2 'Italian socialism was rendered ineffective by its own divisions.' Do you agree?

IV Germany 1890–1914

1. Introduction

Of all the European powers, Germany's power increased the most in the period after 1890. The country had been united only twenty years before, yet by 1900 had become one of the three great economic powers in the world. The massive and rapid economic expansion of the country therefore forms an important area of study for the historian. Equally, the relationship between this economic expansion and the constitutional and political structure of the country has concerned both contemporary and later historians. Was it possible for a highly modernized economy to be governed by an almost autocratic form of government? Thirdly, historians have studied the relationship between the politico-economic structure and the foreign policy of the country. So although this chapter studies these three fields—politics, economics, foreign policy—separately, it is in fact the relationship between them that is of most interest to historians.

2. The Constitutional Organization of the State

Diagram 6 outlines the organization of the German Empire according to the Constitution of 1871:

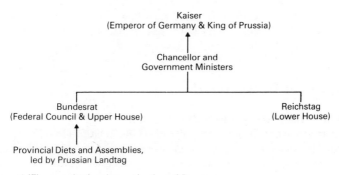

Diagram 6. The constitutional organization of Germany

The Empire technically consisted of four kingdoms, six grand-duchies, five duchies, seven principalities, three free cities and the Imperial territory of Alsace-Lorraine, captured from France in 1871. As the German state was federal, certain local powers remained in the hands of the individual states. Their power in the central government was maintained through the Bundesrat. There were fifty-eight members of this, one from each of the twenty-six states, except for the larger ones which had more. Bavaria had six and Prussia seventeen. The voting system was such that this gave the Prussian members a veto over legislation. The members of the Bundesrat were representatives of their state legislatures and thus bound by their instructions. The Provincial diets and assemblies were therefore of some importance, and the franchise systems in the States significant. These varied considerably. The Prussian Constitution of 1850 established a three-class voting system that assured the nobility of a majority. In the 1908 Landtag elections, 600 000 votes elected six Social Democrats while 418 000 votes secured 212 conservative seats.

Constitutionally, the power to make laws was held jointly by the Bundesrat and the Reichstag. Members of the Reichstag were elected by constituency every five years by all men over the age of twenty-five. In fact, its legislative power was considerably reduced by other aspects of the Constitution. Many revenues were permanent rather than annual, thus reducing the Reichstag's control over the individual ministers. It could be, and was, dissolved by the Kaiser with the consent of the Bundesrat. Consequently, the Reichstag criticized and amended legislation that was proposed by others. Its relationship with the Bundesrat and the Kaiser became critical in the period before the Great War.

The Chancellor and ministers were responsible only to the Kaiser. He appointed and dismissed them, and, as events demonstrated *(see page 71)*, it was very difficult for them to pursue policies with which he was not in complete agreement. Since the Kaiser also had the power to dissolve the Reichstag, his control over politics was considerable. As Prussia dominated the Bundesrat and the Kaiser was also King of Prussia, he could also rely on loyal support there. Moreover, Kaiser Wilhelm II acknowledged the extent of his power and intended to maintain it; in a speech in 1895 he stated, 'It is my wish to uphold undiminished the Right and Fullness of Power founded on history and the constitution.' Wilhelm probably had greater control over the course of events than any other ruler in Europe.

3. Political Background

(a) The Kaiser, the Junkers and the Army
Wilhelm's power was not the result only of his constitutional position but also of his personality. Wilhelm II was twenty-nine years old when he became Kaiser on the premature death (from cancer of the throat) of his father, Frederick III *(see Diagram 7)*. Unlike his relative, Nicholas II of

Russia, Wilhelm keenly anticipated his time as Kaiser. Stories of his childhood and youth are plentiful—of his arrogance and determination to win, of his keeness to fence and play manly games, despite his malformed left arm, of his rudeness to his mother and relatives. There is little doubt that Wilhelm was intelligent; he fully understood political issues and pursued a wide range of interests. Equally, he was an extremely sensitive man, who easily took offence and expected praise for his achievements. Bismark summed up his new ruler well when he complained: 'This new Emperor is like a balloon. If you don't keep fast hold of the string you never know where he'll be off to.' Few had the ability to 'keep fast hold'.

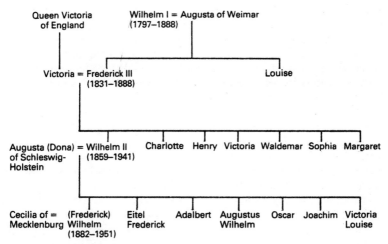

Diagram 7. Family tree of the Hohenzollerns

Two groups of people dominated politics and society in Wilhelmine Germany—the nobility and the army. The two were closely linked by the many nobles who served in the army; in the period 1898–1918, 56% of army officers were titled. The nobles—the 'junkers'—owned enormous estates in the East. Their power was won partly by the Prussian voting system and by their prominent position in bodies like the Colonial League and the Agrarian League *(see page 69)* as well as through their personal positions and contacts with the Kaiser. Equally, the officer class of the army was very influential. There was an army of half a million men in 1890. The troops took an oath of loyalty personally to the Kaiser rather than the State, and money for the army was voted by the Reichstag only every seven years. This enabled the officer corps to avoid civilian control. These officers had great influence in the Kaiser's circle. Count Philip Eulenburg, himself a member of that circle, wrote of Wilhelm II that he

> sucked in like an infant at the breast the tradition that every Prussian officer is not only the quintessence of honour, but of all good breeding, all

culture and all intellectual endowment. How a man so clear-sighted as Wilhelm II could have attributed the last two qualities to *everyone* in guard's uniform has always been a puzzle to me. We will call it a combination of military Hohenzollernism and self-hypnotism.

The Kaiser himself told his troops when they gave him their oath of loyalty: 'We belong to each other—I and the army—we were born for each other and will cleave indissolubly to each other, whether it be the will of God to send us calm or storm.'

(b) Political Parties

There were two main right-wing groups. The Conservatives represented the views of the landowning classes and of Prussia; they were generally supporters of authority and military discipline and were keen adherents of a nationalist foreign policy. As the political party of the Junker class, they were loyal supporters of the Kaiser. The Independent, or Free, Conservatives had similar views and also favoured protectionist economic policies. They were less oriented towards Prussia and farming and more likely to win the votes of wealthy commercial and professional people.

There were also two main 'liberal' parties and a third, smaller, one—the German People's Party. These were not 'liberal' by modern standards in that they were generally nationalist and opposed to the rise of the Socialist party. The National Liberals had been the leading party in the 1870s and had supported Bismarck's policy of 'Kulturkampf' aimed at reducing the power and influence of the Church. By 1890, both they and the Liberal Progressives were losing votes, and were forced to ally with the more conservative parties in the Reichstag to maintain a majority for the right.

(a) Kaisers

1871–9 March 1888	Wilhelm I
9 March–15 June 1888	Frederick III
15 June 1888–9 November 1918	Wilhelm II

(b) Chancellors

1871–18 March 1890	Prince Otto von Bismarck
1890–26 October 1894	General Georg Leo von Caprivi
1894–16 October 1900	Prince Chlodwig zu Hohenlohe-Schillingfurst
1900–14 July 1909	Prince Bernhard von Bulow
1909–14 July 1917	Dr Theobald von Bethmann-Hollweg

Table 16. Political rulers of Germany 1890–1914

German politics were complicated by the existence of the Centre Party ('Zentrum', or Z). The party was founded in 1871 specifically to represent the interests of the Catholic Church and its members. It was opposed to the domination of Prussia and, especially, to Bismarck, because of his anti-clerical policies in the 1870s. Equally, it was concerned by the rise of the parties of the Left. Consequently, it was almost always in the key position of balancing left and right in the Reichstag, particularly as, from 1874, it always had between ninety and 110 seats, making it one of the largest parties *(see Table 17)*.

	1884	1887	1890	1893	1898	1903	1907	1912
Conservatives	78	80	73	72	56	54	60	43
Independent Cons	28	41	20	28	23	21	24	14
National Liberals	51	99	42	53	46	51	54	45
Liberal Progressives	67	32	66	37	41	31	42	42
German People's Party	7	—	10	11	7	9	7	—
Centre Party	99	98	106	96	102	100	105	91
Social Democrats	24	11	35	44	56	81	43	110
Nationalities:								
Poles, Danes,								
Hanoverians and								
Alsatians			38	35	34	32	29	33
Others			7	21	41	22	33	19

Table 17. State of the parties in the Reichstag 1884–1914

The rise of the Social Democratic Party, or SPD (Sozialdemokratische Partei Deutschlands), was the major political phenomenon of the pre-war era. How to treat both the party and its ideas were to be crucial issues for Wilhelm II and his Chancellors. The party had been founded in 1869 by Wilhelm Liebknecht and August Bebel, who were its first members to be elected to the Reichstag. During the 1870s and 1880s their expansion was considerably limited by anti-socialist laws, but some of the more moderate members still won Reichstag seats. Ideological arguments between Marxists, reformists and anarchists divided the membership in its early years.

In 1891 the party voted to adopt the Erfurt programme, which was Marxist. Many members though supported the reformist argument that was best explained by Eduard Bernstein in *Postulates of Socialism* (1898). He argued that, contrary to Marxist doctrine, capitalism was getting stronger. Consequently, the overthrow of the system was becoming harder and change could only be achieved by joining 'bourgeois' Parliaments and governments rather than by total revolution. The revisionist argument was expressed in a motion to the 1900 Congress of the Second International: 'In a modern democratic state, the proletariat must not conquer power by coup, but rather through a long, patient organization of proletarian activity in economic spheres, moral and physical regeneration of the working class, gradual conquest of municipal councils and legislative assemblies'. The motion was defeated, and the SPD rejected reformism. In fact, though, many SPD members did join legislative assemblies. Karl Kautsky, who spoke against the motion at the Congress, and Bebel himself expressed the view of the majority by rejecting reformism in theory but in practice accepting seats in the Reichstag and the provincial diets. Consequently, the SPD won more and more votes and seats, especially as the anti-socialist legislation was relaxed or ignored after 1890. By 1912 it was the largest single party in the Reichstag and had increased its proportion of the vote from 10% in 1887 to 31·7% in 1903.

4. Political History 1890–1914

German history in this period was dominated by the expansion of the economy and by foreign affairs. Domestic political issues were correspondingly less important. The rise of the SPD and socialist ideas, concomitant with the industrial expansion, was regarded as the major problem. Other domestic issues were closely linked to foreign affairs, notably the size of the army and navy and the regulation of overseas trade.

The new Kaiser's enthusiasm to personally determine policy led to an inevitable clash with Bismarck who had, almost single-handed, dictated policy for over twenty years. Two issues divided Bismarck and Wilhelm II. Bismarck wanted to renew the Reinsurance treaty with Russia in 1890 *(see pages 76–7)*; Wilhelm favoured a more clearly pro-Habsburg policy, and suggested the possibility of overtures to Britain. Secondly, in January 1890 the anti-socialist legislation of the 1880s was due for renewal by the Reichstag. The Reichstag opposed the laws and the Kaiser, after initially supporting Bismarck's firmness against socialism, agreed with the deputies. He suggested that an international conference on labour relations should be held, an idea that earned him, temporarily, the title 'Labour Emperor', but which Bismarck regarded as a concession to revolutionary elements. Clearly co-operation was impossible when such fundamental questions divided them. Bismarck was ordered to 'ask permission to resign'; he refused. On 18 March 1890, he was ordered out of office. He was consoled by being made duke of Lauenberg, but infuriated by his unceremonious removal from the Chancery palace.

His successor, General Georg Caprivi, was a Prussian soldier with little political experience, who was expected to do as the Kaiser said. Wilhelm continued his conciliatory policy towards socialism, in the hope that concessions would woo moderates away from extremist policies. A series of legislation was approved to this end. In 1890 Sundays were made a compulsory rest-day and the employment of women and children was limited. A system for the establishment of industrial courts to arbitrate wage claims was set up. The next year the system of factory inspection was tightened up and workers were permitted to elect committees to negotiate with employers on working conditions. However, it was clear that the policy was doing little to win the new proletariat away from the SPD. In 1890 it won thirty-five Reichstag seats (from eleven in 1887) and in 1893 44 *(see Table 17)*. The concessions were actually encouraging support for the SPD; if so few deputies could win this much, how much more could more deputies win? When the French President Carnot was shot by an Italian anarchist in 1894, Wilhelm had second thoughts about socialists, and proclaimed '...forward into battle for religion, for morality and for order against the parties of revolution.' Unfortunately, Caprivi was less co-operative and refused to draft a bill against subversion. Instead he resigned, retiring into obscurity.

During his chancellorship, Caprivi had also made overtures to the left by a series of commercial treaties. These were made with Austria-Hungary, Italy, Russia and a number of smaller powers, and each reduced tariffs between Germany and the country concerned. This facilitated the export of German industrial goods and reduced the cost of agricultural imports; this in turn lowered food prices, which had risen considerably, reaching a peak in 1891–2. However, the policy infuriated landowners, who were forced to reduce their own prices to compete with the cheap imports. In 1894 they organized themselves into the 'Bund der Landwirte' (Agrarian League) which by 1900 had 250 000 members and won considerable concessions on agricultural policy *(see page 71)*.

Caprivi was also responsible for the enlargement of the army. In 1891, Count Alfred von Schlieffen was appointed Chief of Staff. Like his predecessors, he was concerned by the possiblity of a two-front war, especially in view of the end of the conciliatory policy towards Russia. His solution, however, reversed that of his predecessors, and aimed to attack France first. This necessitated an increase in the size of the army. However the Reichstag initially rejected the planned increase—of 84 000 men—and only after being dissolved (1893) did a new Reichstag agree to it. Even then, considerable concessions were made, notably that the period of service for conscripts should be reduced from three years to two and that the Reichstag could debate the army's financial grant every five years instead of every seven. These concessions further infuriated the right-wing, whose opposition to Caprivi was influential in his resignation.

His successor, Hohenlohe, was seventy-five years old, and an ex-Prime Minister of Bavaria and governor of Alsace-Lorraine. He was not expected to oppose the Kaiser's policies, since he seemed to meet the requirements for chancellor that Philip Eulenberg claimed the Kaiser required—'...neither conservative, nor liberal, neither ultramontane nor progressive, neither ritualist nor atheist...'. Hohenlohe himself pronounced that he was 'Imperial Chancellor, not an office boy' but in fact had little influence. In 1894 he proposed the bill against subversion that the Kaiser wanted, but when it was rejected by the Reichstag the issue of socialism was temporarily allowed to drop. Wilhelm made a lot of noise about the need for firmness, but, apart from a bill of 1899 that gave penalties for workers who forced their fellow workers to join a union or go on strike, no action was taken. Instead, the Kaiser planned to win back the support of the middle class, which had been partly lost by the concessions to the workers. The new policy, 'the policy of concentration', emphasized the importance of military expansion and colonial achievements *(see pages 79, 136)*.

Although Hohenlohe remained Chancellor until 1900, the new policies were not implemented on his initiative. Instead, they were produced by a new group of men, who can truly be identified as Wilhelm's ministers. Chief among these was Count Bernhard von Bülow, foreign minister from 1897 and chancellor from 1900–1909. Bülow was only in his forties when Chancellor—a man of Wilhelm's own generation. Little complimentary has been written about him, chiefly because he succeeded in offending most of his colleagues as a part of his game of keeping the Kaiser's favour. His father had been Bismarck's foreign minister, and a diplomatic career in Rome preceded his appointment as foreign minister, The second of the 'new men' was Alfred von Tirpitz, a naval officer who became secretary to the Navy in 1897. Tirpitz was an able organizer and a convincing speaker, who won over both the Reichstag and the German public to the cause of naval expansion. The third major influence on policy was Friedrich von Holstein, a survivor of the Bismarck era. He became a senior adviser in the foreign office in 1878. Balfour has written of him: 'By sitting for long hours at his desk and supplementing his official papers through an extensive private correspondence, he gained a unique familiarity with the minutiae of German foreign policy and with the manner of its executants.' He, like the Kaiser, disagreed with Bismarck's policy towards Russia, and from 1890 onwards found himself Wilhelm II's chief adviser on foreign affairs, even though he only once met him. These three men—Bülow, Tirpitz and Holstein—were the chief influences on government policy in the crucial period at the turn of the century.

The passage of the Navy Laws was the dominant issue in German politics between 1896 and 1900. In 1896 Britain had thirty-three battleships and 130 cruisers; Germany had six and four respectively. The Kaiser and his advisers were convinced that Germany could not attain the status of a world power *(see page 78)* until she too had a navy. To try to equal Britain's fleet was out of the question. Consequently, Tirpitz propounded his 'risk theory', by which the German fleet had to be large enough to damage any attacker sufficiently to make it not worth risking a battle. The Navy Laws were therefore intended to provide the additional ships, men and ports to bring this about. The first Navy Law (1897) proposed the building of seven battleships and nine cruisers before 1904. The Reichstag, often so hostile to military expansion, was won over by Tirpitz. The newly formed Navy League quickly came under his influence and was used to spread the gospel of navalism to the general public. The Kaiser himself explained the need for a fleet at the time of the Boer War; 'I am not in a position to go beyond the strictest neutrality and I must first get for myself a fleet. In twenty years' time, when the fleet is ready, I can use another language.' A second Navy Law, approved in 1900, proposed building three battleships each year over a twenty-year period. The third Navy Law (1906) increased the tonnage of the ships and added six cruisers to the annual programme; it also allowed for the widening of the Kiel Canal to enable ships of Dreadnought size to pass through. By this time, German naval expansion was far beyond the bounds of domestic policy, and had become a key factor in Anglo-German relations *(see pages 136–8)*.

During his period as Chancellor, Bülow concerned himself mainly with foreign affairs, leaving domestic matters to his Interior Minister, Count Arthur von Posadowsky. Broadly speaking, Caprivi's policy of making concessions to the workers was revived. In 1900, accident insurance was extended to more occupations and pensions for the elderly and the disabled were increased. In 1901 Industrial Courts for the settlement of disputes were made compulsory in all towns with more than 2000 inhabitants. From 1903 workers were entitled to receive sickness benefits for twenty-six weeks rather than thirteen, and in 1908 additional restrictions were imposed on the employment of children. On the other hand, when the commercial treaties drawn up by Caprivi *(see page 69)* expired in 1902, they were not renewed. Instead, responding to the pressures of the Agrarian League, agricultural tariffs were restored to their former levels and food prices consequently rose.

Bülow's government faced two internal crises. The first arose in 1906. There had been native risings against German rule in South West Africa, where Catholic missionaries reported that the colonial rulers had treated the natives harshly and dismissed their protests. The Catholic Centre party joined the Social Democrats in criticizing the government and opposing a bill to provide money for the colonial government in South West Africa. Since the Centre party held the balance in the Reichstag *(see Table 17, page 67)*, this amounted to defeat for the government's supporters in the Reichstag. To some extent, Bülow welcomed the opportunity to end the government's dependency on the Catholics. The Reichstag was dissolved and the 'Hottentot' (so-called after the rebellious Africans) election held; it was a lively affair, in which both sides actively criticized the other. The outcome was as Bülow hoped—221 seats for the Conservatives and their allies, 177 to the Centre, Socialists and their allies. This majority was won despite the fact that the centre and left won 3 million more votes than the right as there had been no change in constituency boundaries since 1871. The new coalition of government supporters, known as the 'Blue-Black Bloc' passed some legislation of a conservative nature, such as the extension of the sedition laws, but the Progressives support prevented it from extremism, since they proved almost as moderate as the Centre Party, suggesting (but not winning) an end to the Prussian three-tier franchise system.

The second crisis arose in 1908. On 28 October, an article appeared in the *Daily Telegraph* based on talks between Wilhelm and his English host at Highcliffe in Hampshire. In the article, Wilhelm expressed his great wish for close relations with Britain. He explained how he had supported and helped Britain during the Boer War. He said that the fleet was intended for the protection of Germany's colonies, especially in the Far East, where both China and Japan were a serious threat. It was not to be used against Britain. The article proved to be dynamite, not in England but in Germany. What right had the Kaiser to make such important policy statements? Were they not the prerogative of his ministers? Was it for him to decide that Germany wanted Britain's friendship? Bülow was criticized for allowing the article to be published. He was in a tight corner as he had been sent a proof copy of the article but had passed it on without reading it. He offered his resignation, but it was refused. There followed a period in which the Kaiser was sharply criticized, not only for his high-handedness, but also, not for the first time, for the kind of friends he kept, some of whom were suspected, if not proven, homosexuals. Talk of constitutional changes to reduce the Kaiser's power was widespread, but nothing was done since the Conservative majority in the Reichstag could not agree on any acceptable alternative.

The Blue-Black Bloc collapsed in July 1909. Naval building had incurred enormous expenses. To raise the required money, an inheritance tax and an increase in contributions from the individual states to the federal budget were proposed. The Conservatives refused to support these. The Progressives refused to support anything else. Eventually a Finance Bill was passed with Conservative, Centre and Polish support but Bülow took the opportunity to resign, on the grounds that he no longer had the confidence of the Reichstag. In fact, his relations with the Kaiser had become increasingly difficult and only Wilhelm's difficulty in choosing a successor had kept him in office so long.

Eventually, Wilhelm chose the Interior Minister (since 1907), Theobald Bethmann-Hollweg, of whom he had once said, 'He always knows the answer and tries to instruct me. I can't work with him.' By his own admission, Bethmann knew nothing of foreign affairs, thus leaving Wilhelm greater freedom of action in that field.

The government's relations with the Reichstag continued to prove difficult, since defence and finance, on which left and right had such different views, were the dominant issues. The 1912 election had completely changed the composition of the Reichstag and the Social Democrats, with 110 seats, were now the largest single party. With the newly united Progressive People's Party and the Centre, they could command 243 of the 391 seats. Only the lack of co-operation between these parties gave the government a chance to pass its own legislation. Finance was the greatest problem. The socialists would not countenance any increase in indirect taxation and the conservatives opposed any increase in property taxes. In 1913 a bill for an additional 4000 officers, 15 000 NCOs and 117 000 men for the army, at a cost of a billion marks, was introduced. It was supported by the conservatives, since it was a strongly nationalist measure. However, to meet the enormous cost, a special national defence tax on property (the 'Wehrstener') was proposed. Being a tax on wealth, it was supported by the socialists, even though they opposed the army it was to pay for. Such expediency was the only means to continue government.

In 1913 there was a serious crisis over an incident at Zabern, a town in Alsace. A young lieutenant had not stopped his men treating the townspeople roughly; a lame cobbler was injured. The townspeople demonstrated against the army's actions; they were rounded up by the soldiers and locked in the barracks. There were public and official protests, and the Governor-General appealed to the Kaiser to settle the matter. Only when the Governor threatened to resign did Wilhelm act; rather than punish the soldiers concerned, he had them sent away on manoeuvres. In the Reichstag, all parties but the conservatives joined the protests, but they achieved nothing—even the colonel who was responsible for the town was acquitted by a court martial. The incident forcefully under-lined the superiority of the military, and the inability of civilian authorities to influence them.

Michael Balfour, in *The Kaiser and his Times,* has concluded that 'the atmosphere in Imperial Germany during the wars before the war cannot have been pleasant. The country was being run by an exclusive minority whose strength was waning and whose outlook was becoming increasingly repugnant to the general public.' Neither the public nor their elected representatives in the Reichstag had any influence on events of import-ance. Instead, the Kaiser and his entourage, through the hapless medium of the Chancellor, determined and dictated policy. At the same time, as Perry has written:

> Germany became a state of soldiers and war rather than one of citizens and law. The army not only remained independent of any control other than that of the monarch himself but also through prolonged and universal military service it was able to influence the thinking of the greater part of the German nation. German society was one in which the upper classes were soaked in the ethos of the barrack square, in which social distinction was measured almost entirely by military rank.

Few protested about this. There were strikes, but on purely economic grounds, and they were swiftly settled. The Social Democrats, the likely focus of opposition, were apparently satisfied by the palliative of parlia-mentary power—a power that was illusory. The vast majority of the people seemed content. Economic expansion had provided them with more material benefits than they had ever had before. Their government had made Germany powerful and respected around the world. In any case, harsh punishments were given to those foolish enough to protest.

5. Economic History

The German economy expanded widely and rapidly during the Wilhel-mine period. This section examines the extent of that advance, illustrated as far as possible by statistics. These figures are as accurate as possible, but they are drawn from a wide range of sources and in many cases should be treated as approximations, indicative of a trend, rather than precise details. Secondly, this section makes little attempt to examine the reasons for Germany's rapid economic advance at this time; this is done in the exercise on page 86

Production of crucial basic materials provides one measure of industrial advance. Without such materials, much economic activity—armament manufacture, the expansion of transport facilities, the manufacture of consumer goods—is impossible. Tables 18, 19 and 20 therefore take three such materials, coal, which in the case of Germany includes lignite or brown coal, pig iron and steel. In each case equivalent figures for Britain, the other leading European manufacturer, are included for comparison.

| | Germany | | Great Britain |
	Output	Number of miners	Output
1871	37 900	125 000	118 000
1880	59 100	179 000	149 000
1890	89 100	262 000	184 000
1900	149 800	414 000	228 800
1910	192 300	621 000	268 700
1913	279 000	689 000	292 000

Table 18. Coal Production (in thousands of metric tons) 1871–1913

Some calculations on these figures reveal some more digestible facts. Germany's production between 1890 and 1913 increased by 213% while Britain's rose by 58·6%. Productivity per miner increased consistently throughout the period, with the exception of the decade 1900–10. Overall, in 1871 each miner produced about 300 tons per annum; in 1913 the figure was over 400 tons.

	Germany	Great Britain
1870	1391	6060
1880	2729	7875
1890	4037	8033
1900	7549	9003
1910	14 793	10 380

Table 19. Pig Iron Production (in thousands of metric tons) 1870–1910

	Germany	Great Britain
1870	169	286
1880	660	1320
1890	2161	3637
1900	6645	5130
1910	13 698	6374

Table 20. Steel Production (in thousands of metric tons) 1870–1910

Similar calculations with these tables reveal that pig iron production increased almost eleven-fold in Germany while it almost doubled in

Britain, while steel production rose an incredible 80-fold in Germany and 22-fold in Britain. It was such remarkable increases in these primary industries that provided the basis for Germany's rapid economic expansion before the Great War.

There were also considerable increases in applied and modern industries, most notably the electrical and chemical industries. Siemens had experimented with electric traction in 1879 and by the 1880s the German Edison Company (later AEG) was installing lighting systems. In census returns there had been no category for electrical workers in 1882; by 1895, 26 000 listed themselves in this new category, and by 1907 107 000, of whom more than 30 000 worked for AEG ('Allgemeine Elektrizitats-Gesellschaft'). The value of cable exports rose from £150 000 in 1891 to £2 500 000 in 1908. Similar advances occurred in chemicals. In 1878 only a million tons of sulphuric acid were produced in the whole world; by 1907 Germany alone produced 1 402 000 tons. Ammonia production rose from 84 000 tons to 287 000 tons between 1897 and 1907. The production of crude potassium salts at Stassfurt rose from 906 000 tons in 1881 to 4 607 000 in 1911. Most of these chemicals were sold on the home market, primarily for use as fertilizers.

The increased availablility of modern machinery and the use of fertilizers contributed to expansion in agricultural production. Sugar beet, which requires both of these, provides a good guide for this, and is shown in Table 21.

	Average yield of beet p.a. (tons)	Average yield of raw sugar p.a. (tons)
1866–70	2 500 000	211 000
1889–90	8 722 000	1 110 000
1906–1910	13 423 000	2 116 000

Table 21. Sugar Beet Production in Germany 1866–1910

The yield of sugar per ton of beet increased from one ton of sugar from twelve of beet to one of sugar from six of beet over a forty-year period. There were other agrarian advances. More than four million acres were brought under cultivation for the first time in the last twenty years of the century. Yields of crops and the number of livestock (except for sheep) also increased, although even in 1912 Germany was not self-sufficient in animal products.

The effects of this rapid advance were far-reaching. On the one hand, German workers were likely to be better off than ever before. Their jobs were secure and the material benefits of the new industries reached them, if not immediately, in the form of consumer goods. On the other hand, working conditions were often unpleasant and more and more Germans found themselves crowding into the industrial centres, many of which were concentrated in a single small area. Significantly, the world's first slum clearance programme was undertaken in Hamburg in 1893, while at the same time many German cities were having trams, street lighting and similar amenities installed.

The new conditions stimulated the development of working-class movements. Workers could see both the wealth that they had created for others and the prospect of more material possessions for themselves, each of which encouraged them to demand higher pay. At the same time, their working hours and conditions led them to demand improvements from their employers. Yet the one organ through which they might hope to orchestrate any opposition—the SPD in the Reichstag—was apparently stifled by the franchise system and the constitutional weaknesses of the Reichstag. In such conditions the development of extra-parliamentary forms of protest, and of revolutionary ideas, might have been expected. Consequently, a number of authors have pointed to the likelihood of revolution in Germany during Wilhelm II's reign.

In turn, it has been argued that the Kaiser sought ways to distract his people's attention from this situation and to isolate potential enemies. One way was through the concessions offered to the workers by the Caprivi and Bülow ministries, which can be interpreted as an attempt to win over the moderates. It has also been argued that Germany's ambitious foreign policy was an attempt to capture public support for a government that faced serious difficulties. In this way, opposition to the Kaiser and his ministers could be seen as unpatriotic and the opponents outlawed as extremists while the majority of the people supported the all-conquering government. Similarly, the continued preeminence of the army not only gave the Kaiser a powerful force to quell rebellion but also helped to identify opponents as fringe extremists, since to oppose the army was not just unpatriotic but actually threatened the country's security. Taken to its conclusion, this argument sees the Kaiser's efforts to distract his people from opposition as a critical factor in the events that led up to the outbreak of war in 1914.

6. Foreign Policy

(a) The end of Bismarck's policy
For over twenty years Bismarck had worked to maintain a favourable position for Germany in Europe. Primarily, this necessitated the isolation of France so that the French dream of recapturing the lost provinces of Alsace and Lorraine could not become reality. An alliance of France and her ancient enemy, Britain, was unlikely. Austria-Hungary, both by race and by the treaty of 1879, was a guaranteed friend. Consequently, Russia was the key to Bismarck's policy. Despite the mutual rivalry of Austria-Hungary and Russia in the Balkans, Bismarck was able to keep both on his side during the 1880s. The Reinsurance Treaty of 1887 was the key to this situation; by it, Germany promised to support Russia's claims to the straits *(see page 113)* and to remain neutral in the event of war unless Russia attacked Austria-Hungary while Russia agreed to remain neutral unless Germany attacked France. Bismarck had broken with Wilhelm II over the renewal of this treaty which many, led by Holstein, felt was

incompatible with Germany's promises to Austria-Hungary in 1879. In any case, the Kaiser and his advisers were convinced that the most likely wars in Europe were of Germany against France or of Austria-Hungary against Russia and in neither case could Russia and Germany be on the same side.

Consequently, the dismissal of Bismarck ended Russo-German friendship. Instead, friendly noises were made in Britain's direction, with whom agreement was reached over Heligoland and East Africa in 1890. The following year the Triple Alliance of Germany, Austria-Hungary and Italy was renewed. The discussions and subsequent treaty between Russia and France *(see page 114)* convinced the German generals that they would have to fight a war on two fronts. Their military plans were therefore tailored to this end. The most notorious of these was drawn up by the new chief of General Staff, Count Alfred von Schlieffen, in 1891. This moved the planned attack on France from Lorraine to the Vosges and planned an attack on France before Russia, since it was known that the Russian army would take longer to mobilize. The details of the attack through Belgium, were not, incidentally, brought in at this stage. Significantly, the lines of milito-diplomatic activity were thus drawn up as early as 1894. Of the five major powers of Europe, only Britain was outside the existing agreements; relations with Britain therefore provided the only degree of manoeuvreablility in European diplomacy.

(b) The friendship of Britain

Wilhelm II's attitude to Britain was crucial both to relations between the two countries and to international peace. His attitude was determined largely by his parentage. From his mother he inherited an admiration for English liberalism and the accepted view of English pre-eminence. From his father's family he inherited the strict Prussian military code of behaviour and views on the accepted order of society. In later life he both loved and loathed England. Even in 1911 he told Theodore Roosevelt how he 'adored' England. On the other hand he wrote of 'the same old arrogance, the same old overestimation' of the British. Above all, he was determined to be respected by the British and to win acclaim for what he regarded as his very real achievements.

These influences perhaps explain his peculiar approach to Britain. In 1896 he sent a telegram to the Boer President, Kruger, congratulating him on defeating the Jameson Raid 'without appealing for the help of friendly powers'. Yet in the *Daily Telegraph* interview he was to explain how he had helped the British to defeat the Boers. Again in contrast, he had suggested to Tsar Nicholas in 1897 that they should join together to thwart British plans to expand. Since he seems to have wanted both to befriend Britain and to show her people his own country's strength, it has been suggested that he was trying to show the British that Germany's friendship was crucial to her survival; to frighten them into an alliance. Before 1900, it seemed possible that this tactic might be successful. In 1898 Joseph Chamberlain suggested an Anglo-German colonial agreement, but Wilhelm rejected it on the grounds that Britain was merely seeking an ally against Russian expansion in the Far East. After the turn of the century, the likelihood of an alliance diminished rapidly; Britain's unpopularity over the Boer War and German influence in Turkey being the major stumbling blocks. At the same time, though, the German government believed there was little possibility of Britain reaching agreement with any other major power, in view of their past conflicts, and therefore saw no need to woo Britain too enthusiastically. German naval building was both the final attempt to frighten Britain into friendship and the collapse of that policy, since it had the reverse effect of making the British determined to counter it. Britain's agreements with Japan, France and Russia during the 1900s placed her firmly in the camp of Germany's enemies, and such agreements as were subsequently made were restricted to specific, and minor issues.

Germany's failure to reach agreement with Britain had important effects on the whole of German foreign policy. Given Italy's ambivalence *(see page 134)*, Germany was wholly reliant on Austria-Hungary. This in turn brought Germany increasingly into the disputes over the Balkans. Moreover, the end of British isolation removed the final question mark from international diplomacy and for the first time gave Germany reason to believe that she, and not Britain, was the isolate of Europe.

(c) 'Weltpolitik'

Golo Mann has written that 'great states, that is states which under given conditions regard themselves as great, want to be influential beyond their own boundaries. History confirms this a hundred times.' Such was the ambition of Wilhelm II of Germany. To do this, Germany had to win colonies, so that her influence could be directly brought to bear in different parts of the world. In addition, her power had to be sufficiently respected that she could influence events in Europe even when they did not directly concern her. To achieve either ambition, military power would be required, if not to be used then to exist as a threat—hence the naval and military expansion of the period *(see pages 136–9)*. The German search for world power was to become the dominant issue of world politics and diplomacy after 1900.

This search was encouraged by the 'Leagues'. There were three main leagues devoted to the promotion of Germany's world power—the Pan-German League (established in 1890), the 'Deutsche Kolonial Gesellschaft' ('German Colonial League', founded in 1882) and the Navy League. The Pan-German League, to which some sixty right-wing Reichstag members belonged in 1914, promoted Germany's cause both by the capture of colonies and the establishment of German predominance in Europe. In particular, they hoped that on the death of Franz Josef the German areas of northern Austria-Hungary would be brought under German rule, so fulfilling the old hope for a 'Grossedeutschland'. The Navy League, with its million members, was directly sponsored by the government to promote Germany's claims for a larger navy, while the

Colonial League was more directly concerned with the capture and exploitation of colonies, several of which it actually governed for a time.

(i) Colonial policy

Despite Bismarck's lack of enthusiasm, a number of German entre-preneurs had established interests in Africa and the Far East during the 1870s and 1880s. To protect the interests of their companies, and to protect others from the worst extremes of the companies, colonial armies and the government representatives were sent out. In 1883 'Angra Pequeña', South West Africa, became a German possession when a merchant, Franz Luderitz, raised the German flag there and, after a dispute with Britain over its ownership in 1884, the German government declared it to be a German protectorate ruled by the 'Deutsche Kolonial Gesellschaft' (The German Colonial League). In 1892 it was brought under direct government control. Similarly, the areas in East Africa claimed by Karl Peters came under the German East Africa Company in 1885. In the same year, the German government announced that it had established a protectorate over the land between the Umba and Rovuma rivers in East Africa. For several years parts of this area were disputed with Britain, until in 1890 Germany surrendered her claim to Uganda in exchange for Heligoland. In the same year, the East Africa Company surrendered its sovereignty to the government. Similar events took place on the West coast. In 1884 Gustav Nachtigel proclaimed a protectorate over the coastal part of Togoland and in 1885 a protectorate was established over the Cameroons. Thus Germany's African colonies were at least established before 1890 (see Map 4).

Herein lies the paradox of German colonial policy. For it was during and after the 1890s that the colonial ambitions of Germany reached their peak, and there was much talk of the desirability and necessity of expanding Germanic ideas and people. In 1896 the Kaiser boasted that 'thousands of our countrymen live in far-flung corners of the earth' and that 'German goods, German knowledge, German industriousness, cross the ocean.' The 'Kolonial Gesellschaft' waxed lyrical at public meetings and in the press on the virtues of colonialism. Yet the actual gains were minimal. In 1898 Germany was granted a twenty-five year lease on the port of Kiaochow but her ambitions in the Phillippines were thwarted by the USA. In 1899 the Samoan islands of Savaii and Upolu were taken to-gether with the Mariana and Palau islands. Her other Far Eastern posses-sions had, like those in Africa, been taken in the 1880s—the north-east of New Guinea, the islands of the Bismarck archipelago and the Solomon and Marshall islands.

The neo-colonialism of Germany's relations with the Ottoman Empire proved a little more fruitful. The Berlin-Baghdad Railway was a grandiose and potentially profitable project—a railroad from the heart of Europe to the heart of the Middle East (see Map 8) In 1888 the Turkish govern-ment gave its approval to the first stage of the scheme—from opposite Constantinople to Ankara. This was completed by 1892 and there followed keen competition from the European powers for the right to build the next section. In 1893 the German syndicate that had built the first section won the concession to build a line from Ankara to Caesarea (which was never actually built) and another line through the Southern areas, from Eskis Ehir to Konya. This was completed by 1896, and Baghdad seemed a genuine possibility. There was again competition between the European powers; the Kaiser's visit to Constantinople and the Holy Land in 1898, during which he promised friendship to Moslems throughout the world, was obviously intended to promote the German claim. The French agreed to co-operate with Germany and, despite Russian opposition, the Germans again won the concession—for the line from Konya to Baghdad—in November 1899. The building of this section proved to be less easy, since the British and French governments now refused to co-operate. The railway became, like the naval building, an international issue between Germany and Britain; Germany wanted at least some control over the final section, from Baghdad to the Persian Gulf, while the British claimed the right to control this section. Both therefore looked to the other powers to support their claim. In 1910 Russia agreed to Germany's proposal for international control over the section that was to link up with the Persian Railway and on 15 June 1914 Germany and Britain reached agreement that the Germans were to end their line at Baghdad.

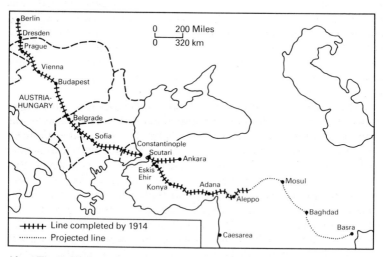

Map 8 The Berlin Baghdad railway

Again, however, the reality of German achievements did not match the aspirations. Much was written in Germany about 'our railway' and the extension of German 'world power' in a new area. In fact, the railways in the Turkish Empire were built by British and French, as well as Germans. The new railway never became the great trade route that it was intended to be, since it took so long to build and it remained cheaper to take the goods by sea. There was some German influence in Turkey—especially through the provision of German officers to train Turkish troops—but it was never paramount, especially after the Young Turk Revolution of 1908.

(ii) Germany and Morocco

German policy towards Morocco falls into no simple category since it encompassed both colonial and European policy. It was therefore an essential part of Weltpolitik.

By 1900 businessmen from several European countries were keen to exploit the resources of Morocco. France, however, who already controlled neighbouring Algeria, hoped for a pre-eminent share of it, and even for a complete takeover. In the Entente Cordiale of 1904 the British had recognized France's interests there and agreed, in secret articles, to the likelihood that it would be partitioned between France and Spain. France obtained similar understandings from Italy and Spain. Germany was neither consulted nor informed of these negotiations, and was technically under the impression that the policy of the European powers was one of 'open door'. The German Foreign Office was of course aware that discussions were taking place and the likely content of them. Bülow and Holstein, initially without the Kaiser's approval, saw Morocco as a means of testing the loyalty of the British to their new ally. If Britain was firmly linked to France, she would support her when Germany challenged France's rights to influence in Morocco. In any case, the Madrid Convention of 1880 had given all the powers equal rights in Morocco. And if France did not want Germans there, she (France) would have to give them somewhere else in exchange. There was nothing to be lost and quite a lot to be gained from challenging France.

In March 1905 the Kaiser visited Morocco. He rode through Tangier on a white charger, a gift from the Sultan that nearly threw him as he was unable to control it with his one good hand. He then visited France's minister there and told him that Germany expected rights in Morocco to which she was entitled. He then visited the Sultan and told him that Germany recognized his independence and reminded him not to introduce European reforms without good reason. He then returned to his ship and left, in the process of which one of the escorting tugs rammed a British vessel.

The repercussions of the visit were not long in coming. Some members of the British and French governments, most notably the French Foreign Minister, Delcassé, saw the crisis as an opportunity for a showdown with Germany, and sought to escalate the crisis. The rest of the French cabinet were less enthusiastic and Delcassé was forced to resign; the Prime Minister, Rouvier, took over the Foreign Ministry. France then accepted the Moroccan (though German inspired) invitation to attend an international conference, and Rouvier contemplated the possibility of offering Germany concessions elsewhere in exchange for a free hand in

Morocco. By the failure of the Anglo-French side to take swift and firm action—a failure that was unavoidable—Germany had won the first round of the diplomatic game.

The conference was convened at Algeçiras in January 1906. Germany now found herself deserted by all but Austria-Hungary and Morocco. France and Britain were supported by Russia and the minor powers present. The German delegation had to be satisfied with a share of the international control of Moroccan finances, while France and Spain were to share the control of the customs and police forces. Far more importantly, Bülow and Holstein had failed to crack the new Anglo-French Entente; if anything, it was strengthened by the experience of a common enemy. Round two was lost and Holstein resigned from the Foreign Office.

By October 1908 Wilhelm had apparently resigned himself to the fact that Morocco would remain French and there was little that Germany could gain there. Shortly afterwards, French troops entered the German embassy in Casablanca, removed three deserters from the Foreign Legion and arrested the secretary for hiding them. German nationalists protested loudly and urged action, but the Kaiser, who thought little of deserters in any case (especially as they turned out to be a Swiss, a Pole and an Austrian), made little of the matter and even reprimanded the diplomat concerned. In February 1909 an end to the arguments over Morocco seemed to have come when an agreement was signed by which Germany acknowledged France's 'special political interests' in exchange for a French promise to respect Germany's economic interests. Morocco's continued independence and territorial integrity were accepted by both sides.

It was the incompetence of the Moroccan 'independent' government that provided the German Foreign Office with a new opportunity for action. In May 1911 the French sent troops to Fez to quell anti-foreign riots. The German government was informed and consulted before they were sent. The German Foreign Minister, Kiderlen-Wachter, was divided between the opportunity to make gains and his anxiety to improve relations with Britain and France. To advance German claims, the gunboat 'Panther' was sent to the port of Agadir in South Morocco on 1 July, ostensibly to protect German citizens in the area, though in fact a petition requesting such protection was only forthcoming when requested by the German Foreign Office via the Hamburg-Morocco Company. Germany demanded the whole of the French Congo as compensation for giving up all claims in Morocco. Lloyd George then claimed that Britain could not be ignored (21 July). Throughout the summer, negotiations continued between Kiderlen and Joseph Caillaux, the conciliatory French Prime Minister, while extremists in both countries, and in Britain, spoke of the likelihood of war. British army manoeuvres were ended and discussions held with the French on the shipment of troops to France. In Germany, von Moltke wrote, 'If we once again crawl out of this affair with our tail between our legs, if we cannot pull ourselves together and take an energetic line which we are ready to back up with the sword, I despair of the future of the German Empire and shall quit.' Saner views prevailed and the Germans reduced their demands. On 4 November agreement was reached: France was to have a free hand, and even a protectorate, in Morocco. Germany received sections of the French Congo, as well as two areas connecting the Cameroons, which was already German, to the important Congo and Ubangi Rivers. The Kaiser congratulated his Chancellor on the success of the negotiations, while the nationalist press thundered, 'Have we become a generation of women?' and Tirpitz pronounced, 'We have suffered a diplomatic check and we must solve it by a supplementary naval bill.'

Morocco became a central feature of Weltpolitik because it combined a variety of aims and interests. It provided an opportunity for colonial expansion, either in itself or through deals with France, swopping control of Morocco for land elsewhere. More importantly, it provided an opportunity to enhance and exploit European aims in relative safety—relative, that is, compared to upsetting the French along their own border or to stirring the Balkans cauldron. France could be humiliated and German greatness demonstrated. Britain could be shown the folly of supporting such a weak ally and the attractions of an alliance with Germany.

(iii) European Policies

Germany's primary aim in Europe was to manoeuvre the alliance system in her favour. Thereby, she would be assured of protection against possible future attack by France and of support in her ambitions for Weltpolitik. Two unalterable facts lay behind her relations with the other powers; events in the nineteenth century had made certain that France would remain her enemy and Austria-Hungary her ally. Germany's relations with Britain and Russia were therefore of great significance. Until 1907, the Kaiser had hopes of an alliance with Britain but thereafter, his efforts centred on Russia since, like Bismarck, he had a low opinion of Russian diplomacy and a high opinion of his own. He believed that through the Tsar he could at least dislodge Russia from her alliance to France. The major effort in this direction came in 1905 when the two emperors met on the island of Björko off the Finnish coast. Nicholas, eager to find friends while his stock at home was so low, not only listened to Wilhelm's proposals but even signed an agreement that promised mutual aid in the event of either being attacked by another European power. The Kaiser told Bülow, 'a great load has been lifted from my dear Fatherland which has finally escaped from the terrible Gallo-Russian pincers.' The ministers of both powers were horrified by the agreement, realizing that it countered their existing treaties with their respective allies, France and Austria-Hungary. Bülow threatened to resign, but it proved unnecessary as the Tsar's ministers told him that the treaty was unacceptable unless France was excluded (i.e. Russia would not be obliged to support Germany if France attacked Germany). Since such an exclusion would destroy the whole point of the treaty, it was never ratified.

After the failure of Björko and the Anglo-Russian Entente of 1907, Germany was left high and dry, allied only to unreliable Italy and crisis-ridden Austria-Hungary. The German reaction was inevitable. Firstly, German press and politicians complained of 'encirclement': the other powers, led by France, had formed a ring of enemies around Germany to prevent her achieving her rightful place in the world power club and, even worse, to help France regain the lost provinces. It was easy for Britain to complain, but how could Germany be expected to survive without a navy when her enemies daily prowled around her?

Secondly, Germany had to make the most of any opportunity to demonstrate her world power prowess, wherever they might arise— Morocco, Turkey and, through her ally and neighbour Austria-Hungary, in the Balkans. At the same time, she opposed any Russian gains in the Balkans, since they would all but close the circle around her. Consequently, in both the periods of crisis in the Balkans (1908 and 1912–13), Germany gave her full support to Austria-Hungary. In January 1909, von Moltke told the Austrian chief of staff, von Hotzendorff: 'The moment Russia mobilizes Germany also will mobilize and will unquestionably mobilize her whole army.' In October 1912 the Kaiser told Franz Josef: 'You can be certain I stand behind you and am ready to draw the sword whenever your action makes it necessary ... whatever comes from Vienna is to me a command.' It was such a 'command' that was to prove so disastrous in the summer of 1914.

7. Bibliography

There are a number of valuable works on Germany, most of which cover not only this period, but also the Weimar and Nazi periods. These include *A History of Modern Germany Vol. 3 1840–1945* by H. Holborn (Eyre & Spottiswoode, 1965), *History of Germany since 1789* by Golo Mann (Chatto & Windus, 1968), *A Short History of Germany 1815–1945* by E.J. Passant (CUP, 1959), *Germany without Bismarck* by J.C.G. Rohl (Batsford, 1967) and *Twentieth Century Germany from Bismarck to Brandt* by A.J. Ryder (Macmillan, 1973). For a slightly different perspective, which includes considerable personal detail about the Kaiser and his court, *The Kaiser and His Times* by M. Balfour (Cresset Press, 1964), is most useful.

8. Discussion Points and Exercises

A   *This section consists of questions that might be used for discussion (or written answers) as a way of expanding on the chapter and testing understanding of it:*
1   Why was the Reichstag so weak?
2   How can the Kaiser be said to have greater control than other European rulers?

3 Was Caprivi a successful chancellor?
4 Why was naval expansion such a key issue?
5 What was the 'risk theory'?
6 What were the motives for the expansion of welfare services?
7 When and why was the Centre Party so important?
8 Why did the *Daily Telegraph* affair become so notorious?
9 What was required of Wilhelm's chancellors?
10 How adequate a guide to economic advance are the statistics provided in Section 5?
11 Why was the Reinsurance treaty abandoned?
12 Explain the Kaiser's attitude to Britain.
13 What is 'Weltpolitik'?
14 Why was Germany so unsuccessful in winning colonies in the 1890s?
15 How clear were Germany's motives in the Moroccan crises?
16 Why was Germany prepared to support Austria-Hungary in the Balkans?

B *This section examines some of the issue raised by the chapter in greater detail:*

1 As a Reichstag deputy—party and date to be specified—describe what you consider wrong with the existing constitutional structure and what reforms you would like to see.
2 Write a report for the Foreign Office expaining how your country is becoming surrounded by enemies and how she can escape the encirclement.

C *This section suggests two ways in which you might compare Germany with other European countries:*

1 Imagine you were a British journalist recently returned from a tour of Germany and France in 1910; record your impressions of the two countries for your readers, paying especial attention to the material and spiritual well-being of the people.
2 Compare the character and approach to ruling of the Kaiser and Tsar Nicholas II.

D *Essay questions:*

1 How acute were the political tensions in Wilhelm II's Germany?
2 Account for the rapid economic advance of Germany before the First World War.
3 Why did Germany embark on such an amitious foreign policy during the reign of Wilhelm II?

9. German Economic Expansion: The Factors and their Importance

Below are detailed a number of factors that influenced the rate and nature of German economic advance at this time.
(1) For each factor, explain how it is likely that it will affect economic growth.
(2) Add any additional factors that are not included in the list below.
(3) Rank the factors into an order of importance, explaining why you have put them into that order.

(i) The expansion of educational facilities
In 1858 the first agricultural school was opened at Hildesheim; by 1910 there were 20 of them. There were also winter agricultural schools—twelve of them in 1870, 240 in 1906. In the last thirty years of the nineteenth century, expenditure on technical education increased five-fold. Those who completed six years of technical education were excused two years of military service and were given officer rank. In 1870 there were more science graduates at Munich University than the total number of science graduates from all English Universities.

(ii) Population growth

	Total population	*Percentage living in towns of more than 2000*
1871	41 059 000	36·1
1880	42 234 000	41·4
1890	49 428 000	42·5
1900	56 367 000	54·4
1910	64 926 000	60·0

(iii) The Banking system
After 1871 the banks were completely free of state control and could lend as much as they liked. The result was an extremely adventurous banking system; for example, the Bank of Essen was even prepared to increase its own capital in order to provide a loan to a coal company. Banks controlled the sale of shares and often owned large numbers of shares. They also used their position to control industrial policy and were instrumental in the formation of a number of cartels. They even financed special research departments in technical as well as financial fields.

(iv) Geographical factors, including availability of resources
Germany occupies a central position in Europe. The flat land in the North facilitates the building of railways. Wide, navigable rivers make the internal movements of goods easier; from Rotterdam to Mannheim are 300 clear miles of the Rhine. There were plentiful resources of coal in the Saar and Ruhr areas, and of iron ore in Alsace and Lorraine. There

were also chemical deposits such as pure rock salt in Prussian Saxony and potash beds at Stassfurt.

(v) The transport system
In 1871 there were 11 000 kilometres of railway; by 1910, there were 61 000 kilometres. Despite this, canals and rivers remained more important, and in 1914 carried more tonnage per kilometre than railways. The merchant shipping fleet was expanded:

	1870	*1900*	*1910–12*
Total tonnage	982 000	1 942 000	3 000 000
Steam tonnage	82 000	1 348 000	2 500 000

(vi) Commercial organization
Many German industries were organized into cartels. These were large controlling companies that either owned the whole of a particular industry, such as coal or steel, in one area (horizontal cartels), or owned all the plants involved in one particular process or industry, such as ship-building (vertical cartels). This control enabled the companies to fix prices and production levels, and do away with the hazards of competition. In 1876 the Rhenish-Westphalian coal owners mutually agreed to lower output by 10%; in 1893 they formed the Westphalian Coal Syndicate; when this joined with the Coke Syndicate and Briquette Union in 1903 it brought half of Germany's coal production under unified control. In 1875 there had been eight cartels; in 1885 there were ninety and in 1905 306.

10. An Essay-planning Exercise

Below is an outline of a system of essay planning that you might find helpful; in this case, you have been given a considerable amount of assistance and guidance, but this can obviously be reduced as your own essay-writing skills develop. It can also be adapted to other titles and types of question *(see page 5)*.

Essay title:
'Who gained, and who lost, as a result of the rule of Wilhelm II in Germany?'
1 What type of question is this? List(s)? Yes/No? Importance? Comparison?
2 Each of the following *might* be included in your answers. Consider each and write down those that you think should be included:

The position of the monarchy	Peasants	The Church
Parliamentary government	Socialists	The economy
Industrial workers	Nationalists	The army
Industrialists	Imperialists	Other countries

3 Now add to this list anything else that you think should be included, but that has been omitted above.

4 Now sort those that you have included into 'winners' and 'losers' by placing a W by all those you think gained and an L beside all those that lost.

5 Next number these into the order in which you intend to write about them—you will have to decide whether to deal with all the winners first, then all the losers, or vice versa, or a mixture of the two.

6 You have now determined (a) what you are going to write about—each to be treated in a separate paragraph—and (b) the order in which you are going to write about them. Next, write the *first sentence* of each paragraph you are going to write. Make them introduce the subject of the paragraph, without being too long, and if possible make each one follow on from the previous one, by the use of words such as 'However', 'On the other hand' etc. Leave several lines between each of these sentences.

7 Finally, in note form, jot down under each of the first sentences the four or five facts that you intend to include in that paragraph to support the view or idea that you have expressed in the sentence. For example, you might have:

Sentence: 'German imperialists had plenty of reason to be pleased with their youthful Kaiser.'

Facts: Encouragement given to Colonial Society
Wilhelm's own speeches on the need for Empire
The provision of an army and navy that could be used to gain land
The gains made after the Moroccan crisis of 1911

(Equally, it might be possible to construct a counter-argument to this paragraph)

8 With these notes as a close guide, you can proceed to writing the essay.

V Russia 1890–1914

(For map of Russia, see page 332)

1. Introduction

The history of Russia has always been dominated by her geography. Her position as the world's largest power has always led to problems of communication, especially in the period before the development of mass communications. In addition, Russia encompasses an enormous range of landscape, soil and people. Large areas in the north and east have until recently been virtually uninhabitable while other regions, the Black Earth areas, are extremely fertile. In turn, the variety has posed an inevitable question for Russian policy makers—is she a Western or European power with the same interests as other such powers or an Asiatic power with interests there? This debate, between the 'Westernizers' and the 'Russophiles', has been further complicated by the variety of nationalities in the Russian Empire. She has been identified as the leading Slav nation but at the same time has both Moslems and Chinese under her rule. These geographical factors have always presented problems for Russian governments.

The organization of this chapter differs slightly from that of other chapters. The sections on political and economic history have been split into two, since it is impossible to understand the problems of the Russian government and the opposition to it without some knowledge of the economic background to the country. Secondly, because of their direct relevance to the events of the revolution of 1905, details of the war with Japan have been included in that section rather than foreign policy.

2. The Constitutional Organization of the State

Until the October Manifesto of 1905, the constitution of Russia was based on the 'Collected Laws of the Russian Empire' compiled by Nicholas I in 1832. Article I of these laws stated that 'The Emperor of all the Russias is an autocratic and unlimited monarch; God himself ordains that all must bow to his supreme power, not only out of fear but also out of conscience.' This did not mean that the Tsar could do as he pleased when he pleased, since his decisions were based on the laws of his predecessors, but he alone did make all final decisions relating to Russia's government, army, economy and foreign relations. All other bodies of government were either administrative, existing only to put the Tsar's policies into practice, or advisory.

There were three such bodies in the nineteenth century. The Imperial Council was to provide the Tsar with expert opinion on any subject he required. The Committee of Ministers, originally eight ministers but by 1900 increased to fourteen, had a similar advisory role, although each minister also had responsibility for his own department, such as finance, war or education. The ministers were responsible only to the Tsar, who appointed and dismissed them. They had the power to issue ministerial statutes with the approval of the Tsar and these had the power of law. The third advisory body was the Senate, founded in 1711 and intended to have a supervisory function over all government. Since the other two bodies, as well as the Tsar himself, were already doing this, it was a superfluous assembly. Consequently, by the legal reforms of 1864, it was transformed into the Supreme Court of the Empire, thus giving it a judicial rather than a political function. None of these three groups could challenge the Tsar's omnipotence, which was reinforced by his position as titular head of the Church.

Alexander II did undertake some reforms in the 1860s. 'Zemstvos' were set up on a county and provincial basis. They were to be local Parliaments, elected by an electoral college system that gave most votes to the richest citizens. The members of each zemstvo were to be responsible for transport, health, education, the poor, famine relief, and the encouragement of agriculture and industry in their area. Zemstvo income came from rates, but much of it was used by the central government. They had no official executive power, but they were to prove a major innovation in the life of the provinces. As zemstvos were set up throughout the country, there were, for the first time, bodies prepared to bring reforms and improvements—hospitals, roads, pavements, schools, sewers and the like.

The 'mir', or village commune, was also established in the 1860s. By the Edict of Emancipation of 1861, Alexander II had ended the system by which peasants were owned by landlords and had no land of their own. The Edict freed them from serfdom and provided them with some land. This land was initially paid for by the State, and the peasants then had to repay the debt. The 'mir' was responsible for collecting these redemption dues as well as taxes. To ensure that peasants would not escape their debts, the 'mir' issued passports and until 1903 no peasant could leave his village without a passport and the consent of the mir. The mir also handled court cases that involved only peasants. In essence, the mir was one method of coping with local issues and controlling Russia's enormous population with minimal expenditure.

3. Political Background: The Tsars

Alexander II (1855–81) was regarded in his time as a reforming Tsar. However, by modern standards, he was reactionary beyond all measure, banning Trade Unions in 1874 and maintaining an enormous army and police force. But by the standards of nineteenth-century Russia, he was indeed the 'Tsar Liberator'. He ended the system of serfdom and gave the peasants their freedom. He reduced censorship. He set up the zemstvos and a new legal system that had juries and trained judges. He ended the arbitrary nature of military service by introducing conscription, and reduced the period of service from twenty-five to fifteen years—six years active service, nine years in the reserves. Ironically, the reforming Tsar was killed by a bomb thrown by a member of the 'People's Will' (or 'People's Freedom') in March 1881—the seventh attempt on his life.

He was succeeded by his son, Alexander III (1881–94). It has been said of him that he set out to undo all that his father had done. He began by publicly hanging six of his father's assassins, and then proceeded with a series of measures to reassert the authority of the aristocracy. The discussions between zemstvo officials and the Imperial Council that had been initiated by the Minister of the Interior, Loris-Melikov, were ended. In 1889 the proportion of peasant votes for zemstvo deputies was reduced; the peasants were to be presented with a list of candidates from whom they could choose. Also in 1889, 'land captains' were appointed in each area; they were virtually governors, since they headed the legal and administrative systems and could overrule the decisions of the zemstvos. In his reforms Alexander III was advised by Constantine Pobiedonotstev, tutor to the Tsar and his son, Nicholas, and Procurator of the Holy Synod. He advised the Tsar to control the education system more closely, to dismiss disloyal judges, to enforce the use of Russian in schools where it was not the local language (such as Poland and the Baltic states), and to force conversions to Orthodoxy. The Jews suffered particularly. The fact that one of the assassins, Hessia Helfmann, was Jewish was used as an excuse for a vicious campaign that forbade them to settle in certain areas and limited their numbers in Universities. Pobiedonotstev pronounced that a third of the Jews in Russia must die, a third emigrate and a third assimilate. In 1891–2 thousands were cleared out of Moscow and forced into ghettoes. Alexander summarized his policies in the Imperial Manifesto of 1885: 'Russian nobles should keep their leading position in the conduct of war, affairs of local administration and courts and in the diffusion by their own example of the rules of faith and loyalty and sound principles of national education.'

Alexander's son, Nicholas (born 1868) *(see Diagram 8)*, was not expected to become Tsar until at least 1910, since his father was only thirty-six when he became Tsar (born 1845). So during the 1890s Nicholas led an easy life as a young army officer, in the company of the ballet dancer Mathilde Kschessinska. In 1893 Alexander fell unexpectedly ill when influenza led to kidney trouble. Suddenly the succession became important; only two years earlier, the Tsar had said of his son: 'he is still absolutely a child, he has infantile judgements.' On 1 November 1894, Alexander died. A week later, Nicholas married Princess Alix of Hesse-Darmstadt, his own choice and originally opposed by his family because she was German. On hearing of his father's death, Nicholas said to his brother-in-law, 'What am I to do? I am not prepared to be Tsar. I know nothing of the business of ruling.'

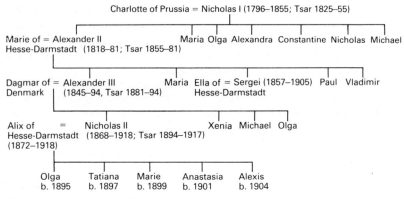

Diagram 8. Family tree of the Romanovs

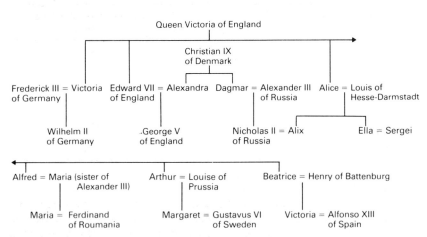

Diagram 9. The Tsar's European relations

Liberal elements, especially among the zemstvo leaders, had high hopes of their new Tsar. However, in his first formal speech, acknowledging the congratulations of the zemstvos leaders, Nicholas said, 'It is known to me that voices have been heard in some assemblies of persons carried away by senseless dreams of the participation of zemstvo representatives in the affairs of the internal government. Let all know that ... I shall preserve the principle of autocracy as firmly and undeviatingly as did my father.' In other ways too the omens were not good. In May 1895 Nicholas was crowned in Moscow, wearing a 9lb. crown that slipped over his nose. That evening, 7000 guests attended a ball in the Kremlin. In the early morning thousands of the poor walked to the outskirts of the city where an open air feast was to be held. Five thousand had arrived when the beer and souvenir mugs arrived; the crowd surged forward when it was rumoured there was not enough beer to go round. The regiment of Cossacks in attendance could not hold them back; 1300 of the poor were killed and hundreds more injured. That night, although he wanted to mourn his people, Nicholas was persuaded to attend the ball at the French Embassy to celebrate his coronation. There, he and Alix, in all their finery, opened the dancing.

4. Economic History

(a) Economic Background

Two factors dominated the economy of nineteenth-century Russia. The population was increasing rapidly and the overwhelming majority of the population were engaged in farming and very few in industry. Table 22 illustrates these points.

Date	Total population (millions)	Percentage of population living in towns of over 5000 people
1730	14	3
1751		7·8
1796	36	
1817	46	
1870	77	
1890	95	
1896		12·4
1900	103	
1913	122	14·6

Table 22. Russian population growth

It is essential to realize that all statistics for Tsarist Russia are extremely approximate; the size of the country and the inefficiency of the bureaucracy, quite apart from the political motives of the Tsars and their successors, are the reasons for this. Two well known English authorities cite the population for 1910 as 111 millions and 153·8 millions respectively.

The emancipation of the serfs in 1861 did little to improve the agricultural efficiency of the countryside. Since landlords could not, or would not, pay labourers and since the peasants could not afford land themselves, almost a quarter of the previously cultivated area fell into disuse. Peasants received very small land holdings, usually of less than ten acres and rarely more than twenty. Inheritance systems reinforced this trend. In some areas, land was inherited in the normal way by the eldest son. In others, the 'obschina', or repartitional, system was used, by which a man's land was redivided on his death on the basis of family size. If his family did not require as much land as they had, then some would be taken by the mir and given to another, larger, family. Given small farms and, except in Black Earth areas, poor soil, it is not surprising that yields were low; about half as much grain per acre as the richest agricultural countries, Britain, Germany and the Low Countries. The rapidly increasing population put great pressure on existing resources of food, especially in times of bad harvest. Famines, in which hundreds of thousands, even millions, died, such as that of the winter of 1891–2, were common.

Industry remained notoriously backward. Most natural resources lay in the East and were not exploited; Russian coal production was less than 5% of that of Britain in the late nineteenth century. Even in the 1890s more than a quarter of Russia's coal was imported. The iron industry also lagged behind the rest of Europe, relying mainly on old-fashioned charcoal forges and importing half of the pig iron that was needed. By all the usual indices—miles of railway track, mechanization in the textile industry, size of the national debt—Russia in 1890 was economically backward.

On the other hand, there had been some industrial progress. Between 1860 and 1876 coal production had risen sixteen-fold and steel production ten-fold. Foreigners had been important in this; the Swedish Nobel brothers had financed oil production in Baku while the Welshman John Hughes had established a coal, iron and rails works in the Krivoi Rog Basin. Railways expanded particularly fast; in 1861 there had been only 1000 miles of railway track—by 1880, there were 14 000. So although the general picture was of backwardness and stagnation, there was advance and expansion in some fields.

(b) Witte's Reform in the 1890s

The advances described above were chiefly due to the initiative of the ministers of finance. These men were instrumental in deciding the extent of taxation and the priorities of government expenditure. Reutern, Minister from 1862 until 1878, had encouraged the first foreign entrepreneurs —the Nobels, Hughes, the textile manufacturer Knoop. Bunge, Minister 1878–86, adopted a laissez-faire attitude to the economy, reducing taxes in the hope of establishing a prosperous peasantry that would provide the demand necessary to stimulate industrial progress. In 1881 he reduced the salt tax, and in 1886 the poll tax, so that taxation was only one-third of what it had been in the 1860s. His policy ran into difficulties because of the military expenditure on the Afghan and Bulgar crises. His successor, Vyshnagradsky (1886–91), adopted an entirely different policy —relentless austerity to build up reserves of capital. Taxation was increased; in years of good harvest, like 1887–8, this policy was successful. But in a time of shortage, such as 1891–2, it was quite impossible for the peasantry to surrender a third of their crops for taxation.

Vyshnagradsky was replaced by Sergei Witte (1891–1900), a mathematics graduate who had risen through the administrative service of the railways. He had the experience of his three predecessors on which to draw, and had a definite plan for the economy, based on the theories of List. Witte planned to establish heavy industry and an extensive railway system, financed by foreign capital. The basis for long-term growth would thus be established. Two subsidiary aims were also necessary—the promotion of technical education and the avoidance of wars, which were so expensive and disruptive to planned economic growth.

The building of railways advanced rapidly. The basic pattern already existed, so Witte's scheme was to extend existing routes to more outlying areas in the South and East, and to improve existing tracks by making them double, by providing more stations, engines and rolling stock. The eastwards expansion through the construction of the Trans-Siberian Railway is usually identified as the major project. The plan was linked to Witte's idea of developing whole new areas in the East by forced resettlement and the development of shipping in the Far East. Construction on the railway was started in 1891 and lasted almost fifteen years. The railway proved so expensive that in places only a single track could be built, and in the end only six trains a day could be run. In fact, the expansion of the railway system in European Russia was far more successful, where the amount of track was tripled and the total mileage covered by some railroad increased by 46%.

Witte also succeeded in attracting foreign capital into Russia. He stabilised the currency by forbidding speculation and amassing gold by high exports of agricultural goods—healthy for the economy, less so for the peasants, all of whose surpluses were removed by taxation. Such was Witte's stringency that by 1897 he was able to put Russia on the gold standard. Table 23 indicates the extent to which foreign capital was attracted into the country.

1893	2 500 000 roubles
1897	80 000 000 roubles
1898	130 000 000 roubles
1913	2 200 000 000 roubles

Table 23. Foreign investment in Russia

Although this trend resulted in large parts of Russian industry being owned abroad, especially in Paris (pig-iron and steel in particular), it did provide much of the required capital. In 1890 only sixty million roubles had been invested in new industries; in 1900 430 million roubles were. It was not surprising that in 1900 40% of all industrial enterprises in Russia had been established in the single decade 1890–1900. (Remember, though, that these figures and statistics are only a guide.)

Education too was encouraged. In 1894 there had been only eight technical schools in Russia. Ten years later there were a hundred, in addition to new polytechnics in Kiev, Warsaw and St Petersburg. The literacy rate rose from 20% in 1890 to 38% in 1914. In many ways, these efforts were inadequate; in the whole decade 1890–1900 only 150 million roubles were spent on education, compared with 120 millions *each year* on railways. However, investment in education was not a popular policy with the traditional autocrats, who preferred an ignorant and subservient populace.

Moreover, war was avoided. Russian expansion in the Far East was not without risks *(see page 110)*, but there were no direct conflicts. Equally, Witte persuaded his master and his colleagues to play down Russia's role in Central Asia and the Balkans, two other potential areas of conflict. The agreement with Austria-Hungary of 1897 *(see page 20)* can perhaps be seen as the result of Witte's influence. In the same year, the Hague Conference on disarmament was held on Russia's initiative. For once, power considerations were made to serve economic objectives rather than vice versa.

Overall, Witte's initial objectives seem to have been achieved. Coal production was doubled; in the Donets basin, it was tripled. Iron production increased five- or six-fold, depending on the area concerned, mainly as a result of the new industrial centres in the South. Russia displaced France as the fourth greatest iron producer in the world and advanced to fifth place in steel production. In the oil industry, production increased ten-fold over the period 1883–1900. In the cotton industry, the labour force doubled and over 200 000 spindles were added each year. The overall growth rate achieved in the 1890s was more than 8% per annum—the highest for any decade in Russia in the nineteenth century. The income from industrial production rose from forty-two million roubles per annum in the period 1888–92 to 161 millions for 1893–97.

Nevertheless, Witte and his system were not without fault or failure. The following criticisms have been levelled at it. Firstly, the dependence on foreign capital left Russia in constant debt to other countries; any crisis in Europe therefore threatened Russian financial stability. About 30% of capital invested in Russia in 1900 came from abroad. The remainder was raised by high indirect taxation and by heavy exactions of crops. Witte took 15% of the crop each year, compared with Reutern's 5%. The result of this was that consumption levels fell by about 25%, the demands of the government being worsened by the requirements of a higher population. Since industrial production was so low, there was no alternative to exporting crops. Usually, grain made up half the total of Russian exports; even in the famine year of 1899 it constituted 42% of the value of exports. As well as ignoring the urgent needs of agriculture, Witte paid little attention to more advanced and sophisticated forms of industry. Modern equipment such as machine tools and electrical goods were imported from the West, making servicing difficult and costs high. Steel works, for instance, often had plenty of modern furnaces, rollers and the like, but only wheelbarrows with which to move the finished steel around the plant. Fourthly, Witte has been criticized for concentrating on showpieces and industries that could demonstrate Russia's might, rather than on essentials. The Trans-Siberian Railway has been criticized on these grounds. Equally, the metallurgical resources of the Ukraine in Western Russia were exploited, but not those of the Urals, where in fact a single mountain could have flooded the iron ore markets of Europe. Ultimately, it is possible to trace the events of 1905 and 1917 to Witte's reforms, since they produced the disaffected peasantry and the urban proletariat who were to be the activists in those years.

In fact, the period 1900–06 was one of depression, in which some of the achievements of the Witte era were undone. In 1902, over 2000 businesses closed, including a third of the great iron mines at Krivoi Rog. However, from the high growth rates resumed after 1906 it may be argued that the momentum gained in the 1890s was not lost.

5. Political History

(a) The Opposition to the Autocracy

The economic spurt of the 1890s imposed great strains on the political and social structure of Russia. The industrial growth rate at that time was higher even than those of Germany and the USA. In the last decade of the nineteenth century, the number of industrial workers in Russia increased by almost a million, producing crises in urban accomodation, new consumer demands and forcing a complete upheaval of the transport system. The shock waves of industrialization spread from the towns to the overburdened peasantry. Moreover, the process of industrialization was artificial—it was imposed by government policy rather than resulting from natural increases in demand. The relationship between the economy and the development of the opposition can be seen in several ways. Firstly, there was direct protest from those who suffered the most—factory workers in terrible slums, starving peasants in the countryside. Secondly, there were theorists who discussed Russia's economic and political future. Thirdly, the economic boom brought increased contact with Western ideas about government and society. Obviously, it is too simplistic to match each of these trends with a separate opposition group; rather each group took features from each trend.

The most moderate of the Tsar's opponents were the 'Westernizers', also known as modernizers and as liberals. These were likely to come from the educated, professional classes and were concerned that Russia should keep up, militarily and economically, with the other great powers. Rapid industrialization was seen as the key to this. The liberals also admired Western democratic processes and hoped to see them emulated in Russia, if only to give their own supporters some influence in government. There was no named group of 'Liberals' making such demands but the zemstvos had liberal views, as did those employed by them—the new 'experts', like doctors, engineers, teachers and lawyers. As their experience of local administration increased, the zemstvos from neighbouring areas met to discuss their common problems and complaints. In 1896 the first Annual Congress of Zemstvo Presidents was held. At this, a proposal for universal elementary education was discussed and plans for a national assembly, a 'zemsky sobor', put forward. After its second Congress the following year, it was banned by the Tsarist authorities as being seditious. In 1902 some of its members were to join the 'League of Liberation', an organization intended to unite the moderate opposition. It is difficult to identify by name many of these men who in 1894 had hoped for so much from their new young Tsar, yet his rejection of their ideas was to prove fatal *(see page 104)*.

The more extreme opposition was fractured into endless groups *(see Diagram 10)*. Many historians have interpreted the history of these groups in different ways, making it difficult to provide a simple account of their development. The great variety of interpretations is hardly surprising, since the Tsar's 100 000 police and 50 000 'security gendarmerie' encouraged secrecy. The following account is intended to be straightforward and may therefore conflict in detail with others.

Diagram 10. The opposition groups in Russia 1870–1905

During the reign of Alexander II, the more extreme opposition can be broadly described as 'populist'. Its members believed that the emancipation of the serfs should lead to the extensive redistribution of the land and increased wealth among the peasantry. Moderate populists believed that this would in turn lead to industrial progress as the result of increased demand and political changes would follow naturally. The extreme populists believed that these processes could be hastened by terrorist activities which would encourage reform and end the hated autocracy. The populists were much influenced by the writings of Peter Lavrov, who hoped for a peaceful social revolution. In *Historical Letters* (1868–9) he wrote that the people must be shown the poverty of their conditions and led to a new society in which they were not exploited. He appealed to the young and educated to educate the masses. Some of them took him more literally than others. In 1874, following a famine in the Volga region, thousands of them went out into the villages to preach the populist message to the peasants. They met with little success, since the peasants understood nothing of their message and in many villages treated them as they had treated other wayside preachers—to mockery, a beating, even a lynching. The government did understand and locked up more than 1500 young populists.

In the next few years, the populists split into more identifiable groups with differing views on the means, rather than the ends, of social and political revolution. In 1876 the 'Land and Liberty' (or 'Land and Freedom') movement was founded. It was a small but well-organized group, whose chief demand was for the land to be handed over to the peasants. It organized demonstrations, and some of its members engaged in terrorist activities. Among their victims were the Governor of St Petersburg, General Trepov, the Crimean War hero General Mezentsov and Prince Kropotkin, governor of Kharkov. In 1879 one of its members even attempted to kill the Tsar.

In the same year, the moderates, led by Plekhanov, formed a new group, the 'Black Partition' (or 'Black Earth Populists'). They were opposed to violence and believed in the gradual education of the peasants into realizing the need for change. Their more extreme colleagues formed the 'People's Will' (or 'People's Freedom') movement, dedicated to hastening the course of events through terrorism. One of their first decisions was to condemn the Tsar to death; it took them seven attempts and nearly two years to carry out the sentence. These two groups remained separate for over twenty years. In 1900 they were reunited when the Social Revolutionary Party was founded as an umbrella party for all those with left-wing views. The new party followed the traditional populist policy of the redistribution of the land as the first priority. It combined the views of the two groups in advocating both a mass move-ment and closely-organized terrorism. Among the victims of the 'Combat Organization', the heirs of the 'People's Will', were two ministers of the Interior, Sipyagin (1902) and Plehve (1904) and the Tsar's uncle and brother-in-law, the Grand Duke Sergei (1905).

The foundation of the 'Emancipation of Labour' group in 1883 was to prove of far greater significance than the populist movements although at the time it went unnoticed. It was founded in Switzerland by a group of ex-populists led by George Plekhanov, Vera Zasulich and Paul Axelrod. Plekhanov was the leading theorist of the group, which for the first time applied Marxist theory to the Russian situation. Marx's works had been translated into Russian in the 1860s, but few saw the relevance of books that wrote of the exploitation of the working class in industrial society to agrarian Russian. It was believed that capitalism would make slow progress in Russia, because of the lack of finance, entrepreneurs and markets and therefore a theory of revolution based on the reactions of the masses to capitalism was inapplicable. Plekhanov dismissed this view and argued that capitalism *would* develop in Russia and that therefore 'the revolutionary movement in Russia can only triumph as the revolu-tionary movement of the workers.'

During the 1880s, the group remained small. As Plekhanov said when its members were once out boating on Lake Geneva, 'If this boat sinks, it's the end of Russian Marxism.' The hostility of the Tsarist regime forced them to remain in Switzerland, and their only influence came through such books as could be smuggled into Russia. In any case, their theories seemed to encourage the industrial development of Russia, rather than destroy it—who but a few intellects could see the sense in apparently making Russia stronger? Even Marx himself was against them. In 1881 he wrote to Zasulich that 'the historical inevitability of the process of economic development is limited to the countries of Western Europe ... The peasant commune is the fulcrum of social development in Russia.'

There were several developments in the Marxist camp during the 1890s. Although the Emancipation of Labour was banned in Russia, Marxism as such was not, partly because of its apparent encouragement of Russian economic development. A number of books expressing broadly Marxist views were published, most notably *Critical Notes on the Question of the Economic Development of Russia* and *Marxist Theory of Social Development* by P. Struve and *The Russian Factory in Past and Present* by Tugan-Baranovsky. As these works were permitted by the government, their authors were known as 'legal Marxists'. In contrast, some of Plekhanov's followers organized illegal groups. One such was the 'St Petersburg League of Combat for the Liberation of the Working Class'. This organized study groups, distributed revolutionary literature and participated in demonstrations and strikes. Among its members was Lenin. At the time, so far as the Tsarist police was concerned, he was but one of many such rebels and was treated in the same way, receiving four years exile in 1898. His colleagues realized that he was somebody rather different; Axelrod wrote of him in 1895: 'I felt I had before me a man who would be the leader of the Russian revolution. He was not only a cultured Marxist, but he also knew what he wanted to do and how to do it.' Kochan has written of him: 'he redeemed the small Marxist groups from possibly ephemeral significance.' While Lenin was in exile, the Russian Social Democratic Party was founded (1898), drawing together the various small groups. Its leaders were almost immediately arrested, and its existence depended on the Swiss exiles, Plekhanov, Axelrod and Zasulich. Two years later, after Lenin's release, the party newspaper, *Iskra* ('The Spark'), was first printed and smuggled into Russia.

The new party was split by arguments between the revolutionaries and reformists, the hard core who wanted to create an elite dedicated to the cause of revolution and those who wanted to change society by gradual, non-violent means. The reformists followed the theories of Eduard Bernstein *(see page 67)* that, contrary to expectations, capitalism was actually getting stronger throughout Europe, and the class struggle was becoming less and less likely. Instead of campaigning for revolution, Marxists should co-operate with existing or future democratic governments to bring about social reform. Lenin himself disliked Bernstein's conclusions but realized (though he never acknowledged it) that a part of Berstein's analysis was correct—the working class could be tamed by improved conditions and so might lack the inclination and will for revolution. In *What is to be done?* (1902), Lenin therefore argued that an elite leadership was more important than ever to keep the proletariat on the revolutionary path.

The second Congress of the Social Democratic Party, which opened in Brussels in July 1903 but later moved to London, saw the resolution of this doctrinal conflict. Essentially, the argument revolved around the issue of party membership; was it to be restricted to an active elite or to be open to all? The decision of the delegates went against Lenin and in favour of open membership by twenty-eight votes to twenty-two. However, Lenin's supporters were successful in the elections to the electoral board of *Iskra* and to the Party's Central Committee. As they constituted a majority, albeit a narrow one, on these bodies, they were known as the Bolsheviks, from the Russian word for 'majority', and his opponents as Mensheviks, or minority. In fact, the divisions were not yet final; in 1904 the Mensheviks won control of the Central Committee and Lenin founded his own rival paper, *Vperyod* ('Forward'). In 1905 the split became permanent when the two groups held separate Congresses, in London and Geneva. Weak and divided, Russian Social Democracy in 1905 was hardly a force to be reckoned with.

One further source of opposition to the Tsars must not be discounted. Less than half the population of the Russian Empire were Russian by nationality. Many of the minority nationalities were strongly opposed to the rule of the Tsar. The Poles, for example, hoped to re-establish their own Kingdom. The Armenians, too, disliked Russian rule and in 1890 founded the Armenian Revolutionary Federation. The Russification policy of the central government under Alexander III encouraged even greater hostility among the minorities. All teaching had to be carried out in Russian, not only in Poland, always a centre of opposition, but also in the German Baltic areas, Finland and Central Asia. The Jews were especially persecuted because of their association with the assassination of Alexander II, and the first of over 200 'pogroms'—attacks on Jews and their property—took place in May 1881. Legal restrictions were also placed on them, so that they were forced to live in towns and were barred from practising law and trading in alcohol. They were even, in 1890, forbidden to vote in zemstvo elections, and their numbers in further education were fixed. In 1897, they formed the 'Bund' to co-ordinate their opposition. Members of the Bund attended the Minsk Conference that attempted to found the Social Democratic Party in 1898.

(b) The 1905 Revolution (see also Documentary exercise, page 118)
The events of 1905 were preceded by a series of decisions and accidents. There were indications of discontent among both the urban and the rural poor. An increasing number of strikes were organized in the cities, especially St Petersburg, as part of a campaign to win reduced hours and better wages. The famines of 1897, 1898 and 1901 worsened the plight of the already desperate peasantry, and in 1902 there were uprisings in the

provinces of Poltava and Kharkov. Thousands of miles away, tension with Japan had reached a new peak. In 1895, Russia had persuaded Japan to give up Port Arthur and the Liaotung Peninsula to her. Subsequent agreements with China had increased Russian influence and a substantial number of Russians had considerable investments in Northern China. This expansion was opposed by Japan *(see page 111)* and there were negotiations about the influence each was to have on the Chinese mainland. A peaceful solution was almost certainly possible, but without the restraining influence of Witte, who had been dismissed in 1900, the Russian Ministers advised the Tsar to ignore it. Plehve, Minister of the Interior, actually welcomed 'a short, victorious war that would stem the tide of revolution'. A Japanese envoy received surly treatment on his arrival at St Petersburg, and Japanese requests for negotiations were ignored. On 8 February 1904 the Japanese fleet torpedoed the Russian fleet stationed in Port Arthur while the Japanese army cleared the Korean peninsula of Russian troops.

The war proved disastrous for Russia's military pride. A second Japanese army was landed on the Liaotung Peninsula *(see Map 10)* and cut off Port Arthur. The Russian armies seem to have fought bravely in spite of inept orders, short supplies and inadequate reinforcements. In March 1905 they were isolated at Mukden and defeated by five combined Japanese armies. In the meantime, Port Arthur had fallen to Japanese troops in January 1905 and in the course of ten months 100 000 Russian troops had been lost. Nicholas was desperate for victory. Had not Kaiser Wilhelm told him, 'It is the great task of the future for Russia to cultivate the Asian continent and defend Europe from the Great Yellow Race'? To avoid such loss of prestige, Nicholas ordered his Baltic fleet to leave Kronstadt. It set sail in October, 1904, fired on British fishing ships on the Dogger Bank by accident, and, barred from the Suez Canal, rounded the Cape with cabins full of coal. On 27 May, 1905, it was sailing through the straits of Tsushima when it was attacked by the Japanese. More than thirty battleships—almost the entire fleet—were destroyed in an afternoon. So much for a 'short victorious war'.

The impact of the war on Russians was riveting. Plehve himself was blown up by a bomb from the Social Revolutionaries in July, 1904, which prompted Nicholas to remark: 'I have a secret conviction that I am destined for a terrible trial'. Two days later his son and heir, Alexis, was born. A week later the remains of the Far East fleet ventured out of Port Arthur; its commander was killed in his flagship, the 'Tsarevich' ('Tsar's son'). Shortly afterwards it was learnt that Alexis had haemophilia. The winter of 1904–5 had already brought discontent and news of the fall of Port Arthur coincided with a strike at the Putilov engineering works in St Petersburg. Spontaneous strikes were called in other cities. By 22 January 1905, 105 000 workers were on strike *(see Table 24)*.

This prompted action from more moderate quarters. Father Gapon, an ex-prison chaplain and head of the Association of Russian Factory and Mill Workers, one of the unions set up by the government to channel

Date		Events in war with Japan	Events in Russia
1904	8 February	Japanese attack on fleet in Port Arthur	
	10 February	War declared	
	1 May	Russian troops defeated at Yalu River	
	30 May	Japanese occupy Darien Siege of Port Arthur started	
	28 July		Assassination of Plehve
	30 July		Birth of Tsarevich Alexis
	6 August	Remainder of Russian Pacific fleet defeated	
	25 August– 4 September	Russians defeated at Liaoyang	
	October	Baltic fleet sent to the Far East	
	November		Zemstvo Congress demands a representative assembly and civil liberties
1905	2 January	Port Arthur surrenders	
	22 January		'Bloody Sunday'— petitioners to the Tsar fired on
	20 February –9 March	Russian Army defeated at Mukden	
	3 March		Tsar promises a 'consultative' assembly and other concessions
	8 March		Foundation of Union of Unions
	27 May	Battle of Tsushima— Russian Baltic fleet destroyed	
	June–August		Widespread strikes and disorder
	19 August		Tsar promises Imperial Duma
	5 September	Treaty of Portsmouth signed	
	20–30 October		General Strike
	26 October		Formation of St Petersburg Soviet
	30 October		Issue of October Manifesto and Witte appointed Prime Minister
	16 December		Arrest of members of St Petersburg Soviet
	22 December– 1 January		Uprising of workers in Moscow suppressed by troops
			Loan with France negotiated
1906	2 May		Witte dismissed and replaced by Goremykin
	6 May		Issue of Fundamental Laws
	10 May		Opening of First Duma

Table 24. Date Chart: The Revolution of 1905

workers' demands, met with zemstvo leaders and Social Revolutionaries. They drew up a petition to present to the Tsar. 'We are not considered human beings ... we are treated like slaves' it began. It requested 'the ending of the war, full civil liberties, a political amnesty and a constituent assembly'. It had 135 000 signatories. On Sunday, 22 January, the petitioners, led by Gapon, proceeded to the Winter Palace, the Tsar's residence in St Petersburg. As they marched, they sang hymns and carried ikons (religious pictures) and pictures of the Tsar. When they reached Palace Square, they were met not by the Tsar, who was not in residence, but by cossacks and dragoons who fired on them. Officially, ninety-six protesters died and 333 were wounded. Probably a thousand died and thousands more were wounded. The Tsar himself recorded that it was a 'painful day' but others were less charitable—Ramsay Macdonald called him a 'blood-stained creature' and 'a common murderer'.

There followed a wave of protests. Almost half a million workers came out on strike. There was more terrorism. On 17 February, the Tsar's uncle, Grand Duke Sergei, the governor of Moscow, was assassinated. In March, the Tsar promised a 'consultative' assembly, religious toleration, language rights for the Polish minority and cancellation of a part of the redemption dues for the peasants. These concessions proved inadequate, and instead unions were set up among groups that had never before been so organized—engineers, teachers, even the peasants. They were co-ordinated into a 'Union of Unions' by the moderate leader Paul Milyukov. As news of further defeats in the Far East—at Mukden and Tsushima—arrived, Nicholas realized that he was in danger of losing what support he had. In August, he repeated his pledges of March, and promised that the 'Duma' or assembly, would be elected, albeit by an electoral college in which the franchise would be based on property ownership. In all but the most right-wing circles the proposal was ridiculed and the protests continued.

The only advance during the summer was peace with Japan. Witte, recalled in the Tsar's hour of need, negotiated with Japan the Treaty of Portsmouth (New Hampshire, USA). By it, Japan received the southern half of the island of Sakhalin and Port Arthur, and Russia acknowledged that Korea was a Japanese sphere of influence. Only a small indemnity was charged and the Tsar could be relieved at the lightness of the terms. Even so, the surrender of territory and, implicitly, of Russian influence in Northern China was hardly a cause of rejoicing, especially in the summer of 1905 *(see Map 10)*.

During the summer the Tsar's position had worsened when his own troops joined the opposition. In June the sailors of the battleship 'Potemkin' had refused to obey orders and had led a mutiny of ships in the Black Sea. A sapper regiment in Tashkent went on strike, ostensibly in protest at the quality of their soup. In the autumn, after the signature of the Treaty of Portsmouth, the situation worsened. A printer's strike in St Petersburg led to what amounted to a general strike; even the Imperial Ballet Company, including Nicholas' one-time lover, refused to dance. As a result of a railway workers' strike in October, communications became almost impossible and the government had little idea of what was happening in outlying districts. Odessa and Kharkov were out of control. Peasants burnt crops and sacked their landlords' homes. In St Petersburg, 500 delegates were chosen by 200 000 workers to form a council, or 'soviet', which organized supplies and emergency measures, as well as deciding policy on the continuation of strikes. For a time, Trotsky was its chairman. Although it has sometimes been identified as the heart of the 1905 Revolution, its policies were in fact fairly moderate and its most extreme appeal was to ask its supporters to refuse to pay taxes and to withdraw their bank deposits.

Witte, on his return from America, convinced the Tsar of the need for more decisive action. Concession plus repression was his recommended formula. On 30 October, having told his mother that he felt 'sick with shame at this betrayal of the dynasty', the Tsar issued the Imperial Manifesto. It promised individual freedoms and the establishment of a State Duma based on a wider franchise than was promised in August. No law would be proposed without the Duma's approval, and the President of the Duma would head a Committee of Ministers. No details of the franchise were included, and it was stressed that the Tsar would retain control of the armed forces. He also upheld the right to raise loans, and thus avoid any Parliamentary control of the budget. The Tsar and his conservative supporters found the plans distasteful, but realized their necessity.

The Revolution was by no means ended by the issue of the October Manifesto. It succeeded in wooing moderates back to the Tsar's side, since they saw the possibility of political reforms on Western lines. It also reinsured the loyalty of the officer class of the army, who could be relied on to repress the remaining opposition. This repression of the more extreme opposition, now more isolated, actually ended the revolution. Trotsky had rejected the Manifesto as 'the police whip wrapped in the parchment of the constitution'. He and other leaders of the Soviet were arrested, and a new uprising in Moscow at the end of the year was put down, though only after considerable bloodshed. Disgruntled troops returning from the Far East were shot, and peasants who continued to burn and destroy farms were ruthlessly suppressed. There were still occasional mutinies among the army and navy, but they too were overcome; the climax of the autumn of 1905 had been passed.

There were many lessons to be learnt from the events of 1905, for both contemporaries and historians. For the revolutionaries, it provided an example for 1917 on timing, tactics and organization. For the liberals, it provided an opportunity for organization that was valuable in the Duma era that followed, when the political parties that emerged resembled the alliances of 1905. To the government, it showed the need for action of some kind, especially in the countryside. Urban workers might be expected to be a source of trouble, but the peasants had usually been loyal to the Tsar. Perhaps the most surprising aspect of the revolution was that the autocracy survived it, although not unscathed. Even before the revolution Witte had said 'the world should be surprised that we have any government' given the problems of the nationalities, the weakness of agriculture and the backwardness of industry. Add to these defeat at the hands of Japan, mutiny in the armed forces and a general strike, and it was remarkable that the Tsar kept his throne. Indeed, as the next year was to show, he kept not only his throne but also his power.

(c) The Era of the Dumas 1906–14

The amendments to the Constitution that resulted from the October Manifesto provided a number of new bodies. The State Assembly, the Duma, consisted of two houses—the Imperial Council and the State Duma. Half the members of the Council were to be appointed by the Tsar, the other half to be chosen by representatives of the wealthier classes. The Duma was to be elected by an electoral college, the members of which were to be chosen by the voters according to their social class. One member of the electoral college was chosen for each 2000 landowners. Property owners in towns had one elector for every 7000 of their number, peasants one for every 30 000 and urban workers one for every 90 000. The members of the Duma theoretically had the power to veto legislation, but as they had little control over government finance and none over the Council of Ministers, which remained responsible only to the Tsar, this power was limited. These arrangements were announced by the Tsar on 6 May 1906, less than a week before the Duma was due to sit. They took the form of a Fundamental Law, in which Nicholas also proclaimed himself an autocrat with control over the army and foreign policy and stated that no alterations could be made to the new arrangements without his approval. Four days earlier, he had sacked Witte, secure in the knowledge that the $400 million loan he had obtained from France would keep him financially independent of the Duma. His replacement was the conservative Ivan Goremykin. The Tsar had seemingly scotched any chance of democratic government before it got off the ground.

Nevertheless, on 10 May 1906, the newly elected members of the Duma met for the first time. 524 had been chosen, but not all of them arrived in St Petersburg for the opening session in the Winter Palace. There were no 'parties' by modern standards, but there were a number of identifiable groups. The Octobrists, who had about forty representatives, took their name from the October Manifesto, which they accepted as providing the right degree of democracy. They were, however, keen to build up Russia's economic strength and establish a wealthy peasantry. The 'Cadets' (Constitutional Democrats), of whom there were nearly 200, had been formed by Milyukov in October 1905. They were the political party of the zemstvo liberals and sought direct and universal suffrage and further redistribution of land in the peasants' favour. The Social Democrats were technically absent, since they had boycotted the elections on the grounds that they were sham democracy. In fact, about twenty of them, chiefly Mensheviks, had ignored the boycott and had been elected. The other members were not affiliated to any particular group. Sixty or so represented particular national groups—Ukrainians and Poles especially—and stood for the independence of their group from the Russian Empire. The other members, about 200 of them, were poorer people with no agreed policy, although about half of them can be identified as a Labour group. The lack of party organization and the few votes that were called makes it difficult to be definite about the numbers and constitution of the different groups.

The first session of the Duma lasted only ten weeks. In that time, the members attempted to win more power for themselves, demanding, for instance, that ministers should be responsible to them not the Tsar and that the Imperial Council should be abolished. They also made a series of demands for nationwide reforms, such as the breaking up of the great estates and the abolition of the death penalty. The experiment in constitutionalism had backfired on the Tsar; he could control the electoral system but not the people who were elected. Rather than give way again, he decided to reimpose his authority. On a Sunday, 22 July, he declared the Duma dissolved on the grounds that it was unable to function. Troops were sent to the Tauride Palace to prevent any meeting continuing. Contrary to his own Fundamental Law, Nicholas set no date for new elections but announced that the next Duma would meet the following February. In protest at this, about 200 Duma members, mainly Cadets, crossed the border into Finland and from the town of Viborg called upon the people to refuse to pay their taxes or to serve in the army. In this instance the timing, issues and proposed means of protest were of little interest to the people, who ignored the call.

The Second Duma differed from the First in two respects. The Social Democrats stood for election, and about fifty of them were elected. Secondly, the Cadets decided to attempt to co-operate with the government. However, they could not prevent other members repeating the radical demands of the First Duma or refusing to co-operate with the government's plans for agrarian reform and the repression of terrorism. Consequently, after three months, the Duma was dissolved on the (false) grounds that a Social Democrat member was plotting to assassinate the Tsar. In an attempt to ensure greater malleability next time, the Tsar altered the electoral quotas. In so doing, he again broke the Fundamental Law of 1906 which stated that it could not be changed without the Duma's approval. The number of electoral college votes for workers was reduced, as was that for the national minorities, while that for estate for estate owners was increased, giving them more than half the seats.

Not surprisingly, the subsequent Dumas, which sat from 1907–12 and 1912–17 respectively, were more obedient. Seton-Watson gives the following membership figures for these two Dumas:

1907: Octobrists 154; other Right-wing 127; Cadets 54; Left-wing 33

1912: Octobrists 121; other Right-wing 145; Cadets 100; Left-wing 23

The Third Duma contained a majority of Octobrists and right-wingers, who gave their approval to Stolypin's repressive measures *(see page 108)*.

The Fourth was also conservative and thus, by 1914, the Tsar had achieved the rubber-stamp democracy that he had wanted. Yet even the conservatives of the Fourth Duma were roused to action by the inefficiency of the government during the war and formed a 'Progressive Bloc' in 1915 to recommend reform. The Tsar's failure to respond to this symbolized the last chance for democracy. Oberlander has summarized the significance of the failure of the Dumas as follows: 'The Tsarist regime was not overthrown, it succumbed to its own inertia. The Russian Parliamentary system was completely undermined by the lack of trust between the Tsarist regime and the First and Second Dumas, which were more or less representative of the people.'

6. Economic History

(c) Stolypin's Economic Reforms

Peter Stolypin became Prime Minister in June 1906. He was only forty-five and had already made a name for himself as governor of Saratov province during 1905, when he had put down revolutionaries with great harshness. He remained a believer in repression. The extra powers granted to provincial governors on his initiative in 1906 (over which the First Duma had been dissolved) resulted in over 100 executions. Nevertheless, Stolypin saw the necessity of establishing Russia as a strong, capitalist state, preferably with the Tsar at its head. To achieve this, he wanted to create a class of wealthy peasants who would provide enough grain for exports while earning enough money to be a consumer class for industrial goods. Those peasants who could not survive would provide the industrial work force. Reforms in this direction should also win new support for the Tsar from the wealthy peasants.

To these ends he introduced the Agrarian Reform Act of 1906 and a series of complex subsidiary legislation between 1906 and 1911. The land captains were abolished and the peasant passport system ended, so that peasants became as free to move around as any other Russian. Far more importantly, the peasant was released from his obligations to the mir and could choose to own his land as an individual rather than as part of the mir. If a majority of members of the mir favoured individual land holding, then the mir was disbanded. When a peasant received his individual land holding, it was in the form of a single farm, rather than parts of land scattered throughout the mir's holding. By 1916, 1·2 million (about 24%) peasants owned their own land, and a further 750 000 applications were waiting a decision. Stolypin also encouraged resettlement, as a result of which about half a million people went to the East with government assistance. The Peasants' Land Bank was extended to make it easier for peasants to set up their own farms. In 1907, redemption payments were ended, by which time 670·3 million roubles had been repaid out of a total due of 2012 million. These measures should have combined to provide a rural revolution.

In fact, they had failed to do so by the time of the political revolutions of 1917. Stolypin had not planned for rapid change; he had said that twenty years of peace would be needed for his measures to have full effect. Stolypin himself died in 1911 from an assassin's bullet in a Kiev theatre; the Tsar and Rasputin were in the audience. As the assassin had been both a revolutionary and a police agent, it is not certain on whose orders he had acted. Stolypin's scheme for ending the mir was ended in 1916, since it was impossible for peasants serving in the Great War to reorganize their land. In any case, Stolypin's reforms had left untouched the 140 million acres held by the nobility and had taken no account of the increasing rural population. Moreover, Stolypin, as Stalin after him, concentrated on reforming the system of landholding as the key to agrarian reform. In other countries, which had undergone a natural rather than an imposed agricultural revolution, innovations (such as machinery and fertilizers) had preceded rather than followed changes in the landholding system. Certainly, Stolypin encouraged new techniques; over 1500 model farms and agricultural schools were set up between 1907 and 1913. However, these were intended to bring changes on the newly created farms rather than bring changes that would *require* new farms. Not surprisingly, crop yields remained at their old levels, about half those of Western Europe. Stolypin's measures had come too little, too late.

7. Foreign Policy

(a) Imperial Policy

(i) Central Asia
During the nineteenth century Russia extended her trading influence and governing control over parts of Central Asia. These are shown on Map 9. Several Russians had undertaken conquests on their own initiative; General Chernayev, acting against official orders, had captured Tashkent in 1865. Next, the three Khanates, previously ruled by the Uzbeks, were captured. The first, Bokhara, was captured as a result of the battle of Dzhizak, Khiva became a Russian dependency in 1873 and Kokand, the third, was taken in 1876. Prince Gorchakov, Russian Foreign Minister, justified these conquests on grounds of security, since each new boundary brought contact with another hostile people. The conquests were also economically valuable, providing minerals and cotton-growing areas. The building of railways after 1880 increased this value and gave them strategic importance. In 1879 the Transcaucasian Railway was started. It reached Merv in 1886, Samarkand in 1888. In 1898 a line from Merv to Kushk on the Afghan border was started.

There was no further expansion after 1890. However, Russian activity in Central Asia remained of diplomatic importance. The British government was concerned that Russia planned to continue their expansion and even threaten British supremacy in the Indian sub-continent. In fact, it would have been extremely difficult for the Russian army to undertake operations on the Indian border, because of the terrain and distances involved. Nonetheless, the Russians exploited British fears; there were crises in 1855–7, 1878 and 1885 which almost led to war. The Russian conquests to the south of Merv and their defeat of the Afghans at Penjdeh frightened the British, and agreement was only reached when Bismarck refused to allow British ships through the straits of Constantinople. Anglo-Russian tension in Central Asia was only ended by the Entente of 1907, when spheres of influence in Persia were agreed on and a buffer zone of 1905 confirmed *(see Map 9)*.

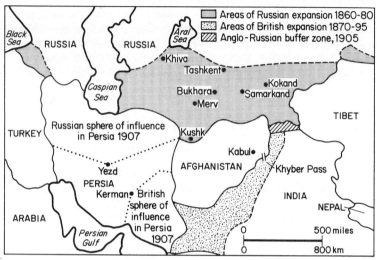

Map 9 Russian expansion in Central Asia

(ii) The Far East

Russia had long been interested in the Far East. Before 1850, Alaska and Kamchatka had been taken *(see Map 10)*. During the 1850s, Count Muraviev, Governor-General of Eastern Siberia, encouraged further expansion, as a result of which the island of Sakhalin and the Kurile Archipelago were occupied. In 1860 the treaty of Peking was signed with China to settle the border between the two countries. The rivers Amur and Ussuri were agreed upon as the frontier, and the next year work was started on the building of the city of Vladivostok. In 1867 Alaska was given up, being sold to the United States for $7 200 000 (about two cents an acre) and in 1875 the Kurile Archipelago was given to Japan in exchange for Japanese recognition of the Russian occupation of Sakhalin.

These early settlements left Russia with two unsatisfactory aspects to her Far Eastern possessions. Firstly, Manchuria remained a Chinese salient in Russian territory; the Russians would have liked to win a border that went from Irkutsk straight to Vladivostok. Secondly, Russia had no ice-free port in the Far East and hoped to gain one. A port on the Korean or Liaotung peninsula would be ideal. Both these ambitions were to lead to crisis and conflict.

Japan's victory over China in 1895 led to extensive territorial gains by the Japanese. They took the Pescadores Islands, Formosa and the Liaotung peninsula. Russia protested that Japan's gains threatened her interests and that she, Russia, was therefore entitled to some compensation. Germany supported this protest, since she was keen to keep Russia occupied in the Far East, rather than the Balkans. As a result, Japan agreed to leave the Liaotung Peninsula to China. In the same year, Russia loaned China 400 million francs and set up the Russo-Chinese bank and in 1896 a treaty was signed by which Russia agreed to defend China. In order to do this, a railway would have to be built across Manchuria and the Chinese agreed to the building of this, the 'Chinese Eastern Railway', by Russian workmen, protected by Russian armed guards. The penetration of Northern Manchuria was well in hand.

Map 10 The Far East

In 1898 Russia won her ice-free port. In 1897 Germany had taken the town of Kiao-chow in retaliation for the murder of two missionaries. Again, Russia demanded compensation for another's gain. China granted Russia a twenty-five year lease on the Liaotung peninsula, including the port of Port Arthur. In addition, the Russians were allowed to build a railway from Harbin to Darien. It is likely that these extensive gains were won by bribing the leading Chinese negotiator, Li Hung-chang.

The next years saw three significant developments in Russian Far Eastern policy. Firstly, negotiations with Japan over the influence of each settled on one particular issue—Japanese influence in Korea. Since 1895 Japan had won such power there that Russia realized she had little chance of winning land or ports there. The Nissi-Rosen convention of 1898 agreed that each power would respect Korean sovereignty and not interfere in the internal affairs of Korea. As far as Japan was concerned, it provided a Russian assurance that they would keep out. Japan offered Russia a free hand in Manchuria in exchange for their free hand in Korea, but Russia had rejected this. Secondly, other European powers acquired railway rights in China. The Boxer Rebellion of 1900 had led to a joint Western force going to China but Russia, keen to maintain her pre-eminence, took the opportunity to occupy all the major cities of Northern Manchuria and increase the number of troops in the railway zone. The other Western powers became concerned by Russia's influence. The Anglo-Japanese treaty of 1902 promised neutrality in the event of a Far Eastern war while Germany supported Russia by declaring that 'the fate of Manchuria was a matter of absolute indifference to Germany'.

Thirdly, the Tsar became increasingly keen to exploit the resources of Manchuria, and, if possible, Northern Korea. His enthusiasm was stimulated by an ex-cavalry officer, Bezobrazov, who persuaded Nicholas to let him have two million roubles to investigate the natural resources of the Yalu River, especially timber. Bezobrazov hoped to use the Russian railway police to guard his men during the investigations, but this was forbidden, and instead he recruited a number of Chinese thugs to act as guards. Their excesses did little to endear the Russians with the Chinese and Japanese in the area.

Japan was obviously concerned by Russia's action. In 1903, the Japanese government offered negotiations and repeated their offer of 1898—a free hand for Russia in Manchuria in exchange for a free hand for Japan in Korea. The Russian government made no reply, and in the meantime appointed Admiral Alexeev, a friend of Bezobrazov, as Regent of the Far East. In October, 1903, they replied to the Japanese offer by saying that Korean independence should be acknowledged by both sides and that the area to the north of the 39th parallel should be neutral. Manchuria was not mentioned. The Japanese rejected the Russian proposals and again asked for the same rights in Korea as the Russians had in Manchuria. Subsequent negotiations during the winter of 1903–4 made no progress, and on 8 February 1904, the Japanese attacked Port Arthur, launching the war that led to Russia's humiliation *(see page 102)*.

After the war, Russia attempted to maintain her influence in Northern China. In 1907, a treaty with Japan settled each nation's fishing rights and the use of the South Manchurian Railway. A secret protocol acknowledged Japan's rights in Korea and Southern Manchuria and Russia's influence in Northern Manchuria and Mongolia. In 1910 Korea was formally annexed to the Japanese Empire and renamed Chosen. After

1911 Russia won from China special interests in Mongolia, setting up a bank and sending military and financial advisers.

(b) European Policies

(i) Russia's position in 1890

In 1872, Russia had joined Germany and Austria-Hungary in the 'Drei-kaiserbund' (Three Emperors League). This was an informal agreement by which each agreed to benevolent neutrality if any of them was involved in war with an outside power. In 1881 this arrangement was formalized into a treaty that was renewable every three years; in the treaty it was agreed that Austria-Hungary should ultimately annex Bosnia and Herzegovina. By 1887 there was considerable opposition in Russia to the renewal of the treaty. This was led by M.N. Katkov in *Moskovskiye vedomisti*, who argued that an alliance with Austria-Hungary restricted Russia's freedom of action in the Balkans, where she could hope to make considerable territorial gains. The German government was also concerned by the treaty, since it seemed incompatible with her promises to Austria-Hungary in 1879, that she would go to Austria-Hungary's aid in the event of war with Russia. Consequently, Russia and Germany signed the Reinsurance Treaty of 1887. By this, each promised benevolent neutrality in the event of the other being involved in war, unless Russia attacked Austria-Hungary, in which case Germany claimed the right to support her ally. Germany also promised to support Russian influence in the Balkans. However, the treaty was not renewed in 1890, for the new German government were concerned that it conflicted with German promises to Austria-Hungary. Only Bismarck had been able to maintain alliances with both the great powers who threatened each other in the Balkans. Consequently Russia was without allies in 1890.

Russia's main interest in Europe in 1890 was in the Balkans, where she hoped to maintain and extend her influence. Bulgaria had accepted Russian friendship until 1885. In that year, Prince Alexander had supported the union of Eastern Roumelia with Bulgaria, thereby annoying the Russian government, who forced his abdication. The new ruler, Ferdinand of Coburg, once again accepted Russia's influence. In addition, Serbia, officially Austria-Hungary's client, looked increasingly to Russia as an ally against Austria-Hungary. Consequently, Russia, which in any case regarded herself as the natural leader of the Slav peoples, had the friendship and support of both the new Balkan powers in the 1890s.

Russia was also keen to see the decline of the Ottoman Empire, by force if necessary. This would not only bring the prospect of territorial gain, but might also resolve the issue of the Straits of Constantinople in her favour. In 1841, Britain, Russia, France, Austria and Prussia had agreed that the straits should be closed to all warships as long as Turkey was at peace. In 1871 this had been revised so that the Sultan could allow warships through if he considered his independence threatened. These arrangements were reasonably satisfactory to Russia as they gave her southern flank a measure of protection, but they also made it difficult for the Russian Black Sea fleet to be used. In 1904–5, this fleet had been barred from the Straits during the war with Japan, so thereafter the Russian government was keen to have the 'Straits Convention' revised so that the Straits were permanently open to her warships.

(ii) The Alliance with France (see pages 134–5)
Russo-French friendship began in the late 1880s. The Russian ambassador in Paris, Baron Mohrenheim, was influential in allaying French fears about the autocracy and financial links began. Bismarck, in 1887, had forbidden German banks to accept Russian securities as collateral for loans, so in 1889 the French took up a 4% loan. In 1890 they took up a second one.

In 1891 the Triple Alliance of Germany, Austria-Hungary and Italy was renewed. Four years earlier Britain had signed the Mediterranean Agreements with Austria-Hungary and Italy, and seemed friendly to the Triple Alliance. France and Russia were both isolated. In July 1891 a French naval squadron visited Kronstadt and the Tsar stood bareheaded while the French anthem was played. On 27 August an agreement was signed promising mutual consultation in the event of possible war; if either was in danger each would agree to 'measures which this eventuality would require the two governments to adopt immediately and simultaneously'. Discussions were initiated on what these measures should be.

In August 1892 Generals Boisdeffre and Obruchev agreed on a military convention which was finally ratified by both sides in January 1894. The details of this were as follows. If France was attacked by Germany (or by Italy and Germany), Russia would provide between seven and eight hundred thousand men against Germany. If Russia was attacked by Germany or by Austria-Hungary and Germany, all available French forces (1 300 000 men) would be used against Germany. These terms were never made public, but during the 1890s it became increasingly clear that the two were committed to each other. In 1896 (and again in 1901), Nicholas II visited Paris, and in 1897 President Faure visited Russia. French loans continued to support and develop the Russian economy.

(iii) Relations with Germany, Austria-Hungary and Great Britain
In 1904–5 the possibility of a Russo-German alliance arose. Germany had failed to come to agreement with Britain and Russian friendship might be valuable not only against Britain but also as a means of securing France's agreement to the permanent accession of Alsace-Lorraine. For Russia, Germany's friendship might provide both security against Austria-Hungary and support for Russian claims in the Balkans and the Straits of Constantinople. In October 1904 the Kaiser suggested a Franco-Russo-German alliance against Britain to the Tsar. Nicholas' immediate reaction was enthusiastic, but he insisted on discussing it

with France before signing anything, while the Kaiser wanted a Russo-German alliance signed before France was brought into the negotiations. The idea was therefore shelved. The following year (in July 1905), the Kaiser entertained the Tsar on board his yacht, the 'Pole Star', and persuaded him to sign the treaty of Björko. By this, each agreed to give full land and sea support to the other in the event of war, and Nicholas was obliged to tell France of the alliance and bring her into it. Bülow disliked the treaty and threatened to resign, while the Russian Foreign Minister, Lamsdorff, when told of it three months later, realized it was not compatible with existing agreements with France. The French Prime Minister, Rouvier, told the Russians there was no need for such an alliance since he wished to maintain Britain's friendship, while Germany's attitude to Morocco made any Franco-German agreement impossible. Consequently the treaty was never ratified and Russo-German relations thereafter worsened.

For a short time, agreement with Austria-Hungary seemed a possibility. After Russia's defeat in the Far East, there seemed little chance of making gains in the Balkans by military action. Consequently, there was some discussion in the Third Duma in 1907 of the possibility of agreement with Austria-Hungary. However, the Bosnian crisis of 1908 and Austria-Hungary's closeness to Germany ended all hopes in this direction *(see pages 139–42)*.

Before the turn of the century, Russia and Britain seemed likely enemies because of their rival ambitions in Central Asia. However, after 1904 they were both allied to France and in 1906 discussions were initiated between the Russian Foreign Minister, Izvolsky, and the British ambassador, Nicholson. On 31 August 1907 a convention was agreed on. Persia was divided into three zones of influence (one British, one Russian, one neutral—*see Map 9*), the position of both powers in Afghanistan was agreed (Russia was to leave and maintain relations with the Afghan government only through Britain), and Tibet was to be under Chinese sovereignty. This convention was the basis of the Russo-British alliance. Germany was given assurances that the agreement was not intended to damage them, and in fact, apart from the Bosnian crisis, Russo-German relations improved considerably. In 1908 an agreement on the Åland islands was signed and in 1910 there was a settlement on the Baghdad Railway. In February 1914 P.N. Durnovo, the Russian ex-minister of the Interior, wrote in a memorandum:'The vital interests of Russia and Germany are nowhere in conflict ... The future of Germany is on the seas where for Russia, essentially the most Continental of the powers, there are no interests at all.'

(iv) Russia and the Balkans

The Balkans were relatively quiet during the 1890s. Both the chief protaganists were involved elsewhere—the Russians in the Far East, the Austro-Hungarians with internal problems. Serbia became increasingly Russophile, and the Austro-Serbian treaty was not renewed in 1895.

Draga Mashin, the wife of King Alexander (1889–1903), was keen to improve relations with Russia. After her assassination with her husband in 1903, the new king, Peter I, of the Karadjordjevic dynasty, was equally pro-Russian. At the same time, Russian influence in Bulgaria remained assured. In 1895 the anti-Russian Prime Minister, Stambolov, was assassinated. The heir to the throne, Prince Boris, was converted from Catholicism to Orthodoxy. In 1902 a military agreement was signed. Russia seemed pre-eminent.

However, the next ten years saw a reversal of Russia's fortunes. In the Bosnian crisis of 1908 *(see page 139)* Russia was unable to back Serbia for fear of German involvement and thus lost some of Serbia's confidence. In the following years, the Russian Foreign Ministry tried hard to create a barrier against further Austrian expansion, particularly encouraging the alliance of Serbia and Bulgaria that was signed in 1912. Unfortunately, while Russia saw this alliance as a way of blocking Austrian expansion, Serbia and Bulgaria saw it as a way of extending their frontiers at Turkey's expense. The treaty was primarily concerned with the division of Macedonia between them. During the Balkan Wars that followed *(see page 142)* Russia found herself again pushed to one side. During the London negotiations of 1912–13, following the victory of the Balkan League, Russia was forced to drop her support for Serbia's demands for a port on the Adriatic. During the negotiations 400 000 extra Russians and 220 000 extra Austro-Hungarians remained under arms in case the negotiations broke down. Then, during the second Balkan War, Russia's original and most loyal Balkan ally, Bulgaria, suffered defeat at the hands of Serbia and Roumania. Therefore, by 1913 Austria-Hungary had made considerable gains in the Balkans at the expense of Serbia and Russia, leaving each resentful and determined not to give way again.

8. Bibliography

There is an abundance of material on Russia. The best introductory books are *The Making of Modern Russia* by L. Kochan (Cape, 1962), *The Decline of Imperial Russia 1855–1914* by H. Seton-Watson (Methuen, 1952) and the older *The End of the Russian Empire* by M.T. Florinsky (Yale, 1931). The standard detailed work, which concentrates on the later period is the six-volume work by E.H. Carr, *The Bolshevik Revolution* (Macmillan, 1950–59).

9. Discussion Points and Exercises

A   *This section consists of questions that might be used for discussion (or written answers) as a way of expanding on the chapter and testing understanding of it:*
1   What is autocracy?
2   What was the Romanovs' approach to the governing of their country?

3 Why was the Russian economy so backward in the late nineteenth century?

4 Comment on Witte's aims for the Russian economy.

5 What were the 'shock waves of industrialization'?

6 What was populism and why was it always in difficulty?

7 Why did so many reject the application of Marxism to Russia?

8 Why was the government so keen on war with Japan?

9 What events amounted to 'revolution' in 1905?

10 Why did the Tsar and conservatives find the concessions of 1905 so hard to swallow?

11 How significant a democratic institution was the Duma?

12 How different were Stolypin's aims and methods from Witte's?

13 Why was Russia keen to expand in Central Asia?

14 Why did Japan's penetration of Korea so disturb the Russian government?

15 Why were the alliances with Germany and Austria-Hungary ended?

16 How important was the Franco-Russian alliance in European diplomacy?

17 Trace Russia's fortunes in the Balkans, 1890–1914.

B *This section is intended to illustrate some of the issues raised by the chapter:*

1 You are appointed adviser to the new Tsar in 1894. Outline for him the chief problems his government is likely to face at home and abroad and possible solutions to them.

2 If you had lived in Russia in 1905, would you have supported the Tsar or his opponents? If the latter, which group would you have joined? Give detailed reasons for your decisions.

3 Write a Foreign Office report outlining the advantages and disadvantages of Russian expansion in the Far East.

C *This section suggests two ways in which you might compare Russia with other European countries:*

1 Read the sections on German economic development *(pages 73, 86)*. Compare Russia's progress, and the methods used to achieve that progress, with Germany's.

2 Compare the imperial aims and achievements of Russia with those of other European powers.

D *Essay questions:*

1 Was Russia a modern industrial power by 1914?

2 Assess the contribution of Witte and Stolypin to the advance of the Russian economy.

3 Why did Tsarism survive in 1905?

4 How powerful was the opposition to the Tsarist regime at the turn of the century?

5 Examine the effects of Russia's ambitions in Manchuria both on Russia itself and on international relations.

10. Documents Relating to the Russian Revolution of 1905

Study carefully the following documents.

A. The Petition of the Workers, Bloody Sunday, 9 January 1905
(Source: A.J. Sack, *The Birth of the Russian Democracy* (1918) quoted in Kertesz p.297)

Sire:

We working-men and inhabitants of St Petersburg . . . come to Thee, Sire, to seek for truth and defence. We have become beggars; we have been oppressed; . . . we are not recognized as human beings; we are treated as slaves. . . . We have no more power, Sire; the limit of patience has been reached. There has arrived for us that tremendous moment when death is better than the continuation of intolerable tortures. We have left off working and we have declared to the masters that we shall not begin to work until they comply with our demands. We beg but little. . . . The first request which we made was that our masters should discuss our needs with us; but this was refused, on the grounds that by law we have no right to make such a request. They also declared to be illegal our requests to reduce the working hours to eight hours daily, to agree with us about the prices for our work, to consider our misunderstandings with the interior administration of the mills, to increase the wages for the labour of women and of general labourers, so that the minimum daily wage should be one rouble per day, to abolish overtime work, to give us medical attention without insulting us, to arrange the workshops so that it might be possible to work there and not find in them death from awful draughts and from rain and snow. All these requests appeared to be, in the opinion of our masters and of the factory and mill administrations, illegal. Every one of our requests was a crime, and the desire to improve our condition was regarded by them as impertinence, and as offensive to them.

Sire, here are many thousands of us, and all are human beings in appearance only. In reality in us, as in all Russian people, there is not recognized any human right, not even the right of speaking, thinking, meeting, discussing our needs. . . . We have been enslaved . . . under the auspices of Thy officials. Every one of us who dares to raise a voice in defence of working-class and popular interests is thrown into gaol or is sent into banishment. . . . Even to pity a beaten man . . . is to commit a heavy crime . . . (a section on the iniquities of imperial officials follows here).

We are seeking here the last salvation. Do not refuse assistance to Thy people. . . . Give their destiny into their own hands. Cast away from them the intolerable oppression of officials. Destroy the wall between Thyself and Thy people, and let them rule the country with Thyself . . .

Russia is too great. Its necessities are too various and numerous for officials to rule it. National representation is indispensable . . . order immediately the convocation of representatives of the Russian land from all ranks, including representatives from the working people. . . . This is the most capital of our requests. . . . Yet one measure alone cannot heal our wounds. . . . The following are indispensable: I. Measures to counteract the ignorance and legal oppression of the Russian people.

1. The immediate release and return of all who have suffered for political and religious convictions, for strikes, and national peasant disorders.

2. The immediate declaration of freedom and of the inviolability of the person—freedom of speech and press, freedom of meetings, and freedom of conscience in religion.

3. Universal and compulsory education of the people . . .

4. Responsibility of the ministers before the people and guarantee that the government will be law-abiding.

5. Equality before the law of all . . .

6. Separation of the Church from the State.

II. Measures against the Poverty of the People.

1. Abolition of indirect taxes and the substitution of a progressive income tax.

2. Abolition of the redemption instalments, cheap credit, and gradual transference of the land to the people . . .

3. The orders for the military and naval ministries should be filled in Russia, and not abroad.

4. The cessation of the war by the will of the people.

III. Measures against the Oppression of Labour.

1. Abolition of the factory inspectorships.

2. Institution at factories and mills of permanent committees of elected workers which, together with the administration, would consider the complaints of individual workers. Dismissal of workers should not take place other than by resolution of this committee.

3. Freedom of organization of co-operative societies . . . and of trade unions . . .

4. Eight-hour working day . . . .

5. Freedom of the struggle of labour against capital, immediately.

6. Normal wages, immediately.

7. Participation of working-class representatives in the working-out of projects of law concerning workmen's State insurance. . . .

Order and take an oath to comply with these requests, and Thou wilt make Russia happy and famous and Thou wilt impress Thy name in our hearts. . . . If Thou wilt not order and wilt not answer our prayers—we shall die here on this place before Thy Palace. We have nowhere to go farther and nothing for which to go. We have only two ways—either towards liberty and happiness or into the grave . . .

B. *The October Manifesto, 17 October 1905*
(Source: F.A. Golder, *Documents of Russian History, 1914–17* (1927) quoted in Kertesz, p.301)

The rioting and agitation in the capitals and in many localities of Our Empire fills Our hearts with great and deep grief. The welfare of the Russian Emperor is bound up with the welfare of the people, and its sorrows are His sorrows. The turbulence which has broken out may confound the people and threaten the integrity and unity of Our Empire.

The great vow of service by the Tsar obligates Us to endeavour, with all Our strength, wisdom, and power, to put an end as quickly as possible to the disturbances so dangerous to the Empire. In commanding the responsible authorities to take measures to stop disorders, lawlessness and violence, and to protect peaceful citizens in the quiet performances of their duties,

We have found it necessary to unite the activities of the Supreme Government, so as to ensure the successful carrying out of the general measures laid down by Us for the peaceful life of the State.

We lay upon the Government the execution of Our unchangeable will:

1. To grant to the population the inviolable right of free citizenship, based on the principles of freedom of person, conscience, speech, assembly, and union.

2. Without postponing the intended elections for the State Duma (which had been proposed by the 'Bulyagin Duma' proclamation of August, 1905 —*see page 104*) in so far as possible, in view of the short time that remains before the assembling of that body, to include in the participation of the work of the Duma those classes of the population that have been until now entirely deprived of the right to vote, and to extend in the future, by the newly created legislative way, the principles of the general right of election.

3. To establish as an unbreakable rule that no law shall go into force without its confirmation by the State Duma and that the persons elected by the people shall have the opportunity for actual participation in supervising the legality of the acts of authorities appointed to Us . . .

C. Manifesto to better the conditions ... of the peasant population, 3 November 1905
(Source: F.A. Golder, *op. cit.*)

. . . The troubles that have broken out in villages . . . fill Our heart with deep sorrow. . . . Violence and crime do not, however, help the peasant and may bring much sorrow and misery to the country. The only way to better permanently the welfare of the peasant is by peaceful and legal means; and to improve his condition has always been one of our first cares. . . . We have decided:

1. To reduce by half, from 1 January 1906, and to discontinue altogether after 1 January 1907, payments due from peasants for land which before emancipation belonged to large landowners, State and Crown.

2. To make it easier for the Peasant Land Bank, by increasing its resources and by offering better terms for loans, to help the peasant with little land to buy more. . . .

D. The St Petersburg Soviet, 13 October–3 December 1905
(Sources: M.J. Olgin, *The Soul of the Russian Revolution* (1917) and A.J. Sack, *op. cit.* quoted by Kertesz, p.303)

(a) Proclamation ending the First General Strike, 20 October 1905 (following the issue of the October Manifesto)

In view of the necessity of the working class to organize on the basis of its achieved victories and to arm for a final struggle for a Constituent Assembly on the basis of its achieved victories and to arm for a final struggle for a Constituent Assembly on the basis of universal, equal, direct and secret suffrage which is to establish a democratic republic, the Council of Workmen's Delegates orders that the political strike be stopped at noon, 21 October. The Council is confident, however, that, should it be required by further developments, the working-men will resume the strike as willingly and devotedly as heretofore.

(b) Proclamation calling the Second General Strike, 1 November 1905, in support of the rebellion of the Kronstadt sailors

> The government continues to stride over corpses. It puts on trial before a court-martial the brave Kronstadt soldiers of the army and navy who rose to the defence of their rights and of national freedom. It put the noose of martial law on the neck of oppressed Poland.
>
> The Council of Workmen's Delegates calls on the revolutionary proletariat of Petersburg to manifest their solidarity with the revolutionary soldiers of Kronstadt and with the revolutionary proletarians of Poland through a general political strike, which has proved to be a formidable power, and through general meetings of protest. Tomorrow, on 2 November, at noon, the working-men of Petersburg will stop work, their slogans being:
> 1. Down with court-martial!
> 2. Down with capital punishment!
> 3. Down with martial law in Poland and all over Russia!

(c) Proclamation of 2 December asking for continued passive resistance of the Russian people.

> The proclamation started by pointing out the main crimes of the Tsar's government, and declared that the downfall of autocracy was the only way forward. To do this, it was declared necessary to remove the Tsar's financial power. To this end, the Manifesto called on the people:
> To refuse payments of redemption instalments and all other fiscal payments.
> To demand that all wages or salaries be in gold and that amounts less than five roubles be paid in hard coin, full weight.
> To withdraw the deposits from the Savings Banks and from the State Bank, demanding all payments in gold.

E. The Fundamental Laws of the Russian Empire, 23 April 1906
(Source: *Jährbuch des offentlichen Rechts* (1908) quoted in *Reading in Modern European History* (1909) by J.H. Robinson and C.A. Beard, and in Kertesz, p.305)

> . . . 4. The supreme autocratic power is vested in the Tsar of All the Russias. It is God's command that his authority should be obeyed not only through fear but for conscience' sake. . . .
> 7. The Tsar exercises the legislative power in conjunction with the Council of the Empire and the Imperial Duma.
> 8. The initiative in all branches of legislation belongs to the Tsar. Solely on his initiative may the Fundamental Laws of the Empire be subjected to a revision in the Council of the Empire and the Imperial Duma.
> 9. The Tsar approves of the laws, and without his approval no law can come into existence.
> 10. All governmental powers in their widest extent throughout the whole Russian Empire are vested in the Tsar . . .
> 17. The Tsar appoints and dismisses the president of the Council, the ministers themselves, and the heads of the chief departments of administration, as well as all other officials where the law does not provide for another method of appointment and dismissal . . .

(As well as these constitutional procedures, the Laws also included a new view of the civil rights of the Russian people. Some of these are included below)

78. Russian subjects are entitled to meet peaceably and without arms for such purposes as are not contrary to law.

79. Within the limits fixed by law every one may express his thought by word or writing and circulate them by means of the press or otherwise . . .

86. No new law shall go into force without the sanction of both the Council of the Empire and the Duma and the ratification of the Tsar.

F. Dissolution of the First Duma, 21 July 1906

(Source: *London Weekly Times*, 27 July 1906, quoted by Robinson and Heard, op. cit.)

We summoned the representatives of the nation by Our will to the work of productive legislation. Confiding firmly in our divine clemency and believing in the great and brilliant future of Our people, We confidently anticipated benefits for the country from their labours. We proposed great reforms in all departments in the national life. We have always devoted Our greatest care to the removal of the ignorance of the people by the light of instruction, and to the removal of their burdens by improving the conditions of agricultural work.

A cruel disappointment has befallen Our expectations. The representatives of the nation, instead of applying themselves to the work of productive legislation, have strayed into spheres beyond their competence, and have been making enquiries into the acts of local authorities established by Ourselves, and have been making comments upon the imperfections of the Fundamental Laws, which can only be modified by Our imperial will. In short, the representatives of the nation have undertaken really illegal acts, such as the appeal by the Duma to the nation.

The peasants, disturbed by such anomalies, and seeing no hope of the amelioration of their lot, have resorted in a number of districts to open pillage and the destruction of other people's property, and to disobedience of the law and of the legal authorities. But Our subjects ought to remember that an improvement in the lot of the people is only possible under conditions of perfect order and tranquility. We shall not permit arbitrary or illegal acts, and We shall impose Our imperial will on the disobedient by all the power of the State . . .

In dissolving the Duma We confirm Our immutable intention of maintaining this institution, and in conformity with this intention We fix 5 March 1907 as the date of the convocation of the new Duma. . . With unshakable faith in divine clemency and in the good sense of the Russian people, We shall expect from the new Duma the realization of Our efforts and their promotion of legislation in accordance with the requirements of a regenerated Russia . . .

To give structure to the discussion of these documents, consider the following questions:

1 What were the complaints of the petitioners and their suggested remedies in A?

2 How realistic were their requests?

3 What does the tone of the petition tell you about the attitude of the people to the Tsar?

4 What did the October Manifesto actually promise?

5 How did the Tsar plan to improve the lot of the peasants? Would this have been adequate?

6 Comment on the tactics of the St Petersburg Soviet to combat the Tsar.

7 As an opponent of the Tsar, compare the petition of the workers and the statements of the Soviet with the concessions made by the Tsar in the Manifesto and the Fundamental Laws of 1906 and the October Manifesto. Write a criticism of the concessions, and indicate what remains to be done.

8 Why did the Tsar dissolve the First Duma?

9 Write a defence of the Tsar's policies during this crisis.

11. The State of Russia in 1914

Historians have frequently debated the importance of the war in the events of 1917. If Russia was a modernized great power by 1914, or at least heading in that direction, then the revolutions of 1917 must be largely attributed to the effects of the Great War. If she was not, then the slide to the collapse of the autocracy was inevitable, war or no war. Consider the evidence presented below:

A. *Number of strikes per annum:*
1910—222
1911—466
1912—2032
1913—2404
1914—4098 (January–July)

B. *Industrial growth rate 1880–1914*
(average per annum)
Russia	3·5%
Germany	3·75%
USA	2·75%
UK	1%

C. *Industrial production in millions of tons 1914*

	Russia	France	Germany	USA	Great Britain	Russian ranking
Coal	36	40	190	517	292	5th
Pig Iron	4·6	5·2	16·8	31	10·4	5th
Steel	4·8	4·6	18·3	31·8	7·8	4th

Russia also ranked second in world oil production, fourth in goldmining.

D. *The revolutionary parties:*
... from 1906 to 1912 the revolutionary movement was undoubtedly in the doldrums. Not the least of its worries were financial—a problem only partially overcome by the use of 'expropriation' tactics. These were the notorious bank raids and hold-ups waged against State and private institutions for the purpose of seizing cash, and at times weapons also. Since this policy gave rise to recurrent scandals, and since the raids were primarily a Bolshevik prerogative, they were an added source of dissension between Bolsheviks and Mensheviks.   L. Kochan, *The Making of Modern Russia*, 1962

E. *Increases in industrial production in Russia* (million puds per annum)

	1860	1876	1900	1909	1913
Pig Iron	18·2	25·2	177	175	283
Steel	0·1	1·1	163	163	246
Coal	7·3	111·3	1003	1591	2214
Petroleum	0·6	10·9	632	563	561

F. *Merchant fleets:*
In 1910 Russia and Finland together accounted for less than 5% of the world's net tonnage. Half of this was sail-powered.

G. *Miscellaneous information:*
Between 1885 and 1914 the proportion of city dwellers rose from 10·6% to 13·3%
Between 1901 and 1907 the Naval Ministry spent 234 million roubles on foreign arms and the War Ministry 111 million
Between 1890 and 1913 the amount of railway track increased from 31 000 kilometres to 62 000 kilometres

H. *Political prisoners:*
I was taken into a room where was stored everything necessary for a convict under sentence. On the floor lay piles of chains; and clothes, boots, etc, were heaped on shelves. From among them some were selected that were supposed to fit me; and I was then conducted to a second room. Here the right side of my head was shaved, and the hair on my left side cut short. . . . A convict was waiting ready to fasten on my fetters. I was placed on a stool, and had to put my foot on an anvil. The blacksmith fitted an iron ring round each ankle, and welded it together. . . . We were taken straight to the railway carriage. I asked my companions the reasons for their banishment, and learned from them that—as in many other instances described to me by people who had similarly been exiled to Siberia—they had simply been accused by the police of being 'untrustworthy'. Literally it means 'of whom nothing good can be expected'. A young man or girl associates with so-and-so, reads such and such books: this is enough to awaken suspicion that the said young man or girl is 'untrustworthy'. The police or the gendarmerie visit, find a suspicious letter or a prohibited book, and then the course of events is certain—arrest, imprisonment, Siberia. It may be scarcely credible that people languish for years in prison, without any pretence of legal procedure against them, simply by decree of an officer of the gendarmerie—most of them fabulously ignorant men.

L. Deutsch, *Sixteen Years in Siberia*, 1905

1 On the basis of *this evidence* alone, how advanced was Russia?
2 Use the rest of the chapter (and any other sources) to find evidence on each of the following aspects of Russia in 1914:
(a) modern democratic institutions;
(b) the state of agriculture;
(c) the quality of leadership, both in the government and its opponents.
3 What other evidence would you require to make a complete judgement?
4 Which *three* pieces of evidence would you regard as the most important in determining how advanced Russia was? Explain.
5 Using all the evidence you now have, write an essay in answer to the question 'Was Russia a modern, industrialized state in 1914?'

VI International Affairs 1890–1914

1. Introduction

(a) General

Inevitably, many parts of this chapter have already been mentioned in the separate national histories, especially in the foreign policy sections. This chapter therefore fulfils two functions. Firstly, it fills some of the gaps left by the other chapters, especially in the area of colonial problems and the crises in the Balkans. Secondly, it puts into order many of those crises and conflicts previously examined. To this end, there is a date chart of the chief events on page 126.

Very broadly, international relations in the pre-war era fall into three periods. During the 1890s most of the conflicts and crises occurred overseas, in the colonies that the great powers had won and sought to extend. Then, roughly during the period 1900–07, the major activity in the field of international relations took place in the formation of alliances and the establishment of military strength. Finally, during the period 1908–14, the major area of concern became, as it had been in the 1880s, the Balkans, and it was here that war broke out, firstly in 1912 and then again in 1914. This breakdown into three periods is an obvious over-simplification, in that there were alliances formed before 1900, colonial crises after 1900 and Balkan problems before 1908. However, the broad pattern may help to provide a framework within which to examine a complex series of trends and events.

(b) Britain and the European powers

Britain played a crucial role in European affairs throughout this period and, as her foreign policy is not examined elsewhere, it is therefore important to consider briefly her aims and attitudes.

Confidence was the dominant characteristic of British foreign policy in the late nineteenth century. The years of expansion at home and abroad confirmed the British people and government in their belief that Britain had attained 'world power' status and therefore was entitled to considerable freedom of action in foreign affairs, and to command the respect of other countries. Since she was an island and her major interests lay at some distance, it was believed that the maintenance of

British power depended on her navy, which should be large enough and powerful enough to protect her world-wide interests.

Her attitude to Europe was based on a set of almost contradictory ideas. On the one hand, British politicians told their European colleagues that European affairs were of no interest to them since Britain was, physically, detached from Europe and upheld her overseas possessions through a navy that was not intended for use in Europe. On the other hand, British statesmen were eager to uphold two principles in Europe. They were concerned by the prospect of any one nation becoming too powerful in Europe and thus, ultimately, providing a threat to British world power. To avoid this, she was keen to maintain a balance of power and to protect each nation's independence if and when it was threatened by possible conquest or defeat. In addition, Britain's own experience and adherence to broadly liberal beliefs led her statesmen to support the claims for national independence by many of the peoples of Europe, especially in the Balkans.

With such guiding principles, it is not surprising that Britain was considerably alarmed by Germany's expansion in the late nineteenth century. By 1900, the German and American domination of the world economy was becoming all too obvious *(see page 38)*. That she was especially advanced in 'modern' industries such as cars, chemicals and electrics was especially noted: such economic expansion could only be the prelude to expansion in other fields. British governments therefore sought ways to both promote her own industries and prevent continued German rivalry. For example, a series of government reports during the 1890s examined the German system of technical education with a view to emulation. As the gap between their respective shares of world manufactures narrowed, and as German political leaders spoke increasingly of the need for world power, so British concern increased. In such circumstances, her opposition to German military and colonial expansion was inevitable.

Table 25. A date chart: International affairs 1890–1914

1878	13 July	Treaty of Berlin: Roumania, Serbia and Montenegro become independent, Bulgaria semi-independent. Russia receives Bessarabia, Batum etc and Bosnia and Herzegovina come under Austrian administration
1879	7 October	Austria-Hungary and Germany sign alliance
1881	18 June	Dreikaiserbund of Austria-Hungary, Germany and Russia formalized into a treaty
1882	20 May	Triple Alliance of Germany, Austria-Hungary and Italy formed
1887	18 June	Reinsurance treaty between Germany and Russia signed
1890		Reinsurance treaty not renewed
1894	4 January	Franco-Russian treaty of alliance finalized
	1 August	Outbreak of war between China and Japan

1895	17 April	Treaty of Shimonoseki ends Sino-Japanese War
1898	28 March	Reichstag approves the First Navy Law
	16 July	Fashoda crisis between Britain and France
1899	11 October	Outbreak of Boer War
1900	12 June	Reichstag approves the Second Navy Law
1902	30 January	Anglo-Japanese Treaty signed
	31 May	Treaty of Vereeniging ends Boer War
	1 November	Secret promise of Italy to France to remain neutral if France attacks Germany following German attack on Russia
1904	8 February	Outbreak of Russo-Japanese War
	8 April	Entente Cordiale concluded between Britain and France
1905	31 March	Visit of Kaiser to Tangier precipitates Moroccan crisis
	5 September	Treaty of Portsmouth (USA) following Russo-Japanese war
1906	16 January	Algeciras Conference following Morrocan crisis
1907	31 August	Anglo-Russian agreement completes Triple Entente
1908	5 October	Bulgaria becomes independent
	6 October	Austria-Hungary announces annexation of Bosnia and Herzegovina—ensuing crisis lasts till March 1909
1911	1 July	German gunboat 'Panther' at Agadir—second Moroccan crisis
	21 July	Lloyd George's Mansion House speech—regarded as a British warning to Germany
	4 November	France cedes areas of central Africa to Germany in return for recognition of France's protectorate over Morocco
1912	May	Italy occupies the Dodecanese Islands
	8 October	Outbreak of First Balkan War
1913	30 May	Treaty of London ends First Balkan War—Turkey cedes land
	1 June	Greece promises aid to Serbia if she is attacked by Bulgaria
	29 June	Outbreak of Second Balkan War
	6 August	Treaty of Bucharest ends Second Balkan War—Bulgaria cedes land
1914	28 June	Assassination of Franz Ferdinand at Sarajevo
	5 July	Kaiser assures Austria-Hungary of support if France and Russia should support Serbia
	20 July	State visit of Poincaré to St Petersburg
	23 July	Austria-Hungary sends 48-hour ultimatum to Serbia
	25 July	Serbia rejects ultimatum; Austria-Hungary breaks off diplomatic relations with Serbia and orders mobilization
	28 July	Austria-Hungary and Serbia at war
	29 July	Russian mobilization begins
	31 July	Russian general moblization ordered; Germany proclaims 'state of danger of war'; Austria-Hungary orders general mobilization
	1 August	Germany mobilizes and is at war with Russia
	2 August	Germany sends ultimatum to Belgium
	3 August	Italy proclaims neutrality; France and Germany declare war on each other
	4 August	Britain sends ultimatum to Germany re: Belgium; Britain declares war on Germany

2. Colonial Conflicts and Rivalries

The Berlin Conference of 1884–5 had settled the principles of European colonization. Each power was to inform the others when it considered that it had established control and settled an area. Thereby clashes between the powers would hopefully be avoided. It was also agreed that a large central belt of Africa should be left as a free trade zone, even though parts of it had already been settled by Europeans. The last fifteen years of the century saw the translation of these principles into practice, in what has become known as 'the Scramble for Africa'.

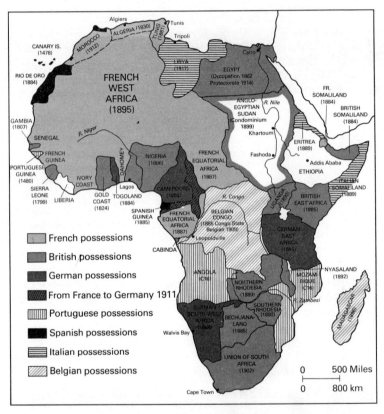

Map 11 European colonies in Africa, 1914

The gains of the separate powers have been separately noted under the Foreign Policy sections of the individual chapters above; there follows therefore a brief summary of the chief territorial gains of the European powers. The German East Africa Company, established in 1888, declared a German Protectorate in central Eastern Africa, while at the same time the German colonies in Togoland and the Cameroons were expanded *(see Map 11)*. Britain disputed Germany's claim to South West Africa but, since there were Germans actually there, could do little about it. In all, Germany acquired a million square miles of territory in Africa between 1884 and 1899, the bulk of it being taken before 1890. In terms of area, France was more successful, winning more than three million square miles. Most of it was in Central and West Africa, where an enormous Empire, French West Africa and French Equatorial Africa, was built up by the expansion of the existing provinces of Algeria, Senegal and Gabon. In the East she claimed part of Somaliland and in 1896 took possession of Madagascar. Italy was less successful, but had won Eritrea and Italian Somaliland and laid claim to Ethiopia. The British had established control over some areas of Africa, such as Gambia and the Gold Coast, before the Berlin Conference, but continued to expand her African Empire after it. She established control in Bechuanaland in 1885, British East Africa in 1888, Rhodesia in 1889, Nyasaland in 1893 and Uganda in 1894. At the same time, her western possessions were expanded and consolidated, while in the North her influence in Egypt was developed. Obviously, throughout Africa, there were considerable areas where possession was disputed and areas claimed by more than one power; it was these issues that were to be settled after 1890.

Africa was not the only area of European expansion: Map 12 shows the acquisitions of the powers in Asia and the Far East. Germany's gains were resticted to islands—parts of New Guinea, the Marshall Islands, the Marianas and Carolines, and a part of Samoa. France won the Marquesa and Society Islands near Tahiti and, on the mainland, established control over Indo-China after 1884. The British already had considerable possessions—Hong Kong, Singapore and India—and to these were added North Borneo and Sarawak in 1888 and later the South Solomon and Gilbert Islands. Both Japan and the United States also took land *(see page 131)*. All the powers had also wrought considerable concessions from the Chinese government during the century, entitling them to a possession of a number of ports and surrounding areas. Russia was also involved in this Far Eastern expansion. Before 1880 she had won large areas of Central Asia *(see page 110)* while her gains and ambitions in Korea and Manchuria brought her into conflict with Japan.

The motives for this swift and thorough expansion of European power in the last years of the century were mixed and complex. In many cases, governments were forced into acting as a result of the actions of individual citizens. Sometimes these were missionaries like David Livingstone, soldiers like the German, Karl Peters, in East Africa, scientists and explorers like Nachtigel in the Cameroons or merchants like Lüderitz in South West Africa. Their actions in setting up mission stations or trading posts, or even in declaring protectorates over areas, often precipitated some kind of government involvement. For example, a government soon became interested in the activities of a trading company if it became involved in difficulties either with the local rulers or with other European traders, especially if there was a possibility of losing face. There were also ideological motives for European involvement. The belief in the superiority of European ideas and culture, from which stemmed the idea of the 'white man's burden', was strong. Missionaries went with the notion of 'Christianizing and civilizing' the natives, while almost all those who went genuinely believed that they would improve the peoples they met. Economic gain was, implicitly or explicitly, an important motive. The new colonies were seen as 'undeveloped estates', in a famous phrase of Joseph Chamberlain, whose cultivation would bring reward for both owners and occupiers. In some cases, such as Egypt, the colonies began as an independent area of European investment in which it became necessary to intervene in order to protect the interests of the investors. Often, the colonies were seen as sources of otherwise expensive raw materials and as enormous new markets for European manufactures. The European expansionism can also be seen as the result of geopolitics. By 1885, almost all the boundaries of Europe were settled and agreed upon. Only the Balkans remained open to question. Expansion by any power in that area was likely to be extremely hazardous, since it was liable to upset the delicate balance between the powers. In contrast, Africa was a huge continent, where gains could easily be made without risking conflict with another European power and, it hardly needs to be said, without great risk to the Europeans involved. Finally, there was an important element of national prestige and 'keeping up with the Jones's' in the scramble for Africa. Prestige at home and abroad was unlikely to be easily won by military victory in Europe, but it could be achieved by victory and expansion overseas. Once one European power won the admiration and respect of its people and rivals in this way, it was hard for the others to resist. These many and mixed motives were rarely clear to the participants in the colonial stampede, whose actions were more often reactions to particular circumstances than clearly rationalized policies.

Inevitably, there were disputes over the borders between the separate acquisitions of the powers. This was especially true of West Africa, where a number of countries had taken possession of coastal areas and then expanded inland. In most cases, the disputed areas were settled by agreement. For example, in 1886 France and Portugal defined the frontier between French and Portugese Guinea, while in the same year Britain and Germany agreed on the borders of Togoland and the Gold Coast. However, there were cases where no agreement was possible. In 1897–98 both Britain and France sought to win control of Western Nigeria. In 1890 an agreement had been signed on the northern limits of British Nigeria. However, the French were eager to link their possessions to the North of this with their colony of Dahomey. French troops were sent to the area and took two towns, Busa and Nikki, in 1897. Britain protested strongly at this action but nothing was done during 1898 when both sides threatened to send more troops to the area. Eventually, a new agreement was reached in June 1898, when a boundary from Northern Nigeria to the coast was drawn, by which France kept Nikki but gave Busa to Britain.

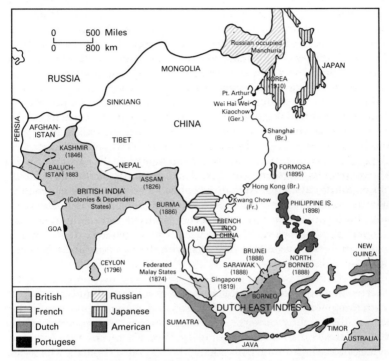

Map 12 European expansion in the Far East

In the same year, British and French interests clashed on the other side of the continent. The Sudan was of considerable importance to both countries, since it lay between the British areas of East Africa and Egypt, and protected the eastern flank of France's western Empire *(see Map 11)*. During the 1880s Britain had lost control of the Sudan and in 1896 General Kitchener set out to reestablish British control. This would restore Britain's economic pre-eminence, facilitate trade and transport for British companies and maintain control of the river Nile, on which Egypt was so dependent. The British were also concerned by possible encroachments into the Sudan by both France and Belgium, who had neighbouring colonies. On 2 September 1898 the Sudanese were decisively beaten at the battle of Omdurman and the British reoccupied Khartoum. However, the French regarded Britain's restoration as a threat to her. With the aid of the Belgian government of the Congo, an expedition under Captain Marchand had been sent out in February 1896 to occupy Fashoda, a fortress in bad repair but strategically placed on the banks of the Nile and thus able to keep the British at bay.

Taking a dismantled steamboat with him, Marchand eventually reached Fashoda in July 1898, where he restored the fort and made treaties with the local rulers. Kitchener, moving up the Nile after his victory at Omdurman, reached Fashoda to find the French flag hoisted in the very heart of territory that was regarded as British. With five gunboats and 2000 men, Kitchener far outnumbered Marchand, whose evacuation of the fort was requested. In Europe, the governments and press of both countries made much of the issue. Britain refused to negotiate until the fort was abandoned. French national pride was at stake; to step down would bring dishonour. In the meantime, Marchand and Kitchener fortunately remained cool, and reached a compromise by flying the Egyptian flag over the fort. By November, the French government was forced to give way since the Dreyfus affair was still at its height, and Russia's refusal to lend support in the event of war made defeat more likely than honour. Consequently, Marchand left the fort and on 21 March 1899 the two countries signed an agreement. France gave up all claims to land along the Nile, in exchange for recognition of her control over the Sahara in the West. France's attempt to prevent British expansion southwards from Egypt had been thwarted and the most serious colonial conflict before Morocco *(see page 81)* ended. Anglo-French rivalry in Africa was only to be ended with the signature of the Entente Cordiale in 1904.

Anglo-German conflicts in Africa were minimal by comparison with the Fashoda crisis. In 1896 the Kaiser sent a telegram to Kruger congratulating him on defeating the Jameson raid 'without appealing for the help of the friendly powers'. The telegram was perhaps intended to frighten the British into friendship *(see page 77)* but had the effect of fuelling public hostility on both sides. Otherwise, apart from the Moroccan crises, Anglo-German relations were less acrimonious. In 1898 they reached agreement over the future of Portugese possessions in Africa. They issued a joint loan to the impoverished Portugese government, whose colonies of Angola and Mozambique were to act as security for the loan. Subsequently, the British negated the treaty by guaranteeing Portugese territory in Africa in 1899. There was bickering between the two powers over the Berlin–Baghdad railway *(see page 80)* as Britain was keen to keep at least a foothold of power in the Middle East, and saw the railway as a threat to this. Ultimately, agreement was reached in June 1914, when Germany promised to end her line at Baghdad and recognized Britain's interests in the ports of the Euphrates.

Central Asia and the Far East posed a far greater threat to peace than Africa. Russian expansion in Turkestan *(see page 110)* brought her in contact with Britain's Indian Empire and Britain wanted to maintain Persia and Afghanistan as buffers to Russian expansion. Between 1885 and 1894 the two reached agreement over most of the borders concerned but their respective influence in Persia itself remained unresolved until the treaty of 1907, by which spheres of influence were defined.

The major clash of interests in the Far East was between Russia and

Japan. This culminated in the war of 1904–5 *(see page 102)*, the only instance of an outbreak of major war resulting specifically from colonial interests. The rival claims of the other powers in the Far East were resolved by agreement. Germany and Britain both laid claim to the Liaotung Peninsula, but reached agreement at the expense of China *(see page 111)*.

The crises over Morocco in 1906, 1908 and 1911 are examined in detail on pages 81–3 and will not be repeated here. However, they do provide an important clue to the nature and importance of the colonial clashes in the pre-war era. In one way, they provided a safety valve through which the great powers could let off nationalist steam without harming each other. The arguments and crises did not directly involve their own nationals or their own territory. This both reduced the temperature of the conflict and made it easier to back down when the crunch came. Moreover, there was sufficient 'empty' territory to provide bargaining power. When Germany traded recognition of France's control over Morocco for thousands of acres of central Africa few German or French people directly benefitted or suffered. Yet if a single acre of Alsace–Lorraine changed hands it could only be at the cost of a European war. However, it is equally possible to argue that the colonial disputes exacerbated relations between the European powers and at least unconsciously encouraged statesmen towards a show-down in which all the issues could be resolved. On the one hand, therefore, the colonial conflicts were an expression of great power conflict but on the other hand they were the cause of it.

3. Allies and Armaments

Countries sought and made allies ostensibly for defensive purposes and the settlement of outstanding disputes between them. An examination of the major alliances made during the period will demonstrate that they were not, openly, formed for offensive purposes to harm or attack other countries. Two factors led to the translation of these defensive alliances into warring factions in the summer of 1914. Firstly, formal treaties of alliance were accompanied by military discussions in which the generals of the countries concerned sought how best to combine their forces. In such circumstances, they inevitably had to decide on the most likely enemies and their most effective ways of defeating the most likely attacks of such enemies. Such hypothetical discussions in fact had the effect of determining who would be enemies, who friends, and how the war would be fought. Complex military plans were drawn up so that troops and materials could be moved with the greatest speed to the most crucial points. These plans in turn fulfilled the second precondition for the translation of defensive alliances into attacking groups—namely, the existence of unalterable mobilization plans that forced politicians into action quickly to name their enemies as aggressors and so justify the mobilization they needed. Thus in the summer of 1914 each power sought to name the other as aggressor and so justify their own declaration of war. It was the military discussions and the mobilization plans, and not the treaties themselves, that were the crucial elements.

Most of the major alliances have already been examined under the foreign policy sections of the countries concerned. There follows, therefore, a brief summary of the terms of the major alliances:

1879: Dual Alliance between Germany and Austria-Hungary. This was renewed every five years until 1918 and provided the basis for each power's foreign policy. It agreed that in the event of either country being attacked by Russia, the other would come to its aid with all its forces. If either was attacked by any other country, then the other would at least be neutral if not lend assistance. If Russia came to the aid of another country that attacked either, then the partner had to come to its aid.

1882: Triple Alliance between Germany, Austria and Italy. This too was renewed every five years up until 1915. Germany and Austria were obliged to come to Italy's help in the event of a French attack on Italy. Italy had to come to Germany's assistance in the event of a French attack on Germany. If any one or two members of the alliance were at war with any two or more great powers, then the member or members of the alliance not involved had to come to the aid of the other or others. If any one of the allies felt forced to declare war on another great power, then the other members should at least preserve benevolent neutrality if not material support. When the treaty was renewed in 1887, Germany agreed to support Italy in North Africa in the event of a Franco-Italian war there and Austria and Italy agreed to the maintenance of the status quo in the Near East, or, in the event of either occupying territory, the other would be compensated. This did not apply to Austria's eventual annexation of Bosnia and Herzegovina. In 1888 Germany and Italy signed a military agreement providing for the use of Italian troops in a war against France, and in the same year the terms of the agreements made thus far were made public, largely as a warning to France and Russia. Although the treaty was regularly renewed (the last time being for six years from 1914), there was a period, mainly from 1902–12, when Germany and Austria had little faith in Italy's loyalty. This was primarily the result of the Franco-Italian agreement of 1902, by which Italy assured France she would remain neutral in the event of France being attacked or of France declaring war 'as the result of direct provocation'. The agreement was not made public, but the friendship between the two was obvious during the years that followed. After 1912, however, Franco-Italian hostility was renewed, largely as a result of the Tripolitanian War *(see page 57)* so the Triple Aliance seemed reunited.

1891–4: Convention and notes leading to Franco-Russian alliance. The treaty between the two was the result of a series of agreements and negotiations. The exchange of notes between December 1893 and January 1894 formally accepted the previously negotiated military convention. It was to remain effective as long as the Triple Alliance was renewed. By it, Russia agreed to provide between 700 000 and 800 000 troops against Germany if she attacked France or if Italy attacked France with German support. In return, France agreed to supply 1 300 000 men against Germany if she, or Austria supported by Germany, attacked Russia. If one or more members of the Triple Alliance mobilized, then both France and Russia should also mobilize. It was also agreed that 'the General Staffs of the armies of the two countries shall co-operate with each other at all times to prepare and facilitate military agreements.' In 1899 the agreement was extended to provide that the balance of power should be maintained as well as the maintenance of peace. The agreements was also made indefinite. In 1912 a naval agreement was added to the previous arrangements, so that the navies as well as the armies of the two countries should work together.

1904: The 'Entente Cordiale' between Britain and France. The treaty's main provisions settled the colonial differences between the two. France accepted Britain's occupation of Egypt, provided that the Suez Canal was free for navigation, while Britain recognized France's interests in Morocco and promised diplomatic support in winning France's demands there. France gave up her claims to Newfoundland in return for some territory near French Gambia. The agreement cannot be regarded as an alliance, as there were no reciprocal arrangements for support. However, it cleared the ground for subsequent negotiations, and in January 1906 military and naval discussions between the two began. Britain refused to promise support in the event of a German attack, but nonetheless agreed to discussions about military co-operation should such co-operation be decided on. This in effect created a 'moral obligation' of Britain to France, although the nearest any formal agreement was made was in November 1912 when an exchange of letters between the foreign ministers, Grey and Cambon, agreed to consult if either country was threatened by attack.

1907: Agreement between Britain and Russia, thus creating the so-called 'Triple Entente' between these two countries and France. This agreement also settled colonial disputes but made no firm commitments on either side. Persia was divided into three separate spheres of influence *(see page 110)* and Russia accepted that Afghanistan was outside her sphere of interest, while Britain promised not to interfere with its domestic affairs. Both accepted China's dominant position in Tibet. In a separate agreement, Britain expressed her support for a revision of the Straits agreements in Russia's favour, while in a third agreement Russia acknowledged Britain's pre-eminence in the Persian Gulf.

In this summary, only those treaties and alliances that were to have direct bearing on the Great War have been included. Thus the Russo-German agreements of the 1880s *(see page 76)* have been omitted, as has the Anglo-Japanese agreement of 1902 and the agreements between the Triple Alliance and Roumania (1882) by which Roumania was protected from Russian attacks.

Although the reasons for the agreements, and even the terms of them, were often innocuous, the end result was clear. After 1907, Europe was clearly divided by two alliance systems. In one respect, this provided the balance of power that many statesmen regarded as essential for the maintenance of peace. On the other hand both blocs had extensive military plans for defending themselves against the other. Inevitably, these defensive plans also included attacks that would lead to widespread declarations of war. For this to come about, the leaders did, though, have to want war; as Italy was to prove in 1914 *(see page 253)* it was possible to avoid war within the terms of the treaties. Consequently, the role of the alliance system in the outbreak of the war is complex and it did not even 'make the war a large one', since almost any of the powers could have avoided their commitments if they so desired.

Similarly, the existence of enormous and well-equipped armies and navies did not necessarily make war any more or less likely. It is difficult to monitor precisely the build-up of these forces, since no power wanted to reveal the extent of its forces to likely enemies. Consequently, the account below is gathered from a variety of sources (hence the different currencies etc) in an effort to bring together a coherent account of the build-up of forces.

The most publicized and potentially dangerous acceleration came in the field of naval expansion. Since Britain held her navy to be vital, any attempt to rival it by another power, particularly Germany, would meet a spirited response. Yet many German statesmen saw naval expansion as the only way to assure Germany of world-power status, since her central position in Europe made the acquisition of overseas colonies essential *(see page 78)*. In addition, only Britain's acceptance of a large and powerful German navy would give her the prestige she so desired. The Navy Laws were therefore intended to provide for this expansion, but in turn they brought responses from Britain, as the chart opposite demonstrates.

Such were the basic elements of a naval race that had widespread repercussions. In particular, rumours about the plans and activities of each side so alarmed the other that attempts at reconciliation between the two were permanently soured. The Haldane mission of 1912 offered Germany support for an extension to her African Empire in return for a halt to naval building, but it came to nothing, as Germany would not stop her naval expansion without concrete compensation. On both sides, the building and plans became almost an obsession that dominated relations between them. In fact, Britain's fleet remained considerably larger throughout the period, as Table 26 opposite demonstrates.

It is less easy to monitor the increases in army size, since this was related to the number of people of the right age for military service and the different regulations regarding length and type of service. Some broad trends can, however, be identified. The German conscription system underwent two major changes. In 1893 the period of service was reduced to two years, but the total size of the standing army was

Date	German naval expansion	British naval expansion
1898	First Navy Law adds twelve battle-ships to existing fleet of seven + larger numbers of smaller ships	
1900	Second Navy Law provides for thirty-eight battleships to be built over twenty years	
1903		New naval base at Rosyth built and Parliament approves plans for the formation of a North Sea fleet
1906 (Feb)		Launching of 'Dreadnought' with ten twelve-inch guns instead of the usual four. Also faster than earlier ships and makes all German ships obsolete
1906 (May)	German government increases tonnage of ships under construction, adds six cruisers to the building programme and plans for the widening of the Kiel canal to take 'Dreadnought' type ships	
1908	Amendment to Navy Law provides for four Dreadnoughts to be built each year up to 1911 instead of three	
1909		As a result of a alarm at size of likely German fleet (Balfour forecast thirteen Dreadnoughts to Britain's twelve by 1911), Britain announces the building of eight Dreadnoughts instead of three
1912 (Mar)	Germany, with nine Dreadnoughts rather than the predicted twenty-one, annouces increases in the number of ships and men and the creation of a third fleet in commission	
1912 (July)		Franco-Russian naval convention and Anglo-French agreement that British ships should be transferred from the Mediterranean to the North Sea and French ships from Brest to the Mediterranean

	Germany	Great Britain
Battleships	33 (+ 7)	55 (+ 11)
Battlecruisers	3 (+ 3)	7 (+ 3)
Cruisers	9	51
Light cruisers etc	45 (+ 4)	77 (+ 9)
Destroyers	123 (+ 9)	191 (+ 38)
Torpedo ships	80	137 (+ 1)
Submarines	23 (+ 15)	64 (+ 22)
Dreadnoughts	13	20

Table 26. Fleet size (4 August 1914) (Figures in brackets indicate number under construction)

increased *(see page 69)* and in 1913 the army was increased by a total of 170 000 men and plans were made to have a war-time army of some five million men. In response to this, both France and Russia increased the length of service; in France, it went up from two years to three and in Russia from three to three and a half. Defence expenditures also increased *(see Tables 27 and 28)*. D.F. Fleming, in *The Origins and Legacies of World War I* (1968) estimates that British expenditure rose from $295 million in 1908 to $375 in 1913, French from $220 million to $410 million and Russian from $300 to $460 million.

Date	Germany Size of army	Size of navy	Total	% of population
1880	401 650	7350	409 000	0·9
1891	511 650	17 000	528 650	1·07
1901	604 100	31 200	635 300	1·16
1911	622 500	33 500	656 000	1·01
1914	791 000	73 000	864 000	1·3
	Great Britain			
1880	198 200	59 000	257 200	0·73
1891	209 000	97 600	306 600	0·8
1901	773 500	114 900	888 400	2·1
1911	247 000	128 000	375 000	0·83
1914	247 000	146 000	393 000	0·85

Table 27. Proportion of population in the armed forces 1880–1914 (from *The Kaiser and His Times* by M. Balfour)

Date	Germany Totale defence expenditure, yearly average (million marks)	% of national income	Great Britain Total defence expenditure, yearly average (million marks)	% of national income
1886–90	510	2·35	626	2·35
1891–5	586	2·59	664	2·29
1896–1900	637	2·4	820	2·3
1901–5	848	2·69	1966	5·33
1906–10	1294	3·23	1220	2·93
1911–13	1468	3·1	1071	2·12

Table 28. Percentage of National Income devoted to defence 1880–1914 (from *The Kaiser and His Times* by M. Balfour)

By a range of indices, therefore, it is possible to identify an 'arms race' between the great powers. However, it is less easy to identify the role that this trend played in the outbreak of the war. Did not this wealth of arms in fact act **as a deterrent** to war, since so many men would inevitably die? Or was it rather an inducement to war, so that the powers could find out what their men and machines were capable of? Or did it merely provide generals and statesmen with the confidence, or even over-confidence, to press their demands on their enemies, in the knowledge and belief that their forces were so strong they would not be attacked?

4. The Balkans

Background information on the Balkans situation in the period can be found on pages 20–22.

(a) The Bosnian crisis
The treaty of Berlin (1878) allowed Austria-Hungary to occupy and administer the Turkish provinces of Bosnia and Herzegovina *(see Map 13)*, that lay on the southern border of Austria-Hungary. Since they bordered Serbia, whose government hoped to win for itself those areas of Austria-Hungary where there was a majority of Serbs, the two Turkish provinces were of great strategic importance to the Habsburgs. In 1881 they won the secret agreement of Germany and Russia to their plan to keep the provinces permanently. However, in 1903, by the Mürzsteg agreement, Austria-Hungary agreed with Russia to maintain the status quo in the Balkans for a five-year period.

During those five years, a number of pressures made some kind of Habsburg action more likely. Events within the Empire *(see pages 15–18)* led the government to believe that it was increasingly urgent to end the opposition of the southern Slav peoples—the Croats, Slovenes and Serbs —to the Emperor's rule. Secondly, the Young Turk revolution of 1908 forced the Turkish Emperor, Abdul Hamid, to accept constitutional government. This made a revival of the Turkish Empire more likely, which in turn threatened Austria-Hungary's occupation of the provinces. Moreover, representatives of Bosnia and Herzegovina were invited to attend the new Turkish Parliament, indicating that the Turkish government had by no means abandoned them. The Austrian Foreign Minister, Aehrenthal, decided that some action was urgently needed. However, the possibility of Russian opposition to Austria-Hungary's annexation of the provinces had first to be removed.

On 16 September 1908 Aehrenthal met his Russian counterpart, Izvolsky, at Buchlau Castle. There, they agreed in principle that if Russia accepted Austria-Hungary's annexation of the provinces, Austria-Hungary would support Russia's claim for a revision of the Straits Convention so that Russian warships could have access to the Mediterranean through the Dardanelles *(see page 113)*. No one else was present at the meeting, and the only written record of what was said was kept by Aehrenthal. Subsequently, two details of the agreement were to be questioned by the Russians; firstly, at what stage the annexation was actually to be announced (i.e. before or after the Russians had seen the other powers) and secondly, whether or not it was agreed to hold an international conference to ratify the changed circumstances in the Balkans.

Map 13 The Balkans 1878–1914

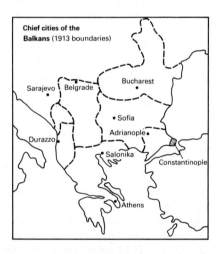

Izvolsky's delight in winning Austria-Hungary's approval for his plans was enough to send him rushing off to the other European capitals to win their approval. After all, Austria-Hungary had most to lose by a revision of the Straits Convention, and once her approval was won the other powers should not be hostile. On 26 September the German Foreign Minister, von Schön, agreed in principle to the plan, but on condition that Germany received some compensation, probably in the form of Russian support for Germany's plans for the Berlin-Baghdad railway. On the 28 September, Tittoni, for the Italian government, agreed to Russia's plans in exchange for Russian support for Italian claims to Tripoli and parts of the Balkans, notably Albania. By 4 October Izvolsky had reached Paris, where he had to win over the French.

Aehrenthal too had been busy. On 23 September he promised Prince Ferdinand Austria-Hungary's support for Bulgaria's independence from Turkey, thus removing another likely source of hostility. Bulgaria, like Bosnia and Herzegovina, had been asked to send representatives to the Turkish Parliament, so the question of her relationship to Turkey was made more urgent. On 4 October Aehrenthal informed Izvolsky in Paris that he planned to go ahead with the annexation. The next day Bulgaria's independence was declared and on the 6 October the annexation of Bosnia and Herzegovina by Austria-Hungary was announced by Aehrenthal.

The announcement had immediate and widespread repercussions. The outraged Turkish government immediately imposed a boycott on all trade with Austria-Hungary and made military preparations. Serbia was equally furious and made military plans. Greece and Montenegro opened negotiations with Turkey and Serbia. In Paris, Izvolsky was powerless. His own government in St Petersburg, denying any knowledge of his secret agreement with Aehrenthal, instructed him to oppose Austria-Hungary and support Serbia. Consequently, he was forced to claim that he had been tricked by Aehrenthal and oppose the annexation. However, his opposition was only half-hearted since he still hoped for Austrian support for revision of the Straits Convention as a form of compensation for the annexation in an international conference. On 9 October Grey (the British Foreign Secretary) told Izvolsky, now in London, that Britain would only support Russia's plans if Turkey agreed to them. Turkey refused to do so. Grey did though agree to Izvolsky's plans for an international conference, which Izvolsky now pressed hard for as the only way of saving face.

By this time, the lines were clearly drawn on both sides. Serbia's troops were mobilized and she and Russia demanded a conference to discuss the annexation and possible compensation for the other powers, especially Serbia and Montenegro. Austria-Hungary refused to accept this and would accept an international conference only to approve the annexation. Germany supported Austria-Hungary but accepted Russia's claims to the Straits provided that she, Germany, received compensation.

On 12 January 1909 Austria-Hungary reached agreement with Turkey, by which Turkey accepted the annexation in exchange for 2 million pounds compensation. Since Turkey was the chief loser by the annexation, this agreement considerably strengthened Austria-Hungary's position. Nonetheless, Serbia's troops remained mobilized. However, Serbia could not act without Russian support, in which case Austria-Hungary would depend on German support. Germany's chief of staff, Moltke, assured his Austrian counterpart, Conrad von Hötzendorff, that such support would be forthcoming—the first time Germany had made such a firm promise to their ally.

This state of affairs remained until 21 March when Germany took the initiative. A note was sent to Russia demanding that she accept the annexation and end her support for Serbia. If she did not reply in the affirmative, 'events would run their course' according to the German note. Izvolsky, presented with an opportunity to escape a war that Russia could not fight, gave way and accepted the note, muttering about the iniquity of the German 'ultimatum'. Ten days later, on 31 March, Serbia sent Austria formal recognition of the annexation and accepted that it did not affect her interests. Significantly, she also promised to stop anti-Austrian propaganda and to be a good neighbour.

The annexation was, in the final analysis, a major triumph for Austria-Hungary and Germany. The Russian government was furious at the outcome and was left more determined than ever not to be forced to give way again. Instead she sought to consolidate her position in the Balkans. She began by helping Bulgaria to pay Turkey the compensation required as a result of the declaration of independence. More significantly, Serbs were outraged by Austria-Hungary's success. More and more extreme groups were formed and were not outlawed by the government. Leading among these was the 'Union or Death' movement, founded in 1911 by 'Apis' (Captain Dragutin Dimitrjević). The movement was known as the 'Black Hand'. It was committed to the liberation of all Serbs living under foreign rule by secret and terrorist means.

(b) The Balkan Wars and their aftermath

In the aftermath of the Bosnian crisis, Russia attempted to construct a Balkan 'bloc' of Serbia, Bulgaria and Turkey as a bulwark to further Austrian expansion. However, she accepted that the difference between the two emerging powers and Turkey were too great and therefore encouraged, in the first place, negotiations between Bulgaria and Serbia. Yet an alliance of these two could be used as well against Turkey as against Austria-Hungary. After initial disagreement over Macedonia, a Serbo-Bulgarian treaty was signed in March 1912. By it, three zones of Macedonia were defined—one each for Serbia and Bulgaria and a third neutral zone. It also included a mutual guarantee of existing boundaries and promised support in the event of a great power trying to take land from Turkey. When, on 29 May 1912, Greece and Bulgaria signed a treaty of alliance, there was born a Balkan League of the four Balkan powers (Serbia, Bulgaria, Greece and Montenegro), each of which opposed both Turkey and the great powers. The great powers realized the likelihood that this League would declare war on Turkey and, in a note of 14 August urged the four to act cautiously.

However, the Balkan powers were not to be denied. Using the frequent outbreaks of rioting in Macedonia as a pretext for action, they mobilized their troops on 30 September 1912 and, on 18 October, declared war. Turkey, already weakened by war against Italy *(see page 58)* was in no state to fight back. The Bulgarian army advanced rapidly southwards and reached the Chatalja lines outside Constantinople by the end of October, where their attack was held. Russia warned Bulgaria against entering Constantinople. In the West, the Serbian army took Northern Albania and reached the coast by mid-November. In the South, the Greek army took Salonika. Apart from three forts and an area of about thirty kilometres outside Constantinople, all European Turkey was in the hands of the Balkan League. On 3 December an armistice was signed between Turkey and Serbia and Bulgaria. Greece remained technically at war.

The great powers, especially Austria-Hungary, had good reason to be upset by the success of the Balkan League. Austria-Hungary and Italy were both totally opposed to Serbia having an Adriatic coastline, and advocated instead the establishment of an independent Albania. In contrast, Russia and France supported the idea of an enlarged Serbia. In late November both Austria and Russia began to mobilize their troops to oppose and support Serbia respectively, while Germany and Britain endeavoured to moderate their allies' demands. Again, Russia was forced to back down rather than risk war, but until March 1913 400 000 extra Russian troops and 220 000 Austrians were mobilized.

On 17 December the peace conference opened in London. Little progress was made as the Turks refused to give up Adrianople and Crete. In fact, they declared war again on 3 February under their new nationalist ruler, Enver Bey. The Turkish army was again defeated swiftly and on 16 April a new armistice was signed following the capture of Adrianople by the Bulgarian army. By the end of May, negotiations were ended and the treaty of London was signed on 30 May. By it, Greece gained Crete, Salonika and much of southern Macedonia, although this was largely inhabited by Bulgars. Bulgaria received Thrace and Serbia won central and Northern Macedonia. Albania became independent from Turkey. These terms were not decided by negotiation between the powers involved but by the great powers, who agreed the terms in advance and then imposed them on the Balkan powers. Consequently, there was considerable dissatisfaction at the terms. In particular, Serbia resented being kept out of the Adriatic coastline, and felt that her share of Macedonia was inadequate. Bulgaria refused to acknowledge that Serbia was entitled to more of Macedonia than had been agreed by the 1912 treaty, and claimed that, under the terms of that treaty, the division of Macedonia should be left to arbitration by the Tsar. On 1 June 1913 Serbia formed an alliance with Greece, their obvious intention being to win on the battlefield what had been denied them in the treaty. Bulgaria had similar intentions.

On 29 June the second Balkan war broke out. The Bulgarian commander, Savov, ordered an attack without receiving government authorization. Even though the Bulgarian government disowned his actions, it was enough for Serbia and Greece to declare war on Bulgaria. Roumania and Turkey joined the war on Serbia's side and the encircled Bulgars were rapidly humiliated. On 10 August the treaty of Bucharest was signed. By it *(see Map 13)*, Bulgaria was forced to give the Dobrudja from Turtukia on the Danube to Ekrene on the Black Sea to Roumania. Serbia and Greece kept possession of those parts of Macedonia that they had captured, leaving Bulgaria a small part of the Aegean coastline around the port of Dedeagach. By a separate treaty, Adrianople was returned to Turkey.

Flushed with success, the Serbs invaded Albania on 23 September, claiming that Albania had raided parts of Western Serbia. Only when Austria-Hungary intervened and demanded a Serbian withdrawal was the invasion ended. Even then, Greek troops remained in Albania until April 1914 when Greece was awarded some Aegean islands in exchange for evacuating Albania.

By the Balkan wars, all the new Balkan powers had made significant gains of both territory and prestige. These gains obviously posed a serious threat to the plans of Russia and Austria-Hungary for the domination, if not annexation, of the Balkans. In addition, the new strength of Serbia posed a serious threat to Austria-Hungary's southern borders. Since neither the great powers nor the combatants saw the Balkan Wars as bringing a final settlement, all sought ways of improving their position in the area. In November 1913 the German general, Liman von Sanders, was sent to reorganize the Turkish army and was made commander of the First Army Corps, based in Constantinople. Russia and France protested loudly at the presence of a German general in such a sensitive area, and a crisis was only averted when the Turks and Germans agreed to reduce his powers. In June 1914 the Tsar, accompanied by his foreign minister, Sazonov, visited Bucharest in an effort to win Roumanian support for Serbia in the event of her (Serbia) being attacked by Austria-Hungary. The Roumanians refused this, but did agree to support and help Russia in the event of the Straits being closed by a Greek-Turkish war. In June 1914 Germany and Austria-Hungary held discussions on future Balkan policy; Austria-Hungary favoured friendship with Bulgaria and Turkey while Germany favoured rapport with Serbia, Greece and Roumania. No decision was reached, and none was needed since events overtook the discussions.

5. The Outbreak of War

In late June 1914, Archduke Franz Ferdinand paid a visit to the provinces of Bosnia and Herzegovina. The trip was ill-planned as it coincided with Austrian army manoeuvres in the area and with the anniversary of the battle of Kossovo when the Serbs had fought valiantly to ward off their Turkish conquerors. The Serbian 'Union or Death' society (or 'Black Hand'), which had been founded in 1911 with the purpose of campaigning, by terrorist means, for Serbia's rights over the provinces *(see page 142)*, were tempted to take the opportunity for a violent protest. In the event, though, it was not the Black Hand that fired the fatal shots. Rather, a group of six young Bosnians, who were not members of the group, planned their own attack on the heir to the throne when he visited Sarajevo on 28 June. Their actual plans fell apart and in the event it was sheer chance that one of them, Gavrilo Princip, was able to reach the Archduke's car and shoot both the Archduke and his wife.

The assassination provided the Austrian government with an excuse for military action against Serbia. The Serbian government could be held responsible in that its officials allowed the assassins through the frontier and in that it knew of the existence and aims of the Black Hand. Before any action was taken, Franz Josef had to be sure of German support. On 5 July an Austrian diplomat, Count Hoyos, took a letter from the Emperor to Berlin. The letter explained that:

> the Sarajevo affair was not merely the bloody deed of a single individual, but was the result of a well-organized conspiracy, the threads of which can be traced to Belgrade; and even though it will probably prove impossible to get evidence of the complicity of the Serbian Government, there can be no doubt that its policy, directed towards the unification of all the Southern-Slav countries under the Serbian flag, is responsible for such crimes, and that the continuation of such a state of affairs constitutes an enduring peril for my house and my possessions.

He also wrote of the necessity to 'eliminate Serbia as a factor of political power in the Balkans'. The implication was clearly that Austria, with German support, would crush Serbia militarily.

The Kaiser, through his Chancellor, replied the following day that Franz Josef could 'rest assured that His Majesty will faithfully stand by Austria-Hungary, as is required by the obligations of his alliance and of his ancient friendship.' This note has become known as Germany's 'blank cheque' to Austria, since it virtually promised German support for whatever action Austria chose to take. It is unlikely that the Kaiser and his advisers realized the full implications of this. Their reading of the situation was that Russia, as before, would not intervene on Serbia's behalf and therefore a local Balkan issue between a great power and a small neighbour would be swiftly and simply resolved.

During the first two weeks of July, the Austrian cabinet debated their policy, and by 14 July had decided on war, even though their envoy to Belgrade, Baron von Wiesner, reported that there was no conclusive evidence of the Serbian government's complicity in the assassination. By the 20 July an ultimatum to Serbia had been prepared, but was not sent until 23 July, to allow the French President, Poincaré, to leave St Petersburg after a state visit. The ultimatum demanded that the Serbian government should publish its intentions to be a good neighbour in its press, that all anti-Austrian organizations should be disbanded, that any anti-Austrian official employees should be dismissed from their posts, that all anti-Austrian propaganda in schools should be ended, that two Serbian officials known to have been involved in the plot be arrested and tried, and that Austrian officials be allowed to join the Serbs in the inquiry into the plot. (The full text of both the ultimatum and the reply can be found in the document books mentioned on page 148.) On hearing of Austria's demands, the Russian government announced that it would not allow Serbia to become a part of the Austro-Hungarian Empire. Austria announced that they did not intend to take over Serbia, but on 25 July the Russian government decided to mobilize against Austria and to declare war if Serbia was attacked.

Initially, the Serbian government decided to accept all the demands in the Austrian ultimatum, but then decided to try to buy time and tempt the Austrian government into negotiation by rejecting just one of the demands. So, on 25 July, they replied in conciliatory terms, but refused to accept the demand that Austrian officials be allowed to play a part in the inquiry. The critical part of the reply reads: 'As far as the co-operation in this investigation of specially delegated officials of the Imperial and Royal Government is concerned, this cannot be accepted, as this is a violation of the constitution and of criminal procedure.' Even before sending the reply, the Serbian government realized that this one point could mean war, and her troops were mobilized. When the reply was received in Vienna, Austria-Hungary mobilized against Serbia. The only remaining question was which countries would feel obliged or tempted to intervene. On 26 July the British Foreign Minister, Grey, suggested that a conference be held to discuss the crisis. Only France supported the idea fully, while both Austria and Germany rejected it. On 28 July war was officially declared, and Austrian forces bombarded Belgrade, thereby ending negotiations between Russia and Austria, although Bethmann Hollweg made a vain effort to renew these the next day. At the same time, he contacted the British government, and promised that Germany would not take territory from either France or Belgium provided Britain remained neutral. Grey replied that his government could not accept such an offer. The actions of the Russian government were critical. On 29 July the Tsar agreed to his government's demands for general mobilization—against both Germany and Austria-Hungary. Then, however, he changed this order to be partial mobilization, against Austria-Hungary alone, when he heard from Berlin that Germany was trying to force Austria-Hungary to lessen their demands. However, this change of plan proved technically impossible, since mobilization plans against both had already been put into effect and men were on the move. On 31 July the German government sent an ultimatum to Russia demanding the withdrawal of forces aimed at her within twelve hours. The Germans also sent enquiries to Paris as to the attitude of France in the case of a Russo-German war, and refused a British request that the neutrality of Belgium be accepted. During the evening of the same day, Austria-Hungary declared a general mobilization. On 1 August the French replied to Germany's enquiry that 'she would be guided by her own interests' and at 3·55 pm her troops were mobilized. Five minutes later Germany's forces were mobilized and at seven o'clock that evening Germany declared war on Russia on the grounds that her ultimatum had expired. On 2 August the British government agreed to help France protect her coast against German attack, while German troops entered Luxembourg and a demand was sent to Belgium that if German troops were allowed through Belgium her neutrality would be respected. The Belgian government refused to accept this. On 3 August Germany declared war on France on the grounds that France had violated the German frontier. German troops entered Belgium, and on 4 August Britain declared war on Germany on the grounds that Belgian neutrality, promised in 1839, had been violated. (By the terms of this treaty, Britain, and the other great powers, had the right to intervene if Belgium's neutrality was violated, but were not obliged to do so.) When Austria-Hungary declared war on Russia on 6 August, all the great powers of Europe, save Italy, were at war with one another.

6. Bibliography

On this complex issue, it is probably best to start by using the standard textbooks listed on page 3. In addition, much of the Open University material, especially Units 5 and 14 of the *War and Society* course, is especially helpful, as it includes primary source material. There is also a pamphlet in the 'Heath Series' entitled 'The Outbreak of the First World War', which includes extracts from a number of different authors. Four more standard texts are *July 1914* by I. Geiss (Batsford, 1967), *Origins of the First World War* by B.E. Schmitt (H.A. pamphlet 39, 1958), *Origins of the First World War* by H.W. Koch (Macmillan, 1972) and *The Origins of the First World War* by L.C.F. Turner (Edward Arnold, 1970). The detailed, but most important, *German Aims in the First World War* by F. Fischer (Chatto & Windus, 1967) is a critical book for more advanced study.

7. Discussion Points and Exercises

A   *This section consists of questions that might be used for discussion (or written answers) as a way of expanding on the chapter and testing understanding of it:*
 1   What effects were Britain's aims and attitudes likely to have on the rest of Europe?
 2   Was Britain justified in her opposition to German expansion?
 3   In what ways was the colonial expansion of the great powers 'the result of geopolitics'?
 4   How serious were the Anglo-French conflicts in Africa?
 5   Why was the Far East the scene of so many conflicts?
 6   What was the importance of the military negotiations that accompanied diplomatic negotiations?
 7   Comment on the advantages and disadvantages of a balance of power.

8 How dangerous was the naval rivalry of Britain and Germany?
9 Why was Austria-Hungary so keen to act over Bosnia and Herzegovina?
10 How close was Europe to war during the Bosnian crisis?
11 What were Serbia's foreign policy aims?
12 What was the chief significance of the Balkan wars?
13 Why was the assassination of Franz Ferdinand such a critical deed?
14 What were Germany's aims during July 1914?
15 Did the treaty obligations of the powers force them to go to war in the summer of 1914?

B *This section suggests two ways of seeing the problems of the period from the viewpoint of different countries:*
1 Write a Russian newspaper editorial of 1908 on the importance and implications of the Bosnian crisis.
2 Examine the arms race, especially the navy race, from the point of view of either an English or a German statesman.

C *This section suggests some ways in which you can compare the roles of the different countries:*
1 Comment on the actual terms of the chief alliances, especially comparing the treaties and obligations on the Central Powers' side with those on the Entente Powers' side.
2 Compare the aims and achievements of Austria-Hungary and Russia in the Balkans.
3 Compare the hopes and fears, and achievements, of the new Balkan powers in the decade before the outbreak of war.

D *Essay questions:*
1 Why were England and France likely enemies in the 1890s, but allies after 1904?
2 To what extent was *either* the arms race *or* the alliance system responsible for the outbreak of war in 1914?
3 Were the problems of the Balkans bound to end in war?

8. The Causes of the Great War: An Exercise

Obviously, there are many documents that are crucial to the events leading up to the Great War. However, I have chosen not to include a document section in this chapter for two reasons. Firstly, it seems that to select a few documents is, in this case, highly misleading as the selection is bound to be subjective. Consequently, it would be necessary to take all the relevant documents. This would be extremely space-consuming, especially when collections of such documents are readily available, notably in *Documents in the Political History of the European Continent 1815–1939* edited by G. Kertesz (Oxford, 1968) and in the Open University's *War and Society* course A301 Unit 5 'Collection of Nineteenth and Twentieth Century Documents Part I'.

Instead of exercises based on documents, I have placed below a variety of interpretations of the outbreak of war from modern authors. Some of these are short extracts from long and detailed theses, and this should be borne in mind when reading them. They should, however, provide a stimulus for discussion and the exercises that follow.

(A) Sir Robert Ensor, *England 1870–1914* (1936):

The disaster had its roots since 1870 in the grand expansion and uncontrolled ambition of the new Germany. Bismarck had sown the seeds through his memorable triumphs for militarism and unscrupulous efficiency . . . After his fall, it grew apace, unchecked by the statesmen and encouraged by the Emperor. In the many-sided quick changing displays of the brilliant William II two features alone never failed—arrogant megalomania and an instinctive preference for methods of violence. These, it is not unfair to say, became the national vices of pre-war Germany; and they made her an object of alarm to every leading nation save her Austrian ally.

(B) M. Howard, 'Reflections on the First World War' in *Studies in War and peace* (1970), quoted in Open University course A301 Unit 14:

Millions of men had to be recalled to the colours, organized into fighting units, equipped with a vast apparatus of arms and services and sent by railway to their points of concentration, all within a few days. The lesson of 1870 was burnt into the mind of every staff officer in Europe: the nation which loses the mobilization race is likely to lose the war. . . . In no country could the elaborate plans of the military be substantially modified to meet political requirements. For the Austrian government a declaration of war was a political manoeuvre, for the Russian government a mobilization was a counter-manoeuvre; but such orders set in motion administrative processes which could be neither halted or reversed without causing a chaos which would place the nation at the mercy of its adversaries . . .

(C) M. Ferro, *The Great War* (1969):

'War guilt' is still an open question. Its solution, obscured by national or other bias, really depends on how it is posed. The role of 'evil genius' behind the explosion no doubt goes to the German leaders, who must be submitted to 'the Judgement of History'—they tipped the balance towards radical solution of the Serbian question, carefully stage-managed its course so as to have a kind of 'perfect crime', deliberately rejected attempts at mediation when the conflict threatened to go further, and deliberately risked this when Russia threatened to intervene. On the other hand, England was 'the apostle of peace'—trying not to aggravate the Austro-Serbian conflict and to ensure that it did not lead to war. Just the same, her policy of conciliation did as much to produce war as the Germans' 'calculated risks'—the Germans, sure that whatever happened England would stay neutral, went further in their adventurous way than they would have done had they known they were wrong.

In comparison with these two contrary attitudes—the effects of which were much the same despite differing intentions—other Powers' roles seem, as time passes, increasingly passive. After Sarajevo the Austrians' singularly artificial rage had more noise than bite—Conrad did want to settle accounts with Serbia, but could be restrained by Germany. In the final analysis Vienna only did what Berlin said—to a degree described, by Fritz Fischer, as 'grotesque'. . . . Sazonov and the Tsar were conciliatory; several times they declared Serbia guilty, and deserving 'punishment'. But the Central Powers rejected these offers. Paléologue (French ambassador to Russia), acting in France's name without a mandate, approved what they did—but in any case the Central Powers had clearly shown that they meant to disrupt the Balkan balance, blackmailing France and Russia into hesitation by threat of continental war . . .

(D) J.R. Western, *The end of European Primacy* (1965):

The war of 1914 was due to the unbearable national tensions within Austria-Hungary and the attempt of that power to escape from them by action dangerous to peace. The continued existence of the Habsburg monarchy as a great power was the thing at stake in the war, at least to start with. To this extent the war was a European rather than a world conflict, and it was 'imperialist' only in the sense that Austria-Hungary had always been a multi-racial state and the subject races were now rebelling against it. But the Austrian crisis could not have grown into a general war among the powers had there not been tensions among them which prevented effective co-operation in the preservation of peace. These tensions were the result of imperial rivalries, and often concerned regions far beyond Europe and hardly touched by the ensuing war.

(E) F. Fischer, *Germany's Aims in the First World War* (1967):

Economic expansion was the basis of Germany's political world diplomacy, which vacillated in its methods between rapprochement and conciliation at one moment, aggressive insistence on Germany's claims the next, but never wavered in its ultimate objective, the expansion of Germany's power.

(F) L.C.B. Seaman, *From Vienna to Versailles* (1955):

As for the widespread view that war was inevitable, that it was due also to the past blunders and to the easy assumption that those blunders could not be rectified or their dangerous consequences postponed. Yet the handling of the Balkan Wars had proved the opposite less than twelve months before August 1914. The whole conception of inevitability in human affairs is often no more than a confession of political incompetence. It implies that tendencies, themselves created by human beings, cannot be checked, diverted or even reversed by human beings. The history of the nineteenth century contains many examples of how 'inevitable' developments can be successfully resisted for a very long time. The break-up of the Habsburg Empire and the triumph of the Revolution had both been regarded as inevitable by Metternich; but neither inevitability had occured by 1900. In 1900 a war between England and the French and Russians had seemed inevitable; but by 1914 they were allies together.

(G) J. Terraine, *The Mighty Continent* (1974):

After 1911 Europe's doom advanced with what now seem to be inexorable strides. The Bosnian crisis of 1909 had ended with the diplomatic defeat of Russia. The Agadir Crisis ended with the diplomatic defeat of Germany. Would either of these great powers, or the blocs to which they belonged, accept defeat again without trying the further test of war? If not, there could only be one result: a continental civil war, continental suicide. It would take a miracle to prevent it.

There was no miracle. National ambition and greed for empire continued to work their mischief. . . . Italy picked a quarrel with Turkey, in order to seize the great Turkish province of Tripoli (now called Libya) . . . in 1911 they managed to defeat the Turks, and so enlarged their Empire, but in so doing they triggered off a more serious train of events.

The weakening of Turkish power was a signal to all her enemies, above all the Balkan states with their deep-seated hatred of the Turks. Now Serbia, Bulgaria and Greece combined to attack Turkey. The result staggered Europe. In seven weeks the Turkish grip on the Balkans which had lasted for five centuries was utterly smashed. And out of the ruin of the once-dreaded Ottoman Empire Serbia emerged as the strongest of the Balkan states, her territory practically doubled. This result was intolerable to the anti-Serb elements in the Austro-Hungarian Empire. The military party urged immediate war against Serbia. And now the perils of the power blocs, and the system of interlocking alliances by which Europe sought security, were clearly seen.

Exercises

1 From your reading of these extracts, it should be clear that there are, broadly, two approaches to examining the outbreak of the war. The first looks particularly at the attitudes and actions of particular countries, and statesmen, and examines its, or their, part in the events leading up to the war. The second concentrates rather on particular concepts or trends, such as imperialism and nationalism, and identifies their role in the causes of the war. Obviously, the two approaches are closely linked and often overlap. Nevertheless, to draw out the distinction in approaches, re-examine each of the passages and explain which of the two approaches it basically adopts, and discuss the merits and defects of each approach to the examination of the causes of the war.

2 Re-examine the views of Fischer, Ensor and Ferro. Put yourself in the position of a German commentator and defend the accusation that the 'disaster had its roots in the new Germany', and demonstrate instead how it was the Entente that provoked the war.

3 What role did the military chiefs play in the outbreak of war—were they a cause of conflict in the first place, an influence on the size of the war, an influence on the timing and sequence of events etc?

4 Compare and contrast the views of Ferro and Western on the role of Austria-Hungary in the outbreak of war.

5 How inevitable was war in Europe in the early twentieth century?

6   The readings and exercise you have completed should have given you some fairly clear ideas about why there was a war in Europe. Below are tabulated what have generally been regarded as the chief causes of the war; where necessary, some additional explanatory notes have been added.

   (i) Germany's desire for world-power. Evidence: her pursuit of colonies; her expansion of trade; naval development; claims that she was being 'encircled' and deprived of her rightful place in world affairs.

   (ii) Germany's support for Austria-Hungary. Evidence: Germany's encouragement of a firm line against Serbia and promises to support Austria-Hungary in the event of war.

   (iii) The alliance system that had developed in the years before 1914. Although the original treaties had been defensive and primarily concerned with colonial affairs, subsequent military negotiations and international crises had welded them into firm commitments that were brought into effect and made a Balkan conflict into, first a European war, and then a world war.

   (iv) Widespread ignorance of what war would be like. There had been no European war since 1871. Authors generally wrote of brightly coloured uniforms, massed ranks of infantry and victorious charges by the cavalry bringing a swift and glorious end to war. In all nations, this encouraged bellicosity.

   (v) The arms race. The development of new and powerful weapons in large numbers undertaken for the purpose of using such weapons, which were not seen as deterrents.

   (vi) The nationalism of the great powers. Evidence: Organizations like the Pan-German League and Navy League pressing for power; the popular press and its enthusiasm for national prestige in all countries.

   (vii) Affronted great power nationalism. Russia had been 'done' by the Bosnian affair, Germany by the Agadir crisis, leaving a conviction that it should not be allowed to happen again, and that a show-down was inevitable.

   (viii) Nationalism of the different nationalities in Austria-Hungary, leading to threats to the stability of the Habsburg Empire. This in turn encouraged Austro-Hungarian leaders to quash firmly any attempt to threaten its power and to seek a swift and easy victory that would reunite the nationalities against a common enemy and, in victory, confer prestige on the Empire.

   (ix) The imperial conflicts of the great powers, leading to frustration and encouraging the view that a show-down was necessary.

   (x) The mobilization plans of the generals which were seen as immovable and essential to success in the war when it came.

Consider each of points (i)–(x) carefully and then judge the importance of each of them on a scale of 1 to 5—5 for a very important cause down to

1 for an unimportant one. You should also add to the list any other contributory causes that you consider necessary.

Examine the inter-relationships between points (i)–(x) and consider the role that each played in bringing about the war.

VII World War I

1. Introduction

A short chapter on the Great War is well nigh impossible. In this chapter, I have attempted to provide two things—a straightforward account of the chief events of the war, painted in bold (and perhaps over simple) lines to show broadly why events happened when and where they did, and a brief analysis of some of the standard problems of interpretation—the role of the navies, the ideas and actions of the generals, and the reasons for Germany's ultimate defeat. To elucidate the account, I have included as many maps as possible. To gain maximum understanding of the events, I suggest that you do not attempt simply to read the chapter, but rather annotate it in conjunction with close examination of the maps.

Obviously, there are as many omissions as inclusions. There is nothing on the war in the air, nothing on Africa, little on the Balkans campaign, little on the war against Turkey, nothing on the home fronts and the changing role of government, nor on the influence of politicians, especially Lloyd George and Clemenceau. In a larger text, such omissions would be inexcusable; in this, I have obviously had to take priorities.

In addition, it is very difficult to write a chronological account of the war. For purposes of clarification, I have broken the chapter down into years, itself a false division, since ideas and campaigns frequently ran on from year to year. Secondly, it is not possible to follow a strictly chronological pattern when the war was fought on so many fronts. For example, the campaigns on the Eastern Front in 1914–15 form a single topic, and have therefore been handled together before examining the Western Front in 1915. It might help you to keep the order of events in mind, and therefore their interactions with each other, to draw out a date chart before reading the chapter and fill it in as you read. This could be divided not only into years, but also separate areas, viz.:

	Western Front	Eastern Front	Balkans	Southern Front	Sea	Others
1914 Aug. Sept. etc						

One final note of clarification: I have referred to the Anglo-French-Russian alliance, and its allies, as the 'Entente' throughout; to call them the 'Allies' can be confusing since it was the Central Powers, Germany and Austria-Hungary, who strictly speaking formed the Triple Alliance.

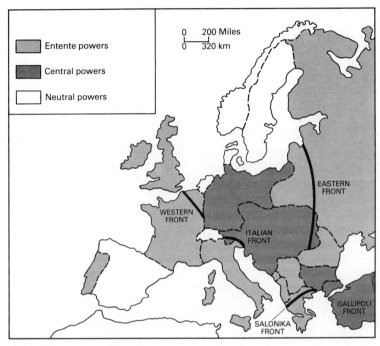

Map 14 Allies and battle fronts

2. The Western Front in 1914

On 4 August the Schlieffen Plan was put into operation. By it, the German armies would attack Northern France through Belgium in a sweeping movement that would ultimately trap the French armies between the German 6th and 7th armies and their own line of forts *(see Map 15)*. The 1st and 2nd armies in the North-west would take the longest route while the 4th and 5th would advance more directly via Luxembourg and Paris would be encircled by the German armies. The opening attack on Belgium was less easy than anticipated, since the forts at Liège held out from 6 to 17 August. Three days later the Germans entered Brussels. The French also put their strategic plan into operation—Plan XVII for an attack into Alsace-Lorraine. By 8 August they had reached Mulhouse; however, it was clear that the German 7th army, hidden in the Hardt forests, would surround and encircle them if they advanced further, and therefore retreat was ordered. Between these northern and southern extremes, the Germans repulsed French attacks in Lorraine and Luxembourg and then advanced. By the beginning of September, they had taken Namur, Montmédy, Soissons, Laon and Rheims. Paris seemed an easy target: the German commander-in-chief, Moltke, said 'in six weeks all this will be over'.

However, the plan had to be adapted from the original in two ways. Firstly, Russia had attacked in the East far sooner than expected; to meet this threat, Moltke sent two army corps from his 2nd and 3rd armies to the East on 25 August. Secondly, the 1st army had altered course in order to help the 2nd army that had met unexpected resistence at Guise. Consequently, its path of advance had moved westwards. Instead of moving around Paris to the East it would now attack Paris from the North-west. In Paris itself, the government moved to Bordeaux and many citizens removed themselves further south. Nonetheless, General Gallieni, now appointed Governor of the city, determined to defend the city. Joffre, the commander-in-chief, formed a 6th army to counter the threat from the German 1st army. They also realized that it would be possible to attack the side of Kluck's 1st army as it passed to the North of Paris in an effort to join with Bülow's 2nd army before it was attacked by the 6th French army.

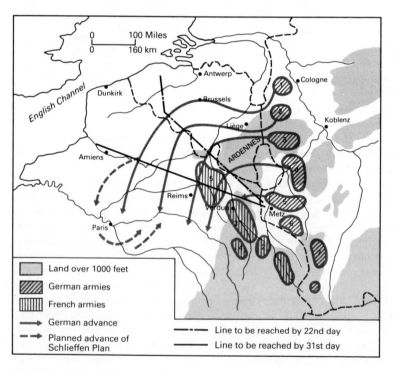

Map 15 The Schlieffen plan

It was this attack that became the battle of the Marne during the period 5–12 September *(see Map 16)*. The French 6th army forced Kluck to retreat, and in so doing Bülow was also forced to move back, in order to avoid the gap between the two armies widening and the possibility of being outflanked. By 12 September, the Germans had withdrawn about forty miles to the North of the river Aisne. This setback made any prospect of implementing the final stages of the Schlieffen Plan impossible for the time being. Moltke was replaced by Falkenhayn as commander-in-chief, and new strategies had to be sought.

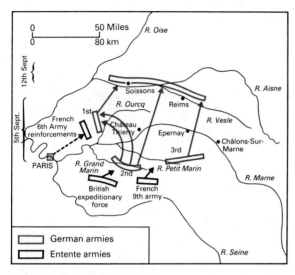

Map 16 Battle of the Marne, 1914

After the battle of Marne, both sides realized that direct confrontation to the North-east of Paris was, for the time being, unlikely to bring results. They therefore sought to find a way behind the others' armies. Since the Vosges made this impossible in the South, they both moved northwards towards the Channel. The ports there were also crucial strategic points, as through them would come additional British forces. From the middle of October to the middle of November there was furious fighting in the northern sector. On 10 October the Germans took Antwerp, and then, moving South, took Ghent, Bruges and Ostend, but their advance was then slowed by the Belgians' flooding of the river Yser. On 29 October the Germans attacked at Messines and Ypres, where, writes Ferro, 'the fighting was among the bloodiest of the war—the London-Scottish losing in a day one-third of its effectives.' The fighting continued for more than three weeks, but neither side made significant gains of territory; both suffered significant losses of men.

With the realization that victory was not to be won in a simple, single glorious victory came the building of defensive works. Even if it was difficult to make significant advances, it was still possible to stop the other side doing so. Thus defensive positions were constructed in the form of interlinking trenches protected by barbed wire and strategically positioned machine guns. From these, the enemy could be seen and attacked at some distance, while unable to attack, given the weapons available (the tactics of trench warfare are discussed further on page 176). Consequently, by the end of November 1914 trenches were dug from the Belgian coast to the Vosges mountains *(see Map 17)*.

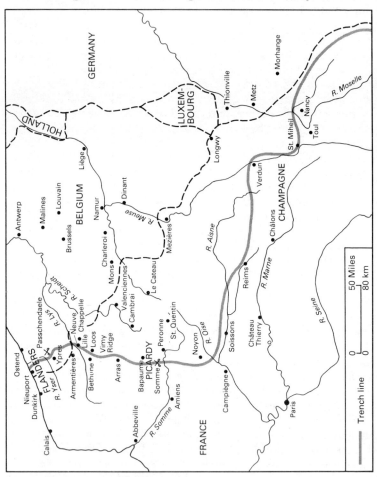

Map 17 The Western Front 1914–18

3. The Southern and Eastern Fronts in 1914–15

On 13 August Austrian troops crossed into Serbia following a heavy bombardment of Belgrade. Until the end of September, the Austrians were forced out of Serbia, and then the Serbs out of Austria. However, the Austrians, although weakened by having to send troops against Russia, eventually defeated the Serbs and, on 2 December, entered Belgrade. They were forced out again after a day, and a fortnight later they were forced out of Serbia, losing more than 200 000 men in the process. The 'swift punitive expedition' against Serbia had proved to be more swift than punitive.

The Russian army expected to take sixty days to be fully mobilized and ready to attack. However, German advances in the West necessitated rather swifter action so Grand Duke Nicholas, the commander-in-chief, sent his men into action without reserves. On 19 August the Russian 1st army under Rennenkampf defeated the Germans under Prittwitz at Gumbinnen in Eastern Prussia. However, the Germans were then re-organized and revitalized by Hindenburg, who replaced Prittwitz. A covering army was left to hold Rennenkampf's army (which could not risk further advance without supplies and reserves) while the rest of the Germans moved South, by foot or by train, to counter the 2nd Russian army, led by Samsonov, which had invaded Southern Prussia. On 29 August the armies met at Tannenburg where 92 000 Russians were taken prisoner in a crushing defeat. Turning north again, the Germans then met Rennenkampf's army in the region of the Masurian Lakes, where another 100 000 Russians were taken prisoner. The lack of co-ordination of the two Russian armies, and the use of uncoded radio messages that allowed the Germans to hear all their plans, had led to the rout of the Russian army in the North *(see Map 18)*.

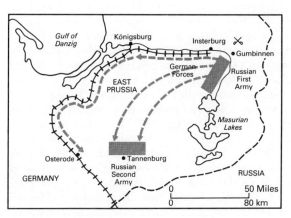

Map 18 Russia's defeats in 1914

Further South, the Russians made considerable advances against the Austrians. At the end of August the Austrian army, advancing towards Lublin, won the battle of Zamosc-Komarov, but almost immediately the Russians counter-attacked and, on 13 September, took Lemberg. This forced the Austrians to retreat and abandon the eastern part of Galicia.

Cracow was now threatened; from there the Russians could advance into Silesia, a crucial industrial area of Germany. It was necessary for the Germans to do something to take the pressure off the Austrians *(see Map 19)*.

German troops under Mackensen advanced as far as Warsaw by 12 October. This attack took the pressure off the Austrians, who were able to relieve the besieged fortress at Przemysl and push the Russians out of the Carpathians. However, a Russian counter-attack forced Mackensen to fall back, as Przemysl was again under siege and, by the end of November, Cracow was under attack. Hindenburg, now promoted to Eastern commander-in-chief, sought extra troops to mount a major offensive against the Russians in Eastern Prussia and so encircle them in central Poland. Falkenhayn was opposed to such plans, believing that it was in the West that the crucial battles would be fought. Consequently, the German attacks in the East were less decisive than had been hoped. Nevertheless, the Germans captured Lodz in early December and in February launched a series of attacks, in which Memel was taken, but the offensive in East Prussia was halted at Augustovo Lakes. To the South, German armies were sent to help the Austrians against the Russians, who were again driven from the Carpathians in early April *(see Map 19)*.

By this time, the situation on the Eastern Front was well balanced. The Russian armies had certainly done all that was expected of them— they had held the German attacks, albeit at the cost of more than a million men, and thus taken pressure off the Western Front. They still threatened Austria-Hungary, for in March 1915 they had eventually taken Przemsyl, with its 120 000 men and 900 guns. The Tsar confidently spoke of a new offensive against Hungary in the summer.

On 2 May an Austro-German offensive was launched in Galicia. By the end of June, more than a hundred miles had been won back, and the whole of Bukovina and Galicia recaptured. In early July a second offensive began, and Hindenburg's aim of catching the Russians in a North–South pincer seemed a genuine possibility, especially in view of the failure of the Gallipoli landings *(see page 163)*. The Austrians attacked northwards, capturing Lublin and Cholm; by early August they were outside Ivangorod. To the far North, in Latvia, the Germans took Windau and Mitau. More importantly, in Poland, Warsaw was captured and then Brest-Litvosk and Grodno. In mid-September the offensive ended with the capture of Vilna, by which time the Russians had lost all of Poland, Lithuania and Courland (Latvia). In the course of so doing, more than 150 000 men had been killed, almost 700 000 wounded and nearly 900 000 taken prisoner. It was decided that a scorched earth policy was needed, so the retreat of the armies was accompanied by thousands of refugees. The incompetence and confusion that led to inadequate supplies of guns, uniforms and food was never before so apparent. Krivoshein, the minister of agriculture, said, 'This vast migration undertaken by the High Command will lead to the abyss, revolution

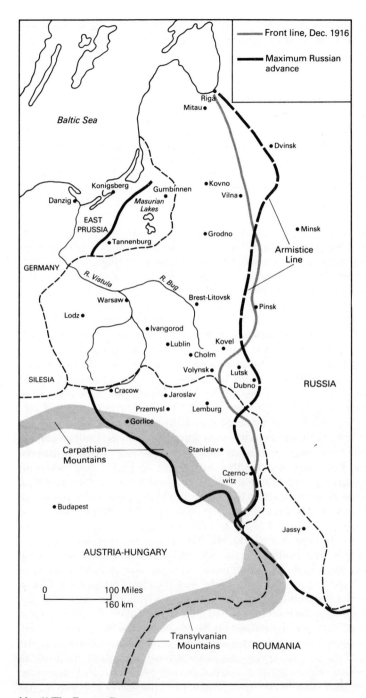

Legend:
- Front line, Dec. 1916
- Maximum Russian advance

Baltic Sea

Riga
Mitau

Dvinsk

Konigsberg
Gumbinnen
Danzig
Masurian Lakes
EAST PRUSSIA
Tannenburg

Kovno
Vilna

Minsk

Grodno

Armistice Line

GERMANY
R. Vistula
R. Bug

Warsaw
Brest-Litovsk
Pinsk

Lodz

Ivangorod
Lublin
Kovel
Cholm

SILESIA
Volynsk
Lutsk
Dubno
Cracow
Jaroslav
Przemysl
Lemburg
Gorlice

RUSSIA

Carpathian Mountains
Stanislav

Czerno-witz

Budapest

Jassy

AUSTRIA-HUNGARY

0   100 Miles
160 km

Transylvanian Mountains
ROUMANIA

Map 19 The Eastern Front

and perdition.' That High Command was now headed by the Tsar himself, who had taken over as commander-in-chief in the midst of the rout, on 5 September.

4. 1915: Weak Point Strategy

Ferro has called 1915 the 'year of weak point strategy'. Although commanders on both sides still believed the decisive battles would be fought on the Western Front, they also realized that such battles would be costly, and that they were not prepared for them. Consequently, all sought alternative ways of striking at their enemy. The focus of the war therefore shifted to other areas and other combatants, most notably in Italy and the Balkans.

Nevertheless, there were still attacks on the Western Front. Joffre in particular was convinced of the value of the offensive, even though his attacks were failing when they had a six to one advantage. In December 1914 it was decided to launch a dual attack in the North from Arras towards Cambrai and Douai and in the South from East of Rheims towards Attigny and Rethel *(see Map 17)*. These offensives were launched in January and again in late February but failed to gain much territory. For their part, the Germans made a new attack on Ypres in late April, using poison gas for the first time. The gas made a considerable impact, the defenders fleeing, but the defence was re-formed and held out. In May a French attack gained six miles to the North of Arras following an enormous bombardment, but in general the summer was quiet, awaiting the promised autumn offensive. This came in late September in Champagne, where the French attacked from Rheims to the Argonne but were held. To the North, the British attacked in Artois, and drove the Germans back towards Lens and Loos before grinding to a halt. In their efforts to catch the Germans in a North–South trap, the French lost nearly ½ million dead and more than a million sick and wounded. At the end of the year, the front lines in the West were barely altered; it was not surprising that generals and politicians sought alternative areas for action.

In Southern Europe and the Balkans, only Serbia had joined the war in 1914. The possibilities for attacks into Austria-Hungary and thence Germany from Italy and the Balkans were obvious to Entente leaders, while for the Central Powers there was the chance to attack Russia through the South–East Balkans. Consequently, both sides courted the uncommitted powers. Turkey had joined the Central Powers in the autumn of 1914 and had attacked Russia across the Black Sea. Russia was keen to win over Roumania and thus open up a second front against Austria-Hungary; however, the Roumanians were not prepared to commit themselves lightly, and it was not until 1916 that they joined the war. The Entente offered Bulgaria much of Thrace and Macedonia, but it was difficult for them to promise too much to Bulgaria, since such gains would be at the expense of Serbia and Greece, who would therefore have to be compensated elsewhere. In fact Serbia was offered Bosnia and Herzegovina and Greece Smyrna. However, the Bulgarians were far more attracted to Germany, who could offer them all they wanted, and who also appeared, in 1915, to be winning. Consequently, in September 1915, the Bulgarians joined the Central Powers and attacked Serbia *(see page 165)*. The loyalties of Greece were less straightfoward; King Constantine was less favourable towards the Entente than his Prime Minister, Venizelos, while both accepted Greece's obligations to Serbia under the 1913 treaty (by which Greece would come to Serbia's aid in the event of attack by Bulgaria). Following complex negotiations, Greece allowed British and French troops to be landed at Salonika, and, in November 1915, declared their benevolent neutrality. During 1915, therefore, the possibilities for action in the Balkans were improved for both sides.

Among the British government there were a number of supporters for such action, led by Churchill, Lloyd George and Lord Kitchener. Their theory was that the stalemate in the West should be left to the French army, while Britain's fresher troops should be used to open up a new front, probably against Turkey. This would, hopefully, have the effect of drawing German troops away from other fronts to help their ally and, given the prospect of territorial gains from Turkey, draw the Balkan states more conclusively into the conflict. Given success, such an attack might ultimately open up a southern front against Austria-Hungary and Germany. The two most likely places for such an attack were Salonika, from where Serbia could most easily be helped, and the Dardanelles, where the Turkish capital, Constantinople, could be captured. Those in favour of such schemes were known as 'easterners' while those who favoured continued major attacks in the West were called 'westerners'. During early 1915, while negotiations with the Balkan states continued, the westerners, led primarily by Joffre, who saw no reason why his men should be left with the hardest task, prevailed. But on 2 January an appeal from Russia to relieve pressure from the Turks in the Caucasus area persuaded the Entente to go ahead with their plans—an operation against the Dardanelles with the aim of taking Constantinople. The westerners though had their way in restricting the size of the force to a single division.

The Dardanelles (or Gallipoli) campaign began on 19 February 1915 *(see Map 20)*. The British navy bombarded the Turkish shore batteries and occupied the island of Lemnos with relative ease. Then on 18 March Admiral de Robeck and a fleet of eighteen ships attempted to enter the Dardanelles through the Narrows. Four of the ships struck mines and sank—the operation was abandoned. It was not until a month later (25 April) that the first British troops were landed—a month that had been well used by the Turks, under the command of the German Liman von Sanders, to prepare their defences and position 100 000 men. Consequently, the British troops (75 000 of them) who landed at the tip of the

Gallipoli peninsula found stiff resistance, as did the ANZAC troops who landed further North. Moreover, the preparations had been poor; there was no disembarkation plan, no detailed maps of the area, no hospital ship near at hand. The troops found themselves trapped between Turkish defences and the sea, and during a summer of fruitless fighting nearly 150 000 were killed or wounded. When a second landing at Suvla behind the Turkish defences failed in August the operation was abandoned and plans made to evacuate the remaining troops, which was eventually done in December and January.

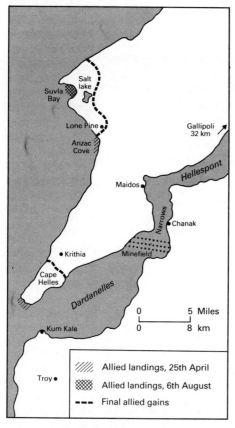

Map 20 The Gallipoli landings

Chronologically, the second weak point to be exploited was the Italian Front. Italy joined the war on the Entente's side in April 1915 following long negotiations that culminated in the secret treaty of London *(see page 253)*. The prospects of Italy providing a major threat to the Central Powers were not good; the Italian chief of staff, Cordona, said: 'The army was virtually in disintegration, so much so that, had Austria attacked us after our declaration of neutrality, it could be said without exaggeration that she would have found us almost defenceless.' There were shortages of guns and ammunition and, as in Russia, plenty of officials to issue orders from afar, few officers in the front line who knew what to do. In the first few months of their war, the Italian army lost ¼ million men. The bulk of the fighting was around the river Isonzo, where the Italian army attempted to dislodge the Austrians from their positions at Gorizia and Tolmino. Four indecisive battles were fought in this area during 1915 *(see Map 21)*.

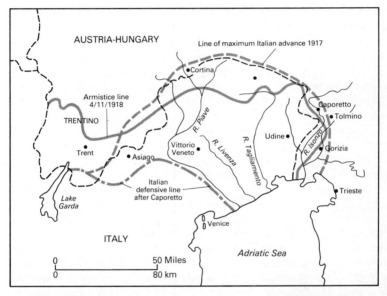

Map 21 The Italian Front

The Central Powers had greater success in their weak point strategy by defeating Serbia. In October a combined Austrian, German and Bulgarian attack was launched against Serbia. Belgrade was captured on 9 October and by mid-November the Serbs were in full flight into Albania. To assist them, an Anglo-French force was landed at Salonika but they were easily pushed back into Greece by the advancing Bulgars, while the Greek government refused to join the war—a state of affairs that was not resolved until 1917. The Serbian army, together with civilian refugees, were led through the mountains to the sea by their 71 year old king, Peter, in a 'Calvary known to few peoples...'. 'Early on they had been giving their weapons for bread, their boots for a slice, their clothes for a few mouthfuls. All looked like walking corpses, at the end of their strength' writes Ferro. The Austrian commander, Conrad, was jubilant at the rapid progress of the Central Powers in the south, and sought to go on to throw the British and French from Salonika. As with

Hindenburg in the East, though, Falkenhayn refused any further commitment on a minor front and withdrew the German forces.

A further weak point attack came in the Middle East. British and Indian troops were landed at the mouth of the Persian Gulf, at Basra, to protect oil supplies in December 1914. In 1915 it was thought that these could be used to dent Turkey's defences by an attack on Baghdad. This attack, led by General Townshend, was launched in June, and by September had reached and captured Kut-el-Amara, despite a lack of supplies. There the force was besieged by the Turkish army from December 1915 until April 1916 and eventually 12 000 British and Indian troops surrendered. They were then forced to march to Baghdad, where they were paraded before the crowds.

'Weak point strategy' had not proved successful. With the exception of the defeat of Serbia and the entry of Italy, the situation at the end of 1915 was little different to the beginning of the year. Neither side had been prepared to commit any real strength to the weak points they attacked. Falkenhayn was always convinced that the Western Front was of paramount importance, and had therefore quashed the schemes of Hindenburg and Conrad. Similarly, the Entente leadership, especially the French generals, was not prepared to commit its forces in any number to distant and potentially more hazardous operations. Consequently, the attacks on weak points were generally weak attacks. Secondly, and more avoidably, these schemes suffered from bad planning and administration— ineptitude in the case of Gallipoli has already been noted. Similar bungles occurred in the Mesopotamian campaign against Baghdad. The port of Basra lacked the facilities to unload many of the supplies that the Entente force had brought; the supplies were taken away again. The soldiers were equipped with rubber soled shoes, which literally melted in the heat of the desert. The only available hospital ship had been despatched to Madagascar, thousands of miles away. Without such regular blunders, it is possible that the strategy might have brought greater success.

5. 1916: The Great Attacks

The strategy of 1915 was almost completely reversed in 1916. Instead, the generals on each side prepared and undertook carefully planned gigantic attacks—Verdun and the Somme on the Western Front, the Brusilov Offensive on the Eastern.

The first great attack was on the Southern Front. Conrad was still convinced that Italy could be easily defeated, thereby freeing additional troops for the Western front. Despite Falkenhayn's refusal to assist in the attack, the Austrians attacked in the Trentino on 15 May, having been delayed by thick snow. They broke through the first lines of defence and captured Asiago, taking 45 000 prisoners, and Arsiero (see Map 21). There, however, the attack had to stop. Italian reinforcements arrived from the Isonzo front while Conrad was forced to move men to the East to counter the Russian attack. He was therefore bound to abandon the captured territory.

The Germans were secure on the Eastern Front by early 1916, and Falkenhayn was therefore able to transfer 250 000 men to the West to assist in the all-out attack he had long planned. Falkenhayn was no longer thinking in terms of an immediate and widespread breakthrough. Rather he sought to attack with sufficient force to draw Entente troops from other parts of the line to defend a single area. This would have a double effect of preventing them from attacking anywhere else and killing more and more troops, weakening both morale and fighting potential. 'The essential question', said Falkenhayn, 'is not to take Verdun...but to pin down the French, pull them towards the battlefield, and since they will have to defend it shoulder to shoulder, we shall bleed them white by virtue of our superiority in guns.' Verdun was chosen as it was in a salient and therefore could be attacked from more than one side.

On 21 February the attack was launched by a bombardment of 1400 guns and a million shells aimed at the right bank of the Meuse *(see Map 17)*. Under the command of Crown Prince William, the German forces advanced and by 25 February had reached Douaumont, only five miles from the centre of Verdun. Joffre, eager to keep as many men as possible further North for his own planned offensive, told Pétain, his general there, to manage with as few men as possible. In consequence, the French forces held on in desperate conditions, with starvation rations, constantly gassed and bombarded and with little knowledge of what was happening around them. To prevent any one group becoming demoralized, Pétain and his successor, Nivelle, frequently altered the forces at Verdun, so that almost three-quarters of the French infantry served at Verdun for a period. This had the double effect of revealing the full horrors of the place to the bulk of the French army. The assaults of March and April were held, but a renewed attack in June resulted in the fall of Fort Vaux and Thiaumont, so that the Germans came in sight of the city. There the attack ended as German forces were more urgently needed to deal with the double allied attack—from British and French on the Somme and the Russians in Galicia. By August, more Germans were dying at Verdun than French, and the captured forts were once again in French hands. In all, some 380 000 French were killed or wounded at Verdun, and almost 340 000 Germans.

Inevitably, the French commitment at Verdun weakened their contribution to the Entente's planned Somme offensive. This attack had been planned in late 1915 and was intended to be a part of a three-pronged Entente assault, coinciding with the Brusilov offensive on the Eastern Front (launched on 4 June) and an Italian attack on the Isonzo (6 August). Despite the reduction in France's contribution, the Entente had almost a two-to-one superiority on the Somme in terms of both men and guns. The generals were convinced that the key to success was the preliminary bombardment; since the bulk of losses were at the hands of concealed guns in enemy trenches, the destruction of those trenches and guns should have made an infantry assault possible. To make certain of this, the bombardment went on for ten days. Then, on 1 July, the main assault was launched with 100 000 troops. The British advanced towards Bapaume, the French Péronne *(see Map 17)*. It was a hot day, the British infantry each carried a sixty-pound pack and advanced at a steady pace up a slight hill. They took the first two lines without much difficulty, but were literally mown down by the next defensive positions. Despite a six-to-one advantage in the early stages, 57 000 British were killed or wounded on that first day. Further South, the French almost reached Péronne, but even by late September only a total of about 125 square miles had been won, and most of that was flattened and destroyed by the bombardment. In all, over a million men died on the Somme that summer—some 400 000 Germans and British, 200 000 French. It seems almost impossible, in the case of the Somme, to explain the incredible tactics that led to more and more men being pushed into an attack that was bound to fail.

The Italian prong of the Entente attack succeeded in capturing Gorizia, on 9 August. Three subsequent attempts to make further advances in the autumn all failed, and about 75 000 men were lost by each side.

As in 1914, the most significant events of 1916 took place on the Eastern Front. The attack was launched on 4 June, a little ahead of schedule in order to bring relief to the Italians. Initial attacks were made in four places, but the heart of the attack was in the Lutsk area *(see Map 19)*. A swift and thorough breakthrough was achieved in the South; Lutsk and Czernowitz were captured with half a million prisoners. In one of the greatest triumphs either side had during the war, the Russians advanced from twenty-five to 100 miles. However, the armies to the North were less successful and failed to capture Kovel or Lemberg and suffered heavy losses at the hands of the Germans, who had been transferred from the West. Despite its tremendous initial success, therefore, the offensive actually increased the misery and discontent of the Russian troops and people. Even so, it had succeeded more than either of the other Entente attacks, in that it drew troops away from Italy, Salonika and the West and caused the Roumanians to join on the Entente's side in the hope of spoils in Transylvania. Roumania declared war on 27 August but was swiftly defeated by an Austro-German attack from the West and a Bulgar-German attack from the South that resulted in the fall of Bucharest in December and the effective end of Roumania's efforts on the Entente's behalf.

'Great attacks' strategy had had little more success than weak point strategy. Despite the millions who died during 1916 the battle lines had changed little, the tactics hardly at all. On both sides there were changes of command but not of ideas. Hindenburg, with Ludendorff as quarter-master-general, replaced Falkenhayn but, despite their earlier enthusiasm for a knock-out blow in the East, they were now convinced that the war would be won and lost in the West. Joffre too was replaced, by Nivelle, the hero of Verdun, who also hoped for a decisive action in the West, based on speed and surprise. 1917 was to show that results were more forthcoming away from the battlefronts, in the streets of Petrograd and the halls of Congress.

6. 1917: The Entry of the United States and the Defeat of Russia

The entry of the United States on the Entente's side was, in fact, of little immediate significance. It came after a period of negotiation in which President Wilson attempted to organize peace talks and after Germany's announcement of the unrestricted use of submarine warfare, which threatened to harm America's trade considerably. This announcement came on 8 January 1917 *(see page 176)*. On the 19 January the US learnt of the Zimmerman telegram, in which the German foreign minister offered Texas, Arizona and New Mexico in exchange for Mexico's support against the United States. The fall of Tsardom in Russia also helped to decide the Americans, for they would no longer be supporting absolutism by joining the Entente. Primarily, however, they were concerned by Germany's successes and the possible damage to American trade, and on 6 April declared war. In the first instance, they could provide little, for the American forces amounted to less than 150 000 in all, and the navy was barely better prepared. Nevertheless, the introduction of conscription in the US at the end of April and the arrival of a token force in July in Paris gave promise of what was to come. The concept of 'holding on till the Americans arrive' was to have a great effect on the thinking and morale of both sides.

On the Western front, the war of attrition found its ultimate expression in the construction of the Hindenburg Line. The German High Command decided to make sure of its defences before launching a new attack. They therefore abandoned Noyon, Bapume, Roye and Lassigny and retreated to the new defensive positions, destroying the area they left and mining the roads. This action was completed during March *(see Map 17)*.

Despite the lessons of 1916, the British and French were still determined to attack. In part this was the result of the continuing and grumbling rivalry between the two allies. Neither would accept a joint command, and both felt their own plans were thwarted by their commitment to their ally. This was especially true of General Haig, who resented being put under Nivelle, and was keen to launch a British attack. This in fact came in April, as part of a joint attack. The British advanced in the Arras region and Canadian troops captured Vimy Ridge; in all about four miles gained. The French attacked simultaneously between the Oise and Rheims, but the Germans knew of the plans and were prepared to thwart them. 40 000 Frenchmen died in the opening days of the offensive, and there was mutiny in the 16th army corps.

Nivelle was dismissed and replaced by his colleague at Verdun, General Pétain. He managed to satisfy the mutineers and executed twenty-three of their leaders, but sensibly decided on a defensive policy until American forces could provide the backing for a new attack. This gave Haig the chance he wanted to win glory for his men, and, despite only lukewarm agreement from Pétain, he launched an attack in Flanders. In early June the British 2nd army pushed the Germans back from the salient at Ypres in the battle of Messines, and in July a new attack was launched there. In this, the battle of Passchendaele (or the third battle of Ypres), nearly ½ million British troops died, many of them Canadians, in a three-month attack that was made wholly impossible by the rain and mud of autumn. French attacks further South intended to relieve pressure on the British were actually more successful, in that they advanced in both the Verdun and Soissons regions. A final assault in the Cambrai region (see Map 17), in which a massed tank attack was used for the first time, made a considerable breakthrough in late November, but the infantry were unable to follow up the attack and were forced back by a German counter-attack. Yet again offensive tactics on the Western Front had proved fruitless.

Eighteen months after Conrad had urged it, Germany decided on an all-out attack against Italy to follow up their victories in the Balkans. The Italians, too, were keen on attack, believing that they could deliver the knock-out blow on Austria, but Haig refused to release troops for such an operation whereas Ludendorff was prepared to let six divisions go. The aim of the Austro-German attack was to cross the Upper Isonzo and push the Italians back to the river Tagliamento (see Map 21). The attack began on 24 October and almost immediately broke through at Caporetto, where ten miles were won on the first day. They were almost able to race the retreating Italians to the Tagliamento and surround them, but the attack was slowed by the need to keep in contact with reserves and supplies. British and French troops were sent to help the Italians, and eventually the line was held on the Piave. In their ignominious defeat, the Italians had lost more than ½ million men, equally divided between prisoners and deserters.

The Central Powers were equally successful on the Eastern Front. Following the revolution in March (see page 325), there was considerable disagreement in Russia as to whether or not the war should be continued. Eventually, the moderate Provisional government decided that it should be. However, the Central Powers were keen to exploit the remaining pacifist sentiment. The Germans therefore made no fresh attacks, though as many troops as before were kept at the front, and the German government did its best to encourage the peace sentiments by returning men like Lenin and Martov to Russia. Having decided to continue the war, the Russian Provisional Government launched a new offensive, again under Brusilov, in Galicia in July. However, this failed, and instead the Russian forces were driven back from Tarnopol, Stanislav and Czernowitz, while to the North Riga was captured. Brusilov was replaced by Kornilov, who then used some of his forces in an attempted counter-coup. The new failures of the army at the front added fuel to the pacifists' fire, and the Bolshevik revolution of November led to peace negotiations and the conclusion of an armistice on 15 December. While details of the peace settlement were discussed, German troops and materials could start to move westwards and reinforce the front line there for a fresh attack.

7. 1918

From the German point of view, the prospects for both victory and defeat were delicately balanced at the start of 1918. On the one hand, one of their main enemies, Russia, had surrendered, releasing men for use on the Western front. The Balkans, with the exception of Greece, had been conquered and Italy all but defeated. On the Western front, Entente attacks had been repulsed and German troops were almost without exception positioned on enemy soil. On the other hand, Germany's allies, particularly Bulgaria and Turkey, hardly inspired confidence, and the longer the war continued the worse this situation would become. Above all, the prospect of American forces arriving in Europe and American industry providing materials for the Entente augured ill; again, the longer the war lasted, the worse the situation would become. Everything pointed to the need for a swift end to the war. The means to this end would be, as always, a knock-out blow on the Western Front, supported by a blockade of the British Isles *(see page 176)*. Ludendorff summed up Germany's position as follows: 'Our situation requires that we should strike at the earliest moment, if possible at the end of February ... before the Americans can throw strong forces into the scale.'

The attack was to be launched primarily at the American and British forces, especially as these had been weakened by the Passchendaele offensive. On 21 March the attack began after a 6000-gun bombardment. From St Quentin, German forces advanced some forty miles, taking Péronne, Bapaume and Noyon. The Entente, faced by a critical situation, reorganized the command structure, so that for the first time there was a single overall commander, the French general, Foch. On 19 April, a second offensive began to the South of Ypres; this too was successful, capturing Messines Ridge and Armentieres. A third attack further South on 27 May was intended as a way of drawing French forces southwards but in fact broke through and reached Soissons. By 30 May German troops were back at the river Marne and less than forty miles from Paris, having created an enormous bulge in the Entente's line *(see Map 22)*. During June further attempts to advance were held up—by the French between Noyon and Soissons and by the Americans at Chateau-Thierry. On 15 July Ludendorff ordered his men to make a final effort to break right through, by an attack across the Marne in Champagne. They succeeded in crossing the river but the French and Americans regrouped, halted the attack and, on 18 July, launched a counter-attack in which both tanks and planes were used. This attack forced the Germans back over the Marne and out of Soissons. Yet again the Germans had been halted at the Marne.

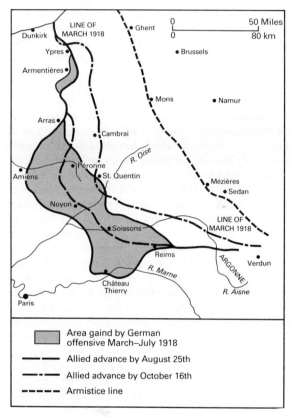

Map 22 Offensive and counter-offensive 1918

For both sides, the critical question was what to do next. The German troops were exhausted, and could not be expected to attack much longer; equally, there was a risk that if they moved back before launching a fresh attack, the Entente would take advantage of it. Foch was keen to follow up his success, but both Haig and Pétain, at last learning, were concerned by the risk of high casualties. Plans were made for a series of attacks on all fronts, intended to be successive and to continue into 1919. As the first part of this, an attack would be launched in the Amiens area.

On 8 August (a day that Ludendorff called 'the black day of the German army') the attack was opened by the British with 450 tanks. They advanced eight miles on the first day, and for the first time in the war captured large numbers of German prisoners without serious resistance. A second attack began on 20 August as a result of which Bapaume, Noyon and Péronne were captured, and Ludendorff ordered a general retreat to the Hindenburg Line. In early September American troops captured 15 000 prisoners in taking the salient at St Mihiel, in one of the most significant victories of all: American troops had succeeded where French had previously failed. By the end of September, the entire line was moving for the first time in the war—Haig's British troops in Flanders, Canadians in Lille and Cambrai, French in Champagne and Americans in the Argonne *(see Map 22)*. Although the advance was slower than Foch had hoped, they were enough to push Ludendorff into resigning (29 September), though his resignation was refused.

With the breakthrough on the Western Front, the successive attacks on other fronts could be launched. In Palestine General Allenby and his British forces defeated the Turks at the battle of Megiddo on 18 September, after which they moved northwards to Damascus and Beirut in early October. On 14 October the Sultan, Mohammed VI, asked President Wilson to arrange for an armistice and when no reply came from him, they negotiated directly with the British forces and signed an armistice on 30 October. From Salonika General Franchet d'Esperey advanced in mid-September and with a combined force of Italians, Serbs, French, British and Greeks attacked eastwards towards Bulgaria, which asked for an armistice on 26 September. In the South, the Italians launched a new attack on 25 September. Austria-Hungary was by now considerably weakened by the defection of the different nationalities, among whom both the Czechs and the Yugoslavs declared their independence from the Monarchy. On 24 October Diaz, who had replaced Cadorna, attacked on a front from Trentino to the Adriatic, and on 30 October won the battle of Vittorio Veneto, where several hundred thousand Austrians were captured while the rest simply left their units and headed for home. In fact, the Austrians had already offered to surrender unconditionally and actually signed an armistice on 3 November. Precipitously, each of Germany's allies had caved in at the very moment their leader was under greatest strain.

German generals and politicians were both convinced of the need for an armistice before their armies were wholly destroyed and incapable of fighting. If it was left too long, they would be forced to accept whatever was offered; if there was still an army, there was still the chance of resistance. On 4 October the German and Austrian governments asked Wilson for an armistice on the basis of the Fourteen Points *(see page 184)*. There followed several weeks of negotiation over the terms; Wilson demanded that all occupied areas should be evacuated and that a democratic government be formed. In the meantime Entente forces continued to advance on the Western Front. On 28 October sailors in Kiel refused to go to sea on a series of raids, and their disobedience was echoed in the other northern ports. When revolution broke out in Munich on 7 November *(see page 288)*, Prince Max of Baden, Chancellor since early October, announced the Kaiser's abdication and sent an armistice commission to meet Foch. In exchange for peace, the Germans were to leave all occupied territory, including that gained by the treaties of Brest-Litovsk and Bucharest, and surrender large amounts of military and semi-military (such as trains) equipment. The terms were accepted and on 11 November the armistice came into force.

8. The Unexpected War: Battle tactics of World War I

The war that was fought between 1914 and 1918 was not the war that had been expected. When the soldiers eagerly went to war in the summer of 1914, they firmly believed that they would be home by Christmas. Both on land and sea, one decisive encounter would settle the issue; for the Germans, a second Sedan, for the British, another Trafalgar. In fact, the length and nature of the war turned out to be wholly different. Technological advances were such that the weapons available demanded entirely different tactics to earlier wars. In addition, for the first time, the war became an economic one, in which battles were won and lost as much by the availability of supplies as by victories in battle.

(a) Naval Warfare
It was at sea that the war turned out most different to that expected. For almost twenty years Britain and Germany had spent millions of pounds developing powerful navies, particularly by building the mighty 'Dread-noughts.' By 1914, Germany had thirteen of these, Britain twenty. Surely they would now be used in the great showdown that would decide the supremacy of the sea, and thus play a decisive role in the outcome of the war as a whole? In fact, they met once, and then but briefly. Quite simply, it was too risky to attempt the great showdown, since both commanders, Jellicoe for the British, Scheer for the Germans, knew that if they lost such an encounter they could be blamed for their country's defeat. Moreover, by mining (a relatively new and rapidly developing means of sea warfare) the entrance to the English channel and by keeping the Grand Fleet off northern Scotland, the British Navy was able to prevent the German High Seas Fleet leaving the Baltic and North Seas. If it risked escape, it risked disaster.

The Germans therefore sought ways of drawing parts of the British fleet away from its base in Scapa Flow so that it could be defeated in parts, until it was small enough to be encountered as a whole. The first attempt at this, in January 1915, resulted in the loss of one German battle cruiser, the 'Blücher', and put off further major attempts until 1916. On 30 May the battle-cruiser squadron under von Hipper moved off the coast of Norway supported by the High Seas Fleet. Again, the British battle cruisers, under Beatty, were sent to investigate, and the Grand Fleet moved out to support him. Two British battle-cruisers were sunk, and Beatty turned to rejoin the Grand Fleet.

The German High Seas Fleet followed him, thereby bringing about the only major naval encounter of the war, the battle of Jutland. Both sides turned and wheeled their fleets in an effort to get the best position, so the battle became confused. Ultimately both main fleets escaped to safety, though both lost ships—the British fourteen ships totalling 112 000 tons, the Germans eleven ships totalling 61 000 tons. Numerically, the Germans could therefore claim victory but ultimately, since the battle decided the German admirals that another major naval engagement could not be risked, it was the British who gained. For it was in the idle, unused German fleet that discontent and, ultimately, mutiny developed.

The only other naval engagements came early in the war and far from Europe. In November 1914 the German East Asia Squadron met a British cruiser squadron at Coronel off the Chilean coast and sank the 'Monmouth' and the 'Good Hope'. To meet this possible danger and avenge the unexpected defeat, a British force, including modern battle-cruisers, was sent to South America where it met and destroyed von Spee and four of his five ships.

There were three main reasons why surface ships played so little part in the Great War. In the first place, as has been noted, the risks were too great. If one side lost its fleet, or even enough of it to give the other a significant numerical advantage, the other would dominate the sea. In turn, this would enable it seriously to damage the trade and supplies of the other and to ship troops and equipment at will, either or both of which would, given the balance of forces on land, enable it to win a decisive overall advantage. Secondly, the development of mines and torpedoes hampered the movement of ships. As with other weapons in the war, the counter to mines—detecting equipment—had not been developed to the same extent. Until such equipment was developed, surface ships were seriously restricted. Thirdly, and most importantly, the use of submarines had a similar effect. Again, no effective counter to them had been developed and they were therefore able to inflict continuous and serious damage on surface ships.

Indeed, it was in this form of warfare—the submarine or U-Boat ('Unterseebooten')—that the bulk of the naval war was fought. At the start of the war, the Germans had only thirty such boats, and even at the end only 130; despite this, they were able to cause sufficient damage genuinely to threaten Britain with defeat. This was possible because the war had, by virtue of its length, become an economic war, in which the continuing ability to bring in supplies, both military and civilian, was critical. Consequently, both sides were anxious to stop such supplies, especially from neutral powers. In August 1914 the British had drawn up a list of contraband goods, and insisted on the right to stop, search and confiscate neutral ships in the North Sea. In February 1915 the German government announced that it was to begin a submarine blockade of Britain and would sink any ships approaching Britain with contraband supplies. There followed the most notorious sinking of all—of the Cunard liner 'Lusitania', with the loss of 1198 lives, of whom 139 were American. It was carrying some arms and munitions and had been warned not to sail. Even so, the sinking provoked a tremendous outcry, especially in the United States, and led, in September 1915, to a declaration by Germany that liners would not be sunk without warning, thus making it possible for civilians to escape. However, this obviously weakened the effectiveness of the U-boat blockade.

The use of the blockade became an increasingly emotive issue in the war. The British were able to stop ships before they entered or while they were in the unmined portion of the North Sea. They could therefore use surface ships and so search them rather than sink on sight. Consequently, they were able to operate an effective blockade *(see page 179)* without killing large numbers of civilians. It was more difficult for the Germans to blockade Britain, since to do so ships had to reach the Atlantic, and therefore avoid the mines in the Channel and the northern North Sea. The only ships capable of doing this were U-boats. Yet it was not practical for a U-boat to stop and search liners and merchantmen; they could only sink them. Consequently, an effective blockade required loss of life, and hence widespread hostility, especially from the United States.

Nevertheless, the German calculations were that unrestricted submarine warfare (i.e. sinking *all* ships approaching British ports) could wreak havoc on the British economy. In 1915 a quarter of a million tons of British shipping had been sunk, in 1916 more than a million and a quarter. Each month the figure rose and Britain, increasingly dependent on overseas supplies of food, could be starved to defeat. It was calculated that 600 000 tons of shipping could be sunk each month. Therefore, on 1 February 1917, unrestricted submarine warfare was announced. In April, 881 000 tons were sunk and the predictions of the German admiralty seemed to be correct. The war would be won by a means that no one had expected. On the insistence of Lloyd George, the British admiralty agreed to adopt a convoy system by which they would escort merchant ships. Although losses remained high, they never again reached the peak of April; by October fifty U-boats were lost and by early 1918 the British were building at a faster rate than they were losing ships. Nevertheless, the submarine had come close to winning the war for Germany.

(b) The generals and trench warfare
The most lasting feature of the Great War, certainly after it ended, was the horror of the warfare on the Western Front. Life in the trenches has been vividly and horrifically described by many authors and film makers, so but a single quote (taken from Ferro) will suffice as a reminder. This describes a trench in Champagne:

> There was a vile stench in the new trenches, to the right of the Epargnes. Rain came down in torrents, so we used bits of canvas we had found stuck

in the trench walls to keep dry. At dawn the next day we saw that the trench had been built in a grave yard; the bits of canvas had been put there to cover bodies and human remains.

Even more horrific were the tactics to try to win territory and ultimately 'deliver the knock-out blow'. Enormous bombardments preceded infantry charges in which literally thousands of men ran, or sometimes even walked, across open ground towards the enemy defences, often carrying a heavy pack only with a single shot rifle and grenades. As they reached the enemy, they were held up by the barbed wire; as they tried to find a way through it, they were shot to pieces in their thousands by machine guns. The question must therefore be asked: why did the generals persist with such tactics and why did so many die?

At the simplest level, technology had again overtaken tactics. The machine-gun was an excellent defensive weapon, that could be set up and camouflaged and used whenever an attack was threatened. Combined with barbed wire, which effectively slowed down attackers, it was lethal. No similarly effective attacking weapon was developed in the early years of the war. Ultimately, the tank would prove to be this weapon, but it was barely used until the last year of the war. The other newly developed weapons were in the artillery field. Whereas guns in the 1880s fired four rounds a minute at a maximum range of two miles, by 1914 an eighteen pounder could fire ten rounds a minute at a range of five miles. Again, these weapons were difficult to use for offensive purposes, since they could not be easily moved to support an attack and were therefore used in preliminary bombardments. This in turn required pinpoint accuracy, which depended on accurate mathematical calculations, the ability to do which was sadly lacking in the armies of the Great War. The new weapons were therefore primarily of defensive value.

A further difficulty was communications. Once an attack had started, only wire, runners or pigeons were available. Wireless was almost non-existent forward of Divisional Headquarters. Thus, commanders had virtually no contact with a battle once it was begun, as wire was easily cut and runners could be hit. In practice, command was left to those in the battle itself.

In contrast to the technology, the training and attitudes of the generals were in the offensive mould. The manuals they had learnt from, and their own limited experience, taught them that battles could only be won by attacking. Moreover, they believed in the 'offensive spirit'; soldiers believe it is their job to attack and overrun the enemy, not sit waiting for him. The way to this end was, it was believed, by a massive attack on a narrow front that would break through and then turn back to encircle the enemy. To achieve this, the men had to take with them enough equipment for the entire operation—hence the need to carry great packs. Common sense argued that if you put enough men in a small area where they outnumbered the enemy they must overcome that enemy and get through to the open countryside behind. Logic dictated it.

This 'logic' disregarded two crucial factors. The entire front was narrow. Consequently it was relatively easy to move reserves from one sector to another and so plug any gaps that were created. Secondly, defences were rarely a single line to be broken; rather, they were complex arrangements involving not just lines of trenches but also machine gun posts in strategic places, large dug-outs, artillery and, often, buildings as well. Often, advancing infantry did break through the first line, and even the second. However, they were then confronted by a third or even fourth line of defence—to turn round and 'encircle' the front lines in such circumstances would have been sheer madness. Instead, they had to go on further and further, continually encountering stiffer resistance as they themselves tired. 'Break-through strategy was better suited to a Staff College blackboard than the battlefield.

In fact, by the end of the war this strategy was abandoned and the later and more successful offensives were conducted in a different way. The first assault of this new type was the Brusilov offensive of the summer of 1916. The bombardment was not limited to a single area, but instead aimed at four different points. This both disguised where the main point of attack would be and disrupted the enemy's efforts to bring reserves up. In fact, the Austrians did not realize that the main attack would come at Lutsk, and sent their reserves to the wrong place. When the attack came, it too came in four places, thereby making 'plugging the gaps' far harder. Subsequent assaults on the Western Front also followed this pattern— most notably Ludendorff's spring offensive of 1918 and the Entente counter-offensive that followed it. Obviously such attacks were much harder to co-ordinate, especially when they involved troops of several nationalities, but they ultimately proved the most effective.

Two further points should be made in defence of the generals. Firstly, they were completely thrown by the scale of the war—in terms of time, geography, and the number of troops. This scale posed supply problems that had never before been contemplated; how was it possible to keep this number of men fully equipped, move them to the right place at the right time, feed them, clothe them? They had all made their initial calculations for mobilization, but thereafter they necessarily had to work from hand to mouth. Some instances will give an indication of the problems involved. The French had underestimated their requirements of guns, cable, radios etc. by about 90%. The French ambassador to Russia reported that the Russians had told him that the Germans could send 400 trains a day to the front, the Russians only ninety (hence the difficulty of following up an attack like the Brusilov offensive). For the Gallipoli campaign, a single 10 000 ton ship was required to take 3000 tons of grain (enough for a cavalry regiment for three months) so that in terms of shipping the transport of fodder took far more space than ammunition. The German army learnt from Barnum and Bailey's circus how best to load and unload a train—by loading from one end and running rails along the carriage floors for the length of the train. Such ideas and techniques would have been beyond the imagination of planners at the turn of the century.

Secondly, the generals were victims of their own backgrounds and attitudes. In Britain and France, the army was not regarded very highly and did not attract the most able elements of society, either in the officer class or among ordinary soldiers. Salaries were comparatively low and budgets tight. With the introduction of conscription, the generals believed that their conscripts were capable of only the simplest manoeuvres, even though many of them were obviously intelligent and able to do far more. However, the generals believed that they were the same 'boneheads' that had joined before the war and treated them accordingly.

Even bearing all these factors in mind, it is often hard to believe that the generals knew what they were doing. Haig's firm belief that he was winning the battle of the Somme when he had just lost 60 000 men seems amazing. 'Lack of offensive spirit', 'not good at attacking in flat country', 'the fighting will of the British race', 'we can break through the German front at will'; all these were said by Entente generals (the first two by Joffre, the latter by Haig and Nivelle) about their men. Even more damaging was the failure of the allies to co-operate. This was equally true of both sides. Both British and French were keen to make the decisive breakthrough on the West while Falkenhayn refused to help the Austrians in the Balkans and Italy. Paradoxically, they were more ready to help their more distant allies—the Russians to help the Italians, the British and French the Russians. Had the co-operation that eventually came in the summer of 1918 come a year earlier, better results might have been achieved.

(c) Germany's defeat

In November 1918 the Germans undoubtedly had had the better of the four years of fighting. In the East the Russians had been beaten and surrendered enormous amounts of territory, having been pushed back from 200 to 700 miles. In the West, the German front line was still on enemy territory when they asked for peace. Her losses were less than those of her enemies. She surrendered not because she had been defeated, but because she knew that she would be. The future was hopeless for Germany.

The entry of the United States had not made an impact but the potential of America's contribution was enormous. Militarily, American troops were arriving at the rate of 300 000 a month by August of 1918; the Germans estimated that they might face an American army of five million men. They were also providing military equipment and assisting in escorting merchant convoys. Even more importantly, the potential American economic contribution was enormous. In the first years of the war, production of coal, steel and iron was almost equal between the Entente and the Central Powers—each produced about 350 million tons of coal and 20 million each of iron and steel. After America's intervention, the Entente production was 841 million tons of coal, 58 million of steel and 50 of iron, while the Central Powers was slightly less than in 1914. From slight economic inferiority the Entente suddenly had a three-fold advantage. Ferro writes: 'American intervention altered the economic terms of the war at the very moment when these were becoming as vital to the outcome of the war as military events or human effort.'

As important as the entry of the United States were the effects of economic decline in Germany itself. This was in part the result of the British blockade on Germany. Obviously, many goods still reached Germany through neutral countries, especially Holland, Denmark and Sweden and it can be demonstrated that German blockhouses were built with British cement. Even so, the slow but steady effects of the blockade were increasingly felt. For example, animal fats were almost unattainable, as what there were were used for making glycerine for explosives. It has been estimated that the Germans were receiving only about a thousand calories a day by the end of the war. German statistics attributed an ever increasing number of deaths to the effects of the blockade—88 000 in 1915, 120 000 in 1916, 260 000 in 1917 and 294 000 in 1918—a total of three-quarters of a million people, as many as the British lost on the Western Front.

German agriculture was hit disastrously by the war. The conscription of agricultural workers hit Germany harder than the other combatant countries, with the result that production fell by up to 70% in some sectors, compared with 50% in Russia and 30–50% in France. Rationing was first organized in Germany, and price controls were brought in in 1916. The production of 'ersatz' (substitute) products increased as the war went on—'K' bread made with potatoes, cloth made out of paper and nettles, shoes with wooden soles. Simultaneously, workers demanded shorter hours because they found it so difficult to work on such small rations. Most importantly, the harvests of 1917 and 1918 both failed, so that production was about half what it had been before the war, as Table 29 below shows.

	1912–13 (pre-war average)	1918
Potatoes	52	26·4
Rye	11·9	7·2
Oats	9·1	4·3
Wheat	4·9	2·5
Barley	3·6	2·1

Table 29. German agricultural production (in million tons)

Rations were reduced accordingly—seven pounds of potatoes, 250 grammes of meat, less than 100 grammes of fats. Again, the economic decline affected Germany's future even more than her present. How could her people keep up their morale and enthusiasm for the war through another winter? Could they even survive it?

In such circumstances, the collapse of Germany's allies and the ultimate failure of the Spring Offensive were but nails in the coffin. Germany's fate was all but sealed before 21 March; only if the offensive actually succeeded, and that meant taking at least Amiens and forcing the Entente to surrender on the Western Front, was there any chance of avoiding a collapse of the Home Front. The last days of September sealed her fate. Between 26 September and 2 October, the Entente launched their fourfold offensive on the Western front, Bulgaria surrendered. Damascus fell, chancellor Hertling resigned, and Ludendorff offered his resignation. On 4 October the German and Austrian governments asked Wilson for an armistice.

9. Bibliography

Most of the numerous books on the Great War have detailed bibliographies that will lead the student to more specialized works, so this selection consists chiefly of introductory works. Of recent books, M. Ferro's *The Great War* (Routledge & Kegan Paul, 1973) and A. Marwick's *World War I* (Units 15–17 of the Open University *War and Society* course) are clearly the best and adopt a rather different approach to the standard textbooks. Of these standards, three are best known: *The Great War 1914–18* by C. Falls (Longman, 1960), *History of the Great War 1914–18* by C.F.C. Cruttwell (OUP, 1936) and *The History of the First World War* By B.H. Lidell Hart (Pan Books, 1972). Also of interest, as they cover areas largely ignored by this chapter are *Gallipoli* by A. Moorehead (Hamish Hamilton, 1956), *The War behind the War 1914–18: the history of the political and civilian fronts* by F.P. Chambers (Faber, 1939) and *The Deluge* by A. Marwick (Macmillan, 1965).

10. Discussion Points and Exercises

A *This section consists of questions that might be used for discussion (or written answers) as a way of expanding on the chapter and testing understanding of it:*
1 Why did the Schlieffen Plan fail?
2 Why did the Western Front develop into a series of trenches?
3 How significant were the defeats of the Russians in 1914?
4 Why was Falkenhayn opposed to the plans for a major offensive in the East?
5 What do you understand by 'weak point strategy'?
6 Why was there so little progress on the Western Front in 1915?
7 Account for the failure of the Gallipoli landings.
8 What could the Central Powers have achieved by victory on the Balkan and Italian front?

9   Were Verdun and the Somme critical battles or just enormous mistakes?

10 What effects did 'waiting for the Americans to arrive' have on the thinking of both sides?

11 Why did the German offensive of 1918 fail?

12 Why did the Germans want to surrender before their armies were crushed?

13 Why was the naval war so different to that which had been expected?

14 Comment on the role of the underwater war.

15 Why was the Brusilov offensive strategically significant?

16 What was the significance of America's entry into the war?

17 How important was the Entente's blockade of Germany?

B   *This section suggests ways in which you can examine some of the problems of the Great War in greater detail:*

1 Write a report either supporting or opposing the 'easterner' argument in 1915.

2 Compare the aims and achievements of 'weakpoint strategy' and 'great attacks' in 1915–16.

3 Examine the relationship between the different fronts of the war, if possible in the form of a diagram or chart.

4 Write a report for the Kaiser in January 1918, outlining Germany's prospects for the year.

5 Write a defence of the tactics employed by the generals on the Western Front.

C *Essay questions:*

1 'In 1914 the war was expected to be over by Christmas, yet by 1918 it was expected to last another two years.' Why were both of these expectations proved false?

2 Why was the Western Front so static and the Eastern Front so mobile?

3 Why did Germany lose the Great War?

VIII The Peace Treaties

1. The Treaty of Versailles

(a) The peacemakers and their aims

When the armistice was signed, few politicians had any detailed conception of what should be done. Usually countries went to war with specific aims: when they were in a position to achieve these aims the fighting stopped and victor made vanquished concede those aims. Yet in August 1914 few of the powers had clearly formulated war aims. When these were formulated, they were generally secret (or at least a censored version was presented to the world), often changed and more easily identified by the actions of armies than the pronouncements of politicians. Fritz Fischer has now shown that Germany's aims were extensive and ambitious. Bethmann-Hollweg's memorandum of September 1914 spoke of the need to weaken France to a state of dependence on Germany and of the construction of a 'Mitteleuropa' of Germany, France, Austria-Hungary, Poland and Scandinavia, with the Low Countries as vassal states. There were also plans to push back Russia and take over a new eastern Empire, part of which would form a defence against the new Russia ('Vorland') and the rest of which, to the South, would be colonized and developed economically by Germany ('Kulturland'). Overseas, an enormous African Empire including the Congo, French Equatorial Africa and parts of West Africa would be created, so satisfying German's need for world power *(see page 78)*. Obviously, these aims differed in detail among different Germans—industrialists and generals were sometimes more optimistic, as in mid–1917, but the overall pattern remained the same.

The aims of the Entente powers were less ambitious. The French sought the return of Alsace–Lorraine and the reduction of German power by the creation of a protective Rhineland Republic, and by the creation of a new political structure in Germany. In consultation with the Russians, it was agreed that Russia should have the straits of Constantinople and Poland should be left as a part of Russia in exchange for Russian support for France's plans to divide up parts of Germany into new states. In March 1917 an agreement to this effect was signed, but almost immediately negated by the revolution. Britain's aims revolved primarily around colonies; it was hoped to take both Germany's and Turkey's, although these would be shared with France and Russia.

In January 1918, Lloyd George enunciated Britain's war aims in a speech to the TUC. He spoke of the need for Germany and her allies to return all the areas they had occupied—Belgium, Serbia, Montenegro, and parts of France, Italy and Roumania, of the creation of a Polish state, of self-government for the nationalities of Austria-Hungary, and of 'reconsideration' of France's losses of 1871, Alsace and Lorraine. Shortly afterwards, Germany's war aims were more clearly revealed in the treaty of Brest-Litovsk in March *(see page 334)* and the treaty of Bucharest in April, signed with the first of the Entente's allies to surrender, Russia and Roumania respectively. By these, Germany and her allies took possession of large areas of Eastern Europe, and Entente politicians could demonstrate the greed of the Central Powers to their people, and the consequent need to make sure of their defeat.

However, it was Woodrow Wilson's ideas that were to form the basis of the peace that was made. This was paradoxical in that America had been the least involved of the Great Powers and had never had any clear aims, except to aid in the defeat of Germany. On the other hand, his plans—the 'Fourteen Points'—were the only coherent outline of what the peace should state, and thus came to play a prominent part almost by default. His ideas were outlined to the American Congress on 8 January 1918. Behind them lay Wilson's view of why the war had started, and he hoped that by eliminating these causes war could be avoided. The alliance system had drawn the powers into a local conflict by virtue of the secret obligations the powers had made to each other: therefore Point 1 asked for 'open covenants openly arrived at'. Secondly, naval rivalry and the determination of Britain and Germany to dominate the seas had led to the arms race: so Point 2 demanded 'absolute freedom of navigation alike in peace and war' (this would also preserve civilian populations from the horrors of blockade). The arms race had extended to the army and ammunitions, so Point 4 stated that 'armaments would be reduced to the lowest point consistent with domestic safety'. Behind the arms race and international hostility lay commercial and colonial rivalry— therefore this too must be eliminated. Point 3 asked for 'the removal, so far as possible, of all economic barriers' and Point 5 for 'an impartial adjustment of all colonial claims'. Finally, there had been no alternative to war, no mechanism for solving disputes: Point 14 therefore asked for 'A general association of nations to be formed to afford mutual guarantees of political independence and territorial integrity to great and small states alike'.

This last would also ensure that the territorial adjustments Wilson planned for in Points 6–13 would be secured. These were:

6. Evacuation of Russian territory by all separate powers and the free determination of her own future.

7. Evacuation and restoration of Belgium.

8. Evacuation and restoration of French territory and the return of Alsace–Lorraine to France.

9. Readjustment of Italy's boundaries 'along clearly recognizable lines of nationality'.

10. Autonomy for the peoples of Austria-Hungary.

11. Evacuation and restoration of Roumanian, Serbian and Montenegrin territory, including access to the sea for Serbia.

12. The Ottoman empire to be broken up—areas of Turkish population were to form an independent Turkey but other areas and peoples 'to be given the opportunity for autonomous development'. The Straits of Constantinople were to be permanently open to all ships.

13. The creation of an independent Poland in all those areas 'indisputably Polish' and this state to have secure access to the sea.

These would seem to be the main territorial changes required to satisfy the Entente's allies and war aims. However, many of them could only be achieved at the expense of existing powers—not only Germany, but also Austria-Hungary and Russia—and even then little seemed to have been done for French security. France and Britain broadly endorsed the plans, but would not accept the clause about freedom of the seas, and demanded that they should also receive some compensation from Germany. Both Germany and Austria-Hungary agreed that the Points could form the basis of the peace, and when they asked for peace in October 1918, asked that it should be based on them.

Yet there were some glaring faults in the Fourteen Points. Most obviously, it would not be possible simply to divide the Habsburg Empire into separate national states. There were more than a dozen such nationalities, and they were by no means neatly segregated into separate areas *(see page 13)*. Secondly, the war was almost certain to be followed by economic hardship among the combatants, who were therefore unlikely to look with favour on the plans to abandon tariffs. In addition, they were more rather than less likely to want to keep large armies at the ready in the period immediately after the war. Electorates would simply not accept widespread disarmament that would make it impossible to ensure and secure territorial changes. Finally, the Fourteen Points hinged on Wilson's interpretation of the causes of the war and the consequent remedies. Were the arms race and commercial and colonial rivalry actually the causes of the war, or were they merely symptoms of an under-lying malaise, a nationalism that would have found its expression in war in any case?

The bulk of the peacemaking was to be done by the 'Council of Four', the leaders of the four great Entente Powers—Britain, France, Italy and the United States. The attitudes of the other three differed considerably from Wilson's idealism. Orlando, Italy's Prime Minister, and Sonnino, his Foreign Minister, were under great pressure from their colleagues and rivals at home to win considerable areas for Italy and so justify the suffering and losses of the Italian people *(see page 254)*. Moreover, they had the treaty of London *(see pages 253–4)* to support their claims to areas of Austria-Hungary, even if the United States had not been a signatory to this treaty. Clemenceau, France's Prime Minister, had endorsed the Fourteen Points, but in secret scorned what he called the 'Fourteen Commandments'. He well knew French feeling—the determination not only to win back Alsace and Lorraine but also to make sure that France could never again be threatened by Germany. He realized that it would be difficult to win any support for the idea of Rhineland Republics, and therefore sought by other means to secure France's eastern frontier. Lloyd George, Britain's Prime Minister, was agreed on the need for redrawing Europe's frontiers but was flexible in his attitude to Germany and her future. However, his flexibility was hampered by the attitude of British people and MPs, who demanded the Kaiser be hanged and that Germany be 'squeezed till the pips squeak'. During the peace negotiations he received a telegram signed by 370 MPs demanding that Germany be forced to pay full compensation.

(b) The history of the peace conference

The Entente blockade of Germany continued until July, 1919. In addition, troops occupied many of the major towns of Western Germany, thereby ensuring that any terms proposed would have to be accepted. This made it possible to bar Germany and her allies from the conference, so leading to subsequent accusations that it was a 'Diktat', a dictated peace. At the same time, Germans continued to starve and the Entente powers spent more than 5 million pounds providing food for the German people. The signature of the armistice was therefore followed by a kind of 'limbo' for seven months until the treaty was signed.

This long delay was caused partly by the fact that it was nine weeks between the armistice and the start of the Conference in January 1919. Once President Wilson had decided to attend personally, he was unable to do so until he had delivered the State of the Union speech in early December, and arrived in Paris on the 19th. There was also an election in Britain on 14 December, as Lloyd George was keen to get Parliamentary approval before going to the Conference. His coalition won a huge majority, based on their promises to punish the Germans and win full compensation from the defeated powers. There was also debate about the best location for the Conference. Geneva was suggested as being neutral, but rejected by Wilson on the grounds that it was 'teeming with Bolshevik sentiments' and therefore potentially dangerous. Paris was therefore chosen as the symbolic centre of Western democracy. To the Germans, it was more symbolic of their victory of 1871. The decision to hold the Conference in Paris also made Clemenceau, out of courtesy, Chairman.

The conference lacked any definite procedure. At one time, it had been planned to hold two conferences, one of the Entente allies and their defeated enemies to deal with immediate matters and a second, at which all powers, including neutrals, would be represented, to deal with more long-term matters. In fact, the great powers could not agree on the details of such an arrangement, with the result that it ended up as a single meeting. Although the treaty was formally signed at Versailles, little discussion took place there; rather, it was undertaken in Paris itself, largely at the Quai d'Orsay, where the French Foreign Office was situated. In all, there were thirty-two states represented, of whom twenty-seven attended the first plenary session on 18 January. Thereafter, there were only a few more full sessions (eight in the first five months) and most of these were purely formal. The bulk of the detailed work was therefore done by the fifty-eight commissions and committees set up to deal with specific matters. All minor powers who hoped to benefit from the treaty had to submit their claims in writing and then appear before the Council to explain them, a time-consuming operation but an unavoidable one. The Council oversaw all the detailed commissions. It at first consisted of ten members—the Prime Ministers and Foreign Ministers of 'the belligerent powers with general interests', namely, France, Britain, America, Italy and Japan. The foreign ministers later split off to form their own council, and by the end of April both Italy and Japan had left the conference, at least temporarily.

The first matter to be discussed was Wilson's Point 14—the establishment of the League of Nations. That this came to the fore was a personal triumph for Wilson, who saw that it underlay all other negotiations. This belief was not shared by his colleagues—Clemenceau was sceptical and Lloyd George was keen to see it kept separate from the treaty itself. It was decided to form a commission to draw up its details and constitution. Wilson became chairman of this, and then, in the middle of February, returned to America. At the same time, Lloyd George went back to London. When they returned in late March, they joined Clemenceau and Orlando in drawing up the bulk of the terms that affected Germany. There was considerable disagreement over this. Clemenceau was under pressure to win the separation of the area on the east bank of the Rhine from Germany and to take the Saar area with its coalfields. He was opposed in this, and eventually forced to accept other forms of security *(see page 188)*. Wilson also opposed his colleagues' demands for compensation, and Italy's claims for land in Dalmatia (a dispute that caused the Italian delegation to go home from 23 April to 6 May). By 7 May the bulk of terms *(see below)* were agreed on and were presented to the German delegation, which objected vigorously that they were not in keeping with the Fourteen Points to which they had agreed. The Council made a few minor alterations and, despite obvious hostility to the terms, the German government decided that they had to be accepted. Their only resistance was to scuttle the entire fleet, which had been taken to Scapa Flow, rather than let their enemies take possession of it. This was done on 21 June, and a week later the treaty was formally signed in the Hall of Mirrors at the Palace of Versailles—where Wilhelm I had been crowned Kaiser in 1871.

(c) The terms of the treaty of Versailles

The final version of the treaty ran to over 200 pages and 440 clauses, including the constitution of the League of Nations. Some of its terms were exceptionally detailed, arranging for transfers of territory. Others were wholly surprising, including provision for the return of astronomical instruments to China, of an African chieftain's skull to Britain and of the leaves of a van Eyck triptych to the University of Louvain. In this section, I have made no attempt to deal with the clauses in the order in which they appeared in the treaty, but rather to pick out the most significant matters in logical order.

The French delegation had to accept a compromise on the issue of security. Foch, putting the most extreme viewpoint, had proposed permanent German disarmament and a Rhineland Republic. Ultimately, it was decided that the West bank and an area fifty kilometres wide on the East bank should become a demilitarized zone. The Entente powers would man the Western bank and the bridgeheads until 1930. In addition, Britain and America gave France a guarantee that they would come to her aid the moment she was attacked by Germany. In the event, the American Senate refused to accept this agreement, and Britain's promise, which had been dependent on America, lapsed too. Consequently, France's search for security was to continue into the 1920s *(see page 241)*. The Saar Basin was to be held by an Inter-Allied force for fifteen years (for the first five of which France was to receive the coal mined there). In addition, France would be protected by restrictions being placed on the size of German armed forces. The army was to be limited to 100 000 men, a quarter of what the British general staff had suggested, and these men were to serve twelve years, thus preventing the establishment of trained men available as reserves. Limitations were also placed on the size and number of guns. The navy was to be limited to six battleships of over 10 000 tons, six light cruisers and twelve destroyers and motor torpedo boats. No submarines or military aircraft were to be built, and the Heligoland base was to be destroyed. The victorious powers explained that these restrictions were imposed 'in order to render possible the initiation of a general limitation of the armaments of all nations'—a general limitation that was never to take place.

Territorial changes occupied a large part of the treaty *(see Map 23)*. France received Alsace and Lorraine, and with them 2 million people and three-quarters of Germany's iron resources. Germany also gave up Eupen, Moresnet and Malmedy to Belgium and Northern Schleswig to Denmark. Her colonies were confiscated and put in the care and control of the victorious powers until such time as they were ready to become independent. This was known as the 'mandate' system, and by it the League of Nations was to oversee the activities of the controlling powers. As well as her colonies, Germany was also forced to surrender her trading rights in Morocco, China, Siam and Equatorial Africa. On her eastern border she had to give up land to the newly independent Poland, created in part also from Russia and Austria-Hungary. Poland had also, by Point 13, been promised access to the sea. This made it extremely difficult to draw a boundary, since the population of that area, from Danzig in the North to Silesia in the South, was mixed. Consequently,

Map 23 Territorial changes after World War I

West Prussia and Posen, both of which contained many Prussians, were given to Poland, thus repudiating for Germans the right to self-determination that was so assiduously applied to other peoples. In other areas it was agreed to hold plebiscites to decide whether they should go to

189

Poland or Germany; as a result, Allenstein and Marienwerder were left in East Prussia, and thus remained part of Germany, while the future of Silesia was not decided until 1921 *(see page 210)*. Danzig presented the greatest problems as it was a largely German town but most of the surrounding area was Polish. It was also at the mouth of the Vistula, which was the key to Polish trade. Ultimately, Lloyd George's proposal that the city should be put under League of Nations control with its foreign policy decided by Poland was accepted as a compromise (a similar arrangement for League of Nations control was made for Memel). As a result of the construction of Poland, Germany lost some 2 million subjects and a wealth of minerals, as well as having one part of their state—East Prussia—separated from the rest by a part of Poland known as the Polish Corridor.

Part of the treaty was designed to make Germany pay for the war damage. The idea of the losing country paying an indemnity to the winner was not new. France had paid Germany 200 million francs in 1871. In the Fourteen Points, Wilson had stated the need to 'restore' Belgium and France and Germany's agreement to this suggested that she had accepted the principle of paying for damage caused. Three aspects of reparations were, though, peculiar. Firstly, the idea of linking the repayment to the idea of war guilt—admitting that it was one country's fault that the war started—was new. This was done by Article 231 of the treaty, the 'War Guilt Clause' which stated that 'Germany accepts the responsibilities of Germany and her allies for causing all the loss and damage to which the Allied and Associated Governments and their allies have been subjected as a consequence of the war imposed upon them by the aggression of Germany and her allies'. Secondly, it was unusual to leave the final sum unfixed. There was disagreement over Germany's capacity to pay; British financiers estimated Germany could pay £24 000 million, whereas the economist Maynard Keynes reckoned that £2000 million was the absolute maximum that could be paid. Lloyd George moaned 'What is a poor politician to do?' while Wilson declared himself 'not much interested in the economic subjects'. As a result, it was agreed to set up a Reparations Commission to decide on Germany's ability to pay. Thirdly, the amount to be paid was intended to cover not only direct damage but also less direct damage, such as the provision of pensions for war widows and orphans in Britain, thus making the total far larger than usual. Until the Reparations Commission drew up a final bill *(see pages 293, 363)*, the Germans were to pay five billion dollars before May 1921. All merchant ships of more than 1600 tons, half of those between 800 and 1600 tons and a quarter of the fishing fleet were to be handed over immediately, and an additional 200 000 tons of shipping was to be built for the Allies each year for the next five years. Other goods, such as coal and timber, were to be delivered to France, Belgium and Italy. The cost of the Allied occupation forced was to be borne by the German government. Such was the cost of 'the aggression of Germany and her allies'.

In fact, Article 231 was to be the source of enormous discontent in later years. So far as Allied leaders in 1919 were concerned, the War Guilt Clause was merely a technical device to justify their charging such an enormous amount. So far as the German people were concerned, and their leaders were keen to tell them, the clause fixed the guilt for the war on Germany in a moral way, and few Germans could stomach being told it was their fault. This interpretation was repeated so often and seemed so obvious that in the inter-war period most Europeans accepted it.

Finally, the 'war criminals' were to be punished. The Kaiser, who had fled to Holland, was to be extradited and tried by special tribunal 'for a supreme offence against international morality and the sanctity of treaties'. In fact, the Dutch government refused to hand him over, as to do so would contravene international law. The surrender of Germans who had violated the 'laws and customs of war' was required, and a long list of war criminals was drawn up. However, the mood of the German people was such that it proved quite impossible to arrest them. The ultimate irony came in 1925, when one of those on the list of war criminals, Hindenburg, was elected President of Germany.

2. The East European Settlements
(see Maps 1 and 34)

The settlement of Eastern Europe was bound to be complicated. The abdication of the last Habsburg Emperor, Karl, on 11 November 1918, led to the separation of Austria and Hungary. Both the new states claimed that they were not the successor to the Habsburg Empire and should not be treated as an aggressor nation as Germany had been, but ultimately both were held to be so and both were charged reparations. In the confused last months of the war, several of the nationalities of the Empire had declared their independence and, in early 1919, arrived in Paris to press their claims. The Entente leaders were all agreed on the need for such 'self-determination', but to put it into practice was to prove more complicated than had been imagined *(see page 195)*. Only one thing was sure—that in the case of disputes both Austria and Hungary would lose out to the new states.

(a) The treaty of St Germain
The treaty of St Germain was submitted to the Austrian government on 20 July 1919 but was not signed until 10 September. By it, the government of the new Republic was held to be the successor of the Empire and was therefore, like Germany, charged reparations and forced to limit her army to 30 000 men. Considerable territories had to be handed over to the new states, whose independence the Austrian government was forced to acknowledge. Bohemia and Moravia went to Czechoslovakia, Dalmatia and Bosnia-Herzegovina to Yugoslavia, and Galicia to Poland. In addition, Bukovina was handed over to Roumania and Trentino, the South

Tyrol and Istria, including the port of Trieste, to Italy. In all, the old Kingdom of Austria had lost over fifteen million of its people, and almost all its industrial area. The only route to prosperity seemed to lie in some kind of economic union with Germany, but this was specifically forbidden by the treaty, unless the council of the League of Nations gave its consent.

(b) The treaty of Trianon

The treaty of Trianon was signed between the Entente leaders and the Hungarian government of Admiral Horthy on 4 June, 1920. No previous settlement was possible because of the frequent changes of government and the continued war between Hungary and Roumania *(see page 217)*. By the treaty, the new Hungarian government was also held to be a successor to the Habsburg government, and was treated as such. She was to pay reparations, limit her army to 35 000 men and hand over war criminals. Like Austria, she was forced to hand over territory to her neighbours, so that in all the old Kingdom lost almost three-quarters of its territory and more than 60% of its people. Slovakia and Ruthenia were given to the new state of Czechoslovakia; Croatia, Slovenia and part of the Banat went to Yugoslavia and Roumania received the rest of the Banat, Transylvania and a part of the Hungarian plain. In addition, Burgenland, the western-most part of the old Kingdom, was given to Austria as it was predominantly German—a decision that was to keep the two new Republics at odds for several years.

(c) The treaty of Neuilly

On 27 November 1919 the Bulgarian government signed the treaty of Neuilly. By it, she surrendered four areas of Northern Macedonia to Yugoslavia, Dobrudja to Roumania, and Western Thrace to Greece, thus losing her Aegean coastline. In addition, she was to pay reparations amounting to almost half a million dollars and limit her army to 20 000.

(d) The treaties of Sèvres and Lausanne

The settlement with Turkey was complicated by the revolutionary changes in Russia, which had previously had claims to Constantinople and parts of Turkey, and by the emergence and ultimate success of the nationalist movement of Mustapha Kemal. In addition, in May 1919 a Greek army invaded Smyrna and an Italian army landed in Anatolia, both of which sought to make gains at the expense of the obviously crumbling government of the Sultan. In August 1920 the Sultan accepted the treaty of Sèvres, by which he gave up all claims to non-Turkish territory. Consequently, the kingdom of the Hijaz became independent, Syria became a mandate of France and Palestine, Iraq and Mesopotamia became mandates of Britain. Armenia was to become independent and Greece received the area round Smyrna (for five years). Eastern Thrace and all the Turkish islands in the Aegean except Rhodes and the Dodecanese, which went to Italy. The Straits were to become international territory and to be demilitarized.

These terms were, however, overthrown as the result of the revival of a Turkish nationalist movement. This received a tremendous boost from the Greek invasion of Smyrna, which was seen as a great insult to national pride. Led by Mustafa Kemal, the nationalists demanded that the Western leaders should guarantee Turkey's frontiers—the Greeks should leave Smyrna and Armenia should remain a part of Turkey. In March 1921, Kemal signed a treaty with the new Soviet government to settle the Russo-Turkish border in the Caucasus, and then turned on the Greeks. By August 1922 he had defeated them and new negotiations took place at Lausanne. By the new treaty, of July 1923, Greece returned Eastern Thrace and two Aegean islands, Imbros and Tenedos, to Turkey. The Straits were to remain demilitarized, but Turkey gained the right to close them to enemy warships in the time of war. The foreign supervision of the Turkish finances was ended and the 'capitulations', the special privileges for foreign governments and individuals, were to be ended. On the one hand the Lausanne settlement can be seen as the first realistic attempt to solve the problem of Turkey by establishing a genuinely Turkish state; but on the other hand it can be seen as the first victory for a leader prepared to use force to get his way over the weakness of the Western powers.

3. Bibliography

Most of the standard textbooks have adequate sections on the peace settlement, but for more detail there are two units in the Open University *War and Society* course—Unit 18 'Collection of Nineteenth and Twentieth Century Documents Part II' and Unit 19 'Between Two Wars'—and a Heath Series booklet *The Versailles Settlement* edited by I.J. Lederer (published by Harrap). It is largely because of the availability of these works that no documents section had been included in this chapter. There is also '*Peacemaking 1919*' by H. Nicholson (Methuen, 1964) which provides a first hand account of the Conference and the most famous critique of the treaty of Versailles, *The Economic Consequences of the Peace* by J.M. Keynes (Macmillan, 1919).

4. Discussion Points and Exercises

A   *This section consists of questions that might be used for discussion (or written answers) as a way of expanding on the chapter and testing understanding of it:*
1   What influences would you expect the war aims of both sides to have on the peace negotiations?
2   How realistic were the ideas behind Wilson's Fourteen Points?
3   Which of the world leaders at the Conference was likely to be most influential?
4   What were the advantages and/or disadvantages of discussing the League of Nations at the start of the Conference?
5   How fair were the terms relating to German disarmament?

6 What problems were likely to arise from the territorial adjustments made to Germany?

7 Was Article 231 necessary?

8 What would the likely reaction of Austria and Hungary to their treaties have been?

B *This section examines in greater detail some of the problems and reactions to the treaties:*

1 It is likely that, in discussion, Wilson's Fourteen Points would have come in for some criticism. If so, draw up an alternative list of 'Points' that might equally have served as the basis of the peace settlement.

2 Put yourself in the position of (a) a French and (b) a German newspaper editor on the day of the signing of the treaty. Write an editorial for your paper on the subject of the treaty.

3 Study the following motion for debate: 'This house believes that the German people were right in regarding the peace settlement as harsh and unfair'. Write a speech either supporting or opposing the motion.

C *Essay questions:*
Many approaches are possible here, so a range of possible titles is provided below:

1 'Far from making the treaty, Wilson in fact destroyed it'. Do you agree?

2 Was there any alternative to the policy of establishing a number of small states in Eastern Europe after the war?

3 'The inadequacies of the treaty of Versailles lay in the conflicts of the Big Three'. Discuss.

4 How justified were the terms of the treaty of Versailles in punishing Germany?

IX The Successor States 1919–39

(For map, see also page 8)

1. Introduction

The 'successor states' are those that 'succeeded' or replaced the Empires of Germany, Russia and Austria-Hungary in Eastern Europe—the new national states of Austria, Hungary, Yugoslavia, Poland and Czechoslovakia. It is also possible to include Finland, the Baltic States and Roumania under this definition, but these have been omitted, primarily for purposes of brevity but also because the history of Eastern Europe is confusing enough to the newcomer when confined to five states, let alone ten.

The chapter has been organized country by country, and within that in the familiar pattern of political history, economic history and foreign policy. This should facilitate contrast and comparison between the countries, and it is on these features that the student should concentrate.

All five states were based on the principle of self-determination and were born at the peace treaties after the Great War. The leaders, especially Woodrow Wilson, hoped that the problems of the nationalities that had beset the Habsburg monarchy could be solved by giving the different peoples the right to rule over themselves. In practice, this did not mean that *every* nationality had its own country, since there were so many nationalities scattered so far and wide *(see page 13)*. In effect it was the larger and more powerful nationalities who won their own states, often in conjunction with a second similar nationality. Thus Czechs and Slovaks joined together to form Czechoslovakia and Serbs and Croats to form Yugoslavia. Even in these cases, it was hoped that the creation of a 'national' state would solve the old problems *(see Map 24)*.

The Versailles peacemakers had other hopes too for the new states. Firstly, they intended that they should be, like themselves, democracies. The democratic powers had won the war, so the new states would replace the tyrranical autocracies with modern, democratic systems. Consequently, each state introduced a democratic constitution and government. The fortunes of democracy were to vary from state to state, but only in one—Czechoslovakia—was it still truly in existence by 1936. Secondly, the peacemakers hoped the new states would act as a 'cordon sanitaire' against the threatened advances of Bolshevism. The new rulers of Russia were preaching the gospel of world revolution, so the new states would act as the first line of defence against such a threat. At the same time, for France, the new states would form a part of a defensive system against Germany. These aims for the new states were to prove heavy burdens, especially by the 1930s when, it has been said, they became 'merely chess pieces shifted by the great powers'.

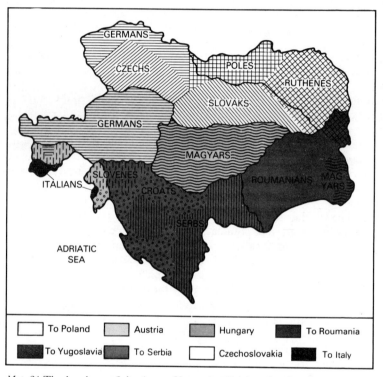

Map 24 The break-up of the Austro-Hungarian Empire, showing the new states and locations of main nationalities

There were, however, differences between the new states. On the one hand there were the 'victor' powers, who had declared their independence before the end of the war and had been invited to participate in the peacemaking. This was the case for Poland, Czechoslovakia and Yugoslavia. In contrast, Austria and Hungary were not victors but rather 'victims' of the Great War. Their creation had not been wanted by their people and the terms of the peace treaties they had to sign were widely resented. While victors were, in general, to seek the maintenance of the arrangements made in 1919, the victims sought their revision. This division into two broad 'blocs' was to prove crucial to international relations, not just in Eastern Europe but throughout the world.

2. Yugoslavia

(a) Introduction

The state of Yugoslavia was constructed by the amalgamation of the Kingdom of Serbia, the semi-independent state of Montenegro and the Croatian, Slovenian and Dalmatian areas of the Habsburg Empire *(see Map 25)*. It therefore contained a variety of nationalities, and this variety provided the major problem for the state in its early years. The two main races were the Serbs and the Croats, and their incompatibility caused endless crises in the 1920s. The Serbs, Orthodox by religion and in many respects an eastern people, were keen to establish a centralized state. The Croats, Roman Catholics and traditionally much more westernized, wanted a federal state in which the different nationalities, or at least the Croats, were free to make their own laws and follow their own customs. Both Serbs and Croats had little sympathy for the other nationalities. The Macedonians were given few rights, while in some areas Magyars and Germans were moved off their farms to provide for landless Serbs. The traditional Habsburg problem of the nationalities was, in the case of Yugoslavia, by no means solved by the creation of a nation state.

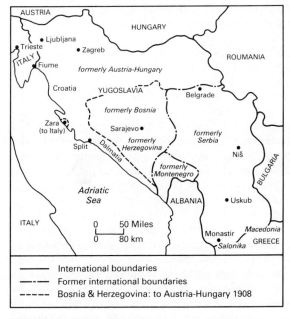

Map 25 The creation of Yugoslavia

(b) Political history

The state was officially created in December 1918 as 'the Kingdom of the Serbs, Croats and Slovenes', the name by which it was known until 1929. The different national groups had held a series of meetings in Zagreb, the

197

Croatian capital, in 1917–18, as a result of which a national council for the 'Yugoslav state' ('yugo' means southern) was formed. Yet when the united state was proclaimed, it was the Serbs who took the initiative, and their king, Peter, who became king of the new state. In fact, Peter's son, Alexander, ruled as regent for his sick and aged father until 1921, when Peter died and Alexander became king.

A Constituent Assembly met in 1920 to draw up a constitution for the new state. The majority of seats in this Assembly were won by the two Serbian parties, the Radicals and the Democrats, and the resulting constitution was largely their work. There was to be a single chamber Parliament, the 'Skupstina', elected by manhood suffrage. To ensure centralization, the country was divided into thirty-three districts, each of which was ruled by a prefect appointed by the central government. The Croats and Slovenes so disliked this arrangement that they boycotted the vote on the constitution, which was approved in their absence.

Politics in the 1920s were dominated by the hostility of the Croat Peasant Party, led by Strepan Radić, to the governments of the Serb Radical party, led by Nikola Pasić. The Croats complained that taxes were too high, that high rank in the army was barred to them and that the central government was overbearing. In 1923, the seventy Croat deputies declared that laws passed in Belgrade had no force in Croatia. In 1924 the Peasant Party was declared illegal as a result of its adherence to the Third International (communism was illegal in Yugoslavia). In 1925 Pasić changed his tactics and invited the Croats to join the government. They did so, but made little effort to co-operate; Radić, now a minister, even referred to his fellow ministers as 'swine' in the Skupstina, and in 1926 they left the government. After Pasić's death in December 1926, it became increasingly difficult to govern the country, as he had been the one politician of real stature. Eventually, in June 1928, a Montenegrin deputy, frustrated by the constant opposition of the Croats to all government proposals, let loose with a revolver in the Skupstina, killing two deputies and wounding three, including Radić. Seven weeks later, Radić died of his wounds. The Croats, more furious than ever, demanded federalization and formed their own government in Zagreb.

King Alexander regarded this as a threat to the unity of the kingdom. To counter it, he proclaimed a royal dictatorship and assumed personal responsibility for the government in June 1929. All political parties were banned, and the Skupstina was replaced by a legislative assembly with advisory powers. The state was renamed Yugoslavia, and the thirty-three districts were replaced by nine larger provinces. Technically, the dictatorship was lifted in 1931, when two political parties were to be allowed, and the party winning most votes would receive two-thirds of the seats. As voting was to be public and oral, and as the government named the candidates, this relaxation did little to please the opposition. The Croats maintained their hostility, and in 1932 there were serious revolts in the Lika. There were plans for these to lead to the declaration of a Croat Republic. Mussolini sent troops to Istria to support this, and only when Alexander told Mussolini that he would regard the proclamation of a republic as a declaration of war by Italy did the revolt subside.

In October 1934 King Alexander was assassinated by a Macedonian revolutionary as he walked along the quayside in Marseilles with the French Foreign Minister, Louis Barthou, who also died. The killer was working with Croats based in Hungary, and their arms had come from Italy. The assassination therefore led to a threat of war between Yugoslavia and Hungary. This was referred to the League of Nations and led to a number of Croats being deported from Hungary. Alexander was succeeded by his eleven-year-old son, Peter II (1934-45). Three regents ruled on his behalf, the senior being his dead father's cousin, Prince Paul. Paul allowed political parties again in 1935, but appointed his own Prime Minister, Milan Stoyadinovič, and was able to keep control. The Croats even won their demands in August 1939 when the state was reorganized on federal lines and six Croats joined the government. However, Paul's government was increasingly identified with the fascist powers, primarily as a result of his foreign policy, although his personal views and internal policies were such that Count Ciano, Italian foreign minister, referred to Stoyadinovič, as follows: 'If he is not a fascist by virtue of an open declaration of Party Loyalty, he is certainly one by virtue of his conception of authority, of the state and of life.'

(c) Economic history
Yugoslavia's economy was dominated by problems. Firstly, most of the country, and especially Serbia, had been at war from 1912 to 1918. Not only were large areas devastated as a result, but also the government was faced by the costs of war debts and reconstruction. Secondly, the country was almost entirely agricultural. In 1930, over 10 million of the 14 million inhabitants derived their living from agriculture. Such industry as there was provided only for the home market, in such fields as textiles and food canning. Thirdly, the new state boundaries disrupted a number of traditional trade routes. For example, Croatia had traded mainly with Hungary, while Macedonia's links had been with the Southern Balkans and Turkey. There was not even a direct railway line from Zagreb to Vienna. The new boundaries meant at least increased tariffs, and, in cases where successor states were hostile to each other, no trade at all.

Despite these problems, there was considerable recovery in the Yugoslav economy in the 1920s. Timber, eggs, pigs and maize, the chief agricultural products, all obtained high prices abroad. Foreign capital, from France, Britain and Czechoslovakia, was received in plenty and some heavy industry, notably steel, was developed. Good harvests were rewarded with high prices, and between 1924 and 1926 there were even export surpluses. As long as world agricultural prices remained high, the Yugoslav economy was safe.

Equally, though, the collapse of world food prices after 1929 wrecked the economy. The depression brought with it industrial unemployment, poverty among farmers who owned their own land, government cuts and sacked civil servants—a pattern that was to become all too familiar in Eastern Europe. The government was forced to look to a wealthy great power for help in recovering. At first, Yugoslavia looked to her ally of the 1920s, France. However, France's links with an attempt to restore the Habsburg monarchy in 1935 and her own problems in the mid-thirties led Prince Paul to look elsewhere. Italy would have been a suitable trading partner, but Mussolini's links with Croatian separatists and the imposition of League of Nations sanctions in 1935 *(see page 278)* made her less attractive. Consequently, both Alexander and Paul looked to Germany, whose own economy seemed strong and who offered favourable terms. Trade agreements were signed in 1934 and in 1936 *(see page 201)* and the quantity of trade between the two increased correspondingly. In 1929, 16% of Yugoslavia's imports came from Germany and 9% of her exports went there; corresponding figures for 1938 were 39% and 42%.

(d) Foreign policy

Inevitably, the collapse of the great empires and the creation of new states led to boundary disputes. Both Yugoslavia and Greece claimed parts of Salonika, a conflict that continued until 1926 when a free zone was created and reinforced by a treaty of friendship in 1929. Yugoslavia's conflict with Bulgaria, whose origins lay in the Balkan Wars *(see page 139)*, simmered on until 1937, when Germany put pressure on Bulgaria to surrender her claims to Macedonia and sign a treaty of friendship.

Yugoslavia's relations with the other successor states were more friendly. Her chief allies were Czechoslovakia and Roumania, with whom alliances were made in 1920 and 1921 respectively, thus forming the so-called 'Little Entente' *(see page 204)*. Although she remained cool towards Austria and Hungary, she signed a treaty of friendship with Poland in 1926 and in 1934 was a signatory to the Balkan Pact, by which Yugoslavia, Greece, Roumania and Turkey agreed to act together in defence.

The problem of relations with the great powers perplexed Yugoslavia as much as the other successor states. On the one hand, she needed their friendship in time of trouble and relied on their economic assistance. On the other hand, she did not wish to become so enmeshed with one great power that her independence and freedom of action were threatened. This was the critical problem that faced all the successor states, and was inevitably posed by the nature of their creation after the Great War. The western powers had intended them to become their clients, but the newly independent powers were keen to avoid this. Poland and Czechoslovakia joined with France in the early 1920s *(see page 241)*, but Yugoslavia was faced with a choice between Italy and France. Geographically and economically, her obvious ally was Italy. However, relations between the two were soured by the dispute over the possession of Fiume *(see page 274)*. This was settled in 1924 by the Pact of Rome, by which Italy received Fiume and Yugoslavia Port Barros; at the same time, the two countries signed a treaty of friendship for five years. This was not renewed in 1929. By then the Yugoslav government had become fearful of Mussolini's intentions as he had established Albania as a client state and supported the Croat separatists. Instead, Yugoslavia looked to France, signing a treaty of friendship that was negotiated in 1926 and finalized in 1927. The treaty was not wholly welcomed, but was seen as the only alternative to encirclement by Italy.

The advent of the Nazis to power in Germany brought another shift in Yugoslav foreign policy in the 1930s. Before travelling to Marseilles in 1934, King Alexander had assured Hitler that he 'would not allow himself to be drawn into a combination against Germany', and Paul repeated this pledge. Paul's subsequent policy was based on three premises—that German friendship would bring economic benefits and protection against Italy; that Italian friendship would bring protection against too great German influence; and that the regimes of Germany and Italy, while harsh, had brought stability and prosperity to their countries. In 1934 a preliminary trade agreement was signed with Germany, to which a second was added in 1936. Then in 1937, shortly before a meeting of the Little Entente powers, a treaty was signed with Italy, by which each agreed to respect the others frontiers, to suppress terrorists and to increase trade. While the Little Entente was the obvious and virtuous way to peace and prosperity, its attractions were increasingly limited in comparison with the friendship of Germany and Italy.

When World War II broke out, Yugoslavia remained neutral. In 1941 Prince Paul announced its adherence to the Axis Pact. Two days later, on 27 March, Paul was overthrown by a coup led by General Mirkovic, and Peter II was made official head of state with a pro-Allied government led by General Simovic. Ten days later the Germans invaded the country and on 20 April occupied Belgrade, forcing the new government into exile.

3. Czechoslovakia

(a) Introduction

Czechoslovakia inherited both the best and the worst of the Austro-Hungarian Empire. Bohemia had been the major industrial area of the monarchy, giving the new state more chance of prosperity than the other new states. However, the boundaries of the new state also contained a wide variety of different nationalities. Of the 13½ million people, less than 9 million were Czechs and Slovaks while 3¼ million were Germans, ½ million Ruthenes and 1 million were Magyars. There were also large minorities of Poles and Jews. This mixture resurrected the traditional problems—relations between the two ruling nationalities and between them and the minorities *(see Map 24)*.

(b) Political history 1918–36

The Czechoslovak state came into being in Paris in October 1918 when a Provisional Government was formed. Thomas Masaryk was its President and Eduard Benes its foreign minister—these two were to dominate the politics of the inter-war era. When the separate Slovak National Council pledged its support to this Provisional Government, the united state of Czechoslovakia was born.

From then until the crisis of 1938, Czechoslovakia was the only example of what the Big Three had hoped for in Eastern Europe—a constitutional democracy, based on a land-owning peasantry and allied to the Western Powers. The assembly that was elected in 1919 drew up a constitution and redistributed the land. Estates of over 250 hectares were forbidden, and the peasants were given land in lots of twenty-five acres. The constitution of 1920 allowed for a President as head of state, to be elected every seven years, and with the power to choose and dismiss ministers. The two houses of representatives were to be elected by universal franchise and a secret ballot with proportional representation. The upper house was given little power and could not even delay measures approved by the lower.

The governments of the 1920s and 1930s were formed from the 'Petka', a coalition of the five main Czech political parties. Masaryk remained President until his resignation and death in 1935, when Benes, until then Foreign Minister, became President. The chief problem that they faced was that of the nationalities. The 1920 Language Law had made Czechoslovak the official language but allowed the nationalities to use their own language in courts and schools where they made up more than 20% of the population. However, the census taken to decide on the proportions in different areas was widely criticized, especially by the Magyars and Germans, who also claimed that they had lost more land and were barred from high office. During the 1920s, relations improved and in 1925 some Germans joined the government and remained members of it. A reform of 1927 reorganized the country into four 'lands'— Bohemia, Moravia-Silesia, Slovakia and Ruthenia—each with its own governor and provincial diet, and so provided a degree of decentralization.

The economic depression brought in its wake political problems that eventually led to the downfall of democracy in Czechoslovakia. The industrial areas of Northern and Western Czechoslovakia, predominantly German in population, were badly hit by unemployment. This brought increased support for the extremist Sudeten Nazi Party. At first, the government was in little danger; Nazi and other paramilitary uniforms were banned and, in 1932, some members of the party tried for treason. Events in Germany and continued economic distress led to increasing support for the party, now renamed the 'Sudetendeutsche Partei' and led by Konrad Henlein. During 1933 and 1934 it organized protests and demonstrations, and in the 1935 elections won forty-four seats, becoming the second largest party in the lower house. Press attacks on the government reinforced the party's complaints, and Henlein demanded equality and cultural freedom for the Germans. Then, in 1936, Henlein declared the loyalty of his party to National Socialism and demanded autonomy for his 'group', rejecting government concessions as 'empty promises'. As other nationalities—Poles, Magyars, Slovaks and Ruthenes—followed the German lead in demanding more from the government, Czech democracy looked increasingly endangered.

(c) Economic history
Czechoslovakia was the one successor state that had the makings of a flourishing economy. More than 80% of many of the industries of Austria-Hungary—linen, silk, hemp, glass and cotton—were sited in the boundaries of the new state. There were plentiful mineral resources in Silesia and Bohemia *(see page 18)*, which had been the centre of Austria-Hungary's heavy industries. Even Slovakia, a predominantly poor and mountainous area, had timber and paper works. Bohemia and Moravia both contained rich agricultural lands. With these advantages, Czechoslovakia managed to avoid both the inflation crises of 1919–23 and the dependence on foreign loans that beset the rest of Eastern Europe.

Consequently, the 1920s saw considerable expansion and prosperity. In 1925 Czechoslovakia was one of only three nations involved in the war that had regained and overtaken its 1913 levels of manufacture. New factories were opened and, protected by high duties on imported goods, markets were found both at home and abroad. As long as other countries could afford to purchase Czechoslovak industrial and agricultural products, property was assured.

The depression was therefore a shattering blow to Czechoslovakia's economy. The immediate reaction of the central European states was to increase tariffs and restrict amounts of imports. Demand for Czechoslovakian goods fell, and unemployment came to the industrial areas. The only social groups to avoid the worst effects of the depression—the very rich who returned to self-sufficiency and the very poor who were paid in kind—were few and far between in Czechoslovakia. Even worse, the major industrial areas were in the West—in the Sudetenland where the German minority lived.

(d) Foreign policy 1918–36
Czech foreign policy was dominated by three issues—relations with Poland, friendship with France and dependence on the Little Entente. To these can be added, in the 1930s, a fourth—fear of her great neighbours, Germany and Russia.

The borders drawn up at Versailles created friction with Poland. Both countries claimed the area around Teschen, which was occupied by Czech troops for a time, before it was divided by the Conference of Ambassadors in 1920. The town itself was awarded to Poland but the nearby coalfields and suburb of Freistadt to Czechoslovakia. Both also claimed small areas in the Tatra mountains—Orawa and Spits, both of which were eventually divided. During the mid-1920s, the two countries drew closer together, signing three agreements in 1925 to settle outstanding disputes. However, Pilsudski was a long-time opponent of Czechoslovakia, and once he came to power in Poland *(see page 207)* there was little hope of further agreement.

Czechoslovakia signed treaties with both the great power 'patrons' of Eastern Europe, Italy and France, in 1924. The treaty with Italy did not commit either country to support the other, whereas that with France stated that each should help the other to defend the status quo. Moreover, it was supported by a treaty of Mutual Guarantee signed in 1925. This formed a part of the Locarno agreements *(see page 369)* and stated that France would guarantee Czechoslovakia's frontiers while Germany promised that any disputes over the frontier would be submitted for peaceful arbitration rather than by violence. This alliance with France provided one cornerstone of Czech security in the 1920s.

The other was provided by the 'Little Entente', of which Czechoslovakia can be seen as the originator and leading member. She had co-operated with Yugoslavia in some of the negotiations of 1919, especially in opposition to the restoration of the Habsburg monarchy. To this end, they signed a treaty in August 1920 promising mutual assistance in the event of attack by Hungary or an attempt at restoration. When, in 1921, ex-emperor Karl appeared in Hungary to try to regain his throne, Czech troops were mobilized and Yugoslav reserves called up—moves which helped to force Karl to back down. Also in 1921, a Defensive Convention was signed by Czechoslovakia and Roumania (and by Yugoslavia and Roumania), thus forming the tripartite 'Little Entente' (a title first coined by a Hungarian journalist as a term of derision). The Entente was subsequently strengthened, most notably in 1929 when the treaties became automatically renewable and the first joint military conference was held, and in 1933 when a Permanent Council and Secretariat were formed and it became 'an international community with a distinct personality'. Throughout, Benes was the leading advocate of the system as the basis of Czechoslovakia's defence and prosperity, although he was increasingly aware of Yugoslavia's unreliability.

The advent of Hitler and the simultaneous emergence of the 'Sudetendeutsche Partei' threatened to show up the weakness of the Czech security system. It was therefore bolstered by an agreement with the Soviet Union in 1935 which provided for mutual consultation in the event of a threat of war against either and a promise by each 'immediately to give the other aid and assistance' if attacked. This agreement was only to come into effect if France also came to the aid of the country attacked. 1938 was to prove the importance of this condition.

(e) The end of Czechoslovakia 1937–9

The Czech government continued to oppose the rise of the 'Sudetendeutsche Partei' by force. In October 1937 a meeting at Teplitz was broken up by the police. Henlein replied by encouraging his supporters to further violence, to such an extent that elections had to be postponed and public meetings forbidden. Hitler's speech of 20 February 1938, in which he promised protection to Germans living outside the Reich, provided further encouragement. On 24 April the 'Sudetendeutsche Partei' held its annual conference at Karlsbad, where Henlein made eight demands of the government—the chief of these were for self-government for Germans in an area to be defined, and protection for other Germans. Germans were also to have 'full freedom to profess German nationality and the German world outlook'. The government appealed to France to assist in the maintenance of the status quo, but both France and Britain encouraged Benes to give way to the Sudeten demands. There is some evidence that had he given way at this time, Hitler would have put pressure on Henlein to be satisfied, thereby at least postponing the destruction of the state. Hitler told Mussolini on 6 May that 'cantonization' (i.e. division into semi-independent areas) 'might put off the solution for several years'. Benes chose not to. He issued the Nationalities Statute, promising 'self-government for the minorities and their proportional employment by the state'. He also mobilized some troops and sent them to the border, on the strength of rumours of an impending invasion. The rumours were false, and Hitler, furious at the claims that he had been forced to abandon invasion, issued the directive: 'It is my unalterable decision to smash Czechoslovakia by military action in the near future'. 1 October was fixed as the latest date for this.

Throughout the summer, the Sudetens' campaign for autonomy, or rather separation, continued. The German press argued that the Czech government was threatening peace by its unreasonableness, Henlein visited London and Benes even promised to give way to the Sudeten demands, once they were set down in writing, which they never had been. The crisis reached its climax in September. On the 12th Hitler, for the first time, made an outright demand for self-determination for the Czechs. There were riots in the Sudetenland. Martial law was declared. Henlein 'fled' to Germany for safety. Since Hitler's tone was threatening and France and Russia had both guaranteed Czechoslovakia's frontiers, a general European war was threatened. To avert this, Chamberlain made his three visits to Hitler *(see page 390)* and, on 29 September, the Munich Conference was held.

The Conference was attended by the German, Italian, French and British leaders. Russia and Czechoslovakia were not represented. Hitler's demands were met—immediate surrender of the predominantly German areas (the Sudetenland) with the military and economic establishments therein unharmed. An international commission would supervise the evacuation of these areas by non-Germans during the period 1–10 October. It would also arrange for plebiscites in areas where there were large German minorities, a condition previously regarded by the British as 'unacceptable'. Britain and France guaranteed the remainder of Czechoslovakia against unprovoked attack, and Germany and Italy promised to join the guarantee 'once the question of the Polish and Hungarian minorities had been settled'.

As a result of this agreement, Germany was ceded 10 000 square miles and 3½ million people, of whom less than a million were German *(see Map 26)*. Poland was awarded Teschen and Hungary took South Slovakia. In all, Czechoslovakia lost some 5 million people (of a total of 15 million) and 16 000 square miles (of 45 000). Throughout, the Czech government had opposed the concessions and had kept its army mobilized. But the attitude of Britain and France made any kind of military action hopeless. On 5 October Benes, for long the target of the Germans, resigned and a new government was formed. Slovakia and Ruthenia (renamed Carpatho-Ukraine) were given autonomy and the state had a central government and three 'sub-governments'. The central government President was Emil Hacha and Rudolf Beran, an old opponent of Benes, was Prime Minister. He promised to co-operate with Germany and to this end, communism was banned and anti-semitic laws introduced.

Map 26 The dismemberment of Czechoslovakia

The final crisis in the life of Czechoslovakia was born of a dispute between the central and Slovak governments, and had little to do with Germany. On 9 March 1939 the Prague government dismissed the Slovak Prime Minister, Tiso, on the grounds that he was about to declare the independence of Slovakia. Czech troops went to Bratislava, and the Slovaks appealed to Hitler. Hitler decided the time for action had come, and he announced his support for, and protection of, an independent Slovakia. He also invited Hacha to Berlin, and on 15 March, told him that German troops were about to invade Czechoslovakia in large numbers. Hacha, with the destruction of his country as the only alternative, ordered his forces not to oppose the German advance. Bohemia–Moravia (the Czech lands) became a Protectorate within the German Reich, Slovakia an independent state 'under the protection of the Reich', and Ruthenia, already occupied by Hungarian troops, was ruled by a government chosen by Hungary.

4. Poland

(a) Introduction

Poland was the largest and most populous of the successor states, having a territory larger than Italy and a population of 27 millions. Of these, only 18 million were Poles, 4 million were Ukrainians, more than 2 million Jews, 1 million White Russians, 1 million Germans and a million others. An even more acute problem than this variety of nationalities was the hostility of Poland's neighbours. All of them—Germany, Lithuania, Russia and Czechoslovakia—were dissatisfied by the frontiers decided at Versailles. Consequently, Polish affairs were largely dominated by her relations with these powers.

(b) Political history

The formation of the state was extremely complicated. During World War I, Poland had been partly occupied by both the Central Powers and Russia, each of which had supported a provisional government. There was also a provisional government in Paris. Therefore when the Polish Republic was proclaimed on 3 November 1918 there were three potential governments. By January 1919 they had agreed on Marshal Joseph Pilsudski as provisional head of state (until a Constitution was approved) and Paderewski as Prime Minister and Foreign Minister.

The constitution was formally adopted in March 1921. It gave most power to the 'Sejm', or lower house, which had drawn it up. The deputies were concerned that Pilsudski, who had been a socialist revolutionary before the war, might try to establish a dictatorship. Consequently, the constitution gave little power to the President—he was not even able to dissolve Parliament. The actual consequence was not as intended— Pilsudski simply refused to become President. The constitution also allowed for an Upper House, but its power was limited to the delaying of legislation. The first 'Sejm' also introduced legislation to limit the size of agricultural holdings—sixty hectares in industrial areas, 100 in agricultural—but this was never passed and a more moderate law—180 hectares in agricultural areas—was approved in 1925.

The early years of the Republic were troubled. The chief problem was inflation *(see page 208)*, and the governments tried endless remedies, including the issue of a new currency and the imposition of wage restraints. Each attempted remedy aroused the opposition of some members of the ruling coalition—with fourteen parties in the 'Sejm' all governments were coalitions—so that Prime Ministers came and went with alarming frequency. Between 1919 and 1926 thirteen separate cabinets were formed, each of them resting on a coalition as shaky as the last. Not surprisingly, many people, especially among the armed forces, felt that democracy was creating more problems than it solved.

In 1926 Marshal Pilsudski decided to act. When he had refused the Presidency, he had retained the post of Chief of General Staff until 1923, when he refused to serve under Prime Minister Witos, leader of the

Peasant Party. He had then technically retired, but many Poles and many army officers still looked to his leadership. On 11 May 1926, the day after Witos formed his third Cabinet, Pilsudski published an attack on the new government. The next day he led three regiments into Warsaw; the government ordered the army to oppose them, but many of the troops deserted to Pilsudski and on 14 May Witos' government resigned. From then until his death in 1935 Pilsudski was in effect ruler of Poland, although he refused to serve as President and was only briefly Prime Minister (1926–8). For the rest of the time, from his positions as Minister of Defence and Inspector General of the Army, he ruled through his friends, President Ignatz Moscicki and Prime Minister Casimir Bartel.

Parliamentary government was effectively ended in 1930. Until then, the left-wing Parties, who had gained in the elections of 1928, opposed the government consistently in the 'Sejm', where Pilsudski's supporters held less than 30% of the seats. In 1930 Pilsudski dissolved the 'Sejm', had eighteen opposition leaders imprisoned and ordered fresh elections. In these, with the full support of the government and the army, Pilsudski's 'Non-party Bloc for Co-operation with the Government' won 247 seats, an absolute majority.

Pilsudski's death in 1935 did little to alter the de facto dictatorship. Shortly before his death a new constitution had limited the franchise for 'Sejm' elections and made Senators indirectly elected or nominated. The opposition boycotted the elections of 1935 in protest at this, so government supporters won a large majority. After Pilsudski's death, Moscicki remained President and the new head of the armed forces was Marshal Rydz-Smigly. Their government ignored the left's protests about high unemployment, and if anything introduced more right-wing policies. Anti-semitism, widespread in Tsarist days but ended by laws of 1927 and 1931, was reintroduced, and the government announced its intention to 'Polonize the minority nationalities'. When deputies elected an opponent of the government, Slawek, as leader of the 'Sejm', the government dissolved it and, in 1938, exerted considerable pressure to get its own supporters elected. Undoubtedly, many Poles were hostile to their government by this time, and civil war was a possibility.

(c) Economic history

From an unpromising start, the Polish economy recovered well by the late 1920s, but was then badly hit by the depression.

The majority of Polish people earned their living from farming. In most areas, farming methods were old fashioned and yields were low. Industry was confined to a few areas—only Upper Silesia, won in the plebiscite of 1921, was an extensive industrial area. During the early 1920s, inflation reached incredible heights, prices being multiplied by 2 500 000 (compared with 1 000 000 000 in Germany). The governments' attempted remedies—expenditure cuts, wage freezes and increased taxation—only worsened the plight of the poorer working people. There was also a rapid population increase throughout the twenties, reaching nearly ½ million per annum (1·7%). Although some of this was siphoned off through emigration, there were still more people to be fed each year. Consequently, small farms were divided again and again, so that by 1931 65% of all land holdings were less than five hectares.

Nevertheless, the mid-1920s saw some industrial expansion. American gold was generously lent, allowing Poland to obtain foreign loans and balance her budget. The British miners' strikes also helped, allowing Poland to sell her coal to previously British markets, most notably in Scandinavia. The new port of Gdynia was built to avoid Polish goods having to go through Danzig, as a result of which more and more trade was sent by sea. Between 1925 and 1928 Polish industrial production rose by 38%, the greatest increase in Europe, excluding Russia, in the period.

Poland remained primarily dependent on the export of agricultural goods, especially crops, for a favourable balance of trade. She was therefore hard hit by the slump in world food prices after 1929. To combat this, imports were reduced, tariffs raised and the familiar pattern of industrial unemployment and rural poverty followed. The government encouraged the building of new factories to produce goods that were previously imported, but there was simply insufficient government money available to counter a widespread fall in the standard of living. This in turn led to the government being more and more unpopular, and to the use of suppression to end this opposition.

(d) Foreign policy

Almost all the demands of the Polish delegation were met by the treaty of Versailles. They were promised 'all territories inhabited by indisputably Polish populations' and 'a free and secure outlet to the sea'. These were both provided for, though, on Lloyd George's insistence *(see page 190)*, Danzig was put under League of Nations control. Two areas of East Prussia—Allenstein and Marienwerder—were returned to Germany as the result of plebiscites *(see page 190)*, and the fate of Silesia was left undecided. Nevertheless, Poland's wishes were basically satisfied, leaving her neighbours dissatisfied. The solution of these disputed frontiers was to occupy several years.

The most serious quarrel was with Russia. The Big Three had fixed Poland's eastern frontier on the Curzon Line *(see Map 27)*. The Poles demanded that the boundary of 1772 should be restored, and in an effort to win this invaded Russia in April 1920. Polish and Ukrainian troops, led by Marshal Pilsudski, rapidly overran the Ukraine and reached Kiev. The Russians counter-attacked and by the end of June had reached the outskirts of Warsaw. French troops under General Weygand now came to the aid of the Poles and by late September had forced the Russians back over the river Nieman. An armistice was signed and in March 1921 the treaty of Riga was concluded, by which Poland gained about 100 miles of Russian territory and three million people.

A plebiscite to determine the future of Upper Silesia was held in March 1921. Overall, the voting was 60% in favour of Germany and 40% for Poland; however, there was no clear geographical division between the groups, as Germans tended to dominate the towns and Poles the country-side. The result therefore referred to a committee of experts, while irregular Polish troops under Korfanty tried to settle the matter by force. The area was subsequently divided between the two countries *(see Map 28)* to the mutual dissatisfaction of each—Germany received three times as much land as Poland, but Poland received fifty-three coal mines to Germany's fourteen.

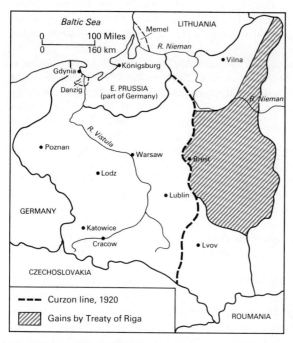

Map 27 The creation of Poland

The area around Teschen was disputed with Czechoslovakia *(see Map 28)*. Fighting there in 1919 was supposed to be ended by a plebiscite, but neither country would agree to this. In July 1920 the Conference of Ambassadors ended the argument by dividing the area.

The town of Vilna was disputed with Lithuania. During the war with Russia in 1920, it was seized by the Polish general Zeligowski and there-after remained a part of Poland. The Lithuanians made constant efforts to win back the town, and both governments refused to accept any compromises offered by the League. Eventually, in 1923, the League recognized Poland's occupation of the city, and a permanent scar was left on Polish–Lithuanian relations.

With such hostile neighbours, Poland inevitably sought security further afield. In February 1921 a treaty of alliance was signed with France, which provided that each should come to the aid of the other in the event of being attacked. This was followed by an alliance with Roumania, providing for mutual aid in the event of attack by Russia, but Poland's refusal to promise assistance in the event of war between Roumania and Hungary led Roumania to look instead to Yugoslavia and Czechoslovakia. Consequently, the alliance with France remained the basis of Polish security, and France supplied loans for reconstruction and rearmament in the 1920s.

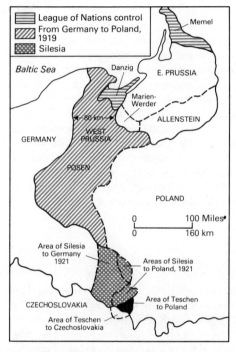

Map 28 Poland's Western frontier

However, especially after the treaty of Rapallo in 1922 *(see page 296)* and the Locarno settlement, the government increasingly felt that France alone was sufficient. Pilsudski's Foreign Minister, Beck, personally suspected France's willingness to act and felt that Poland had been sold out by the Locarno treaties—France had secured her own frontiers by *not* guaranteeing the eastern ones *(see page 369)*. The recovery of the Soviet Union posed a possible threat to the lands previously gained from Russia, and a non-aggression pact signed in 1932 gave Poland some assurance that her eastern frontier would not be threatened by attack. Hitler in Germany posed a far greater threat, especially after Danzig came under Nazi control in 1933. Pilsudski contemplated an invasion of

Danzig, but France advised against it and Hitler's tone was placatory. In fact, largely through Beck's influence, a ten-year non-aggression pact was signed with Germany in 1934. Although the Polish government realized that Hitler had not abandoned his plans for the annexation of Eastern Europe, they hoped to gain time and, as Beck said, 'perhaps induce France to take more account of Poland'. In fact, the major effect of the pact was to breach the system of combined East European opposition to Hitler.

German friendship proved of brief advantage in 1938. In the aftermath of the Munich agreement, Poland demanded, and received, the area around Teschen from Czechoslovakia.

However, after the Nazi take-over of Czechoslovakia in March 1939, Hitler changed his tune. He demanded that Danzig should be given to Germany and that Germany should be allowed to build a road and railway across the Polish corridor, in return for a guarantee of Poland's frontiers and a renewed non-aggression pact. These demands were rejected, and instead Poland won a guarantee of aid in the event of attack from both Britain and France. In reply to this, Hitler renounced the 1934 non-aggression pact and encouraged Nazis in Danzig to further violence. Frontier incidents became commonplace, and German troops arrived in Danzig. In August, the Nazi leader in Danzig, Albert Forster, announced 'the hour of deliverance is near', and the signature of the Nazi–Soviet Pact *(see page 392)* removed the last restraint on Hitler's attitude towards Poland. Britain repeated her pledges to Poland, while Hitler repeated his demands; on 1 September, German forces attacked Poland.

5. Austria

(a) Introduction
Austria was the most unfortunate creation of the peacemakers. The industrial centres of the old Empire were now in Czechoslovakia, leaving a predominantly agricultural country with a semi-industrial capital— Vienna—where a third of the 8 million population lived. The new boundaries made trade difficult, and there was constant political conflict between the socialist capital and the more conservative countryside. At least the age-old nationalities problem was absent, but it had been replaced by a new nationality problem, in that the vast majority of Austrians were Germans and desired union with Germany itself, not only for political but also economic ends. But this 'Anschluss' was forbidden by the treaty of St Germain *(see page 191)*.

(b) Political history
On armistice day, the last Emperor, Karl, abdicated leaving a political vacuum until the meeting of the Constituent Assembly in February 1919. This assembly, in which the majority of seats were shared between the leftist Social Democrats and the conservative Christian Socials,

voted that Austria should be part of the German Reich. This she remained until the signing of the treaty of St Germain in September. As this forbade the union, the state's name was changed from 'German-Austria' to the 'Republic of Austria'. Even then, the issue of union was not over, for the provinces of Salzburg and Tyrol voted for union in 1921 and only Allied threats put an end to such talk. The Assembly also drew up a constitution. This gave limited powers to a President and included proportional representation for parliamentary elections. It was also federal, leaving considerable power with the separate provinces, the 'Lander'.

The first governments of the Republic were faced by acute economic problems. Food shortages and the flood of refugees into Vienna were helped by League of Nations emergency services. Prices rose twenty-fold, and further League aid, in the form of a loan of 650 million gold crowns, was needed. In May 1922, a Christian Social, Ignaz Seipel, became Chancellor (Prime Minister) and set about the task of furthering economic recovery. In exchange for the League loans, he agreed to cuts in government expenditure, which led to the dismissal of nearly 100 000 public officials, and a renewed promise that Austria would not attempt to give up her independence—i.e. reunite with Germany—for at least twenty years. Seipel remained in office until 1929 (except during 1924–6), supported by a parliamentary coalition of Christian Socials and Pan-Germans, who gave up their desire for immediate 'Anschluss' in exchange for economic security and protection against a possible communist threat. At the same time, the government of Vienna remained in the hands of the Social Democrats, who introduced social welfare and housing schemes quite in contrast to the general economic stringency.

By the late 1920s there was open conflict between supporters of the left and right. Each had their own uniformed armies—the 'Heimwehr', technically local border guards, on the right and the 'Schutzband' on the left. In July 1927 demonstrations by Viennese workers following the acquittal of three right wingers for the alleged murder of two socialists led to eighty-five deaths and hundreds wounded. A general strike was called and in turn put down by the army. In 1928 the various local Heimwehr groups joined together to 'suppress ruthlessly any attempt to set up a Red Dictatorship'. Seipel resigned in 1929 and his successors had even less control over extremists; the Heimwehr announced their intention of holding a 'march on Vienna', and there were more deaths and injuries in a demonstration in Styria. Supported by Mussolini, the Heimwehr adopted a fascist programme including 'the rejection of democracy and Parliament' in 1930. The financial crisis of 1931 (*see page 214*) worsened the situation, while governments came and went with increasing frequency, five cabinets being formed between 1929 and 1932.

In May 1932 the Christian Social Engelbert Dollfuss formed a new Government. He tried to curb the extremists by banning both the 'Schutzband' and the Nazi party, to which Hitler retorted by fining any German who visited Austria a thousand marks. Dollfuss' supporters had a majority of only one in Parliament, making the passing of legislation difficult. He therefore announced that Parliament was dissolved while a new constitution was prepared by the government, which would rule by decree in the interim. He also proclaimed the creation of a paramilitary 'Fatherland Front' to replace the 'Heimwehr'. In secret talks with Mussolini he made plans for a government putsch to introduce an authoritarian regime pledged to keep Austria independent.

These plans were never fulfilled. In February 1934, following government searches for arms among workers in Linz, the 'Schutzband' ordered its members to 'actively resist the government'. There was considerable fighting in the countryside and in Vienna, where workers' flats were bombarded. In all, over 300 people died in three days of warfare. Many socialists were arrested, and the Social Democrat party was outlawed. On 1 May, the new constitution was introduced. It increased the powers of the Chancellor and planned for the introduction of a corporate state. However, these plans were not completed by the time of Dollfuss' death. In July 1934 he was shot and left to bleed to death by Nazis in an attempted coup. The coup was put down in a few days and a new government, led by Kurt Schuschnigg, was formed.

Schuschnigg's policies were in most respects similar to Dollfuss'. Conscription was reintroduced in 1936. Prince Stahremberg, leader of the 'Heimwehr', was removed from the Vice-chancellorship, and Schuschnigg proclaimed himself 'Führer of the Fatherland Front'. In 1936 he toyed briefly with the idea of restoring the Habsburg monarchy, but Britain and the 'Little Entente' powers made forceful protests. Despite Schuschnigg's apparently firm line, Nazi demonstrations continued, and 1938 was to show where the real power lay.

(c) Economic history

Austria was the worst affected of the successor states in both the economic crises of the inter-war era. In the inflation crisis, the value of the Austrian crown fell to one fifteen-thousandth of its pre-war value in 1922. The situation was only saved by the massive loan organized by the League of Nations and financed by Britain, France, Italy and Czechoslovakia. Even then, considerable hardship was caused by the need for salary cuts and dismissals to help balance the budget. Only in the later 1920s were there some signs of recovery—Seipel encouraged agricultural improvement and the building of hydro-electric stations (which reduced Austria's dependence on imported coal), while an increase in tourism provided welcome foreign capital.

The depression hit Austria at a time when political extremism has already begun. In an attempt to ease both the economic problems and reduce the political tension, the government announced, in March 1931, its plans for a customs union with Germany. This sent France and her allies into a flurry of activity, for it seemed to be the first step towards the dreaded 'Anschluss'. To 'encourage' Austria to think again, the French government withdrew their funds from the main Austrian bank, the

'Creditanstalt'. This bank financed many industries, the Savings Bank and the city of Vienna's reserves; it now announced that it no longer had sufficient capital to pay its creditors, and was taken over by the government's National Bank. Creditors then began to withdraw their funds from this bank. Only France had the capital available to support the National Bank, and she demanded a renunciation of the customs union *and* foreign control of Austria's finances in return for her support. The Bank of England provided the National Bank with a short-term loan to overcome the immediate problem, but by September the government had agreed to withdraw their plans for the customs union. Instead, in July 1932, Austria accepted a loan of 300 million schillings from France, and agreed to French control of her finances and to make no effort to unite in any way with Germany for twenty years. In the meantime, the depression had had its usual effects on the bulk of the population—widespread unemployment and impoverishment.

(d) Foreign policy

In the early years of the Austrian Republic, the issue of Anschluss dominated foreign affairs. Its overwhelming economic advantages, together with the fact that it fulfilled the principle of self-determination that had been applied to the rest of Eastern Europe, persuaded most Austrians of its necessity and desirability. Even after it had been forbidden by the treaty of St Germain, many still hoped for a change of heart on the Allies' part. Therefore no agreements were made that might offend Germany or support the opponents of 'Anschluss'. The treaty of Lana was signed with Czechoslovakia in 1921, by which each agreed to neutrality and to respect the other's frontiers, and Austria received a loan. Even this was too much for the Pan-Germans, who withdrew their support for Schöber's government in protest at this tacit acceptance of the peace settlement. The treaty was not renewed in 1926. Consequently, Austria remained uncommitted during the 1920s. She could not look to France, since she led the victors not the victims, nor to Italy, who had committed treachery in 1915 by joining the Entente powers and who had then 'stolen' the South Tyrol. Even Hungary was not a suitable ally, for the two had disputed Burgenland, an area of Eastern Austria inhabited by Germans but formerly a part of the kingdom of Hungary. It had been given to Austria in the peace treaties, but occupied by Hungarian irregular forces in 1921 and finally settled by a plebiscite in December 1921, by which all but Oldenburg remained with Austria.

During the 1930s Austria's isolation was ended, and friendship with Hungary and Italy developed. Mussolini was keen to overcome Austria's hostility to Italy, and used the friendship of Hungary to do so. Hungary provided arms for the 'Heimwehr' and, in 1933, signed a commercial treaty with Austria. Thereafter, Dollfuss visited Rome several times, culminating in a trip in March 1934 (immediately after the near civil war) when the 'Rome Protocols' were signed by Austria, Hungary and

Italy. The three governments agreed to consult together on matters of mutual interest, to respect each other's independence and to trade together. Most notably, Austrian timber would be traded for Hungarian wheat. These agreements placed Austria firmly in the camp of the revisionist powers.

The attempted coup by Austrian Nazis in 1934 obviously highlighted relations with Germany. After it, Hitler was keen to reestablish the respectability of Nazism in Austria and made no protest when Schuschnigg's government pursued the assassins and dissolved some Nazi orgnizations. He then sent von Papen to Vienna to negotiate the future relations between Austria and Germany, and personally announced that he had no intention of annexing Austria. The negotiations reached fruition in a pact of July 1936, by which Germany recognized Austrian independence and Austria promised that her policy 'should always be based on principles corresponding to the fact that Austria had acknowledged herself to be a German State.' Even if the pact did not provide permanent security for Austria, it at least gave her time and its recognition of the Rome Protocols left Italy with some influence.

However, the continued activity of Austrian Nazis, and Hitler's public statements about Austria, alarmed Schuschnigg. During 1937 he approached both Czechoslovakia, with whom there had been some negotiations in early 1936, and Hungary, with a view to arming himself against Hitler. The approaches came to nothing and served only to infuriate both Hitler and the Austrian Nazis.

Hitler's active participation in Austrian affairs came to a head in 1938. Acting on the premise that Schuschnigg had broken the 1936 pact, Hitler summoned him to a meeting on 12 February, and there berated and abused him. His actual demands were much the same as before—the Nazi Seyss-Inquart should be Minister of the Interior and responsible for security. Schuschnigg agreed to this, but was now convinced that Hitler planned more. The latter's speech of 20 February, promising to protect Nazis outside the Reich had led to riots in Graz. Schuschnigg decided firm and fast action was needed. On 9 March he announced that three days later a plebiscite would be held to ask the people to vote for (or against) 'a free and German, independent and social, Christian and united Austria, for peace and work and equality for all who confess themselves loyal to People and Fatherland'. Put in these terms, and with the Fatherland Front's assurance that they would make certain the vote went the right way, Schuschnigg was confident of victory.

Hitler was furious and ordered his troops to be ready to march on 12 March. Göring was put in charge of negotiations, and he won from President Miklas both postponement of the plebiscite and Schuschnigg's regignation. Seyss-Inquart was appointed Chancellor, by which time German troops were on the march. Göring had ordered Seyss-Inquart to telegram for them to 'prevent bloodshed'. On 13 March Austria was proclaimed a 'province of the German Reich', a decision endorsed by a plebiscite of 10 April, in which over 99% voted in favour of the Union.

The opposition had already been rounded up (76 000 of them in Vienna alone) and Nazi policies introduced, most notably anti-semitism, the dissolution of Trade Unions and the introduction of public works.

6. Hungary

(a) Introduction
The Hungarian part of the Habsburg Empire had traditionally been dominated by Magyar landowners who owned huge estates on which grain was grown. After independence, the main theme of political life was the attempt of these landowners to keep control at the expense of the peasants and the more radical, fascist elements. In addition, the landowners had to cope with the opposition of the other nationalities, who made up almost half the 8 million population and, as before, resented Magyar domination.

(b) Political history
In November 1918 a Hungarian Republic was proclaimed with Count Michael Károlyi, a Magyar landowner, as President. He was immediately faced by an invasion in the North by Czechs and another in the East by Roumanians. In March 1919 he resigned in favour of a Socialist-Communist government, which was dominated by the Bolshevik Béla Kun. It was hoped that Kun's friendship with Lenin would bring Russian aid in the war against Roumania. No such help came, and the Western allies, keen to see the end of Bolshevism in Hungary, did nothing to stop the Roumanian army. In August 1919 Roumanian forces occupied Budapest and Kun and his colleagues fled. For several months thereafter there was no recognized government.

In these circumstances, Hungary fared badly at the Peace Conference. Austria, Yugoslavia, Czechoslovakia and, chiefly, Roumania won their claims against Hungary. 700 000 Magyars ended up in Slovakia, two million in Roumania and lesser numbers in Austria and Yugoslavia (*see page 197*).

Following Kun's departure, his enemies, in the form of troops led by Admiral Horthy, last commander-in-chief of the Austro-Hungarian Empire, took their revenge on all suspected Bolsheviks. Eventually, elections were held in January 1920. The Social Democrats boycotted these, in protest at Horthy's viciousness, and the new Parliament was dominated by the Smallholders Party (mainly medium and small farmers) and the conservative Christian Nationals. The Parliament declared that the acts of the Károlyi and Kun regimes were null and void, that King Karl had abdicated but that the monarchy continued to exist and that Horthy was to act as regent until the issue of the monarchy was finally resolved.

Throughout the 1920s the governments of Hungary were dominated by the question of revision of the treaty of Trianon. They were convinced of the need to revise the frontiers, and foreign policy was conducted with this end in view *(see page 220)*. In addition, many Magyars wanted to see the Habsburg monarchy restored to the throne. During 1921 King Karl made two attempts to regain his throne. The Prime Minister, Count Istvan (Stephen) Bethlen, was opposed to the restoration. Although conservative by nature, Bethlen feared the international repercussions of restoration. Consequently, Karl's second attempt was halted by Hungarian government troops and he was forced into exile in Madeira. On the orders of the British government, a Dethronement Act was passed to prevent a further attempt. When Karl died in April 1922, the hopes for restoration went with him, since his son was only eleven years old.

Thereafter, Bethlen was able to ensure the power of the conservative landowners. The franchise was revised, so that only 27% of the population were able to vote, and even then voting was open. Socialists were muzzled by a deal in which Bethlen agreed to release Union funds and imprisoned socialists in return for official Socialist support. There was some land reform, in that ½ million hectares (of a total land area of 8 million) were redistributed, but the promised second instalment was never released. While economic conditions improved, as they did during the 1920s, Bethlen was secure.

As elsewhere, the economic depression brought political change. Bethlen resigned in 1931. His successor, Count Gyula (Julius) Károlyi, was forced to make drastic cuts in government expenditure to satisfy the League of Nations, which had taken control of Hungary's finances. He resigned in September 1932 and was replaced by Captain Gyula Gömbös, a very different type of politician to the ultra-conservative landowners who preceded him. He was a radical right-winger, determined to restore the former boundaries of Hungary, using an alliance with Fascist Italy as the means to the end. One of his first actions was to visit Rome and sing the Duce's praises. Gömbös' extremism was curbed by the composition of his Parliament, which had been elected in 1931 on Bethlen's franchise. Horthy, still regent, only allowed fresh elections in March 1935, but at these Gömbös' supporters, despite a minority of votes, won 166 seats to the opposition's fifty-one. Thereafter Gömbös was freer to pursue his own policies, but only until his death on 6 October 1935—one week after a visit to Hitler in which he agreed 'to co-operate more closely with Germany'.

There followed three governments that each lurched away from, then towards, the fascists. The conservative Darányi formed the first. He tried to end extremism by a combination of repression and 'thunder stealing'; for example, legislation to limit the number of Jews in the professions was introduced. Nonetheless, the Hungarian National Socialist Party, led by Ferenc Szalasi, was founded in October 1937. Darányi's successor, Béla Imrédy, began by arresting Szalasi and seventy-two supporters. However, the Anschluss of March 1938 brought the Nazis as neighbours, and Imrédy's policies were more circumspect. More restrictions on the Jews were brought in, limiting their numbers in the professions and business, and he made friendly noises in Germany's direction. Imrédy also planned to launch a 'Movement', complete with banners and uniforms, but his enemies succeeded in bringing him down by discovering some Jews among his ancestors. The next Prime Minister was another conservative, Count Paul Teleki. He gave up the idea of a 'Movement', but did not withdraw Hungary from the anti-Comintern Pact. In addition, he kept to his predecessor's promise to withdraw Hungary from the League of Nations. He was also afraid to act against the Nazi Party, which won fifty-three seats in the elections of May 1939 (they previously had six). By the outbreak of war, the Hungarian government had truly tied itself in Nazi knots—knots that Teleki himself escaped by suicide in April 1941.

(c) Economic history

At the end of the war Hungary's distress was not as great as that of Austria, for she was at least self-sufficient in food. Nonetheless the invasions of 1919 destroyed communications and industry and thus created unemployment. The new boundaries removed the bulk of her raw materials and forced the disbandment of the army, while inflation on the grand scale was suffered during 1921–3.

During the 1920s the Hungarian economy made a considerable recovery from this sorry start. In 1924 she received a loan of 250 million gold crowns from members of the League in exchange for a promise to obey the treaty of Trianon and pay reparations. The loan encouraged the investment of private capital, which in turn facilitated the building of new factories, mines and roads. These provided employment and helped to relieve overpopulation in the countryside. With high protective tariffs, farmers and landowners prospered as long as there were buyers overseas. Industrial production almost trebled between 1921 and 1928, while the number of factory workers rose from 137 000 to 236 000.

There were, however, fatal flaws in the Hungarian economic structure. Almost all capital investment came from overseas, and she was forced to borrow more to repay the interest on existing loans. Almost all her exports were agricultural, so she was dependent on world agricultural prices for a favourable trade balance.

Consequently, when these prices fell in 1929 and the loans came to a halt, Hungary's economy was badly affected. The League was asked for help, and this led to extensive spending cuts and the consequent fall of Károlyi. The League kept contol of the budget until 1938. Meanwhile, the familiar economic and political repercussions followed, while the government looked to its strongest neighbour, Germany, for assistance. By 1938 40% of Hungary's foreign trade (both imports and exports) was conducted with Germany—more than double what it had been in 1929 *(see page 311)*.

(d) Foreign policy

The dire circumstances of Hungary at the end of the war have already been noted *(see page 217)*. The invasions by her neighbours forestalled any attempt to win more favourable boundaries by military action or even appeals to principle. Consequently, Hungary was left with a single aim in foreign policy—the revision of the treaty settlement. Promises to the contrary, such as that made in 1924 in return for the League loan, were regarded as time-gainers. In addition Hungary regarded the 'Little Entente', whose members had all gained Hungarian land, as a block to revising the new boundaries and therefore sought to destroy it. In 1926 negotiations for a treaty of friendship and arbitration were held with Yugoslavia. To have won this treaty would have blown a triumphant hole in the 'Little Entente', but in fact Yugoslavia delayed the negotiations and nothing came of them.

Hungary was herself wooed by Mussolini, and in 1927 a treaty of friendship and co-operation was signed between Italy and Hungary. This treaty remained the basis of Hungary's hopes for treaty revision. Arms were sent from Italy, and she was allowed special port facilities at Fiume. When some of the arms were discovered in transit in 1928 there was a brief international outcry. During the 1930s the dispute over the Burgenland was forgotten and instead Hungary became friendly with Austria. A commercial treaty was signed in 1933, and in 1934 both countries were signatories of the Rome Protocols *(see page 215)*. This brought Austria, Hungary and Italy together in a revisionist bloc against France's 'clients', the 'Little Entente' and Poland. It also provided a protective alliance against German expansion southwards, particularly for Austria; Hitler himself regarded it as such.

Gömbös was keen to cultivate Germany's friendship, for both commercial and ideological reasons. The commercial treaty signed in February 1934 allowed for Hungarian goods to be exchanged for German manufactured ones, and led to an expansion in the trade between the two *(see page 219)*. Shortly before his death, Gömbös promised to 'co-operate more closely with Germany', and secretly to introduce a one-party system and put the Hungarian army 'at the service of the dynamic German forces'. Gömbös' death ended this rapprochement, and for a time there was agreement with the 'Little Entente' powers; the Bled agreement of 1937 renounced the use of force between the Entente and Hungary and settled the position of Magyar minorities in the Entente countries. However, Germany's friendship offered far more chance of frontier revision, and in 1938 Hungary's demands for the Magyar areas of Slovakia were added to Germany's for the Sudentenland. In November 1938 she received 5000 square miles of South Slovakia, to which were added the Carpatho-Ukraine (Ruthenia) in March 1939. The next month she joined the anti-Comintern Pact and resigned from the League of Nations, thereby confirming her close links with the Axis Powers.

7. Bibliography

As the chapter you have just read suggests, I consider the problems of Eastern Europe between the wars important, not only in their own right but also because of their role in the outbreak of World War II (*see chapter XIV*) and their political problems and development. Most standard textbooks do not, however, devote much attention to them, and it will be necessary to go to a more detailed work for further study. The two most readily available are *Independent Eastern Europe* by C. A. Macartney and A. W. Palmer (Macmillian, 1962) and *Eastern Europe between the Wars 1918–41* by H. Setson-Watson (CUP, 1945).

8. Discussion Points and Exercises

A   *This section consists of questions that might be used for discussion (or written answers) as a way of expanding on the chapter and testing understanding of it.*

1   Why was it so difficult to satisfy all the demands of all the nationalities?

2   What principles lay behind the decisions on which nationalities to satisfy, and which to leave dissatisfied?

3   Why was it so difficult to reconcile the Serbs and the Croats?

4   What was the significance of the assassination of King Alexander?

5   Why did the depression ruin the Yugoslav economy?

6   Why were relations with the Great Powers such a problem for Yugoslavia?

7   How successful was the Czech government in the 1920s?

9   How did the future look for Czechoslovakia in 1934?

10   Could the Czech government have prevented its dismemberment in 1938–9?

11   What were the chief problems confronting the Polish government in the 1920s?

12   Was Pilsudski a dictator?

13   Why was it so difficult for the Polish (and other East European) government to solve the problems of inflation?

14   Why was Poland involved in so many border disputes?

15   What did Pilsudski and Beck hope to achieve by the non-aggression Pact with Germany?

16   Why was 'Anschluss' so attractive to Austria?

17   Why did the left v. right conflict develop so early in Austria?

18   What did Dollfuss aim to do?

19   Why was it so long before Austria found allies?

20   Comment on Schuschnigg's policies towards Germany.

21   Why was the political scene so confused in Hungary in 1918–22?

22   How did the Magyar landowners secure their pre-eminence in the state?

23   Was Hungary a fascist state in the 1930s?

24   Why were Hungary and Italy so close?

B *This section is intended to examine the role and problems of Eastern Europe in greater detail:*

1 Write a report for the French or British Foreign Office in the late 1920s on the progress and prospects of the successor states since their birth.

2 Put yourself in the position of either Benes or Schuschnigg in 1937–8. Write a report for your cabinet outlining the problems that your country faces in relation to Germany and the possible courses of action that you and your government might take.

C *This section suggests two ways in which you might compare the Successor States with other times and other places:*

1 Compare the extent and nature of the nationalities problem after 1919 with what it had been before 1914.

2 Compare the economies of the successor states with the economy of the Austro-Hungarian Empire and the economy of France in the 1920s.

D *Essay questions*

1 What did the peacemakers hope for from successor states and to what extent were their hopes fulfilled?

2 'The essential factors for stable parliamentary government simply did not exist in Eastern Europe after World War I.' How true is this view?

3 'Economic problems, not political changes, were the source of Eastern Europe's problems.' Do you agree?

9. A Comparative Exercise

This exercise compares the different states of Eastern Europe, and it is assumed that you have read the chapter thoroughly and made notes on it. The exercise should also help you to begin to consider many of the concepts and ideas that came to the fore in Germany and Italy in the inter-war era. In some ways, it will help to have already studied chapters XI and XII, but equally this exercise is intended to act as an introduction to those chapters. You will already have made a useful start on comparing the successor states in some of the discussion points, especially 'Was Pilsudski a dictator?' and 'Was Hungary a fascist state?'. This exercise differs from previous ones in that it is part essay and part activity, and requires you to work as you read it.

In comparing these states, it is clear that in all of them a democratic form of government was set up but did not survive till the outbreak of the World War II. However, before considering this, it is essential to decide (a) what we mean by a 'democratic form of government' and (b) what we mean by the 'ending' of a democratic form of government. If this sounds easy, then consider the position of a state that has a limited franchise, or open elections, or even universal franchise and secret ballot but widespread police or army involvement at election time. With these in mind, answer question *1* below.

1 When can it be said that a democracy has come to an end?

2 Draw a chart like the one below and complete it:

Country	Constitutional arrangements after World War I	Date and nature of ending of democracy	New form of government
Yugoslavia			
Czechoslovakia			
Poland			
Austria			
Hungary			

Having established that democracy, in the normally accepted sense of the word, had ended in all but Czechoslovakia by the mid-1930s, we can consider *why* democracy failed. In particular, we shall consider the extent to which democracy was doomed by weaknesses inherent in the new states and the extent to which it was weakened by problems faced in the inter-war period. To do this, study and answer the next set of exercises.

3 Consider each of the following factors that contributed to the weakness of democracy and that existed *before* 1919. Having considered each, put them in what you consider an order of importance, and explain *how* each made democratic government more difficult. For each, give examples from the successor states that you have studied. In addition, if you think there are factors that have not been included here, add them for yourself.

(a) The determination of dominant groups to maintain their pre-eminence in politics.

(b) The absence of established political parties.

(c) Peasants formed the majority of the population, and they had no experience of political participation, having been ruled by autocracies.

(d) Economic weaknesses of the states, so that all political parties were interest groups.

(e) Democracy was imposed on the new states rather than evolving from within the country.

4 Now similarly consider these factors that developed in the inter-war era and again rank them in order of importance and add details.

(f) Immediate post-war economic problems, especially inflation, and the difficulties of democratic governments in dealing with them.

(g) The constant pressure of diplomatic problems.

(h) The effects of the Great Depression of the period after 1929 and the difficulties in dealing with them.

5 Which played the more important part—the inherent problems or the arising ones?.

Detailed work and discussion of these factors should enable you to understand the relationship between political structures and economic problems better than before, and you ought now to be able to write on the subject (such as essays 2 and 3 in section D of the Discussion Points and Excercises). This next question should help to round this off.

6 Why did democracy survive longer in Czechoslovakia than the other states?

The second major similarity between the successor states, again with Czechoslovakia as the exception, is that in each the governments of the 1930s were right-wing. In Yugoslavia, Prince Paul signed treaties with Hitler and Mussolini, while opposition leaders were locked away. In Poland, the governments of the 'Camp of National Unity' preached anti-communism and the Polonization of minorites. In Austria, the government had a private army—the 'Heimwehr'—and Schuschnigg declared himself 'Führer of the Fatherland Front'. In Hungary, the Prime Minister, Imrédy, was forced out of office by his own anti-semitic policies. In addition, each of the regimes was well supported by the army, the aristocracy and the Church, traditional supporters of right-wing regimes, and each introduced policies of an illiberal and reactionary nature.

However, there were major differences between these regimes and the fascist regimes of Italy and Germany. Both Hitler and Mussolini boasted of the *revolutionary* nature of their parties, while the East European rulers tended to boast of the *conservatism* of their governments. Horthy, the regent of Hungary, said that he used to ask himself how the old emperor, Franz Josef, would have thought before he approved bills. There was no place for the Church and the aristocracy in the new, dynamic regimes, whereas the 'authoritarian' governments wanted to keep or return power to these traditional groups. Genuine fascists, such as the Hungarian Szalasi, were locked away.

7 To examine these ideas, draw out and complete a chart like that below. Under it, while a conclusion, in particular examining whether or not you agree with the ideas expressed above.

Country	'Authoritarian' leaders	'Fascist' leaders	Government policies of a 'fascist' type	Government policies against fascists
Yugoslavia				
Czechoslovakia				
Poland				
Austria				
Hungary				

8 With the help of chapters XI and XII, write in greater detail on the differences between the governments of Eastern Europe and those of Italy and Germany.

The third main similarity between the states is that each failed to withstand the might of Hitler's Germany. They had been set up in part to resist the advance of communism but in the event they were unable to prevent the advance of Nazism. Yugoslavia and Hungary gave way, in the first instance, by alliance, while Austria, Poland and Czechoslovakia were more or less militarily defeated. The reasons for this failure is therefore critical, and question *9* examines these.

9 Below are listed four possible reasons why the successor states proved weak in the face of Hitler. List them in order of importance, expanding on each of them and adding additional reasons that you consider important:
(a) weakness of Western and other great power allies;
(b) disagreements between successor states making the establishment of effective 'blocs' impossible;
(c) the lack of effective leadership;
(d) nationality problems both within and between the successor states
—i.e. self-determination was doomed to failure in any case.

X France 1919–40

1 Introduction

(a) General

French governments in the inter-war period have been heavily criticized. A period of 'anxiety, survival, and, finally, collapse' writes one author, L. Derfler. Another, J. M. Roberts, writes: 'social stagnation and political stalemate seemed to dog one of the most vigorous of pre-war cultures'. While Eastern European nations changed rapidly, Russia was transformed and Germany and Italy revolutionized, nothing of lasting note happened in France until her conquest in 1940. One problem for the historian is therefore to establish why France was so stagnant in this period.

This chapter provides a good example of the falsity of dividing chapters between politics, economics and foreign policy. In the period 1922–4 especially the three became inextricably interwoven as governments were preoccupied with the problem of making Germany provide the economic means to French prosperity by paying reparations. Nonetheless, since the divisions seem valid and helpful for much of the period, I have maintained them.

(b) The effects of the Great War

France's suffering as a result of the war that was fought largely on her soil can be enumerated with the following examples:

Deaths: 1 385 000 soldiers: 250 000 civilians.

Wounded: 700 000 seriously (120 000 permanently disabled); over two million others.

Buildings: 300 000 houses destroyed; a further 300 000 damaged. 6 000 public buildings and 22 000 factories and workshops damaged or destroyed.

Farming: 1 360 000 head of livestock killed or confiscated. Five million acres of land (not all farmland) damaged.

Bare statistics like these give an impression of the tasks facing the French government and people in 1919. They do not, though, tell the human stories of the effects the war had on people. Of all Frenchmen aged between twenty and thirty-two in 1914, over half had been killed. With thousands more injured, it was likely that every French family lost relatives or friends as a result of the war. Even if they did not, the sight of the wounded on the streets, the war memorials and crematoria or the damaged buildings were reminders.

Under such circumstances, it was not surprising that two emotions dominated the thinking of both government and people—revenge and security. The first of these, revenge, took two forms. One was that those who had caused France's suffering should suffer themselves; the other that they should pay for the damage caused. Since Germans had fought Frenchmen on French soil, it had to be Germany's fault. Since it was the fault of Germans, Germans must pay. Thus ran the train of thought in France, and Britain, at the end of the war. Again, since Germany had invaded France, French security could only be assured by protective measures against Germany. To Clemenceau and Foch, who led the French delegation to the peace conference, this meant at least the annexation of the Rhineland, if not the permanent military occupation of it. Such were their demands.

In fact, France's security was assured in rather different ways. The Rhineland was to be occupied only temporarily, but to be a permanent demilitarized zone, and Britain and the USA promised to come to France's aid in the event of attack *(see page 188)*. This guarantee actually came to nothing because the American Senate refused in 1920 to agree to the promises their President had made at Versailles.

The French desire for payment, and the suffering of Germany, was more satisfactorily achieved. The 'lost provinces' of Alsace and Lorraine, together with their rich mineral resources, were returned to France. The coalfields of the Saar were given to France for five years. The Turkish and German colonies of Syria, Lebanon and parts of Togoland and the Cameroons were given to France as mandates. Above all, France was to receive reparation payments from Germany. The sum was not fixed in 1918, but it promised to be large; figures of over £10 000 million were discussed, of which France was to receive more than half. Even if, in 1919, the security settlement was not quite as France had hoped, the prospects of receiving recompense seemed good.

2. Political History

(a) Constitutional changes

There were no important alterations to the constitution of the Third Republic. Several issues were debated in press and parliament, but nothing came of them. Poincaré, when President from 1913 until 1920, especially bemoaned the weakness of his office. Both he and his successor, Millerand, had more influence over the appointment and dismissal of ministers than their predecessors—a tendency which was ended by Herriot forcing Millerand to resign in 1924, *(see page 232)*. Neither, however, was able to win enough support for the right of the President to dissolve Parliament to get anything actually done. Equally, suggestions that the President should be popularly elected rather than chosen by the Chamber and Senate were discussed, but no more. Generally, therefore, it would be true to say that Parliamentary sovereignity was upheld.

On the other hand, the power of the government (i.e. Prime Minister and Cabinet) was increased by Parliament's willingness to grant it decree powers. This was the power to make laws by decree, 'règlements de nécessité', rather than by the vote of Parliament. Such powers had been given to ministers during the war. After it, they were frequently granted to deal with particular problems, especially financial. The practice came to a halt in the late 1930s, when both Blum and Chautemps were refused them. This was partly as a result of the abuse of the system by Laval when Prime Minister in 1935; he issued some 500 decrees, many of them by no means 'de nécessité', such as that forbidding foreigners from keeping racing pigeons.

The only constitutional alterations affected the voting practices for Chamber elections. These did not, incidentally, include giving women the right to vote; this was not done until 1944. In 1919, an adaptation of the 'scrutin de liste' system was reintroduced. Instead of voting for one member for their 'arrondissement', voters were presented with a list of candidates for the whole 'départment', a much larger unit. Again, a two-ballot system operated. This meant that those candidates in the 'départment' who did not receive a majority on the first ballot could go forward to the second. Obviously, if like-minded candidates could agree which stood the best chance of winning, some would drop out to leave the field clear. The system therefore favoured the parties which were best able to make such arrangements: in 1919 this was the right wing, in 1924 the left. For the 1928 (and subsequent) elections, the single-member constituency system was restored.

(b) Political parties

The underlying attitudes towards politics in the Third Republic remained the same after the war. That is to say, voters were less interested in the party that they voted for, and more interested in the person. Similarly, party discipline remained as loose as before. Table 30 showing party membership of the deputies cannot be taken as an accurate, strict, interpretation since deputies could easily vote with one block on one issue and another on another. This is especially true of those right of centre, where there existed a multiplicity of parties, united only by their opposition to social reform, their horror of communism and their desire for a strong, nationalist, foreign policy.

In addition, the Radical party remained faithful to 'Alain's' dictum that resistance to the powers-that-be was more important than the use of power to reform. The Radicals represented those who feared the power of central government to tax them and make laws that harmed them. They were, par excellence, the party of opposition. Paradoxically, they were also a party of government for many of the inter-war years, since they held the balance between left and right. This paradox goes far to explain the inaction and sterility of politics in the inter-war era.

There were some important developments on the left of politics. Here, too, incidentally, party discipline was far stronger. The annual congress of the Socialist party, the SFIO, at Tours in December 1920, marked a crucial turning point. The party had to choose whether or not to join the Bolshevik inspired Third International. The majority chose to do so, and thus renamed themselves the PCF, 'Parti Communiste Française'. By so doing, they agreed to take their instructions from Moscow and work directly and wholeheartedly for the revolution. This meant no co-operation with the 'old official "social democratic" or "socialist" parties, which have betrayed the braver of the working class'. A minority refused to pursue this line, and remained as the SFIO under the leadership of Leon Blum, dedicated to evolutionary socialism.

Broadly, the political pattern of the inter-war years was right, left, right, left, left *(see Table 30)*. However, on each occasion when the left won a majority—in 1924, 1932 and 1936—they were unable to maintain control over affairs until the next election. In each case—in 1926, 1934 and 1938—they surrendered their power to the right. This failure of the left to govern when elected provides a second source of stagnation in French politics, and the reasons for this failure form a major area of study.

	1919		1924		1928	1932	1936	
Right of centre parties	430	*Bloc National*	256		320	253	215	
Radicals	86		139	*Cartel des Gauches*	113	155	109	*Popular Front*
Republican socialists	26		43		40	36	55	
Socialists	68		104		101	129	147	
Left-wing socialists	—		—		5	11	—	
Communists	—		26		14	12	72	
Total number of deputies	610		568		593	596	598	

Table 30. Membership of the French Chamber of Deputies 1919–40

(Note that the size of the groups can vary even within the same parliament, and therefore the figures are only approximate.)

(c) Political chronology

French voters in the election of November 1919 were, like other West Europeans, terrified by the rise of communism. The Bolshevik successes in Russia, the Spartacist revolt in Berlin and Béla Kun's brief reign in Hungary all pointed to the impending overthrow of western society as it had been. To protect themselves against this, they voted for those who promised firm action and were not themselves tainted by an association with communism. Right-wing deputies, many of them ex-servicemen, therefore predominated. The 'Bloc National', the broad right-wing coalition, won 338 seats, with another ninety-two deputies who would support them but were not directly committed to the coalition. The SFIO won only sixty-eight seats, losing almost half the deputies they had had in 1914. The belief that the left was responsible for France being unprepared for war in 1914 and that their supporters would be 'soft' on Germany in the continuing negotiations, especially over reparations, also contributed to the demise of the Left.

In the Presidential election of January 1920, Clemenceau was defeated by Paul Deschanel. Despite admiration for Clemenceau's contribution to victory in the Great War, many senators and deputies feared that he would be too strong a President—too keen to involve himself in government affairs and take independent action. In addition, some right-wingers had always been suspicious of him because of his declared opposition to religion. Deschanel was therefore chosen and Alexandre Millerand, a one-time socialist but more recently the founder of the 'Bloc National', became Prime Minister. This arrangement only lasted until September, by which time it had become clear that Deschanel was unbalanced (he was found wandering on a railway line in his pyjamas); he was persuaded to resign. Millerand took his place and, after the Chamber refused to accept Millerand's first nominee, Leygnes, Briand became Prime Minister (see Table 31).

Alexandre Briand was to head five ministries in the inter-war years. He had started his political life as an extreme socialist in the 1890s. Thereafter he had joined the reformist wing of the socialists, had played an important part in the separation of Church and State in 1905 and had joined the Cabinet in 1906. In 1910 he had apparently renounced his socialist background by breaking the general strike. Nonetheless, he remained one of the more flexible members of the 'Bloc National', adopting a moderate attitude towards Germany. It was his view that an impoverished Germany isolated from the rest of Europe was a danger to France and instead he worked for reparations from a restored and accepted Germany.

Reparations dominated the early 1920s. It has been estimated that the war had cost 150 000 million francs. In consequence France had massive debts with her allies, which were increased by additional borrowing to pay for reconstruction. Moreover, the two most obvious sources of income were unfruitful—her two chief debtors, Russia and Roumania, refused to repay while taxation within France was widely avoided. Direct taxes had only been introduced in the years before the war but were fixed at very low rates and produced only a fraction of other countries. Therefore reparations were crucial to the French economy.

The former President, Raymond Poincaré, had headed the Allied Reparations Committee. Like Briand, he was to play an important part in inter-war politics. He was born in Lorraine (but not in the area taken from France) in 1861 and was a long-time opponent of Germany. He wanted as much in reparations as possible and, unlike Briand, was prepared to use force to get it. When Millerand made concessions during the negotiations for reparations in 1920, Poincaré resigned as President of the Committee and headed the opposition in the Senate. In April 1921 the sum was fixed at 132 billion gold marks, of which France's share was to be 52%. In 1922 Briand agreed that this was perhaps too much and gave his approval to a planned European conference to review reparations. This concession appalled the parliamentary right and President Millerand personally informed Briand of this disapproval, at which Briand resigned.

(a) Presidents

Date of taking office	Name	How term ended
18 February 1913	Raymond Poincaré	Served full term
18 February 1920	Paul Deschanel	Insane—forced to resign
20 September 1920	Alexandre Millerand	Forced to resign by Herriot
11 June 1924	Gaston Doumergue	Served full term
13 June 1931	Paul Doumer	Assassinated
6 May 1932	Albert Lebrun	Served full term and re-elected but resigned 10 July 1940

(b) Prime Ministers

Date of appointment	Name	Date of appointment	Name
14 June 1914	Réné Viviani	13 December 1930	Theodore Steeg
27 August 1914	Réné Viviani	27 January 1931	Pierre Laval
31 October 1915	Aristide Briand	23 February 1932	André Tardieu
12 December 1916	Aristide Briand	4 June 1932	Edouard Herriot
19 March 1917	Alexandre Ribot	20 December 1932	J. Paul Boncour
18 September 1917	Paul Painlevé	31 January 1933	Edouard Daladier
16 November 1917	Georges Clemenceau	24 October 1933	Albert Sarraut
19 January 1920	Alexandre Millerand	22 November 1933	Camille Chautemps
3 September 1920	Georges Leygnes	30 January 1934	Edouard Daladier
16 January 1921	Aristide Briand	9 February 1934	Gaston Doumergue
16 January 1922	Raymond Poincaré	10 November 1934	Pierre Flandin
14 June 1924	Edouard Herriot	1 June 1935	Fernand Buisson
17 April 1925	Paul Painlevé	6 June 1935	Pierre Laval
29 November 1925	Aristide Briand	25 January 1936	Albert Sarraut
23 June 1926	Aristide Briand and Joseph Caillaux	3 June 1936	Léon Blum
20 July 1926	Edouard Herriot	23 June 1937	Camille Chautemps
24 July 1926	Raymond Poincaré	28 January 1938	Camille Chautemps
28 July 1928	Aristide Briand	12 March 1938	Léon Blum
11 November 1928	Raymond Poincaré	10 April 1938	Edouard Daladier
2 November 1929	André Tardieu	21 March 1940	Paul Reynaud
21 February 1930	Camille Chautemps	17 June 1940	Henri Pétain
2 March 1930	André Tardieu		

Table 31 Political leaders of France, 1919–40

Poincaré succeeded him, and there followed a period of attempting to get reparations by force. Germany's disobedience of the provisions of the treaty of Versailles in signing the treaty of Rapallo with Russia in 1922 (it should have had Allied approval) and her stated intention to end repayments, led to the invasion of the Ruhr industrial area by French and Belgian troops on 23 January 1923. The German workers responded by refusing to work or obey French orders. Until September, the Ruhr was the scene of much unpleasantness. French engineers and miners were sent in and had some success in exploiting the resources there, to the anger of the German government, and this helped to create the massive inflation *(see page 293)*. Some German civilians were killed and wounded, both as a result of the passive resistance policy and an attempt to create an independent Rhineland Republic. The effects of the inflation and the apparent ability of the French to exploit the area for themselves led the German government to agree to resume payments. Poincaré had won a mighty victory—his government, without the aid of allies, had forced Germany to give way.

The victory was, however, to prove less mighty. Poincaré agreed to hold an international conference on reparations, rather than deal independently with Germany. This conference led to the Dawes Plan for reparation repayments, named after the American general who headed the commission. It put reparations on a sliding scale; Germany's payments each year were to be assessed on her ability to pay and no overall annual sum was fixed. In addition, the Allies were to take partial control of the German bank and the United States was to loan 800 million gold marks. So although France was once again to receive German money, she could not be certain of how much, which made it difficult to make economic plans based on income from Germany. Also, France was not to be the only country responsible for getting that money.

The 1924 Chamber elections were won by the 'Cartel des Gauches', a broadly left-wing electoral coalition *(see Table 30)*. The Communists were not included, and the Socialists, although supporting the government, did not serve as ministers. Their victory in the light of Poincaré's apparent success in 1923 needs explaining. Many Frenchmen were actually frightened by the occupation of the Ruhr, for it once again raised the spectre of war on France's eastern frontier. They were also opposed to the apparently dictatorial approach of the government in its use of decree laws and the tax increases it had brought in 1923. In addition, the left-wing parties were better organized for the election, in that they had agreements over withdrawing after the first ballot *(see page 228)*.

The new Prime Minister was Edouard Herriot, a Radical and mayor of Lyons. His first action was to remove Millerand from the Presidency for his active support of the right in the election campaign. He did this by refusing to severe under Millerand. The President knew that if he appointed anyone else, the 'Cartel des Gauches' would defeat that appointee in the Chamber. He therefore resigned and was replaced by the moderate Radical, Gaston Doumergue.

However, Herriot's ministry was short-lived. Since the war, the value of the franc had fallen against the dollar and the pound, and this trend was accelerated in the mid-1920s. In 1922, there were thirty-five francs to the pound, in 1924, seventy francs and 243 by 1926. The different elements of the Cartel could not agree on a solution to this problem. The Socialists suggested a levy on capital to take the wealth from the rich—a suggestion that met with horror in more conservative circles. In the meantime, government borrowing from the Bank of France simply devalued the currency even further. In July 1926, therefore, the Radical government, once again led by Herriot after various alternatives *(see Table 31)*, resigned and Poincaré again became Prime Minister.

He formed a government of National Union, which included five former Prime Ministers and members of all parties bar the Socialists and Communists. Parliament once more gave him decree powers, and he used these to end the ever-decreasing value of the franc. Its value was fixed at only 20% of its pre-war value, at fifty to sixty francs to the pound. This was done by cutting public expenditure and increasing both taxes and the efficiency with which they were collected. Although the measures were harsh, they were seen as necessary, and Poincaré's policies received public endorsement in the elections of 1928, which increased his majority *(see Table 30)*. The new Chamber continued the policies of retrenchment, repudiating 80% of their debts to holders of government bonds. Nonetheless, the late twenties were seen as good years, with economic stability and social progress—after years of indecision, a national insurance scheme for old age pensions and sickness benefits was finally approved in 1928 and came into effect in 1930. There was also security overseas and firm leadership, even though Poincaré resigned from ill health in 1929 and died in 1934.

As elsewhere, though, the depression brought back political instability and extremism. The 1932 election showed a swing to the left, and Herriot again became Prime Minister. However, he was forced to resign when he refused to repudiate France's debts to the USA. He was succeeded by a succession of short-lived ministries—six between June 1932 and February 1934 (there were eighteen between 1930 and 1936). In such conditions, many felt that democracy was a weak form of government and looked instead to bodies that promised action, and above all, firmness. This led to increased support for the 'Leagues', fascist and semi-fascist groups seeking to emulate the revolution that Mussolini had brought about in Italy. The oldest of these was the nationalist 'Action Française', founded in 1905, by Maurras and Daudet. Added to it were the 'Croix de Feu' movement, originally for ex-servicemen, led by Colonel de la Rocque; the 'Camelots de Roi'; the 'Jeunesses Patriotes' of Pierre Tattinger, the champagne magnate; and 'Solidarité Française' of the perfumier Coty. These movements differed in their origins. 'Action Française' was more traditional, Catholic and authoritarian while those founded later, like 'Solidarité Française' (1933) and the 'Parti Populaire Français', were more avowedly supporters of fascism. All, however, were united in their opposition to the weak deomcracy provided by the Third Republic, in their support of anti-semitism and in their desire for a strong, nationalist, foreign policy. These view are well expressed by the official aims of the 'Jeunesses Patriotes': 'to defend the National Territory against the dangers of internal revolution, to increase public prosperity and to improve our public institutions'.

This extremism came to a head in 1934. Serge Stavisky was a Jewish night-club owner and financier, with many friends and contacts in the government. In December 1929 he had disappeared when a warrant for his arrest on charges of fraud was issued. He then managed to avoid arrest again in 1933 when he formed another highly doubtful company. When he was eventually found, he was dead. The government said that he had committed suicide as the police entered the room. Others said he had been shot by the police to avoid the public hearing how he had been protected by his influentual friends for so long (as they would have done if the case came to trial). Either way, it was apparent that his shady dealings had only been possible because he had been protected by others—policemen, judges, even politicians. The old question of the Panama scandal was raised once again—what kind of a government was it that allowed people who protected crooks like Stavisky in its numbers? Such an issue was a godsend to the Leagues, who organized demonstrations to protest against the corruption and inefficiency of the government.

The new Prime Minister, Daladier, decided firm action was needed. He sacked the Paris Chief of Police, Chiappe, for his failure to prevent the riots and demonstrations of the Leagues. The Leagues responded by organizing a huge demonstration for 6 Februrary 1934, the day that Daladier was to present his new government to the Chamber. A huge gathering assembled in the 'Place de la Concorde', and set off to march to the Chamber. The police refused to allow the demonstrators there, and opened fire on them. Fourteen rioters and one policeman died and 1435 demonstrators were injured. Daladier resigned, the first Premier to resign as a result of mob action. Gaston Doumergue, the former President, formed a government of National Union, and managed to prevent further violence, partly by introducing right wingers into his cabinet.

The most lasting effect of the riots was the uniting effect it had on the left wing. The two trade union movements—the 'Confedération Générale du Travail' and the communist 'CGTU' (U = Unitaire)—which had split in 1921, joined in organizing a twenty-four hour strike on 9 February to protest against the fascists. In July, the Socialist and Communist parties signed a 'United Action Pact' promising to co-operate and organize joint public meetings. The change in Comintern policy that allowed communist parties to form electoral agreements with 'bourgeois' parties also encouraged co-operation. The Communists therefore joined the already united Radical and Socialist parties to form the 'Rassemblement Populaire', or 'Popular Front', with its formula of 'Bread, Peace and Liberty' to save the Republic.

The elections of May 1936 brought victory to this combination *(see*

Table 30). The Popular Front's programme had four major planks, and it was over these issues that the election was fought. It promised to dissolve the 'Leagues' and corruption in public life. It offered support to the League of Nations and collective security—support that had been clearly lacking in the Abyssinian crisis *(see page 278)*. Thirdly, it promised economic reforms, such as the reduction of hours, government spending on public works programmes and nationalization of the Bank of France. Finally, it promised increased revenues from taxes, both by increasing income taxes and (again) the efficiency with which they were collected. This package of reforms brought together all the problems that France had faced since 1919 and attempted to remedy them. The victory of the Front indicated that at last French voters wanted change, rather than the familiar short-term remedies of decree laws. On 3 June 1936 the first ever socialist government was formed by the leader of the SFIO, Léon Blum. It was dependent on the support of the Radical party, members of which joined the government, and the communist party, who, following Comintern instructions, did not accept ministerial posts.

The new government was immediately faced by 1½ million workers in occupation of the their factories. These occupations were not organized by the CGT or CGTU but were more local demonstrations of the worker's desire for immediate action for reform. In response, Blum organized a conference between the CGT and the employer's organization, the 'Conféderation générale de la Production Française' at the Hotel Matignon. The so-called 'Matignon Agreements' reached there went some way to bringing reform. Wage increases ranging from 7% to 15% were agreed and a system for worker's representatives to negotiate directly with factory managers was established. A forty-hour week and compulsory holidays with pay were introduced. A National Wheat Board ('Office du Blé') was set up to control grain prices and distribution and the Bank of France and the armaments industry were brought under greater government control. The 'Leagues' were banned, but tended only to reorganize themselves and re-emerge with new names. Nonetheless, many of the promises seemed to have been fulfilled and France at last had social and economic reform.

However, the Popular Front government of Blum lasted barely a year and was unable to carry through many of the longer term reforms, such as public works, that were promised. There were a number of reasons for this. Firstly, the French economy was still relatively depressed in 1936 and wage increases and shorter hours were inappropriate at a time when increased production was urgently required. In addition, many of the richer were strongly opposed to Blum's measures, notably the nationalizations, and withdrew their capital. This in turn reduced the amount available for investment, and accelerated inflation. Thirdly, the international situation pushed the different elements of the coalition apart. The Communists wanted France to help the Republicans in the Spanish Civil War. Blum agreed with them, but the Radicals were strongly opposed to intervention. Blum was also keen to maintain Britain's friendship in the face of German expansionism, and Britain too opposed intervention. Faced with opposition from his own supporters on the Spanish question and refused emergency economic powers by the Senate, Blum resigned.

During 1937–8, the Popular Front remained in government, first under Chautemps, then Blum again. However, its inability to deal with either the economic or the international problems led to its replacement by a Radical government under Daladier in April 1938. He remained Prime Minister until the fall of France in 1940, a period dominated by international crises and the outbreak of war. At home, he was given the decree powers that had twice been refused to Blum, and he used them to devalue the franc and end the strikes that broke out when Blum's second government ended. He also revised some of the reforms of 1936 in an effort to remedy France's financial problems. The forty-hour week was modified, a move that led to a general strike in November 1938, which was in turn put down by threats of severe punishments. Daladier's government had lost the support of the left and was dependent on the right-wing parties. Once again, France had reverted to the situation of political bitterness and short-term solutions.

3. Economic History
(See also above, pages 230–36)

French governments were dominated by the problem of where to get money from, especially in view of the enormous expense of the war. There were three major sources of income available—taxes, loans and reparations. Income tax was introduced only in 1917 and even then was never a major source of income. Thomson describes it as follows:

> The more conservative parties opposed it (income tax) on grounds of 'fiscal inquisition'—the old fear of excessive government power and the State's gaining overmuch control over the family and individual income. Evasion of taxation, among all classes but especially by the peasants, became widespread and rampant. Again, the practical effect was a half-hearted compromise typical of the parliamentary Republic as its least virile—retention of income tax but weak application of it against the most powerful blocs in the electorate.

There were plenty of indirect taxes but they never realized sufficient to meet the government's needs. Consequently, loans and reparations became more important. Reparations were at first seen as the solution to France's financial problems in the immediate post-war era and only after 1924 was it appparent that they would never be so. Therefore loans from foreign governments became crucial, but they too were dependent on others—on the confidence of French and overseas investors in the economy. Such confidence was not always forthcoming.

The fourth alternative was inflation. By increasing the amount of money in circulation, the government could provide for its own needs.

However, this also had the effect of reducing the value of the currency. Consequently, French governments were caught between allowing inflation as a temporary solution to cash shortages, as in 1919–25, and halting inflation to avoid the franc becoming worth less. Twice in the inter-war period—in 1928 and 1937—the franc was devalued.

Despite the problems of the period 1919–25, there was considerable recovery and expansion in the French economy during the 1920s. The devastated regions of the North-east were rehabilitated and steel, iron and chemicals all expanded. The car industry, which had really come into being during the war, continued its expansion, producing some 200 000 cars each year. Taking 1913 as base year with an index of industrial production of 100, it had fallen to 60 in 1916 and reached 140 by 1930. Similarly, trade in 1930 had an index of 166 and even agriculture, the weakest element in the economy, had reached 110.

Nevertheless, the depression hit France as elsewhere. Although her greater self-sufficiency protected France for a little longer than other European countries, the index of production had fallen 34 points by 1932 (compared with 1928). If the depression arrived late, it also lasted longer, 1935 being the worst year for unemployment, when 425 000 were out of work. The international moratorium on debt and reparation repayments had a significant effect on government income, which fell by 33% between 1929 and 1935. Most importantly, the effects of the depression were such that they made Blum's reform efforts almost impossible, since increased government expenditure, higher wages and shorter hours were incompatible with industrial depression.

4. Foreign Policy

(a) Imperial policy

France's empire was the second largest in the world, with a population of 100 million. Nonetheless, it remained relatively in the background of French political and economic issues between the wars, partly because of its own unimportance and partly because of the overwhelming importance of other issues. Its own unimportance can be seen by Map 4—the bulk, territorially, was in Northern and Central Africa and relatively unprosperous. Indeed, colonial trade only accounted for about 15% of total French commerce in the inter-war era. Nonetheless, many of the lands held by France—in North Africa, the Middle East, Madagascar, Indo-China and the West Indies—were of considerable strategic importance. In addition, they all demonstrated the problems of colonial ownership that Britain experienced to a far greater extent.

The North African possessions—Algeria, Tunisia and French Morocco —illustrate both these points of economic irrelevance and strategic importance. The strategic importance of these possessions was particularly obvious in the construction of a railway from French Morocco to Tunisia. This was completed in 1933 and would enable French troops to get from Tunisia to Moroccan ports on the Atlantic without going through the straits of Gibraltar. France was keen to further establish her own pre-eminence in these areas, while the national groups were equally keen to press their own claims. In Tunisia, for example, France ceded some oases in the South to Libya (and thus Italy) but also tried to strengthen her hold by a nationality law (1921) making children of any nationality born in Tunisia French. This law was brought before the International Court by Great Britain and subsequently amended to give such children a choice of nationality.

Opposition groups emerged in each of these colonies. In Tunisia, the 'Destour' party campaigned for self-government, a degree of which was won in 1922 when the economic administration was reorganized on a system of councils on which both French and Tunisians sat. In French Morocco, peace was maintained for a long time by the French governor, Louis Lyautey, until his resignation in 1925. This was in stark contrast to Spanish Morocco, where Abd-el-Krim was a highly successful enemy of Spanish rule—the French even provided 150 000 troops to assist in defeating him in 1925–6. In 1932, the French were faced by opposition in their own part of Morocco, partly as a result of the disastrous consequences of the depression there which had led to a lower demand for phosphate. Troops were sent to the Atlas region to occupy Tafilet, the head-quarters of the tribesmen concerned. Far more significantly, a group of young Moroccans presented a 'Plan for Moroccan Reforms' in 1934. Whereas tribesmen were merely opposed to French rule, this group were genuinely nationalist in their desire for self-government. There was a serious nationalist uprising in September 1938 and troops and planes were rushed there and arrested leaders. Albert Sarraut was appointed chairman of a new commission for co-ordination for North Africa with the intention of strengthening the French position there. The next month Tunisia became the centre of a new crisis when Italy made loud demands for its cession, which were ended by Daladier's refusal to consider them and a visit to Tunisia where he was widely welcomed by the Arabs. In Algeria there was less open opposition to French rule in the inter-war period, though there too a National Party developed. Hostility to France increased during the depression when there was also serious anti-semitism, the climax of which came in 1934 when riots in Constantine between Jews and Moslems led to several deaths. The French possessions in North Africa were, however, considered a great asset, chiefly because of their strategic value.

France's other possessions in Africa were extensive, and were increased by the mandates received from Germany after the war. The inter-war period was largely one of consolidation in these areas, which had mostly been French possessions for some time. In general, therefore, some form of assembly or council was established in each colony, giving the native populations some control over economic affairs but leaving the French governor in overall control. For example in Madagascar, the administration was reorganized in 1924, providing for an increase in native officials and giving the Governor-General economic and financial councils, composed equally of natives and Europeans, to advise on public works and the budget.

There were efforts to end slavery and to introduce education, especially primary, and training for particular skills. Colonial courts, if not already set up, were established. Railways and roads were built in many of the colonies as part of a more general effort at economic exploitation of the resources of the area. In 1921, Albert Sarraut, then minister of the colonies, proposed a grandiose scheme for the development of West Africa, involving building eight ports, twenty railways, widening rivers, providing water supplies for cities and so forth. Although much of the work was initiated in the 1920s, the 1930s were poor years, for the products of the colonies fell in value, as they were chiefly agricultural raw materials—bananas, peanuts, cocoa—which were harmed by the world fall in prices. Obviously, this situation led to some hostility to French rule, but it never reached sufficient heights to require more than police action.

France's Middle East possessions were less peaceful. As a result of the War and Peace Conference, France was given the mandate of Syria, which was formed into a separate state in 1920. France's control over Syria was opposed by the Syrians, who proclaimed their independence with Faisal as King. This situation was not accepted by Britain and France, and French troops were sent to Damascus where King Faisal was deposed, and Syria reorganized under a French Commissioner. In 1925 a People's Party was organized and demanded independence. In addition, the Druses, a Moslem people who thought that France favoured the Christian inhabitants of Syria, organized a revolt and controlled many areas in 1925 and even occupied the capital, Damascus. The French were left in control of only Lebanon and Beirut. The insurrection was suppressed during 1926, but with considerable harshness, especially when the French bombarded Damascus. Even then, France's troubles were not over. In 1928 a constituent assembly was summoned by the French but drew up a constitution which removed French control. The assembly was therefore adjourned by the Governor-General, Henri Pousot. He introduced his own constitution, by which Syria was to be a republic with a parliament elected every four years. In the first elections of 1932 French pressure ensured that the Parliament was moderate and Ahmad Ali Bey el-Abed was chosen President with French approval. The French then made moves to withdraw from their mandate. At first, there was opposition to France's plans, which included an alliance with France for twenty-five years and French control of foreign policy, the army and finance. In January 1936 there were riots, demonstrations and a general strike, when the French governor banned the Nationalist party. Eventually, in September 1936, France withdrew from both Syria and Lebanon, signing a treaty of friendship with each and making no claims for future French control.

The 1920s were boom years for French Indo-China, with considerable investment and new companies being founded. Between 1924 and 1929 over two million francs were invested, mainly in rice, rubber, tea, coffee, textile and cement works. However, the economic crisis hit Indo-China hard, with rice prices halved and exports overall reduced by 25%. Measures were taken to improve the situation, but the economic decline was fuel to the claims of those who wanted either a greater say in government or complete independence. Even in the 1920s a bomb had been thrown at the Governor-General and there had been student riots. The climax of the opposition was reached in 1930, when several provinces—Vinh, Ha-tinh and Annan—fell under rebel control and only in 1931 was peace restored. The opposition prompted considerable reforms in education, agriculture (loans for farmers), tax and government, where natives replaced Europeans in both the assemblies and the administration. These was a decline in open opposition, but there remained two important sources of nationalism—European-educated students and the communists, who had inspired the violence of 1930.

(b) European policies

As noted above, some aspects of French foreign policy are inextricably linked with domestic affairs and have already been studied. This is especially true of the occupation of the Ruhr, further details of which will be found on page 232.

French foreign policy in the inter-war years was determined within a complicated framework of conditions that made most decisions reactions to the actions of others rather than French initiatives. Thomson, in *Deomcracy in France since 1870*, has explained these circumstances in the following passage.

> The pre-war dual system of alliances had gone, and neither a truly collective system nor a French diplomatic network had fully taken its place. Instead, there grew up a triangular structure of diplomatic relations, from which three different alliance groups could at any time appear. It was this, more than any one national policy, which determined the constant uncertainty and tensions of the inter-war years in Europe.
>
> In the West were the two democratic Powers of Britain and France, anti-revisionist in interests but not in concord as to foreign policy, save for a short period after 1924. In central Europe were Germany and Italy, each for different reasons a revisionist Power, hostile in spirit to the League and to the western democracies, after 1933 both fascist and after 1936 in alliance. In the East, the Soviet Union, at first ostracized and hostile to all her western neighbours, but later emerging into open participation in European affairs. Relations between any two of these groups inevitably affected the third. Any drawing together of the first two, as at Stresa or Munich, looked like an anti-Soviet bloc. Any 'rapprochement' between the western democracies and Russia, as when Russia joined the League in 1934, meant 'encirclement' for Germany and to a less degree Italy. Any sign of German-Soviet co-operation, as at Rapallo or in the Nazi-Soviet Pact of 1939, made the democracies fear a union of single-party states

against democracy. Although each shift of these alignments was due to particular national policies, it equally meant that the foreign policy of the third side in the triangle was at that moment dictated by events. The result was twenty years of extreme political instability in Europe, and the emergence of a system of great alliances even more nerve-racking than in the years before 1914.

This passage illuminates a great deal about international relations between the wars, and will be referred to again in chapter XIV. For the time being, it is of value in demonstrating the constraints that existed on any French actions.

Neither the French government nor people were satisfied by the security arrangements provided by the treaty of Versailles. Clemenceau and his successors had little faith in the League of Nations as a mechanism for preventing wars and felt they had been sold out in the provisions for the Rhineland *(see page 188)*. When the American Senate refused to ratify the American guarantee to France, and thus Britain's guarantee, which had been dependent on America's, also lapsed, the French government felt forced to find alternative sources of security. This was the basic aim of French foreign policy throughout the 1920s. One way to its achievement was through alliances with other powers. To this end, an alliance was formed with Belgium in 1920. This was followed by a succession of treaties with East European countries—with Poland in 1921 and then with each of the 'Little Entente' powers—Czechoslovakia in 1924, Roumania in 1926 and Yugoslavia in 1927. These provided for mutual aid in the event of unprovoked attack, and gave each side a measure of security against their potential enemies—Germany, Russia and, in the case of Yugoslavia, Italy. At the same time, France refused to consider disarmament, thereby disrupting the League's efforts to organize a conference and giving Germany a justifiable grievance.

Hand in hand with the question of security was the problem of Germany's reparations. France's ability to afford security measures and, simultaneously, Germany's inability to do so, depended on the regular and continued payment of reparations. Even before the sum was fixed there had been a crisis, leading to Poincaré's resignation. This led to brief period in 1921–2 when Briand was foreign minister. These two men—Poincaré and Briand—dominated French foreign policy in the 1920s. While the one—Poincaré—was determined to extract all he could from Germany, if necessary by the use of force, the other was prepared to accept reductions and alterations and to treat Germany as more of an equal in international affairs. Briand's more conciliatory policy led to his resignation in 1922. At the Cannes conference of January 1922, he agreed to plans for a large international conference, at which Germany and Russia would be present, to discuss the reparations issue. His agreement was won by a British promise to renew their guarantee of French security. However, President Millerand himself informed Briand that this agreement was unpopular and against France's interests, and as a result Briand resigned his post.

He was replaced by Poincaré, and there followed two years of harshness against Germany. The highpoint of Poincaré's policy was the occupation of the Ruhr during 1923 *(see page 232)*. However, the victory of the 'Cartel des Gauches' in 1924 and Herriot's agreement to the Dawes plan, signalled the end of this harsh policy and a return to moderation.

Briand became Foreign Minister again in April 1925 and remained in the post until January 1932, even when Poincaré was Prime Minister. As Foreign Minister, he was the vital counterpart to Stresemann *(see page 297)* and was instrumental in bringing the era of peace known as the 'Locarno honeymoon'. In 1925–6 he, together with other European ministers, negotiated the Locarno treaties by which France and Germany accepted the Versailles boundaries between their countries *(see pages 297, 369)*. In 1928, he and the American Secretary of State, Kellogg, drew up the 'Pact of Paris', by which the sixty-two signatory countries renounced the use of war as a means for the settlement of international disputes. He also supported Germany's membership of the League of Nations and signed the Geneva Protocol, committing his country to compulsory arbitration of disputes *(see page 368)*. Many Frenchmen saw his friendship and agreement with Stresemann as tantamount to treachery and a threat to French security—the aged Clemenceau, in his last book *Grandeurs et Misères de la Victoire* (written in 1926) was highly critical of Briand. These fears were to some extent allayed by the development of a permanent defensive line, authorized by Painlevé, Minister of War in 1929, but began under his successor, André Maginot, after whom they were named. An intricate and extensive defensive system, built around the idea of a permanent and immovable concrete 'trench system', was to be constructed from the Swiss border to the Ardennes forest. Consequently, by 1930, most Frenchmen could be reasonably satisfied with the prospects for future French security. Briand had made the outbreak of war less likely, and if it did come France had the allies and the defences to survive it.

His successor, Louis Barthou, returned to Poincaré's policy of security through alliance rather than appeasement. After Hitler became Chancellor of Germany in 1933, Barthou sought 'to forge a new and more powerful ring of Continental alliances around Germany with which to supplement the now insufficient "small ring" in Central Europe and to balance the effects of Germany's impending rearmament'. He supported Russia's entry to the League, and opened negotiations with her that culminated in the Franco-Russian Pact of May 1935, concluded after his death. He sought to strengthen and consolidate the 'Little Entente' powers and looked at the possibilities of friendship with Italy. If this was to be achieved, he had to bring an end to the long-standing enmity between Italy and Yugoslavia. To this end, he welcomed King Alexander of Yugoslavia to Marseilles in October 1934. Negotiations never began, for both men were assassinated on the quayside.

Pierre Laval continued Barthou's policy of seeking Italian friendship.

In January 1935 they signed an agreement over African matters—the status of Italians in Tunis and the financing of the Ethiopian railway. This paved the way to the Stresa agreement between Britain, France and Italy in June 1935, by which each agreed to oppose 'any unilateral repudiation of existing treaties'. Thereafter, Laval became more conciliatory. He did not object to the reintroduction of conscription in Germany and delayed the ratification of the agreement with Russia of 1935 on the basis of Hitler's hostility to it. The Italian invasion of Ethiopia signalled the end of French opposition to the European dictators.

There was little support among deputies for the imposition of sanctions on Italy and Laval, eager to find a middle course and end France's involvement in the crisis, drew up the Hoare–Laval pact with his British opposite number *(see page 278)*. Laval was forced to resign in the aftermath of this (in January 1936) and from then onwards French policy became increasingly dependent on British attitudes and actions.

On the pretext that France's ratification of the Franco-Soviet Pact, on 27 February 1936, contravened the Locarno agreements, Hitler sent troops into the Rhineland in March 1936. The caretaker government of Albert Sarraut felt unable to act against this blatant contravention of the Versailles treaty without the certainty of British support, and this was not forthcoming. Subsequently, French foreign policy was more hamstrung than ever, as the presence of Hitler's troops just across the Rhine made free action almost impossible. Indeed, French foreign policy was haunted by two fears—the fear that Hitler would unleash the full force of his armies and the fear that too clear a policy would meet strong opposition within France, even to the extent of civil war. It was this second fear that influenced Blum's Popular Front government into choosing a policy of non-intervention in the Spanish Civil War. Although Blum and his ministers supported the Republicans, they realized that many other Frenchmen openly supported Franco and to commit his government would bring the risk of even more open opposition to it.

Nonetheless, the new Prime Minister, Daladier, assured the Czech government in May 1938 that France would stand by the promises of her treaty of 1925. When, in September, the Czech army was mobilized to counter the German threat, a million French soldiers were also mobilized. However, it was the British Prime Minister, Chamberlain, and not Daladier who took the initiative in the crisis, and the French who followed his lead at the Munich conference. For a time, French policy became more conciliatory than ever: in December 1938 a pact was signed with Germany declaring the inviolability of their mutual frontier and the promise of consultation to establish a peaceful means of settling disputes. This was in part a reaction to the deterioration of Franco-Italian relations. The Italian press contained numerous claims to Tunisia and Corsica at this time, and as a result Daladier visited the two colonies in January 1939 to reaffirm France's determination to keep them.

After the German occupation of Czechoslovakia in March 1939, French foreign policy again followed the British lead and lurched back to defiance. During the summer, negotiations were held with the Soviet Union with a view to an alliance, and it was in the midst of these negotiations that the Nazi-Soviet Pact was announced *(see page 315)*. When Germany invaded Poland on 1 September, the French army was mobilized but, significantly, the declaration of war was not announced until 3 September, following six hours behind the British declaration of war.

5. The Fall of France
(See also pages 246–52)

On the outbreak of war, over 5 million Frenchmen were mobilized. There was little of the wild enthusiasm for war that there had been in 1914, but nevertheless there was a quiet optimism that the Maginot defences would be more than equal to their task. Certainly, there were weaknesses and shortages of equipment, especially aircraft, that the government attempted to remedy during the 'phoney war' period of winter 1939–40. For example, the government took greater control over war industries; women and colonials were brought in to supplement the workforce in factories; and a sixty-hour week was introduced.

On 10 May 1940 Germany's forces attacked Belgium, Holland and Luxembourg. To the consternation of the British and French generals, lightly-armoured troops moved swiftly into the Ardennes forest, which had been left lightly defended. On 12 May German forces crossed the river Meuse at, symbolically, Sedan. By 21 May the French and British troops had been pushed back to the coast, whence, at the beginning of June they were evacuated from the beaches. In the midst of the rout, the French government had brought back the aged General Weygand as commander-in-chief and General Pétain as deputy Prime Minister. Both counselled armistice, seeing no future for France as long as the United States remained neutral and the Soviet Union was with Germany. In contrast, Prime Minister Reynaud felt that all was not lost, even if France itself fell—there was still the Empire and the fleet.

On 10 June Italy declared war and her forces invaded Southern France. The same day the Government left Paris and, joining the flood of French civilians moving southwards, went first to Tours and then to Bourdeaux. On 16 June Reynaud realized the hopelessness of the military situation; he resigned and was replaced by Pétain. The eighty-five year-old Premier broadcast to the nation his intention to seek an armistice, though his Under Secretary for War, General de Gaulle, went to England and broadcast *his* intention to continue fighting. On 21 June the armistice was signed in the same railway carriage in the forest of Compiègne that the Germans had surrendered in at the end of World War I. The terms of the armistice were moderate. All French troops were to be immediately demobilized, though the fleet was to remain intact but under Axis control. Germany would take control of the northern part of the country, though it would continue to be administered by Frenchmen.

The southern part of the country would remain under French control through the government of Pétain, based in the spa town of Vichy. In a matter of weeks, the Third Republic had been defeated. A few weeks later it was symbolically buried by a new constitution that gave extensive executive powers to the head of state, Marshal Pétain. At last France would have the controlling power at the top that she needed so badly.

6. Bibliography

Most of the books mentioned at the end of Chapter II *(page 45)* include discussion of the inter-war period as well as the pre-war era. To these might be added *The French Economy* by T. Kemp (Longman, 1972) and the Heath Series booklet *The Fall of France* edited by S.M. Osgood (Harrap).

7. Discussion Points and Exercises

A *This section consists of questions that might be used for discussion (or written answers) as a way of expanding on the chapter and testing understanding of it:*

1 What kind of leadership did France need after World War I?
2 Why did the SFIO do so badly in the elections of 1919?
3 Why was Clemenceau not elected President after his great war leadership?
4 Why was the French economy in such dire straits in the mid-twenties?
5 Why was democracy threatened in the early thirties?
6 What was the significance of the Stavisky affair?
7 Were the aims of the Popular Front realistic?
8 What were the issues that split left and right in the late thirties, and how bitter were the divisions?
9 Were France's economic problems insoluble?
10 What was the value of France's Empire?
11 Why did France look to Eastern Europe for allies?
12 Was it possible for French foreign ministers to pursue policies of both appeasement and alliances for security in the 1930s?
13 How possible was an agreement with Italy?
14 Why did France becomes so dependent on Britain in foreign policy?
15 Which course of action was most realistic in June 1940—Pétain's, Reynaud's or de Gaulle's?

B *This section is intended to illustrate some of the problems faced by the government:*

1 As a newspaper editor, write an editorial on either the virtues and vices of the Versailles settlement or the virtues and vices of Briand's approach to the German problem.

2 Write a report for the French Foreign Office in the early 1930s outlining the problems facing France and possible solutions to them.

C *This section suggests two ways in which you might compare France with other European countries in the same period:*
  1 Compare the constitutional structure of France and Germany in 1930 by examining the powers and role of the President, the Prime Minister and Cabinet and the legislature. Comment also on political parties in each.
  2 Compare the foreign policies of France and the 'Little Entente' powers, examining both their aims and the means to those aims.

D *Essay questions*
  1 Compare and contrast the careers and achievement of Briand and Poincaré.
  2 Why was little achieved and so little changed in France between the wars?
  3 'French foreign policy was doomed to failure by its constant changes of direction.' Discuss.

9. An Exercise on the Fall of France

France's swift and humiliating defeat at the hands of Germany was a subject for much emotional debate both at the time and afterwards. Obviously, military failure was the immediate cause of the defeat, but what lay behind it? Was it that French parliamentary leaders had provided ineffective leadership, as was suggested by the Vichy régime, who put some of them, including Daladier and Blum, on trial at Riom in 1942? In fact, their defence was so convincing that blame subsequently shifted to the military leaders of France. In this exercise, we shall first examine in general the broad reasons for France's failures and then the views of the four leading ministers of the time—Laval, Pétain, Daladier and Blum.

In the first place, France's defences were inadequate. Great faith was put in the Maginot Line, with the result that little else was done. It had been intended to link the Maginot Line to the coast by a series of tank traps, but in fact these were never completed, partly as a result of a shortage of concrete and disagreements over design details. In any case, the French had made the same mistake as in 1914, in thinking in terms of the war before: the Maginot Line was the trench to end all trenches, when technological advance in the form of tanks and aeroplanes had made trench warfare obsolete. There were other military failings. At the top, Generals Gamelin and Georges found it difficult to agree, or even to decide which had the ultimate command. Neither generals nor civilians were prepared to take the initiative in the early part of the war. German generals expressed their amazement that France made no attack on their weak western defences while they were attacking Poland. But French military thinking was locked to the idea of defence. In addition, the French feared that any positive action would bring a swift German attack and civilian casualties. For this reason, Daladier, as minister of Defence, opposed British plans to mine the river Rhine and persuaded the British to mine Norwegian waters instead. In the event, this action heralded the German assault on the West anyway.

However, military failings were ultimately only the expression of other failings. For example, France lacked the economic support necessary for a modern army fighting a massive war. Industry had always lagged behind her European competitors, and even in the 1930s a third of the French workforce was engaged in agriculture. Moreover, the depression had hit France later than other countries, with the result that her industrial production, down some 20% in 1938 compared with 1928, was inadequate.

More importantly, many Frenchmen saw little purpose in fighting Germany in 1940. After all, the World War I had brought little reward for the losses suffered, and the years between had been, if anything, even worse than before the war. On an individual level, many Frenchmen who had fought, or died, in the World War I, had sons or sons-in-law of military age by 1940. Many of them saw no reason why their sons should suffer what they themselves had been through.

In addition, there were political mistakes and inadequacies. There had been endless changes of government, making any coherent or complete programme of reform almost impossible. The only government that had attempted genuine change—the Popular Front—had been dogged and defeated by opposition from both sides. Parliamentary government had largely been superceded by decree laws; for thirty-five of the seventy-seven months between 1934 and 1940 there was decree law. Employers and business had considerable influence in government and had prevented the proposals of the Matignon Agreements coming into full effect. Above all, there were no political leaders of genuine stature. Clemenceau, Poincaré and Briand, the giants of the Great War and the 1920s, were gone, and their successors had none of their determination, vision or ability to win over supporters and opposition. Blum, Daladier and Laval were pale shadows, buffeted from policy to policy by interest groups and other powers.

With these ideas in mind, study the following documents:

A. Pierre Laval—Speech to the National Assembly, Vichy, 10 July 1940 (extracts) from *Le Figaro* 29 February 1952, translated by S. M. Osgood and printed in *The Fall of France* by S. M. Osgood.)

> Some have charged that the proposal the Government is about to bring before you amounts to a repudiation of the parliamentary regime. Let me say loud and clear that this is not so. The Government's proposal is much more than that. It is the repudiation, not only of the parliamentary regime,

but of everything that was and can no longer be. . . . There was too little awareness in France, beyond a few official platitudes, that certain policies and formulas had to be avoided if the peace were to be preserved. Remember? It is permissible to call someone a thief, a crook or a pimp. But the one irreparable insult, the insult of insults was to call someone a fascist. Ah yes! The fact is that anti-fascism was the starting point of all our domestic and foreign policies. . . .

France was overly fat and happy. She used and abused her freedom. And it is precisely because there was an excess of freedom in all fields that we find ourselves in the present straits. It is also a fact—I say this sadly because a great calamity has befallen us—that the existing institutions cannot be allowed to survive a disaster of this magnitude. Without wishing to impassion the debate, let me remind you that too much freedom in our schools contributed to our demise. One word was forbidden in our schools, the word 'Patrie'. Take a look at our neighbours. Italy was once on the verge of anarchy. One could walk the streets only at the risk of being assaulted by a mob bent on seizing power. In Germany, defeat had brought on misery, and misery, in turn, had brought on chaos. Well, what did these two neighbours do? They restored the idea of the fatherland. They began by teaching their youth to love their country, and that one's country is the family, the past, the village where one was born. These are the values which the schoolteachers failed to instil in our children.

The Constitution we have in mind is not reactionary. Both the current state of affairs in France and the temperament of our people preclude a longing for, or return to the past. We must plan ahead for the future. We must give the working class something more than the right to vote. The workers must be able to enjoy tangible rights under the impartial supervision of the State. Both agricultural and industrial workers will receive full recognition for the amount and quality of their work. There will be only one aristocracy, an aristocracy of the intelligence. . . .

Let me say, to avoid the possibility of any misunderstanding, that in virtue of the full powers you are about to grant Marshall Petain, the role played by the Chambers will necessarily be reduced. But his Government reserves the right, and intends to enlist the help of regularly appointed parliamentary committees. . . . We have no intention of becoming the slavish imitators of any other country, because this would mean that we were no longer worthy to call ourselves Frenchmen, that we had lost all pride in our race. Do you know why, above all, we are bringing up this proposal for a new Constitution? It is to obtain for France, I will not say the best, but the least harmful possible peace terms. Bear this in mind when you come to the public session.

B. Marshal Pétain—'Speech of 11 October 1940'
(From *Quatre annees au pouvoir* by Philippe Pétain (1949) translated by S. M. Osgood and printed in *The Fall of France* by S. M. Osgood.)
Frenchmen!

Four months ago, France suffered one of the most thorough defeats in her history. This defeat was caused by many factors, not all of which were of a technical nature. In truth, the disaster was simply the reflection, on a military plane, of the weaknesses and defects of the former regime. Many of you, however, as I well know, loved that regime. Because you exercised that the right to vote every four years, you considered yourselves to be free citizens in a free state. I will thus surprise you by saying that, to an extent unparalleled in the history of France, the State was at the mercy of special interests during the past twenty years. It was taken over in various ways, successively and sometimes simultaneously, by coalitions of economic interests, and by teams of politicians and syndicalists falsely claiming to represent the working class.

The succeeding majorities represented the temporary ascendancy of one or the other of these two factions. The majority's sole concern was all too often to eliminate the minority. When these struggles led to an impasse, one resorted to yet another dupery: the formation of a so-called 'Government of National Union'. A coalition of divergent political opinions does not make for coherence; a reservoir of 'good will' does not necessarily translate itself into 'one will'. These swings of the pendulum, this modern-day vassalage, had far-reaching effect. Everything pointed to the impotence of a regime which repudiated its very principles by resorting to emergency decree powers in the face of every serious crisis. War and defeat merely hastened the coming of the political revolution toward which the country was eventually headed. Hindered by such domestic political considerations, the regime was, for the most part, incapable of formulating and implementing a foreign policy worthy of France. Inspired in turn by a paranoid nationalism or a doctrinaire pacifism, characterized by lack of understanding and weakness—at the very moment when our victory called upon us to be at once generous and strong, our foreign policy could only result in disaster. It took us approximately fifteen years to fall into the abyss to which it inexorably led. One day in September 1939 without even daring to consult the Chambers, the Government declared war. This war was all but lost in advance. We had been equally incapable of avoiding or of preparing for it.

Today we must rebuild France on a heap of ruins.

The new order can in no way whatsoever imply a return to the mistakes which have cost us so dearly. Nor should it take on the features of a kind of 'moral order', or of a revenge for the events of 1936.

The new order cannot be a servile imitation of foreign experiments—though some of these experiments are not without sense and beauty. Each people, however, must conceive of a regime suitable to its temper and genius.

A new order is an absolute necessity for France. Our tragedy is that we shall have to carry out in defeat the revolution which we were not even able to realize in victory in peace, in an atmosphere of understanding among equal nations.

C. Edouard Daladier—'Why France Went to War'

(From *Les Evenements survenus en France de 1933 à 1945, Témoignages et documents receuillis par la commission d'enquête parlementaire, Rapport—Annexes (Depositions)* (1947) translated by S. M. Osgood and printed in *The Fall of France* by S. M. Osgood.) (Extracts)

Had she taken a different course, had she bowed before Hitler, France would not only have been dishonoured but she would have acted against her best interests. Again, in spite of what followed, I insist we had no alternative. If we had not gone to war, France would have earned the contempt of the democratic world. Neither Great Britain nor the United States would ever again have been willing to sign the least pact with us. And, in the final analysis, we would not have avoided war. What would Hitler have done once he had gobbled up Poland's chief resources? These are only hypotheses. One does not rewrite history. But, if I may be allowed to speculate, what would Hitler have done? Would he have crushed Poland and gone on to attack Russia in the spring of 1940? It is by no means certain that in the spring of 1940, Russia would have been able to parry the first onslaught and turn the tide of battle as she did toward the end of 1941. The fortunes of war are subject for debate, but it is a fact that not a single country in the world was able to stop the German army at its borders. And, although Russia was saved by the courage of her soldiers, the tenacity of her people, and the strength of her industry, the fact remains that in the beginning she lost two thousand kilometres of her richest, most fertile, and most industrialized territory to the German army.

Had Germany jumped on Russia in the spring of 1940, can you imagine the French Government asking the French people to go to her help? After the Nazi-Soviet Pact? After the publication of the secret clauses of that Pact? One may hypothesize further that before he attacked Russia, Hitler would have demanded guarantees from France. Are you so sure that there would not have been a government in Paris, ready to give him these guarantees in order to avoid war? These are good questions to ponder in ones solitude.

For my part, I believed then as I do now, and I shall try to get you to share this conviction, that France was initially capable of resisting, if not of invading and defeating Germany. I feared that we might well have been pushed back in some areas of the front. But I did not for a moment envision the possibility of military collapse. In my mind, this collapse was due less to deficiencies of a technical or material order, than to faulty military doctrines, and even more to the difference between the doctrines of the two armies, and to the tremendous strategic surprise which was sprung at the time.

I am not here to prosecute the military leaders. They prosecuted me at Riom, and that is reason enough for me not to want to do so. But if you study the campaign, you will see that the General Staff expected the German attack to come through Holland and Belgium. In 1914, we had expected the attack to come on the right bank of the Meuse. This time it was expected to come in Holland, in Northern Belgium, and on the left bank of the Meuse. That is why the largest and best equipped divisions of the French army were moved to the North. Two or three days later, it became apparent that the invasion of Holland and Belgium was only a diversionary manouevre.

On 12 May I went to the Château du Câteau, in Belgium, to ask the King of Belgium to place his army under French command. I travelled by car in broad daylight, and stopped in almost every town. I saw the French motorized units pass by. I saw French soldiers park their trucks, tanks, and armoured cars at every crossroad and public square, and jump out, in violation of all regulations, to fraternize with the Belgian people . . .

The essence of the strategic surprise was that the bulk and the most powerful elements of the German army attacked not on the left bank of the Meuse, but on the right bank from Namur to Sedan, at the centre of our line, and to the rear of the French forces that had been moved forward. The

German documents now in our possession prove that the enemy attacked at that point because he knew full well that this was the weakest link on our line of defence.

D. P. Reynaud—'The Failure of the Parliamentary System'
(From *La France a sauvé l'Europe* (1947) translated by S. M. Osgood and printed in *The Fall of France* by S. M. Osgood.) (Extracts)

'The regime led the country to ruin', said Marshal Pétain, in a radio address on 4 April 1934. Following his lead, the Vichy press invariably accused the parliamentary regime of having been responsible for the defeat. Why then were we defeated? 'Because we did not have enough arms or allies', said Pétain, in a broadcast from Bordeaux on the morrow of the débâcle. True enough, but let us suppose for a moment that France had been ruled, between the wars by an absolute monarchy with Pétain as King. . . . Would we have had a tank corps? We have already seen that Pétain did not even want a single armoured division. Would we have had a single air attack wing? We have already seen that he discounted the role of air power in battle. Would we have had a pact with Russia, the only alliance capable of saving us? We have seen that he had publicly taken a stand against such an alliance. On the question of armaments, Maurras was content to proclaim to the four winds: 'We must give our military leaders what they want!' The trouble was that they did not want anything! . . .

What is the greatest complaint about the parliamentary regime? Instability. Instability at the Ministry of War? From December 1932 to May 1940, with an exception of an interlude of two years and four months, we had the same Minister of War. Instability of Command? From 1917 to 1940, we had only Pétain, Weygand and Gamelin—three Commanders-in Chief in twenty-three years!

Did Parliament ever refuse to provide the necessary funds for national defence, be it for fortifications or armaments? It always granted all requests in full. Did Parliament refuse to lengthen the period of service? The Chamber doubled it on the very day the request was made. The truth is that we were defeated because, during the interwar period, both the succeeding Governments and Parliaments failed to fulfil their functions. Was this due to institutional weaknesses? Or can we lay the blame at the door of the politicians? Can we blame the framers of the Constitution of 1875 for not having inserted a clause to the effect that when one is the weaker party, one seeks a powerful ally? For not having specifically stated that once one has chosen weak allies, one must maintain an army capable of attacking their would-be aggressors?

Let us look rather at the Governments. I have already shown that the three distinguishing characteristics of our military policy, originally formulated by Marshal Pétain, were ignorance, cynicism and incoherence. This policy was endorsed by succeeding ministers of War. Yet the very essence of parliamentarism is the supremacy of the civilian branch over the military establishment. . . . In a debate over our inability to fortify the path traditionally followed by the invaders of France, because our Ministers of War 'adopted the views of Marshal as a matter of principle', I had occasion to remark that the military policy of France should no more be left to the soldiers than our financial policy be left to the Inspectors of Finance, or our foreign policy to the diplomats. Such questions must be settled by states-

251

men—with the help, of course, of the technicians. . . . By delegating entirely to our top soldiers the task of formulating and implementing our military policy, they deprived the country of a statesmanlike strategy. Our military policy was incoherent because it was never thought out at the highest plane. . . .

The Parliament was also to blame, in that it sanctioned economic, diplomatic and military policies that were equally incoherent. A Parliament should no more be a rubber stamp than a wrecker of ministries. Its essential task is to study, approve or disapprove, and supervise the implementation of the various programmes brought before it by the Executive branch. This is an important and difficult role which demands more knowledge and hard work than the framing of an insidious amendment designed to ensure the defeat of a bill and perhaps the government itself. This primary task was simply not performed. What did Parliament do, in 1933, when Hitler came to power, *Mein Kampf* in hand? It voted the reduction of the French army's officer corps by one-sixth. . . . Why could not the Armed Forces Committee of each Chamber have said to successive Ministers of War: 'You are raising a defensive army. You think in terms of concrete, continuous front, and firepower. Yet France is committed to come to the defence of Poland and Czechoslovakia in case of German aggression. How are you going to attack Germany with a defensive army? Should Belgium be attacked, our army will have to fight an open-field campaign. Such an eventuality is all the more likely, since the Maginot Line is but another inducement for the Germans to take the traditional invasion path to France which runs right through Belgium. How are you going to fight such a campaign with a defensive army? Will the French army push its concrete before it, as Malcolm's army, in Macbeth, carried the trees of Birnam Wood?' Could not these same parliamentary committees have told these same ministers: 'Your policies are incomprehensible. You claim that you are raising a defensive army, yet it is being equipped with too few anti-aircraft guns, anti-tank guns, and anti-tank mines to match the offensive weapons of our potential enemy.' . . . All the National Defence Committees should have concluded in unison: 'The ministers must devise new doctrines or we will replace the ministers.' Then, and only then, would the parliamentary regime have functioned. The appeal of all this incoherence was that it represented the path of least resistance. But it would never have carried the day without the endorsement of the 'Victor of Verdun'. whom the Republic canonized until he turned round and strangled it. This surrender to the Marshal amounted to the quasi-dissolution of Parliament. . . France's misfortune was not that she was saddled with a Parliament, but that hers was not worthy of the name. . . . We were defeated because the parliamentary regime failed to function.

Having carefully read and discussed these four views on the fall of France, answer the following questions:

1   To what and/or whom does each of the authors attribute France's weakness in 1940?

2   Why does each of the authors adopt his particular standpoint— what were the personal and political motives underlying their explanations?

3   Which of the four explanations seems most plausible, and what additional evidence would you require to support your view?

XI Italy 1919–39

(For map, see page 50)

1. Background: Italy and World War I

From the outbreak of war until May 1915 Italy remained neutral. Prime Minister Salandra explained this on the grounds that Austria's action against Serbia was offensive, while the Triple Alliance was a defensive alliance and therefore Italy was entitled to remain neutral. During the winter of 1914–15, Italian politicians and people argued over the relative merits of each side and of continued neutrality. Obviously, the war provided an opportunity for Italy to settle her major dispute—the areas of Austria-Hungary with large Italian minorities—and the argument was therefore over how these could best be won. Foreign Minister Sonnino claimed that Article VII of the Triple Alliance promised Italy compensation to balance any Austrian gains in the Balkans, and he persuaded the German government of this. However, it was not until 10 May 1915 that the Germans persuaded the Austrian government to accept these demands (the cession of Trentino and the South Tyrol and some Adriatic islands). By this time, those who favoured Italy joining France and Britain had equally won considerable concessions in the case of Austria's defeat. In the secret treaty of London (26 April 1915), the Allies agreed that, in return for Italian military assistance, they would help in the fight against Austria, and, when victory was won, Italy could have Trentino, the South Tyrol, Gorizia, Gradisca, Trieste, Istria, parts of Dalmatia, the Adriatic islands, extensions to Libya (as Tripolitania was now known), Eritrea and Somaliland and a share of any war indemnity—all if Italy declared war within a month *(see Maps 29 and 30)*.

On 3 May Salandra denounced the Triple Alliance. On 20 May, Parliament voted by 470 to seventy-four in favour of intervention, although previously only seventy deputies had been committed to the war. Nationalist demonstrations were encouraged to ensure popular support —100 000 were amassed for the largest of these in Rome. Three days later war was declared on Austria-Hungary but was not declared on Germany until 28 August 1916.

Italy's war record was not impressive, and both ministers and generals rose and fell fast. On 12 December 1916 Salandra was replaced by Paolo Boselli, who himself resigned following the defeat of his army at Caporetto in October 1917, to be replaced by Vittorio Orlando *(see page 170)*. 217

different generals were appointed in the space of two years, few victories of note were won, and by the time of the armistice the treaty of London seemed less of a diplomatic triumph for the Entente than it had in 1915. This became even more obvious during the Paris Peace Conference. For it was soon clear that the promises made in the treaty of London conflicted with Woodrow Wilson's plans for national self-determination (Wilson, of course, had not been a signatory of the treaty of London). Hence the Italian delegation found their claims publicly denounced by Wilson on 24 April 1919 and, led by Prime Minister Orlando, left the Conference in high dudgeon, only to return uninvited to make sure they got something, on 5 May. Ultimately, Italy did gain a considerable amount of land from the treaty of St Germain with Austria—Trentino, the South Tyrol, Trieste and Istria all became a part of Italy—but there were no colonies, no money and only some of the land they had hoped for: 9000 square miles of it, and a population of 1·6 million, in exchange for 600 000 dead, massive war debts and a huge increase in the cost of living.

Map 29 South Tyrol and Trentino

2. Political History

(a) 1919:–21
Not surprisingly, the war and its aftermath left the government with little prestige, for Italians had taken a mighty blow to their self-esteem in

the previous four years. During 1919, this unpopularity, both with the government and with the system of government, was shown in a number of ways. Firstly, Prime Minister Orlando lost support and resigned in June 1919 when only seventy-eight deputies voted for him out of more than 500. Then, on 12 September 1919, Gabriele D'Annunzio, a poet and ardent nationalist, led an army of volunteers into the city of Fiume on the Dalmatian coast and claimed it for Italy since the majority of the population were Italian. D'Annunzio's supporters wore black shirts and used the straight arm salute, and proclaimed music to be the state religion. Their occupation of Fiume, which lasted for fifteen months, showed both that there were groups of people who were prepared to take the law into their own hands, and that the government was prepared actually to let them do so. The government's only attempt to get them out before December 1920 was to invite D'Annunzio to join an experimental flight from Rome to Tokyo. D'Annunzio replied by hiring an

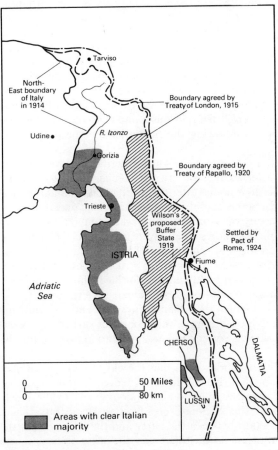

Map 30 Italy's north-east Border, 1915–24

aeroplane and dropping a chamber-pot of carrots on to the Parliament building in Rome. The government of Nitti chose to leave the rebels in Fiume and it was only in December 1920 that they were finally ousted by the army, leaving without a fight. The Fiume incident foreshadowed what was to come not only in the salutes and uniforms, but also in the attitude of the government to lawbreakers. For it became a commonplace of Italian political life in 1920–22 that the government took no action against right wingers who used violence to remove elected governments and install their own.

A third indication of disillusion with the existing political structure and parties was the development of the socialist party, the PSI, in 1919–20. The party grew in size from 50 000 before the war to 200 000 in 1919 and trade union membership in the Confederation of Labour from ½ million to 2 million. With the increased membership came increased activity: 1½ million strikers in 1919, compared with 300 000 before 1914. Even more notably, the PSI controlled twenty-six of the sixty-nine provinces and some 2000 town councils, on whose buildings flew not the tricolour of Italy but the red flag of socialism. Moreover, in the general election of November 1919, the socialists won 156 seats, when previously they had held fifty; they were not only the largest political party in Italy, but also the most organized. This increased popularity of socialism was obviously a sign that many new voters were not attracted by the old alternatives. It was, though, even more than that, for the 1919 party Congress at Bologna had rejected reformism and chosen instead to join the Third International, following the revolutionary line dictated by Moscow.

The strikes and the adherence to the Third International were not the only indications of a leftward trend. In the confusion of 1919, many peasants returning to their homes after the war had taken land that had belonged to landlords. Sometimes the land was taken in anger, following a struggle; sometimes it was simply taken because nobody seemed to own it. Either way, these seizures of land were given official recognition by the government in the Visocchi decree of September 1919 and the Falcioni decree of April 1920. Workers on strike, a powerful revolutionary socialist party, government approval for illegal land grabbing— what was Italy coming to? Respectable Italian society, used to the formality of elections in which their man always won and governments were always respectable conservative coalitions, not surprisingly wondered what their world was coming to—was revolution just around the corner?

There were two further indications that the old way of government was under attack. Pope Benedict XV lifted the ban on Catholics participating in elections, thereby giving a tremendous boost to the newly formed Catholic party, the 'Popolari' or Christian Democrats. There was no official connection between the party and the Church, but the leader was a Sicilian priest, Don Sturzo, and the party obviously won support from churchgoers, and won over 100 seats in the 1919 election—

another new political force. In fact, though, the 'Popolari' was never a united party as its members ranged from traditional, monarchical Churchmen at one end to virtual Marxists at the other. Their one common ideal was opposition to anticlericalism, which was represented by the major coalition bloc in Parliament, the Liberals and Democrats gathered around Giolitti. This opposition was to prove fatal in that it prevented these two groups—the 'Popolari' and the anticlericals—uniting and forming a moderate alternative to either socialism or fascism.

Month of appointment	Name
March 1914	Antonio Salandra
June 1916	Paolo Boselli
October 1917	Vittorio Orlando
June 1919	Francesco Nitti
June 1920	Giovanni Giolitti
July 1921	Ivanoe Bonomi
February 1922	Luigi Facta
October 1922	Benito Mussolini

Table 32 Italian Prime Ministers 1914–43

The final, and apparently least important indication of opposition, was the foundation of the 'Fascio di Combattimento' by some fifty malcontents on 23 March 1919. They were an assorted lot, ranging from the syndicalist Bianchi to the monarchist de Vecchi via the futurist poet Marinetti, who suggested that the Pope should be dropped into the Adriatic. They put up candidates for the 1919 election, but fared disastrously, winning no seats at all. Even their leader, Benito Mussolini, could only win 2% of the vote in Milan, less than 5000 votes against 170 000 for the Socialists.

However, 1920 and 1921 were to see the upsurge of this tiny group so that it rivalled the Socialists. In the summer of 1920 Giolitti's government (Giolitti had first formed a government almost thirty years earlier) faced ½ million workers sitting in in factories following a lock-out in the metallurgical industry in protest at low wages that accounted for only 9% of total costs. In fact, union leaders were taken by surprise by this sudden, spontaneous, revolutionary outburst and soon persuaded the workers to give in in return for higher wages. But this outbreak and the continued discussion of the impending revolution that it gave rise to led to further fear among the opponents of socialism, many of whom now joined Mussolini's 'Fascist' party. In the winter of 1920–21 these men, organized into 'squadre d'azione' (squads of action) by local leaders ('ras') like Balbo in Ferrara and Grandi in Bologna, began a campaign of violence against Socialists that led to some 200 dead and 800 wounded in the period between December 1920 and May 1921. The government did little to prevent the violence, and instead saw it as a cheap way of curbing the rise of socialism, though by the spring of 1921 the clashes had reached riot proportions. Nonetheless they had succeeded in their aim of disrupting the progress of socialism.

At the party Congress at Livorno in January 1921 the PSI split into a revolutionary and a reformist wing, a move welcomed, if not actually forced, by the Fascists.

The increasing support for the Fascists was also reflected in the election of 15 May 1921. For it, Prime Minister Giolitti invited them to form a part of his right-wing electoral alliance, thereby promising them, for the first time, some influence in the government as well as in the streets. The Fascists did well in these elections, as these figures show. (These figures are not wholly accurate, as different researchers disagree on the precise affiliations of some deputies):

Extreme Nationalists	10		
Fascists	35	} 184	Government bloc
National Bloc (Giolitti)	139		
Radicals (Liberal Democrats)	68	} 175	Potential centrist
'Popolari'	107		opposition
Reformists	29		
Socialists	123		
Communists	15	} 176	Left opposition
National minorities	9		

From May to July 1921 Giolitti was to govern on the basis of this coalition but within a year there were to be thirteen different groups in Parliament. Since the deputies fell into three approximately equal groupings, the Fascists' thirty-five seats were crucial, since their defection to the opposition would make government very difficult. This situation, as a powerful force in Parliament despite only having thirty-five of the 535 seats, took Mussolini by surprise. His immediate reaction was to become a respectable participant in government; he even signed a 'peace treaty', 'the pact of pacification', with the Socialists to end their mutual violence. However, his lieutenants in the provinces disliked this curb on their power and protested against it, in reply to which Mussolini actually resigned as leader; but in November he accepted their demands for continued hostility and tore up the pact.

(b) 1921–2: The Fascists take power

The economic conditions of the period did much to encourage support for both the extremist parties, the Fascists on the one hand and the Communists and PSI on the other. As a result of Italy's war debts and problems of reconstruction, the lire was devalued and prices rose about 50%, while wages remained at their pre-war levels. In such circumstance, the working-class voters were attracted to the left-wing parties in the hope of pressing for wage claims. In some cases, they took action on their own behalf by striking and, in some cases, occupying factories. In turn, this raised the spectre of revolution and increased the attractions of the Fascists for the middle class and all those who owned property and feared socialism. The Fascists alone seemed to offer the firm action to prevent revolution that many Italians saw as the only alternative to Bolshevism.

From December 1921 to November 1922 both Fascist violence and short-lived governments continued. Fascist thuggery became ever more efficient, and the Socialists claimed that in the two years before October 1922 3000 of their supporters had been killed by the Fascist squads, who had suffered only 300 fatalities themselves. Giolitti, faced by Fascist opposition in Parliament, was forced to resign on 26 June 1921. His successor, Ivanoe Bonomi, was a reformist Socialist, and formed a government with Radical and 'Popolari' support; since the one was clerical and the other anti-clerical, he was walking a political tightrope, from which he fell in February 1922. It was four weeks before the king could persuade anyone else to take over, and the lot fell to Luigi Facta. Mack Smith has described him as follows: '. . . a timid, ignorant provincial lawyer who had risen in politics by seniority alone. His appointment was at first taken almost as a joke. . .'. His government was defeated by the desertion of the 'Popolari' in the summer of 1922, but on 1 August he again became Prime Minister when no other could be found; as Mussolini himself said: 'No one wanted or was able to seize power.'

The very day that Facta formed his new ministry, the unions began a general strike. The strike was called in an effort to force the government to take some action against the Fascist violence. The Fascists had won control of a number of cities, and had even driven the communist town council of Bologna out of office in May 1922. Even worse, the government had still failed to act, despite the availability of 240 000 armed forces, 65 000 police and 40 000 militia. When they did act, as at Sazana in June 1921 when 500 Fascists were put to flight by the police, the measures were effective. Yet subsequently, the governments had not bothered and even an order of December 1921 to provincial prefects to suppress the Fascists was ignored. At the end of their tether, the strike was called by Socialists to try to force the government into action. The strike played right into Mussolini's hands, for yet again the bogey of socialist revolution was raised. The Fascists promised that they would end the strike even if the government would not. On 2 August they acted against the strikers in Ancona, Genoa and Leghorn and the next day entered Milan; after three hours of street fighting, they entered the offices of the socialist newspaper, *Avanti*, smashed the presses and burnt the buildings to the ground. The Socialist administration of Milan was then attacked and the triumphant Fascists were addressed by D'Annunzio. When the transport workers continued their strike, the Fascists simply took over the trains and ran them themselves.

By the late summer, Mussolini had determined that the Fascists had the power to take over the government, although the means to that end were undecided. On 13 August the party congress gave its approval for his efforts to win power by peaceful rather than violent means. Consequently, his first aim had to be new elections to increase Fascist representation in Parliament and so give greater weight to his demands for power. The incumbent government of Facta looked fragile and it was expected that, after the parliamentary recess of the summer, a new coalition would be formed under one of the accepted parliamentary leaders—Giolitti, Salandra or Orlando. Members of Facta's coalition were spread along a spectrum from those who favoured the forceful suppression of Fascism to those who sought the inclusion of Fascists in the new government. This latter group dominated the congress of liberal politicians held at Bologna on 8 October to form a new party which stated its intention to 'steer firmly to the right'. Consequently, there was in the government itself a faction prepared to accommodate the Fascists.

There were still a number of potential obstacles to Mussolini. The most obvious were the King and the army. Victor Emmanuel himself had little time for the Fascists. However, many of his advisers, including the Queen Mother, Margherita, and his cousin, the Duke of Aosta, a general in the war and hero of the nationalist right, were known to be Fascist sympathizers. Mussolini himself tried to allay the King's fears, and in speeches explained that the King had nothing to fear from him. In the final analysis, the King's role was to prove decisive. The loyalties of the army, whose support would be critical in the event of a Fascist uprising, were uncertain. On the one hand, many young officers openly supported the party and one of its generals, De Bono, was a leading member of it. On the other, most soldiers had little time for Fascism and accepted that their loyalty was to Crown and State. To reinforce this, the Minister of War, Soleri, ordered the dismissal of officers who attended Fascist meetings in army uniform and the instigation of disciplinary action against De Bono.

Another possible source of opposition was D'Annunzio. He resented Mussolini's new found support and still hoped to find a role as national saviour. He was a close friend of Facta, with whom he discussed ways of keeping Mussolini out of power. The two decided on a national rally on 4 November (the anniversary of Italy's war victory) at which D'Annunzio and Facta would together address a meeting of ex-servicemen, and appeal for peace, order and national unity. In this alliance of moderation and the hero of war veterans lay the greatest threat to Mussolini.

By mid-September much of North Italy was under Fascist control through their domination of local government. The problems of unemployment and strikes required immediate action that would be easier if the party also has control of the national government, while the semi-military blackshirted 'squads' needed action to prevent disaffection. At the end of the month, Mussolini went on a tour of the North, in which he made his intentions clear: 'Our programme is simple: we intend to govern Italy', he told the crowds at Udine. Under such a threat, Giolitti seemed the one politician with the support and experience to prevent a violent Fascist take over. All the moderate parties and Facta himself promised their support for him and by early October negotiations for him to form a new government were almost complete. The plan was for a multi-party coalition including the Fascists, to be formed when Parliament reassembled and prepared for fresh elections in the spring. Mussolini, however, made it clear that he would only join such a coalition if it was formed *before* Parliament reassembled (i.e. before the planned rally of 4 November) and provided that elections were held sooner than the spring. Parliament was not due to meet again until 7 November, and Facta was concerned about his own ability to cope with the Fascist Party Congress planned for 24 October and the rally of 4 November. Both could easily result in violence, and Facta urged Giolitti to act quickly.

Both the Fascists and the government prepared for the possibility of violence. On 16 October, the Fascist leaders met and drew up plans for a march on Rome. The 'quadrumviri'—Balbo, Bianchi, De Vecchi and De Bono—were appointed to lead and co-ordinate these plans. Mussolini hoped that violence would not be needed, but that the threat of it would be enough to precipitate a crisis that would bring him to power peacefully. On the same day, he met D'Annunzio and reached agreement over union recognition in the Genoa docks (a major cause of dissent between the supporters of the two men) and so reduced the likelihood of opposition from that quarter. For his part, Facta sounded out the army leaders, Diaz and Badoglio, who assured him that 'the army will do its duty if it is necessary to defend Rome'. Badoglio thought that 'ten or twelve arrests' would be enough to crush the Fascists. Between 19 and 25 October the Rome garrison of 2500 was reinforced and plans for blocking the bridges and roads into the city drawn up. Police and troops guarded the stations as Fascist delegates passed through the city en route to the Party Congress in Naples.

On the first day of the Congress, Mussolini announced that they would join the government only if they were given five cabinet posts, including the Foreign Ministry. At a march past of 60 000 supporters, Mussolini announced that it was only a matter of days and even hours before the government was theirs. The plans for the march on Rome were finalized; three columns of marchers were to descend simultaneously on the city on 28 October. Mussolini repeated his pledge that they did not intend to confront the army but that Rome would be reached 'at all costs'. Mussolini then returned to Milan, where he continued negotiations with Giolitti through the mediation of Lusignoli, the prefect of Milan. De Vecchi, Grandi and Ciano were sent to Rome to act as Fascist spokesmen in the capital, and the scene was set for Mussolini's final triumph.

On 26 and 27 October, the Fascist leaders in Rome told Facta, Salandra and the King that their party was on the point of seizing power by force. Facta's ministers urged resignation, but the King refused to appoint a new Prime Minister 'under threat of violence'. He was told of the defensive plans for the city and approved them. On the night of 27/28

October squads of Fascists seized control of town halls, post offices and stations in many towns of Northern Italy, unopposed by local officials or police. They did not, however, take possession of the major cities of Turin, Genoa and Bologna and their hold in Florence and Milan was not assured. At 12.30 am on 28 October the military authorities were put in overall charge of public order throughout the country. Facta had an audience with the King at 2.30 am, in which the King approved a manifesto whereby the government announced 'its supreme duty to defend the state at all cost, by all means and against all who violate its laws.' At 5 am the cabinet met and approved the manifesto and the firm measures taken to put down the uprising, so at 7.50 am a state of siege was announced, to commence at midday. By 9 am the government's manifesto was appearing on buildings throughout Rome. The trainloads of Fascist supporters were stopped at checkpoints and the main body of intending marchers—some 20 000 of them—were stopped fifty miles from the city when confronted by 400 policemen. Only two of the three columns, with a mere 5000 men between them, had reached their assembly points, where they waited for action, hungry, ill-equipped and soaked by torrential rain. In Rome 28 000 troops and police awaited their arrival.

At 9 am Facta drove to the palace to get the King formally to authorize the state of martial law. He refused to sign it. For some reason, he had changed his mind since earlier that morning—a change that was criti—cal for the future of Italy but is difficult to understand, given that the Fascists stood little chance if they continued their attempt to win by force. After World War II, Victor Emmanuel explained that he thought there were 100 000 Fascists outside the city, and only 8000 troops to stop them; in fact, there were about 30 000 of each, but the king never asked the military commander of Rome, Pugliese, for an estimate. It is also possible that he feared his cousin, the Duke of Aosta, and thought that he might lead the revolution against him. Above all, he feared a civil war, especially as he was not convinced of the army's loyalty. One account is that General Giraldi told him, when asked what the army would do, that 'the army will do its duty, but it would be better not to put it to the test'. This conversation took place between 5 am and 9 am. In addition, he certainly did not see a refusal to sign as tantamount to giving power to Mussolini. When Facta resigned, at 11 am on 28 October, Victor Emmanuel went through the motions of consulting all political parties, but by the evening had persuaded his old adviser, Salandra, to form a government. Salandra agreed to this only on condition that Mussolini would join the government.

At first it seemed likely that Mussolini would agree. Salandra negotiated with De Vecchi, Grandi and Ciano and agreed that there should be four Fascists in the new cabinet. However, in the early hours of 29 October, Mussolini rejected the offer. He had not gone to the trouble of organizing a national insurrection for the reward of four cabinet posts. In the morning Salandra told the king that he was unable to form a government, leaving Victor Emmanual with little choice. During the day Mussolini was contacted again, and that evening he caught the night train from Milan to become Prime Minister of Italy. On 30 October the bedraggled columns of blackshirts, their numbers swelled by the scent of triumph, were allowed into Rome. There were some outbreaks of violence —thirteen deaths were reported from the working-class San Lorenzo district—but in general the army prevented trouble. The blackshirts marched past the King on the balcony of his palace and then past Mussolini outside his hotel. Their 'march on Rome' had gone ahead, but it was of little significance; Mussolini had taken power at the end of a telephone while they were waiting around.

3. Political History 1922–39

(a) The Fascist takeover

Mussolini took power in the same way that many of his predecessors as Prime Minister had done—as the leader of a coalition, of Fascists, Catholics, right-wingers and even Social Democrats. However, he did not intend that he should continue to follow in their footsteps, either in length of service or as a coalition. His first steps towards establishing greater power were taken in November, 1922. On the 16 November the Chamber gave him a vote of confidence by 306 votes to 116 in a massive reversal of his previous fortunes and on the 25th the King gave him dictatorial power to restore order and introduce reforms. As this power was due to last only until 31 December 1923, Italians could still believe that they were living in a constitutional democracy, since after that date Mussolini's government would again be accountable to Parliament.

However, 1923 was to see the further erosion of constitutionalism. In January the Fascist squads were transformed into the 'MVSN', a volunteer militia for national security, who took their oath to the state, and not to the King, as their predecessors, the now disbanded Royal Guard, had. This provided Mussolini with what amounted to a private army of 300 000. Throughout the year, there were changes of personnel in key jobs, like the police force, the prefectures and local government, while in March a new group of Senators, including several leading Fascists like De Bono, was created. Then in November—a month before the emergency powers expired—the Accerbo electoral law was debated. It was brought before Parliament rather than introduced by decree because of its importance and because it affected Parliament's composition; yet while it was debated black-shirted troops strolled ostentatiously around the building, armed with pistols and daggers. By this law, the party that received the largest number of votes in an election, provided that it won at least 25% of the votes, would automatically receive two-thirds of the seats in the Chamber, while the rest of the seats would be divided proportionally. In theory, it would put an end to the succession of weak coalition governments that had for so long plagued Italian politics, and for this reason it was supported by Parliamentarians like Giolitti and Salandra. In practice, since they controlled both the blackshirts and the Ministry of the Interior that ran elections, it gave massive power to the Fascist party.

The elections of April, 1924, showed just this. A number of right-wing and liberal politicians, such as Orlando and Salandra, joined the Fascist electoral alliance, thereby adding respectability to the movement. The Communist party attempted to organize a united opposition alliance but the other parties suspected them of duplicity, so that there were six different opposition groups. In the election, the Fascists and their supporters won about two-thirds of the votes (4½ million) and the divided opposition one-third (2½ million). The new composition of the Chamber was as follows:

Government supporters		Opposition parties	
Fascists	375	Popolari	39
Independent Liberals	15	Reformists	24
Social Democrats	10	Socialists	22
Peasant Party	4	Communists	19
	—	Sardinians	2
	404	Dissident Fascist	1
			—
			107

With such a majority, it was not only hard to prevent Mussolini and the Fascists doing as they liked, but also it provided the King with an excuse to take not action against the Fascists, whatever they did. After all, had not the people shown their overwhelming support for them?

The murder of Giacomo Matteotti on 10 June 1924 at first threatened Mussolini's power but was then used to further consolidate it. Matteotti was a Socialist deputy who had openly criticized Fascism in a book, 'The Fascists Exposed', in which he gave details of case histories and acts of violence by the blackshirts. In the Chamber, he asked why it was that the Fascists were proud of the fact that Italians alone were incapable of running their own affairs and had to be ruled by force. Shortly afterwards, he was murdered by the Fascists, with the most obvious complicity of the leadership. The moment to question Mussolini's leadership seemed to have arrived; the King, however, refused to act, seeing that the only possible alternative was socialism, which he disliked and which would lead to violence. Some politicians (but few of the leaders like Giolitti or Orlando) led by Ancola, who made a final forty minute speech listing the crimes of Fascism (he too was murdered in 1925), walked out of the Chamber and set up their own assembly. This was known as the 'Aventine secession'. Mussolini himself denied all knowledge of Matteotti's murder and dismissed all those remotely implicated. Having done so, he then turned on the opposition, introducing press censorship on 1 July and banning meetings by all opposition parties on 3 August.

When the secessors tried to return to Parliament in 1926 they were told that they had forfeited their seats by 'an unconstitutional and clearly revolutionary secession'. What might have been a genuine opportunity to attack Mussolini's position turned out to be no more than a momentary setback.

From then on, it became increasingly difficult to oppose the Fascist regime. In 1925, the 'Legge Fascistissime' was passed, by which further press controls were imposed, Freemasonry and other secret organizations forbidden and local government controlled through Fascist appointed 'podestas'. The constitution was altered by a new fundamental law, by which the Prime Minister became head of state and responsible only to the king, and not to the Chamber. This position was made unchallengeable by the law of 31 January 1926 by which government by decree (by Mussolini) was authorized, thus destroying any existing myth of constitutional democracy. Over 100 000 decree laws were to be enacted in the next seventeen years. A new electoral law was brought in in May 1928; by this, universal suffrage was abolished and the franchise restricted to those over twenty-one who paid taxes of more than 100 lire. The electorate was reduced from 10 million to 3 million. In elections, the names of potential candidates would be submitted by unions and employers to the Fascist Grand Council, who would then choose 400 candidates; their names would then be submitted to the electorate who would either support or reject the whole 400. The first election held on these terms was in March 1929. Surprisingly, 136 000 voted against the listed candidates, but the remaining 2 864 000 voters were obedient to the cause. By the 1930s, 'Il Duce', as Mussolini now called himself, was unstoppable.

Why was there so little opposition to Mussolini? First, many Italians had little reason to dislike him, but rather considerable reason to like him. After all, had he not brought them stability, money, jobs, and a new pride in their country? And if they were among his supporters, did they not get a uniform, a belief in something and even entertainment? As Albertini, a Liberal senator, said: 'Mussolini has given the government freshness, youth and vigour, and has won favour at home and abroad. . . . He has saved Italy from the socialist danger which has been poisoning our life for twenty years.' Even abroad he was admired. Winston Churchill, after an hour's interview in 1927, spoke highly of him and Lloyd George admired the corporate state.

Secondly, such opposition as there was in Parliament was divided and weak. Many of the old-style liberals, who had generally provided the ministries from 1870 to 1922, readily confessed that he seemed better able to govern the country than they had been, and many of them, like Giolitti (who died in 1928) and Orlando, had served their time and wanted only a quiet life. Indeed, these political leaders can be blamed for failing to oppose him until it was too late, and then too ineffectively. Giolitti and Orlando only joined the opposition in November 1924, while Nitti had taken refuge in Paris in 1923. The rest of the opposition generally regarded each other as more of a threat than Fascism; reformist Socialists vied with the majority socialists, while both were suspicious of the Communists. When they did act collectively—in the Aventine secession—they merely provided the King with an excuse to ignore appeals against Mussolini on the grounds that the Chamber gave no lead.

Thirdly, for those who did oppose him the penalties were severe. There were a number of assassination attempts—three in 1926 alone, including one by an Irish noblewoman, Violet Gibson—but Mussolini's person was then declared inviolable and the death penalty was used even for contemplating an attempt on his life. For anyone considered a possible opponent, there was, in the first instance, the unofficial action of the squads, whose treatment ranged from the standard dose (a litre) of castor oil, to eating live toads in public or having your head shaved and painted in the national colours. There was an enormous police force, which included the 'OVRA' or secret police. Known enemies of the regime, if left alive, were kept under surveillance in remote villages, or sent to the camps on the Lipari islands. The most notable active opponent was Carlo Roselli, who was stirred into action by Matteotti's murder. After escaping from the Lipari Islands, he edited the leading opposition paper *Justice and Liberty* from Paris, where there were a number of voluntary exiles. Roselli, though, after a brief excursion to the Spanish Civil War in 1936, suffered the fate so common to Mussolini's enemies when he was assassinated. It is difficult to gauge the true measure of opposition to the regime, which was efficient at disguising it, as this description illustrates:

> The crowds which cheered Mussolini's speeches in Tuscany and Lombardy last summer are quoted as evidence of his popularity among the masses; the reports did not mention that fifteen train-loads of blackshirts followed him to swell the ranks and overawe the crowd, that workshops were closed and the men driven to his meetings under pain of dismissal, that his arrival at each town was preluded by the arrest of suspects by the hundred.

(b) Fascism in theory and practice

The Manifesto of the Fascist party of 6 June 1919 *(see page 282)* and the programme adopted by the Fascist Party Conference at Rome in November 1921 throw interesting light on the programmes and ideas of the party. In 1919, the party's political and economic proposals were radical and socialist. The monarchy was to be abolished and a constituent assembly called to draw up a new constitution. The workers were to be brought into industrial management and a wealth tax to be introduced. Church property was to be confiscated and an 85% tax was to be levied on war profiteers. These proposals were clearly left-wing, while the party's foreign policy was openly nationalist. Like Hitler's, Mussolini's first declaration of principles was a mixture of socialism and nationalism.

However, the party programme of 1921 makes very different reading. No proposals about the constitution were included, no wealth tax mentioned, no attack on the Church was made ('the freedom of the Church must be guaranteed') and the representation of the workers was to be restricted to 'personnel matters' only. Two years later, when in power, the Fascists halved death duties and ended a commission of enquiry into war profiteers. In other words, Mussolini had discovered that the appeal of his party was not to the working class, but to men of property, who owned something and were frightened by talk of revolution. Fascists therefore posed as the defenders of this property and had, apparently, become conservative nationalists.

In fact, neither Mussolini nor his supporters attached much importance to political manifestoes. As Mack Smith has written:

> Fascist policy was built up by a wholesale borrowing of ideas, the intention being to make the regime look progressive and yet sound. Measures and ideas did not need to be consistent, so long as they were popular, showy, easy to administer, preferably non-commital, and pre-digested enough to need no extra thought or definition.

In his first speech to the Chamber as Prime Minister, Mussolini told the deputies that there was no lack of programmes, but rather a lack of the will to put those programmes into action. This, then, was Mussolini's promise—action, not words, by a man strong enough to implement them. Hence Fascist propaganda concentrated not on what they were going to do about the economy, the constitution or whatever (they fully realized that few people read manifestoes anyway), but on the strength and power of the party and its leader. The result was pictures of Mussolini working in the fields, Mussolini's 'hypnotic stare' (he was never pictured smiling) and his autobiography with its emphasis on virility and the ability to 'will' things to happen. Mack Smith again summarizes this:

> . . . any reception in Mussolini's gigantic marble study was always carefully staged to humble the visitor. His most important quality was that of being a stupendous poseur. His mixture of showmanship and vulgarity appealed to the common people, who liked to hear of his adulterous relationships and illegitimate children because he then became more human and virile. They were not allowed to know about his ill-health or use of eye-glasses, and foreign journalists would be expelled if they mentioned his ulcer, let alone if they hinted at syphilis.

Consequently, historians cannot expect to see in Mussolini's Italy a clear cut programme being put into action. As Hitler was to promise simply to make Germans proud and employed, so Mussolini promised only to make Italy great again. Therefore we should look for pragmatic measures with this aim in mind. Once the Fascist party was established in power, there was little that could be strictly described as 'political policy', since most of what needed to be done to make Italy great lay in the economic or imperial sphere.

There was, however, a spate of legislation in the period 1936–8. As Mussolini became increasingly under Hitler's influence, a number of Nazi-style measures were introduced in Italy. Hitler returned to Germany from a visit to Italy in 1937 promising that he would 'Prussianize

Italy'; shortly afterwards the Italian army began marching the goose-step (renamed the 'passo Romano' or Roman step), although, as Marshal De Bono pointed out to the Duce, it was not best suited to make Italian soldiers look fearsome, as their average height was only 5′ 4″. The following year saw the introduction of anti-semitic laws, by which foreign Jews were barred from Italian schools, all Jews who arrived in Italy after 1919 were to leave within six months, Jewish teachers lost their jobs and marriage between Italians and Jews was forbidden. These laws were enforced despite the fact that there were only 56 000 Jews in Italy (0·1% of the population), many of whom were members of the Fascist party. It was not surprising that Hitler referred to Mussolini as his 'Italian gauleiter'.

(c) Relations with the Church

The Lateran treaties of 11 February 1929 were a major achievement of Mussolini's government, since they solved the long standing problem of the united kingdom of Italy—the hostility of the papacy. The actual Lateran treaty restored to the Pope the right to rule over the 108·7 acres of the Vatican City, an area carved out of the centre of Rome, in full sovereignty; that is, there was to be no challenge to any laws or powers he might create within the boundaries of that City. Previously, he had had all his temporal power (i.e. right to rule as a king over an area, as opposed to spiritual power—his control over men's hearts and minds) removed. Added to this treaty was a 'Concordat', or agreement, which theoretically defined the role of the Church in the Fascist state. Catholicism was to be the state religion, Church marriages were to be recognized as legal by the State, and religious instruction was to be given in both primary and secondary schools. For its part, the papacy gave up any claims to rule temporally over any area beyond the Vatican City, and agreed that the State could object to any bishop or archbishop on political grounds. To seal the agreement, the papacy was paid 750 million lire in cash and 1000 million lire in government bonds.

In theory, these agreements should have been a triumph for both sides. For the Pope, it gained a restoration of temporal power, albeit limited, a large amount of money and an important place for the Church in society, as a result of its continued importance in education and religion. For the Fascists, it won international prestige as the only government who could solve a sixty-year-old dispute, and it won the support of traditional Catholics who had been opposed to all constitutional governments of Italy.

In fact, relations between the two did not remain as friendly as they should have done. It soon became obvious that the agreements about marriage, education and the appointment of bishops were merely conveniences to win over the Pope, and in fact the State did much as it liked. Pope Pius XI did his best to reassert the role of the Church in education, as it came more and more under the wing of the Fascists. In 1931, a Catholic youth organization, 'Catholic Action', was set up, and through this the Church was able to wield some influence over the young. Ultimately, however, the Church did benefit from the 1929 arrangements, for they at least protected it from the kind of persecution that Hitler meted out to its German counterpart.

(d) Education and leisure

At first, Italian schools maintained considerable freedom over their curricula and methods. The 1923 Education Act, the work of the Sicilian philosopher, Gentile, stressed the importance of a humanist education and suggested that philosophy be taught at all levels. Thereafter Mussolini stressed the need for reforms of a Fascist nature with more stress on discipline and loyalty to the State, less on individual differences. To these ends a number of reforms were brought in by the various Ministers of Education (eight in all) that he appointed and dismissed. 'Fascist culture' became a compulsory subject, and mixed schools were ended. Textbooks came under the scrutiny of the party. History, in particular, suffered. In 1926, 101 out of 317 history texts were banned, and in 1936 a single history textbook became compulsory, in which dates started at 1922 ('anno primo') and the section on World War I described how Italy had saved Britain and America from imminent defeat. Introductory reading books were also suitable cases for treatment, as these extracts from books for eight-year-olds illustrate:

> The eyes of the Duce are on every one of you. No one can say what is the meaning of that look on his face. It is an eagle opening its wings and rising into space.

> How can we ever forget that Fascist boy who, when near to death, asked that he might put on his uniform and that his savings should go to the party?

Even so, results were not what they might have been, for the 1931 census still reported 20% illiteracy (48% in Calabria), while the 1936 census gave no figures on this at all.

Equally, children's leisure times was considered an important area for Fascist activity, and in 1926 a youth organization, the Balilla, was founded. (It took its name from a Genoese boy who was supposed to have thrown a stone at Austrian soldiers in 1746.) The movement's symbols were the book and the rifle and new members took its oath, '. . . to follow the orders of the Duce and to serve the cause of the Fascist revolution with all my might, and, if necessary, with my blood.' The organization also had a creed, which ran as follows:

> I believe in Rome the Eternal, the mother of my country, and in Italy her eldest daughter, who was born in her virginal bosom by the grace of God; who suffered through the barbarian invasions, was crucified and buried, who descended to the grave and was raised from the dead in the nineteenth century, who ascended into heaven in her glory in 1918 and 1922, who is seated on the right hand of her mother Rome; who for this reason shall come to judge the living and the dead. I believe in the genius of Mussolini,

in our Holy Father Fascism, in the communion of martyrs, in the conversion of Italians and in the resurrection of the Empire.

The Balilla was only for boys; girls joined the 'Little Italian Girls'. Then, as the 'Child's Guide to Fascism' explains:

> From the age of eight to fourteen the boy as a member of the Balilla is trained both physically and morally; on reaching fourteen he passes into the Avanguardisti, while as a youth of eighteen he can take his place with the Fascist Levy in the ranks of the National Fascist Party.

The leisure-time of adults was considered equally important, for when not at work they might be tempted to think about or even criticise the regime. To avoid this, the 'Dopolavoro' organization was founded. This was an umbrella organization for recreation, and in 1932 it controlled 1350 theatres, 8265 libraries, 2208 dramatic societies, 3324 brass bands and 2139 orchestral societies. It also organized holiday cruises, authorized football referees (under the chief referee with his gold whistle) and licensed players. Even the Olympic Games committee had to be affiliated to the party, while in 1939 the Italian lawn tennis association ordered its international players to wear the Fascist uniform and make the Fascist salute when their opponents offered to shake hands.

4. Economic History

The Italian economy was reorganized by Mussolini to increase the influence of the State without destroying capitalism. Since Mussolini discovered that his support came from those with property and wealth (rather than, as he originally expected, those *without*), his economic policy had to satisfy them. At the same time he realized the need for increased state intervention if the economy was to make any real progress.

The economy was therefore organized into what was known as the Corporate State. Each occupation was to form two syndicates, one for workers and one for employers, which would meet both separately and jointly to create agreements on wages, hours and conditions of work, rights of dismissal and the like. Such agreements would be binding on both sides and thus, hopefully, put an end to the appalling record of wage disputes that had so beset the Italian economy both before and after World War I. To further this end, the Vidoni Palace Pact of 1925 forbade strikes. In all, there were twenty-one separate categories of syndicate for trade and industry; all metal workers, for example, were grouped in the ninth category while the sugar beet industry was represented by the fifth category. A twenty-second category was set up to represent professional people and artists. Each of the syndicates was under the control of a representative of the Fascist party, and all were under the Ministry of Corporations, founded in 1926 with Mussolini himself as minister. In 1930, a National Council of Corporations was set up, wherein workers, employers and the party were represented. The Council was to plan, regulate and control production. In 1933, Mussolini announced plans for it to become a legislative assembly to replace the Chamber so that the laws of the country would be determined by representatives of the economic interests directly, rather than by political representatives of those economic interests. The corporate state and its development were closely studied by other European powers, who seriously saw it as an alternative to total state control, with its links to communism, and the wayward boom and bust nature of capitalism.

The Corporate State had both advantages and disadvantages for Italy and Italians. Certainly, the workers lost their right to free collective bargaining, and the use of the strike as a weapon in this. Equally, the chaos of the post-war years was avoided. Close state control helped to save the lire from devaluation after the Wall Street Crash. Instead, Mussolini simply ordered all workers to take a cut in wages. On the other hand, the new system created an enormous and often inefficient bureaucracy, which may have helped to ease unemployment, but cost a great deal for what it achieved. The *Economist* commented in 1935:

> The new corporative state only amounts to the establishment of a new and costly bureaucracy, from which those industrialists who can spend the necessary amount can obtain almost anything they want, and put into practice the worst kind of monopolistic practices at the expense of the little fellow who is squeezed out in the process.

Equally, corruption increased as time went on. Even mock factories were built in order to get a state subsidy, while Mussolini's friend with interests in the Carrara marble mines made a healthy profit from the new public building programme.

In the field of agriculture, Mussonlini's economic policy achieved much. The great propaganda campaign, the 'Battle for Grain', featured pictures of the Duce in the fields or at the wheel of a tractor; on 21 April, which was made into a public holiday to rival May Day, he distributed gold, silver and bronze stars to the most productive farmers. New land—notably the Pontine Marshes and the Volturno Valley—was brought under cultivation. The overall result was that the production of wheat increased by 50% between 1922 and 1930 and doubled in the whole period 1922–39, so that wheat imports could be reduced by 75% between 1925 and 1935. Even so, wheat remained the third largest import, with over 500 million lire being spent on it in 1933, while the cost remained high because of the subsidies to farmers. In addition, much of the marginal land given over to wheat production was not actually suitable for it (e.g. hillside terraces) and would have been better suited to olives or fruit. Thirdly, little attempt was made to alter the traditional pattern of land-holding so that a small number of very wealthy landowners remained in control of a huge bulk of very poor labourers. In 1930, about fifteen families held a total of over a million acres, while more than half of the land cultivated was owned by less than 20 000 estates. Nonetheless, considering Italy's backwardness up to this time, some credit must be given to Mussolini's agricultural policy.

Much was done for Italian industry. At first, this was left in private hands though it was encouraged and partly controlled by the State through subsidies. The Fiat company, for example, produced 80% of Italian cars, and involved itself in mining, cement, smelting and the newspaper business. Electrification, subsidized by the government, proceeded apace, increasing fivefold between 1917 and 1942. Modern industries, notably the Edison Electric Comany, Montecatini Chemicals and the Pirelli Rubber Company, also thrived, while new oil refineries were built at Bari and Leghorn. In 1933, the Institute for the Reconstruction of Industry was set up and the State took over direct control of many banks and heavy industries, in an attempt to help the economy through the depression. As with agriculture, much was achieved but Italian industry still remained comparatively backward. Table 33 below illustrates the dependence on imported raw materials and the failure to export industrial products, except for textiles.

Imports (in million lire)		Exports (in million lire)	
Raw cotton	737	Fruit and garden produce	1091
Coal and coke	685	Raw and artificial silk	820
Wheat	504	Cotton fabrics and yarn	676
Machinery	365	Cheese	241
Wool	361		

Table 33. Main Italian imports and exports 1933

Communications were greatly encouraged by the Fascist state, partly because of their prestige value. The well-known boast of Mussolini that he had at least made the trains run on time was supported by the electrification of 5000 kilometres of railway. The building of the mighty 'autostrade' (motorways), carving their way through mountains and over valleys, was also encouraged, though many minor roads were neglected as a result. This was a good example of priority being given to a project that could be used for military purposes, and could be seen by all the world, taking priority over what was most beneficial economically. Two mighty ocean liners—the 'Rex' and the 'Count of Savoy'—were also built to ensure that Italy could hold her own in international shipping. Equally, great pride was taken in the achievements of Major de Bernardi, who set world speed records in a Macchi seaplane powered by a Fiat motor in 1927 and 1928.

A more doubtful aspect of Mussolini's economic policy was the 'Battle for Natality', or Births, launched in 1927. Mussolini was convinced that a populous nation was a powerful nation (e.g. Germany before the World War I) and therefore determined to increase the population to 60 million, from 37 million in 1920. To this end, high taxes were introduced for bachelors and prizes were given to the most prolific mothers—ninety three of them who had between them produced 1300 children received the Duce's personal congratulations in 1933. Although the net reproduction rate (the number of live births per every thousand women of child-bearing age) did rise, reaching 1·131 in 1935–7, the battle was not entirely succesful—in 1932 there were less than one million live births in Italy for the first time since 1876, and by 1940 the population had only reached 43·8 million. Much of this increase was due to a decline in emigration, mainly the result of a change in policy by the American authorities. In 1920, 350 000 Italians had emigrated to America; in 1921 the USA introduced limits on immigration and by 1924 only 4000 Italians went to the States each year. The major trend in population was, in fact, the shift to the cities from the countryside. The population of Rome increased between 1921 and 1931 from 690 000 to over a million. It is equally notable, though, that the shift in population led primarily to an increase in bureaucrats and professional people, rather than industrial workers, for heavy industry remained backward throughout the period, as Table 34 illustrates.

(a) Pig iron output (annual production in million tons)

	1900	1918	1930	1940	
Italy	—	0·3	0·5	1·0	
USA	14	39·7	32·3	43	(world leader)
Germany	8·5	11·9	9·7	13·9	(European leader)
Belgium	1·0	—	3·4	1·8	
Luxemburg	1·0	1·3	2·5	1·0	

(b) Steel output (annual production in million tons)

	1900	1918	1930	1940
Italy	0·1	0·3	0·5	1·0
USA	10·4	45·2	41·4	60·8
Germany	6·6	15·0	11·5	19·0
Belgium	0·7	—	3·4	1·9
France	1·6	1·8	9·4	4·4

Table 34. Italy's place in the World Economy 1900–40

Although, therefore, both agriculture and industry were improved under Mussolini's rule, Italy remained well down in world terms. In addition, two major criticisms can be made of his policy. Like his predecessors, Mussolini did nothing to solve the traditional problems of the Italian economy—the dualism and the overwhelming poverty of the South *(see page 50)*. If anything, his policies accentuated the dualism. Secondly, as the depression lifted, the emphasis in the economy shifted to military and semi-military production, primarily to help with the imperial missions described below, but in the process disrupting the normal growth of the economy.

5. Foreign Policy 1922–39

(a) European policies 1922–35

'My objective is simple, I want to make Italy great, respected and feared', said Mussolini, thus providing the only real guidelines to his aims in foreign policy. Italy's humiliation in and after World War I, and the nationalist wave on which he climbed to power, was bound to make for a nationalist foreign policy, wherein any available means would be used to demonstrate Italy's return to greatness. He did, however, face the traditional problems of Italian foreign policy *(see page 53)* of powerful and hostile *(to each other)* northern neighbours. Although Mussolini would never have admitted this to be a problem, it did require him to protect his country against possible French or German hostility, which involved the subsidiary aim of securing influence in the Balkans to ensure that he could at least balance the influence of these potential enemies there. As these first two aims were, to some extent, achieved during the 1920s, Italian foreign policy became increasingly expansionist in the 1930s, aiming not only at control of the Mediterranean, but also at an African empire.

Italy's 'renewed greatness' was first demonstrated soon after Mussolini became Prime Minister. On 21 August 1923 General Enrico Tellini and four other Italians on his staff were assassinated while working for the boundary commission of the Conference of Ambassadors (a body set up to complete the detailed territorial arrangements of the treaties of 1919) on the border of Greece and Albania (they were actually in Greece). Without waiting for further news or explanation, Mussolini demanded from the Greek government a full apology and 50 million lire compensation. Greece appealed to the League of Nations, who referred the matter to the Conference of Ambassadors. In the meantime, on 31 August, as soon as the Greeks had rejected Italy's demands, Mussolini ordered his navy to bombard the island of Corfu, on which marines were then landed. The Conference of Ambassadors tried to push Greece into apologizing and, if a commission of enquiry found evidence to support Italy's claim that the assassins were Greek, pay the compensation. Under pressure from Britain, Mussolini agreed on 27 September to withdraw his forces and in exchange received the 50 million lire. The exercise had not been wholly successful (for example, Italy had responded to pressure from the Conference and had not received the full apology) but the Italian press made much of it as the triumphant return of Italy to the international scene as a nation who got her way.

During the 1920s Mussolini was also able to secure influence in, and prestige from, the Balkans. In 1924 the Pact of Rome was signed with Yugoslavia, by which Italy received the long-disputed town of Fiume, though a part of it, the suburb of Susak, went to Yugoslavia, along with Port Barros *(see Map 30)*. Two treaties with Albania, in 1926 and 1927, firmly established Italian influence in Albania, which was extended thereafter by loans, military agreements and arrangements for Italy to receive Albanian oil. This marked the first stage in Mussolini's efforts to establish Italy in the Balkans, where the 'Little Entente' of Czecho-slovakia, Roumania and Yugoslavia was so closely tied to France, Italy's likely enemy *(see page 204)*.

Further to this end, and in order to maintain an independent state between himself and his other possible enemy (Germany), Mussolini cultivated the friendship of Austria and Hungary. In 1927 a treaty of friendship was signed with Hungary and in 1930 a similar treaty with Austria. Relations with Austria became even closer after Hitler came to power in Germany, and it was Mussolini who provided the arms and money for the Austrian Chancellor's private army, the 'Heimwehr'. In March 1934 Mussolini achieved his objective of creating a counter to the French-backed 'Little Entente' with the signing of the Rome Protocols, when Dollfuss and Gömbos of Hungary visited Rome. The Protocols arranged for increased trade links and a common foreign policy between Italy, Austria and Hungary. Shortly afterwards, in July 1934, Mussolini's Austrian policy was put to the test when Dollfuss was murdered by Nazis. Mussolini acted fast, sending troops to the border with Austria as an obvious threat to Hitler not to intervene. When Hitler backed down, Mussolini could claim a minor triumph. Incidentally, the friendship of Bulgaria was also cultivated, reaching a peak in 1929 when the daughter of King Victor Emmanuel, Princess Giovanna, married King Boris. ·

During the 1920s Mussolini realized that he could not yet attempt to have the Versailles settlement revised in his favour and needed the friendship (or at least an absence of hostility) of France and Britain. Therefore in 1925 he went to Locarno and signed the treaties guaran-teeing the Franco-German and Belgo-German frontiers, and in 1928 was a signatory of the Kellogg–Briand Pact *(see page 369)*. In particular, he drew closer to Britain, seeing her as a possible friend in any future con-flict, though privately resolving to end British power in the Mediter-ranean. Agreement was reached over the frontier between Libya and Egypt, and discussions were held on the possibility of British aid for railway building in East Africa. During the 1920s, therefore, Italy remained a member of the League of Nations, and acted as a good citizen of Europe.

Hitler's advent to power in Germany obviously altered things con-siderably. Mussolini was delighted to see a fellow traveller in power, and saw the potential of a German alliance against Britain and France to revise the 1919 settlement; on the other hand, he was wary of having Germany too close, i.e. in Austria. In April 1933 Goering and Papen visited Rome, but all the visit achieved was German agreement to the Four Power Pact—Mussolini's brainchild to have a pact of the four great powers, Italy, Germany, France, Britain to keep the peace in Europe, thus replacing the League. It was actually only ever signed by Germany and Italy (on 15 July 1933). June 1934 was to see the crucial meeting of the two dictators, when Hitler visited Venice. Unfortunately, the meeting got off to a bad start as Hitler had been told that Mussolini would be in civilian clothes. He was therefore infuriated to be welcomed by Mussolini in full dress uniform when he was in a suit. Then Mussolini refused to have an interpreter, despite his German being very poor, so it is likely the meeting meant little to either. The crisis following the death of Dollfuss a month later worsened things further, so that in 1934–5 Mussolini was far from being an ally of Hitler. Indeed, in April 1935, Mussolini even attended the Stresa Conference, called by France to consider what action to take over German rearmament and to guarantee the independence of Austria. Italy joined the declarations and protests, largely to avoid British and French hostility to Italian imperialism but partly in genuine hostility to Germany.

(b) The Abyssinian crisis

'We have a right to empire as a fertile nation which has the pride and will to propagate its race over the face of the earth, a virile people in the strict sense of the word', said Mussolini. In the 1920s, the Italian empire was hardly promising. Libya was territorially the heart of the empire, but only some 2000 Italians had settled there, and by 1930 it was costing over 500 million lire per annum, compared with 107 million in 1921. In fact the two smaller Italian colonies, Eritrea and Italian Somaliland, looked more promising, for they bordered on to Ethiopia (Abyssinia), one of the few remaining independent kingdoms of Africa *(see Map 31)*. During the 1920s, therefore, Italy took special interest in Abyssinia, sponsoring her membership of the League in 1923 and signing a treaty of friendship in 1928. However, it became clear that the ruler, Haile Selassie, did not intend to allow his country to be dominated by one modern power—in 1930 he signed a treaty with Japan—and Mussolini considered the possibility of war to force Abyssinia under Italian control.

The incident that was subsequently used as the 'casus belli' by the Italians took place in December 1934. Ual-Ual was an oasis on the border of Abyssinia and Italian Somaliland, marked on Italian maps as being in Abyssinia, but the Italians claimed the right to use it. Some Italians therein were fired on and killed in the oasis in December 1934. Mussolini demanded an apology and compensation from Abyssinia. The Abyssinians in turn insisted on an investigation, to which the League of Nations agreed in May, 1935.

In the meantime, Mussolini made preparations for his attack, both by building up forces and sounding out the attitude of Britain and France. Already, way back in 1906, Britain and France had agreed that a part of Ethiopia should be a minor sphere of Italian influence. Now, in January 1935, Pierre Laval, the French Foreign Minister, while on a visit to Rome, gave part of French Somaliland to Italy and sold to Italy France's shares in the Abyssinian Railway. Clearly, France was not going to oppose Italy although later Laval claimed he had given his support only to Italy's economic plans, not military ones. Similarly, the British made no mention of Abyssinia when they met Mussolini for the Stresa Conference in April, while in June, Eden, on behalf of the British government, offered the Abyssinians a corridor to the sea through British Somaliland if they gave Mussolini part of Ogaden—an offer rejected by Mussolini. In the summer, Italian troops under Generals De Bono and Graziani arrived in Eritrea—five regular army divisions, five blackshirt divisions, and two native divisions. In July, the League's investigators reported that neither side was to blame for the incident at Ual-Ual since both believed the other was on its territory. This did not satisfy Mussolini, who continued to make noises about his intentions, as a result of which a meeting between the British, French and Italians was held in Paris on 16 August. At this meeting, Italy was offered the opportunity to develop Abyssinia, provided that the Abyssinians agreed. The Italians rejected the offer, since they were unlikely to get that agreement, and by now Mussolini had decided on war.

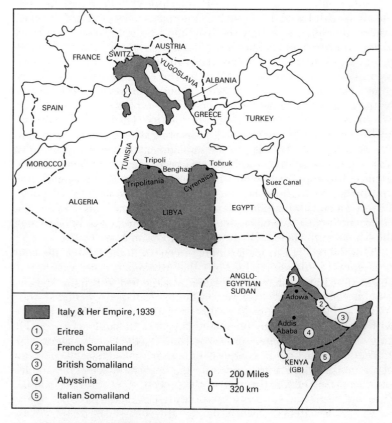

Map 31 Italy and her Empire: 1939

On 3 October 1935 Italian troops attacked from Eritrea and on 6 October captured Adowa, thus avenging the defeat of 1896 *(see page 54).* The next day the Council of the League condemned Italy as the aggressor and arranged for economic sanctions to be imposed on Italy; no arms were to be carried to Italy, and no goods to be bought from her. Oil, coal, iron and steel were all excluded from the ban, and the Suez canal was not closed to Italian shipping. Nonetheless, the Italian press made much of this 'harsh' measure, and Italians were persuaded to give up their wedding rings and other valuables to provide much-needed cash. By the time the sanctions were brought in on 18 November, the Italian army had already captured Makallé and Marshal Badoglio, a regular soldier, had replaced the Fascist De Bono as commander. He had already reorganized his troops to take advantage of the mountainous countryside and brought in air support and introduced poison gas.

During the winter, Britain and France made various efforts to end the fighting. In December, the British Foreign Secretary, Sir Samuel Hoare, en route from a holiday in Switzerland, stopped in Paris and discussed the affair with Laval, his French counterpart. They proposed the partition of Abyssinia, with Italy receiving the northern and southern thirds to add to Eritrea and Italian Somaliland respectively, and a rump state being left in the middle. Before the plan was put to either of the protaganists, the press found out about it. There was a great outcry in both countries, for here were the two leading countries in the League of Nations, which was based on the principle of opposing aggression, prepared to give way to the aggressor country. The plan got no further; on 18 December Hoare resigned, prompting King George V to remark 'No more Hoares to Paris'. At the same time, a British naval squadron was sent to Alexandria, and France, Greece, Turkey and Yugoslavia all promised to support, diplomatically at least, any action against Italy that Britain took. However, indecision was the keynote of British policy, for to act against Mussolini was to drive him into the arms of Hitler, and before any action was taken, the attention of Europe was refocussed on the Rhineland, wherein Hitler sent his troops in March 1936.

With the rest of Europe far more interested in the Führer, the Duce proceeded in Abyssinia. In April the Abyssinian army was heavily defeated at Lake Ashangi, and Haile Selassie fled to Britain, knowing that his country was beaten. On 5 May the Italian army entered Addis Ababa and four days later Abyssinia was formally annexed and became, with Eritrea and Italian Somaliland, a part of Italian East Africa. The king of Italy became emperor of Abyssinia. To the Duce's chagrin, only 1537 Italians died in the conquest—not nearly enough for the purposes of national sacrifice or to 'harden the national character'. The conquest complete, the Italians then began the process of pacification, building forts and roads and suppressing native attacks, on the basis of 'ten eyes for an eye'. On 19 February 1937 the viceroy, General Graziani, was the subject of an assassination attempt (which failed), which was followed by a brutal round-up of all possible opponents, including Ras Desta Demtu, the leading native opponent, who was captured and publicly executed. Thereafter, the colony was reasonably peaceful and in 1938 even Britain and France recognized Italy's ownership.

The conquest of Abyssinia was regarded as a major triumph in Italy, ranking alongside the Concordat of 1929. Mussolini had said 'the Italian character has to be formed through fighting', and fighting it had had. Nonetheless, little else was gained, for the party officials and bureaucrats moved in, making the colony as corrupt and profitless as the mother country; in 1939, only 2% of Italy's trade was with her colonies. The Italian population of New York was still ten times greater than the Italian population of Italian colonies.

(c) European policies 1935–9

When the Spanish Civil War broke out in July 1936, Mussolini was immediately active in providing Franco and the Nationalists with men and equipment, on the grounds that he could not allow a communist government to be formed in the Mediterranean. At first, volunteers were sent and their presence kept secret, but then a film of the capture of Malaga by the Spanish fascists was shown in Rome and the audience did not take long to recognize the Italian number-plates! In fact, nine battalions under General Roatta took part in the attack on Malaga—a total of some 70 000 men—a commitment, coinciding as it did with the settlement of East Africa, that proved very expensive and necessitated devaluation and a special levy. Moreover, it produced considerable tension with Britain, for Mussolini was supplying submarines to attack shipping carrying Russian goods in the Mediterranean, as a result of which British, French, Greek and Danish cargo ships had all been sunk. Therefore in 1937 the Nyon Conference was held to discuss patrolling rights and Italy was granted a zone to patrol. This allowed Mussolini to provide Franco with what he required fairly freely. Yet again Britain paid a heavy price in trying to woo Italy away from Germany.

In fact, Italy was inevitably drawing closer and closer to Germany. On 25 October 1936, the two reached agreement over Austria—to maintain its independence. Mussolini referred to this as the 'Rome-Berlin Axis, around which can revolve all those European states with a will to collaboration and peace.' Thereafter, relations became closer and closer. In September 1937, Mussolini visited Germany, where he was suitably impressed by the massive displays, the 800 000 crowd that applauded him and Hitler's flattery in referring to him as his 'teacher of fascism'. In November Italy joined the Anti-Comintern Pact, and in December withdrew from the League. Even the 'Anschluss' was not opposed in March 1938. Hitler sent a special envoy, Prince Philip of Hesse (who was married to Victor Emmanuel's daughter) to explain his actions to Mussolini. Hitler thanked the latter suitably after Austria had, to the annoyance of many Italians, been swallowed by Germany. In May 1938 Hitler visited Rome and Mussolini, determined to impress, had the houses en route white-washed and 6000 possible opponents arrested. Hitler was not at first impressed, finding the King, with whom he stayed, tiresome, but later mellowed as the navy put on a display in Naples harbour and the crowds roared their approval in Florence. Again, in

September 1938, Mussolini triumphed in Europe when he brought together her leaders at the Munich Conference to settle the Czech crisis without resort to war *(see page 391)*. Nonetheless, it was increasingly clear that he was little more than Hitler's sidekick.

Partly to correct this impression and show his independence, Mussolini organized the invasion of Albania in April 1939. The invasion had little other purpose since Albania was all but controlled by Italy anyway, but it might show the world that Italy was still a 'virile nation'. In fact, the invasion was a shambles. There was no Albanian army to stop the four divisions of Italian troops, and King Zog fled before they reached the capital, Tirana, which they then proceeded to loot. The Italian press were not even sure whether they were supposed to report that their men had overcome fearful odds or that they had been welcomed as liberators from the vile dictator Zog.

The chief effect of the episode was to show Mussolini how unprepared he was for a real war. He admitted as much to Goering, who attended Victor Emmanuel's coronation as King of Albania. Nonetheless, in May 1939, apparently infuriated by an American paper's report that Ribbentrop had been booed by a crowd in Milan, he suddenly decided to draw closer still to Germany, and ordered the foreign minister, his son-in-law Ciano, to conclude a formal alliance. This treaty, known as the 'Pact of Steel', tied the two so closely that Italy was committed to join Germany in any war, be it aggressive or defensive. Unknown to Mussolini, plans for the attack on Poland were already afoot. When Hitler informed him of these plans on 25 August, Mussolini replied that Italy was not ready for war, and when asked what he needed, asked for an enormous quantity of supplies, including 10 000 tons of lead and 150 Anti-Aircraft batteries—in other words, enough to ensure Hitler would not want to call on Italy's help. When Poland was invaded, therefore, Mussolini was in a quandary—Italy was not prepared for war, yet 'the Italian character has to be formed by fighting'. He could not admit to being neutral, so he called Italy 'a non-belligerent power' until June 1940, by which time Hitler had convinced him of the need to fight and could see the advantages of using Italian troops in North Africa.

Mack Smith has argued forcibly that Mussolini's foreign policy was inconsistent and haphazard. 'Mussolini's violent changes of policy', he writes

> were sometimes accepted on his own valuation as brilliant strokes of Macchiavellian deceit, part of a superplan which the fullness of time would reveal, but Ciano's diary now confirms that they were rather a pathological symptom. At one moment he vetoed the Anschluss and began to fortify the Brenner; at the next he struck an attitude and announced to the world that he was standing beside Germany in shining armour. At one moment he was ranting against Hitler and hoping that the Russians would beat Germany; then in a matter of days he suddenly changed when a recollection of Chamberlain reminded him how contemptible were the pluto-democracies.

This is perhaps to exaggerate, for Mussolini's policies were consistent in their ends, if not their means. It would, though, be true to say that his policies were extravagant—both literally (by 1939, annual expenditure exceeded income by 28 039 million lire) and metaphorically (who else could claim that 'by a single order and in a few hours I can mobilize 8 million bayonets'?). Incidentally, in June 1940, only one and half could be mobilized!

6. Bibliography

The two books recommended at the end of Chapter III (page 61) both cover the later period as well as the pre-war era. In addition, there is the biography, *Benito Mussolini* by C. Hibbert (Longmans, 1962), *Fascist Italy* by A. Cassells (Routledge, 1969) and *A History of Italian Fascism* by F. Chabod (Cedric Chivers, 1974). Of the standard texts listed on page 3, Perry has a particularly useful section on the nature and ideas of Fascism.

7. Discussion Points and Exercises

A *This section consists of questions that might be used for discussion (or written answers) as a way of expanding on the chapter and testing understanding of it:*

1 What did D'Annunzio hope to achieve by his expedition to Fiume?
2 List the reasons for the expansion of socialism in Italy after World War I.
3 Why was the split between the 'Popolari' and the right-wing parties so important?
4 Explain the failure of the government to act against right-wing violence 1919–22.
5 How much planning went into Mussolini's moves to increase his power 1922–5, and to what extent was he simply an opportunist?
6 Explain the attitude and actions of the King towards Mussolini.
7 Why was the Ballilla creed so openly stolen from the Christian church?
8 Why did the Church come to agreement with such an obviously anti-Christian party?
9 Why was the Corporate State regarded as such an innovation?
10 Why was corruption so common?
11 How much was genuinely achieved for the Italian economy?
12 Explain the importance of the Balkans in Mussolini's foreign policy.
13 In what ways would Mussolini have wanted the Versailles settlement revised?
14 Comment on the relationship between Hitler and Mussolini.
15 How consistent were Mussolini's policies, both at home and abroad?
16 Why are historians so cynical about Mussolini?

B   *This section is intended to illustrate some of the features of the Fascist regime in a rather different way:*

1   Put yourself in the position of a traditional conservative Italian, who had supported Giolitti before World War I, yet by 1922 was keen for Mussolini to be made Prime Minister. Explain to an interviewer what made you do this.

2   The 'fascistification' of education seems somewhat ludicrous; to what extent was it necessary or successful? If you feel you have insufficient data to answer this, then explain what evidence you would require.

3   Write two newspaper editorials on the day after the invasion of Abyssinia began. One should be for an Italian Fascist paper, the other for a French paper.

C   *This section suggests two ways in which you might compare Italy with other countries:*

1   Much is made of Italy's experience 1914–19 as being responsible for the rise of Fascism. Compare this experience with that of other European countries. What does this explain about the rise of Mussolini?

2   Compare the role of left-wing parties in Mussolini's rise and consolidation of power with the role of similar parties in Germany at the time of Hitler's rise.

3   Compare and contrast the domestic achievements of Hitler and Mussolini.

D   *Essay questions*

1   How far did the peace treaties satisfy Italy's war aims?

2   What were the main reasons for the rise of Fascism in Italy?

3   What may be said in defence and approval of Mussolini's rule in Italy?

4   Examine the relationship between Italy and the rest of Europe during Mussolini's term as Prime Minister.

8. Documents Relating to Fascist Italy

A. The Fascist Programme (1919)
(Source: Count C. Sforza *Contemporary Italy* (1946) quoted in Kertesz, p. 386.)

> 1. A Constituent National Assembly will proceed, as the Italian Section of the Constituent International Assembly of the peoples, to a radical transformation of the political and economic bases of the life of the community.
> 2. Proclamation of the Italian Republic. Decentralization of the executive power; autonomous administration of the regions and communes entrusted to their respective legislative organization. Sovereignty of the people, exercised by universal suffrage of all citizens of the two sexes; the people retaining the initiative and the veto.

3. Abolition of the Senate. Abolition of the political police. The Magistrature to be elected independently of the executive power.

4. Abolition of all titles of nobility and all orders of knighthood.

5. Abolition of obligatory military service.

6. Liberty of opinion and conscience, of religion, of assembly, of the press.

7. A system of education in the schools, common and professional, open to all.

8. The greatest attention to social hygiene.

9. Suppression of incorporated joint stock companies, industrial or financial. Suppression of all speculation by banks and stock exchanges.

10. Control and taxation of private wealth. Confiscation of unproductive income.

11. Prohibition of work of children under the age of sixteen. An eight-hour work day.

12. Reorganization of production on a co-operative basis and direct participation of the workers in the profits.

13. Abolition of secret diplomacy.

14. An international policy based on the solidarity of the peoples and on their individual independence within the framework of a federation of States.

B. Proclamation by the Quadrumvirate 26 October 1922

(Source: B. Mussolini, *My Autobiography* (1939) quoted by Kertesz, p. 387.)

This was the order given to the Fascists to embark on the March on Rome. The Quadrumvirate was a committee of four generals presided over by Mussolini himself.

Fascisti! Italians!

The time for determined battle has come! Four years ago the National Army loosed at this season the final offensive, which brought it to victory (the battle of Vittorio Veneto). Today the army of the Black-shirts again takes possession of that victory, which has been mutilated, and going directly to Rome brings victory again to the glory of that capital. . . . The martial law of Fascism now becomes a fact. By order of the Duce all the military, political and administrative functions of the party management are taken over by a secret Quadrumvirate of Action with dictatorial powers.

The Army, the reserve and Safeguard of the Nation, must not take part in this struggle. Fascism renews its highest homage given to the Army of Vitttorio Veneto. Fascism, furthermore, does not march against the police, but against a political class both cowardly and imbecile, which in four long years has not been able to give a Government to the nation. Those who form the productive class must know that Fascism wants to impose nothing more than order and discipline upon the nation and to help to raise the strength which will renew progress and prosperity. The people who work in the fields and in the factories, those who work on the railroads or in offices, have nothing to fear from the Fascist Government. Their just rights will be protected. We will even be generous with unarmed adversaries. Fascism draws its sword to cut the multiple Gordian Knots which tie and burden Italian life. We call God and the spirit of our five thousand dead to witness that only one impulse sends us on, that only one passion burns within us—the impulse and the passion to contribute to the safety and greatness of our country.

Fascisti of all Italy! Stretch forth like Romans your spirits and your fibres! We must win! We will.

Long live Italy! Long live Fascism!

C. The Establishment of the Dictatorship 1925_6
(Source: Rappard's *Source Book on European Government*, quoted by Kertesz p. 389.)
(a) Law on the powers and Prerogatives of the Head of the Government, 24 December 1925.

1. The executive power is exercised by H.M. the King through his government. The Government consists of the Prime Minister, Secretary of State and the Ministers Secretaries of State.

The Prime Minister is Head of the Government.

2. The Head of the Government. . . . is appointed and recalled by the King and is responsible to the King for the general policy of the Government . . .

3. The Head of the Government . . . directs and co-ordinates the activities of the Ministers, settles disputes among them, calls meetings of the Council of Ministers and presides over them . . .

6. No bill or motion may be submitted to either of the Houses of Parliament without the consent of the Head of the Government.

The Head of the Government has the power to request that a bill, rejected by one of the Houses of Parliament, be voted upon again three months after the first vote. In such cases the vote is by ballot without previous debate . . .

(b) Law on the Power of the Executive Branch to make Decrees having the Force of Laws, 31 January 1926

1. By Royal Decree, after deliberation in the Council of Ministers and hearing in the Council of State, regulations having the force of laws may be issued concerning the following, even in matters heretofore regulated by law:
   (i) the execution of laws;
   (ii) the use of powers belonging to the executive branch;
   (iii) the organization and functioning of of the State administration and of their personnel; the organization of public institutions and concerns . . .

3. By Royal Decree, after deliberation in the Council of Ministers, regulations having the force of laws may be issued in the following cases:
   (i) when the government is empowered and delegated to do so by law . .
   (ii) when the case is exceptional by reason of its urgency or absolute necessity; whether or not a case is exceptional shall be judged only by Parliament.

In cases referred to in paragraph (ii) . . . the Royal Decree shall contain a clause providing for presentation to Parliament for ratification; the Decree ceases to have effect unless it is submitted to one of the Houses of Parliament for ratification and this shall be done not later than at the third session after the publication of the Decree . . .

D. The Establishment of the Corporate State, 3 April 1926
The law quoted below, the 'Law concerning the Legal Discipline of
Collective Labour Relations' is regarded as laying the foundations of the
Corporate state in that it established compulsory associations for both
trades and the professions under the control of the government. It also,
in clauses not quoted below, banned strikes and lock-outs.
(Source: Rappard's *Source Book on European Government*.)

1. Associations of employers and of workers, intellectual and manual, may
be legally approved under the following conditions:
   (i) In the case of associations of employers, that the employers volun-
       tarily registered as members employ at least 10% of the workers in
       the trade and district which the association represents; in the case of
       associations of employees, that the employees voluntarily registered
       as members include at least 10% of the workers in the trade and
       district which the association represents.
   (ii) That, besides protecting the economic and moral interests of its mem-
       bers, the association effectively carries out plans for the insurance,
       instruction and moral and patriotic education of its members.
   (iii) That the director of the association gives proof of his ability, morality,
       and unswerving loyalty to the nation.
3. The associations referred to . . . shall consist either of employers only or
of employees only.
   Associations of employers and those of employees may be united by
means of central co-ordinating bodies with a common hierarchy of higher
officers . . .
5. Legally recognized associations have legal personality and legally represent all the employers, labourers, employees, artists or professional
men of the particular class for which they are formed within the territorial
limits of the association, whether they are registered as members or not . . .
   Only legally recognized associations may appoint representatives of
employers or employees to all councils, corporations or other bodies in
which such representation is provided for by law.
6. Associations may be communal, district, provincial, regional, inter-
regional or national. . . .
   Whenever a national confederation shall have been recognized . . ., the
recognition of federations or associations which do not form part of these
confederations shall be prohibited . . .
10. Collective labour contracts made by the legally recognized associations . . . are obligatory on all employers, employees (etc) in the classes
referred to in the contracts or represented in the associations . . .
   The central co-ordinating bodies . . . may establish . . . general norms
and conditions for labour, valid for all employers and employees of the
class to which the said norm refers . . .
13. All controversies arising as to the regulation of collective labour relations, whether they concern the application of collective contracts and
other existing regulations, or whether they concern demands for new
labour conditions, are subject to the jurisdiction of the Courts of Appeal
acting as Labour Courts . . .
17. Only legally recognized associations have the right to take action in
disputes arising out of collective labour contracts, and such action must be

taken against legally recognized associations, when they exist; otherwise against a trustee specially appointed by the President of the Court of Appeal . . .

Only legally recognized associations can represent in Court all the employers or employees of the class in the district for which they are formed . . .

Exercise Relating to Documents

1 Examine document A.
 (a) Would you describe the planned programme as left-wing or right-wing? Explain your reasons for this.
 (b) To what extent was the programme altered by the time the Fascists were in power?
 (c) Why do you think these changes were made?
2 Examine document B.
 (a) Explain the references to Vittorio Veneto in this.
 (b) What arguments did Mussolini use to persuade people to support him?
3 Examine documents C.
 How did these laws of 1925–6 give Mussolini power?
4 Examine document D.
 (a) What were to be the duties of the newly-formed associations?
 (b) Why were there to be separate organizations for employers and employees?
 (c) Compare the functions and restrictions on these organizations with those normally imposed on Trade Unions.
5 Compare documents C and D with document A.

XII Germany 1918–39

A. The Weimar Republic 1918–33

1. Political History

(a) The German Revolution and the Weimar Constitution

The early years of the German Republic were politically confused. Moderate politicians, such as Erzberger, Müller and Bauer, were eager to put aside the war and its international consequences, and work hard at the establishment of a democratic republic to replace the imperial autocracy. They were opposed by two large minorities. On the one hand right-wingers loathed the idea of Germany becoming a republic in which the government was responsible to the elected representatives of the people, and actively agitated for the restoration of the monarchy. The Kaiser's abdication was, however, welcomed by many of his supporters, since it meant that the approbium associated with the defeat and peace settlement would be attached to the new republican government, so paving the way for the Kaiser's restoration. On the other hand, left-wingers saw the confusion at the end of the war as an ideal time for the establishment of a communist regime. The left wing was split into a number of groups. At the most extreme were the Spartacists, led by Rosa Luxemburg and Karl Liebknecht, and the Independent Socialists (USPD) led by Kurt Eisner. The majority socialists remained the Social Democrats (SPD) led by Friedrich Ebert and Philipp Scheidemann, who had much in common with the moderates like Erzberger of the Centre Party. The early years of the Republic witnessed a struggle for power between these different groups.

Before the end of World War I, the old order had gone and plans for the future had been laid. In April 1917 the Kaiser had announced the end of the three-class voting system in Prussia and the introduction of equal, direct and secret suffrage. Bethmann Hollweg, long-serving Chancellor, was allowed to retire in July 1917, and was replaced by George Michaelis (July–October 1917) and Count Georg von Hertling. Hertling's resignation on 30 September 1918 was an indication of the desperate plight of Germany *(see page 180)*. His successor was the liberal Prince Max of Baden; it was he who persuaded the Kaiser to abdicate on 9 November, after which he went to Holland, where he lived to hear of the German invasion of France in 1940. Immediately after the end of the war—on 25 November—a conference of representatives from the state governments was held and agreed on the election procedure for a National Constituent Assembly. This met in February 1919 at Weimar to draw up a new constitution.

However, this orderly transition of power was only surface deep. During the same period—the winter of 1918–19—there were a number of uprisings and claims to be the true government. In early November the sailors of Kiel had mutinied, stating 'further than Heligoland we will not go'. Their revolt was supported by workers, soldiers and sailors in other cities, where revolutionary councils were set up. On 7 November Eisner led the revolt in Munich, where an independent socialist republic of Bavaria was proclaimed. Three days later the SPD and USPD took control of Berlin, and Prince Max resigned in favour of Ebert. There followed a struggle for power within the socialist movement. The Spartacists, eager for the violent overthrow of capitalism and the swift establishment of the dictatorship of the proletariat, hated the apparent tardiness of the SPD, which extended the welfare system and introduced the eight-hour day, but would do no more.

The struggle came to a head in January 1919 when the Spartacists tried to take control in Berlin, with the support of the USPD. On 6 January a proclamation was issued deposing Ebert's government and announcing the establishment of a new revolutionary government. Ebert had already won the support of the army, by agreeing with General Groener to oppose Bolshevism (the 'Ebert–Groener Pact'), and used troops to suppress the revolt. Rather than use regular forces, bands of volunteer forces, known as 'Freikorps', were formed. There followed a week of vicious street fighting, in which, to the anger of the Ebert government, Luxemburg and Liebknecht were murdered while under arrest. By 15 January the rising had been put down and Berlin was again under SPD control. Over the next months there were to be other revolts and disturbances. Eisner was murdered by monarchists. In April 1920 a new Bavarian Soviet Republic was proclaimed in Munich, and survived until October, when it was bloodily suppressed by the 'Freikorps'.

In the meantime, the orderly business of government continued. On 31 July 1919 the new constitution was adopted. It had been prepared by the National Assembly elected in January, which was predominantly moderate (see Table 35). The extreme left wing had boycotted the elections. The SPD won 163 seats, the Centre party eighty-eight, the Democrats seventy-five, the right-wing Nationalists forty-two, the Independent Socialists twenty-two and other parties thirty-one. The assembly chose Ebert as President and Scheidemann as Chancellor. He resigned in June, however, in protest at the peace treaty, and was succeeded by Bauer. The most important points of the new constitution were as follows: the President was to be elected every seven years. He was to appoint the Chancellor, who in turn appointed the cabinet, which should command majority support in the Reichstag. The President had the power to suspend the constitution and the Reichstag in times of emergency. The Reichsrat was to be composed of delegates from the eighteen states, and had the power to delay but not veto legislation. The Reichstag deputies were to be elected every four years by all men and women over twenty-one from party lists drawn up for the whole country, rather than to be individual members or representatives of particular districts. The election was to be run on lines of proportional representation—each party won one deputy for every 60 000 votes cast for it. The Reichstag was to initiate and approve legislation, and was regarded as the soveriegn body of the new republic.

Party	Jan 1919	June 1920	May 1924	Dec 1924	May 1928	Sept 1930	July 1932	Nov 1932	Mar 1933
NSDAP Nazis	—	—	6·6 (32)	3·0 (14)	2·6 (12)	18·3 (107)	37·3 (230)	33·1 (196)	43·9 (288)
DNVP Nationalists	10·3 (44)	14·9 (71)	19·5 (95)	20·5 (103)	14·2 (73)	7·0 (41)	5·9 (37)	8·3 (52)	8·6 (52)
DVP People's Party	4·4 (19)	13·9 (65)	9·2 (45)	10·1 (51)	8·7 (45)	4·5 (30)	1·2 (7)	1·9 (11)	1·1 (2)
DDP Democrats	18·6 (75)	8·3 (39)	5·7 (28)	6·3 (32)	4·9 (25)	3·8 (20)	1·0 (4)	1·0 (2)	0·9 (5)
Z Centre	(91)	13·6 (64)	13·4 (65)	13·6 (69)	12·1 (62)	11·8 (68)	12·5 (75)	11·9 (70)	(74)
}	(19·7)								(11·2)
BVP Bavarian People's Party		4·3 (21)	2·2 (16)	3·7 (19)	3·0 (16)	3·0 (19)	3·4 (22)	3·1 (20)	(10)
SPD Socialists	37·9 (165)	21·6 (102)	20·5 (100)	26·0 (131)	29·8 (153)	24·5 (143)	21·6 (133)	20·4 (121)	18·3 (120)
USPD Independent Socialists	7·6 (22)	17·9 (84)	0·8 —	—	—	—	—	—	—
KPD Communists	—	2·1 (4)	12·6 (62)	9·0 (45)	10·6 (54)	13·1 (77)	14·3 (89)	16·9 (100)	12·3 (81)
Others*	1·5	3·4	9·8	7·8	14·1	13·9	2·8	3·4	4·3
Percentage of electorate voting	82·7	78·4	76·3	77·7	74·6	81·4	83·4	79·9	88·0

* This includes a number of parties, such as the right-wing Agrarian League and Saxon County People's Party, and of moderate parites like the German Middle-Class Party and the Christian Social Party.

Table 35 Voting patterns for Reichstag elections expressed as percentages of votes cast— 1919 Constituent Assembly election included

(Figures in brackets are numbers of Reichstag seats won)

The first elections were held in June 1920. The coalition that was then in power, led by Hermann Müller after Bauer's resignation in March, was defeated and replaced by a coalition of the People's Party ('Deutsche Volkspartei'), the Centre Party and the Democrats, to be led by the Centre party leader Fehrenbach (see *Tables 35 and 36*). In fact, it was the SPD, Centre and Democrats who formed most of the governments of the 1920s. They were known as the 'Weimar Coalition' and were, together with the DVP, the parties most willing to try to make the new political and international circumstances work. The SPD and Centre parties were survivals from Wilhelmine Germany, while the Democrats had been founded in November 1918 and combined the Progressive Party and the left wing of the National Liberals. The DVP had also been founded in 1918, predominantly from the right wing of the National Liberals, but under Stresemann's influence came to support the Weimar Republic in the 1920s.

Date of appointment	Name	Party
10 November 1918	Friedrich Ebert	SPD
11 February 1919	Philipp Scheidemann	SPD
23 June 1919	Gustav Bauer	SPD
26 March 1920	Hermann Müller	SPD
25 June 1920	Konstantin Fehrenbach	Centre
4 May 1921	Joseph Wirth	Centre
14 November 1922	Wilhelm Cuno	Non-party
12 August 1923	Gustav Stresemann	People's Party
23 November 1923	Wilhelm Marx	Centre
15 January 1925	Hans Luther	Non-Party
17 May 1926	Wilhelm Marx	Centre
13 June 1928	Hermann Müller	SPD
27 March 1930	Heinrich Brüning	Centre
31 May 1932	Franz von Papen	Non-party
2 December 1932	Kurt von Schleicher	Non-party
30 January 1933	Adolf Hitler	Nazi

Table 36 Chancellors of the German Republic 1919–45

(b) Opposition and elections 1920–24

Extremist opposition to the government continued. On 13 March 1920 monarchists led by Kapp and von Lüttwitz, who had been instrumental in suppressing the Spartacists, seized control of government buildings in Berlin and forced the government to flee to Stuttgart. This uprising— 'the Kapp putsch'—could not maintain control, as the unions declared a general strike and on 17 March the rebels surrendered. In fact, the government barely punished their leaders for fear of losing valuable right-wing support. Two days afterwards a Spartacist revolt in the Ruhr district was put down with great ferocity by government forces. The following year the right-wing struck again by assassinating Matthias Erzberger, Germany's representative on the Reparations Commission, and in 1922, they murdered Walter Rathenau, a leading Jewish industrialist and member of the cabinet. After this outrage, the government made membership of monarchist organizations a criminal offence (30 June 1922).

During the inflation crisis of 1922–3 *(see page 293)*, governments came and went with alarming frequency. In November 1922 Joseph Wirth, who had succeeded Fehrenbach in May 1921, resigned. His replace-ment, Cuno, lasted till August 1923 when Gustav Stresemann, leader of the People's Party, formed a 'Grand Coalition' cabinet assured of support by the SPD, Centre and Democrat parties as well as the DVP. This government was faced by the continued hostility of the right who, led by Hitler and Lüdendorff, tried to take over the government of Bavaria in the Beer Hall Putsch of 8–11 November. The uprising, though at one time supported by about 4000 National Socialists, was put down by troops, and the leaders imprisoned. Again, though, the prison sentences were short, as the judicature showed its fear of the right. Stresemann's ministry lasted only until 23 November, when William Marx of the Centre Party formed a new coalition.

In 1924 there were two Reichstag elections. In May, the right wing made considerable gains *(see Table 35)*, and the centre-left parties all lost votes. However, the December elections, which followed the introduction of the Dawes Plan and the stabilization of the currency *(see page 294)* saw the recovery of the SPD, although the party did not rejoin the government until 1928, thereby making life difficult for the DVP–DDP–Centre coalition as it could not command a Reichstag majority. In 1925, a member of the Nationalist DNVP was included in the Cabinet for the first time, perhaps indicating a shift away from the right wing's consistent opposition to the new government. 1925 also saw a presidential election following Ebert's death. None of the seven candidates won an overall majority on the first ballot, which was headed by the Nationalist Karl Jarrès with the socialist Otto Braun second. For the second ballot, the SPD and Democrats supported the Centre party candidate, Wilhelm Marx, who won 13 751 615 votes. The communists refused to accept him and their own candidate, Ernst Thalmann, won just under 2 million votes. This split in the left and centre allowed the right's candidate, Field Marshal Paul von Hindenburg, to win with 14 655 766 votes.

(c) Recovery and collapse 1924–32

Despite the economic recovery after 1924 *(see page 294)*, there was a distinct rightward trend in this period. In November 1925 the Prussian state government donated large areas of land to the ex-Kaiser. The following May, Luther's cabinet resigned, following instructions that the old imperial colours should be restored to the diplomatic service. In September 1927 President Hindenburg, in a speech dedicating the Tannenburg monument, repudiated German responsibility for the outbreak of war in 1914. The old ways, briefly forgotten in the problems of the early twenties, were resurfacing.

Nevertheless, the Reichstag elections of 1928 showed a leftward shift, and Hermann Müller formed a Grand Coalition cabinet. This government overcame nationalist opposition to win approval for the Young Plan *(see page 294)* but resigned shortly afterwards when Müller realized that Hindenburg would not grant him emergency powers to bring in social legislation. The new Chancellor, Heinrich Brüning, was leader of the Centre Party, and his cabinet contained members of all the Coalition parties except the SPD. It did not command a majority in the Reichstag. Consequently, the budget was authorized by Hindenburg's decree, and the President then dissolved the Reichstag when it refused to approve the budget by 256 votes to 193. The elections that followed in September 1930 saw a swing away from the moderate centre parties and towards the extremes for the first time since May 1924. Even more alarming, it was the Nazi party that now took the votes on the right rather than the DNVP or nationalists. This tendency was reinforced by the presidential elections of March 1932 when two right-wing candidates—Hindenburg and Hitler—each won a huge number of votes (over 18 million and 11 million respectively) while the single left winger, the communist Thalmann won less than 5 million. In the second ballot, Hindenburg defeated Hitler by 6 million votes.

By this time, parliamentary government had all but ended and most laws were passed by decree under Article 48 of the Constitution *(see page 299)*, which allowed the President to give the Cabinet emergency powers. Between 1929 and 1932 over 100 laws were introduced in this way, while only twenty-nine were passed through the Reichstag in the normal way. In May 1932 Brüning resigned when Hindenburg refused him such powers to divide the bankrupt East Prussian estates into allotments on which 600 000 unemployed could be resettled. Franz von Papen's new cabinet was to be responsible only to the President, and not to the Reichstag. In June the ban on Hitler's Nazi storm troopers (the 'Sturm Abteilung'), effectively the Nazi private army, was lifted. There followed the inevitable clashes between left and right, in the midst of which the socialist government of Prussia was dismissed by the Chancellor. Prussia was put under martial law as nothing could be done to stop the SA's violence. In the elections of July, the Nazis won 230 seats—some ninety short of an overall majority—but because Hitler refused to enter a coalition without himself as Chancellor, the Papen government remained in office. On 12 September a motion of no confidence was passed by 512 votes to forty-two in the Reichstag, and fresh elections were held in which the Nazis lost slightly while the Communists gained. Papen resigned on 17 November but again Hitler refused to become Chancellor, this time because Hindenburg refused to grant him decree powers. Consequently, General Kurt von Schleicher formed another cabinet that was to be responsible only to the President, but he lasted only until 28 January; he resigned when Hindenburg refused to grant him emergency powers. This time Hitler did accept the Chancellorship. *(See pages 304, 318)*

2. Economic History

The Weimar Republic was faced with two major economic crises, one at the start of its life, the other at its end. The first was the consequence of the Great War and the treaties that followed it, the second the consequence of the great depression. Each crisis demonstrated Germany's close connections with the economies of the rest of the world.

The Great War left Germany broken and half starved. It did not end for Germany until July 1919, when the Allied blockade was lifted on the signing of the treaty of Versailles. By that time, over a ¼ million people had died of starvation. The 1918 harvest had been disastrous, leaving crop yields low and forcing prices up sevenfold compared with 1914. Moreover, the peace treaties deprived Germany of three-quarters of her iron ore resources, a quarter of her coal and 15% of her arable land. Much of her merchant shipping fleet had to be surrendered. In addition, the government would have to find money for the recovery of industry and agriculture.

The Germans' burdens were compounded by the Allies' demands for reparations. These were only finalized by the Reparations Commission in April 1921, and were fixed at a grand total of 132 million gold marks (about £11 000 million). More than half of this would take the form of cash payments to the countries that had suffered, the rest would be paid in goods. For example, Germany was expected to deliver 375 000 tons of coke to France each month, despite the fact that all German industry had been badly hit and did not regain its 1914 output figures until the 1930s. The first cash payments were made in August 1921 but at the end of that year the government announced that it would not be able to make the payments scheduled for January and February 1922.

This announcement met a mixed reaction. Lloyd George sought some kind of international agreement, to which end the Genoa Conference *(see page 364)* was held. However, the American government put pressure on its European debtors to repay, and there was a widespread view that Germany was just squealing in an attempt to avoid continued payments. At the same time, the governments of Wirth and Cuno made little effort to limit the amount of notes being printed. As a result, the number of notes in circulation rocketed, and the value of the mark simultaneously plummetted. In 1918, the rate of exchange was about 20 marks to the pound; by the time of the worst inflation in late 1923, the rate was 20 000 *million* marks to the pound. Notes of enormous value—100 000 marks—were printed and were needed for even the smallest purchases. Stories illustrating the plight of the German people are plentiful. Wages were collected daily, often in wheelbarrows. The price of a cup of coffee could double in the time it took to drink it. A lecturer refused to lecture because her fee would not cover the cost of the fare to the hall. Many people, especially in rural areas, resorted to a system of barter. At the same time, French and Belgian forces occupied the Ruhr district *(see page 232)* and the policy of passive resistance that was used to combat them reduced production and ultimately cost German industry twice as much as the annual reparation payments. The extent of government blame for the inflation crisis was obviously an important issue, both to contemporaries and historians. On the one hand, many argued that it was simply a device to escape reparation payments, while on the other it can be argued that the desperate state of the economy and the entirely new circumstances of the 1920s posed impossible problems for the German government.

The crisis was ended by two measures, one undertaken by the Stresemann government, the other by the American government. The German government appointed Hjalmar Schacht as special currency commissioner. On 15 November 1923 he introduced the 'Rentenmark', a mark theoretically secure because it was based on a mortgage of all land and industry to the tune of 3200 million gold marks. Each 'Rentenmark' was exchangeable for one trillion old marks. This new currency was used as a temporary measure until August 1924 when the reformed Reichsbank began to issue its own new notes. At the same time, the Minister of Finance, Hans Luther, introduced government economies, including the dismissal of 700 000 government employees. The American inspired Dawes Plan was implemented in 1924 to ensure recovery. By it, the Reichsbank was reorganized under Allied supervision. Germany was to receive a loan of 800 million gold marks, mainly from the United States. The system of reparation payments was altered, so that the total was reduced and the period for repayment increased. Germany was to pay one billion marks per annum (£50 million) for the next five years, after which it would be increased to 2½ billion (£125 million) per annum. The plan was put forward on 9 April 1924 and accepted by the Reichstag a week later. It would at least bring respite from repayments at the highest levels.

The next five years saw considerable economic recovery. The prospect of industrial expansion under Allied supervision attracted capital back to Germany. Loans to the value of 25½ billion marks were received between 1924 and 1930, mainly from America. At the same time 22·9 billion marks were repaid in reparations. These were again revised in 1929, by the Young Plan. This allowed for a 59-year schedule for repayments, at an average of 2·05 billion marks per annum. It also allowed for a possible deferment of payment in times of economic hardship, when two-thirds of the sum could be left aside. During the late 1920s, German industry almost regained its pre-war levels of output, despite the loss of resources. By 1927, coal had reached 79% of its 1913 level, pig iron 68% and steel 86%. There was a large increase in the number of industrial cartels. Agriculture did not make a similar recovery, and yields generally remained low. There was little change in the pattern of agricultural landholding. In 1919 more than 20% of cultivated land belonged to less than 1% of landowners; despite the redistribution planned for in 1919 only ½ million hectares were released as a result of right-wing opposition in the Reichstag. Prices rose only slowly, and, significantly *(see page 320)*, the plight of small farmers was barely improved. Nevertheless, there was considerable hope for the German economy by the end of the 1920s.

However, the world depression affected Germany badly. The flow of foreign capital, on which industrial recovery depended, dried up, and much of it was withdrawn. By 1928, Germany had been borrowing over 5 billion marks each year, yet by 1931 the Reichsbank had no foreign currency and in three weeks £50 million worth of gold was taken out of the country. Some banks were forced to close, and many thousands of Germans lost their savings. Foreign trade was badly hit by the rapid trend to economic nationalism and the consequent increases in tariffs. Between 1929 and 1932 the value of exports fell from £630 million to £280 million and imports from £670 million to £230 million. With little capital and shrinking markets for their goods, industries inevitably had to contract their businesses and sack workers. Even in the winter of 1928–9 there had been over 2 million unemployed. By the following winter there were over 3 million, and by 1932 over 6 million. At the same time, the government Grand Coalition, of all the moderate parties from the DVP to the SPD, were unable to agree on what measures to take. At one extreme, the DVP argued for the need for stringency and cuts in public spending, while the SPD demanded action for the unemployed in the form of additional welfare benefits and increased government spending. President Hindenburg felt unable to grant emergency powers to a government so divided in its views, with the result that inaction was the chief policy. In such circumstances, voters inevitably looked to the more radical parties for solutions.

3. Foreign Policy

Weimar foreign policy falls broadly into two periods. Until the early 1920s, the government was virtually told what to do by the Allies, and had the final quarrels of the Great War settled for it. From 1921, Wirth and his successors sought to restore Germany's place in world diplomacy and to find agreements that would lead to economic recovery and the restoration of Germany's true frontiers. Both periods were dominated by the treaty of Versailles, of which Hiden has written: 'If the constitution may be regarded as the framework for the internal developments of the Weimar Republic, it would seem self evident to see the Versailles treaty as the framework in which the country's external relations had to develop'. Almost every German was agreed on the need to revise the treaty; in particular, the new eastern frontiers (see Maps 23 and 27) had to be readjusted in Germany's favour. They were less agreed on the means to revise the treaties. At one extreme, the Nationalists wanted swift and forceful action as soon as there were enough troops to do something, while more moderate politicians were prepared to work longer and through diplomacy.

After signing the treaty of Versailles, there were a number of actions that Germany was forced to take. On 22 September 1919 the government was forced to remove provisions for the representation of Austria in the Weimar constitution and promise to respect Austrian independence. It also had to order German troops under General von der Goltz out of Latvia. A number of territorial changes were made as the result of plebiscites and League of Nations decisions. In 1920 Schleswig-Holstein was partitioned between Germany and Denmark as the result of a plebiscite. (This was the result of finally applying the terms of the treaty of Prague of 1866.) French troops were sent to Upper Silesia and remained there until the plebiscite and League of Nations' division of 1921 *(see page 210)*. In the same year Allenstein and Marienwerder in East Prussia were restored to Germany as the result of a plebiscite, but Eupen and Malmedy, where the majority of the 600 000 people were German, were awarded to Belgium by the Allies. Danzig was taken under League of Nations control, thus ending, more than two years after the armistice, most of the post-war border issues.

One potential route to the revision of the treaty was through the friendship of Russia. Both countries had been rejected by the rest of Europe, both being barred from League of Nations' membership. Both were territorially harmed by the recreation of Poland. Both saw the creation of a string of new East European states, sponsored by France, as a possible threat. Germany foresaw the possibility of using areas of Russia for the military training and production that she regarded as essential but which had been barred to her by the treaty. German industry required new markets; Russian industry needed capital and foreign knowledge. Consequently, discussions were held during 1920 and in May 1921 a Provisional Commercial treaty was signed between the two. Germany was cautious for fear of Allied disapproval, but the two were brought closer together by the Poles' gains in the Upper Silesian plebiscite and France's hard line against Germany at the Genoa Conference in 1922. The treaty of Rapallo was signed in 1922 by which both Germany and Russia gave up all claims for war damages from each other and promised each other special treatment in economic matters. This was backed up by the treaty of Berlin, of 1926, by which each promised to continue to maintain good relations. The Russian friendship was supported by most German political parties, except the SPD, who feared it would lead to greater support for their communist rivals.

During the early 1920s relations with Britain and France were inevitably soured by the reparations issue. As early as March 1921 the Allies occupied the Rhineland towns of Dusseldorf, Duisberg and Ruhrort because of alleged German failures to comply with the treaty terms. This was a significant move, for it convinced Chancellor Wirth, and his successors, of the need for the policy of 'fulfilment'—that is, to fulfil the terms laid down by the treaty and by so doing show how impossible they were for Germany and thus bring about a mood in which Germany could more profitably ask for revision. Before this policy was fully put into effect came the inflation crisis and, in January 1923, the French and Belgian occupation of the Ruhr. This had been undertaken despite British opposition, although all the allies were agreed that the Germans had defaulted on their repayments of coal. When the troops entered the area, the German government immediately refused to make any more repayments and the workers and management in the Ruhr area refused to co-operate with the French authorities. Mines, factories and railways were put under French military control in an effort to secure some production, but the refusal of the workers to co-operate made the French task a difficult one. To have fired on the unarmed workers would have created an international outcry. There was in fact some fighting as the French endeavoured to declare an independent Rhineland Republic, but the local opposition forced the French to abandon this idea. On 26 September the passive resistance policy was, on government orders, ended as the French had indicated their willingness to come to agreement and support for it was proving too expensive. Consequently, it was agreed to investigate the entire question of reparations, the outcome of which was the Dawes Plan *(see page 294)*.

After 1923, the policy of fulfilment was more or less closely adhered to until the 1930s. Its chief architect was Gustav Stresemann, Chancellor for a brief time in 1923 and thereafter Foreign Minister until his death in 1929. The Ruhr invasion and its aftermath had perhaps made the Allies less rigorous in their hostility to Germany, and this made Stresemann's task of winning at least partial revision of the treaty easier. The climax of 'fulfilment' came in 1925, with the agreements reached at Locarno in October and finalized in London on 1 December, and normally referred to as the 'Locarno treaties'. Germany accepted her borders with Belgium and France, and these were guaranteed by agreements involving Britain and Italy as guarantors, which would take effect when Germany joined the League of Nations. Germany also agreed to arbitration in any future border quarrels with Poland and Czechoslovakia. However, since these were not given the same guarantees as the Western frontiers, the Germans felt there was still hope of revision in the East. The Locarno treaties marked a genuine breakthrough in relations with Britain and France, for in December 1925 they evacuated the occupation zone on the left bank of the Rhine and in the autumn of 1926 Germany was accepted as a member of the League. She was also given a permanent place on the League's Council, although this was delayed by the opposition of Spain and Brazil. In 1927 the Allied Commission of Military Control left Germany (it had been posted to guard against German rearmament) and the Rhineland occupation forces were reduced by 10 000. In 1929 Germany became a signatory of the Kellogg–Briand Pact *(see page 369)* and in 1930 the Allies left the Rhineland. Stresemann's policy had achieved much—Germany was once again a free agent in European affairs and there was a good chance of further concessions and revision.

The policy of fulfilment raised considerable questions. It was generally popular in Germany, although the Nationalists were hostile to anything that smacked of co-operation with the League of Nations, which they regarded as nothing more than an instrument for imposing the terms of the treaty of Versailles. Others argued that it was not possible to pursue a policy of friendship with both the Western powers and Russia, and that alliance with Russia was a more profitable route to treaty revision in the East. From a different viewpoint, Stresemann has been criticized for double-crossing—on the one hand supporting a policy of friendship to the Western powers, and willingly accepting their loans, while on the other sending men and money into the Soviet Union for military purposes. Given that his aim was treaty revision, he was in fact pursuing his end by the two means best open to him, for the forces in preparation would give Germany the teeth she required to force some concessions. The extent of German preparations in Russia is interesting. A fighter pilot training base was set up at Lipetsk in 1924, where by 1933 more than 100 pilots a year were trained, while a tank school was opened at Karma in 1929. A considerable number of men were trained, but little equipment was made; for example, there were only some ten tanks and less than seventy planes available in 1931. Nevertheless, a start had been made, and enough men trained to provide the basis of a fighting force.

5. Documents Relating to the Weimar Republic

A. The Weimar Constitution, 11 August 1919
(Source: *British and Foreign State Papers*, vol. cxii (1919), quoted in Kertesz, p. 406.) This is an edited version, but includes the most significant parts of the document.

This constitution has been framed by the united German people, inspired by the determination to restore and establish their Federation upon a basis of liberty and justice, to be of service to the cause of peace both at home and abroad, and to promote social progress.
1. The German Federation is a Republic . . .
5. The executive power is exercised in Federal affairs through the institutions of the Federation in virtue of the Federal Constitution, and in State affairs by the officials of the State, in virtue of the Constitution of the States.
6. The Federal Government has the sole legislative power as regards: 1. Foreign relations. 2. Colonial affairs. 3. Nationality, right of domicile, immigration, emigration and extradition. 4. Military organization. 5. The monetary system. 6. The customs department, as well as uniformity in the sphere of customs, trade, and freedom of commercial intercourse. 7. The postal and telegraph services, including the telephone service.
13. Federal law overrides state law . . .
20. The Reichstag is an assembly composed of the deputies of the German people.
22. The deputies are elected by the universal, equal direct and secret suffrage of all men and women above the age of twenty, upon the principles of proportional representation . . .
25. The President of the Federation may dissolve the Reichstag, but only once for any one reason. The general election will take place not later than sixty days after the dissolution . . .
41. The President of the Federation is elected by the whole German people . . .

47. The President of the Federation has supreme command over all the armed forces of the Federation.

48. In the case of a State not fulfilling the duties imposed on it by the Federal Constitution or the Federal Laws, the President of the Federation may enforce their fulfilment with the help of the armed forces.

Where public security and order are seriously disturbed or endangered within the Federation, the President of the Federation may take emergency measures necessary for their restoration, intervening in case of need with the help of the armed forces. For this purpose he is permitted, for the time being, to abrogate, either wholly or partially, the fundamental laws laid down in articles 114, 115, 117, 118, 123, 124 and 153.

The President of the Federation must, without delay, inform the Reichstag of any measures taken in accordance with paragraphs one and two of this Article. Such measures shall be withdrawn upon the demand of the Reichstag . . .

52. The Federal Government consists of the Chancellor of the Federation and the Federal Ministers.

53. The President . . . appoints and dismisses the Chancellor, . . . and, on the latter's recommendation, the . . . Ministers.

54. The Chancellor . . . and the . . . Ministers require, for the administration of their office, the confidence of the Reichstag. Any one of them must resign, should the confidence of the House be withdrawn by an express resolution.

56. The Chancellor . . . determines the main lines of policy, for which he is responsible to the Reichstag. . . .

60. A Reichsrat is formed for the representation of the German States in Federal legislation and administration . . .

68. Bills are introduced by the Federal Government or by members of the Reichstag.

69. The introduction of bills by the Federal Government requires the consent of the Reichsrat.

76. The Constitution may be altered by legislation. But decisions of the Reichstag as to such alteration come into effect only if two-thirds of the legal total of members be present, and if at least two-thirds of those present have given their consent . . .

114. Personal liberty is inviolable. No encroachment on, or deprivation of, personal liberty by public authority is permissible, unless supported by law.

Persons who have been deprived of their liberty shall be informed—at the latest on the following day—by what authority and on what grounds the deprivation of liberty has been ordered; opportunity shall be given them without delay to make objection against such deprivation.

115. The residence of every German is a sanctuary for him, and inviolable; exceptions are admissible only in virtue of the laws . . .

117. Every German has the right, within the limits of the general laws, to express his opinion freely by word, writing, printed matter or picture . . .

123. All Germans have the right, without notification or special permission, to assemble peacefully and without arms . . .

124. All Germans have the right to form unions and societies, provided their objects do not run counter to the penal laws . . .

153. Property is guaranteed by the Constitution . . .

B. The Treaty of Rapallo, 16 April 1922
(Source: *British and Foreign State Papers*, vol. cxviii (1923 pt. 2), quoted in Kertesz, page 461.)

1. The two governments agree that the settlement . . . of the questions arising from the time when a state of war existed between Germany and Russia shall be effected on the following basis:
(a) The Parties renounce mutually all compensation in respect of the costs of the war and of war losses . . . also . . . all compensation in respect of civilian losses caused . . . by the so-called exceptional war legislation or by compulsory measures taken by State Departments on the other side.
(b) The public and private legal relations between the two states . . . will be settled on the basis of reciprocity.
(c) Germany and Russia will mutually renounce all compensation in respect of costs incurred on both sides for prisoners of war . . .
2. Germany renounces all claims arising from the application up to the present of the laws and measures of the Russian Socialist Federal Soviet Republic to German nationals or their private rights and to the rights of the German Reich and States in regard to Russia . . . provided that the government of the RSFSR does not give satisfaction to like claims but forward by other states.
3. Diplomatic and consular relations will immediately be resumed. . . .
5. Both governments will endeavour reciprocally to meet the economic needs of the other side in an accommodating spirit . . .

C. The Occupation of the Ruhr (1923)
(Source: E. R. Huber, *Dokumente zur deutschen Verfassungsgeschichte* vol iii, translated by G. Kertesz.)

1. Directive on Passive Resistance, 19 January 1923
The action of the French and Belgian Governments in the Ruhr area constitutes a gross violation of international law and of the treaty of Versailles. As a consequence all orders and ordinances directed to German officials in the course of this action are legally invalid. The Governments of the Reich, of Prussia, Bavaria, Hessen, and Oldenburg therefore order all officials not to obey the instructions of the occupying forces, but only the ordinances of their own Governments. . . .
2. Proclamation calling off Passive Resistance, 26 September 1923
On 11 January French and Belgian troops occupied . . . the German Ruhr territory. Since then, the Ruhr territory and the Rhineland have had to suffer much oppression. Over 180 000 German men, women, old people and children have been driven from house and home. Millions of Germans no longer know what personal freedom is. Countless acts of violence have accompanied the occupation, more than one hundred fellow Germans have lost their lives, and hundred are still languishing in prison.

A spirit of justice and patriotism rose against the unlawfulness of the invasion. The population refused to work under foreign bayonets. For this loyalty and constancy . . . the whole German people give them thanks.

The Reich government undertook to do what it could for the suffering compatriots. An ever increasing amount of the means of the Reich has been claimed by this task. In the past week support for the Ruhr and the Rhineland amounted to 3500 billion marks. In the current week a doubling of this sum is expected. Economic life in Germany, occupied or unoccupied, is disrupted. Perseverance in our present course threatens the terribly serious danger that it will be impossible to establish a stable currency, to maintain economic activity, and thus even to secure a bare existence for our people.

In the interests of Germany's future as well as the interest of the Rhineland and the Ruhr this danger must be averted. To save the life of the people and of the State we face today the bitter necessity of breaking off the struggle . . .

D. Appeal of the SPD Executive, 28 March 1930
(Source: E. R. Huber, *op. cit.*)

In 1928 the Grand coalition of SPD, Centre, BVP, DDP and DVP had formed a government, which lasted for almost two years. In the document below the SPD leaders explain their reasons for ending support for this coalition.

The struggle over unemployment insurance has led to an open crisis.

Securing support for the huge army of . . . unemployed is and remains the aim of Social Democracy, a reduction of benefits is the aim of the 'Deutsche Volksparteri'.

This contrast led to the crisis.

Last year already there was a strong attack on unemployment insurance. Social Democracy and the trade unions . . . defeated it. They were successful in maintaining unemployment benefits. But the social reaction was not satisfied. The social reaction wants to destroy unemployment insurance, so that necessity will force the worker to accept reductions in wages withou opposition . . .

The attack of the 'Deutsche Volkspartei' is not only against unemployment insurance. It is directed against the whole of the social welfare activity of the Reich, States and municipalities, and thus against the basis of the existence of the working class. . . .

E. A View of the Weimar Republic
(Source: F. Ernst, *The Germans and their Modern History* (1966), quoted in Hiden.)

In our high school in Stuttgart, as, indeed, in most of the secondary schools in Germany after 1918, a noticeable rightist trend prevailed, which most of the teachers followed, at least those who spoke to us about politics. We believed that it was the stab in the back alone that had prevented a German victory; we had one Pan-German history teacher who defended this worst form of the legend. We were convinced that one could be patriotic only on the rightist side. We repeated the stupid jokes, which were then circulating among the middle classes, about President Ebert and his wife, which were supposed to prove their unworthiness. In fact, the Eberts succeeded, with quiet dignity, in regaining a sympathy for Germany under the most trying conditions—in a world in which public opinion was dominated by Germany's wartime enemies. About this, however, we heard nothing, and we read nothing about it in our rightist middle-class press. We did not know what the actual situation of the war had been in 1918; we were taught to hate the British and French and to despise the Americans. . . . We did not see that socialist workers had also sacrificed their blood for Germany—for a country that had never really given them a chance. We were not meant to suspect that the leading classes of Imperial Germany had made serious mistakes, and that these had jeopardized the victory . . . as much as the trend on the left had. We were brought up for a world that no longer existed, and we took up nationalistic slogans, while the Republic of which we were trying to make fun was trying to pull the waggon out of the mud.

After graduation, many of our class joined the 'black army'. It was at this point that I, a student . . . in Stuttgart, . . . saw how wrong they were. Thus, at eighteen, I became immune to the allurements of Hiterism and could observe the rise of the Weimar Republic with keen interest.

F. Inflation

(a) (Source: A memoir of Dr Freda Wunderlich quoted in G. Bry, *Wages in Germany 1870–1945* (1960), and quoted in Hiden.)

As soon as I received my salary I rushed out to buy the daily necessities. My daily salary, as editor of the periodical 'Soziale Praxis'. was just enough to buy one loaf of bread and a small piece of cheese or some oatmeal. On one occasion I had to refuse to give a lecture at a Berlin city college because I could not be assured that my fee would cover my tube fare to the classroom, and it was too far to walk. On another occasion, a private lesson I gave to the wife of a farmer was paid somewhat better—by one loaf of bread for the hour.

A friend of mine, a clergyman, came to Berlin from his suburb with his monthly salary to buy a pair of shoes for his baby; he could only afford a cup of coffee. The Zeiss works in Jena, a non-profit firm, calculated the gold mark equivalent of its average wage paid during a week in November 1923 and found that weekly earnings were worth four gold marks, less than a sixth of pre-war levels.

(b) (Source; Willi Frischauer, article in *The Daily Telegraph*, 1974.)

Most mornings in the autumn of 1923, the courtyard of the Reichsbank resembled a factory dispatch area. Lorries queued to load sacks of newly issued banknotes, none lower than 100 000 marks. So great was the demand for notes that 100 private printers were pressed into service to help the bank's thirty contract firms to produce the money. At local banks, messengers stood by with trolleys and laundry baskets to cart away the weekly payrolls. Soon the value of the currency fell so low that it was more profitable to sell notes in bulk as old paper than rely on their purchasing power— not that there was much to purchase. A point was reached when notes ordered by the Reichsbank a week earlier were worthless by the time they were delivered and were promptly consigned to the cellars where they were shredded and pulped. Upstairs, in the bank's elegant boardroom in the first week of November 1923 the Reichsbank's ageing and ailing President, Dr Rudolf Havenstein, confronted his directors with a situation report which listed the amount of money in ciculation: 400 000 billion marks or, to quote the precise and mind boggling figure—400 338 326 350 700 000 000.

Drained of working capital and raw materials, the German economy faltered. Only the printing presses continued their macabre rotations until they ran out of paper for banknotes. Shortages became so acute that prices rose beyond intelligible calculations. Newspapers published 'multiplicators' relating the day's prices to the pre-war rate. At the end of 1922, the multiplicator for bread was 37 000. This was only the beginning. Denominations of notes already verged on the fantastic; 10 000 marks notes turned up as 100 million marks. The effect on daily life was devastating. With 28 million marks in his pocket a young friend who was a composer could not afford a newspaper (price: 300 million marks) or the tram fare. When he collected his year's royalties, they did not cover the milkman's bill for the week. Frustrated and hungry crowds plundered food stores, the police making common cause with the rioters. Political extremists harassed the Weimar Government which was powerless to control events. Inflation had watered the seed of political distcontent and disintegration.

The runaway inflation ended suddenly and undramatically. It was halted by the so-called Helfferich Plan, providing for the wealthy landowners to underwrite a new currency, and the technical skill of Dr Hjalmar Schacht, owner of the National and Darmstadt Bank, who implemented it. Schacht introduced the new Rentenmark and, by simply chopping off 15 noughts, reduced the value of the dollar at a stroke from 4·2 billion old marks to 4·2 Rentenmark (later Reichsmark). Dr Havenstein, the father of inflation, retired and Schacht took over as Reichsbank President.

Exercise on Documents

1 Examine document A.
   (a) Explain the federal nature of the Weimar government.
   (b) Comment on the relationship between the President and the Reichstag.
   (c) What were the implications of Article 48?
   (d) Draw a diagram to demonstrate the relationship between the different government bodies.
   (e) What promises about personal liberties did the Constitution make?
2 Examine document B.
   To what extent did the signatories of the treaty commit themselves to each other?
3 Examine document C.
   (a) What reasons did the government give for ordering passive resistance?
   (b) What reasons did the government give for ending passive resistance?
4 Examine document D.
   Why did the SPD desert the Grand Coalition in 1930?
5 Examine document E.
   (a) How different does the atmosphere of Weimar Germany seem from the atmosphere of Wilhelmine Germany?
   (b) What light does this document throw on class attitudes in Weimar Germany?

6   Examine documents F.
    (a) What effects would the inflation crisis have had on the attitude
         of German people to their own government and to the other
         European powers?
    (b) What groups of people would have especially suffered during
         the crisis?

B. The Nazi State 1933–9

1. Political and Constitutional History

(a) The capture and consolidation of power

It is not possible to speak of Hitler's 'seizure of power', nor of 'the end of
the Weimar Republic'. Hitler did not seize power, but was appointed
Chancellor, constitutionally, by President Hindenburg. The Weimar
Republic came to an end as early as May 1932, when von Papen became
Chancellor responsible only to the President, or as late as August 1934,
when Hitler became President. On 30 January 1933 Hindenburg
appointed Hitler as head of a cabinet that was predominantly composed
of Nazis but also contained two Nationalists. Hugenberg and Seldte.
and was dependent on other parties, including the Centre, for a majority
in the Reichstag. Consequently, Hitler's political priority was to secure
power for himself and the Nazi party.

By refusing to co-operate with the Centre Party leader, Kaas, Hitler
precipitated Reichstag elections, which were to be held in March, 1933.
The election campaign itself was used to extend Nazi power and influence. Goering, as Prussian Minister of the Interior, recruited 50 000
'police' auxiliaries to assist in the maintenance of law and order. These
recruits, most of whom were attached to one of the Nazi private armies,
the SA ('Sturm Abteilung') and the SS ('Schutz Staffel'), had only to don
a white arm band to assume authority. Among the orders they received
from Goering was the following: 'Police officers who make use of firearms
in the execution of their duty will, without regard to the consequences of
such use, benefit from my protection: those who, out of a misplaced
regard for such consequences, fail in their duty will be punished . . .
failure to act will be regarded more seriously than an error due to taking
action.' The new era had arrived.

On 27 February 1933 the Reichstag building in Berlin was burnt to the
ground. Hitler blamed it on the 'anti-democratic' Communist Party,
and argued that an uprising was planned. President Hindenburg therefore allowed a decree that suspended or adjusted many civil liberties:

> restrictions on personal liberty, on the right of free expression of opinion,
> including freedom of the press, on the rights of assembly and association;
> violations of the privacy of postal, telegraphic and telephonic communica-
> tions . . . are permissible beyond the limits otherwise prescribed.

The young Dutchman, van der Lubbe, who started the fire was tried and executed. Many KPD members were arrested and the party's efforts in the elections severely hampered. It was claimed that the fire was a KPD plot. Subsequently, it was believed that the Nazis started the fire deliberately as an excuse for a purge on the communists, but recent investigations have suggested that van der Lubbe, an unstable character, started the fire on his own initiative.

Apart from his anti-communism, Hitler's election programme was simple 'I ask you, German people, that after you have given the others fourteen years you should give us four.' In the event, it was not necessary to win an overall majority, since Hitler was assured of continued Nationalist support. The Nazis did win a larger percentage of the vote than ever before *(see Table 35)* and increased their vote by 5½ million, while the KPD lost 1 million votes and the SPD 66 000. The membership of the new Reichstag was as follows: Nazis 288 seats, DNVP fifty-two (making a total of 340), DVP two, DDP five, Centre seventy-four, BVP ten, SPD 120, KPD eighty-one, others seven. If all the opposition combined, it could muster more than 290 votes, though the DVP and DDP were unlikely to join all the others. In any case, the Nazi–Nationalist combination opened proceedings by outlawing the Communist party, which gave the Nazis an overall majority without Nationalist support.

The most vital bill debated and approved by the new Reichstag was the 'Law for Removing the Distress of People and Reich', normally known as the Enabling Bill, debated on 23 March 1933. This law would give the government powers for four years (until 1 April 1937) to enact laws without consulting the Reichstag, including the right to go against the Constitution and make treaties with foreign powers. Since it was a law that amended the Constitution, it had to be approved by a two-thirds majority in the Reichstag, which had to have a quorum of two-thirds for the debate. The SPD therefore considered defeating the bill by boycotting the debate, but to prevent this a procedural change was introduced by which all Reichstag members were counted present unless specifically excused. While the bill was debated in the Kroll Opera House (the temporary home of the Reichstag), SA and SS members were in the corridors and galleries in force. As the SPD leader Wels spoke against the bill, the SS chanted 'We want the Bill—or fire and murder'. The bill was passed by 441 votes to ninety-four, all the votes against being cast by member of the SPD. Hitler then turned swiftly on his enemies; the SPD was dissolved on 10 May, Trade Unions were banned in the same month, and in July the Catholic parties were declared illegal. As the DNVP had already dissolved itself, the Nazis had no difficulties in declaring themselves the only legal party on 14 July 1933.

The only remaining opposition was to be found among the SA and among right-wing nationalists. Many of the latter had hoped to use Hitler to win power for themselves. Papen, whom Hitler appointed Vice-Chancellor, said 'in two months we'll have pushed Hitler into a corner so hard that he'll be squeaking.' Hitler himself was well aware of their plans and in February 1933 said: 'the reactionary forces believe they have me on the lead. I know that they hope I will achieve my own ruin by mismanagement. . .'. At first, Hitler used right-wing support to gain respectability at home and abroad. The high point of this was reached in the ceremony in Potsdam Garrison Church on 21 March 1933 to mark the opening of the Reichstag. On the anniversary of Bismarck's opening of the first Reichstag of the German Empire in 1871, Hitler entered the Church alongside the President, the generals in their imperial uniforms and his own symbols of the new Germany, the SA and the swastikas. In his speech to the President, Hitler said:

> By a unique upheaval, in the last few weeks our national honour has been restored and, thanks to your understanding, Herr General-Feld-Marschal, the union between the symbols of the old greatness and the new strength has been celebrated. We pay you homage. A protective providence places you over the new forces of our Nation.

Equally conciliatory were the Concordat with the Vatican (July 1933) and the German withdrawal from the League of Nations (October 1933). Both were likely to win support from traditional Germans and opponents of Weimar.

However, their support for Hitler was shortlived. The DNVP, which had committed political suicide by voting to ban the KPD, was forced to dissolve itself on 27 June 1933. The following February all monarchist organizations were banned. A number of right-wing leaders were removed in the 'Night of the Long Knives' (30 June–2 July 1934). Ex-Chancellor General von Schleicher and his wife and the Centre Party leader, Erich Klausener, were among those who died. The last survivors of the traditional right were Blomberg, the minister of war, and Fritsch, commander-in-chief of the Reichswehr, who were not dismissed until February 1938. Until then, their presence in the government was useful in assuring the support of the army; but after their dismissal the war ministry was abolished and Hitler took personal command of all armed forces. With them went sixteen other generals, thereby ending any presence of the traditional right in Hitler's government.

Hitler's left-wing supporters were mainly to be found in the SA, the 'Sturm Abteilung'. Röhm, their leader, still sought the economic revolution promised by a nominally socialist party. This was talked of as the 'second revolution'. He and his Brownshirts also felt that they had not been given the jobs and responsibilities that they felt they deserved as Hitler's earliest supporters. Hitler regarded this wing of his party as a threat and, in the 'Night of the Long Knives', had them removed. Röhm and Gregor Strasser, the two most prominent left-wing National Socialists, were murdered, as were many others. On 3 July, Hitler himself admitted to seventy-seven victims, although it is likely that several hundred died.

A month after this 'Great Purge', Hitler assumed complete control of Germany. On 1 August 1934, with Hindenburg a dying man, Hitler announced, in the 'Law concerning Head of State', the amalgamation of the offices of Chancellor and President in the new title 'Führer and Reichskanzler'. The next day the 87-year-old Hindenburg died, and Hitler assumed his new title. The same day Blomberg agreed to a new oath of allegiance for the army: 'I swear by God this holy oath, that I will render unconditional obedience to the leader of the German Reich, Adolf Hitler, supreme commander of the armed forces and that, as a brave soldier, I will be ready at any time to stake my life for this oath.' All soldiers had now sworn loyalty, not to the state, but to one man. The same month a plebiscite approved Hitler's assumption of the Presidency and of sole executive power. His position was unassailable, de facto and de jure.

(b) Constitutional policy

After the passage of the Enabling Law and subsequent legislation, the Weimar organs of government either ceased to exist or became rubber stamps for Hitler's dictatorship. The separate states lost all effective power in April 1933 when eighteen Nazi 'Statthalter' (Commissioners) were appointed, with full powers over local government officials. On 30 January 1934 the 'Law for the Reconstruction of the Reich' abolished the Reichsrat and all State Diets, thus making Germany a national rather than a federal state. Locally, state governments and local Nazi party groups (the 'Gaue') increasingly became one and the same.

The Reichstag and Cabinet suffered similar fates. Elections for the Reichstag were held in November 1933. Only Nazis were permitted to stand, so the only means of opposition was to cast an invalid ballot paper. Despite intimidation, 3 million voters did this, but even so 92% of the voters voted for one of the named Nazi candidates. In any case, the Reichstag was impotent after the Enabling Law, and met only to hear speeches from Hitler. The cabinet, too, had little influence; most of them heard of the outbreak of war in 1939 from a radio newscaster rather than their Führer.

Legal processes were also altered. Traditional concepts of right and wrong were replaced by considerations of the welfare of the State and the Nazi party. In May 1934 the People's Court was established. It could only try citizens for treason, which was given a wide definition. Proceedings were secret and appeals could only be made direct to the Führer. The normal penalties were execution or a term in a concentration camp.

(c) Religious policy

Nazism and the Church were inevitably at odds, since the virtues each stressed were in contradiction to each other. Though Hitler at first paid lip service to Christianity, to friends he stated that it was important for Germany to choose between 'the Jewish Christ creed with its effeminate pity-ethics, or a strong heroic belief in God in nature, in God our own people, in God in our destiny, in our blood. . .'. There were semi-religious aspects in Nazism itself, with its emphasis on rites and ceremonials, and neo-pagan movements were encouraged.

The Catholic bishops feared a second 'Kulturkampf' against their Church. They also, like most old conservatives, misunderstood Hitler's regime and were deceived into believing that Hitler meant only to restore German greatness and stability. Consequently, a written agreement with Hitler seemed a harmless way of guarding their Church. For Hitler, such an agreement would win him international prestige and forestall criticism from the clergy. In July 1933 an agreement, or Concordat, was reached in Berlin between von Papen and Pacelli, the Papal Nuncio in Berlin and subsequently (1939) Pope Pius XII. The Concordat assured the Church religious freedom, promised it that bishops could communicate with Rome, that pastoral letters could be published and that the Pope could continue to appoint bishops, though after consultation with the government. Church schools would not be harassed. In return, Catholic bishops were to swear an oath of loyalty to the state, the Christian Trade Union and the Centre Party would be dissolved, and clergy would promise not to participate in politics.

In fact, the agreement was almost immediately ignored. Bishops' letters were interfered with, church schools were taken over and charities were restricted. Open conflict came in 1935 when some priests were tried for allegedly breaking currency regulations, and in 1936, when some monks were accused of immorality. Late that year, several bishops attacked Hitler from their pulpits, and in 1937 Pope Pius XI attacked Hitler in the encyclical 'Mit bremender Sorge', as a result of which the Nazi campaign against the Catholic Church continued.

The Protestant Church was muffled in a different way. Until 1933 the Protestant churches were organized in separate 'Landeskirchen' in twenty-eight different areas, each with its own structure and hierarchy. However, in the Church elections of 1933 the 'German Christians', an evangelical group with Nazi backing, won considerable support. As a result, the separate churches were amalgamated into a single, national, Church, known as the Evangelical Church. Non-Aryan priests were removed from office. Ludwig Müller, the Nazi candidate, was elected to be the first 'Reichsbischof' with authority over all churches. In September 1935 the Protestant Church was brought under closer state control when a minister of Church affairs, Hans Kerrl, was appointed and given decree powers.

There was opposition to the Nazi takeover of the Protestant churches. By December 1933 there was a group of 600 priests, led by Pastor Niemoller, who organized themselves into the Confessional Church. After a brief effort at reconciliation, the Nazis decided to persecute this group and in 1937 arrested 800 of its members and made the Confessional Church illegal. Niemoller himself was arrested in July 1937, acquitted in March 1938 but taken back to concentration camp anyway.

(d) Racial policy

The origins of Hitler's ideas on race lie in the theories of earlier authors such as Gobineau and Houston Chamberlain. They pointed to the biological struggle between different races, and the inevitable superiority of the Aryans, as the one truly civilized race. The mission of the German people was to strengthen the Teutons, the purest form of the Aryan race, and to rule over the inferior races, especially the Slavs, to the East. Hitler's addition to the theories was anti-semitism. In his eyes, the Jews were not simply an inferior race, but a counter-race who aimed to destroy the Aryans by inter-marrying with them and thus polluting their blood. The origins of Hitler's anti-semitism lie in his years in Vienna before the Great War and in his view of the home front during that war, when he felt that the Jews were predominant among war profiteers. Equally, his anti-semitism was a deeply felt personal conviction and was not a great vote-catcher. During World War II, he was quite prepared to divert valuable resources of men, money and equipment to his campaign against the Jews, even when these were needed elsewhere. For example, trains that were needed to transport troops were used instead to take Jews to the concentration camps. Nor was anti-semitism a major reason for his popularity. In a 1934 survey by T. Abel into the reasons why people joined the Nazis, more than 60% never even mentioned anti-semitism among the reasons. (The survey was run as an essay competition on 'Why I joined the Nazis' lines, and there were 1000 entries.)

After Hitler became Chancellor, active measures against the Jews were soon introduced. Jewish officials were quickly dismissed, and from 1 April 1933 there was a boycott of Jewish shops. The Civil Service Law of 7 April forced the retirement of all non-Aryan officials of the national, state and municipal governments. This included semi-public servants such as notaries and teachers. At the same time, propaganda of a pseudo-scientific nature began; for example, films were made showing the inevitability of biological struggle and the superiority of some animals, and, by association, some races, over others. On 15 September 1935 the Nuremberg Laws removed German citizenship from all those with one or more Jewish grandparents. Such people were also forbidden to marry Aryans. The high point of the pre-war anti-semitic campaign came in 1938. In June Jews were required by law to register all property within two weeks. Then in November a German embassy official in Paris was murdered by a seventeen-year-old Jewish boy. On the night of 9–10 November, 'Kristallnacht', Jewish shops all over Germany were looted, their schools, homes and synagogues burnt, and Jews themselves murdered or at least beaten up. This was followed by further laws. It became impossible for a Jew to own a business, to go to the theatre or cinema, to drive a car, or even attend school. All Jews had to wear the star of David in public as a means of identification. The government levied a fine of a billion marks on the entire Jewish community, to be paid by a 20% tax on all property worth over 5000 marks. Many Jews realized that they had to leave the country, but many more were left behind to face the 'Final Solution' of death in the gas chambers during World War II.

(e) Control over individuals

The Nazi state permeated every corner of life in Germany in the 1930s. To even the least enthusiastic, there could be no escape from the public parades, the flags, the uniforms, the bands, the propaganda films and radio shows. The success of this extensive control and machinery is exemplified by the way in which a complete reversal of policy such as the Nazi-Soviet Pact was readily accepted by public opinion. It was almost impossible for anyone over the age of ten to avoid membership of some Nazi organization, usually uniformed. Boys and girls, whose teachers would be politically 'reliable', and whose textbooks, especially in history and biology, would have been Nazified, were expected to be members of the 'Hitlerjügend' (Hitler Youth) or 'Bund deutscher Madel' (League of German Girls). Men aged eighteen to twenty-five were expected to do two years national service and six months in the 'Arbeitdienst' working on public works. Almost everyone was a member of an organization connected to their work; George Ley's 'Deutsche Arbeitfront' replaced trade unions, Darre's 'Reichsuerhstand' was for farm workers, and there were similar organizations for lawyers, doctors and the like.

Under this relatively harmless front lay the sinister side of Nazi control. The SS was founded in 1925 as Hitler's personal bodyguard. In 1929 Heinrich Himmler took charge of it, and built it up from a group of 200 to an elite of 5000 men. Himmler was also head of the secret police and of the Bavarian Police and in April 1934 took control of the Gestapo, technically the Prussian secret police. He thus became 'Reichsführer' of the SS with control over all secret police. He then made the SS an independent organization within the Nazi party, with responsibility only to Hitler. The SS had eighteen concentration camps under its authority to which political prisoners were sent. Even so, the extent of the Nazi terror should not be exaggerated. At the end of 1936 there were less than 10 000 prisoners in these camps and in 1938 five camps were actually closed. The numbers went up again following the renewed attack on the Jews in 1938, but even in 1939 there were only 25 000 prisoners, a fraction of the number of Stalin's victims in Russia. Only after the outbreak of war were the camps transformed to become the centres of genocide. Nonetheless, the existence of the camps remained as a threat to anyone who might contemplate opposition, while at a local level the extensive 'Gau' structure provided plenty of officials and semi-officials to spy on possible opponents.

2. Economic History

The Nazi programme before 1933 befitted a nominally socialist party. It called for the abolition of unearned incomes, a state share in industrial profits and a degree of state control over large businesses. However, this programme was never implemented. When he became Chancellor, Hitler forbade discussion of economics within the party and appointed an orthodox financier, Kurt Schmitt, as economics minister.

Hitler considered economics subordinate to politics. 'Let them own land or factories as much as they please', he said, 'the decisive factor is that the state through the party is supreme over them, regardless whether they are owners or workers ... our socialism goes far deeper ... it establishes the relationship of the individual to the state, the national community ... why need we trouble to socialize banks and factories? We socialize human beings.' Nevertheless, Hitler recognized that labour posed two important problems for him. Firstly, trade unions still opposed some policies, and could easily ally with the left wing of his own party. He therefore placed himself symbolically at the head of the working class, proclaiming 1 May to be Labour Day and speaking to a rally of workers. On 12 May Trade Union leaders were arrested and their buildings taken over. On 17 May unions, strikes and lockouts were forbidden and the Nazi Labour Front was set up to supplant unions.

The second problem was unemployment. In 1933 there were 6 million unemployed Germans—one-sixth of the working population—and much of Hitler's support had come from his promises to end unemployment. 'History will judge us', he said, 'according to whether we have succeeded in providing work.' The reduction of unemployment was the official aim of the first Four-Year Plan of 1932–6, which succeeded in finding work for some 5 million of the unemployed. This was achieved by a variety of methods. The public works schemes that had been started by von Papen and Brüning were extended into the 'Arbeitdienst', which undertook afforestation and water conservation schemes, as well as semi-military programmes like the building of barracks and motorways, the renowned 'Autobahnen'. Regulations were introduced to provide more work. For example, machines were not to be used for road-building as long as a surplus of labour was available. Other ways in which the problem was tackled were through the expansion of the party and national bureaucracies and, in March 1935, the introduction of conscription. Marriage allowances for women helped to remove some women from the job market. By 1938, Hitler could claim that there was a shortage of labour in Germany, and that the GNP had risen 100% between 1933 and 1937.

The aim of the second Four-Year Plan, launched in 1936, was autarky, or economic self-sufficiency. Goering was placed in overall charge, though Hjalmar Schacht, the Reichsbank President who had headed the economy since 1933, remained in part control until he resigned in 1937 and was replaced by Walter Funk. It was hoped that autarky would make Germany totally independent of world enonomic trends. This was in part a reaction to the disasters of 1929–32, when Germany had been so badly hit as a result of her association with the rest of the world's economy. In addition, many countries were already boycotting trade with Germany as a protest against her anti-semitic policies, so autarky was in part a necessity. Thirdly, autarky would be essential in the event of war. In order to minimize imports and increase exports, bilateral agreements were made with some of the Balkan countries *(see page 200, 219)*, by which Germany exchanged manufactured goods for raw materials. At the same time, it was hoped to reduce raw material imports by increasing the use of low grade ores and synthetic materials. For example, the Hermann Goering steel works at Salzgitter was built specifically for the use of low-grade ores. Overall, the plans for autarky were less successful than hoped; by 1939, synthetic oil production had only reached 45% of its planned levels and over 30% of raw materials were still imported.

Even so, much had been done for the economy and for the workers by 1939. Even taking account for propaganda, production levels undoubtedly increased and the unemployment problem was solved. The workers may have lost some freedoms and may have been paid low wages (real wages never went above the 1930–32 levels), but in many respects they were better off. The 'Kraft dürch Freude' ('Strength through Joy') organization offered stable rents, paid holidays, cheap theatres, subsidized holidays to Italy and Norway, convalescent homes and sports facilities. German farmers, as long as they were Aryan and obedient, were certainly better off, having security of tenure, easy credit and high prices for their products. 'If the German workers lost some freedom, the most important freedom was the freedom to starve'.

However, this was not simply a Nazi economic miracle. In the first place, the German economy, like the rest of the world's, was beginning to recover by 1933, and Hitler's predecessors had themselves begun this recovery. Secondly, the recovery was dependent on complete state control and involved government restrictions and directives that would have been quite unacceptable in a democracy. Thirdly, the financial background to the recovery was unsound. Since no capital was invested from abroad, most money was raised by loans within Germany, many of them forced. Moreover, Germany's balance of trade deficit was so large—432 million marks in 1938 alone—that by normal standards Germany could be adjuged bankrupt throughout the period of Hitler's chancellorship.

3. Foreign Policy

Four chief aims underlay Hitler's foreign policy. Behind all his actions was the hope and intention that Nazism would be extended, either by more and more areas coming directly under German control, or by the establishment of more and more independent governments adhering to Nazi principles. Secondly, he planned to defy and revise not only the terms of the treaty of Versailles but also the spirit of the treaty. He told party leaders in 1928:

> . . . in so far as we deliver the people from the atmosphere of pitiable beliefs in possibilities which lie outside the bounds of one's own strength—such as the belief in reconciliation, understanding, world peace, the League of Nations and international solidarity—we destroy these ideas.

Thirdly, Hitler intended to unite all the German speaking peoples of central Europe into a great Reich. Finally, he intended to undertake conquests in the East to provide 'Lebensraum' ('living-space') for his new Reich, which would require raw materials, especially of wheat and oil, and workers for the more menial tasks from these Slav areas. Such a plan fitted neatly with his racial theories.

As the Kaiser with his fleet, so Hitler with his army. He realized that he could not pursue foreign policy aims that contradicted the aims of other countries without an army to enforce (or threaten to enforce) his plans. So in March 1935 conscription was introduced, providing a force of ¾ million soldiers, supported by 1 million reservists, by 1939, when comparable figures for Britain were less than ¼ and less than ½ million respectively. In addition, many of the public works undertaken during the Four-Year plans were of a military nature, such as the provision of the Autobahns to facilitate troop movements. In some respects, therefore, the rearmament programme was no more than a part of the overall solution to the unemployment problem. In others, it was a bluff, providing Hitler with the illusion of strength, rather than the reality; for example, there is little doubt that the force that entered the Rhineland in 1936 *(see below)* could well have been stopped, while many of the trucks used in March 1938 broke down en route to Vienna. Nonetheless, by 1939 Hitler had a large, well-equipped fighting force at his disposal.

Before the army was of any strength at all, Hitler set about the preliminaries necessary to the achievement of his foreign policy aims. In October 1933 he withdrew Germany from the League of Nations and the Disarmament Conference, to the overwehlming approval of the German people, which had been sought in a plebiscite. During 1934 three steps were taken to prepare the ground. On 26 January a non-aggression pact and an agreement to respect existing frontiers for ten years were signed with Poland *(see page 212)*. This removed a possible threat in the East while he acted in the South and blew a hole in the side of France's security network *(see page 241)*. On 19 June, Hitler went to Venice and held formal talks with Mussolini for the first time *(see page 275)*. During July, the Austrian Chancellor, Dollfuss, was murdered by Nazis; it is possible that Hitler hoped this would be enough to install a Nazi government in Austria. Yet the extent to which Hitler was in control of Nazi parties in other countries is difficult to judge. At this time, he was prepared to await the outcome; when the putsch failed, he was ready to condemn the participants—had it succeeded, he would have been equally ready to capitalize on it. Later, he faced the same problem in Danzig and in the Sudentenland, where Forster and Henlein respectively were eager to hasten events, and Hitler to some extent put the brakes on them. Even taking account of the failure of the Austrian Nazis, the agreements with Poland and Italy were valuable foundations.

Further preparations were made in 1935. In March, Hitler denounced the Versailles terms on German disarmament and announced his intention of introducing conscription. Italy joined Britain and France in protesting at this violation of the treaty, but no action was taken. In June, Hitler calmed British fears by signing a naval agreement, by which he promised to limit the size of the German navy to 35% of that of Britain. Britain's agreement to these terms was another blow to France's security system.

As well as preparations, 1935 also saw the first achievement of Hitler's aims. On 13 January a plebiscite was held in the Saar Basin under League of Nations supervision. This was in accordance with the terms of the treaty of Versailles, which had put the area under League control for fifteen years. Over 90% of the voters were in favour of reunion with Germany, rather than union with France or continued League super-vision, and on 1 March the Saar joined the Reich. The unification of German-speaking peoples had begun and, like so many subsequent actions, had been achieved by purely legal steps.

On 6 March 1936 German troops once again occupied the Rhineland. This contravened not only the treaty of Versailles but also the Locarno agreements *(see page 369)*, which had both forbidden the stationing of troops in that area; the occupation was, therefore, quite in contrast with Hitler's victory in the Saar. It is important to realize that the move did not involve 'winning' land, or reuniting Germans, for the Rhineland had never been 'confiscated'—it was simply to be kept free of troops. There seems little doubt that in sending troops there Hitler was testing his enemies—the men that were sent were by no means crack divisions and could well have been forced to retreat by a show of strength by the British and French. France was 'between governments' *(see page 387)* and was not prepared to act without British backing; the troops went in during the week-end, and the British, as Hitler well knew, were not prepared to act till the Monday, by which time any action would be that much harder. The ultimate reaction was as Hitler had hoped—official protests followed by debate about the validity of the original treaty terms that banned German forces from a part of their own country. These seeds of doubt about the morality of the Versailles settlement were to prove invaluable.

While progressing towards the achievement of one aim—the renuncia-tion of Versailles—Hitler continued to prepare himself for others by the formation of alliances and agreements with friends and neighbours. On 11 July, he agreed to respect Austrian independence in return for 'a policy befitting a German state' *(see page 216)*. On 25 October, following the visit of the Italian foreign minister, Ciano, to Berlin, the Berlin–Rome Axis was signed *(see page 279)*. On 18 November Hitler recognized Franco's regime in Spain and a week later signed the Anti-Comintern Pact with Japan, technically an agreement to join together to stop the spread of communism, but in effect an extension of the alliance with Italy, since Italy joined the pact in November 1937. With these allies at his side, Hitler seemed increasingly invincible, especially in view of the continued isolationism of the United States and the position of the Soviet Union. Britain and France realized the difficulty of their position, and in

1937 Lord Halifax visited Berlin in the hope of discovering Germany's objectives and suggesting a peaceful settlement, while the French foreign minister, Yvon Delbos, visited France's eastern allies (Poland, Roumania, Yugoslavia and Czechoslovakia) to try to strengthen the alliance that Hitler had so weakened.

After 1937, Hitler achieved each of his first three aims before 1939, while his efforts to achieve the fourth—'Lebensraum'—led to the outbreak of war in September 1939. In March 1938 he succeeded in uniting Germany and Austria by the 'Anschluss', thereby reuniting German people and extending Nazism *(see page 312)*. During the summer he campaigned for the German-speaking Sudetenland area of Czechoslovakia, which was finally won in September and October of that year after the Munich Conference *(see page 205)*. Once again, the German Reich had been extended and the Versailles settlement overturned. In March 1939 the rest of Czechoslovakia was taken and Memel re-attached to Eastern Prussia. Each of these achievements helped to fulfil the original aims, and each was completed without the use of troops but rather with the agreement or the compliance of the Western powers. In the case of both Austria and the Sudetenland, they were again ready to reconsider the terms of the Versailles settlement and see in them the unfairness of applying the principle of self-determination *(see page 195)* to other powers but not to Germany. In the case of Czechoslovakia itself, the British and French were defeated not by argument but by the sheer impossibility of taking action against a power that had already entrenched itself in the country. It is significant that it was after this, in March 1939, that Britain and France offered guarantees to Poland to help protect her frontiers.

After his success in Memel, Hitler made new demands on Poland and, significantly, found new justifications for his actions. On 28 April, in reply to a letter from President Roosevelt asking for assurances that Germany would not attack thirty-one named countries and for discussions on disarmament, Hitler denounced his naval agreement with Britain of 1935 and his agreement with Poland of 1934. He claimed that the British guarantee to Poland threatened to 'encircle' Germany and was contrary to his existing agreements. He now began detailed preparations to put into practice his aim of 'Lebensraum', which would be most difficult and face most opposition. In May he signed bilateral non-aggression pacts with Denmark, Latvia and Estonia, and strengthened the alliance with Italy. He continued to demand Danzig and the right to construct a road and railway across Pomorze (the 'corridor'), and by late June German 'volunteers' arrived in Danzig and set up a 'freikorps'. Then, on 23 August a non-aggression pact with Russia was signed. This was a complete contradiction of principle for both sides, since Hitler's stand against the communist threat had been a crucial factor in his success in the early 1930s, and he had been the architect of the Anti-Comintern Pact. Self-interest overrode principle for both sides (for the Russian point of view, *see pages 353, 392)*. Agreement with Russia gave Hitler freedom of action in the East, since he no longer had to fear Russian aid for Poland. Consequently, on 1 September he launched his attack on Poland, hopeful that, yet again, the British and French would not stand by their international agreements and let him have his way. This time he was proved wrong.

There is a danger in examining Hitler's foreign policy of imposing on it a pattern that did not exist in Hitler's mind. He certainly had the aims outlined in mind, and he had expressed them in detail in *Mein Kampf* in 1924. However, whether he still saw them as realistic ten years later, or whether he had a definite plan for their achievement, is less certain. For in some respects Hitler was the great opportunist, whose skill lay in his ability to exploit a situation and to time his actions to perfection. His timing was well illustrated by the Rhineland crisis of 1936, his opportunism by the 'Anschluss' of 1938. Yet whether he planned to take Austria in that way at that time, or whether he planned to reoccupy the Rhineland before looking to the South and the East, is to surmise. Certainly, he realized that the winning of 'Lebensraum' would be the hardest aim to achieve, and would have to wait till he had achieved a position of strength, but here again he completed and perfected the means to the end at the last minute. The agreement with Russia was not a long-held plan, but an opportunity created by the inability of France and Britain to come to agreement with the communist government. Like his other opportunities, Hitler exploited it to the full.

4. Bibliography

Most of the works recommended at the end of Chapter IV *(page 84)* also include chapters on the Weimar and Nazi periods. In addition, *The Weimar Republic* by J. W. Hiden (Longman, 1974) is most useful, and includes an extensive selection of documents. There are vast quantitites of books on the Nazi regime, of which the most helpful for the student are probably *Hitler: A Study in Tyranny* by A. Bullock (Penguin, 1969), *The Nazi Revolution* edited by J. L. Snell in the Heath Series (published by Harraps) and *The Burden of Guilt. A Short History of Germany 1914–1945* by H. Vogt (OUP, 1965).

5. Discussion Points and Exercises

A *This section consists of questions that might be used for discussion (or written answers) as a way of expanding on the chapter and testing understanding of it:*

1 What immediate problems confronted the Weimar government?

2 Compare the Weimar constitution with the constitution of Wilhelmine Germany.

3 Why was there so much opposition to the Weimar government in its early years?

4 Examine and explain the results of the elections of 1924.

5 Why was agriculture left behind while industry recovered in the 1920s?

6 Comment on Russo-German friendship in the 1920s.

7 What was 'fulfilment'?

8 Why were governments 'President cabinets' and not responsible to the Reichstag after 1930?

9 What steps did Hitler take in 1933 to secure his own position?

10 Examine the attitude of the Nationalist politicians to Hitler.

11 Why did Hitler turn against the SA?

12 In what ways was Germany a 'totalitarian' state?

13 What was Hitler's attitude to the army?

14 Why was there so much violence and terror in Nazi Germany?

15 What effects did Hitler's religious and racial views have on his support at home and abroad?

16 Was the search for autarky inspired by economic or political motives?

17 Did Hitler make any genuine economic achievements?

18 How different were Hitler's foreign policy aims from those of the leaders of Wilhelmine Germany before the World War I?

19 Would Hitler have ended his demands if Poland had given way?

20 What was the significance of the Nazi-Soviet Pact?

B *This section suggests ways in which you might examine Germany's history in a rather different way:*

1 Put yourself in the position of a leader of the Weimar Coalition in 1928. Record your feelings about the achievements of the coalition to that date, and your views of the likely future.

2 Write a British Foreign Office report in May 1933 on the likely impact on European affairs of the rise of Hitler.

3 Pur yourself in the position of a German who had served in the Great War and lived through the 1920s. Describe your views of the Weimar Republic and of Hitler, explaining why you have chosen to support or oppose him.

C *This section suggests two ways in which you might compare Germany with other countries:*

1 Compare the German economy 1919–33 with those of Eastern Europe in the same period.

2 Compare the planned programmes and actual policies of the Fascists in Italy and the Nazis in Germany.

D *Essay questions*

1 Account for the failure of the Weimar Republic.

2 Examine and explain the changes that Hitler made to the machinery of government.

3 To what extent was the Versailles treaty a critical factor in framing Hitler's foreign policy and assuring its early successes?

6. Why Did Hitler Win Power?

This is intended to offer one interpretation of Hitler's rise to power, and should be used as a discussion document rather than as a definitive interpretation. Obviously, there are many omissions and inadequacies, and it is hoped that readers will identify and expand these for themselves.

The birth of democratic government in Germany in 1919 was the culmination of a trend that had developed throughout the life of the German Empire. Between 1871 and 1912 the nationalist and imperialist parties lost support, while the left-wing parties, especially the Social Democrats, won increasing support. By the years before the outbreak of World War I, the right wing was still in power only by virtue of its close connections with the Kaiser and its dominance at the Imperial Court. This trend towards the left, and with it support for a less autocratic form of government, continued in the elections for the Constituent Assembly of 1919. This is illustrated in Table A, in which the parties have been amalgamated and the percentage vote for each group simplified to the nearest whole number.

	1871	1912	1919
Right	53%	26%	15%
Centre	35%	29%	39%
Left	3%	35%	45%

Table A. Percentage of votes cast for different groups for the Reichstag and Constituent Assembly

The democratic constitution of the Weimar Republic was not therefore a historical aberration, imposed upon an unwilling German people by the bullying allies, but the clear culmination of a long-term trend.

However, the new Republic, and democracy, lost support rapidly and considerably in the early years of its life. Saddled with responsibility for the treaty of Versailles and faced with political extremists, the Weimar government was soon in difficulty. This was reflected in the elections of 1920, when the two right-wing parties, the DNVP and DVP, won almost 30% of the vote. There followed even more problems for the new government—inflation, the Franco-Belgian invasion and the continued political violence that resulted in nearly 400 political murders between 1919 and 1923. The elections of May 1924 well reflected the electorate's disillusion with the Weimar government. In particular, as Table B shows, the extremist parties did far better than before, the Nazis winning over 6% of the vote and the Communists over 12%. After only five years, the future for democracy in Germany looked bleak, and the Kremlin concluded that Germany was, again, ripe for revolution.

Yet the period after 1924 saw a considerable recovery in the fortunes and popularity of the Weimar governments. Industrial output recovered,

318

in some fields regaining the pre-war levels even though Germany was 13% smaller. In the diplomatic field, the Locarno treaties were signed and Germany was accepted as a member of the League of Nations. These achievements were again reflected in the elections of the period, as Table B demonstrates:

	1920	May 1924	Dec 1924	1928
Nazis	—	6½%	3%	2½%
Right (DNVP, DVP)	29%	29%	31%	23%
Weimar Coalition (DDP, Z, BVP, SPD)	48%	42%	49½%	50%
Communists	2%	12½%	9%	10½%

Table B Election results 1920–28, expressed as percentages of the votes cast

This new found stability was destroyed by the depression. Because of its dependence on foreign loans, Germany was worse hit than any other country, with unemployment reaching a high point in 1932, when about one in three of the adult male population of Germany was unemployed. The future for Germany seemed hopeless—what country was going to lend money to Germany in such circumstances? Germans looked from their immediate economic grievances to their other grievances. Why was Germany so hard hit? Because of the dependence on foreign loans. Why were they so dependent on others? Because of the crisis of 1923. Why had there been a crisis then? Because of the reparations charged through the hated 'Diktat', the treaty of Versailles, that all patriotic Germans so hated. To many ordinary Germans, all the old wounds that had apparently healed in the 1920s had been opened up once again.

These circumstances gave rise to massive new support for the Nazi party, although it was still not in a majority when Hitler became Chancellor. Table C below illustrates this final change.

	1930	July 1932	Nov. 1932
Nazis	18%	37%	33%
Right	11½%	7%	10%
Weimar coalition	43%	35%	36%
Communists	13%	14%	17%

Table C Election results 1930–32, expressed as percentages of the votes cast

The Communists maintained a fairly steady support, if anything gaining slightly from the SPD, as Table 35 on page 289 demonstrates. Support from the Nazis came from two chief sources. One group was those who had not bothered to vote before; the turnout in 1930 was 7% higher than in 1928, and another 2% up in 1932. Secondly, those who had previously

319

voted for the right-wing and moderate right parties—the DNVP, DVP and DDP—shifted their allegiance. Again, this is better demonstrated by the more detailed Table 35. Between 1928 and 1930 the DNVP lost 7% and the DVP 4% of their votes. Those who were already dissatisfied with the Weimar government now crossed to the Nazis. Who exactly were these voters, and what was it that particularly attracted them away from their parties to the novelty of the Nazis?

Firstly, it is clear that Hitler's support did not come from the places he expected it to. His original power base, and the scene of the attempted putsch of 1923, was Munich, the capital of Bavaria. In the early 1920s, this had indeed been the centre of his support. In the 1924 election, the Nazis had won more than 10% of the vote in only four consituencies, three of which—Upper Bavaria, Lower Bavaria and Franconia—were in Bavaria. Yet between 1930 and 1933, when the Nazi vote averaged well over 30%, not one of these three recorded an average vote of over 40% for the Nazis. Only Franconia averaged over 35%, while in Lower Bavaria the Centre party won 47% of the votes. Hitler's supporters at the time of his rise to power were to be found away from Bavaria, the original power base.

Equally, he found little support in the cities. Until 1928, Hitler assumed that he would win votes among unemployed and threatened factory workers. But that year the Nazis won only 1.4% of the vote in Berlin, and did little better in other major cities. Significantly, after the 1928 elections, Hitler ordered his touring speakers to brush up on their knowledge of farming problems and get out into rural areas.

For it was in the countryside that the new support for the Nazis lay. An analysis of voting figures shows four or five constituencies where the Nazis won a consistently high percentage of the votes in all the elections between 1928 and 1933. These were Schleswig-Holstein, East Prussia, Mecklenburg, East Hanover and Frankfurt (Oder). All were predominantly agricultural areas, with few major cities, and situated well away from the major industrial area. They were inhabited mainly by middle-class—'Mittelstand'—farmers, the owners of middle-sized farms with few workers outside the family and largely dependent for a living on the sale of agricultural products in local markets. They were likely therefore to be hard hit by the national cash shortage that the depression produced.

A second group of enthusiastic Nazis was the young. In 1931, 60% of the 118 000 students supported the Nazi Student Movement, and in 1932 the students of Berlin University—traditionally a left-wing centre —voted for a majority of Nazis. It was the young who provided many of the members of the SA and SS, both of which expanded rapidly during the depression period. Membership of the SA rose from less than ½ million in the late 1920s to 1½ million by 1933, while it is recorded that the SS had ten applicants for every vacancy, and that a quarter of its members held doctorates. Again, it is easy to see a link between the young and the depression. The lack of jobs made the future hopeless for them, and their qualifications would prove worthless: at least the Nazis offered the prospect of a change.

Thirdly, Hitler's support came from Protestants rather than Catholics. In predominantly Catholic areas, Bavaria and the western borders, the Centre party and the Bavarian People's Party (BVP) recorded consistently high support, even in the elections of 1932. This resulted partly from traditional Catholic hostility to the central government—a hostility that was born out of the 'Kulturkampf'—but also from the high degree of organization among Catholics. Two million Catholics were members of either the 'People's League for Catholics' or the 'Catholic Youth Organization' in 1930. In contrast, Protestants were less well organized and tended to fall easier prey to Nazi charms.

Having established *who* gave their support to Hitler, either through the ballot box or membership of party organizations, it is worth examining briefly *why* they did so. His likely supporters had more reason than most Germans to have suffered the effects of the depression, and therefore were likely to be disenchanted with the existing moderate alternatives. They were unlikely to be attracted by the Communist alternative. In the case of farming people, there was the risk that their land would be lost if the Communists came to power and in the case of students communism offered little special reward for their extra qualifications. In addition, they were often already supporters of right-wing parties and therefore likely to be attracted to the nationalist aspects of Nazism. They were disillusioned with their own parties links with Weimar democracy; the DNVP had had members of the government since 1925. Yet even accepting all these factors, how could they come to support such a plainly nasty party as Hitler's?

Hitler himself was by no means 'nasty' in their eyes, but rather, an attractive and intelligent leader. Much of our analysis of his rise to power has been hampered by our moral outrage at what he later did, and by the evidence that has been used to produce a picture of his early life. It is now clear that much of this evidence about his days as a down-and-out was gathered by a journalist called Heiden from a tramp called Hanisch, who had met Hitler in a Viennese dosshouse while he, Hitler, was trying to avoid conscription in the Austrian army. Hanisch was prosecuted by Hitler for theft, so it is hardly surprising that he painted an unflattering picture. There is little doubt that in the circumstances of the depression Hitler's simple explanation of Germany's ills and the simple solution that he offered, were exactly what the bulk of German people felt was needed in 1930.

The ideology of the Nazi party blended many traditional German beliefs and ideas. It included the 'volkisch' tradition of Austria and Southern Germany, which asserted not only the racial superiority of the people but also their right to dominate others. It also took on the Prussian traditions of militarism and discipline that promised firm leadership and an established order, both values that held special attractions in the early 1930s. To these traditional German ideas was added anti-semitism, but this, as Abel's survey of 1934 showed *(see page 309)*, was not a major factor in attracting people to the party. Nazism rather offered an apparently cogent alternative to the existing confusion, an alternative that not only promised different policies but also a return to the traditional Germanic values that had been deserted by Weimar.

XIII Russia 1914–39

1. The Revolutionary Period

(a) Russia in World War I

Russia was even less prepared for the rigours of the Great War than the other European powers. The general staff had anticipated a twelve-week campaign. There were no reserve officers, the artillery available was out of date. Communication and co-ordination problems abounded; there were seventy-two different aircraft types, twelve of them Russian made, but a lack of suitable trained officers and fuel—some mechanics, in an effort to make the fuel lighter, even watered it down. Aircraft from France arrived at Murmansk and were taken across the snow in parts by dog sleigh. Railways were such that in many places there were several lines arriving at a town but only one leaving it. The result was hundreds of thousands of soldiers sitting on station platforms, quite content with their daily ration of a pound of meat and endless supplies of vodka, but doing little for the war effort. In Western Russia, few lines ran North/South (though plenty East/West), making communication between the different sections of the front a criss-cross affair. Moreover, the economic requisites for modern warfare were lacking. In terms of sheer manpower, there were only some 3½ million industrial workers in a population of 115 million. Statistics of production for key industries like iron, steel and coal *(see page 123)* illustrate the likely weaknesses of the economy. It was to prove almost impossible to provide the quantities of such goods that were to be needed for shells, weapons, uniforms, transport, radio and all the vast and complex needs of a mass army. In addition, Russia's dependence on foreign loans to provide the finance for industry inevitably left a gap of capital during wartime. The omens were not good.

Militarily, the war proved to be the expected disaster *(see pages 158–62)*. In three months of 1914 the Russian army lost 151 000 men killed, 683 000 wounded and 895 000 prisoners. The lack of proper preparation came to the fore when thirty-seven divisions of cavalry were put into action, necessitating endless train loads of fodder for the horses. Not surprisingly, equipment frequently failed to arrive in the right place at the right time, giving rise to the tales of one rifle between three soldiers and German advances being held up by the mounds of Russian dead. During 1916 some of the supply problems were overcome and the army fared better *(see page 168)* but the underlying weaknesses remained. For example, no NCO class had been created (largely for fear of its potential to organize opposition) so all depended on the officer class, many of whom had been promoted for their wealth and connections rather than efficiency. Equally, the Russian dependence of her Western allies left her lacking not only in military support campaigns, most notably Gallipoli, but also supplies: in 1916 the French were able to deliver only fifty-six planes of an order of nearly 600.

If the war went badly at the front, it went even worse at home. Obviously, the industrial needs of an army of millions necessitated economic reorganization. To this end, some 80% of factories were taken over and run by the State, and extra men drafted in from the country-side to operate them. Unfortunately, the men brought in were not trained for the tasks required of them and output actually fell by about 50%. At the same time, as a result of military service and moving men, the area of land under cultivation fell by 20%. Florinsky has pointed to the vicious circle of economic problems that confronted the Tsar's government—labour shortages, food shortages, increased demand for goods, an inadequate transport system, the disruption of foreign trade and the decline in government revenue (caused in part by the prohibition on the sale of alcohol, a government monopoly). Each problem was of itself sufficient to threaten a government—together they were overwhelming.

Moreover, Nicholas II seems to have been quite unable to control the situation, and actually exacerbated it by wrong decisions. In 1915 he dismissed his uncle, Grand Duke Nicholas, and assumed the post of commander-in-chief for himself. This had two disastrous consequences. Firstly, it identified him directly with the failures of his forces, so that he bathed in their reflected failure. Secondly, it took him away from Petrograd, as St Petersburg had been renamed because of its Germanic sound, and left the court in the hands of his wife, Alexandra. She in turn relied for advice on Gregory Rasputin, the 'holy man' who was able to alleviate, at times, the haemophilia of her son, Alexis. He took the opportunity, until his assassination in December 1916, to promote himself and his own circle. In addition the Tsar appointed aged and incompetent ministers from this circle. In February 1916 the seventy-five year-old Ivor Goremykin was replaced as Prime Minister by the sixty-nine year-old Boris Stürmer, who also took over the foreign ministry. He was widely rumoured to be pro-German, giving people and army little faith in their government during 1916.

The major problem by this time was inflation. Prices had reached astronomical proportions, especially as wages did not keep pace. Table 37 details some of these. Overall, food prices increased more than five-fold between 1914 and 1917. In 1916 the secret police even discovered that banks were storing sugar in their vaults, such was its value. By 1917, less than 10% of factory workers in the Novy Lessner district of Petrograd received what was regarded as the minimum living wage of 200 roubles a month, while more than half of them received less than 100 roubles a month. Not surprisingly, workers became increasingly discontent and strikes increasingly common, as Table 35 illustrates.

	Pre-war price	Price in January 1917
Bag of rye-flour	6 roubles 50 kopecks	40 roubles
1 pud (3·1 lbs) wheat flour	2 roubles 50 kopecks	16 roubles
Bag of potatoes	1 rouble	7 roubles
1 lb meat	10–12 kopecks	60–70 kopecks

Table 37 Price inflation in wartime Russia

Year	Number of strikes	Number of strikers
Aug–Dec 1914	68	34 752
1915	928	553 094
1916	1284	1 086 345
Jan–Feb 1917	1330	

Table 38 Strikes in Russia 1914–17

(b) The March Revolution

A police report in Petrograd of early 1917 read as follows:

> The impossibility of obtaining goods, the loss of time spent queueing up in front of stores, the increasing mortality rate because of poor housing conditions, the cold and dampness resulting from lack of coal . . .—all these conditions have created such a situation that the mass of industrial workers is ready to break out in the most savage of hunger riots.

It continued:

> Forbidding changes of employment from one factory to another and from one job to another has reduced the workers to a chattel state, good only for common fodder. Restrictions on all meetings, even for the purpose of organizing co-operatives or canteens, and the closing of unions are the reasons why the workers led by the more educated and perhaps the more revolutionary among them, adopt an openly hostile attitude to the government and protest against the continuation of the war.

In such conditions, the outbreak of a series of strikes culminating in bread riots on 8 March was no great surprise. The surprise was the failure of the forces of law and order to curb the riots, and the support for the strikers that came from the respectable elements of society—the white-collar workers, the liberals, the zemstvo men. Herein lay the difference between 1917 and 1905. Then they had been ready to follow and obey—now, when a Cossack officer ordered his men to fire on demonstrators on one of the bridges, they refused, and turned on their officer.

Why did these groups now oppose the Tsar? For the soldiers, nearly three years of war had been enough. They no longer had any faith in their officers to lead them to any kind of victory. Moreover, many of them had for the first time been brought together with other men and trained in the ways of soldiering. As a result, they at last had the ability to make a meaningful stand against the Tsarist regime, when before their lack of training and weapons made them easy prey. For the whitecollar workers, inflation had done more than anything else to convince them of the need for change; few knew what they did want, but many knew what they did *not* want—the Tsar. The wealthy were less affected by the economic rigours of the time, but had other, powerful, reasons for deserting the Tsar. They were certainly disillusioned by the court circle that had power, if for no other reason than that they were excluded from it. They had expressed their views in the Duma in 1916, but had then been ignored, winning only the dismissal of Stürmer. In addition, some realized that the likelihood of a revolution increased daily. If there was to be a change their best place was at the head of it. Hence, in 1917 there was a serious plot to replace the Tsar by Prince Lvov (or Milyukov) hatched by a wide range of wealthy men, like the industrialist, Terschenko, Duma leaders like Guchkov and Kerensky, generals like Brusilov and Alexeyev. Only the turn of events prevented it reaching fruition.

The revolutionary parties played little part in the March Revolution. The Bolsheviks were weak both in their numbers and influence. There were probably no more than 10 000 of them. When they called for a strike in Petrograd in February 1917 to commemorate the opposition of Social Democrats to the war, the workers refused to strike. Almost all the leaders were in exile—Lenin and Radek in Switzerland, Litvinov in London, Stalin in Siberia. Bukharin and Trotsky in the United States. Only when the new Provisional Government declared an amnesty did they begin to return to Russia. As Ferro has written, 'paralyzed by their differences, the revolutionaries were unable to bring about the downfall of Tsarism, and it was finally the state itself which contributed most effectively to fulfil the revolutionaries' dreams.'

Nevertheless, when Nicholas II abdicated on 15 March, his brother, Michael, refused to take the throne, leaving a power vacuum that was in part filled by the revolutionaries. The official government was taken over by the Provisional Government, intended to last only until a new constitution was drawn up by an elected Constituent Assembly. The Provisional Government, led by Prince Lvov, contained predominantly liberals, such as the new Foreign Minister, Milyukov, but also three right-wingers and a single Menshevik, Alexander Kerensky, as Minister of Justice. However, this new government was no more able to deal with the overwhelming problems than its predecessor had been. Consequently, local organizations were formed to try to deal with some of these. Among these re-emerged the Soviets on the lines of 1905 *(see page 105)*, elected by workers, soldiers and ordinary people. In places they organized food supplies and controlled the post and telegraph. The Petrograd Soviet was the largest and best known, but it did little at first to oppose the Provisional Government, since much that the government did—the political amnesty, Finnish independence, the confiscation of land—was its own policy. It did, however, ensure its own power by the issue of 'Order No. 1', which took power from the army officers and instructed soldiers only to obey itself.

	Date	
1916	18 November	Meeting of Duma attacks government incompetence
	24 November	Stürmer replaced by Trepov as PM—strongly repressive policy against opposition implemented
	30 December	Assasination of Rasputin by Prince Yusupov and others
1917	8 March	Riots and strikes in Petrograd
	10 March	Mutiny of troops in Petrograd
	11 March	Duma refuses to be dissolved by the Tsar
	12 March	Duma sets up a Provisional Government under Prince Lvov
	14 March	Petrograd Soviet issues Order No. 1 depriving army officers of all authority and giving power to those elected by officers and men
	15 March	Nicholas II abdicates in favour of his brother, Michael, who himself abdicates in favour of the Provisional Government
	30 March	Provisional Government confiscates imperial and monastic lands
	16 April	Return of Lenin, Zinoviev, Radek and other Bolsheviks to Petrograd
	14–16 May	Lvov reshuffles government, dismissing Guchkov and Milyukov and bringing in more Mensheviks and Social Revolutionaries. Kerensky becomes Minister of War
	29 June–28 July	New military offensive in Galicia. Initially successful but the Russians driven back and Brusilov replaced by Kornilov
	16–18 July	Bolsheviks attempt to seize power in Petrograd but fail. Trotsky arrested; Lenin flees to Finland
	20 July	Resignation of Lvov and Kerensky becomes Prime Minister
	9–14 September	Attempted counter-coup by General Kornilov almost succeeds. Kerensky uses Bolsheviks to help defeat it, releasing many, including Trotsky, from prison
	October	Bolsheviks win majorities in the Soviets in Petrograd and Moscow
	6 November	Bolshevik revolution. Sailors, Red Guard soldiers and supporters take possession of government buildings and the Winter Palace
1917	7 November	All-Russian Congress of Soviets meets and approves the Bolshevik seizure of power
	25 November	Elections held for Constituent Assembly
	15 December	Armistice signed with Central Powers
	30 December	Foundation of the 'Cheka'—the 'Extraordinary Commission to Combat Counter-Revolution' (secret police)
1918	18 January	Opening session of Constituent Assembly
	19 January	Constituent Assembly members dispersed by Bolshevik troops

(Dates are by the Western calendar; until February 1918 the Russian calendar was thirteen days behind the Western calendar—thus the March and November revolutions are known as the February and October revolutions in Russia.)

Table 39. Date Chart: The period of revolution in Russia, 1917

(c) The Summer of 1917

The identity of interest between Soviets and government did not last for long. In April Lenin returned from Finland, via Germany, whose government foresaw that Lenin could disrupt the Russian war effort to the extent of surrender. He would have no compromise, and on the day he returned he announced his plans for the future (known as the 'April Theses') to the assembled ranks of Bolsheviks. He said that the war must be ended by the overthrow of the capitalist system, co-operation with the Provisional Government ended, the Soviets controlled by Bolsheviks and banks, land, factories and transport taken over by those Soviets in the name of the State. At first, his colleagues were terrified by his extremism, but by the end of April his policies had been endorsed by a conference of the party.

In the meantime, the Provisional Government struggled. At first, it continued to take part in the war. When a letter from Milyukov to Russia's allies to this effect was made public, Milyukov was forced to resign and the reformed Cabinet which now contained six socialists of various hues, pursued a less definite policy. Russian troops continued to fight but nothing was said of how long or to what end this would go on. The land policy proved even less successful. The expropriation of Tsarist estates was announced but nothing was done about the other estates. Consequently, many families in the countryside simply took the law into their own hands and took over the estates: by July over 1000 were taken. This in turn affected the army. Soldiers heard of what was happening at home, and, anxious not to be left out, simply deserted the army and went off to stake their claim. First Lvov and then Kerensky as Minister of War were trapped. Russia's promises to her allies were such that military obligations could not be ignored (even though Wilson was asked to relieve Russia), yet the soldiers had little desire to fight, and every desire to get home. Hence the Galician offensive, despite its initial success, failed and the German army simply rolled the Russians back *(see page 170)*.

This failure, combined with continued inflation, unemployment and desertion, led to demonstrations in Petrograd on 16 July. The outbreak was not Bolshevik-inspired, but, seeing the possiblity of chaos again, they tried to lead the movement as a way of toppling the Provisional Government. Instead, Kerensky was able to command enough support to suppress the riots and show the Bolsheviks to be unpatriotic and pro-German. The Bolshevik paper, *Pravda*, was banned and most of the Bolshevik leaders fled or were imprisoned. Lenin himself went to Finland. If Kerensky, now Prime Minister, could rally support for genuinely non-Tsarist policies, his chances of keeping the Bolsheviks out were bright.

Paradoxically, it was the right wing that gave the Bolsheviks new strength and hope. For in September, General Kornilov, army commander-in-chief, attempted to march on Petrograd, end the Soviet and cleanse the Provisional Government of socialist elements. His march from Moscow failed miserably, largely because many of his men deserted en route, partly in response to a continued Bolshevik, Menshevik and Social Revolutionary propaganda campaign. In the capital, Kerensky released Trotsky and other Bolshevik leaders in an effort to unite his supporters against the threat of a counter-coup from the right. Its effect was to restore the Bolsheviks as patriots in the eyes of the people. They alone were 'unsullied' by connections with Tsarism and the war, and soon after the Kornilov episode had won control of both the Petrograd and Moscow Soviets.

Lenin now returned to the border town of Viborg, and encouraged his colleagues to plan for the uprising called for in the 'April Theses'. The Central Committee of the party approved the plan on 20 October and a Military—Revolutionary committee of the Petrograd Soviet was established to draw up detailed plans, under the chairmanship of Trotsky.

(d) The November Revolution

During the last weeks of October, plans for the coup were carefully made and 6–7 November fixed as the date. On the evening of the 6th, Lenin arrived at the party's headquarters, the Smolny Institute in Petrograd, to find everything carefully organized and ready. Early the next morning sailors on the battleship 'Aurora' opened fire on the Winter Palace across the river Neva. This was the signal for action. More than 20 000 troops were committed to the Bolsheviks. They now occupied the important strategic points of the city—stations, electrical power stations, main roads, the banks—almost without opposition. Only the Winter Palace remained untaken that day, guarded as it was by 100 cadet officers. During the night of the 7–8, Bolshevik troops moved up to surround it and got into the grounds. Early the next morning they moved in, again without a struggle and arrested the ministers of the Provisional Government, apart from Kerensky who had already fled. To all external appearances, little had happened and little changed. Key points in the city were still guarded by troops, and the problems of prices and the war remained.

The evening of 7 November saw the first significant change. The second 'All-Russian Congress of Soviets' met and recognized both the end of the Provisional Government and the legality of the new 'Council of People's Commissars' (as the Bolshevik leadership called itself) as the government. This recognition was opposed by some of the congress, especially the Mensheviks, but the Bolsheviks and leftist Social Revolutionaries were able to command a majority. Having won approval for his government, Lenin, as its President, addressed the Congress. He told it of his government's first two decrees. The first asked 'all the warring peoples and governments to open immediate negotiations for an honest democratic peace'. The second abolished all private property in the form of landowners, Church and Royal estates and took it into State ownership. It was to be distributed to the peasants by local soviets. At a stroke, Lenin had, apparently, fulfilled two of his three promises to the people—peace and land. The third promise bread was less simply achieved.

In fact, the pronouncements of the leadership could have little effect on events. So far as peace was concerned, Lenin had asked for peace involving no exchange of land or reparations, and negotiations for this would take time. In the meantime, he had offered an armistice, and this came into force in mid-December. With regard to the land decree, Lenin was doing no more than acknowledging what had already, in many areas, happened: that is, the peasants had taken the land. Nevertheless, it was a significant move in two respects. Firstly, it assured the Bolsheviks the support of the peasantry; their opponents were unlikely to win favour for a land policy that promised the return of landlords or the removal of their newly-won land. Therein lay the Bolsheviks' problem for the next twenty years. They were now struck with a landowning system in which the peasants *owned* their plots, but, because of the population, those plots were tiny and therefore inefficient. The struggle of the Bolsheviks and their successors to promote a productive agricultural sector without offending the peasants was to prove a continuing and insoluble problem.

Moreover, the distribution of the land did not win the Bolsheviks votes in the elections for the Constituent Assembly in mid-November. The Council of People's Commissars could not avoid holding these elections, since the Assembly had been a major policy aim throughout the year. Some 90 millions were enfranchised for the elections but less than half voted. Their votes confirmed the fears of the Bolshevik leadership. They won 175 seats. Their allies, the leftist Social Revolutionaries got a further forty. However, opponents of the Bolsheviks were in a large majority— 370 right-wing Social Revolutionaries, fifteen Mensheviks, seventeen Cadets. The rest of the seats—about eighty—were won by representatives of the various minority nationalities, few of whom supported the Bolsheviks. There was no way the Bolsheviks would win a majority in a democratic vote.

Consequently, the Assembly was broken up by Red Guards, the Bolsheviks' main military force, the day after it met. Lenin explained it away as representing 'true democracy', since the Bolsheviks knew genuinely what the people wanted and had no need of elected assemblies to tell them. To others, it went against all they had fought for and objected to in Tsarism. All the parties except the left Social Revolutionaries were confirmed and determined in their hostility to the new form of dictatorship.

2. Lenin's Russia

(a) The Civil War, 1918–22

By early 1918 the Bolsheviks controlled only the North-western area of the Russian Empire, that is, the two great cities, Petrograd and Moscow, together with the areas between and around them. Elsewhere, a confusion of opponents and governments existed. Some of these were based on the minority nationalities, many of whom, such as the Lithuanians, Moldavians and Ukrainians, declared their independence. In other areas, leaders of the anti-Bolsheviks, or 'Whites', formed armies with the aim of establishing a power base and advancing from it to the Bolshevik stronghold. In addition, Russia's former allies sent troops to Russia with two aims in view—to continue the Eastern front across Germany and to help to defeat Bolshevism, which they saw as a potential threat (did it not promise 'world revolution'?) and which had told them it would not repay Russia's debts. The fourth and final anti-Bolshevik force was the Czech Legion, 30 000 men originally captured by the Russians in the war against Austria-Hungary, and now in central Russia. The 'civil' war was therefore the efforts of these varied and disparate forces to defeat the Bolsheviks, and their success in withholding those attacks and eventually defeating them *(see Map 32)*.

The first attack came from the South, from the area of the Don Cossacks. In December 1917, three generals—Kornilov, Denikin and Alexeyev, formed a White Army there. They launched their first attacks in early 1918, but Kornilov was killed in battle and they made little headway. In the spring of 1918 the three Caucasian states—Georgia, Armenia and Azerbaijan—declared their independence and held off a Bolshevik attempt to conquer them and win control of the oil fields there. In early 1919 Denikin's White Army advanced northwards but was then pushed back to the Black Sea where, during the summer of 1919, he won control of Kiev and Odessa and was within 250 miles of Moscow before a new Bolshevik attack forced him to resign. His successor, General **Wrangel**, won back control of much of Southern Russia during 1920, and only after the defeat of Polish forces in October 1920 was a new Bolshevik offensive launched, which forced him to abandon Southern Russia and take his army to Constantinople. Thereafter, Soviet Republics were set up in Georgia and Armenia; in 1922 these, together with Azerbaijan, were combined to form the Transcaucasian Soviet Socialist Republic.

This southern war was a confused and intermittent affair. Denikin's army had at first been popular with the peasants, but his troops were ill-disciplined and too ready to take advantage of the chaotic conditions to benefit themselves. They were also equipped by the British and French, thus giving them the label of being unpatriotic. Nor was this the only force—there were also local partisan groups and a Ukrainian nationalist army, led by Petliura. Given this confusion, the Bolsheviks were to some extent able to ignore this southern area until it genuinely threatened them *(see Map 32)*.

The same could not be said of the East. Here, the Czech Legion posed a major threat to the Bolsheviks. The legion had been formed before the revolution and planned to get to Vladivostok and then back to the West. They asked the Bolsheviks for help in this scheme but when none was forthcoming turned against them, and thereafter received financial help from the Western Entente and joined local White groups. By June 1918

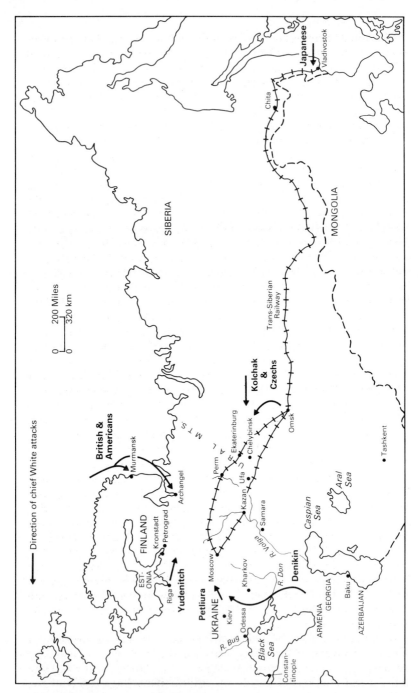

Map 32 The Russian civil war, showing places mentioned in text and (→) directions of chief White attacks

the Legion had control of the Trans-Siberian Railway and all the towns along it from Vladivostok to the Volga. In November the independent Siberian government that had been set up at Omsk by rightist Social Revolutionaries and Mensheviks was ousted by the Whites, whose leader, Admiral Kolchak, previously commander of the Black Sea fleet, was declared 'supreme Ruler of Russia'. His White army, together with the Czechs, advanced westwards taking Perm and Ufa and threatening both Kazan and Samara; this forced Trotsky, the Bolshevik Commissar for War, to hurry to Kazan to organize the defences. By April 1919 they had reached their furthest point West, and a Bolshevik counter-attack was launched to the South by the former Tsarist officer, S. Kamenev. Kolchak was defeated at Chelyabinsk and then, in November, at Omsk. He resigned and handed over to General Semenov: by February he (Kolchak) had been captured and executed by the Reds, while his armies simply disintegrated into the countryside. The Whites' hopes in the Far East were left in the hands of the Japanese, who kept control of Vladivostok throughout the war, leaving it only in October 1922, by which time it had become the last city in White hands. In fact, for almost two years the Reds had simply left Vladivostok alone, setting up a buffer state, the 'Far Eastern Republic', based at Chita, between themselves and the Japanese.

The civil war in the North and West was even more confused. In January 1918 the British had landed troops at Murmansk, theoretically to keep an eye on German troops in the East. In August, British and French forces took Archangel and set up a government there under Chaikovsky. During 1919 there was considerable fighting between Red troops and these allied forces, but neither Britain nor America was prepared to send more troops or money to Russia. This was hardly surprising, since the armistice to end four years of war had only recently been signed. Consequently, in the autumn, the allies abandoned both Archangel and Murmansk, which were quickly taken by the Reds.

To the South of this, German troops occupied the Baltic States and White Russia until mid-1919. Then a White force, backed by the British, was set up in Estonia under General Yudenitch. In October 1919 this army launched an attack on Petrograd and reached the suburbs of the city. For a time Petrograd was virtually cut off, but Yudenitch had neither the forces nor the equipment for a long siege. Trotsky again arrived to inspire the defence of the capital and Yudenitch, unable to either besiege Petrograd or advance, was forced to retreat, in the process of which his forces dispersed. During 1920, the Soviet government recognized the independence of Finland and the three Baltic States, ending possible hostility from those areas.

In January 1918 the Ukraine had declared its independence from Russia and a moderate Socialist government had been set up. In February 1918 this government had signed a separate peace treaty with Germany and Austria-Hungary. Immediately, the Bolsheviks had attacked but had been defeated by German forces, who then took control of the Ukraine themselves. They established a more right-wing government led by General Skoropadsky, who was himself displaced by the Ukrainian Socialists under General Petliura in November 1918. In February 1919 the Red Army took Kiev, only to be removed by Denikin *(see page 33)* in August, recapture it in December and then be attacked by a Polish army under Pilsudski. In May 1920 he captured Kiev but the support he had hoped for from the Ukrainians was not forthcoming and by December the Bolsheviks had retaken the city and driven the Polish forces back across the River Bug. On 28 December the Soviet government recognized the independence of the Ukrainian Soviet Government, which two years later joined the Union of Soviet Socialist Republics.

Objectively, the victory of the Reds over the multifarious groups that attacked them was a military miracle. In early 1918 it controlled a minute proportion of the country and completely lacked the troops and equipment to fight a many-fronted war against enemies receiving aid from the West. The Tsar had himself depended on these for his equipment; where were the Reds now to get theirs? By their control of the industrial centres, they were able to utilize the factories to provide arms and equipment. At the same time, Trotsky, as Commissar for War, organized the Red Army. It had started as a volunteer force, but was converted into a regular army of conscripts with strict discipline. 30 000 former officers of the Tsarist army were brought in by Trotsky to provide expertise and leadership. In contrast, the various enemies were divided in their intentions. The nationalities, many of whom were socialists, wanted only what they had always wanted—independence from the centre. The White leadership, on the other hand, wanted to win control of that centre. The hopes of the allies were at first grandiose: in December 1917 Britain and France had divided Russia into spheres of influence for their future control. Once the war with Germany was ended, there was little desire or incentive to continue a war in the farthest (and coldest) parts of Europe. In addition, the participation of the Allies and the behaviour of the White armies undoubtedly gave the Reds additional support among ordinary people—were they not defending the homeland from acquisitive foreigners?

(b) The Treaty of Brest-Litovsk, 1918

Following Lenin's offer of peace in November 1917, an armistice with Germany was signed on 15 December 1917. The peace treaty that followed was finally ratified by the Congress of Soviets only in March 1918. In the meantime, Trotsky, who acted as the chief negotiator, had delayed the final terms for as long as possible, in the hope that either revolution in Germany and Austria-Hungary would topple the Emperor or that the Allies would come to Russia's aid. Both hopes proved illusory.

Negotiations opened on 3 December 1917 at Brest-Litovsk. Kuhlmann represented Germany, Czernin Austria. On Christmas Day, these two accepted the original Russian request for a peace with no annexations of land and no financial indemnities, if the Western allies agreed to the same principle within ten days. Trotsky appealed to the West to agree, but no reply came. The German delegation therefore put forward the demands of its government. These had been formed by the general staff and demanded extensive annexations, with the hope that the extra land would provide the military needs for food and equipment. Trotsky baulked at the prospect and for ten days refused to negotiate. Then, on 9 February 1918 the new Ukrainian government signed a separate treaty and Trotsky left Brest and declared the war ended with no peace being signed. The Germans responded by a fresh declaration of war; they took Dvinsk, Dorpat, Reval, Pskov and Narva, and were only 100 miles from Petrograd when Lenin ordered a resumption of negotiations. On 3 March 1918 Trotsky signed the Treaty of Brest-Litovsk.

By it, Russia surrendered the Western part of their country, Estonia, Latvia, Lithuania and Poland were given up to Germany and Austria, and areas in the Southern Caucasus to Turkey. Finland, Georgia and the Ukraine were to have their independence recognized. 6000 million marks were to be paid as reparations. Since the areas surrendered represented the wealthiest regions of Russia, more than a third of the population and

Map 33 The Treaty of Brest-Litovsk, 1918

farming land and 80% of her coal mines were lost. All the gains that the Russian Empire had made in the West over several hundred years were lost *(see Map 33)*.

Not surprisingly, the peace treaty created splits in the government. The Central Committee of the Bolshevik Party accepted it by 7 to 4, and the left wingers, led by Bukharin and Radek, left to pursue a more revolutionary line. The leftist Social Revolutionaries ended their support for the Bolsheviks. Lenin's answer was that Russia could take no more war. Moreover, he said, the treaty was only a temporary measure, since the inevitable and promised revolution in Germany (and in the world) would soon come and in its aftermath all comrades would renounce their gains ill-gotten by war.

(c) Economic Policy

(i) 'War Communism'

The early economic measures of the new government were the result of practical rather then theoretical considerations. That is to say, they were less inspired by Marxist doctrines about State ownership than a practical desire to alleviate the acute economic problems and satisfy the military requirements of the civil war. The land decree of 1917 *(see page 329)* has already been mentioned. Among the other early measures were the nationalization of the banks and of war industries, together with a State monopoly of the grain trade. Each of these resembled measures that other countries involved in the war had taken. During 1918 other industries were nationalized, first sugar, then oil and in June a decree that legally made all industries nationalized, though in fact it was some time before this was actually, and gradually, undertaken.

As the civil war progressed, the problems for the Bolsheviks increased. Paper money, already worth about a tenth of its pre-war value, lost all value, and wages were for a time paid in kind. In their efforts to keep up the war effort, the commissars took power to send workers wherever they were needed, be it in the army or industry. Private wealth and trade were banned. The overwhelming problem was food. The peasants had just taken land for the very first time. Now the government urgently needed their grain to feed the workers and fighters. To this end a decree of 1919 ordered the peasants to hand over to the State any grain surplus to what was needed for subsistence. In consequence, the peasants simply reduced their production so there was no surplus. By 1921 only about half as much stock was kept and half as much land cultivated as there had been in 1913. Little food arrived in the cities, and the only prospect of a livelihood lay in the countryside. City workers in their thousands simply left and went into the country, to join the thousands of soldiers returning from their wars.

Yet it was in the city that occurred the spark that forced action on the government. In March 1921, shortly before the Tenth Bolshevik Party Congress opened in Petrograd, the sailors of the Kronstadt naval base outside Petrograd, joined by some of the Red Army, refused to obey their officers and called for a new revolution that gave genuine freedoms—of speech, of assembly, of private trade. Trotsky decided firm action was needed and sent his men across the frozen Bay of Finland to bring the rebels to order. There followed ten days of fighting in the midst of snow storms before the rebels surrendered.

This outburst, together with the peasant's active refusal to take part in grain requisitioning, convinced Lenin of the need for change. Agriculture lay at the heart of the problem. The peasant farmers had somehow to fulfil four functions. They had to provide food enough for both themselves and the workers in the cities. They had to provide enough to export and so provide foreign capital to finance the purchase of machinery for industry. They had to provide raw materials like flax and cotton for industry and, finally, they had to become the consumer class—the sector of the population with enough cash to stimulate demand for industrial goods. Such were their functions in the eyes of the government. Yet to the peasant farmer the only function was to provide himself and his family with enough to eat, and something to spare to sell. The extra money thus earned would help him to enlarge his farm and improve life for his children. The Bolshevik government had done the one and only thing it could to win the peasants' support—it had given them land they could own and farm for themselves. Anything else it did—especially anything likely to give the peasants less control over his own property—would alienate rather than endear it.

(ii) 'New Economic Policy'

Lenin's new policy of March 1921 was primarily aimed at the peasants in an effort to regain their support and give them an incentive to produce more. The requisitioning of surplus grain was ended and instead an agricultural tax introduced, to be paid in kind until 1923 and thereafter in cash. The amount to be paid was a fixed proportion of the surplus, hence the more that was produced, the greater the peasant's share of his own surplus. In addition, this surplus could be privately traded, at first only at local markets but then through middle-men, known as 'Nepmen', to the towns. By 1923, some three-quarters of trade was controlled by private individuals, 14% by the state and 10% by co-operatives.

The 'New Economic Policy' (NEP) was not restricted to agriculture. Industry and trade were restored in part to private enterprise, although the types of works and businesses in private hands tended to be small and local. The State retained control of what Lenin called 'the commanding heights'—heavy industry, the transport system and banking. Thus, as Kochan has shown, the average number of workers in State-owned firms was over 150, in private firms only two.

NEP had considerable success in its immediate aim of restoring the economy to something like its pre-war level. In 1920–21 there was a great drought in the Volga region to add to the ravages of war and civil war that had all but destroyed the economy. Thereafter, though, there was a considerable recovery in living standards and production levels. Table

40 below illustrates this recovery. However, these figures should be taken as very approximate since both Tsarist and Soviet statistics are prone to exaggeration and it was obviously extremely difficult to obtain accurate figures of production during the years of war and civil war.

	1913	1921	1922	1923	1924	1925	1926
Grain (million tons)	81·6*	37·6	50·3	56·6	51·4	72·5	76·8
Pig iron (million tons)	4·2	0·1	0·2	0·3	0·75	1·5	2·4
Electricity (million Kwh)	1·9	0·5	0·8	1·1	1·5	2·9	3·5
Steel (million tons)	4·2	0·2	0·4	0·7	1·1	2·1	3·1
Cotton fabrics (million metres)	2582	105	349	691	963	1688	2286
Sown area (million hectares)	105·0	90·3	77·7	91·7	98·1	104·3	110·3

(* 1913 had been a particularly good year for the harvest.)

Table 40 Production figures in Russia. 1913–26

This table well illustrates not only the achievement of NEP but also the desperate state that Russia had fallen into by 1921. For example, the grain harvest of 1921 was only 46% of that of 1913—by 1926 it had recovered to be 94% of the pre-war level. Pig iron had fallen to less than 5% of its pre-war level; by 1926 it was back to 57%. Electrification was the one area in which a positive advance was made, due largely to Lenin's personal interest and enthusiasm.

Nevertheless, NEP was not without its problems or faults. Above all, it shelved rather than solved the agrarian crisis. Undoubtedly, as long as farms remained small, uneconomic units, the levels of production needed for a genuine advance would never be reached. By returning to a private trade system the immediate problem had been solved but at some time a fundamental reorganization would be needed. Equally, all other sectors of the economy were under fairly strict state contol, so that the town worker could still be ordered where to go, and how much he could be paid and so forth, while his country colleague was free to produce as he liked. This paradox was unsatisfactory, not only on economic but also ideological grounds.

(d) The Soviet Constitution and the Communist Party
The constitution was drawn up in 1918 and adopted by the fifth All-Russian Congress of Soviets in July of that year. Diagram 11 below illustrates the chief components of the governmental system.

The All-Russian Congress met for only about one week in each year and was therefore far too cumbersome a body to act as a genuine executive body. Equally, its Central Executive Committee was too large to meet regularly. Therefore, genuine executive power lay primarily with the Council of People's Commissars. The franchise was, incidentally, universal; but, as the diagram shows, the factory workers received more generous representation than country dwellers. The 'non-labouring' bourgeois classes, including the clergy, were disenfranchised. All elections were open: there was no secret ballot.

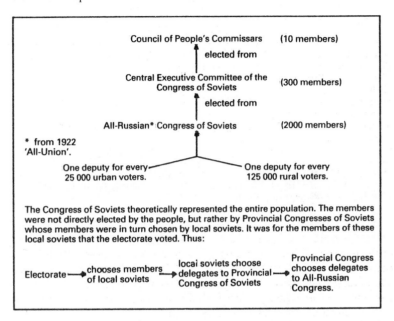

Council of People's Commissars   (10 members)

↑ elected from

Central Executive Committee of the   (300 members)
Congress of Soviets

↑ elected from

All-Russian* Congress of Soviets   (2000 members)

* from 1922
'All-Union'.

One deputy for every   One deputy for every
25 000 urban voters.   125 000 rural voters.

The Congress of Soviets theoretically represented the entire population. The members were not directly elected by the people, but rather by Provincial Congresses of Soviets whose members were in turn chosen by local soviets. It was for the members of these local soviets that the electorate voted. Thus:

Electorate → chooses members of local soviets → local soviets choose delegates to Provincial Congress of Soviets → Provincial Congress chooses delegates to All-Russian Congress.

Diagram 11 The Soviet government

The crucial factor in this democratic constitution was the role of the Communist Party, as the Bolshevik Party renamed itself in March 1918. The Party had, at the time of the Kronstadt mutiny, banned not only all other political parties, but also any opposition or discussion within itself, such as Bukharin and Radek had shown over the peace treaty *(see page 336)*. Until then, too, the Mensheviks and the Social Revolutionaries had both functioned. Not only was the opposition banned (a ban enacted by the 'Cheka'—the secret police) but also the party was enlarged and restructured. From being an élite in 1917 it had 431 000 members by 1920 and over ½ million by 1921. It now took additional powers in the army, in factories and in local government, where party members not only voiced the views of the Party but also took the action to put them into practice. The Party too had a structure that paralleled the official governmental structure of the State, as Diagram 12 shows. At each level of government, therefore, there was an equivalent organ of the Party. Not surprisingly membership of the two was frequently identical, especially in the higher echelons.

The Communist Party ensured its own authority by a campaign of terror beginning in July 1918. In that month, the Tsar and his family (there is now some doubt about the fate of his wife and daughters, though not his son) were murdered in the cellar of the house where they were kept at Ekaterinburg by local Bolsheviks fearful of the advance of Kolchak's White Army. The next month two attacks by opponents led to the full counter-attack by the Bolsheviks. A Jewish girl, Dora Kaplan, attempted to assassinate Lenin himself while Uritsky, the head of the Cheka in Petrograd, was shot dead. In retaliation 1500 people in Petrograd were shot dead. There is no doubt that this led to a widespread terror campaign, a part of which formed merely one aspect of the civil war. Prisoners in that war (on both sides) were killed as a matter of course, while the Cheka singled out more obvious opponents—landlords especially—as one way of encouraging the compliance of others. The Kronstadt mutiny led to a renewed terror. All those taken prisoner there were executed and others suspected of similar sympathies were imprisoned. Again, the resolution of March 1921 to forbid dissension within the party resulted in over 100 000 expulsions from the party. Only with the ending of the civil war and the start of the economic recovery in 1922 did the 'Red Terror' relax.

Political bureau (Politburo)

Central Committee of the Communist Party (Praesidium)

Party Congress

Local Communist Party groups

Diagram 12 The structure of the Communist Party

The final touches to the political organization of the Soviet Union came in December 1922 when the Union of Soviet Socialist Republics— the Russian, Ukrainian, Byelorussian (or White Russian) and Transcaucasion Republics—joined together. In government, the 'All-Russian' Congress of Soviets now became 'All-Union' Congress, and in the Party organization a similar 'All-Union' structure was formed. The separate republics maintained some control, especially in the social and cultural fields, and each had its own congress, but in practice the important decisions were still made at the centre.

(e) Foreign Policy 1920–24

The conclusion of the Civil War did not mean the end of war for the new state. The Polish invasion of the Ukraine in 1920 was repulsed *(see page 334)* and Lenin then decided to continue his advance. There were two reasons for this. Firstly, the Russo-Polish border had constantly been in dispute and it was in the Russian tradition to land-grab from Poland whenever and wherever possible. More importantly, Lenin hoped that the time had come for the advance of communism beyond the boundaries of Russia, as had been hoped and promised for so long. The new states of Eastern Europe were relatively unarmed, while Germany was weaker than ever—surely the time was ripe to at least sow the seeds of international revolution? The Polish armies were swiftly pushed back and in August 1920 the Red Army was outside Warsaw. Here, with considerable French aid and the guidance of General Weygand, the Poles fought back and the Russians were forced to retreat and leave their new conquests *(see page 209)*. The gamble had failed, and the West had had its only victory in Russia. In March 1921 the treaty of Riga was signed defining the frontier *(see page 210)* and leaving resentment on both sides of it.

Before 1924, the Soviet Union could look for little help, trade or friendship from the Western powers. Their participation in the Civil War had left each suspicious and convinced that the war between communism and the West was not over. In March 1919 the Third Communist International ('Comintern') had been founded with the express intention of spreading communism around the world and organizing the overthrow of the Western governments. For their part, the Soviets could fear the West's intentions following the construction of the 'cordon sanitaire' and the signing of treaties between France and the new East European countries. Nevertheless, given its perilous economic condition, the Soviet Union needed trade with the West to help build up industrial expertise. The first step in this direction was taken in March 1921 when an Anglo-Russian trade treaty was signed. In May a similar treaty was signed with Germany. Then in April 1922 Soviet delegates attended the Genoa conference on economic problems; this was the first sign that the Bolsheviks were prepared to co-operate with the West. However, the French government demanded that the Soviet government should repay the debts of Tsarist Russia to France. The Soviets refused. For two years there was little contact, until on 1 February 1924—after Lenin's death—Great Britain recognized the communist government and she was followed shortly afterwards by Italy and France.

Soviet policy was not, however, aimed simply at friendship and trade. Lenin certainly hoped that, postponed though it was, the great international revolution would still come. In the meantime it had been postponed and therefore all that could be done was to foster the most favourable conditions for the future. To this end, the Western powers should be divided so that they should not unite against revolution. Lenin was remarkably perceptive in seeing that a Russo-German alliance would be the way to uphold these divisions. He realized that the Versailles treaty had alienated Germany from the rest of Europe and that agreement with Russia would, for Germany, be a way of maintaining the divisions of the capitalist West.

The treaty of Rapallo (6 April 1922) was the basis of Russo-German friendship. By it, the two 'pariah nations' as Lloyd George called them, agreed to cancel all territorial claims against each other and to co-operate economically *(see pages 296, 364)*. A supplementary commercial treaty of 1925 and a treaty of friendship and neutrality (the treaty of Berlin) of 1926 further consolidated the alliance. By secret agreements German factories producing military goods were built inside Russia, thus enabling the Germans to get round the military terms of Versailles and the Russians to see Western military technology. By earlier arrangements, several German companies worked in Russia, especially in mining. Until the early 1930s Russo-German friendship proved of considerable mutual advantage, but it also provided the Western powers with severe embarrassment.

3. Stalin's Russia

(a) Ideological Conflict and the Emergence of Stalin
The mid-twenties were a time of ideological reassessment among the communist leadership. The revolution had been won in Russia and the state reorganized; what of the future? Lenin himself was increasingly disturbed by what he saw around him. Much of the idealism of the movement was gone; for example, the minority nationalities were no better treated than they had been by the Tsars. Far from being a state in which people *wanted* to help each other and work for the creation of a socialist utopia, the Soviet Union had become a state in which people were bullied into working for the State. An enormous bureaucracy had been created to bully them. In an article of January 1923, 'On Co-operation', Lenin wrote of the 'uselessness' of 'the machinery of state' and the paradox of revolution occurring first in the least-industralized European state. He wrote of the need for a 'cultural revolution' to educate the people into the need for the revolution that had already happened. Then, in his last article, 'But Fewer But Better' (March, 1923), he wrote that the 'state apparatus' was 'deplorable not to say disgusting'. This was an attack on the 'Rabkrin', a body of workers and peasants established to inspect the civil service, and by 1923 under Stalin's control. Yet Lenin's disillusion with his new state was ultimately of less importance than the conflict between his successors.

In March 1923 Lenin suffered his third major stroke, as a result of which he lost the power of speech; from then until his death in January 1924 the struggle between his likely successors was the real issue. Four men were genuine candidates for the succession. Trotsky, organizer of the revolution, victor of the civil war and Lenin's right-hand man, was the most likely. Zinoviev, also a close colleague of Lenin and head of Comintern, and Kamenev, one-time President of the Central Executive Committee, were also possible candidates. Stalin, General Secretary of the Party Central Committee, Commissar for Nationalities and Rabkrin was immensely powerful within the party but had not been one of the leaders in 1917 and had been verbally attacked by Lenin.

Between 1923 and 1925 Kamenev, Zinoviev and Stalin were united in their opposition to Trotsky. There were many issues that divided them and were debated in private and semi-public (Party Congresses) in these years. The size of the bureaucracy, the extent that dissent should be allowed within the party, and the solution to the continuing agricultural problem were all key issues on which it was possible to see the case for several alternatives. Above all, what of the promised world revolution? To Trotsky, a revolt in Russia alone was a contradiction of the theses of both Marx and Lenin; the revolution had to be both permanent and world-wide if the Soviet Union was to be secure. All resources and efforts should be directed to that end. Only then could the Soviet Union itself be safely built up. In contrast, Stalin argued for 'socialism in one country'. Russia had to be established as a powerful socialist country, strong enough to defend herself from attacks and to lead the attack to the rest of the world. Apart from the political argument, there was also the personal conflict. Stalin was the unimaginative official, who had worked his way up from humble beginnings to the top by hard work and loyalty. Trotsky was the Jewish intellectual who had spectacularly thrust himself forward and brought honour to himself. The two had little liking for each other. liking for each other.

During 1924 and 1925 Stalin and his allies openly attacked Trotsky. In October 1924 Stalin publicly referred to Trotsky's correspondence of 1913 in which he referred to Lenin as 'a professional exploiter of everything that is backward in the Russian workers' movement'. In 1925 Trotsky fell ill and, partly voluntarily, resigned as Commissar of War and took a less important post in the council of National Economy. The next dispute was between Stalin and his former allies on the agricultural issue. There was still a grain shortage and the peasants still demanded more concessions. Stalin supported the motion at the 14th Party conference to cut the tax on grain by 25% and make it easier for farmers to lease land and employ labourers. Again, agriculture had won a concession from communism. Kamenev and Zinoviev opposed the motion. It was carried by 559 votes to sixty-five. The elections for three new members of the Politburo also went Stalin's way. All three new men, Molotov, Voroshilov and Kalinin, were his supporters.

During 1926 and 1927 a new alliance of Trotsky, Zinoviev and Kamenev made a final effort to oppose Stalin, on the grounds that he led the bureaucracy against the interests of the peasants. However, the 15th Party Conference of October 1927 endorsed Stalin's policy of 'socialism in one country'. All three opponents were removed from the Politburo. In December 1927 they planned to circulate a memorandum to the conference; fearing it would not be allowed, they had it printed secretly. Members of 'OGPU' (as the Cheka had become) found the presses. All three, together with seventy-five colleagues, were expelled first from the Central Executive Committee and then from the Party. Subsequently, Trotsky was expelled from Russia in 1929, while Zinoviev and Kamenev remained in Russia until the purges and show trials of the 1930s (see page 350).

Stalin's power was not yet unchallenged. The winter of 1927 and 1928 saw further grain shortages that convinced Stalin of the need for an end to NEP and a new agricultural policy. However, leading Party members, with whom he had allied in 1925, were wedded to the moderate idea of a wealthy peasantry. Prominent among these were Bukharin, editor of the Party paper *Pravda*, Tomsky, head of the unions, and Rykov, chairman of the Council of People's Commissars. During 1928 the Comintern Conference condemned reformism. A debate on agriculture in the columns of *Pravda* followed, in which rich peasants were condemned. Bukharin wrote in their defence, but in February 1929 he and the others were accused, with Kamenev, of plotting against Stalin's campaign against wealthy peasants. All three nominally supported Stalin but by the end of the year all three had left the Party. Stalin's fiftieth birthday at the end of that year was celebrated with massive demonstrations and huge street portraits.

Stalin's emergence as unchallenged leader was primarily the result of his manipulation of his official posts and his ability to identify himself as a genuine successor to Lenin. As General Secretary, Stalin controlled an enormous power machine. Directly under him, he had over 700 officials and local party secretaries were appointed directly by him. The secret police came under his authority, as did the youth movement, 'Komsomol', founded in 1927. There were separate sections in the secretariat for press, statistics, village affairs, education and the like. Thus the General Secretary, largely through his power of appointment, could build up vast local and national bases of support. If his appointees and supporters voted for him in the Party Conference, he was likely to win. Lenin had written against Stalin before his death, saying that he should be removed as General Secretary and replaced by someone 'more tolerant, more loyal, more polite and more attentive to the needs of comrades'. Stalin ignored this criticism and on 26 January 1924, at a special congress of the Party to pay tribute to Lenin, spoke in uncharacteristically emotional terms of the dead leader. Later, he was able to show that his policies of gradual change and 'socialism in one country' were in the Leninist tradition. For example, when he sided with Bukharin against Kamenev's campaign for agrarian change, Stalin quoted Lenin's statement of 1919 that 'there is nothing more stupid than the idea of compulsion with reference to economic relations with average peasants'. Time was to show that Stalin's pursuit of Lenin came from convenience rather than conviction.

(b) Economic Policy

(i) Introduction

'Socialism in one country' inevitably meant that Russia must be strengthened. Despite the ravages of seven years of war, production had almost reached pre-war levels by the mid-1920s. However, the population had increased by 20 million in the same period. In 1921, Lenin had said,

'We are in a condition of such poverty, ruin and exhaustion . . . that everything must be set aside to increase production.' Much had been achieved, but much more lay ahead. Stalin's victory ensured that maximum efforts and resources would be given to the expansion and strengthening of Russia herself rather than an effort to propagate the revolution elsewhere. Stalin best expressed this in a famous speech of 1931:

> It is sometimes asked whether it is not possible to slow down the tempo, to put a brake on the movement. No, comrades, it is not possible! The pace must not be reduced. . . . To do this would mean to lag behind; and those who lag behind are beaten. Russia has too often been beaten for her back-wardness. She was beaten by the Mongol Khans, by Turkish Beys, by Polish-Lithuanian Pans, by Anglo-French capitalists, by Japanese barons —she was beaten by all—for her backwardness. . . . We are fifty or a hundred years behind the advanced countries. We must make good this gap in ten years. Either we do it or they crush us . . .

Thus the decision was taken and the orders sent out. In December, 1927, the 15th party Congress ordered 'Gosplan' to draw up a five-year plan for development of the whole economy. 'Gosplan' was the State Planning Commission, founded in 1921 to set up a single economic plan for the whole country. By 1927 it had developed regional offices and a considerable bureaucracy, but was more an advisory and surveying body, producing reports on progress and possible developments, than an executive body. The orders of that 15th Congress were to change that status.

(ii) The Collectivization of Agriculture

The same congress also ordered the transformation of agriculture and the destruction of the wealthy peasant class, the 'kulaks'. The import-ance of agriculture has already been noted (see page 337); in a period of rapid industrialization its primary functions were to be the provision of food that was plentiful—to be exported for foreign goods—and cheap—to provide the town workers with bread. The existing agricultural struc-ture could not fulfil these terms. The vast majority of farms were far too small to utilize modern equipment. The larger farms, those owned by the kulaks, could use such equipment. However, this would mean that only a sector of agriculture was producing surpluses for the towns and could therefore demand the price it liked. In addition, it would maintain and encourage the existence of a group of wealthy farmers, made rich by private enterprise. This would be a severe ideological embarrassment to a regime committed to the ending of private ownership. A third requisite determined the government's attitude. This was the collection of grain in the countryside and its distribution to the towns. Although total grain production remained fairly stable (see Table 40) the amount reaching the towns was less and less. Even before 1914 a quarter of grain production reached the towns, in 1925, only 13% left the countryside. Many of the problems were undoubtedly administrative, such as a shortage of trained

345

clerks and of scales, but it was obviously difficult to collect from a large number of small farms. Such therefore were the problems—low production, the emergence of a capitalist class, the difficulties of collection.

Stalin explained his solution to a conference of agronomy students:

> There are two solutions. There is the capitalist way, which is to enlarge the agricultural units by introducing capitalism in agriculture. This way brings the impoverishment of the peasantry and the development of capitalist enterprises in agriculture. . . . There is . . . the socialist way, which is to set up collective ('kolkhoz') and State farms. This way leads to the amalgamation of small peasant farms into large collective farms, technically and scientifically equipped, and to the squeezing out of the capitalist elements from agriculture.

Only thus would agriculture be reformed to provide the needs of industry in terms of food, exports, and labour through the movement to the towns of excess labourers in the countryside.

The 15th Party Congress gave its approval to Stalin's plans and asked for voluntary collectivization and limited the kulaks' power to rent land out and hire labourers. However, 1928 proved that a mild approach was inadequate. The quantities of grain reaching the towns was lower than ever, partly because of the old problems and partly because the low price it fetched there, which was fixed by the government, encouraged farmers not to send it. The government blamed the kulaks. Civil servants were sent to search out hoarded grain. Kulaks who refused to surrender their produce were imprisoned. Poorer peasants were encouraged to criticize the richer and to take their land from them. Collectivization remained voluntary and had some success. In June 1927 there were just under 15 000 collective farms, a year later 33 000 and by June 1929 57 000. These contained over a million families and might have augured well. However, there were well over 100 million peasants in all and those who had volunteered to join collectives generally had little land or equipment to put into the new enterprises.

By the summer of 1929 Stalin had decided on a policy of compulsion, both in the destruction of the kulaks and in the creation of the collectives. 'We have passed', he said in December, 'from a policy of confining the exploiting tendencies of the kulaks to a policy of liquidation of the kulaks as a class.' The winter of 1929–30 was the worst period of forced collectivization. By March 1930 over half the peasant farms had been brought into collectives, from a mere 4% in October 1929. 25 000 Party officials, sometimes aided by police and army, did most of the work themselves, simply ordering the kulaks to comply. When they refused, the poorer farmers were 'encouraged' to simply seize the land, animals and equipment. To avoid this, the kulaks frequently burnt their own homes and crops and killed their animals. It has been estimated that about half the animal population of the Russian countryside died in this way between 1929 and 1933.

In March 1930 an article by Stalin himself, 'Dizziness from success', appeared in *Pravda*. In this he wrote that, for all but the kulaks, collectivization was purely voluntary. After a short initial 'drop-out' in which the peasants took Stalin's statement literally and left the collectives until reminded by Party officials that this was not desirable, the proportion of peasants living in collectives increased more steadily, reaching about 70% by 1934. At the same time, some of the rigidity was relaxed, so that collective farms could sell any produce surplus to their quota openly. Small plots for vegetables and a few animals could be kept privately. Also the mechanization programme got under way. Motor Tractor Stations were set up to provide the machines which specialists and mechanics needed, and winter farm schools were set up in new districts.

Nonetheless, the period of rapid collectivization was turbulent and destructive. The loss of cattle and livestock has already been noted; in the worst affected area, Kazakhstan, 83% of cattle, 87% of sheep and 89% of horses were destroyed. The loss of human life was also enormous. Obviously, figures of this were not published, but it has been estimated that some 7 million people were either killed or deported either to labour camps or new factories. The efforts of the kulaks to destroy their crops and the destruction of sown areas in the open conflict between kulaks and poor peasants resulted in famine conditions in some areas, most notably the Ukraine, 1932–3.

	1928	1929	1930	1931	1932	1933	1934	1935
Grain (m. tons)	73·3	71·7	83·5	69·5	69·6	68·6	67·6	75·0
Cattle (m. head)	70·5	67·1	52·5	47·9	40·7	38·4	42·4	49·3
Pigs	26·0	20·4	13·6	14·4	11·6	12·1	17·4	22·6
Sheep and goats	146·7	147·0	108·8	77·7	52·1	50·2	51·9	61·1

Table 41. Agricultural Production in Russia 1928–35

(iii) Industry and the Five-Year Plans

The rapid industrialization of Russia was always regarded as a major priority. Only when it had machines and materials could Russia be strong enough to defend itself against the continuing threat from the rest of the world, and act as the springboard for world revolution. Everything else was subservient to this need. As Stalin had said in 1931:

> If you do not want our socialist fatherland to lose her independence, then you must in the shortest time liquidate backwardness and develop the present Bolshevik tempo. . . . We are 50 to 100 years behind the advanced countries. We must make up this gap in 10 years. Either we do this or they will crush us.

'Gosplan's' officials produced extensive and detailed plans for every industry and area. Overall, the aim was to triple production in the heavy industry sector—coal, iron, oil steel—and double it in other sectors. To help all areas of industry electrical output was to be increased six-fold. Plans for agriculture and social development such as the expansion of hospitals and education were also included in Gosplan's strategy. The scheme was launched in October 1928.

The achievements of the first two five-year plans (1928–32 and 1933–37) were impressive. Table 42 below gives an indication of the sheer scale of this achievement.

	1926	1928	1933	1937
Gross industrial production				
(m. roubles)	11·1	18·3	43·3	95·5
Electricity (mld kwh)	3·5	5·05	16·6	36·2
Pig iron (m. tons)	2·4	3·3	6·2	14·5
Steel (m. tons)	3·1	4·0	5·9	17·7

Table 42(a). The achievements of the Five-Year Plans (outline)

In 1932, nearly half the machine-tools in use in Russia had been installed since 1928. Overall production was up by 118%, there were over 200 000 students in higher education and nearly a million at secondary technical schools. The Urals and the areas beyond it were exploited for the first time, the most famous such plant being the ironworks and blast furnaces at Magnitogorsk. Specific areas became specialist producers of goods most readily available to them, such as the oil of the Caucasus, the iron of Krivoi Rog, the tractors of Kharkov. The existing cities expanded and new industrial cities like Voronezh and Novosibirsk, previously provincial centres, were doubled and trebled in size. In the factories workers received basic education for the first time.

The campaign for industrialization was conducted as a war upon backwardness. 'Gosplan', the high command, sent out its orders for levels of production to specific areas and they in turn translated them into detailed requirements for each plant. On this local level, managers received the orders of the level of production required, and had to achieve it as best they could. Plan requirements and achievements were published in the factories for all to see, and, as in wartime, constant propaganda urged the workers to ever higher efforts. There were medals, literally, for the highest producers and penalties for those who failed to achieve. Obviously, such constant supervision and threat put pressure on many managers to falsify figures and take short-cuts in production. Nevertheless, the battle had to be won and, especially in comparison with the achievements of Western Europe at the same time, it apparently was.

This battle mentality had other, less pleasant, implications. The conditions of work and, especially, of living were neglected to a point of near disaster. Certainly factory workers newly arrived in an area lived in shanties that would have compared unfavourably with pre-revolutionary times. Consequently, a high degree of compulsion and suppression of complaint were required. Again, as in war, failures were rarely admitted and always underplayed, so it is difficult for the Western historian to truly assess the impact of the plans. It is certain that the targets of the first Plan were not achieved in many areas, most notably in iron and steel production, where production reached about 60% of what had been planned, but then the ambitions were so great that this is hardly surprising. Equally, however, a warlike sense of patriotism made many workers accept hardships and renew their efforts in a way that would never have normally been possible.

The planners learnt from their errors and in many respects the second Plan was more successful than the first. 'Gosplan' officials had been hoping for improved harvests, a greater share of world trade and a fall in military expenditure, none of which materialized, during the first Plan. However, the first year of the first Plan had proved so promising that it was decided to complete the Plan in four years instead of five and increase the targets. In fact, their optimism proved false *(see Table 42b)* and 1933–34 was regarded as a year of relaxation before a renewed effort. Consequently, the second Plan was slightly less optimistic, involved less administrative shuffling, and was more successful. This was especially true of the years 1934–6, by which time many of the new plants were in operation and less machinery had to be imported. In 1932 78% of machine tools had to be imported; by 1937 only 38%. Equally, however, the second Plan had to be adjusted to increase defence expenditure, which became the first priority of the third Plan. In addition, after two good years, 1937 showed a considerable slowdown, especially in the metallurgical industries, partly as a result of the purges *(see below)*. Nevertheless, not only were production figures increased, but also, to some extent, worker's conditions. Malafayev was calculated that while prices rose by some 80%, wages more than doubled, and that goods and shops were more readily available to workers.

		First plan planned 1932–3 first version	1932–3 optimal	actual 1932–3	Second plan planned 1937	1937 actual
	1927–8					
Electricity (mKwh)	5·05	17·0	22·0	16·6	38·0	36·2
Coal (m. tons)	35·4	68·0	75·0	64·3	152·5	128·0
Oil (m. tons)	11·7	19·0	22·0	21·4	46·8	28·5
Pig iron (m. tons)	3·3	8·0	10·0	6·2	16·0	14·5
Steel (m. tons)	4·0	8·3	10·4	5·9	17·0	17·7
Employment	11·3	14·8	15·8	22·8	28·9	26·9

Table 42(b). The Five-Year Plans and their achievement (details)

(c) Political History

The warlike atmosphere of Russia in the 1930s extended into the political sphere. There were three particular aspects to this. Firstly, as with all nations in wartime, the leadership became increasingly identified in one person and he was regarded as more and more infallible. Secondly, any oppposition was ruthlessly suppressed. Thirdly, some constitutional alterations were made to facilitate rapid decision making.

(i) Stalin's leadership

Stalin's portrait first appeared in *Pravda* in 1929. For the next twenty years, his speeches and pronouncements were given all the more familiar media treatment to show him as the great leader and to spur his people on to greater and greater achievements. Not for Stalin the 'fireside chat' approach, but rather the cultivation of a distant 'Big Brother' figure whose pleasure was a reward and whose anger was to be avoided. Other cult figures were drawn not from Stalin's entourage, whose anonymity was to be carefully preserved, but rather from the ordinary people, the workers who had achieved more than their norm and whose portraits appeared outside works canteens. Best known of these figures was Alexei Stakhanov, the miner who could hew ten tons of coal in the time most men managed one. Thus the great worker was glorified and the great leader's distant magic preserved.

(ii) The purges

The purges of the mid and late 1930s were the climax of putting down opponents. As early as 1930 a group of technicians and managers were brought to trial for sabotage and mismanagement. After this, many managers and local officials were tried for their failures, and the Communist Party itself was purged of thousands of 'unfaithful' members. These early trials and purges provided an excuse for the failures of the 'war' on backwardness and aroused the patriotism of the work force against self-confessed fifth columnists. The seventeenth Party Congress of January 1934 congratulated itself on the success of its economic measures and its hopes for the future.

However, the same year saw the start of an extraordinary campaign against any possible dissidents. On 1 December Nikolayev shot and killed Serge Kirov, head of the Leningrad Communist Party and a close colleague of Stalin. Stalin immediately ordered his secret police, OGPU, to intensify their investigations of all possible opposition and his judges not to expect any pardons of those sentenced to death. Those responsible for Kirov's death were secretly tried and executed while many other possible dissidents were deported. In 1935 the campaign took on a new turn. Kamenev, Zinoviev and several other onetime leaders were tried for treason and imprisoned. In August 1936 they were brought out of prison and accused of plotting with Trotsky and other powers to overthrow the Soviet State. Sixteen men publicly confessed their guilt, to the amazement of Russians as well as the rest of the world, and were executed. Yagoda was replaced as head of OGPU by Yezhov and a renewed campaign ensued. In January, 1937 thirteen more prominent Bolsheviks, including Karl Radek, were executed and others imprisoned. Political commissioners were appointed to watch over the army, and that June, one Marshal, Gamarnik, was reported to have committed suicide while another, Tukhachevsky, commander-in-chief of the army, was executed together with seven other top ranking generals. All had confessed to conspiring with Japan and Germany against the USSR. The real climax came in March 1938 when twenty-one leading Bolsheviks, including Bukharin, Rykov and Yagoda were similarly accused and executed. By 1939 only two of Lenin's Politburo—Trotsky and Stalin—survived and every important branch of Soviet life had been affected. Of the 1966 delegates of the seventeenth Party Congress in January 1934, 1108 had been arrested and only fifty-nine lived to attend another Congress. Lower down the hierarchy, untold thousands died or were deported. The 'Chief Administration of Corrective Labour Camps and Labour Settlements', set up in 1934, had established a string of camps in the distant corners of Russia—camps whose notoriety has since been established by the writings of Alexander Solzhenitsyn.

To a degree, the trials fulfilled some of the functions of the early trials of 1930. They reminded the people of the penalties of opposition and they provided scapegoats for the setbacks in the economic war. However, the scale of the purges in sheer numbers and the expense and trouble incurred in getting confessions and putting on the show trials in which the confessions were made, seem totally excessive if these were the sole motives. There can be little doubt that Stalin was genuinely afraid of rivals toppling him; after all, if he had done it to Trotsky, why shouldn't others do the same to him? Moreover, his targets—the leaders of politics, of industry, of the armed forces and of diplomacy—were calculated to ensure his supremacy over all sections of Soviet life by his ability to appoint virtually unknown successors who would follow his lead. Given Stalin's personality, the knowledge that the rest of the world was still opposed to his country and the military atmosphere, the purges may be in part explained if not understood.

(iii) The new Constitution
A new constitution came into effect in December, 1936. Its chief difference from that of 1922 was its reflection of the growing size and multiplicity of the Russian state. The four republics of 1922 *(see page 340)* became eleven, the additions being mainly in the East. The new Federation consisted of Russia, the Ukraine, White Russia, Azerbaijan, Georgia, Armenia, Turkmenistan, Uzbekistan, Tedjikistan, Kazakhstan and Kirghistan. To recognize this new federation in the organs of government, the Congress of Soviets, known as the Supreme Soviet, was divided into two parts known as the 'Soviet of the Nationalities', in which representation was proportional between the different groups, and a 'Soviet of the Union'. The Central Executive Committee remained to act while the Congress was not in session. In addition, the electoral system was altered so that no groups were disenfranchised, the secret ballot was introduced, and elections to the Soviet of Nationalities and Soviet of the Union were to be direct. Stalin called it 'the most democratic constitution in the world'. The Communist Party remained the only legal political group.

(d) Foreign Policy 1924–39

Soviet foreign policy remained complex and, at times, contradictory. The Soviet leadership was convinced that a showdown with the capitalist West was inevitable, and preparations for this had to be made. Equally, Germany was still at the very heart of Russian ambitions; she was the most likely 'bad apple' in Western Europe, yet she also was the one power near enough and potentially strong enough to attack Russia. Thirdly, Soviet policy was frequently determined not by her actions but by the actions of others towards her. As long as France, Italy and Britain were prepared to be friendly, Russia could continue to trade and build up her strength, but if they turned, her policy had to be reconsidered.

Such a situation arose in 1927. First Italy supported Roumania's territorial claims to Bessarabia, then Russian advisers were thrown out of China by Chiang Kai-shek. In May, Britain ended diplomatic relations following a series of episodes, some genuine, others false, of Soviet propaganda and spying in Britain. In the space of a few months the elaborate negotiations of the Lenin era were shattered and once again the Soviet Union was isolated and threatened.

There followed a period of retrenchment in which Russia again became accepted in the international community. This was largely the work of Maxim Litvinov, Deputy Commissar for Foreign Affairs under Chicherin, and then Commissar. In December 1927 he announced a policy of complete disarmament. In the next year Russia was a signatory of the Kellogg Pact *(see page 369)*. By 1929 he had established friendly relations with most of Russia's Western neighbours, and Poland, Roumania, Latvia and Estonia (joined later by Lithuania, Turkey, Persia and Danzig) signed with Russia the Litvinov Protocol which promised not to resort to war in the case of disputes. In 1933 the Protocol became a multilateral treaty of non-aggression. At the time of collectivization and the socialist drive, peace was apparently assured.

Germany, however, once more became the problem. Until 1932 trade continued unabated and Russia, as a result of a new trade agreement of 1928, took over 30% of German machinery exports and German engineers were sent to aid the industrialization programme. However, the warning lights were on and the Soviet leaders became more and more concerned by talk of union with Austria and the appointment first of Conservative Chancellors like Papen and then of Hitler. These were not the men who would provide the Soviets with a route into Western Europe, or a defence against attack from the West. The Russo-German trade continued— almost half Russia's imports in 1932 came from Germany—but at the same time a new policy towards the West was adopted. This became even more urgent with the advent of Japanese expansionism in the Far East. In 1935 the Russians were forced to sell their share of the Chinese Eastern Railway; Japan's signature of the Anti-Comintern Pact in November 1936 led to even more open conflict along the Russo-Manchurian border. Peace, or at least assurances of assistance in the case of war, was essential in the West. A series of initiatives were taken in this direction, and these are detailed below:

Feb.–July 1932: for the first time, the Soviet Union took an active part in the Disarmament Conference; previously their delegates had opposed and delayed negotiations.

November 1932: a non-aggression pact with France. The USA recognized the Soviet government, in exchange for which the Soviet government promised not to spread propaganda in the USA.

May 1934: the non-aggression pacts with Poland and the Baltic states became ten-year agreements. In fact, Poland's signature of a non-aggression Pact with Germany in January 1934 had effectively brought Poland into Germany's camp, and provided a great threat to the Soviets.

June 1934: Agreements reached with Czechoslovakia and Roumania, by which the Soviet Union acknowledged the loss of Bessarabia.

September 1934: Russia joined the League of Nations and became a permanent member of the Council. Litvinov took an active part in the League's affairs and supported France's plans for an East European agreement to parallel the Locarno agreements in the West.

May 1935: Alliance with France, by which each promised assistance in the case of unprovoked attack. In the same month, an alliance with Czechoslovakia was signed, by which Russia agreed to come to Czechoslovakia's aid in the event of attack, as long as France also did so.

July 1935: The Third International instructed communists in 'bourgeois' countries not to oppose military expansion, in view of the increasing threat from the fascist powers.

The next three years witnessed the failure of these initiatives. Certainly the Western powers accepted Russia's about-turn, but were not prepared to welcome her and co-operate in military planning in the way that was actually needed if a real defence against Nazism was to be erected. Although the threats of world revolution had been repudiated in Moscow, they had not been forgotten in the West. Equally, the Third International's decision actually backfired on the Soviet Union; freed from their promises to the Soviet Union, Western communist parties suddenly found new support *(see pages 235, 379)*. To many this was an indication that Russia's pronouncement was actually a plot. Consequently, France and, particularly, Britain, played lip service to Russia's friendship, but their policy which, in the final resort, was what mattered, took little account of it.

During 1936–9 the Soviet Union saw international affairs going more and more against her. Germany, united with Austria, moved eastwards and took Czechoslovakia. Stalin was left out of the Munich Conference; Mussolini took Abyssinia; Franco won Spain. Litvinov had certainly asked for international action, or at least discussion, in March 1938 and in March 1939 with a view to action against Germany, but in both cases his suggestions were dismissed by Britain. Not surprisingly, Stalin was disillusioned by his adherence to collective security. Pro posals for an alliance with Britain foundered and finally collapsed in the summer of 1939 when no agreement could be reached by an Anglo-French-Russian military conference on how Russia could be used to defend Poland. Litvinov, architect of peace, had been dismissed in May 1939 and his replacement, Molotov, was ready to put Soviet policy once again into reverse.

On 23–24 August 1939 Molotov and his German counterpart, Ribbentrop, reached agreement on Russo-German policy. Germany could rely on Russia's benevolent neutrality when she invaded Poland, in exchange for which Russia would be rewarded with a share of Poland and the Baltic states. By the Nazi-Soviet Pact, Russia once again had an opportunity to launch a new assault of the capitalist West, albeit at the risk of German influence *(see pages 315–6)*.

4. Bibliography

Obviously, there are numerous works on this subject. Most of those recommended at the end of chapter V *(see page 116)* continue to at least the revolutionary period. In addition, there are two booklets in the Heath Series—*The Russian Revolution and Bolshevik Victory* by A.E. Adams and *The Stalin Revolution* by R.V. Daniels. Other useful introductory works include *Lenin and the Russian Revolution* by C.E. Hill (English UP, 1947) in the 'Teach Yourself History' series, and the paperback *A History of Soviet Russia 1917–1929* by E.H. Carr (Penguin, 1966). More advanced works include *The First Fifty Years* by I. Grey (Hodder & Stoughton, 1967), *Economic History of the USSR* by A. Nove (Allen & Unwin, 1968) and the two biographies entitled *Stalin* by I. Deutscher (OUP, 1949) and A. Ulam (Allen Lane, 1973).

5. Discussion Points and Exercises

A *This section consists of questions that might be used for discussion (or written answers) as a way of expanding on the chapter and testing understanding of it:*

1 Why was Russia so ill-prepared for World War I?
2 What misjudgements did the Tsar make during the war?
3 Why was it that even some of the nobility deserted the Tsar in 1917?
4 Who started the March Revolution?
5 Was Lenin offering a coherent policy in the summer of 1917, or just playing on the weakness of the Provisional Government?
6 Could the Provisional Government have taken Russia out of the war?
7 Comment on the achievements of the Bolsheviks in the summer of 1917.
8 What was the 'All Russian Congress of Soviets'?
9 Why did the Bolsheviks do so badly in the elections for the Constituent Assembly?

10 Why was the Civil War such a confused affair?
11 Construct a date-chart to illustrate the events of the Civil War in different parts of the country.
12 Why did the Bolsheviks win the Civil War?
13 Comment on the terms of the Treaty of Brest-Litovsk.
14 Was NEP a success?
15 Why was agriculture the key problem for all Soviet governments?
16 Why did the Communists ban other parties, and how was this ban justified?
17 Why were the Western powers so hostile to the Soviet government?
18 Explain Lenin's feelings about his new state in 1923.
19 How did Stalin become undisputed leader of Russia?
20 Why was Stalin so opposed to the kulaks?
21 How successful was collectivization?
22 Why was the emphasis in the Five–Year Plans on heavy industry?
23 Examine the reasons for the purges.
24 Was Russia 'the most democratic country in the world' after the issue of the new Constitution?
25 What principles guided Russian foreign policy after 1924?
26 Examine the Russian reaction to Hitler's rise to power in Germany.

B *This section suggests three ways of examining Russia's problems from a number of points of view:*

1 As a foreign observer in Petrograd in May 1917, write an outline of what you consider the likely course of events to be over the next few months.
2 As a Bolshevik adviser, write a report on the tactics and policies required to win the civil war.
3 If you had been a member of the Politburo in 1926, would you have supported Stalin or Trotsky in the struggle for the leadership? Give details of the reasons for your decision.

C *This section suggests two ways in which you might compare Soviet Russia with other times and places:*

1 Compare Russia in 1924 with Russia in 1913, by means of a chart or diagram.
2 Compare and contrast the style of leadership provided by Lenin and Stalin with that of Hitler and Mussolini.

D *Essay questions:*

1 What problems did the Bolsheviks face after seizing power in 1917 and why were they able to overcome them and remain in power?
2 Examine and explain the shifts in Soviet foreign policy between 1919 and 1939.
3 Assess the achievements of Stalin's economic policies.

6. An Essay-writing Exercise

The four exercises below are intended to help you practice the skills required in essay writing by breaking them down into a number of parts, and by allowing you to work on a number of titles, rather than just one.

1. You might be asked to write an essay on the reasons for the Reds victory in the Civil War. Below are listed three sentences that might form the first sentences of paragraphs in answer to this question. In each case, list four pieces of data—facts, statistics etc—that might be used to support the assertion made by the opening sentence.
    (i) Trotsky's leadership was one of the Reds' greatest assets.
    (ii) The Reds' control of the industrial centres was also to their advantage.
    (iii) On the other hand, the divisions of the White leaders and armies seriously hampered their efforts to overcome the Bolsheviks.

2. Another essay might ask you to assess the character and abilities of Lenin as ruler of Russia. Construct four sentences that would serve as first sentences of paragraphs for such an essay. Make sure that each is an important point that can be supported by evidence, but do not include that evidence.

3. A third question might ask 'Was Stalinism necessary?' Below are listed three sets of data that might be used in paragraphs in answer to this question. In each case, write a first sentence that might accompany each of these sets of data and then write the paragraph concerned, utilizing the data given here.
    (i) Russia's agricultural production before 1928 *(see page 338)*
    Communication and collection difficulties in the Russian country-side
    The needs of the cities
    Ideological undesirability of the kulak class
    (ii) 'We are 50 to 100 years behind ...'
    Production levels of Russian heavy industry in 1928 *(see page 348)*
    Heavy industry as the basis for all development
    (iii) Treatment of opposition to collectivization
    The show trials
    Labour camps
    The number of deaths in the purges

4. A fourth essay might require you to examine the changes of direction of Soviet foreign policy, and the reasons that underlay such changes, in the inter-war period. Construct and write any three paragraphs for this essay. Make sure each contains an assertion and evidence to support it. They do not have to be successive paragraphs, and should not include an introduction or conclusion.

7. Stalin: an Exercise in Debate

Stalin is obviously one of the most controversial figures in twentieth-century history. To illustrate this controversy, there are listed below six statements about Stalin and his policies. For each statement list the *evidence* that might be used to (a) support the statement and (b) refute it.

(1) The needs of the Russian economy made the policy of collectivization essential.
(2) Stalin understood the Russian people better than his predecessors.
(3) The purges were entirely unnecessary.
(4) Stalin put his own interests before those of his country.
(5) The Russian people were better off under the Tsar than under Stalin.
(6) It was in his foreign policy that Stalin truly revealed the turncoat nature of his policies.

Obviously, you will find that in doing this exercise you are often not simply listing evidence, but also expanding on the sentiments expressed in the statement. Nonetheless, it should prove a useful exercise both in the evaluation of evidence and in the consideration of motives.

XIV International Relations and Crises 1919–39

1. Introduction

International relations in the inter-war period were more complex than ever before. They can conveniently be broken down into a number of periods, as below, although these are obviously false in many respects. To assist your overall understanding of the period, it may help to construct an outline date chart on which you can chart the major events of the period. This will especially demonstrate the coincidence of events in different parts of Europe (and the world); this was particularly important in 1936. Secondly, to get some idea of the shifts in attitude between the different countries, it may help to construct four 'friendship/ enemy charts' (one for each of the periods 1919–24, 1925–30, 1930–6 and 1936–9) on which the attitudes of the different powers to each other can be charted below. Where two countries are obviously close to one

1919–24	Fr.	Ru.	GB.	It.	Ger.	EE.I	EE.II
France	/			0		+ 3	
Russia		/					
Britain			/				
Italy	0			/			
Germany					/		
East Europe I (Poland. Cz.,Yugo.)	+ 3					/	− 3
East Europe II (Hungary, Austria)						− 3	/

another, for instance by signing an alliance, score +3 in the appropriate boxes (e.g. France and East Europe I). Where countries are clearly enemies, score −3 (e.g. East Europe I and East Europe II). Use the intervening numbers (−2, −1, 0, +1, +2) to record degrees of friendship; for instance, France and Italy, although both members of the League Council, were not friendly, especially after 1922. Obviously, this is a very crude device, but four completed charts should reveal some important trends.

The Spanish Civil War has been included in this chapter for several reasons. Its European significance is such that to have written a separate chapter on it would have led to considerable repetition within this chapter. Moreover, it coincided with a number of crucial events and trends elsewhere that together altered the whole complexion of international relations after 1936. To take account of its importance, a separate 'Discussion Points and Exercises' section has been included, so that it could form an individual area of study.

2. 1919–24: The Settlement of the Peace Treaties

(a) Introduction

Four issues dominated Europe in the immediate post-war period. The treaties signed at the end of it had left a number of unresolved problems, chiefly concerning the boundaries of Eastern Europe. These problems were mainly settled either peacefully or, in some cases, forcefully by 1924. The second issue was European security. Both France and the East European nations felt that the treaty settlements had left them vulnerable and sought ways of making themselves safer. Economic problems were inevitable in the aftermath of the war, and the early 1920s saw, for the first time, international efforts at co-operation to solve these. Finally, there were efforts, some of them planned, others less so, to ensure that the disaster did not happen again and that peace was to stay.

Three factors underlay and hampered all the efforts of statesmen to deal with these problems. By a vote of 11 November 1919 the United States Senate had refused to ratify both the Treaty of Versailles and the agreement to guarantee France's security *(see page 241)*. Instead, the American government embarked on a policy of isolation, involving themselves in European and world affairs only rarely and when directly affected. The Senate vote had also meant that the USA was not a member of the League of Nations, since membership was incorporated in signing the Treaty of Versailles. The second factor that underlay international affairs was the continued suspicion and hostility between France and Germany. Many Frenchmen believed that Germany would be keen to gain revenge and would attempt to win back at least Alsace and Lorraine. Equally, the peace settlement outraged the majority of the German people, and their determination to overthrow its terms, by force if necessary, became a dominant feature of the 1920s. Thirdly, the situation in Russia added a new dimension to international relations. At first, its major influence was in involving the European powers in the Civil War *(see page 331)*. Even before it became clear that the Communist government could survive and rule, the West European powers sought ways of protecting themselves from the threatened communist advance. Throughout the 1920s, and even the 1930s, Russia's position was to be crucial since it added a third side to international relations. On the one hand were the Western powers and their allies who had won the war and devised the treaties. On the other were the defeated powers of central Europe, eager to revise the treaties. Russia seemed at some times to be on the one side, at others the other; each change, or possible change, brought international repercussions *(see page 240)*. These three factors were to lie behind many of the crises and problems of the inter-war period.

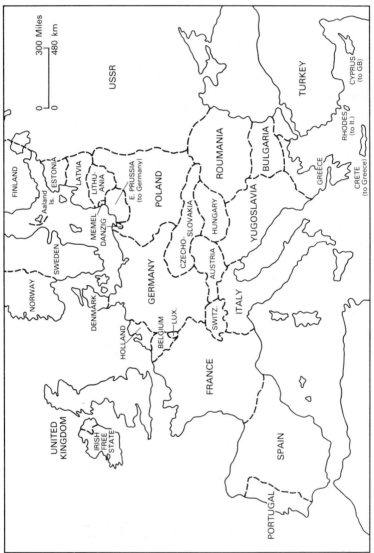

Map 34 Europe in 1923

(b) The settlement of border problems resulting from the treaties

These problems have already been examined under the national histories of the countries concerned. The table below therefore only summarizes the major issues and their resolutions.

Dates	Countries involved	Issue and resolution	Page references
1919–22	Poland and Lithuania	Possession of the town of *Vilna*. Won by the Polish army in 1919 but by the settlement of Poland's eastern border by the Curzon line, Vilna was taken from Poland. It was then won by the Red Army in June 1920 but in August was taken by Lithuania. It was retaken by by a Polish army in October and eventually a plebiscite organized by the Poles decided in favour of the city being united with Poland (8 January 1922). Lithuania refused to accept the settlement, but was unable to do anything about it.	210
1919–20	Poland and Czechoslovakia	Both countries claimed the area around the town of *Teschen*. In January 1919 Czech forces seized the town and there were serious clashes in the area during that year. In July 1920 the area was divided between the two countries by the Conference of Ambassadors. (This was a body consisting of the ambassadors of the great powers in Paris, together with a representative of the French Foreign Office, appointed to settle disputes arising from the peace treaties.)	210–212
1919–20	Poland and Russia	The efforts of the Polish government to push their frontier eastwards resulted in war between the two countries. This war fluctuated both ways and was eventually settled by the treaty of Riga (March 1921) by which Poland made considerable gains.	209–211 341
1919–21	Austria and Hungary	Both countries claimed the area of *Burgenland*. By the peace treaties it had been given to Austria, as most of the people were German. However, Hungarian troops occupied it and only left after a plebiscite organized by the Italians in December 1921. By it, most of the area was assigned to Austria, although Hungary kept possession of Oldenburg.	215
1919–24	Italy and Yugoslavia	Both countries claimed the town of *Fiume* which was occupied by Italian forces led by the poet Gabriele D'Annunzio in September 1919. The	255–256 274

361

		issue was initially resolved by the treaty of Rapallo (November 1920) by which Fiume became independent and Italy was given a number of the Dalmatian islands. But in March 1922 the town was again taken over by irregular Italian forces and eventually, in July 1924, Yugoslavia gave up her claim to the city and received Port Barros in exchange.	
1919–22	Poland and Germany	The mineral rich area of *Upper Silesia* had been left undecided by the peace treaties as it contained a mixed population. A plebiscite of March 1921 was indecisive and in August 1922 the Conference of Ambassadors referred the matter to the Leagues of Nations, whose council accepted a partition scheme that had been drawn up by a committee of experts. By this, Germany received a larger part of the area but Poland won the richer mineral areas.	208–211 256

Table 42. Post-war problems of Europe

(c) The settlement of French and East European security

After America's rejection of the guarantee to protect French security in November 1919, France sought alternative means of protection. As the newly-created East European countries also felt vulnerable, surrounded as they were by powerful enemies, their interests coincided with those of France. The result was the construction of the alliance system by which France's security was linked to that of Eastern Europe. The foundations of this system were laid by the treaty between Czechoslovakia and Yugoslavia of 14 August 1920 *(see page 200)*. This was initially a defensive treaty against Hungary, but was to become the basis of the 'Little Entente'. Chronologically, the next agreement was the treaty between France and Poland promising each other assistance in the event of either being attacked. This formed the northern arm of France's East European defences, which was always kept separate from her southern arm—the 'Little Entente'—because of the mutual hostility and suspicion between Poland and her southern neighbours *(see pages 209–12)*. During 1921 the 'Little Entente' was completed by treaties between Roumania and both Czechoslovakia and Yugoslavia. It also survived its first test when it successfully opposed (by mobilization) the attempts of former King Karl to regain his throne in Budapest. The 'Little Entente' was first linked to France by the Franco-Czech treaty of January 1924 which provided for mutual aid if either was attacked without provocation. Subsequent treaties between France and Roumania (1926) and France and Yugoslavia (1927) tightened these ties and, on the face of it, secured both France and the East European powers against possible attack.

These treaties were to be crucial to the future security of Europe and it was ultimately an agreement between Poland and the Western powers that led to the outbreak of war in 1939 *(see page 392)*. Consequently, they are worth assessing a little more closely. To what extent did France really believe that the military strength of Poland, or Czechoslovakia, would genuinely cope with either a German or a Russian (or, at worst, a combined Russo-German) attack? Or did the French government really undertake the negotiations, and the treaties, as a way of satisfying its own conscience, and the protests of its people, in the aftermath of the American let-down? For their part, did the East European powers hold out much hope for the French to come to their aid if and when the communist advance began? Italy in 1914 and the USA in 1919 had shown that formal treaty arrangements were open to interpretation and could be used to justify both involvement and non-involvement in disputes. The 1930s were to show the same thing with more devastating effects. Consequently, the treaty arrangements of the 1920s were, to some extent, a sham; as long as the prevailing mood in Europe was peaceful, such treaties gave the semblance of security. However, in the face of the very threats that they were designed to combat, they were to be shown to be only as powerful as their signatories.

(d) International economic issues
Two closely related economic issues dominated the early 1920s. All the combatants had suffered, to a greater or lesser degree, economic dislocation and, both during the war and in the period of reconstruction that followed it, had incurred enormous debts, partly to each other, but chiefly to the USA. Secondly, all the victors hoped to repay their debts, and continue their plans for reconstruction, through the reparations they were to be paid by the defeated powers *(see pages 230, 236)*. When the payment of these monies was not immediately forthcoming, the economic plans of the victor states were overthrown and alternatives had to be sought. It was to seek such alternatives, and to try to salvage something from the reparations, that a series of international conferences were held.

At the Peace Conference, the final sum of reparations had not been settled, and a Reparations Commission had been set up to finalize this. During 1920 and 1921 a number of conferences were held with this aim in view. At Spa, in July 1920, Germany submitted a series of suggestions relating to the extent and methods of payment, which included plans for payment in kind. At the same time, the allies agreed to apportion the payments in the ratio France 52%, British Empire 22%, Italy 10% and Belgium 8%. Further conferences were held at Paris, in January 1921, and London, in February and March 1921, to examine more detailed proposals. Germany was supposed to have begun payments, to the tune of 5 billion dollars, before the final sum was fixed, and in March 1921 was claimed to be behind with her payments, although, using different figures, this was denied. The arguments and negotiations were ended by the decision of the Reparations Commission, which was reached on

27 April 1921. Germany was to pay a total of 132 000 million gold marks (£6600 million or $33 000 million). At the reconvened London conference two days later, it was decided that the first 1000 million marks were to be received by the end of May. In fact, this money was not received until the end of August, and only then after a threat to occupy the Ruhr area and a loan from London bankers.

By this time, it was clear that the economic reconstruction of the victor powers, and the repayment of debts, was less simple than had been hoped. Consequently, there followed a number of conferences intended to examine Europe's economic problems in as wide a context as possible. The first of these was held at Genoa between 10 April and 19 May 1922. Significantly, representatives of Germany and Russia attended, indicating a willingness to forget the quarrels of the immediate post-war period in the search for a genuine and lasting answer to Europe's economic problems. In fact, the conference had unexpected consequences. The Western powers refused to moderate their demands for reparations from Germany, while France insisted that the new Russian government should repay its predecessor's debts. Therefore, Germany and Russia felt as isolated and rejected as before and on 16 April signed the treaty of Rapallo *(see page 296)*. Nevertheless, there was one optimistic sign in the aftermath of the conference: on 31 May the Reparations Commission postponed all further payments from Germany for the rest of the year in view of the serious financial problems in Germany.

A second international conference was held in London in August 1922. It followed a British proposal of 1 August to cancel all debts to her, and end her demands for reparations, if a general economic settlement could be reached, including America cancelling her debts from the European powers. If the USA would not do this, then Britain would have to insist on sufficient payments to repay the USA. The American government stated that, in its view, the debts to her were quite a separate issue to reparations and that they still stood. At the Conference, therefore, France still sought repayment. Poincaré said that the postponement of payments could only continue if France received 'productive guarantees', including the exploitation of German mines in the Ruhr area and 60% of the profits of German dye factories on the left bank of the Rhine. This demand brought sharp disagreement with Britain and the Conference broke up.

A second London conference met in December 1922. This time, the new British Prime Minister, Bonar Law, agreed to cancel the debts to Britain, even if America continued to require repayment. However, this had no tangible effects as Poincaré still sought German reparations, and these, in total, far outweighed France's debts to Britain. One final effort to alter France's attitude was made at the Paris conference of 2–4 January 1923, when Britain and Italy proposed that Germany's repayments could be staggered by them being paid in government bonds. This too was rejected; the French government, with the support of the French people, remained adamant in their demands for cash payments supported by tangible payments in kind, such as coal and timber. Consequently, after Germany had been declared in default on coal deliveries by the Reparations Commission on 9 January 1923, French and Belgian forces occupied the Ruhr area and remained there until the autumn, faced by a policy of passive resistance from the local population *(see page 232)*. The reparations issue was ultimately resolved only by the intervention of the United States when, in April 1924, the Dawes Plan provided for the stabilization of the German currency and the issue of a loan of 800 million gold marks to Germany to enable her to reconstruct and repay reparations *(see page 294)*. Significantly, the European powers had not been able to resolve their economic problems for themselves.

(e) The maintenance of future peace

The chief hopes that the deluge of 1914–18 would not be repeated lay in the League of Nations. The League had been proposed in Wilson's Fourteen Points and its constitution (the 'Covenant') formed an integral part of the treaty of Versailles. By it, a structure and organization was provided not only to ensure that peace would be kept, but also that glaring denials of human rights should be eradicated. The organization of the League is summarized in Diagram 13 below.

Diagram 13. The organization of the League of Nations

The Assembly was to be the heart of the League's activities. All members—the forty-one original members had risen to fifty by 1924 and sixty by 1934—were represented in the Assembly, where each had an equal vote. For important decisions, such as the imposition of sanctions, the vote of the members had to be unanimous, thus ensuring that any important action was not controversial. The Assembly admitted new member states and decided on the financial contributions of the different members. Technically, the Assembly met only once a year, so a Council was formed to remain in permanent session and to take immediate action in a crisis. It had to report on and explain its actions to the Assembly, and was therefore accountable to it. Originally, there were eight members of the Council. Four of them, the four great victor powers—Britain, France, Japan and Italy—were to be permanent members of the Council, while the other four, to be elected by the Assembly, were to be temporary members. The number of temporary members was raised to six in 1922 and to nine in 1926. The Secretariat, headed by a Secretary-General, was to service both the Assembly and Council, as well as the League's other departments, with information, records and accounts. It would provide the interpreters and civil servants needed to run the new organization from its headquarters at Geneva. Under the authority of the Assembly and Council, an International Court of Justice was convened at the Hague to deal with purely legal disputes between member states.

Numerous other bodies, usually referred to collectively as 'Special Departments', dealt with particular problems or topics. The ILO (International Labour Organization) was the largest of these, having its own separate organizational structure. Governments, workers and employers were all represented on the ILO, which endeavoured to improve and standardize working conditions and employer–worker relations throughout the member states. There was a Mandates Commission to supervise the control of the mandated territories *(see page 188)*; a Drugs Department to attempt to end drugs trafficking; a Health Department; a Slavery Commission; and a Refugees Department, among others. Between them, these new bodies would hopefully bring the better world that was promised after the 'war to end all wars'.

The League had a number of means of maintaining international peace. When they joined the League by signing the Covenant, the members agreed to Article 10 of the Covenant, which stated: 'The Members of the League undertake to respect and preserve against external agression the territorial integrity and existing political independence of all Members of the League'. Further articles of the Covenant— articles 16 and 17—committed the members to take action against any member regarded as an aggressor by the League. In the first place, they were to sever trade relations (i.e. impose economic sanctions) and, if required 'contribute to the armed forces to be used to protect the Covenants of the League'. The keynote, therefore, was to be collective action by all members against an aggressor power.

In its early years, the League did seem to be fulfilling some of its promises. Several minor international issues were successfully dealt with. In 1921 Yugoslav troops were forced to leave Albania and the disputed ownership of the Aaland islands between Sweden and Finland *(see Map 34)* was resolved when the islands were given to Finland on condition that they established an independent government there. Also in 1921 the issue of the ownership of Upper Silesia was ended by a League decision *(see page 210)*. At the same time, League officials took over the administration of several areas that had created problems at the peace treaty. The 'free cities' of Danzig and Memel and the disputed territory of the Saar all came under the administration of League personnel. Equally, the Special Departments of the League seemed to be making progress. The Health Department worked on the control of epidemics in Eastern Europe; the Refugees Department, headed by the Norwegian explorer Fridtjof Nansen, gave considerable assistance to Austrian refugees in Vienna and to Greeks in Thrace and Asia Minor. Financial help was provided for the Austrian government. The ILO won action on child labour in Persia, where it had long been the practice to employ very young children in making carpets.

The League was also to organize the promised
great powers. However, little was actually done by
1926, although there were some other steps towards di
chief of these were taken at the Washington Conference, v
12 November 1921 until 6 February 1922. It was convened i.
States and had two main purposes—to consider naval armam.
examine peace in the Far East. A series of agreements resulte.
By the 'Four-Power Pacific Treaty', the USA, Britain, France and pan
mutually guaranteed each other's rights in the Pacific islands and promised to consult with each other if these rights were in any way threatened.
Secondly, by the Shantung treaty Japan returned Kiaochow to China.
Thirdly, two Nine-Power treaties, signed by the previous four plus
Holland, Belgium, Italy, China and Portugal, guaranteed China's territorial integrity and administrative independence. They also repeated
the 'Open Door' principle, by which all powers had equal rights of access
to China. Fourthly, a Naval armaments treaty was signed. By it, the
signatories agreed not to build any warships over 10 000 tons with guns
over 8'' over the next ten years. It also established a 'naval ratio' by
which the USA and Britain were allowed 525 000 tons of capital shipping
to Japan's 315 000 and France's and Italy's 175 000 tons. These were the
first tentative steps towards disarmament.

Despite the optimism surrounding the foundation of the League and
the first armaments treaty, there were several disquieting signs in the
early 1920s. These particularly surrounded the political activities of the
League of Nations. For example, the League Commissioners in the Saar,
headed by a Frenchman, angered the German population in the area by
calling in French troops to quell a strike in 1923 and by issuing a decree
which included penalties for criticizing the Commissioners or the peace
treaties. Similarly, the settlements in Vilna and Upper Silesia were
adequate but left a number of unresolved problems. Most disturbing of
all was the Corfu incident of 1923 *(see page 274)*. Mussolini had clearly
acted forcefully before the true criminals were known and had threatened to withdraw from the League when Greece appealed to it, and
had still come out as the winner in the dispute. If such an important
member of the League as Italy could treat it with such disdain, what
were the prospects for the League in a really important case?

Equally, some of the flaws of the League were already becoming
apparent. Three major powers were not members. The USA had opted
out, and both Germany and Russia had been barred from membership
on the insistence of Clemenceau and Wilson. Yet the very essence of the
League was the collective action of its members; such action was inevitably hampered by the absence of such powerful countries. Not only
might their forces be needed in a crisis, but also their actions were less
controllable as long as they were outside the League. Since the United
States still played an important role in European affairs, especially with
regard to German reparations, League membership seemed to some
extent irrelevant. Moreover, the absence of these three great powers left

...hip of the League to Britain, France and Italy. These three ...een the victor powers and the creators of the Versailles settlement. ...ncreasingly, as in the Saar, the League was seen simply as their method of enforcing that settlement, rather than providing a neutral body that would judge impartially.

Nevertheless, the years of 1919–24 did see genuine achievements and genuine progress. Although there were still areas of disagreement over borders, there was none of the confusion that had reigned, especially in Eastern Europe, immediately after the war. There were still tremendous economic problems, but at least, through the ministrations of the League and the actions of the USA, there was less of the earlier chaos and starvation. Despite its weaknesses and problems, the League seemed to have made genuine progress in several areas and fields. Finally, the Washington Conference, despite Japan's resentment of its outcome, gave some promise of future disarmament.

3. 1925–30: 'Fulfilment'

These years have been described as the 'era of fulfilment' because of Germany's new attitude to the terms of the treaty of Versailles *(see page 296)*. Instead of working consistently for their revision, the German governments now agreed to fulfil their terms. In a more general way, too, the second half of the 1920s fulfilled the hoped and promise of the first half in bringing a period of peace and disarmament. The Geneva Protocol, the Kellogg–Briand Pact and the Litvinov Protocol all provided, in a variety of forms, the promise of peace and an end to war as the means for solving disputes. The Locarno treaties of 1925 reinforced the Versailles settlement and seemed to secure peace between the two most likely enemies in Europe, France and Germany. Germany's admission to the League of Nations in 1926 brought her back into the international community and into the disarmament talks. By the signed promises to renounce war, by the Locarno treaties and by the disarmament talks, a new era of peace could be hailed. Yet in each of these there was a weakness that would prove to be a fatal flaw.

In October 1924 Ramsay MacDonald, the British Prime Minister, brought forward the 'Geneva Protocol' and the League of Nations recommended its members to sign it. It attempted to overcome two of the League's weaknesses—the absence of the great powers and the difficulty of deciding which country was the aggressor in a dispute. The document was drafted by the Czech, Eduard Benes, and the Greek, Nicholas Politis. Those who signed it agreed that they would submit any disputes to arbitration and accepted that the 'aggressor' was the country which refused to go to arbitration. Since it also involved the signatories in mutually enforcing its provisions, a number of nations feared that it might involve them in distant disputes that were nothing to do with them. When the new Conservative government in Britain rejected the protocol in March 1925 it was dropped, although the idea of providing a form of reinforcement to the League Covenant remained.

The Locarno Conference of October 1925, and the four treaties that resulted from it on 1 December were regarded by Britain and France as the conclusion of the West European security system. Germany, France and Belgium signed treaties of mutual guarantees of the Franco-German and Belgo-German frontiers. These guarantees were in turn guaranteed by Britain and Italy *(see page 297)*. Significantly, they agreed to intervene if *either* side broke the treaties; Germany was no longer treated differently from the other powers. Also at Locarno, Germany signed arbitration treaties with each of France, Belgium, Czechoslovakia and Poland. By these, the separate powers promised to submit future frontier disputes and claims for land to arbitration. However, Germany would not agree to mutual frontier guarantees with Czechoslovakia and Poland. Instead, their boundaries were secured by treaties of mutual assistance with France. By these, Poland and Czechoslovakia promised France assistance if she was attacked by Germany, and France promised them aid if either was attacked by Germany. Herein lay the fatal flaws of Locarno—while Germany's *Western* borders were agreed and re-signed, her eastern borders were left less secure since they were not the subject of a revised agreement.

Nonetheless, Germany's relations with the rest of Europe did seem to be improving *(see pages 297–8)*. Under the guidance of Stresemann, she seemed to be following a more pacific policy. In the spring of 1925, French troops left the Ruhr and fresh discussions were held with the French government on the future of the Rhineland. Following the Locarno settlements, Germany's membership of the League was proposed in March 1926. However, both Spain and Brazil opposed her membership, since their places on the Council were in jeopardy. This opposition was overcome during the summer and on 8 September Germany was admitted to the League and given a permanent place on the Council, introducing (said Stresemann) 'a new era of co-operation among nations, a time of real peace'. Shortly afterwards, on 31 January 1927, the inter-allied Commission of Military Control in Germany came to an end. Thereafter, any problems relating to German armaments were to be referred to the League.

Germany's new role seemed to be further reinforced when, in February 1929, she became a signatory of the Kellogg–Briand Pact. This was the brainchild of the American Secretary of State, Frank Kellogg, and his French counterpart, Foreign Minister, Aristide Briand. It was first signed in Paris (and is therefore sometimes known as the Pact of Paris) on 27 August 1928. The signatories renounced the use of aggressive war as a means of solving disputes. In all, over sixty nations were to sign it, and the ninth Assembly of the League (September 1928) endorsed it by approving a general motion for conciliation and arbitration. In Eastern Europe, the Pact was mirrored by the Litvinov Protocol of February 1929. This was signed in Moscow by Russia, Poland, Roumania, Estonia and Latvia, and, like the Kellogg–Briand Pact, renounced the use of war for the settlement of disputes. These pacts contained obvious weaknesses since there were no provisions for any kind of sanctions against those who broke them, and no definition of 'aggressive war'.

A further contribution to the continuing peace was made by the 1929 Young Plan for reparations. The thinking behind the plan was to reduce the continuous pressure on Germany to pay a large amount each year. In future, all settlements were to be made to a new 'Bank for International Settlements' at Basle, at which all the separate nations in receipt of reparations were represented. Germany was to continue annual payments until 1988, with the annual sum being increased gradually for the first thirty-six years. Only 660 million marks *had* to be paid each year and the remainder of the payment could be postponed for up to two years; this would, hopefully, enable Germany to overcome any temporary economic problems. The planned annual sum of 1707 million marks was less than Germany had been paying under the Dawes Plan. Hopefully, reparations would no longer be a major issue, since France would still receive the money she demanded but Germany would not be put under continuous pressure. The Plan was put forward on 7 June and subsequently discussed at an international conference at the Hague during August, after which it was accepted by both sides. As a result of German acceptance of the scheme, the Allies agreed to evacuate the Rhineland by June 1930.

Throughout the second half of the 1920s disarmament talks were undertaken under the auspices of the League of Nations. In May 1926 the first meeting of the Preparatory Commission for the Disarmament Conference was held. All the major powers apart from the Soviet Union were represented on this Commission, which met frequently over the next few years. The Soviet Union joined the talks in 1927, and in November 1927 their Foreign Minister, Maxim Litvinov, proposed that all powers should disarm immediately and completely—a proposal that was rejected by the other powers as an attempt to open the way for communist expansion. The final meeting of the Preparatory Commission was held in November 1930. It approved, by a majority vote which was opposed by both Russia and Germany, a convention to be discussed at a full disarmament Conference in February 1932. A part of the convention stated that all military claims and rights guaranteed by previous treaties should stand. In other words, the restrictions on German armaments imposed by the treaty of Versailles would remain in force, whatever was decided about the military strength of the other powers. Herein lay the flaw in the disarmament plans—Germany was still to be treated differently.

As well as the League's disarmament talks, there were also conferences on naval strength. In 1927 a meeting between Britain, Japan and the United States at Geneva failed to reach further agreement on their relative strength of smaller naval vessels and submarines. However, at the London conference of 1930 a treaty limiting the size and use of submarines was signed by France, Italy, Britain, Japan and the United

States. The latter three also agreed to scrap some warships by 1933 and settled their previous dispute on tonnages of smaller ships, although a let-out clause allowed any one of them to build up their forces beyond the agreed limits if they felt it necessary.

During this period considerable progress had been made. Russia and Germany had, to varying degrees, returned to the international fraternity. The Franco-German border settlement had been reinforced. Numerous nations had signed pledges not to fight each other. A disarmament conference had, against odds, been planned for 1932. Despite these very real achievements, underlying problems remained. All the pacts and protocols had failed to overcome the original problem of the League Covenant: its failure to define an aggressor nation or devise satisfactory means to deal with such an aggressor. France's attitude to disarmament in general, and to Germany's military strength in particular, loomed large over any future conference. Above all alse, a question mark hung menacingly over Germany's eastern borders.

4. 1930–36: Weaknesses in the League System

(a) Background: the international economic crisis

The collapse of the world economy following the Wall Street Crash threw the plans of the 1920s into disarray. Each country was threatened with disaster if its factories could not sell their goods. They could not be sold overseas since other countries could not afford to buy them nor to risk threatening their own products by supporting others. Consequently, every country imposed high duties on imports in an effort to protect their own industries. At the same time, they were unable to repay their debts to each other at a time when they needed as much capital as possible to help their own failing economies.

There were some international efforts to solve these common problems, particularly insofar as they affected debts between different countries. In 1931, President Hoover of the USA (the country most affected by the inability of others to pay) proposed a one-year moratorium on all payments between countries. This was to include not only the inter-allied debts, but also the reparations. This proposal, made in June, followed the collapse of the Austrian 'Creditanstalt' and of the Austrian economy. The French government initially opposed the moratorium but in July accepted it.

In June of the following year (1932), representatives of the leading nations met at Lausanne in an effort to reach agreement on reparations. The Western powers (Britain, France, Italy, Belgium and Japan) agreed to accept German reparation repayments in the form of government bonds to be deposited with the Bank for International Settlements and sold later. However, this settlement was dependent on America's acceptance of continued postponement of debts to her. In December 1932 the American Congress refused to accept this, so the Lausanne agreement lapsed and, in theory, Germany returned to repayments under the Young Plan. In fact, the Nazi government denounced that Plan—and reparations—and no more was paid. Equally, America barely gained from her intransigence, since less than $3000 million out of a total debt of over $10 000 million was ever repaid. A further effort at international agreement at the London Conference of June 1933 tried to settle the currency instability but failed.

Thereafter, the governments of Europe were faced less by the economic crisis and more by the new attitudes that had followed in its wake. In many European countries—most obviously Germany—there were new regimes determined to solve not only the economic problems but also international issues in a radical fashion. Most of the 1930s were occupied by these radical solutions and the efforts of the moderates to deal with them.

(b) The failure of the League of Nations

(i) The failure of collective security
The League of Nations was faced by aggressive action by a major power for the first time in 1931. In late September, Japanese forces occupied the important Manchurian towns of Mukden, Changchun and Kirin on the pretext that their commerce was threatened by explosions on railway lines. By February 1932 they had taken control of South Manchuria. Between January and March some 70 000 Japanese troops were landed at Shanghai and forced the Chinese to retreat and to end their boycott on Japanese goods. Manchuria was renamed 'Manchukuo' and Changchun became 'Hsiu-ching' (New Capital). Henry Pu-Yi, who had been forced off the Chinese throne in 1912, was reinstated as Emperor, but ruled entirely through Japanese officials. This was exactly what the League had been intended to prevent. One member country had attacked another member country and used its superior military strength to get its way. The actions that it, and its supporters, took were therefore critical.

On 8 December 1931 the League set up a Commission of Inquiry, on the suggestion of Japan. The Commission, headed by the Englishman, Lord Lytton, began its enquiries while, for their part, America took some action: on 7 January 1932 American Secretary of State, Henry Stimson, informed the signatories of the 1922 agreement *(see page 367)* that his country would not recognize any territorial claims made by armed forces, as it would contravene the Pact of Paris. Lytton's Commission reported on 2 October 1932. It stated that Japanese military action had not been undertaken for purposes of self-defence, nor had the establishment of Manchukuo been in response to a local desire for independence. The Commission recommended the establishment of an autonomous Chinese administration with international advisers and police. It also stated that Japan's economic interests in the area should be recognized. On 24 February 1933 the League officially accepted the Commission's report and called for its implementation. However, the Japanese rejected the report and, on 27 May, withdrew from the League. This was, in a sense, the moment of truth for the League: how would it deal with a member who rejected its decision? In adopting the Lytton report, the League had also followed Stimson's plan to refuse to recognize Japan's occupation, but when Japan ignored this, no further action was taken. During the 1930s, more and more Japanese troops were moved into Manchuria in an effort to pacify the area and it was only during World War II that any military action was taken against the Japanese, by which time the League had effectively ceased to exist.

With hindsight, it is easy to condemn the weakness of the League in dealing with Japan. However, the actions of the member countries were, at the time, quite understandable. With its high ideals, the League could not act immediately the invasion took place—the facts of the case had to be investigated and blame apportioned before any action could, morally, be taken. Yet by the time the Lytton report had been written and presented to the Assembly, it was far too late to take any action. Not only were Japanese troops relatively secure by this time, making any military action more difficult, but also the Western powers would have found it hard to justify, especially to their electorates, the need to send their armies thousands of miles to 'punish' the Japanese for what they had done almost two years earlier. Distance itself was an additional handicap. Now, we can see the links between what happened in Manchuria in 1931–3 and what was to happen in Europe in 1939, but at the time the notion that 'if collective security is not used effectively in Manchuria there may be a European war in ten years time', would have seemed faintly ludicrous. Moreover, the only two powers near enough and strong enough to take effective action—the USA and the USSR—were not members of the League.

There are a number of parallels between the Manchurian affair and the second major test of collective security through the League, the Italian invasion of Ethiopia in 1935. In each case, a leading League member was in fact the aggressor. In each, the country that it attacked was relatively weak and could only have resisted with considerable military assistance from League powers. Yet in each the sympathies of the members were, broadly, more likely to lie with the aggressor. In the case of Manchuria, few Westerners had much sympathy for China, which had, only thirty years before, openly opposed them. In the case of Ethiopia, both Britain and France were far more concerned to preserve Italy's friendship than to defend an African country. After all, they had spent much of the nineteenth century conquering parts of Africa for themselves. Finally, in each case the distance of the dispute made it very difficult for Europeans to see any necessity for them to intervene. Tragically, each of these coincidences and accidents made it all the easier for a collective security system to fail.

Perhaps learning from their experiences in Manchuria, the League acted more quickly when Italian forces invaded Ethiopia in 1935 (*see page 277*). During the summer, the League had investigated both Italian and

Ethiopian claims following their clash at Ual-Ual in December 1934 and were aware of Italy's plans by the autumn of 1935. Consequently, on the day that Italian troops invaded—3 October—the League Council met and declared that Italy had broken Article 12 of the Covenant by which member countries agreed not to 'resort to war within three months' of a dispute being referred for arbitration. The Italian–Ethiopian quarrel had technically been referred to arbitration by the Council in September. On 7 October Italy was declared aggressor and on 18 November representatives of fifty-one member states voted to apply sanctions to Italy. By this, they imposed a prohibition on the import of Italian goods and an embargo on arms sales and financial assistance to Italy. Although certain goods could still be sold to Italy, including steel and oil (partly because of the threats that Mussolini made if these were barred), this was the harshest action that the League had ever taken against an aggressor.

By the end of the year, even firmer action was threatened. British naval forces were prepared in Alexandria and France, Yugoslavia, Greece and Turkey all agreed to support British action against Italy. However, the prevailing mood in Britain was that the League should act as a whole, not through a single member state, and that sanctions were the most effective form of combined action. Again, a peaceful formula was sought and, apparently, found in the Hoare–Laval Pact *(see page 278)* which proposed that most of North and South Ethiopia should be given to Italy. This, and the furore that surrounded its exposure, only served to weaken the League's position since it revealed that the two leading members of the League—Britain and France—were prepared to give way to Italy. In early 1936 the League debated further action, including the imposition of oil sanctions and the closure of the Suez canal. Since it was likely that such moves would result in war with Italy, no agreement could be reached and nothing further was done. By March 1936 the European powers were far more concerned by Hitler's troops in the Rhineland, and the Italians were left to complete their conquest of Ethiopia, which was finished by May. Thereafter, the League's claim to act as the defender of small nations against aggression sounded hollower than ever. It had been foiled by its own morality—the need to make sure that it was acting fairly and with the support of all its members had delayed it and weakened it to the point of ineptitude.

(ii) Disarmament

In addition to its wider failings in international conflicts, the League also failed in its hope to achieve widespread disarmament. Yet again, coincidence played its part in this. During the 1920s when countries were at least prepared to make concessions, the League had succeeded, albeit painfully, in setting up a Disarmament Conference. Its planned first meeting was for February 1932, by which time the effects of the economic crisis had put countries more on the defensive than ever.

At this first meeting, which opened at Geneva on 2 February 1932, sixty nations were represented, including the USA, USSR and Germany. While the latter demanded equality of armaments, the French refused to consider any reduction in their armaments until their security was assured. In an effort to break the deadlock, President Hoover of the USA proposed that all national forces should be divided into 'police' and 'defence' components and that only the latter should be reduced—by one third. This proposal too was rejected and the meeting broke up inconclusively in July.

The second meeting of the Disarmament Conference, on 2 February 1933, assembled with greater optimism. In December 1932 the USA had persuaded the four leading European powers—Britain, France, Italy and Germany—to sign an agreement by which they promised 'not in any circumstances to attempt to resolve any present or future differences between them by resort to force'. At the new conference, a French proposal for very limited disarmament was rejected. For Britain, Ramsay MacDonald proposed that all European armies should be reduced by 500 000 men and that France and Germany should be allowed armies of equal strength. The United States supported these plans, but the new German government objected to her 'storm-troops' being included. In June the conference was adjourned to meet again in October. In the meantime, Britain, France, Italy and the USA agreed to a four-year freeze on armaments, at the end of which Germany would be allowed equality of armaments. Germany, however, insisted on being allowed more arms immediately and in October announced that she was withdrawing from the Disarmament Conference and from the League itself. The Conference did reconvene, between 29 May and 11 June 1934, but no decisions were reached. With Germany's departure, France's determination to maintain her forces was more intransigent than ever. Germany's formal denunciation of the Treaty of Versailles' restrictions on her armaments in March 1935, followed by the re-introduction of conscription *(see page 313)*, marked the end of any hope of disarmament. Significantly, Hitler's pretext for the expansion of her army was the failure of the other powers to disarm, as the treaties of 1919 had planned, and the growth of the French and Soviet armies.

(iii) The effects of the League's failure

As the weakness of the security system of the 1920s became apparent, so countries reverted to agreements and alliances of the pre-1914 type in an effort to insure that they at least would be secure. In February 1933 the 'Little Entente' was reorganized and formed a permanent council. Also in 1933 Mussolini proposed a 'Four-Power Pact' of Italy, Germany France and Britain to replace the cumbersome and slow League, but the scheme came to little as the four could only rarely reach agreement. In February 1934 the Balkan Pact was signed by Greece, Roumania and Turkey. Although it was weakened by Bulgaria's absence, it did represent a genuine effort by the Balkan powers to protect themselves against the great powers without recourse to the League of Nations. The entry of

Russia into European affairs in 1934 reflected her growing fear of Germany *(see page 353)*. In September 1934 she joined the League of Nations, and reinforced this by a five-year alliance with France, signed on 2 May 1935, by which each promised help in the event of an unprovoked attack. Until 1936, Italy also sought protection against Germany: in April 1935 Mussolini met with British and French representatives at Stresa, forming the so-called 'Stresa Front' against Germany and in March 1936 joined them, and Belgium, in denouncing Germany's re-occupation of the Rhineland. Thereafter, though, despite the efforts of Britain and France to keep her with them, Italy moved increasingly towards Germany. 1936 was in many respects the key year for international relations. It saw the discrediting of the League in the aftermath of the Ethiopian affair and the joining together of Germany and Italy in the Axis Pact of October, so that Europe was yet again aligned in two great power alliances. The 'concert of power' had yet again been replaced by a 'balance of power'.

5. The Spanish Civil War 1936–9

(a) Background: Spain 1923–31

Spain had remained neutral during World War I but nevertheless suffered many of the problems of the combatants. King Alfonso XIII (1902–31) was faced by considerable left-wing opposition, both from the Trade Unions, grouped together in the CNT ('Confederación Nacional del Trabajo'), and the Socialist party, the UGT ('Unión General de Trabajadores'). In the North-east, there was a considerable movement for home rule in Catalonia, the main industrial area of the country that had been boosted by additional trade during the Great War. Barcelona, the main city of Catalonia, was the centre not only of the campaign for autonomy but also of left-wing opposition. This had reached its peak in 1909, during the 'Semana Tragica' ('Week of Tragedy'), when more than twenty churches and thirty convents had been destroyed in a week of class warfare. Economically, Spain was one of the poorest countries in Europe. Like Italy, it was divided between the industrial North-east and the rest of the country which was predominantly agricultural. In these farming areas, there were vast differences between the small peasant holdings and the enormous estates known as 'latifundia'. On these, there were many landless labourers, known as 'braceros', over two million of whom sought seasonal work and often earned less than £30 a year. In the field of foreign affairs, Spain had suffered a setback in 1898 when she lost her Pacific colonies in the war with America. Even worse, in 1921 a Spanish army of 20 000 were defeated at the Battle of Anual in Spanish Morocco by an army of Riffians led by Abd-el-Krim. Twelve thousand Spanish soldiers died, and such was the outrage in Spain that a Parliamentary committee was set up to investigate the defeat, although its findings were not published. All in all, Alfonso's government was faced by widespread opposition and problems.

In an effort to provide firm government to overcome these, General Miguel Primo de Rivera seized power in September 1923. With the King's approval, he used troops to take control of Barcelona and then, for a time, introduced martial law. The Cortes (Parliament) was dissolved, the press censored and the jury system suspended. This lasted until December 1925 when the dictatorship was formally ended, but in effect Primo remained in power as he was appointed Prime Minister over a cabinet of generals. His regime was able to secure peace in North Africa, as an agreement with France in 1925 brought French assistance in the battle against Abd-el-Krim, whose forces were defeated by 1927. Primo was also able to bring some improvements in industrial relations by establishing compulsory arbitration boards for the settlement of wage disputes. However, there was considerable opposition to his dictatorial rule. In 1929 some army officers at Ciudad Real revolted, while a number of universities were closed down in an effort to end the opposition of their staff and students. In January 1930 Primo, now a sick man, resigned and died in March, having failed to bring any lasting changes.

He was succeeded as Prime Minister by General Berenguer. He granted an amnesty to political prisoners, dissolved the assembly set up by Primo and promised elections. However, this did little to stem the tide of opposition, now chiefly aimed at the King himself. There was considerable support for a republic to be set up, and this became more vocal after the ending of censorship in September 1930. In response to the widespread criticism, King Alfonso announced that elections would be held in March 1931.

In fact, the municipal elections were not held until April. They resulted in a landslide victory for the Republicans, led by Alcalá Zamora. The King left the country, although he said he would not abdicate until public opinion was clear. Zamora set up a provisional government and on 28 June elections were held for representatives for a Constituent Assembly to draw up a new constitution. These too gave a huge majority to the Republicans and their allies and the monarchy was doomed. In November, the Constituent Assembly, through a special Committee, found Alfonso guilty of high treason, confiscated his property and forbade his return.

Through the new constitution of December 1931, Spain was transformed from a monarchy, supported by Church and army, into a republic. The Upper House was abolished and the single chamber Cortes was to be elected by universal suffrage every four years. The head of State, the President, was to be chosen every six years by an electoral college that consisted of the Cortes and an equal number of electors chosen directly by the electorate. Army officers and clergy were barred from the Presidency. Most radically, there was to be religious freedom, and Church and State were separated. There was to be no compulsory religious education, and the property of the church was nationalized. The Jesuits were dissolved and their property seized. Equally dramatically, the government was given the power to take over large estates and to nationalize public service industries. Spain was to become a modern socialist state.

(b) Republican Spain 1931–6

The next five years witnessed a variety of reactions to this new structure and constitution. Zamora had resigned as Provisional President in October as a protest against the legislation reducing the Church's influence, but in December he was re-elected President. His Prime Minister was Manuel Azaña, who was immediately faced by opposition from both left and right. In August 1932 General Sanjurjo took over Seville in the hope of arousing conservative opposition to the government, but was forced out by troops loyal to the Republic. In January 1933 there was an anarchist uprising near Barcelona, followed by widespread strikes organized by the extreme left. Azaña used troops to put down this movement, which inevitably lost him support. Azaña had also been forced to give way to the Catalans, whose leaders had won support for their home rule plans in a plebiscite in August 1931. As a result, Catalonia was given its own flag, President and parliament—a move that inevitably led to similar demands for autonomy from other national groups, such as the Basques. By mid-1933 Azaña had enacted a series of harsh measures in an effort to end the opposition to his government and once again the press was censored, the police enlarged and 9000 CNT members imprisoned.

Azaña himself resigned in September 1933 and his supporters were defeated in the first regular parliamentary elections, held in November 1933. Although in total the left-wing parties won more votes, they won only some 20% of the seats in the Cortes to the right's 44%. There followed a series of weak coalition governments that were as harassed as Azaña's had been. In December 1933 an anarchist-backed uprising in Barcelona was only put down after ten days of fighting. Elections in Catalonia in January 1934 were won by the left and Catalonia remained the centre of left-wing opposition to the central government. In April there was a further strike in Barcelona and in October, following the formation of Lerroux's new government *(see below)*, a general strike was called. On 6 October President Companys of Catalonia declared Catalonia independent, as a result of which troops were sent to the region and Catalonia's autonomy suspended. Simultaneously, the unions in the Asturias, where a communist state had been declared, were attacked by troops. Three thousand of the protesters died and another 70 000 were wounded in a campaign of bloody suppression, led by Spanish troops normally stationed in North Africa.

Lerroux's government that was responsible for this campaign of oppression was a coalition between the monarchists and the new 'Popular Action Party' ('Accíon Popular'). This party was predominantly Catholic and was opposed to the anti-clerical laws passed in December 1931 and May 1933 (when an Associations Law had abolished church schools and nationalized church property). It was led by Gil Robles and, apart from its close links with the church, incorporated many features of the regimes of Italy and Germany, such as a youth movement and great stress on the leadership qualities of Robles. In March 1935 he and his two supporters in the Cabinet left the government in protest at the pardoning of nineteen of the Asturian miners' leaders who had been sentenced to execution. His enthusiasm for harshness against protesters had in fact slightly back-fired, as the viciousness against the Asturian miners had resulted in more public sympathy for the left. After Robles' departure, Lerroux's cabinet survived until September 1935, when it was again followed by a series of coalitions.

The Cortes elections of February 1936 inevitably brought a showdown between left and right. On the one side were those who wanted a more Liberal policy towards the workers, a continuation of anti-clericalism and the restoration of Catalonia's autonomy. These were generally supporters of the Republicans, Socialists, Syndicalists and Communists, who formed an electoral alliance known as the 'Popular Front'. Ranged against them were, broadly, the parties of the right—Conservative, Republican, Monarchists and 'Popular Action', who favoured harshness against strikers, the reintegration of Catalonia and the restoration of the Church's pre-eminence in Spanish society. More than ever before, the split between left and right was clear. The promise of an amnesty for strikers and protesters was enough to win the Popular Front a decisive victory. Azaña formed a new government and began by declaring an amnesty for strikers and plans for the restoration of Catalan autonomy. In April, President Zamora was removed from office on a vote of the Cortes, and in May Azaña was elected President.

By this time, there was considerable chaos throughout the country. The re-introduction of the anti-clerical laws brought widespread oppos-ition from the right. The government's promise of land reform was pre-empted by many peasants, who simply seized land from their landlords, bringing even further hostility from the right. On the other hand, left-wingers felt that social reform was taking too long and there were still many strikes. Azaña wanted to form a temporary dictatorship to restore order but before anything was done events overtook him. On 17 July an army revolt, led by officers, at Melilla in Spanish Morocco was supported by garrisons at Cadiz, Seville and other leading towns.

(c) The outbreak of the war

In the first instance, the rebelling army chiefs had no clear programme beyond the overthrow of the Popular Front government and the restor-ation of law and order. The army was traditionally more involved in politics in Spain than in other European countries, and had, like the Church, been especially hard hit by the reforms of the Republican government. The number of officers had been reduced by more than half and, significantly, one of the leaders of the revolt, General Mola, had been sacked as chief-of-staff in March 1936. Another leader, General Sanjurjo, had led an uprising in 1932 but he died in an aeroplane crash at the very start of the war. The third leader, General Francisco Franco, had also suffered at the hands of the Republican government, being dismissed as governor of the Canary Isles in March 1936.

The army revolt rapidly developed into civil war when the government kept control of the garrisons of Madrid and Barcelona and endeavoured to regain control of the rebellious areas. Those loyal to the government soon became known as 'Republicans' while supporters of the rebels were called 'Nationalists'. The divisions between them were, or at least seemed to be, even clearer than those that had divided the electorate in the Cortes elections in February. To the Nationalists, the Republican regime had been too influenced by the Communists, had destroyed the economy, had failed to keep order and had led an attack on the traditional pillars of Spanish society, the monarchy, the Church and the army. For their part, the Republicans were supported by Communists, Socialists and others who approved of the attacks on those traditional bastions. These apparently clear divisions were to be a significant factor in the widespread interest in the war overseas.

(d) The course of the war

The chief events of the war are summarized in the date chart opposite and on Map 35.

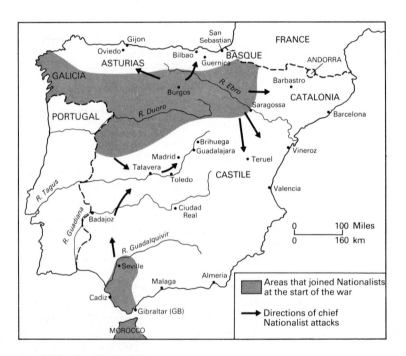

Map 35 The Spanish Civil War

1936	17 July	Army revolts in Melilla, Cadiz, Seville, Saragossa, Burgos, Toledo and Oviedo.
	30 July	Rebel generals establish 'Junta of National Defence' at Burgos.
	15 August	Nationalists capture Badejoz and advance up the Tagus valley through Talavera and Toledo.
	4 September	Popular Front government, led by Largo Caballero, formed in Madrid with support of left-wing parties and Basque and Catalan nationalists.
	12 September	Nationalists capture San Sebastian.
	1 October	Nationalists appoint General Franco as 'Head of Spanish State'.
	6 November	Nationalists begin the siege of Madrid and the government moves to Valencia. Heavy siege of the capital, chiefly from the air but also including fighting in the outskirts, fails to capture it.
	18 November	Germany and Italy recognize Franco's government although joining Britain and France in the policy of non-intervention.
1937	8 February	Nationalists capture Malaga but fail to take the road that links Valencia and Madrid.
	18 March	Republicans defeat Italian forces fighting for the Nationalists at Brihuega.
	26 April	Town of Guernica bombed.
	17 May	Caballero replaced as Prime Minister by Juan Negrin of the Socialist party.
	18 June	Nationalists capture Bilbao after weeks of fighting and heavy air attacks.
	21 October	Nationalist forces take Gijon, thereby conquering all the Asturias and bringing North-west Spain under Franco's control.
	28 October	Republican government moves from Valencia to Barcelona.
	28 November	Franco announces his intention to blockade the entire Spanish coast from his base on Majorca.
	5 December	Beginning of Republican counter-attack around Teruel, which was captured on 19 December.
1938	15 February	Nationalists recapture Teruel and begin an attack towards the sea.
	15 April	Nationalists capture Vineroz on the coast and thus split Republican areas in Catalonia from those in Castile.
	23 December	Beginning of Nationalist attack into Catalonia, forcing Republicans back towards Barcelona.
1939	26 January	Nationalists capture Barcelona and then take all of Catalonia, forcing 200 000 Republicans into France.

27 February	Britain and France recognize Franco's government.
28 February	President Azaña resigns
6 March –28 March	The Republican's army in Madrid revolts and forces Prime Minister Negrin out of office. A 'National Defence Council' led by General Miaja formed, its aim being to win 'peace with honour'. The Communists oppose this, which leads to a further civil war in Madrid itself before Miaja defeats the Communists and tries to negotiate with Franco. Franco refuses to offer terms and Miaja surrenders unconditionally. On 28 March Madrid and Valencia surrender to the Nationalists, and Miaja and his colleagues flee.
1 April	USA recognizes Franco's regime.

(e) The nature of the war and the reasons for Franco's victory

The most outstanding feature of the war was its savagery and brutality, for which each side was responsible. The Church suffered appalling losses at the hands of the Republicans: more than 6000 priests, nuns and monks were killed, while in the Barbastro region more than 80% of clergy died. The most notable single incident was the bombing of Guernica. On 26 April 1937, this small town near Bilbao was bombed by Heinkels and Junkers for three hours in the late afternoon. The number of dead has been variously estimated at 100 to 1600. Equally horrific was the destruction of property in the town; only about one house in ten was left undamaged. Because of the involvement of German planes, the raid was attributed to the Nationalists, although more recently evidence has been produced to suggest that it could have been a Republican effort to win support. Throughout the war, few prisoners were kept, and little mercy shown to local populations caught up in the war. Horrific propaganda photographs, showing wounded and dead children in particular, were produced by both sides for foreign consumption. Many authors, most notably George Orwell and Ernest Hemingway, have described the circumstances and horrors of the war. The Nationalists estimated that a million people died during the war, though Thomas has suggested 500 000 as a more accurate figure, of whom about 100 000 can be attributed to disease and malnutrition rather than violent death.

Ultimately, Franco and the Nationalists won because of their greater unity and superior supplies. All right-wing groups supported his campaign for a return to stability. The Church was an especially powerful ally as it was able to use its influence throughout the country. In contrast, the Republicans' supporters were divided into a number of disparate groups. Even before the outbreak of war, Anarchists and Communists had little time for each other, nor for Socialists or Republicans. In some ways, they had provided as much opposition to the Republican government as the right. Paradoxically, it was the right who were united in a cause and the left that was left defending an inept status quo.

Franco's forces received far more aid from Germany and Italy than the Republicans got from either Russia or international groups. Not only did Hitler and Mussolini send men and military equipment to the Nationalists' assistance, but also supplies of food and raw materials. Nor was it only these powers that helped Franco; the American Texas Oil Company, for example, gambled on a Nationalist victory and was prepared to supply Franco in the hope of winning profitable contracts later.

Moreover, Franco was inevitably at an advantage in what was pre-dominently a conventional war. His colleagues and officers were far more experienced in matters of tactics and supply than the 'People's Army' which, although it was well organized, lacked military expertise. The 'International Brigade', made up of Republican sympathizers from a number of European countries, exemplified the innocent enthusiasm of the loyalists, although Russian technicians and advisers did something to redress the balance. It was the International Brigade who decisively defeated Italian Nationalist forces near Guadalajara in March 1937. Apart from this, though, the Republicans were at an obvious disadvantage and their successes, such as the recapture of Teruel in December 1937, were short-lived.

6. The Spanish Civil War and its European Context

(a) European powers and the war

On the outbreak of war, Azaña appealed to the French Popular Front government of Leon Blum for arms and assistance against rebels. However, involvement in the Spanish war would have proved political dynamite in France *(see page 235)* in 1936. It could certainly only be undertaken if victory was assured, and this could only be if Britain was prepared to intervene. If this happened, then it seemed likely that Germany and Italy would come in on Franco's side. In turn, this increased the likelihood of the war spreading to other parts of Europe. Not only did both France and Britain want to avoid this at all costs, but also they hoped to keep Mussolini away from Hitler *(see page 242)*. To have openly supported the Republicans would have risked far too much for Britain and France.

Consequently, the British and French governments announced their policy of non-intervention, and endeavoured to win support for this policy from other countries. In all, twenty-seven nations were represented on the 'Non-Intervention Committee' that sat in London. Although participant countries agreed to impose a ban on supplies to the warring factions, they were not opposed to individual citizens of their countries going to fight as volunteers. Although the committee attempted to introduce a scheme to supervise their policy, it failed to prevent supplies reaching both Nationalists and Republicans from outside supporters.

Although they were members of the Non-Intervention Committee, Germany and Italy both gave aid to Franco, at first secretly but later openly. As far as the Nazi government of Germany was concerned, involvement was a sound investment—Hitler hoped to win supplies of Spanish minerals for his factories after Franco had won. In addition, Goering, as Luftwaffe chief, saw the possibility of using the war as a testing ground for his men and equipment. Consequently, a special squadron, known as the 'Condor Legion', was sent to Spain and proved a considerable asset to the Nationalists. It was used not only in bombing raids but also to link the nothern and southern armies of the Nationalists by air in the early part of the war *(see Map 35)*.

Italy's involvement, although secret at first *(see page 279)*, was ultimately far more extensive. Between 50 000 and 75 000 Italian troops were sent to fight with Franco, compared to about 10 000 Germans. In March 1937 they suffered a considerable setback when they were defeated at Brihuega, especially as the victorious Republican forces included other Italians. This in fact encouraged Mussolini to increase his involvement in an effort to win back lost prestige, although, as Thomas has written: 'Mussolini got no real advantage from the war, but it satisfied his ego to see Italy waving a big stick in the world again.'

During 1937 there was considerable European tension over Mediterranean shipping as a result of Germany and Italy's involvement in the war. A German vessel, the 'Deutschland', believed to be carrying supplies for the Nationalists, was attacked by Republican planes. In retaliation, four German ships bombarded Almeria and Germany, joined by Italy, demanded that the non-interventionist powers should investigate the attack on the 'Deutschland'. Germany and Italy then refused to continue manning (or to recognize) the 'neutrality patrol' that the Non-Intervention Committee had organized off the Spanish coast to prevent supplies reaching Spain. As a result, during the summer of 1937, France seriously considered openly supporting the Republicans.

At the same time, a number of British ships, including warships, were attacked by submarines of unknown origin in the western Mediterranean. Between 10 and 14 September 1937, a conference was held at Nyon to discuss the situation. As a result of this, the western Mediterranean was divided into separate patrol zones, and nine different countries, including Italy, agreed to share the supervision of these zones. Relations were further improved as a result of the Anglo-Italian agreement of April 1938, by which Mussolini agreed to withdraw all his troops from Spain at the end of the war, and immediately withdrew about a quarter of them.

Stalin was eager to avoid Russia becoming involved in the war. It coincided with a change of policy towards the rest of Europe *(see page 353)*, by which Stalin hoped to improve the communist image in Western Europe. Extensive commitment in the war would not only tarnish this image but would also prove extremely expensive and difficult to maintain. Nonetheless, Stalin was unable to entirely ignore a struggling left-wing government, especially as it was receiving aid from other European Communist parties through the International Brigade. Consequently, Russia supplied advisers and materials to the Republicans for a time, but ended its aid before the end of the war.

(b) Spanish fascism and European interest in the war

There was widespread interest in the war throughout Europe, and many individuals volunteered to fight for both sides. To some extent, they were attracted by the prospect of adventure in what seemed to be an exciting war, a view that was encouraged by the newsreel coverage of the war and the extensive propaganda undertaken by both sides. To many young men, it offered an escape from the drudgery and, in many cases, lack of prospects in their own country.

However, the main reason for interest in the war was that it seemed to represent the inevitable conflict between left and right. On the one side were the forces of progress, opposed to the power of the Church, landowners and army and keen to establish a modern socialist state. On the other were those who wanted to uphold these traditional bastions of power and, it seemed, introduce a fascist state. They were supported not only by the Spanish Fascist party, the 'Falange', but also by the leading European fascists, Hitler and Mussolini. The Spanish Civil War seemed to represent the Armageddon of fascism against communism. Many of the young men who fought and died there genuinely believed that they were serving the cause of one or other of the great creeds.

In fact, this interpretation of the war was a massive over-simplification. It resulted chiefly from German and Italian involvement on Franco's behalf, which inevitably identified his side with fascism. It was also in part a consequence of the sheer bloodiness of the war; men could not, it was thought, treat each other so vilely for the sake of a purely domestic quarrel. Yet the origins of the war *(see pages 378–80)* were purely Spanish, and Franco's identification with the other fascists was in many respects illusory.

The Spanish Fascist party was one of many small political groups in the early 1930s. It had been founded as the 'Falange Española' and was led by José Antonio Primo de Rivera, son of the former dictator. In 1934 it joined with the JONS ('Juntas de Ofensiva Nacional Sindicalista'), a similar party that favoured strong central government, a nationalist foreign policy and the dissolution of the Communist party. The new joint party was officially known as the 'Falange Española de las Juntas de Ofensiva Nacional Sindicalista', usually abbreviated to 'Falange'. Although their leader, José Antonio Primo de Rivera, was elected to the Cortes, the total party membership was only 2300. Party broadsheets were printed and parades held, wearing blue shirts, but in effect the party was no more than one of many small right-wing groups. In the elections of 1936 no member won a seat in the Cortes and in total the party received only some 40 000 votes. More than half the party members were under twenty-one. The Popular Front government gave the group a little glamour by imprisoning its leaders, but it was not even sufficiently regarded by the right-wing to be informed of the planned army revolt.

After the outbreak of the war, the Falange joined the Nationalists where possible. In many areas they were locked away, and José Antonio became the movement's first martyr when he was shot dead. In April 1937 Franco ordered the merger of the party with the monarchist Carlist party into a new party, the 'FET' ('Falange Española Tradicionalista') which he adopted as his own party. Yet from the very outset this party could not be identified with its apparent counterparts in Italy and Germany. Most of the government ministers were generals and monarchists and the only ministry run by a Falangist was the ministry of propaganda. The new regime supported, and was supported by, the Church, which was given back its control over education, a policy totally abhorrent to the genuine Fascists. Even the party's name was a contradiction: a fascist party could not be 'traditional' *(see page 224)*. José Antonio himself had, in a letter from prison, warned against 'the establishment of a false, conservative, fascism without revolutionary courage and young blood'. Franco's new regime was to be exactly that— conservative fascism that looked back to the good old days rather than forward to a new future.

Yet if Franco was not at heart a fascist, why did he call his own political party by the fascist name and thereby invite identification with European fascism? At the start of the war, Franco needed foreign aid badly—he had an army, but no navy or air force, and was fighting a two-front war. The only likely sources of help were Hitler and Mussolini, and both he and General Mola (his co-leader subsequently killed in an air crash) sent to Hitler for help, their respective envoys embarassingly arriving separately. Given his dependence on foreign fascists, Franco could hardly disband the party in Spain itself. Nevertheless, he was eager that it should not be too influential, and consequently swamped it with his own conservative supporters.

At the end of the war, Franco announced that Spain had joined Germany, Italy and Japan in the Anti-Comintern Pact. Yet again the appearance was different to the reality. By the end of June 1939, all German and Italian forces had left Spain, after taking part in the victory parade. Thereafter, Franco again kept his distance from his powerful allies. On 3 September he indicated that he did not plan to become involved in the dispute over Danzig and Poland and Spain remained neutral throughout the war. Although it provided minerals to Germany (until 1944) and a refuge for Germans at the end of the war, Franco's contribution to the Axis war effort was hardly that of a committed fascist.

The Spanish Civil War was, therefore, a tragic mirage. It gave the appearance of being the great left against right struggle that had been brewing since before World War I. Those who went there to fight in this belief actually fuelled this appearance and attracted others. Yet in fact it was a Spanish conflict on lines similar to that which brewed but never boiled over in France. And household squabbles are notoriously the most vicious and unpleasant.

7. 1936–9: Appeasement and War

Hitler's foreign policy aims have already been examined *(see page 312)*. This section therefore assesses the reactions of the rest of Europe to his aims and his efforts to translate them into reality. Although these aims were clear enough and had been expounded both in *Mein Kampf* and subsequent speeches and statements, Hitler had left himself with considerable freedom of movement over both the details of his plans and the methods by which they were to be put into practice. For example, he had never delineated precisely what his enlarged Reich would encompass, nor exactly how far the eastern 'Lebensraum' would stretch. Consequently, he could have claimed that he had achieved his first goal when Germany and Austria were united, or, as he in fact did, reiterate that this was only the start. Equally, he never explained precisely in what order, at what time or by what method he intended to achieve his aims. As A.J.P. Taylor has written, he was a 'man of daring improvizations; he made lightning decisions and then presented them as the result of long-term policy'.

Hitler's first 'daring improvisation' was the re-occupation of the Rhineland in March 1936 *(see page 314)*. His excuse for sending troops once more in the forbidden area was that the ratification of the Franco-Russian alliance *(see page 242)* gave birth to an aggressive alignment in contravention of the Locarno treaties, as a result of which Germany was no longer bound by those treaties. Militarily, his troops could easily have been forced out, since France, Poland and Czechoslovakia could have mobilized almost 200 divisions against Germany. However, Hitler's reading of the political situation was accurate. The re-occupation took place on 7 March, at a time when France was between governments. The caretaker Prime Minister, Albert Sarraut, could not risk decisive action without the support of the Chamber. Although the French Foreign Minister, Flandin, was keen to attack, the French Generals, like their German counterparts, did not want to risk an attack across the Rhine as their men could too easily be cut off from a retreat. Moreover, the British government was not prepared to act swiftly. They were concerned by the possibility of a repeat of the 1923 Ruhr occupation and, in some cases, had considerable sympathy with the German viewpoint—it was their territory, surely they should be allowed to station their troops on it? The most the British offered was two divisions after fifteen days. Hitler subsequently spoke of the forty-eight hours after the march as 'the most nerve-racking in my whole life'. With hindsight, the reoccupation takes on considerable significance as the first of a number of steps that led inevitably to war. In fact, even if France and Britain had acted decisively, there is no guarantee that Hitler would have been thwarted. The Germans had, almost for the only time, rallied behind the Weimar government in 1923 and could well have done again in 1936 if Britain and France had sent troops into Germany.

Britain, France and Belgium protested vigorously at the re-occupation but did no more. They were joined in their protests by Italy, the last time that Italy showed opposition to Germany. Italy's conquests of Abyssinia had begun her isolation from the rest of Europe, while her part in the Spanish Civil War *(see pages 277, 384)* pushed her even further from Britain and France and towards Germany. The signature of the Rome–Berlin Axis in October 1936 *(see page 279)* finally ended any hope of a common West European front against Hitler and divided Europe clearly into two camps.

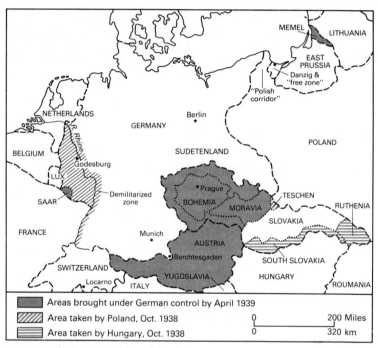

Map 36. German Expansion in Central Europe 1936–9

Hitler's victory in the Rhineland brought him three assets. Firstly, he had undertaken the operation against the advice of his generals, thereby giving him prestige and encouraging him to overrule them again. Secondly, he was able to demonstrate the 'softness' of Britain and France: an exercise that would also be repeated. Thirdly, it enabled him to order the construction of the Siegfried Line on Germany's western frontier which he called 'a barrier across Germany's front door which will leave her free to sally out eastwards and southwards by the other ways'.

388

As if in realization that the horse had bolted in 1936, Britain and France sought to lock the stable door in 1937. On the one hand, they began to strengthen themselves and their allies. Rearmament programmes were undertaken on a larger scale than before, with Britain concentrating especially on her air defences. The French foreign minister, Delbos, visited France's eastern allies in December 1937 *(see page 315)* in an effort to stir them into common action and, if possible, form a united front against Germany. In the event, he found little sympathy for the idea, and Yugoslavia and Poland in particular were keen to maintain their freedom of action. On the other hand, the Western democracies sought ways of satisfying Hitler. In November, Lord Halifax, on behalf of the British Cabinet, visited Germany. Hitler's grievances over Danzig, Austria and Czechoslovakia were sympathetically received, and the possibility of their joining the Reich was discussed.

This policy—of accepting and rectifying genuine German grievances —has become known as 'appeasement'. It had many supporters in Britain and France and, at the time, had considerable merits. The memory of the World War I inspired many Europeans to feel that it should never be allowed to happen again. This feeling was especially strong in the thirties, when many of those who had suffered or survived in 1914–18 had sons who were of military age and would be the first to suffer if it happened again. In addition, many people, especially in Britain, felt that Germany had been harshly, even unfairly, treated in 1919, a feeling that was well exploited by propaganda. The view that all nationalites except the Germans had been given the right of self-determination was especially strong. Thirdly, the obvious divisions of Eastern Europe meant that Russia's help would be needed in defeating Germany. Many conservatives in Britain and France were very sceptical of an alliance with Russia which might lead to communists coming, armed, into Western Europe where they might, at the very least, contaminate British and French troops with their revolutionary ideas. 'Better Hitlerism than Communism' was a powerful argument, especially in France, where fear of left-wing ideas was especially strong *(see pages 229–36)*.

Appeasement has subsequently been discredited because it failed to prevent the outbreak of war in September 1939. We know now that a policy that involved applying reasoned arguments and accepting stated agreements was not successful when applied to Hitler, who accepted neither reason nor agreements. In the 1930s, though, he was able to project an image of a reasonable statesman—an image that was taken as reality by Western politicians. In addition, appeasement was at times only a front as Britain and France continued to rearm in case appeasement failed. Yet Hitler could easily point to the contradiction of a government that preached goodwill and appeasement while building up its armoury.

Hitler's annexation of Austria in March 1938 *(see page 312)* created remarkably little interest in the rest of Europe. Italy, whose interests were most threatened, was preoccupied in Spain and Mussolini was won over before the move was made *(see page 279)*. France, again, was between governments and, in any case, would have found it difficult to act without Britain and Czechoslovakia which would, in turn, have brought Hungary into the conflict. Despite Churchill's warnings to the House of Commons, the British government did no more than make an official protest. Many Europeans felt that the 'Anschluss' did no more than provide Austrian Germans with the self-determination that they had been deprived of in 1919 and campaigned for ever since.

In April, Italy returned briefly to a policy of friendship with Western Europe, perhaps in an effort to counterbalance Hitler's increasing influence. On 16 April 1938 an Anglo-Italian Pact was signed. By it, Britain recognized Italy's rule over Ethiopia and agreed to persuade other states to do the same. In exchange, Mussolini agreed to withdraw Italian forces from Spain at the end of the war and to end her propaganda against Britain in Arab states. However, Hitler's impressive and much-hailed visit to Rome at the beginning of May redressed the balance and showed where Italy's true allegiance lay.

When Czech troops were mobilized against Germany in May 1938 *(see pages 205, 315)*, Britain and France supported Czechoslovakia diplomatically, while Russia promised to stand by her 1935 agreement with Czechoslovakia. Throughout the summer, Britain and France attempted to mediate between Germany and Czechoslovakia, trying to get Hitler to moderate his demands and the Czechs to consider giving up the Sudetenland.

Hitler's Nuremburg speech of 12 September 1938, in which he said that 'the Germans in Czechoslovakia are neither defenceless, nor are they deserted, and people should take notice of that fact', precipitated the final crisis over Czechoslovakia. Hitler had again gambled on Britain and France not being prepared to fight, and their friendly noises during the summer suggested that he was right. On 13 September the British Prime Minister, Neville Chamberlain, announced his intention to fly to Germany to see Hitler. On 15 September, while the Sudetenland was under martial law and the Nazi leaders in Czechoslovakia had fled to Germany, Chamberlain met Hitler at Berchtesgaden. Hitler demanded the Sudetenland be annexed to Germany on the grounds of self-determination. On 18 September, Chamberlain conferred with the French Premier, Daladier, and Foreign Minister, Bonnet. They agreed that all areas where more than half the population was German should be ceded to Germany, while the borders of the rest of Czechoslovakia should be internationally guaranteed. They then (20 September) rejected the Czech government's suggestion that the frontiers be submitted to international arbitration, on the lines suggested by the Locarno treaties, and forced the Czech government of Sirovy to accept their scheme.

On 22 September, Chamberlain met Hitler for the second time. At Godesberg, Hitler rejected the Anglo-French scheme and upped his price for peace. He demanded the immediate annexation of German areas (with military bases and factories intact), plus plebiscites in areas with German minorities, to be held by 25 November under German–Czech or international supervision. Since this would increase both the area and value of land that Czechoslovakia would have to give up, Chamberlain refused the demands. The Czech government mobilized all its forces: the French called up over ½ million reserves. Daladier and Chamberlain met again and agreed to support Czechoslovakia's resistance. Chamberlain was joined by the American President, Roosevelt, in calling for an international conference. Mussolini, bound to support Hitler but quite unprepared for a European war *(see page 280)*, joined the call and apparently persuaded Hitler to agree to it.

On 29 September the Munich conference was convened *(see page 205)*. The leaders of the four great powers of Western Europe conferred all afternoon and evening and, just after midnight, reached agreement. Hitler won his final demands, in that the German areas would be evacuated by 10 October and plebiscites held under international supervision in other areas. The borders of the Czechoslovak state would be guaranteed by all four powers *(for details see pages 205–6)*. On their return from Munich, the leaders were initially hailed as peacemakers. However, doubting voices were soon heard in Britain and France. The last democracy in Eastern Europe had been abandoned to Hitler and, even if the grounds for fighting (Hitler's occupation of the German areas of Czechoslovakia) were weak, war would inevitably come in the end and sooner was better than later. In the event, the conference was followed by a flurry of diplomatic activity to take account of Germany's new strength and the collapse of the 'Little Entente' and France's chief eastern ally. On 16 November the Anglo-Italian Pact of April was officially put into effect, again reflecting Mussolini's hesitancy over German friendship. On 26 November Poland and Russia renewed their non-aggression pact *(see page 353)* and Poland sought agreements with the Baltic and Balkan states. On 6 December France and Germany signed a pact agreeing to their existing frontier and to consult peacefully over any disputes. Yet again, the explosive mixture of appeasement and alliance was being concocted.

The German occupation of all Czechoslovakia in March 1939 marked a crucial turning point *(see page 212)*. Thereafter, the Western powers were convinced of the need to act more firmly to prevent the German conquest of Eastern Europe. In the case of Czechoslovakia itself, any military action was out of the question, since Hitler was already safely entrenched in much of it, and was secure from both Austria and Hungary to the South and West. On 15–16 March Czechoslovakia came under German rule; on 17 March Chamberlain at Birmingham asked 'is this a step in the direction of an attempt to dominate the world by force?', prompting the German ambassador in London to report to Hitler that 'it would be wrong to cherish any illusions that a fundamental change has not taken place in Britain's attitude towards Germany'. On 21 March Hitler annexed Memel. Three days later Britain and France agreed to resist any German aggression in Holland, Belgium or Switzerland, and on 31 March Chamberlain said that Britain would stand by France in guaranteeing Poland's frontiers. When Mussolini attacked Albania on 7 April, Anglo-French guarantees were also given to Greece and Roumania. On 26 April Britain introduced six-month universal military conscription for the first time ever. On 28 April Hitler denounced the German-Polish pact of 1934 *(see page 212)* and on 22 May the Rome–Berlin Axis became a full scale political and military alliance known as the 'Pact of Steel'. The era of appeasement was over and the battle lines drawn. As Hitler told his generals on 23 May, 'We cannot expect a repetition of the Czech affair. There will be war. Our task is to isolate Poland. The success of this isolation will be decisive. . . there must be no simultaneous conflict with the Western powers'.

In the summer of 1939, the Soviet Union became the critical power. If Britain and France could win her to their side, Hitler could be thwarted; whereas if Germany could neutralize her, Hitler's task would be relatively easy. Between June and August Britain and France negotiated with the Soviets. Russian representatives insisted on an alliance and a military convention, a degree of commitment that Britain and France were not prepared to give to the communist power. The Russians also hinted that they should be given the Baltic states and insisted on the right to send troops across Poland in the event of a German attack on Poland. Throughout the 1930s Poland and Roumania had consistently refused to allow any plans for Russian troops to enter their countries. Consequently, the negotiations reached a deadlock, leaving the Russians (obviously a principal target for Hitler's 'Lebensraum') feeling that they were being deserted. Britain and France, eager to avoid Russia becoming too involved in Eastern Europe, felt that agreement would eventually be reached and that, in any case, Communist Russia would never agree with Nazi Germany.

Nazi Germany had far more to offer to Russia. Confident that Russia would ultimately be beaten anyway, the German government not only offered a peace pact but also land in Eastern Europe. Molotov, the Russian Foreign Minister who had replaced the long-serving and pro-Western Litvinov in May 1939, negotiated with Ribbentrop during August. On the 20th they announced the conclusion of a trade agreement and, on 21 August, announced that they were about to sign a non-aggression pact, which was signed two days later. Only the first part of the agreement was made public, by which each agreed not to attack the other and to remain neutral if either were attacked by a third power. The second, secret, part of the pact settled the division between the two powers of Poland, and accepted that Lithuania and Vilna should go to Germany and Finland, Estonia and Latvia should go to Russia. This, the 'Moscow–Berlin' or 'Nazi–Soviet' Pact, was a shattering blow to the peace hopes of Britain and France.

It met with immediate reaction. Britain and France hastened their military preparations and, on 24 August, Britain and Poland signed a pact of mutual assistance. Since 20 August, Hitler had made increasingly loud demands for the annexation of Danzig and the right to construct a road and railways across the Polish Corridor *(see page 212)*. He also demanded that a plebiscite should be held in the Corridor with a view to its being returned to Germany. The leaders of America, Britain and France all appealed to Hitler for peace, but by 28 August military plans were well advanced as Hitler refused to moderate his demands. British naval ships were recalled to their bases, while in Germany rationing was introduced. On 29 August Hitler demanded that a representative of the Polish government should meet him in Berlin within twenty-four hours. On the 30th Polish troops were partially mobilized. On the 31st the German government published a sixteen-point plan to Poland, but it was refused without being seen. On hearing of this, the Russian government ordered mobilization against Poland. On 1 September German forces attacked Poland. Even then, Britain and France, through Italy, agreed to negotiate, if German troops evacuated Poland. Hitler rejected this offer and ignored an Anglo-French ultimatum demanding withdrawal. As a result, Britain and France declared war on Germany on 3 September.

8. Bibliography

All the general works referred to in the introductory bibliography *(see page 3)* have sections on this subject which should prove adequate when studied in conjunction with the individual countries concerned. The most important single work on the subject is *The Origins of the Second World War* by A.J.P. Taylor (Hamish Hamilton, 1961). It was written in 1961 and has since aroused considerable controversy, much of which has been summarized in *The Origins of the Second World War: A Symposium* edited by E.M. Robertson (Macmillan, 1971). The relevant documents for the period are to be found in the two volumes of *Speeches and Documents on International Affairs 1918–37* by A.B. Keith (OUP, 1938) or in 'Collection of Nineteenth and Twentieth Century Documents Part II', published by the Open University as Unit 18 (Block VI of the *War and Society* Arts Third Level Course.) Other works that may be of assistance include: E.H. Carr, *International Relations between the Two World Wars, 1919–39* (Macmillan, 1947); E.H. Carr, *The Twenty Years Crisis* (Macmillan, 1961); G.M. Gathorne-Hardy, *A Short History of International Affairs 1920–39* (OUP, 1950); M. Gilbert, *Britain and Germany between the Wars* (Longman, 1964); W.M. Jordan, *Great Britain, France and the German Problems 1919–39* (OUP, 1943); F.P. Walters, *History of the League of Nations* (OUP, 1952).

On the Spanish Civil War, the accepted authority is H. Thomas, *The Spanish Civil War* (Eyre & Spottiswoode, 1961). Professor Thomas has also written more briefly on the subject, for example in Purnell's *History of the Twentieth Century*. G. Brenan, *The Spanish Labyrinth* (C.U.P., 1950) is also useful.

9. Discussion Points and Exercises

(a) General

A *This section consists of questions that might be used for discussion (or written answers) as a way of expanding on the chapter and testing understanding of it:*

1 Explain the meaning of each of the following: guarantee; mutual aid; arbitration; pact; protocol; preparatory commission; plebiscite; alliance.
2 How important to international relations were the changed circumstances of Russia?
3 Could Franco-German hostility have been ended?
4 Were the border disputes of 1919–24 of importance?
5 Why did the victor states put so much stress on reparations?
6 How realistic were the hopes of the League of Nations?
7 How significant were the Locarno agreements?
8 Was the Kellogg–Briand Pact of any real value?
9 Why did the economic crisis of 1929–31 so change international relations?
10 Could the League of Nations have stopped the Japanese in Manchuria?
11 Why didn't League members take military action against Italy, 1935–6?
12 How clearly was Europe divided into rival armed camps in 1937–8?
13 Why was Hitler allowed to send his troops back into the Rhineland?
14 Would the Western powers have been justified in declaring war on Germany as a result of Germany's occupation of the Sudetenland?
15 Why was the occupation of Czechoslovakia in March 1939 a turning point?
16 Why did Britain and France fail to reach agreement with Russia in 1939?
17 Why did Britain and France declare war on Germany in September 1939?

B *This section examines the problems of the period from a number of points of view:*

1 Examine and assess the Locarno agreements from the point of view of: (a) France, (b) Poland, (c) Germany.
2 Examine and assess the Manchurian crisis from the point of view of: (a) Italy, (b) Great Britain.

C *This section examines the problems of the period in greater detail:*

1 Write a report for the League of Nation's Assembly in 1929 outlining the League's achievements in its first ten years and what its plans for the future should, in your opinion, be.
2 Explain, in the form of a paper for the British Foreign Minister, why so little progress was made in the field of disarmament by 1933.
3 Outline the arguments for and against appeasement.

D *Essay questions:*
1 What hopeful signs for peace in Europe were there in 1929, and what signs of danger?
2 Why did Britain and France not oppose Mussolini's actions in Abyssinia and Spain more forcefully?
3 Was appeasement justifiable? Why did it eventually fail to keep peace in Europe?

(b) The Spanish Civil War

A *This section consists of questions that might be used for discussion (or written answers) as a way of expanding on the Spanish Civil War and testing understanding of it:*
1 Why was King Alfonso so unpopular by the late 1920s?
2 Comment on the new constitution and laws of 1931.
3 Was 'Acción Popular' a fascist party?
4 Why were there strikes in Spain even when the left were in power?
5 Why did the North and East continue to support the Republic?
6 Why was the war so brutal and vicious?
7 Could the Republicans have won the Civil War?
8 Why did Britain and France continue their policy of non-intervention after Germany and Italy were helping Franco?
9 Was the Spanish Civil War really an epic 'left against right' struggle?
10 What did Franco hope to achieve by the formation of the FET?

B *This section suggests a way of comparing Spain with other countries:*
1 Compare the problems that Spain faced in the 1920s, and the solutions to them, with those experienced by other European countries.

C *This section suggests ways of examining events in Spain from a different point of view:*
1 As a government adviser (to either a Republican or a right-wing government), write a report outlining some solutions to Spain's problems.
2 As a member of the International Brigade during the Civil War, outline your reasons for going to fight in Spain.

D *Essay questions:*
1 Why was there such widespread interest in the Spanish Civil War?
2 Was the Civil War an expression of European problems or a purely Spanish crisis?

10. An Exercise on the Causes of World War II

Below are six different interpretations of the causes of the Second World War. Examine each carefully and expand upon it for yourself. In particular, assess whether you consider each to be a root cause that really lay behind the start of the war, or a secondary cause, that may have encouraged the war or affected the timing of its outbreak, but was not a fundamental reason for it. Also, assess whether each interpretation presents the view that the war was inevitable and unavoidable or the view that it could have been prevented, and if so how. Having done this, rank the interpretations offered into what you consider their order of importance and assess whether, between them, they offer a valid and sufficient explanation of the outbreak of war.

1   The policy of appeasement encouraged Hitler to continue his plans for the expansion of the Reich. In particular, the attitude of the Western powers at Munich confirmed his opinion that they would not go to war with Germany in defence of an East European power.

2   Nazism meant war: once Hitler had come to power in Germany, a European war was inevitable as the aims and creed of Nazism were bound to conflict with those of other countries. One or more of these would ultimately attempt to resist Hitler.

3   The erection of a series of weak states in Eastern Europe, especially ones that could not even agree with each other, brought about the war as it meant there was no state, or 'bloc' of states, to oppose Hitler in the very area that he had stated he planned to conquer.

4   The unavoidable failure of the League of Nations in Manchuria and Ethiopia meant the end of collective security and, consequently, a return to the principle 'might is right'.

5   Agreement between Britain and France and the Soviet Union would have prevented the outbreak of war. This agreement proved impossible only because of the fear and suspicion of communism in government circles in Britain and France, who must, therefore, take responsibility.

6   The origins of the World War II lie in the treaty of Versailles. The penal clauses of that treaty inevitably meant a hostile Germany that would, given the opportunity, attempt to redress her grievances.

XV An Outline of World War II in Europe

1. Introduction

This chapter is intended only to provide an outline of World War II in Europe; to do more would require more space than is justified in a book of this nature. However, this does mean that it leaves out far more than it includes, and should be taken to be a background against which more detailed study can be undertaken. To assist this, a detailed bibliography *(see page 432)* has been included. In particular, I have included nothing on the war against Japan in the Far East, even though it involved some European powers, France and Holland slightly, and another, Britain, extensively. Another important omission is any detailed study of the European countries under Hitler's rule—of Vichy France, of the occupied countries, the resistance movements, the treatment of the Jews. To present an outline study of these features would be inadequate and too great a generalization, so I have pointed in the bibliography to suitable books. Thirdly, I have included very little on the role of the air forces and the navies during the war. Finally, I have neglected the crucial conferences and meetings between the leaders of the great powers, Churchill, Roosevelt and Stalin, that were to play such an important part in the formation of the post-war world.

World War II was entirely different from World War I. In the 1914–18 war, the Western front became a double line of trenches along which a series of battles were fought, while on the East, after a short-lived Russian success, Germany's armies were almost entirely victorious. Between 1938 and 1940, Germany (and Russia) conquered a series of countries one after the other. There followed an almost complete lull in the fighting in Europe between June 1940 and June 1941, after which the focus of attention shifted to the Eastern front, with continued success for Germany. Until 1942 the Axis forces (Germany, Italy and Japan) were almost entirely successful and achieved all their objectives. In that year, they suffered three major setbacks at the hands of the Allies (USA, USSR, Britain); in the Far East, the Japanese aircraft carriers were held for the first time at the battles of Coral Sea and Midway, in Russia the German army was defeated at Stalingrad, and in North Africa the German and Italian armies were defeated at El Alamein. Thereafter, the history of the war was almost exactly the reverse of the first two years, and 1943–5 saw a series of defeats for the Axis forces. Although this pattern is an over-simplification, it does help to put some of the events into focus and to demonstrate the linear nature of the events of the war.

Obviously, a war fought on several fronts is difficult for the student coming to it for the first time to follow. It might, therefore, help to construct a date chart of the main events split, like that for World War I *(see page 154)*, into the different fronts where the war was fought. This will especially help to demonstrate the inter-relations of the wars on different fronts. Secondly, a series of sketch maps should be of great assistance in understanding the war. Those in the text are as detailed as possible, but for purposes of clarity it has not been possible to show the movements and counter-movements of the armies in, for instance, North Africa. Thirdly, it should be noted that some of the questions in section 7 will be difficult to answer without reference to additional materials.

2. The Russo-German Conquest of Europe

(a) The First Attacks: Poland and Finland

The Polish army was numerically superior to its German attackers, having over 2 million men at its disposal. However, it was badly lacking in modern equipment and methods of transport. For example, it had eleven cavalry brigades and even its infantry often had to march long distances from the railheads. Heavy artillery and aircraft were in particularly short supply—there were only 377 aircraft available, less than a fifth of those available to the Germans. Its military plans were chiefly defensive—to form a line to the north of Warsaw to hold the German attack from East Prussia and wait for the help of the Western allies *(see Map 37)*.

Germany had two army groups each split into two, under the overall command of von Brauchitsch, allocated to the attack on Poland. In the North, they were to attack South from East Prussia and East across the Corridor, and in the South from Silesia towards Lodz and Cracow *(see Map 37)*. On 1 September, an early morning air assault attacked airfields, army bases and railways, so disrupting the movement of Polish troops. The air attack was followed by the advance of the infantry and armoured divisions, some of which reached fifty miles into Poland within forty-eight hours. This type of attack—a massive aerial onslaught followed by fast moving infantry—was known as 'Blitzkrieg' or 'lightning-war', and was to be used elsewhere later.

By 7 September the South-western corner of Poland, Silesia, was overrun and Lodz had been taken. In the North the German forces were approaching Warsaw and the four different German armies were close to meeting up. On 10 September the Polish High Command ordered a general retreat to the South-east, in the direction of Roumania, leaving defensive groups on the rivers Vistula and San. This retreat was undertaken efficiently, but was completely nullified by Russia's attack on

Poland, which was launched on 17 September. As a result of this, Polish forces in Lvov found themselves attacked by both Germans and Russians, and the situation became increasingly hopeless. Warsaw was heavily bombarded, both by air and artillery. Once the main water-works were destroyed, on 23 September, the situation became desperate as incendiary bombs could not be stopped. On 28 September peace negotiations began, and on the 30th German troops entered a smouldering Warsaw. Although the fighting continued in some areas until 5 October, the Poles, with no direct assistance from their Western allies, were defeated.

Map 37 The conquest of Poland, 1939

Germany and Russia then divided the spoils. Germany annexed Danzig and over 30 000 square miles between East Prussia and Silesia. A further area of 39 000 square miles was not taken directly under German rule, but was known as the 'Gouvernement General', and was administered under German control. Russia took over some 77 000 square miles of Eastern Poland and over 22 million people including many White Russians. The Nazi-Soviet Pact had borne fruit within little more than a month.

However, Stalin had little faith in Hitler's promises in the Pact, and was eager to build a buffer between himself and the enlarged Germany.

To this end, a series of treaties were made with the Baltic states. Estonia and Latvia both agreed—they had little option—to allow Russian troops and ships to be stationed in their countries. Lithuania made a similar agreement but did gain something, the town of Vilna, in exchange. The Finnish government were less compliant in the face of more extensive demands, including cessation of the Karelian isthmus between Lake Ladoga and the Gulf of Finland *(see Map 38)* and on 28 November the Russians declared war. Finland appealed to the League of Nations, as a result of which the Soviet Union was expelled from the League on 14 December—its last, pathetically defiant, act against an aggressor.

Map 38 The campaigns against Finland and Norway, 1939–40

The Russo-Finnish war lasted through the winter until 12 March 1940. The Russian army found considerably stiffer opposition than they had anticipated. The chief attack, across the Karelian Isthmus, met heavy resistance on the defences of the Mannerheim Line (named after the Finnish commander-in-chief). A number of Russian divisions were lost further North, in attacks towards Oulu and the Arctic Road (from Tornea to Petsamo), being surrounded and starved out in freezing conditions. Only in the furthest North, in an attack from Murmansk to Petsamo, were the Russians immediately successful. Reinforcements and heavy artillery were moved up towards the Mannerheim Line, and in early February a new offensive was launched, as a result of which the main line of defence was reached in early March. On 6 March peace negotiations began, and on 12 March they were concluded at Moscow.

As a result of the treaty, the USSR won what they had earlier demanded. They took seventy miles of the Karelian Isthmus and an area around Sortavala to the North of Lake Ladoga. Various other smaller areas, including a right of way to Sweden, were taken, as well as the city of Viborg and the naval base of Hankö. Although some Finns advocated continuing war, the government decided to accept the terms. They had received little material assistance from the Western allies and, despite the initial difficulties of the Russians, were up against a much stronger enemy who had fought competently in difficult conditions.

(b) The Phoney War and the Defeat of Norway

After his easy victory in the East, Hitler was expected to turn his attentions to the West and attack France. His initial targets were expected to be Holland and Belgium, as the Maginot Line would preclude any direct attack across the frontier. Hitler laid plans for his army to move westwards in the late autumn, but in the event he postponed the assault until the following spring.

As a result, the winter of 1939–40 saw little military activity in Western Europe and was christened the 'phoney war' by American journalists. In Britain and France, the governments prepared for the type of war they expected to come. Industry and agriculture came under more direct government control in the expectation that the war would again be a long one and that economic production would be crucial. In varying degrees, rationing was introduced. Propaganda machinery was established to counter that already existing in Germany, and RAF planes were employed to drop leaflets over Germany. Most strikingly to British civilians, children were evacuated to the countryside so that they would avoid the expected bombing raids. As thousands streamed out of London and other major cities, air raid defences were constructed and civilians enlisted in fire and police services. Britain braced herself for the attack to come. Nothing happened, and many of the evacuees returned to their parents.

On the continent, the French army advanced to the outermost defences of the Siegfried Line. The French commander-in-chief in the North, General Gamelin, decided that he did not have sufficient forces to launch a major assault on the Line, so they remained cautiously in front of it. In fact, during the attack on Poland, the German defences in the West were slight, but by early October had been considerably reinforced by troops moved from the East. This made the French troops increasingly vulnerable, and they were secretly withdrawn to the safety of the Maginot Line and a German attack from the Siegfried Line on 16 October found only a light defence of cavalry troops. The French army, supported in the North by a British Expeditionary Force under General Gort, was ready and waiting for the German assault.

Only at sea was there any activity that amounted, in popular eyes at least, to warfare in the winter of 1939–40. The German navy had no High Seas Fleet comparable to 1914 but, learning the lessons of World War I, had a considerable fleet of U-boats. With none of the declarations or warnings of that earlier war, these immediately began a campaign of unrestricted attacks in which not only combatant but also neutral shipping was sunk.

Two specific incidents gave the Allies' press and public something to shout about. On 13 December the German 'pocket' battleship, the 'Admiral Graf von Spee', was attacked by three British cruisers, the 'Ajax', 'Achilles' and 'Exeter' off the Atlantic Coast of South America. Although she put the 'Exeter' out of action, she was considerably damaged and limped up the River Plate to Montevideo to make repairs, while the British cruisers awaited her return. The Uruguayan authorities gave her a time limit in which to leave but, before this expired, the ship was taken out of port and scuttled on 17 December. The second British triumph came on 19 February 1940. A German auxiliary cruiser, the 'Altmark', with 299 British prisoners on board, was known to be in Norwegian waters on the West coast. The British destroyer 'Cossack' went into the fjord where the 'Altmark' was and, to the annoyance of the Norwegian government, freed the prisoners from the ship.

Norway was in fact the next scene of action. It was thought to be strategically crucial to both sides, since control of its Western coast would provide Germany with naval and air bases from which to attack not only the North Sea and Atlantic, but also Britain itself. Similarly, the Germans regarded it as a possible Allied base for attacks into Germany. Consequently, both sides were eager to take Norway to prevent the other taking it. It did have additional value for Germany, as supplies of Swedish iron ore had to be transported through the Norwegian port of Narvik for the seven months of the year that the North of the gulf of Bothnia was frozen.

Before attacking Norway, Germany occupied Denmark. The Danish government, with few defences, realized that their position was impossible and, on 9 April 1940, allowed German troops to occupy the country.

On 7 April, German ships were seen to be moving northwards and, although their destination was not definite, it was thought that this was the expected attack on Norway. Consequently, the next day, the British and French governments announced their intention of mining Norwegian coastal waters to prevent German landings, even though such action was in breach of Norwegian neutrality. On 9 April, German troops were landed to attack the five main ports and cities of Norway: Oslo, Bergen,

Trondheim, Stavanger and Narvik *(see Map 38)*. Norwegian resistance was greater than had been expected and two German cruisers were damaged or sunk. However, the German landings succeeded in capturing their objectives and, crucially, took all the major airfields.

The most successful opposition to the German landings came in Narvik, in the far North. There, between 10 and 13 April, British ships succeeded, in two attempts, in destroying eight German destroyers and, on 18 April, landing a combined force of British, French, Polish and Norwegian troops. This force captured an airfield through which it could be supplied, and on 27 May recaptured the town itself. However, it was held only for a short time before the Allied forces, with no hope of extending their reconquest, had to be withdrawn in early June to reinforce their colleagues in Northern Europe. Unfortunately, the only victorious force in Norway left under a cloud as four ships were sunk during the evacuation.

After the initial German successes of 9 April, King Haakon VII had negotiated with the German government, and his government agreed to resign in favour of a more pro-German one. However, the King refused to accept the German nominee, Major Quisling, as Prime Minister, and he and his government chose to continue fighting.

As the German forces controlled most of the South of the country, the key to resistance lay in British and French assistance. Between 16 and 18 April British troops, with half a French brigade, landed at the ports of Namsos and Andalsnes in an effort to attack and recapture Trondheim from North and South. However, the troops in this area could not be adequately reinforced and supplied as the airfields were in German hands. Consequently, on 27 April, the Allied forces were withdrawn from central Norway. Despite their shortlived success in Narvik, they had failed to prevent the German occupation and, by 10 June, all opposition was ended. As in Poland and Finland, the Germans had won without great difficulty, and their morale and prestige continued to rise.

In both Britain and France, these victories led to a change of government. In both, public opinion and the elected representatives expressed their discontent at the lack of Allied support for both Finland and Norway. It is unlikely that any British or French government would have risked a wholesale commitment in the far North, where their forces would be hard to supply and easily cut off, and would have resulted in a weakening of their defences in France. The changes in government were therefore as much symbolical as practical, indicating a change of mood as much as of commitment. In France, the Russian victory in Finland led to the downfall of Daladier, who was replaced by Paul Reynaud on 20 March, although Daladier kept his place in the Cabinet. In Britain, Chamberlain was replaced as Prime Minister on 10 May by Winston Churchill, long-time opponent of appeasement and a consistent enemy of Hitler. Both the new governments were broad coalitions, including both conservatives and socialists.

(c) The Low Countries and France

Throughout April 1940 Holland and Belgium expected to be attacked and prepared themselves for it. Both based their defensive systems on the plentiful rivers and waterways of their countries, the flooding of which, supported by troop action, was to hold up the enemy. The Dutch hoped to defend their major cities—Rotterdam, Amsterdam and the Hague—by this method, while the Belgians hoped to hold invaders along the Albert Canal and River Meuse *(see Map 39)*. However, both countries depended on small armies that were made especially vulnerable by their lack of artillery and air support.

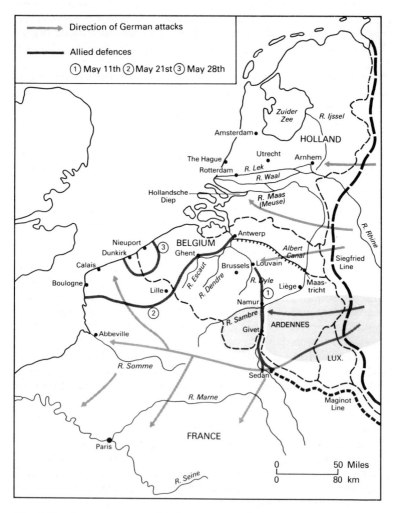

Map 39 The German conquest of the Low Countries and France, 1940

On 10 May, German troops attacked both Holland and Belgium (Luxembourg was also immediately occupied, and in 1942, annexed to Germany). The Dutch defensive system was broken within three days, when the capture of the bridgehead at Arnhem was followed by the capture of the bridges across the Maas (Meuse) estuary at Hollandsche Diep. On 14 May Rotterdam was systematically bombed from the air, and a part of it almost completely destroyed. The lesson was obvious: if the Dutch did not surrender, other cities would suffer similarly. That evening Dutch forces were ordered to cease fire, and Queen Juliana and her family fled to Britain.

The Allies had far more hope of defending Belgium. Their defence was to be based to the west of Liège on a line from Sedan to Namur and then to the river Dyle *(see Map 39)*. It was to be held by Belgian forces in the, North, British in the centre and French in the South. As in World War I, a defensive line from North to South, but now linked to the Maginot Line, would hold the German attack.

However, the German attack was to be of an entirely different type. Falls, in *The Second World War*, describes the German tactics as follows:

> German tactics in attack were designed to pierce a deep system of defence at several points by armoured columns on a narrow frontage, covered by dive bombers and supported by motor-borne infantry employed to widen the breaches. Once through the defences one column would converge upon another to envelop a section of the defence, which would then be mopped up by infantry.

A continuous defensive line would find it extremely difficult to counter such an attack without permanent entrenchments of the type constructed on the Maginot Line.

By 11 May the Allied forces were in position and ready to withstand the German onslaught. However, on 14 May—the very day of the Dutch surrender—the Germans made a vital breakthrough in the South. The southernmost part of the line, from Sedan to Namur, had been entrusted to the weakest of the French forces, the 9th Army, as it was well protected by the Ardennes and therefore least likely to be attacked. So when Rundstedt's armoured forces came through the Ardennes they met little resistance and soon found themselves in open country to the South and West of Sedan. The threat was obvious; if this hole was widened, German forces could pour through it and cut off the Allied troops in Belgium.

To counter this danger, the Allied defensive line retreated to the River Escaut on 16–18 May, abandoning both Brussels and Antwerp to the Germans. Yet by 26 May their escape to the South had been cut off when the German army approached the French coast and captured Boulogne. Lord Gort, leader of the British Expeditionary Force, and General Weygand, who had replaced Gamelin as French commander-in-chief on 18 May, contemplated an attack to their South to break the German line from Sedan to the coast. This could be joined by a northern attack by other French armies from the Somme. In the event, it was decided that such an attack was unlikely to succeed and instead the retreat towards the sea continued. At midnight on 27 May, King Leopold III surrendered Belgium to the Germans, realizing the hopelessness of his situation but simultaneously worsening the plight of his allies. Gort decided that evacuation by the sea was the only way out, and to facilitate this constructed a final defensive line in a semi-circle from Nieuport to Dunkirk.

Between 28 and 31 May this was constructed. For the next three days and nights the Allied forces were evacuated by sea from Dunkirk. As German aircraft had destroyed the harbour and piers, the troops had to be taken literally from the beaches. In all, nearly 900 ships were used in the operation, of which only 222 were naval ships. Another ninety were passenger or merchant ships, but the large bulk were smaller craft, often sailed across the channel by their owners. In all, some 200 000 British and 140 000 French were rescued in what became known as 'the miracle of Dunkirk'. A battered and depleted army, leaving its equipment in Belgium, was returned to Britain. General Weygand was left to organize the defence of France. New defensive lines were constructed along the rivers Seine and Aisne, but in many cases the French forces were dispirited and eager to avoid the enemy. Their movement was seriously hampered by refugees, and they were completely overwhelmed by the aerial superiority of the Germans. Although there were five RAF squadrons in France from 7 June, the British government refused to commit all their reserves to the defence of France. With hindsight, this decision can be seen to be right, but at the time it was obviously unpopular in France.

On 5 June the German armies attacked southwards from Abbeville to Sedan *(see Map 39)*. By 10 June—the day that Mussolini chose to declare war on France—they had crossed the river Seine. Paris was obviously threatened, and the government, joined by thousands of Parisians, moved southwards—first to Tours and then, on 15 June, to Bordeaux. *(See page 244)* *(See page 244)* The next day Reynaud resigned and Marshal Pétain, who had been brought into the government a month before as Vice-president of the Council, took over. His new government was known to want peace, and on the night of 16–17 June he contacted the Germans. For three days the Germans continued to push southwards, but then replied to the French request for peace. On 22 June the French accepted the armistice terms, although Hitler did not order a cease fire until two days later. This was because Italian forces had attacked Southern France on 22 June and Hitler did not wish to end his war with France until the Italians agreed to an armistice, which they did on 24 June.

The armistice was signed in the same railway carriage in Compiègne that had witnessed the German surrender in 1918. By it, the Northern and Western part of France, from Geneva to Bourges and Tours and then South to the Pyrenees, was to be occupied by the Germans. This meant that Germany took direct control of all the country's ports and of the northern industrial region. The rest of the country was to continue under the rule of Pétain, whose government was to be based at Vichy. French troops were to be demobilized and the navy disarmed. Germany claimed the right to take over all the defences and weapons she required in good order, and all German prisoners were to be returned, though French prisoners were to remain under Germany until a peace treaty was concluded. The armistice with Italy required France to demilitarize both her own southern area and ports and those in the French colonies in Africa.

Two further events marked the death throes of the Third Republic. General Charles de Gaulle, who had briefly been head of Reynaud's Military Cabinet, went to London when Pétain took over. On 18 June he broadcast his refusal to accept surrender and on 23 June announced the establishment of a Provisional National Committee, under his leadership, to work for the liberation of France. Secondly, the British government were by no means satisfied by the arrangements for the French fleet. Although disarmed, it continued to exist and could easily be used by Germany or Italy. Consequently, on 3 July, French ships in British ports were taken over, while the fleet at Oran, in Algeria, was asked to either join Britain or comply with British orders. The German authorities ordered Admiral Darlan to refuse these instructions. Consequently, the British naval force opened fire and either sunk or captured the French fleet with extensive loss of life. This incident, although apparently un-avoidable, caused considerable ill-feeling, especially in French colonies.

(d) The Battle of Britain
The fall of France opened a new phase in the war. It left Britain alone against Germany. The likelihood of this had already led the British government to look across the Atlantic, and in early June an agreement had been reached for the supply of American war material on the understanding that the British government both paid for it and arranged its delivery (the 'cash and carry' system). Significantly, the first American goods—over ½ million guns, from rifles to light artillery—arrived just before France capitulated. Hitler, having achieved his primary objectives, hesitantly offered peace to Britain in a speech to the Reichstag on 19 July when he appealed to the 'reason and common sense of Britain'. It was very soon clear that a resolute Britain had no intention of accepting a Hitler-dominated Europe.

Hitler therefore pressed ahead with his plans for an attack on Britain. 'Operation Sea Lion', as it was known, was to take place in the autumn. It was thought unlikely that the main British fleet, stationed at Scapa Flow in Northern Scotland, would threaten his invasion force, as it could be held in the northern North Sea by German naval forces, including U-boats. The main threat to ships and barges crossing the channel would come from smaller craft, protected by air escort, and directly from aircraft. Consequently, before the invasion could be undertaken, the British fighter aircraft that threatened it had to be destroyed; it was to this end that Goering's 'Luftwaffe' launched its attacks.

During July and early August channel shipping and south coast ports, such as Portland and Dover, were attacked. Then, from 12 August onwards the fighter bases and factories were attacked by bombers. The success of their missions depended on the ability of their fighter escorts—usually Messerschmidt 109s and 110s—to keep RAF fighters at bay while they destroyed their targets. These assaults, which reached their peak in early September, failed in their major objectives. The British fighter force, despite growing desperately short of pilots, was not destroyed, and in fact shot down almost twice as many enemy aircraft as they lost. Statistics in this respect are obviously unreliable—not only was it often difficult to be certain of the damage inflicted on an enemy but also both sides took an optimistic view of their success in an effort to boost morale. The British had two great advantages in the battle. The Spitfire, although only providing about one-fifth of the fighter force, was technically superior to the Messerschmidt, and by the increasing use of radar, the British fighters were able to go directly to their targets rather than staying in the air.

On 7 September the battle took on a new complexion. The attack shifted from the airfields to the major ports and cities. London docks were seriously damaged in the first of these raids, and the city's power supplies badly hit. More than 300 Londoners died and over 1000 were seriously hurt. 15 September marked a further turning point. Two German attacks that day, one in the morning and a second in the afternoon, were launched, each with about 250 aircraft. At the time, it was estimated that 150 of these were shot down; even with the revised and more likely figure of fifty-six, it was a loss rate that could not be sustained. Thereafter there were fewer daylight raids and from early October almost all the German attacks were night-bombing raids on cities. Hitler was no longer preparing the ground for invasion, but rather attacking the civilian population in an effort to destroy morale. London, together with ports like Bristol and Southampton and cities like Birmingham and Coventry, all suffered heavily. By the end of 1940 over 20 000 civilians had died in the raids, and during the next year another 19 000 were to die. Nonetheless, the invasion had been postponed and the resolve of the British to go on fighting had not been destroyed.

The battle of Britain was a major influence in bringing the United States closer to Britain's aid. On 2 September, 1940 the USA agreed to provide fifty destroyers to help in guarding convoys in exchange for the right to use naval bases in British colonies near the USA. In November it was agreed to standardize some military equipment and to co-operate in arms development. By January 1941 Britain had used up her credit in America, and the 'cash and carry' system was seriously jeopardized. Instead, Congress approved the 'Lend-Lease' system, by which the President was permitted to supply any state 'whose defence the President deems vital to the defence of the US'. The act was approved in March and a month later the first supplies of food arrived in Britain.

3. The Widening War

(a) Africa and the Balkans

The battle of Britain marked the end of the first phase of the war. Until September 1940 Germany had not been checked and had brought much of Europe under her control *(see Map 40)*. In fact, her victorious progress was to continue, but no longer in a single 'victory-by-victory' style in which each conquest was followed up by another. Instead, the war widened into a number of fronts, the most critical of which, to both sides, was the Russian. Because of its importance, this has been treated separately, but the other fronts have been summarized in the chart on pages 411–16.

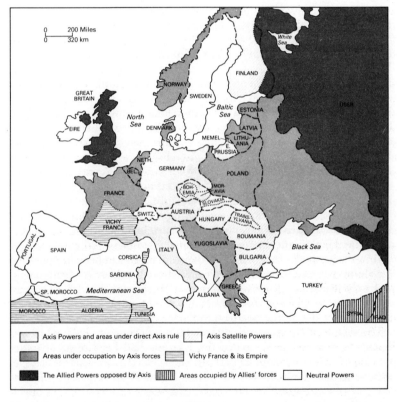

Map 40 Europe at the height of Axis expansion, October 1942

There was remarkably little fighting in Europe during the year from June 1940 to June 1941. Hitler had achieved his first major objectives and Western and Central Europe had, for the first time ever, been practically united under a single ruler *(see Map 40)*. His interests in South-east Europe and the Balkans were peripheral, since they neither posed a major threat nor offered any great rewards. In addition, they would have been quite unable to withstand any concerted military attack, especially as Hungary was already sympathetic to Germany. Consequently, both Roumania and Bulgaria sought an accommodation with Hitler, while resistance in Yugoslavia was shortlived. Greece posed slightly more problems as it successfully resisted Mussolini's troops, but it too had succumbed by the spring of 1941.

The fighting in Africa revolved around Italy's two main colonies, Libya and Italian East Africa. Both bordered British spheres of influence and the temptation to expand into these was too great. In the case of East Africa, the result was a relatively short war in which, for the first time, Axis forces (albeit Italian ones) were decisively defeated. In the case of Libya, Mussolini's decision to attack Egypt was to have far more important consequences that were ultimately to lead to his downfall.

(b) The Invasion of Russia (1941–March 1943) and the Entry of the USA

Hitler had formally issued orders for the invasion of Russia in December 1940. It had always been a part of his plans to capture the South of European Russia and take its rich cornfields and raw materials. Nor had he ever intended to share his hegemony of Europe with another ruler— especially not a communist one. After his easy victories throughout Europe, including the supposedly crack French army, the ill-equipped Russians would be easy prey; the temptation was too great to resist. His advisers, on the basis of intelligence reports and the performance of the Russian army in Finland, suggested that an eight-week campaign should be sufficient to reach Moscow and bring the Soviet government to its knees. Consequently, he saw no need to rush into 'Operation Barbarossa', as it was known, and British fears that the attack would come in May 1941 were proved wrong. Even so, their warnings had been little heeded by Stalin, who continued to believe that Hitler would defeat Britain first.

In the event, 22 June was chosen as the fateful day. The German attack was launched on three fronts that would, it was hoped, eventually stretch from the White Sea to the Black Sea *(see Map 41)*. One prong, assisted by Roumanian forces, attacked through Southern Poland towards Kiev: its ultimate goals, when the Ukraine had been brought under German control, were the Don Basin and even the Caucasus oil fields. A second attack was launched through the Baltic States and aimed to take the city of Leningrad (as Petrograd had been re-named). It was to be helped by Finnish forces in the North, who hoped that their assistance might lead, once again, to freedom from Russian influence. The third, central, prong of the attack was to go via Minsk and Smolensk towards the capital, Moscow. In all, the Germans had a similar number of men to the Russian defenders, over 150 divisions each, but were better equipped and enjoyed air superiority. They also had two of the new 'Panzer' divisions of light and completely mechanized troops. *(Continued, page 417)*

Date	Balkans and east Mediterranean	Middle East	North Africa	East Africa	The War at Sea
1940					
26 June	USSR demands Bessarabia and Northern Bukovina from Roumania. They were ceded and occupied by Soviet troops				
6 August				Italian forces invade British Somaliland and conquer it	
17 August					Germany declares total blockade of Great Britain. In fact, this was already in operation and throughout 1940 and 1941 Britain fought the Battle of the Atlantic— the effort to continue to bring supplies from the USA, despite German U-boat and
30 August	Under German and Russian pressure, Roumania and Hungary reach an agreement by which most of Transylvania was ceded to Hungary. King Carol of Roumania replaced by his son, Michael V				

surface attacks. In both years over 4 million tons of shipping, most of it British, was sunk. Eventually the U-boats were combatted, by the continued use of escorted convoys and anti-submarine devices, especially detection equipment

8 September	Roumania forced to cede Southern Dobrudja to Bulgaria	
13 September		Italian attack on Egypt launched from Libya. By the 16th had reached Sidi Barrani (*see map 42*) and then stopped to reassemble
8 October	German troops enter Roumania	
28 October	Italian troops invade Greece from Albania. British troops sent to Greece	
13 November		British aircraft from the carrier 'Illustrious' destroy three Italian battleships at Taranto
20 November	Hungary joins the Axis	
23 November	Roumania joins the Axis	
3 December	Greek victory in Albania, pushing Italian forces back and forcing Germany to send 50 000 troops to their aid	
8 December		British counter attack

1941

5 January	recaptures Sidi Barrani and moves into Libya	
15 January	Italians at Bardia surrender	British attack from Sudan and Kenya into Italian East Africa
22 January	Capture of Tobruk by Allies	
7 February	Benghazi captured: in the counter-attack more than 100 000 Italians captured	
26 February		Mogadishu, capital of Italian Somaliland, captured
1 March	Bulgaria joins Axis and German troops occupied Sofia	
25 March	Yugoslavs sign Axis Pact but then Paul overthrown (*see page 201*) and new government of Simovic declares its neutrality	
30 March		
3 April	Italian forces, reinforced by German troops under	Battle of Cape Matapan—three Italian cruisers and two destroyers sunk between Greece and Crete

6 April		Rommel, re-enter Libya. British forces weakened by 60 000 men going to Greece	Addis Ababa falls to British and (5 May) Haile Selassie reinstated	
14 April	Surrender of Yugoslavia	Germans reoccupy Sollum and Bardia		
17 April		Tobruk surrounded and beseiged		
20 April				
23 April	Surrender of Greece			
27 April	48 000 British troops evacuated from Greece			
2 May	Iraqi artillery bombard British troops stationed in Iraq, leading to British counter attacks			
18 May			Battle of Amba Alagi in Ethiopia—British forces from North and South converge and force Italian Commander-in-Chief, Duke of Aosta, to surrender. By November all Italian East Africa pacified	
20 May	German paratroopers invade Crete			
27 May	Remaining British			German battleship 'Bismarck' sunk
31 May	British forces enter			

414

		Baghdad	
4 June	forces in Crete evacuated to Cyprus and Egypt	British troops enter	
8 June		Mosul: armistice signed and pro-British government installed Combined allied attack on Syria, which had been used as a base for German and Italian aircraft	
18 June		German treaty with Turkey by which each promised to respect the other's territory	
22 June			German attack on Russia
14 July		Armistice with Syria giving British right to occupy both Syria and Lebanon	
28 August		Pressure on Iran by British and Russians results in Iranian government agreeing to British and Russian forces being stationed there	
18 November			British counter attack launched into Libya, and on 11 December Tobruk relieved.

7 December

1942
27 May

Benghazi again taken

Axis attack launched: Tobruk taken 21 June and advance into Egypt halted at El Alamein: followed by a four-month lull

Japanese attack on Pearl Harbour

As soon as the German campaign began, the Soviet Union was assured of the support of Hitler's other enemies. On 12 July an alliance was signed with Great Britain, whose government persuaded even the Poles to assist their usually hostile neighbour. The main agreement between the Soviet government and its Western allies was signed on 1 October 1941. By it, both Britain and the United States agreed to supply Russia with war materials for nine months. Subsequently, on 11 June 1942 the United States extended her lend-lease arrangements to Russia, and eventually sent 11 billion dollars' worth of goods to the Soviet Union. Despite considerable transport difficulties (to avoid the problems involved in reaching the northern port of Murmansk, many supplies were sent through Iran), over 3000 tanks and more than 4000 planes were eventually supplied by the Western allies.

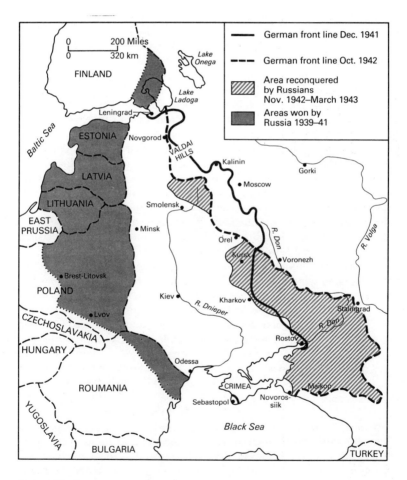

Map 41 The Eastern Front, 1939–43

Initially, however, they could provide little help, and Hitler's forecast of an eight-week campaign seemed justified. By mid-August his forces were approaching Odessa and Kiev in the South and had taken Smolensk in the centre. In the North, the Baltic States had fallen almost immediately, and by early September German forces were outside Leningrad. The city was to be besieged for the next two winters, through which supplies were brought across the frozen Lake Ladoga and thousands of inhabitants died of starvation. Despite this hold-up in the North, the southern wing of the German army continued its advance. During September most of the Ukraine was taken. On 16 October Odessa fell; on the 26th Kharkov. The Crimean peninsula was invaded, and by the end of October all of it except the city of Sebastopol was taken.

In the centre, a huge offensive was launched towards Moscow during October. It stretched from Orel some 200 miles northwards to the Valdai Hills. At first, it was successful and reached the surroundings of Moscow itself. There, however, it was held by the Soviet army under the command of General Zhukov. In November, General von Brauchitsch launched a new attack, in an effort to take the city before the full rigours of the Russian winter. He failed to do so, and on 7 December decided to end the offensive and hold his position until spring. For his pains, he was relieved as commander-in-chief and Hitler himself took personal control.

Despite their territorial gains, the German army had not been as successful as it appeared. Everywhere it had been met with fierce resistance; it was not for nothing that Russians referred to World War II as 'The Great Patriotic War'. Thousands of prisoners had been taken, and thousands of Russians killed. Yet nowhere did the German armies receive succour; rather, the civilians, often in company with any serviceable equipment and materials, were evacuated and the Germans forced to bring up their own equipment over enormous distances. Over 25 000 miles of railway track had to be either rebuilt or converted to German gauge in the central region alone. Moreover, the German troops suffered badly during the winter of 1941–2. Their equipment was not suited to the harsh Russian winter: boots were too small for extra socks to be worn, and vehicles could only be kept from freezing up by burning fires under them, so wasting valuable fuel. During the winter, there were many Russian attacks on isolated German garrisons, and they even succeeded in retaking Kalinin. Nevertheless, the Germans survived the winter and were once again ready to take the offensive in May.

By the time they did so, the whole balance of the war had been altered by the Japanese raid on Pearl Harbour on 7 December 1941. Until then, Japan's expansion had gone virtually unopposed. In 1932 Japan had occupied Manchuria *(see page 372)* and had thereafter extended her rule southwards into China itself. In October 1941 French Indo-China (now Vietnam) had been conquered. In the same month the new government of General Tojo made threatening noises towards the United States, saying she should end her embargo on trade with Japan and stop supplying the Chinese with arms and equipment. These threats, though noted, were not taken seriously, as it seemed far more likely that Japan would extend her Empire southwards into Dutch or British areas before attacking any American possessions. Consequently the raid came as an almost complete surprise and over 2000 Americans were killed and another 2000 accounted missing or wounded. Eight battleships and three cruisers were either sunk or severely damaged, and almost 200 aircraft destroyed.

The attack had the immediate effect of solidifying the alliances on both sides. On 8 December America's declaration of war on Japan was accompanied by a British declaration of war. On 11 December Germany and Italy declared war on the USA, and signed a full military alliance with Japan. Why Hitler chose to do this remains a mystery; that he did so was ultimately to prove a decisive factor in the outcome of the war. Only the Soviet Union stayed out of the mutual declarations of war, having signed a mutual non-aggression pact with Japan earlier in 1941. However, she did join the United States and Britain (and their allies) in signing a joint declaration pledging an all-out war against all their enemies and agreeing not to make a separate peace. This was signed on 1 January 1942. Britain, fighting alone only six months before, had been joined by the world's two greatest industrial powers. In the first instance, though, this had little effect as the Americans were by no means prepared for a war in both Europe and the Far East, and the Japanese were able to continue their advances, taking Hong Kong, Singapore and the Philippines by the spring of 1942.

For 1942, Hitler adopted different tactics in Russia. Instead of attacking on all three fronts, it was decided to restrict the offensive to the southern front. This had been the most successful area and, if it continued to be so, might be expected to draw troops from the North, so facilitating the German attacks there. More importantly, it contained the rich industrial area of the Don Basin and the oilfields of the Caucasus. Ultimately, German forces might be able to take the Caucasus and march south-westwards to link up with Axis forces from North Africa to take the Middle East in a mighty pincer movement.

In May, a new offensive in the Crimea resulted in the capture of Sebastopol. A Russian counter-attack led by Marshal Timoshenko to the south of Kharkov on 12 May was held after a week. Then, between 10 June and 2 July three German attacks were launched along a front from Kursk to the south of Kharkov (see Map 41). The Russian armies were forced to retreat, losing many men. In one attack to the North-west of Kharkov the Germans claimed to have taken more than 200 000 prisoners. The northern part of the attack was held at Voronezh on the Don, but further South the Germans made rapid progress. By mid-August they had advanced over the Don and into the Caucasus, taking their first oilfield, at Maikop, on 9 August. The advance into the Caucasus, which would not only provide petrol supplies for the Germans but also deprive the Russians of them, then had to be slowed. Until the city of Stalingrad to the North could be taken, and with it the Don and Volga, there was a risk that the German forces in the Caucasus could be cut off and isolated.

On 14 September the first German forces reached the outskirts of Stalingrad. They were to remain outside the city until the end of January, having encountered some of the stiffest resistance of the war. Thomson has described the battle as 'a sort of Verdun in reverse—an objective so vital for Germany to win that she poured in her men and material extravagantly, only to lose both to no avail'. As the German Sixth Army fought snipers among the streets and ruins of the city, so General Zhukov, transferred South from Moscow, moved three armies around the outside of the city. The first attack, from the North-east, was launched on 21 September and the second, from the South, on 1 October. The German army was trapped in a pincer, with the city in front of it and Russian armies in its rear. All efforts to extricate it from its dilemma were repulsed and on 31 January 1943 General von Paulus and his surviving 80 000 men surrendered.

At the same time, there were other Russian successes. In the North, the Germans were driven back from Lake Ladoga, and the siege of Leningrad, an even more epic struggle than Stalingrad, was lifted. Although the Germans successfully withdrew their forces from the Caucasus, they were driven back on a wide front in the South. During February, the Russians recaptured Kursk, Rostov and Kharkov, and had either killed or taken prisoner ½ million Germans during three months. Even though General Manstein managed to take back Kharkov on 15 March and end the Russian drive, the change in the situation was clear. German forces had been driven back over 200 miles and, for the first time in Europe, the boot was on the other foot.

4. The Mediterranean Counter Attack

(a) The Allied Conquest of North Africa
In the summer of 1942 Axis forces were also successful in North Africa (*see page 416*). The attack that was launched in late May took 20 000 prisoners in Tobruk on 21 June and had advanced along the coast to take Bardia. The British forces decided to form their defensive line at El Alamein, seventy miles West of Alexandria (*see Map 42*). This was an excellent defensive position as it was bounded on one side by the sea and on the other by the Qattara Depression, a salt-pan through which tanks could not advance. Consequently, outflanking manoeuvres were impossible, and the British were left with only a thirty-five mile front to defend. When Rommel launched his first attack on this on 1 July, it was repulsed, although the British were still relatively weak; they were soon reinforced by men and equipment from Egypt. The next major German assault—on 31 August—did advance fifteen miles in the South but was held when it attempted to turn northwards towards the Alam Halfa ridge.

By this time, the Allied leaders had decided on a dual attack in North

Africa. One thrust would come from the British 8th Army led by Montgomery through the El Alamein region while the other would come from landings in French North Africa and advance eastwards through Tunisia and Libya. However, the defensive advantages of El Alamein inevitably made it a difficult area in which to attack. It was only possible to advance through a direct frontal assault, which involved passing through German minefields.

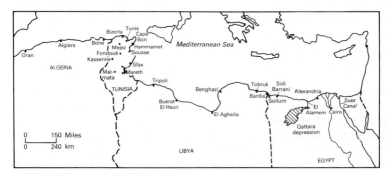

Map 42 The war in North Africa

On 23 October the attack was launched with a heavy bombardment. Two routes were made through the minefields in the northern sector and, after heavy fighting, the British broke through on 3 November, taking some 30 000 prisoners, many of them Italian. Many tanks were destroyed or abandoned by both sides, but in this respect the British were at a considerable advantage, having recently been reinforced with 500 American Sherman tanks. Rommel retreated in the first instance to El Algheila but by mid-January had been forced back to Buerat, 250 miles to the West. On 15 January this position was attacked and by the 23rd the first of Montgomery's troops reached Tripoli.

The Anglo-American landings in the North-west had taken place on 8 November 1942. A convoy of 850 ships had been needed to transport the force, which was split into three. The force that attacked Casablanca on the Atlantic coast met considerable opposition, but the landings at Oran and Algiers were easier. As expected, there were considerable political repercussions as a result of landing Allied troops in French territory. Darlan, the Vichy head of state in North Africa, was kept in power by the Allies, to whom he promised support. He was disowned by the Vichy government and, after his assassination on 24 December, was replaced by an Allies' appointee, General Giraud. As a result of the invasion, and ostensibly to guard against an attack on the southern coast, the Germans occupied Southern France and removed Pétain's regime, but the French fleet at Toulon was scuttled on 27 November when the Germans attempted to take it over.

From Algiers, the British arm of the invasion force advanced to Bone but was held in its efforts to conquer Tunisia. Following an Axis counter-attack, the line stabilized through Mejez and Foudouk by early 1943. An Axis attack in mid-February succeeded in taking the Kasserine Pass, but it was held for only four days. Rommel's forces in Tunisia were faced by the dilemma of a two-front attack which, to the outside observer, they would eventually lose. However, it was critical for them to delay defeat for as long as possible so that Allied forces were tied up in North Africa and Germany's own eastern defences could be prepared. In the event, they held out until May 1943. On 20 March the British attacked the Mareth Line (a French-built defensive line in Southern Tunisia) by a flanking movement through the Matmata Hills. By the end of March the Line had been taken, and during April Montgomery's force advanced up the coast, taking the ports of Sfax and Sousse. At the same time, the Allied forces in the West had taken the Fondouk Pass and opened the way for a final assault on Tunis and Bizerta.

By this time, the remains of the Axis forces in North Africa were considerably outnumbered. They had about 200 000 men to the Allies 300 000, had only a tenth of the number of tanks and were desperately short of air support. Nonetheless, they were well equipped with anti-tank defences and hoped to hold out for a considerable time. In the event, the final attack lasted little over a week. It was launched on 5 May from both West and South of Tunis, and rapidly took Bizerta, Tunis, Hammamet and the Cape Bon Peninsula. On 13 May the Italian commander-in-chief, Marshal Messe, ordered the surrender. Some 250 000 men were captured in the Tunisian campaign alone. In all the Axis powers had lost nearly a million men, 8000 aircraft and 2½ million tons of shipping in the North African fighting. Mussolini's dreams of an Italian Empire in · Africa were dead, as were Hitler's hopes for the domination of Egypt and the Middle East. Instead, the Allies had reopened the southern Mediterranean to shipping and had made possible attacks into Southern Europe.

(b) The Invasion of Italy

The Allies' leaders had agreed at the Casablanca Conference in January 1943 that the invasion of Italy should follow victory in North Africa. They had accepted that any attempt to reconquer France should not be made before 1944: such an attack was seen as the key to victory in Europe, and should therefore only be undertaken when enough men and materials had been prepared to ensure success. In the meantime, something had to be done in Western Europe to help the Russians on the eastern front. Churchill described Italy as the 'soft under-belly of Europe' from which further attacks could be made, at first by air, into central Europe and Germany itself.

During June, the islands of Pantelleria and Lampedusa were captured after heavy fighting, and on 10 July, British and American forces were landed in Sicily. More than 2000 ships transported 160 000 men there from Tunisia. American forces were landed on the South-west of the island and British on the South-east. Syracuse and Augusta were quickly captured, and by 22 July half the island had been retaken. However, there was considerable resistance at Catania and it was not until 18 August that both British and American forces converged on and captured Messina *(see Map 43)*. By this time, more than 60 000 Germans had managed to cross to the mainland, with a smaller number of Italians, to fight another day.

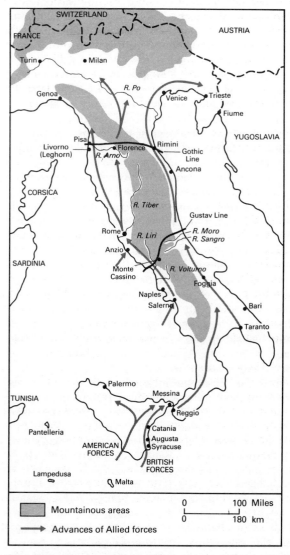

Map 43 The Conquest of Italy, 1943–5

However, by the time of the capture of Messina there had been considerable political developments. On 24 July, Mussolini was sum-

423

moned to appear before the Fascist Grand Council, which had previously acted as his rubber-stamp. He was severly criticized, sacked by King Victor Emmanuel (25 July) and subsequently arrested and kept under guard. His place as Prime Minister was taken by Marshal Badoglio, who had, in agreement with the King, decided on the necessity of an armistice. Italy had already lost over a million men, and the future was only too clear—Germany and Britain would fight their way up the Italian peninsula bringing only further destruction. An armistice would at least protect them from one side. Negotiations opened in August and on 3 September a secret act of surrender was signed at Algiers. Allied forces then crossed the straits of Messina. On 8 September the surrender was made public, and the following day American forces landed at Salerno. Two days later the Italian fleet surrendered to the British at Malta.

As expected, the Germans did not accept this all too easy surrender. German forces occupied Rome and, having rescued him from imprisonment, installed Mussolini as head of a 'Republican Fascist' government in alliance with Germany.

Following their crossing to the mainland, the British forces moved to the eastern side of the peninsula, where they were supported by further landings. With relative ease, they advanced through the East-coast ports and across the Foggia plain. During November they succeeded in crossing the rivers Sangro and Moro but were then held up. On the West coast, the American landings at Salerno were faced initially by considerable difficulties and it took them five days to break out from their beachhead. Having done so, they took Naples on 1 October and by mid-November had crossed the Volturno. However, the Allies' hopes of reaching Rome by Christmas looked over-optimistic. Kesselring, the German Commander, realized that by judicious use of the mountainous terrain, the advancing Allies could be held up and so constructed the 'Gustav Line' to the South of Rome through the Appenines, incorporating in it the famous monastery at Monte Cassino (see Map 43).

Throughout the winter, the Allies made little progress in the mountains where heavy rain added to the considerable transport difficulties. In an effort to go round the defences, Allied forces, mainly American, were landed at Anzio on 22 January. The landing was initially successful but it was then decided to strengthen the position before breaking out. During this time, the Germans made a number of counter-attacks which threatened to force the Allies out; only in mid-February was the position secured.

In the mountains, a massive bombardment was launched on Monte Cassino on 15 March. It was subsequently shown that the ancient monastery, birthplace of the Benedictine order, had not been a key defensive position and its destruction was unnecessary. On 11 May a new offensive was launched both in the mountains and up the valley of the Liri. In the former, several key points were captured by Polish forces and by French colonial troops from the Atlas mountains. On 23 May Kesselring ordered the retreat from the Gustav Line and on 4 June the

Allies entered Rome, having linked up with the forces from Anzio. By 12 August Florence had fallen and the Allies were in control of Italy South of a line from Leghorn and Ancona.

However, the final conquest of Italy was not completed until 1 May 1945. Kesselring constructed a second defensive line—the 'Gothic Line' —which held through the winter of 1944–5, although by this time the Allies were more concerned with France and Northern Europe and made no real effort to take Northern Italy. In April 1945 a new offensive drove the Italians across the Po and occupied all of the North. Mussolini attempted to escape to Switzerland but was found and summarily executed by Italian anti-Fascists.

The conquest of Italy had brought the Allies several advantages. Obviously, it eliminated Italian troops not only from Italy but also from other fronts. It also occupied up to twenty-six divisions of German troops which might otherwise have been available in France or Russia at a crucial time. In addition, it provided the Allies with bases for bombing raids into the Balkans, Southern France and Central Europe, which would otherwise have been out of their range.

5. The Defeat of Germany

(a) The Eastern Front 1943–5

After the Russian successes of early 1943, a German counter-attack was expected. It duly came on 5 July in the form of a combined attack from North and South on the Russian salient around Kursk *(see Map 44)*. The attack from the South advanced rapidly, but that in the North was held and the offensive petered out. On 12 July the Russians launched their own offensive against the German salient around Orel, attacking it from both East and North. At first the attackers advanced very rapidly but were then slowed and eventually took Orel on 5 August. The eventual success of the operation confirmed the Russian generals in their belief that they could now move to the offensive and it was decided that these should be launched at various points in order to force the German defenders to move from one place to another to reinforce their line. These Russian offensives, apart from minor set-backs, were almost entirely successful and not only drove the Germans out of Russia but also provided a launching pad for a Russian attack into Germany. In order to record this advance as simply and briefly as possible, it has been catalogued in the date chart below, which should be studied in conjunction with Map 44.

1943 23 August   Russian offensives launched. In the North, advanced towards Smolensk (captured 5 September); in the South, reached the river Dnieper on a 400-mile front by October.

6 November	Kiev recaptured and Russian forces advance seventy miles over the Dnieper. A German counter-attack, led by Manstein, recovers some twenty-five miles of this advance but is then held.
1944 January–February	In the North an offensive from Leningrad removes the German siege forces and (on 20 January) reaches Novgorod. In the South, Russian forces advance towards the river Bug, forcing the Germans to withdraw their most southerly forces. On the Dnieper, ten German divisions are trapped near Cherkassy (17 February) and 50 000 men either killed or captured.
March–April	Russian forces cross the Dniester and enter (pre-war) Poland. They are also close to the Roumanian and Czech borders. In the South Odessa taken on 10 April and during April and early May the Crimea is recaptured.
10 June	Offensive in northern-central sector liberates to 1939, the Mannerheim Line immediately broken and Viborg taken. _
June–July	Offensive in northern-central sector liberate Vitbsk and Minsk (6 July).
July–October	In Poland, the advance from the South leads to capture of Lvov, Brest-Litovsk and Lublin but the advance halted outside Warsaw. As a result, the Germans turn on the Polish supporters in Warsaw and crush them; there is considerable political outcry at the failure of the Russians to provide them with more aid. In the North, the Russian advance through Latvia reaches the Gulf of Riga. A German counter-attack reopens communications with German forces in Estonia in late August, but soon afterwards Russian troops reach East Prussia.
24 August	Roumania surrenders. A week later Russian troops enter Bucharest and Roumanian forces join the Russians in marching up the Danube towards Yugoslavia.
8 September	Bulgaria surrenders and Soviet troops enter Sofia. A pro-Russian government established and Bulgarian forces also join the attack on Yugoslavia.
20 October	Belgrade liberated by Russians and their new allies. Yugoslav resistance forces, at first divided between those under the conservative Mihailovic and those under the Communist Tito, play a large part in occupying German troops and in leading the liberation.

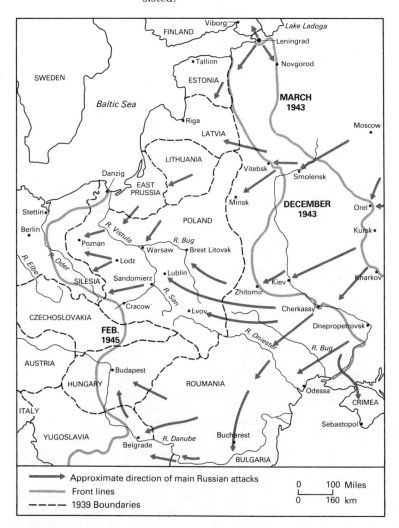

Map 44 The Eastern Front, 1943–5

1945 12 January   Three-pronged Russian assault on Poland laun-
            ched. Marshals Koniev (from Sandomierz),
            Zhukov (on the Vistula) and Rokossovsky (further
            north) advance in conjunction, while East Prussia
            also invaded from the East. Warsaw falls on 17
            January, then Cracow and Lodz taken. Zhukov's
            forces reach the Oder and by mid-February

| | Koniev's forces are in the Silesian industrial area. By 20 February Russian forces are within thirty miles of Berlin. |
| 20 April | Russian troops enter Berlin and the centre of the city is bombarded. |

Throughout the advance, the Russians had concentrated on the southern front although it was ultimately in the North—through East Prussia and Poland—that the decisive battles were to be fought. This concentration on the South was chiefly because it was easier to attack there and success was more assured. It was also the result of Stalin's determination to ensure that the East European states—Bulgaria, Roumania, Yugoslavia and Hungary especially—would be loyal to the Soviet Union after the war.

In view of Russia's singular failure to resist Germany's attacks in 1941, her spectacular successes in 1943–5 demand explanation. The ability of the Russian soldiers not only to survive but also to attack during the winter was a major asset and their sheer courage and fortitude should not be discounted as a major contributory factor in Russia's success. The Russians also developed highly effective and efficient artillery that was considerably superior to their enemy's. The staff organization and administration of the Russian armies were considerably improved as the war went on. Obviously, the assistance of America and Britain *(see page 417)* was a considerable asset. However, the great achievement of the Russian government has been described by Falls as follows:

> . . . they had put into the field a mass army of many millions with so relatively a high standard (of equipment and mechanization). They had combined so far as was humanly possible, mass, which commonly stands for a low scale of efficiency, with the most modern type of equipment; and had made a remarkable success of the venture.

(b) D-Day and the Reconquest of Europe

The Allies' leaders had always accepted that victory in Europe would finally be achieved by the reconquest of France and subsequent invasion of Europe. The code name for the plan—'Operation Overlord'—implied the importance that was attached to it.

Preparations for the attack were the most elaborate ever. Since the Battle of Britain, British and, later, American planes had bombed targets of strategic importance in Germany. During 1943 this had taken on a new form with, in general, American Flying Fortresses striking precise targets in day-light raids and British Lancasters bombing cities at night. Many cities, especially Berlin itself and the cities in the western industrial areas such as Essen and Dortmund, suffered extensive damage, although industrial production was not decisively harmed until 1944. In the first months of that year the bombing campaign was intensified, and German military targets in France were also attacked. By the end of the war, the Germans had received over 300 tons of explosive for every ton dropped on Britain.

More immediately, intricate plans were drawn up and special equipment devised. Originally, it was planned to have a three-front attack, but, on Montgomery's insistence, it was expanded to five. The Normandy coast from Caen to the Cotentin peninsula *(see Map 45)* was chosen as the best site as the landing troops would be least likely to encounter concentrated opposition in the first instance, as they would have done at the most obvious point—the Pas de Calais. Under the overall control of the American General Eisenhower, troops were dispersed in secret camps along the British South and East coasts. In the hope of confusing the enemy, cardboard camps were even constructed in the Dover area so that the expected attack seemed likely to come from there. To overcome the problems of supplying the landing forces, artificial harbours, known as 'Mulberry Harbours', which could be transported in sections and erected across the channel, were built. To provide fuel, pipelines under the Channel (PLUTO = 'Pipe Line Under The Ocean') were to be laid. In all, some 10 000 planes, eighty warships and 4000 other craft were to be needed for the invasion, all of which had to be prepared and assembled in the right place. Drawing on their experiences in North Africa, Sicily and Italy, the Allied leaders assembled the largest and best equipped invasion force ever seen.

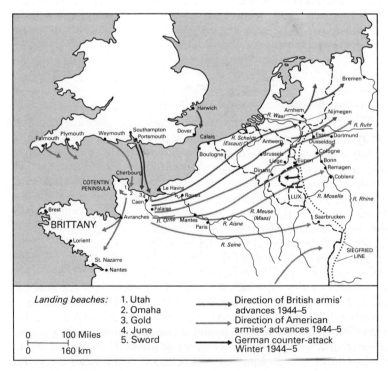

Map 45 The D-Day landings and reconquest of northern Europe

To gain maximum advantage, the landings had to take place when there would be half tide on the beaches forty minutes after first light—conditions that could only be met three times a month. Consequently, Eisenhower decided to go ahead on the night of 5 June despite poorish weather as the forecast was for an improvement. German intelligence had broken the code used to French resistance workers and actually knew of the invasion, but refused to believe it was the main attack because the weather was so poor, and believed it to be only a raid. A diversionary attack was made in the Pas de Calais region while 60 000 men, supported by airborne landings and a massive bombardment of the German defences, were landed in the five chosen areas (codenamed Utah, Omaha, Gold, Juno and Sword) on the morning of 6 June.

The initial landings succeeded in establishing the beach heads that were needed. Within a week 300 000 men had been landed and in the first 100 days of the operation, over 2 million men, 450 000 vehicles and 4 million tons of equipment had reached France. The plan was for the American forces to capture the Cotentin Peninsula and the port of Cherbourg and then, leaving some forces to recapture Brittany, turn towards the North-east and advance to the Seine, South of Paris. The British forces would attack towards Paris itself and the two armies would then move forward in parallel. The first three weeks were to be spent in establishing stores and providing the means to break out. The Americans were able to move first, reaching the West side of the Cotentin Peninsula on 18 June and Cherbourg a week later. The port was captured on 27 June but had been so damaged that it was several weeks before it could be used. The British forces had hoped to break out by 3 July, but were in fact delayed. On 9 July, after a severe struggle, Caen was captured and, on 18 July, the British launched a major offensive.

During July and August, the Allied offensives proceeded as intended. The Americans had taken Avranches and despatched one division to Brittany and were able to concentrate on their advance north-eastwards. They were delayed by a counter-offensive to the west of Falaise, which the Allies turned to advantage by turning back northwards and trapping the Germans in the Falaise region. On 19 August the Americans reached the Seine at Mantes. By this time, their advance was supported by Franco-American landings at Toulon in the South of France, which then moved northwards to join the main attack. On 26 August the Allies reached Paris, and De Gaulle and the Free French forces marched into their capital. By this time, some forty of the sixty defending German divisions had been destroyed or seriously damaged; they had suffered about 500 000 casualties and abandoned 10 000 vehicles. The end appeared to be nigh.

On 1 September Eisenhower assumed personal control of the land forces from Montgomery, as had been planned. He intended all his forces to advance simultaneously on a broad front, in contrast to the British general's preference for a mass attack in one region to break through. This led, both at the time and later, to considerable debate and, in Montgomery's opinion, to 'several unco-ordinated fronts'.

In early September, the advance continued but then the Allies were held up through the winter. In the North, Brussels was liberated on 2 September and, on 4 September, the vital port of Antwerp was captured undamaged, although it could not be used until November as the Germans still controlled the estuary of the river Scheldt. On 8 September, Liège was taken, by which time the Americans had reached the Moselle. On the 12th the first American forces crossed into Germany in the Eupen area. By this time, the Allies were finding the co-ordination and supply of their forces increasingly difficult. However, it was decided to attempt to secure crossings of the vital rivers of Holland—the Maas, Waal and Lower Rhine—so that Allied forces could be moved northwards and thence into Germany through the weakest northern defences of the Siegfried Line.

To this end, Allied paratroopers were landed at Arnhem while land forces advanced towards Nijmwegen. The operation was launched on 17 September. Although the land forces managed to capture bridges across the Maas and Waal, they failed to reach their colleagues at Arnhem soon enough, and they had to be withdrawn without capturing the crossing. Of the 9000 who had been landed, less than 2500 escaped in what has become one of the heroic battles of the last year of the war.

During the winter, the Allied advance found both the defences of the Siegfried Line and the ravages of the weather a considerable handicap. Although the Rhine was reached in early December, the Allied forces were spread over a wide front, and von Runstedt saw the opportunity to take advantage of this. He hoped to be able to advance northwards from the Ardennes towards Liège and, ultimately, Antwerp. On 16 December the attack began and German forces advanced up to fifty miles into Allied held territory by Christmas. Thereafter, though, he was unable to extend his advance as Allied re-inforcements were rushed northwards and better weather enabled American planes to bomb the Germans. In the event, Von Runstedt lost over 200 000 men either killed or as prisoners and the 'Battle of the Bulge' proved to be the last German counter-attack, not the first.

By March 1945 Germany was under attack from both sides. In the East the Red Army reached the Baltic in Pomerania and had made further advances in Hungary and Silesia. At the beginning of April Russian troops were in the suburbs of Vienna and on 16 April Zhukov launched what proved to be the final attack on Berlin from the Oder. In the West, the final battle in front of the Siegfried Line from the Nijmegen bridgehead was launched on 3 February. On 6 March American forces reached Cologne and the next day took the bridge across the Rhine at Remagen intact. Thereafter it proved easier than expected to cross the Rhine and by mid-April the Allies were able to advance at about forty miles a day. Only because the Allies had pledged themselves to demand an unconditional surrender and Hitler had pledged never to give in did the war continue. On 25 April the fate of Germany was sealed: Berlin was surrounded, and Russian and American troops met up at Torgau. On 1 May Hitler's death was broadcast to the German people; he had committed suicide in his bunker the night before. Admiral Doenitz took over and, on 7 May, the official surrender was signed, although in many areas local commanders had already given up. On 8 May President Truman and Prime Minister Churchill announced the victory in Europe (V–E) to their people, and the next day Stalin told the Russians their war was over.

6. Bibliography

There are hundreds of books on World War II. I have therefore restricted this list to those that are most readily available and most likely to be of use. All of them contain bibliographies which will refer you to more detailed works and to works on more specialist aspects. Of the text books listed on page 3, the best on this topic are Wood and Roberts, both of which have sections on German-occupied Europe.

The best introductory book on the war as a whole is *World at War* by Mark Arnold Forster (Collins, 1973), which was originally the book accompanying a television series of the same name. It contains extensive illustrations and highlights all the important features of the war, illustrating them with personal memories that are often taken from interviews for the television series. An older but valuable outline is provided by C.B. Falls in *The Second World War* (Methuen, 1948), while a more recent work is *History of World War II* edited by A.J.P. Taylor and compiled by S.L. Mayer (Octopus books, 1974). This is adapted from the magazine series 'History of the Twentieth Century' and contains many colour pictures and diagrams and chapters by separate authors not only on military but also political and social aspects of the war. A.J.P. Taylor has also produced *The Second World War: An Illustrated History* (Hamish Hamilton, 1975, also published by Penguin). Another recent work, and one that includes documents, is *The Ordeal of Total War 1939–45* by G. Wright (Harper Torchbooks, 1968).

For greater detail, the four best known works are the six-volume *The Second World War* by W.S. Churchill (Cassell, 1948–52), *The Second World War 1939–45: A Strategical and Tactical Study* by J.F.C Fuller (Eyre & Spottiswoode, 1954), *History of the Second World War* by B.H. Lidell Hart (Cassell, 1970 ed.) and *The Struggle for Europe* by Chester Wilmot (Collins, 1952). All of these contain detailed studies of the war, but tend to concentrate on the military fortunes of the nations involved. Some books that may help you with different aspects of the war include: Robert Aron, *The Vichy Regime* (Putnam, 1958); A. Dallin, *German Rule in Russia* (Macmillan, 1957); M.R.D. Foot, *Resistance: An Analysis of European Resistance to Nazism 1940–45* (Eyre Methuen, 1976); E. Kogon, *The Theory and Practice of Hell* (Secker & Warburg, 1950) on concentration camps; A. & V.M. Toynbee (eds), *Hitler's Europe* (OUP, 1954).

7. Discussion Points and Exercises

A   *This section consists of questions that might be used for discussion (or written answers) as a way of expanding on the chapter and testing understanding of it:*

1   Why was Poland so easily conquered?

2   Why did Britain and France provide so little assistance to Poland and Finland?

3   Was the capture of Norway of any real importance to either side?

4   Should Britain have committed more of its reserves to the defence of France?

5   Why didn't Germany occupy the whole of France?

6   Explain why the Battle of Britain was fought in the air.

7   Why was Europe almost at peace from June 1940 to June 1941?

8   Why did Hitler and Mussolini declare war on the USA in December 1941?

9   Why was Russia so easily defeated in 1941?

10 How decisive was the battle of Stalingrad?

11 Why was there war in North Africa?

12 Account for the Allied victory in North Africa 1942–3.

13 Was the conquest of Italy worth the cost in men and equipment?

14 Why was the southern front in Russia so mobile while the centre and North were so static?

15 Why was the reconquest of France and the invasion of Germany from the West necessary?

16 Why were the Normandy landings so immediately successful?

17 Was the Arnhem operation a justifiable risk?

18 Why did Germany not surrender earlier?

B   *This section consists of questions that examine events of the war from the point of view of different countries:*

1   Write an editorial for a French newspaper in April 1940 outlining France's role in the war to date and her prospects for the future.

2   As an adviser to the American President, outline the alternative strategies facing the Allies in Europe after their victory in North Africa and the attitude of Britain and the other allies to them.

3   Write an article for a Russian newspaper at the end of the European war in May 1945 examining the separate roles of Russia and the Western allies in the war as a whole.

C   *Debate and discuss the validity of each of the following statements:*

1   'The RAF saved Britain in 1940'.

2   'Hitler's decision to attack Russia was both ill-founded and fatal'.

3   '1942: year of decision'.

4   'The Normandy landings were a triumph of administrators, not soldiers'.

D *Essay questions:*

1 Why was the Western Front in 1939–40 so different to the trench warfare of World War I?

2 Why was Hitler so successful between 1938 and 1940?

3 Account for the initial failures but subsequent success of the Soviet Union in World War II.

4 Was Hitler responsible for Germany's defeat?

Index

Caporetto, battle of (1917)   170, 253
Caprivi, Georg Leo von   66, 68–9, 71
Carol II, King of Roumania   411
Caroline Islands   42, 129
'Cartel des Gauches'   229, 232, 242
Casablanca, conference at (1943)   422
Caserio, Santo   34
Casimir-Perier, Jean   36, 37
Catalonia   376–87 passim
Cavaignac, Louis   30
Centre party (Germany)   66–7, 71,
     289–92 passim, 304–6
Chaikovsky, Nicholas   333
Chamberlain, Houston   309
Chamberlain, Joseph   77–8, 130
Chamberlain, Neville   243, 390–3, 403
Chambord, Count of   26
Champagne   158, 162, 171
Chautemps, Camille   228, 231, 236
'Cheka'   327, 339, 340
Cherkassy, battle of (1944)   426–7
Chernayev, Mikhail   109
Chiang Kai-shek   352
Chicherin, Giorgi   352
China   102, 111–3, 367, 372–3
Chotek, Sophie   12
Churchill, Winston   163, 265, 390, 403,
     422
Ciano, Count Galeazzo   199, 261–2, 314
Clemenceau, Georges   29, 30, 35, 36, 37,
     154, 186–7, 227, 230–1, 242, 247
Colonial League (Germany)   65, 78–9
Combes, Emile   37
Comintern   341
     See also Anti-Comintern pact
Communism:
     in France   229, 232;
     in Italy   264;
     in Germany   287–8, 304–5;
     in Russia   339–57
     See also Bolsheviks
Companys, Luis   378
Concordat (1929)   268–9;
     (1933)   306, 308
Condor Legion   384
'Confédération Générale du Travail'
     (CGT)   35–6, 234–5
Conference of Ambassadors   274, 361, 362
Confessional Church   308
Congo   41, 83
Conrad von Hötzendorff, Count Franz
     141, 165–7, 170
Constantine I, King of Greece   163
Constantinople (Straits Convention)   9,
     110, 113–4, 139–42, 183, 192–3
Corfu   50, 271, 367
Coronel, battle of (1914)   175

Corporate State (Italy)   270–3, 285–6
Corradini, Enrico   57
Cotentin Peninsula   429–30
Covenant (of the League of Nations)   366,
     374
Cracow   160–1, 398–9
Creditanstalt, collapse of   214–5, 371
Crete   140, 143, 414–5
Crispi, Francesco   52–4
Croatia   8, 12–18, 20–2, 192, 197–201
'Croix de Feu'   233–4
Cuno, Wilhelm   290–1, 293
Curzon Line   209–11
Czech Legion   331–3
Czechoslovakia:
     before 1919   6–24, 191–2;
     1919–39   201–6, 217;
     and France   241, 243–4;
     and Italy   275;
     and Germany   315, 361, 362–3, 369,
         389–91;
     and Russia   353;
     and World War II   426–8
Czernin, Ottokar   334

Dahomey   41, 128–31 passim
'Daily Telegraph' incident (1908)   71, 77
Daladier, Edouard   231, 234, 236, 238,
     243, 246–7, 249–51, 390–1, 403
Dalmatia   8, 17, 187, 191, 197, 253–5
D'Annunzio, Gabriele   57, 255–6, 259,
     260–1
Danzig   189–90, 209, 211–2, 296, 313–6,
     366, 393
Daranyi, Koloman   218
Dardanelles   58, 139–40, 163–4
     See also Constantinople
Darlan, Jean-Francois   407, 421
Daudet, Léon   233
Dawes Plan   232, 242, 291, 294, 297, 365
De Bono, Emilio   260, 261, 263, 268,
     277–8
De Gaulle, Charles   244, 407, 430
Delbos, Yvon   315, 389
Delcassé, Théophile   43–4, 81
'Delegations' (Austria-Hungary)   9–10
Denikin, Anton   331, 334
Denmark   188–9, 315, 402
Depretis, Agostini   52
De Robeck, John   163
Déroulède, Paul   43
Deschanel, Paul   230, 231
'Deutschland' incident (1937)   384
De Vecchi, Cesare   257, 261–2
Diaz, Armando   173, 261
Dimitrjevic, Dragutin   142
     See also Apis

437